Media/Society

Industries, Images, and Audiences

Fifth Edition

David Croteau

Virginia Commonwealth University

William Hoynes

Vassar College

Los Angeles | London | New Delhi
Singapore | Washington DC

Los Angeles | London | New Delhi
Singapore | Washington DC

FOR INFORMATION:

SAGE Publications, Inc.
2455 Teller Road
Thousand Oaks, California 91320
E-mail: order@sagepub.com

SAGE Publications Ltd.
1 Oliver's Yard
55 City Road
London EC1Y 1SP
United Kingdom

SAGE Publications India Pvt. Ltd.
B 1/I 1 Mohan Cooperative Industrial Area
Mathura Road, New Delhi 110 044
India

SAGE Publications Asia-Pacific Pte. Ltd.
3 Church Street
#10-04 Samsung Hub
Singapore 049483

Acquisitions Editor: Matthew Byrnie
Associate Editor: Nancy Loh
Editorial Assistant: Gabrielle Piccininni
Production Editor: Melanie Birdsall
Copy Editor: Ellen Howard
Typesetter: C&M Digitals (P) Ltd.
Proofreader: Theresa Kay
Indexer: Ellen Slavitz
Cover Designer: Michael Dubowe
Marketing Manager: Liz Thornton

Printed in the United States of America

Library of Congress Cataloging-in-Publication Data

Croteau, David.

Media/society : industries, images, and audiences / David Croteau, Virginia Commonwealth University, William Hoynes, Vassar College. — Fifth Edition.

pages cm
Includes bibliographical references and index.

ISBN 978-1-4522-6837-8 (pbk. : alk. paper)
1. Mass media—Social aspects—United States.
2. Mass media—Political aspects—United States.
I. Hoynes, William. II. Title.

HN90.M3C76 2014
302.23—dc23   2013032389

This book is printed on acid-free paper.

SUSTAINABLE FORESTRY INITIATIVE

Certified Chain of Custody
Promoting Sustainable Forestry
www.sfiprogram.org
SFI-01268

SFI label applies to text stock

17 18 10 9 8 7 6 5

Brief Contents

Detailed Contents

3 Political Influence on Media 72

6   Social Inequality and Media Representation   187

9   Media Technology   294

Preface

We live in a society that is saturated by media. For most of us, the Internet, print, television, radio, music, and film are central parts of our daily lives. In addition, it is impossible to understand most social and political issues today without understanding how the media influence the perception and discussion of these issues. It is no surprise, then, that understanding the relationship between media and society is an important topic across many disciplines.

We are pleased that the first four editions of *Media/Society* helped to introduce thousands of students to a sociologically informed analysis of the media process that promoted such understanding. Building on that success and the helpful comments we have received from a variety of instructors, we are happy to offer you this fifth edition of *Media/Society*.

A "BIG PICTURE" APPROACH TO STUDYING MEDIA AND SOCIETY

The purpose of this book is to provide a framework for understanding the media process and to explore the elements of that process by reviewing some key examples of media research. This book is likely to be of special relevance for students of mass communication, sociology, political science, journalism, cultural studies, and American studies.

We have found that teaching about media works best as a collaborative process. Most students bring a great deal of media experience to the classroom. They have been readers, viewers, listeners, and players all their lives. In many cases, they are producers of media, including creating blogs and websites, shooting and sharing pictures and video, writing for school-based newspapers and magazines, doing production or on-air work for school news broadcasts, recording musical performances, and more. Their knowledge and experience often result in lively and insightful classroom discussions. Their awareness of the latest popular media products and trends often outpaces our own.

What students generally lack, though, is a broader framework for understanding the relationship between media and society and a sense of the historical evolution of media. Those are our contribution to the classroom. In teaching about media, we try to build on our students' experiential knowledge by providing resources to help them gain new insights about the media. A part of this involves putting the most recent media developments in a broader theoretical and historical context. Another part involves developing skills for critically evaluating both the conventional wisdom and our own often taken-for-granted assumptions about the social role of media. In short, we step back and put the ever-changing world of media into perspective, providing students with tools to think critically about media today—and tomorrow.

This fifth edition of *Media/Society* has at least four distinct features that continue to make it unique among media texts.

- A sociological framework

- An integrated, "big picture" approach to media of all types

- Emphasis on the social, political, and economic forces shaping media

- Current examples that connect broader theory to everyday life

First, our approach is sociological. By this, we mean that our emphasis is on the "big picture," examining relationships between the various components of the media process. In the first chapter, we present a model of media and society (see Figure 1.5) that identifies the key relationships among the media industry, media products, audiences or users, technology, and the broader social world. One of the central points of *Media/Society* is that we need to understand media, in all their complexity, in social terms.

Second, because our approach emphasizes the sociological "big picture," we integrate a wide variety of topics into our discussion. Our analysis explores both different dimensions of the media process (production, content, and audiences or users) and different types of media (film, music, news, television, books, the Internet, etc.). We do not fragment the study of media by separating chapters by individual medium; convergence of media technologies has made this kind of medium-specific approach untenable. Instead, we emphasize an integrated approach to studying media of all types. The issues we examine are also diverse. They range from how government regulates the media to how audiences actively construct meaning; from how media personnel do their jobs to how changing media technology is having global repercussions; from how the economics of the media industry shape media products to how media products might influence audiences; from the portrayals of race, class, gender, and sexuality in the media to the news media's impact on the world of politics. This diversity allows readers to see connections among media issues that are often treated separately. In addition, it allows instructors to use this text as a comprehensive survey of the field while tailoring supplementary readings to highlight issues of particular interest to them.

Third, our sociological focus on social relationships highlights the tension between constraint and action in the media process. For example, while we must understand the influence of the media industry in our society, we must also recognize how economic and political constraints affect the media. While we should be alert to the potential influence of media products on audiences, we must also recognize how audiences actively construct their own interpretations of media messages. While we ought to pay attention to the influences of technology on the media process, we must also see how social, economic, and political forces have shaped the development and application of technology. Examining these tensions helps us gain a more balanced and nuanced understanding of the role of media in society.

Finally, with updated examples in the fifth edition, this book aims to be current and accessible. The particular details of current media debates change rapidly, but the types of debates that are occurring date back to the very origins of mass-mediated communication. Therefore, our analyses are historically grounded but highlight current media issues, such as the implications of so-called Web 2.0, regulation of the Internet, the concentration of media ownership, portrayals of the LGBT community in the media, the challenges facing contemporary journalism, the explosion of mobile devices, and the growth of globally circulating media. By drawing on recent examples, we concretize our broader theoretical points about media and society. We hope our approach will help make the text accessible and engaging for students and instructors alike.

REVISIONS FOR THE NEW EDITION

This fifth edition will be comfortably familiar to those instructors who have used the previous editions of *Media/Society*. The organizing framework and underlying sociological model remain the same throughout. We have retained our consideration of classic studies, added discussions of select new studies, and provided up-to-date material about the ever-changing media landscape. This edition includes new, revised, or expanded discussions of

- Ownership. Changing patterns of ownership concentration, including the further concentration of the music industry to just the "Big Three" players.

- Media Audiences. Audiences as media producers, media fans and fan communities, and the transition from audience to user.

- Users. The changing ways that people use the media—often challenging traditional broadcast models—including the expanding role of mobile devices, the rapid growth of streaming video, the popularity of the "second screen," and the trend of "binge" television viewing.

- Privacy and Surveillance. Discussion of the gathering of Internet user data by corporations is supplemented with additional material on NSA and other government surveillance.

- Changing Media Professions. How technological changes, convergence, and the 24-hour news cycle have transformed the work of journalists, and the changing world of book publishing.

- Copyright and Piracy. Debates surrounding copyright and pirating of media content.

- Representation. Race/ethnicity, gender, class, and sexuality in television, film, and journalism. The section on representation of the LGBT community, in particular, has been revised and updated, with new material.

- Media and Politics. The role of media in recent political events, with examples from the 2012 U.S. Presidential campaign, the Occupy movement, and the Arab Spring.

- Global Consequences. A substantially revised section on the debate over "cultural imperialism" and a new section on European cultural policies.

In addition, we have made two pedagogical changes:

- Discussion Questions. By popular demand, we've added a few discussion questions at the end of each chapter to prompt thinking about some of the key issues discussed in the chapter. More such questions can be found on the accompanying website, http://www.sagepub.com/croteau5e.

- Online Resources. Some of the biggest changes for this edition are digital and are found online in a free-to-use website that accompanies this book, http://www.sagepub.com/croteau5e. In particular, we've moved there what had been an appendix with many online resources related to media education, policy, research, and activism.

While these revisions will help ensure that the details in *Media/Society* remain up-to-date, they also serve to reaffirm the timeless nature of the analytical framework and core questions presented in the earlier editions of *Media/Society*. By understanding this framework and focusing on these questions, students will be well equipped to assess media developments long after they have left the classroom.

Acknowledgments

We would like to take this opportunity to acknowledge the people who have helped make the five editions of this book possible. We are grateful to Kassia Arbabi, Henry Bartlett, Johanna Buchignani, Matthew Dillard, Dave Gray, David Hurley, Marilyn Kennepohl, Caroline Lee, Kristin Monroe, Corrina Regnier, Mollie Sandberg, Jacinthe Sasson-Yenor, Heather Tomlins, and Kate Wood for their research assistance. Thanks to Clayton Childress for his valuable suggestions during the early stages of preparing the fourth edition and to Stefania Milan for her contributions to the fourth edition. We would also like to thank Pine Forge founder Steve Rutter for his assistance and encouragement on the first two editions of the book. We appreciate the support and assistance of the staff at SAGE as we prepared this new edition. We are grateful to the many SAGE and Pine Forge reviewers, who have provided very helpful comments on previous editions of *Media/Society*:

Terri L. Anderson, *University of California, Los Angeles*

Ronald Becker, *Miami University–Ohio*

Vince Carducci, *College for Creative Studies*

Victor P. Corona, *Polytechnic Institute of New York University*

Jiska Engelbert, *Erasmus University Rotterdam (The Netherlands)*

Paul Mason Fotsch, *New York University*

Donna L. Halper, *Lesley University*

John Hochheimer, *Southern Illinois University–Carbondale*

Aniko Imre, *University of Southern California*

Nick Jankowski, *University of Illinois at Chicago*

Dana Kaufman, *DePaul University*

Gholam Khiabany, *London Metropolitan University*

Osman Koroglu, *Fatih University*

Martin Lang, *Gustavus Adolphus College*

Linda Levitt, *Stephen F. Austin State University*

Eric Louw, *University of Queensland*

Michael H. McBride, *Texas State University–San Marcos*

Ryan Moore, *Florida Atlantic University*

Lisa M. Paulin, *North Carolina Central University*

Jeff Ritter, *La Roche College*

Gabriel Rossman, *University of California–Los Angeles*

Matthew Schneirov, *Duquesne University*

Fred Turner, *Stanford University*

Phyllis S. Zrzavy, *Franklin Pierce University*

We would also like to thank the students who have taken our media courses over the years. Their questions and concerns have provided wonderful fuel for thought.

Thanks to Ben and Nick Hoynes for providing their father with a continuing lesson about the complex role of the media. Finally, special thanks, as always, from David to Cecelia Kirkman and from Bill to Deirdre Burns—for everything.

PART I

Media/Society

CHAPTER 1

Media and the Social World

The media surround us. Our everyday lives are saturated by the Internet, television, radio, movies, recorded music, newspapers, books, magazines, and more. In the 21st century, thanks in part to the proliferation of mobile devices, we navigate through a vast mass media environment unprecedented in human history. Yet our intimate familiarity with the media often allows us to take them for granted. They are like the air we breathe, ever present yet rarely considered.

This book invites you to step back and seriously consider the mass media and the issues they raise. It asks you to put your everyday media activities into a broader social, political, and economic context to better understand them.

Let's take the simple act of watching television. Nothing could be easier. Sit yourself down and click; it's on. Click, change the channel. Click, click, click. . . . Most of us do it almost every day without thinking much about it. But what if we stepped back to look at television in a broader context? What would we find?

Or take the Internet. Facebook, YouTube, Wikipedia, Tumblr, Twitter, Google, Instagram, Yahoo, and a thousand other sites and services compete for our attention, while the latest "hot" trend garners endless hype. "Revolutionary," "ground-breaking," "a new era in communication"—this is the sort of language that has long surrounded the Internet's evolution. But again, what happens if we pause and take a look with a more critical eye? What do we see?

One thing we see is change. The technology and models for producing and delivering media content are constantly evolving. The "old" television networks no longer dominate as they once did. Hundreds of cable and satellite channels vie for the attention of a fragmented audience. Online streaming services like Netflix and Hulu, video-on-demand, digital video recorders (DVRs), and smartphones offer content delivery options that enable people to choose what and when they watch, making old-fashioned television programming a fading relic of the past. The Internet is changing even faster. The expanded bandwidth offered by fiber optics has enabled more sophisticated, higher-quality video and audio, while mobile devices have created new ways to access and use the Internet.

But if we focus only on change, we risk missing the forest for the trees. That's because, surprisingly, when we step outside of our routine media habits and move away from all the media hype, we also find that some enduring questions and issues face all types of mass media. From the printed page (or e-book) you are reading, to the television program you watch (on a TV, computer screen, or cell phone), to the world of cyberspace, we can examine all of these by asking some fundamental questions:

- How—and by whom—are media products created?
- Why are some images and ideas so prevalent in the media while others are marginalized?
- What impact are media having on our society and on our world?
- How has growth in media influenced the political process?
- What should be the government's relation to regulating the media?
- How do people use and interpret the media?
- How do new media technologies develop, and what is the effect of technological change?
- What is the significance of the increasing globalization of media?

These questions and others like them are not simple to answer. Indeed, one of the arguments in this book is that popular answers to such questions often overlook the more complicated dynamics that characterize the media process. But these tough questions raise important issues with which we need to grapple if we are to understand the mass media and their increasingly important place in our society.

THE IMPORTANCE OF MEDIA

The equipment that provides access to electronic media is everywhere (see Figure 1.1). Radio (99%) and television (96%) have a nearly universal presence in U.S. households (Nielsen 2013a; U.S. Census Bureau 2012). Many U.S. households have cable (49%), fiber optic (8.3%), or satellite (29%) television service. DVRs (42%), DVD or Blu-ray players (80%), and game consoles (42%) are also common (Nielsen 2013b). Adults in the United

States are equipped with a vast array of media technology, including a cell phone (91%) or smartphone (56%); a desktop (58%), laptop (61%), or tablet (31%) computer; and about two-thirds (65%) have broadband Internet access at home (a dramatic increase from just 3% in 2000). MP3 players (43%) and e-readers (26%) are also popular (Pew Internet and American Life Project 2013; see Figure 1.2). Teens aged 12 to 17 have rates of cell phone (78%) and smartphone (37%) ownership that are nearly as high as adults, and 93 percent of teens own or have access to a computer at home (Madden et al. 2013).

Many Americans quickly embrace new technology, thereby continuously changing the media landscape. For example, the proliferation of mobile media devices—cell phones, MP3

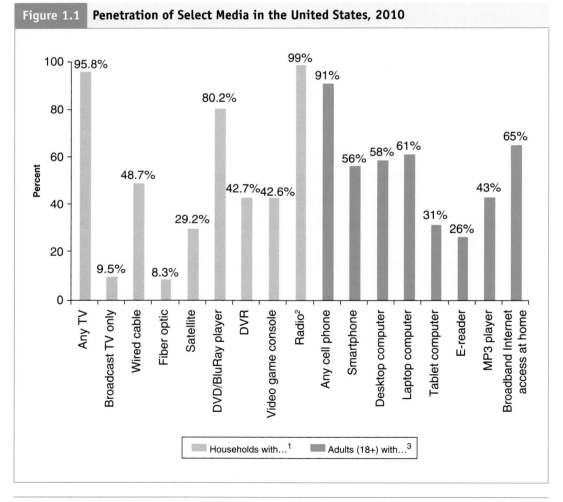

Figure 1.1 | **Penetration of Select Media in the United States, 2010**

Sources: [1]Nielsen (2013b); [2]U.S. Census Bureau (2012); [3]Pew Internet and American Life Project (2013).

players, tablet computers, and the like—has made it easier to access media products anytime and anywhere and has led to a decline in the use of desktop computers (see Figure 1.2). The growth of Internet-based video streaming services has also led to an uptick in the number of "Zero-TV" households that do not access television programs through the traditional avenues of over-the-air broadcasts, cable, or satellite. Three-quarters of these households have a television set, and many of them stream video on the Internet to their television sets or watch video on mobile devices. Though Zero-TV homes are still fewer than 5 percent of U.S. households, over half are made up of young adults under age 35 and likely signal an emerging trend. The growth of such households is likely to continue; and in the fall of 2013,

Figure 1.2 **U.S. Adult Ownership of Media-Related Devices and Broadband Internet Access, 2006–2013**

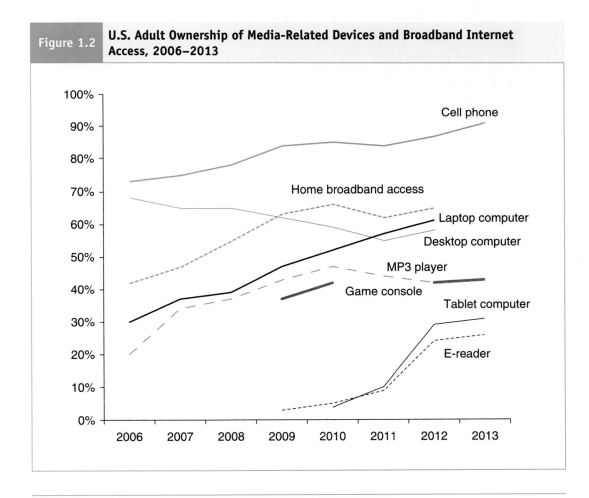

Source: Pew Internet and American Life Project (2013).

Notes: Data from multiple surveys in a single year were simplified. Data was not available for all categories in all years.

Source: © Ed Kashi/VII/Corbis.

Media are so central to our daily lives that we often use more than one form at a time. Multitasking is common, and media devices—many of them portable—are deeply integrated into social life.

Nielsen—the dominant company in media audience measurement—began counting such homes in their television ratings for the first time (Nielsen 2013a).

Whatever devices they use, Americans spend an enormous amount of time watching, listening to, reading, or otherwise using these various forms of media. For example, Nielsen estimates that, on average, Americans spend more than 5 hours a day watching television: 4 hours and 39 minutes on live TV and 25 minutes on "time shifted" television (recorded programs watched later). Over the course of a year, that adds up to more than 76 days of TV viewing! Imagine someone sitting in front of a television set 24 hours a day for two and half months! Every year, that's how much TV the typical American watches.

Media use among young people is also extensive, though reading print has been declining (see Table 1.1). One study found that young people 8 to 18 years of age devoted more than 7.5 hours a day to entertainment media, including television, music, computers, and video games. Because they often *multitask*—using more than one form of media at a time, such as listening to an MP3 player while surfing the web—young people managed to access 10 hours and 45 minutes of media content during those 7.5 hours (Rideout, Foehr, and Roberts 2010). With such vast exposure to media, it can be argued that the media have become the dominant social institution in contemporary society, supplanting the influence of older institutions, such as the educational system and religion.

Our media and our society as we know it are fused: media/society. One way to recognize the importance of the media in our lives is to imagine life without the media. Imagine that you wake up tomorrow in a sort of twilight zone parallel universe where everything is the

Table 1.1	Media Use by Young People 8–18 Years Old, 1999–2009		
Among all 8- to 18-year-olds, average amount of time spent with each medium in a typical day:			
	1999	*2004*	*2009*
TV content	3:47	3:51	4:29
Music/audio	1:48	1:44	2:31
Computer	:27	1:02	1:29
Video games	:26	:49	1:13
Print	:43	:43	:38
Movies	:18	:25	:25
TOTAL MEDIA EXPOSURE	7:29	8:33	10:45
Multitasking proportion	16%	26%	29%
TOTAL MEDIA USE	6:19	6:21	7:38

Source: Rideout, Foehr, and Roberts (2010).

Notes: **Total media exposure** is the sum of time spent with all media. **Multitasking proportion** is the proportion of media time that is spent using more than one medium concurrently. **Total media use** is the actual number of hours out of the day that are spent using media, taking multitasking into account.

same except that media do not exist: no television, no movies, no radio, no recorded music, no cell phones, no computers, no Internet, no books or magazines or newspapers.

If the media were eliminated, nothing else would be the same. Our entertainment would be different. We would not watch sports on TV, catch videos or stream programs online, or go to a movie for fun. We would not listen to recorded music for relaxation. We would not use our cell phones to call or text friends. We would not post news and information about ourselves—or communicate with others—on social networking sites, blogs, or other Internet forums. Our understanding of politics and the world around us would be different because we would not have newspapers, television, magazines, websites, and books to explain what is happening in our communities and beyond. Even our perceptions of ourselves would probably be different, because we would not have television characters and advertising images to compare ourselves against. For example, we might not concern ourselves so much with the latest fashions, music, or cars if ads did not imply that we should be concerned with such things.

With no television, no recorded music, no movies, no radio, and no Internet, we would have a great deal of time on our hands. We would probably spend much of it interacting with other people. We might entertain ourselves by playing music or playing games. We might attend meetings and lectures or hold discussions on politics and current events to learn what was going on. We might take up hobbies or learn new skills to pass the time. Our social lives—how we interact with other people—would also change in the absence of media.

Of course, changes would reach well beyond our private lives. The behavior of politicians, business executives, and leaders in other fields would change without media. Government would operate differently. Without advertising, business would be fundamentally different. Education, religion, and every other institution would also be different without media, as would social movements and citizens' organizations.

Given the pervasiveness of the media and their significance in our lives and in society, it's surprising to realize that the mass media are relatively new phenomena. Most forms of mass media are still in their infancy. Before we go any further in our discussion, we should take a brief look at the history and meaning of *mass media*.

THE RISE OF MASS MEDIA

The word *media* is the plural of medium. It is derived from the Latin word *medius,* which means *middle.* The communication media are the different technological processes that facilitate communication between (and are in the middle of) the sender of a message and the receiver of that message. In this book, we will sometimes use the term *reader* or *user* rather than *receiver* or *audience* because we want to highlight the active role of audiences in interpreting the messages they receive and, increasingly, in generating media content of their own. People "read" the sound and pictures of media messages just as they read the words of a written media message. Reading implies actively interpreting media messages. The same media product might mean very different things to two different people. For example, a music video of a popular new artist may elicit very different responses from a 15-year-old fan of the band and a parent concerned about stereotypically sexist images that might be present in such videos. The media product—the video—is the same, but different "readers" interpret it in very different ways. In studying media, then, it's important to consider readers because they do not simply swallow the messages presented in the media.

Sociologists call the process of actively creating meaning in this way the *social construction of reality*. This means that, while reality exists, we must negotiate the meaning of that reality. A student who sports a series of prominent tattoos is an objective reality. However, different people will interpret such body art in different ways. Is it a sign of conformity to a fad? A rebellious political statement? A playful snubbing of mainstream norms? A disgusting mutilation of the body? Or is it just an act of personal expression? The meaning of the tattoos must be constructed by those observing them. The same is true for the meaning of media messages. That is why the audience, or "readers," is such an important part of the media process.

One of the biggest changes in recent years is that, increasingly, audiences are also *users* of media; they contribute content to the platforms created by media companies. These include a product review on Amazon, a Facebook update, a video on YouTube, photos via Instagram, music posted on a Tumblr blog, a tweet, a comment or tag on a news item, a post on a hobby forum, a "mash-up" audio recording, or one of countless other ways that users can now create their own content and make it available to others via the Internet. Such user-generated content blurs the line between media producer and consumer.

Our primary concern in this book is mass media, that is, media that reach a relatively large audience of usually anonymous readers. Writing a letter, sending an SMS text message, or placing a telephone call involves the use of different communication media; but scholars generally do not consider these to be mass media because messages in such media have a single, intended, known recipient. You know the individual who will receive your letter, text, or phone call. Mass media producers, though, have no way of knowing exactly who—or how many people—will read their book, watch their television program, buy their CD, or "hit" their Internet home page. The difference between mass media and other forms of communication is not always simple or clear-cut. As noted, the distinctions have become blurred with the introduction of new technologies. Many Internet platforms enable ordinary users to reach *potentially* a large audience. However, in reality, the vast majority of what is posted on Facebook pages, blogs, and video sharing sites is seen by only a handful of people—often friends and acquaintances we already know. Our primary concern in this book is the generally recognized mass media of print, film, radio, television, sound recordings, and the Internet.

The Print Medium

When American revolutionaries founded the United States, there was only one form of mass media: print. (See DeFleur and DeFleur 2009; and McQuail 2010 for summaries of the rise of mass media.) The technology for printing dates back to the beginning of the 15th century, when inventors in Korea first created the cast metal type that made printing possible. In 1450, Johannes Gutenberg made printing more practicable by converting a winepress into the first printing press with movable type. While the technology evolved, media content changed little. Reflecting the power of the Church in Europe at the time, the Bible, which scribes had previously hand copied, was the book most often produced by early printers. Thus, as was true for later changes, social forces other than technology determined the direction of media development (see Figure 1.3).

For several centuries, print media—in the form of books, newspapers, and pamphlets—served as the only means for reaching a wide audience from a distance. However, the need for physical distribution limited print media products (unlike later electronic media). News, for example, traveled only as fast and as far as a horse, train, or ship could carry it. It routinely took four to eight weeks for information to travel from Europe to the United States. Even distances that we now perceive to be quite short—from New York to Washington, for example—were separated by a vast communication gulf. The only way to communicate across such distances was for messages to travel physically between the two locations. While improved transportation technology increased the speed of communication throughout the 19th century, in the years immediately preceding the development of the telegraph, it still took several days for news to travel from one city to the next (see Figure 1.4). Both routine and extraordinary information, from holiday greetings to news of the outbreak of war, traveled at a slow speed difficult to imagine today.

Not until the 1840s did the technological innovation of the telegraph allow for near instantaneous communication over long distances that were physically wired together. For the first time, there was a separation between transportation and long-distance communication. Since it did not reach a large audience, the telegraph was not a mass medium, but it did speed up the dissemination of information through newspapers. Reporters could send news stories instantaneously over a long distance to newspapers that would then print and distribute the story locally. The invention of the telephone in 1876 opened the way for more widely accessible personal long-distance communication as well as facilitating the work of reporters.

Sound Recording and the Film Medium

In 1877, Thomas Edison developed the phonograph, which marked the beginning of the first new mass medium since print. In 1887, phonograph records were introduced and, later, other forms of sound recording proliferated. In 1948, the long-playing (LP) 33 1/3-rpm record was launched by Columbia Records and became the recording industry standard for more than 30 years. Magnetic tape originated in the 1920s and became most popular in its easy-to-use cassette form, introduced in the 1960s. In the early 1980s, sound recording went digital, and the compact disk (CD) emerged as the dominant recording format. By the late 1990s, digital file formats, such as MP3, were allowing music to be more speedily distributed via the Internet and stored on mobile MP3 players, such as the iPod. Since 2011, digital music has made up the majority of music sales, outselling CDs and vinyl; in addition, streaming audio services, such as Spotify, Pandora, and Rdio, enable audiences to hear a vast array of music without purchasing any specific tracks.

In 1895, Auguste and Louis Lumière invented the cinematograph, which subsequently led to "moving pictures." While the need to assemble a viewing audience in a particular location limited the reach of this new medium, movies proved to be enormously popular. By 1912, 5 million Americans a day were attending the cinema. Fifteen years later, the introduction of the first "talking picture" made moviegoing even more accessible and popular. By the late 1970s, videocassette recorders (VCRs) allowed people to purchase or rent movies to watch in their own homes. They also enabled users to record television broadcasts and to film their own home videos.

In 1997, the digital video disk (DVD) was introduced, marking the shift of film to digital formats. Increasingly, digital cameras and related software made it relatively easy for the general public to record and edit their own movies. By the mid-2000s, websites such as YouTube and Vimeo provided accessible spaces for the upload of these amateur films. Meanwhile, commercial films were increasingly available via Internet streaming options, such as those provided by Netflix, Hulu, and Amazon.

Broadcast Media

In the first decade of the 20th century, innovations leading to the rise of radio presented new opportunities for communication. Radio was the first broadcast medium, and it introduced a new element to the media equation. No longer did media producers have to physically distribute their products (for example, to newsstands, bookstores, or movie theaters). Nor did the public have to travel physically to these locations to have access to mass media. Now, communicators could use the airwaves to transmit a media product directly to anyone who owned a radio receiver. Communicators could now cast media messages broadly.

Broadcasting made another advance with the introduction of television. When the Pioneer Corporation introduced the first television sets to the United States in the 1940s, their advertising boasted, "We bring the revolution home" (Tichi 1991: 12). They were not exaggerating. In the span of less than 10 years, between 1946 and 1955, television sets made their way into 65 percent of American households (Spigel 1992).

In 1998, with television in nearly all American homes, the first digital television broadcasting began. However, faced with the slow sales of digital television sets, stations had little incentive to invest in new digital broadcasting equipment. At the urging of

Figure 1.3	**Time Line of Media Development**

Year   *Media-Related Event*

100   Papermaking develops in China and spreads through Asia and the Arab world by the year 600

700   Arabs carry Chinese techniques for papermaking to the West

1000   Moveable type made of clay used in China

1400   Moveable metal type developed in Asia

1450   1456 Gutenberg perfects moveable metal type and handpress in Germany; the Bible is printed

1600   First newspapers appear in Germany, France, and Belgium

1700   1702 London's *Daily Courant* is the first daily newspaper

1800   1833 Mass-circulation media begin with the first *penny press* newspaper, the *New York Sun*

1837 Telegraph is first demonstrated

1850   1876 First telephone message sent by Alexander Graham Bell

1879 Edison patents the electric light

1884 Eastman perfects roll film

1894 Motion pictures are invented and the first films are shown to the public

1895 Radio messages are transmitted by Marconi

1900   1920 First regularly scheduled radio broadcasting begun by KDKA in Pittsburgh

1927 The *Jazz Singer* is the first feature-length film with synchronized speech

1933 TV is demonstrated by RCA

1937 First digital computer created from telephone parts

1941 First commercial TV is broadcast

1946 The first mainframe computer is invented at the University of Pennsylvania

1949 Network TV begins in the United States

1950   1956 Videotape recording (VTR) is invented

1957 Sputnik, world's first communication satellite, is launched by USSR

1961 San Diego cable operator is the first to import television signals from another city
    (Los Angeles) for distribution to subscribers

1969 First nodes of the computer Internet are created in a Pentagon plan to establish a
    decentralized communications system that can withstand nuclear attack

1970 Early (and expensive) videocassette recorders (VCR) introduced

1971 Invention of the microprocessor

1975 The first microcomputer is marketed; fiber optics transmission begins; HBO begins
    transmitting programming to cable TV systems by satellite

1977 Qube, the first interactive cable system, begins in Columbus, Ohio; 200,000 VCRs sold;
    more affordable machines enter the market and sales boom

1982 Audio compact disk (CD) introduced

1990 World Wide Web (WWW) started as simple user interface for a wide variety of data types

1994 First cyber stations (radio stations on the Internet) appear

1997 Digital video disks (DVD) first introduced

1998 Digital television broadcasting begins

(Continued)

Figure 1.3	(Continued)

1999
- Compact MP3 files makes music downloads more practical
- Netflix launches DVD-by-mail subscription service; adds streaming in 2007

2000–2001
- Satellite-based digital audio radio services begin to grow with the launch of XM radio
- Wikipedia is launched and becomes a major collaborative resource
- Apple's iPod is introduced
- Microsoft Xbox introduced, beginning competition with Sony's Playstation

2002
- Friendster, an early social networking site, is founded; MySpace (2003) and Facebook (2004) later follow
- The Blackberry smartphone is introduced, supporting web browsing, texting, and e-mails; the iPhone (2007) later becomes a market leader
- Popularity of web logs—blogs—continues to grow

2003
- The term *Web 2.0*, coined in 1999, is increasingly used to refer to different web applications that facilitate user interaction, collaboration, and information sharing
- Skype peer-to-peer Internet telephone network is introduced

2004
- Flickr photo sharing site is launched
- Podcasts become more popular and easier to find and download
- Google launches project to digitize millions of books

2005
- YouTube, a video posting website, is founded

2006
- First Sony e-reader is introduced, followed by Kindle (2007) and others
- Twitter microblogging service is founded

2007
- The combination of easy-to-use video cameras, video sharing sites, and growth of social networking contributes to the rise of viral videos
- Hulu website launched to stream commercial television programs and movies

2008
- Google announces initiative to digitize old newspaper archives

2009
- Social networking sites reach new peak of popularity

2010
- Apple's iPad helps spark revival in the dormant tablet computer market

2011
- Digital music purchases make up a majority of all units sold, surpassing physical (CDs, vinyl, etc.) sales for the first time ever

2013
- Google Glass is introduced, signaling the emergence of "wearable technology"—in this case in the form of glasses

Sources: Crowley and Heyer (1991); Jost (1994a); Rogers (1986); Shedden (2010); and media accounts.

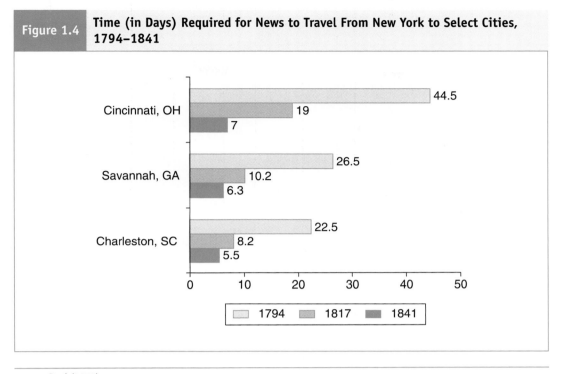

| Figure 1.4 | **Time (in Days) Required for News to Travel From New York to Select Cities, 1794–1841** |

Source: Pred (1973).

manufacturers and broadcasters, the government intervened and ordered all television stations to convert to digital signals by June of 2009. This marked yet another medium making the shift to the universal digital format. Digital television programming can be easily stored on DVRs for later "time-shifted" viewing, delivered "on demand" via cable and satellite services, or streamed via the Internet.

The development of broadcasting fundamentally altered patterns of media consumption by creating the possibility of a largely privatized and individualized media experience. Consuming media or other forms of entertainment were often social activities, such as attending movies or going to concerts. These public activities were replaced, or at least supplemented, by television, video, and DVD rentals, and recorded music, which people usually experience in the privacy of their own homes. More recently, the social dimension of television viewing has been revived through social networking. For example, fans and critics often use Twitter to deliver commentary during live television broadcasts.

Digitization, the Internet, and Mobile Technologies

The rise of computing technology changed the media landscape in a variety of important ways. First, media content could now be created in digital form, stored in the 1s and 0s of computer code. This meant that traditionally distinct forms of media—text, image, audio, and video—now converged. In digital terms, there is no difference between a movie, a recorded song, a family snapshot, and an e-book chapter; they are all collections of digital

Model 17K7—Big 17 in. screen... Mahogany or Limed Oak Cabinet.

TV adds so much to family happiness

There's more fun in television than any other family-shared entertainment...comedy, music, sports, drama and educational shows everyone enjoys. Make sure your family gets all this TV fun on the set that brings you every show at its best—Motorola TV

PHOTO-PERFECT PICTURES THAT COST YOU LESS
Now—sit close up or far away and enjoy sharp, clear pictures—the product of Motorola's "years ahead" circuit design and advanced engineering features. There's a Motorola to fit your home and pocketbook—from budget-priced table models to luxurious TV-Radio-Phonograph combinations—all with the Motorola Built-in-Antenna. Compare—you'll agree—no other offers you so much quality at such low cost.

☑ "GLARE-GUARD" SCREEN

☑ FASHION AWARD DESIGN

☑ CAMERA VIEW PICTURES ☑ "MUSIC LOVER" SOUND

☑ "DEPENDA-BILT" CHASSIS ☑ TWO SIMPLE CONTROLS

you get all these features only in **Motorola TV**

SEE YOUR CLASSIFIED DIRECTORY FOR YOUR NEAREST MOTOROLA DEALER... specifications subject to change without notice

When manufacturers first promoted television, they promised a wide range of benefits for the family.

information. Media devices were no longer distinct either. A vinyl record can only be played on a phonograph. A digital recording can be created, copied, distributed, and played on any computerized device with appropriate software: desktop computer, MP3 player, cell phone, and the like.

Second, digitization changed the world of media production as well. Authors replaced the pen with word processors. Filmmakers turned to digital video recording and editing techniques. Musicians manipulated recordings in software programs. And, in some cases, media creation for different platforms merged. For example, journalists now routinely create content suitable for their newspaper's print edition as well as for broadcast and online distribution; the distinctions between different media have become far less significant (Brooks et al. 2012).

Third, the rise of the Internet provided an unprecedented global platform on which digitally based media content could be distributed and consumed. The Internet made it easier to distribute media content, to share it, and to find new media content of all sorts. Previously, separate devices—books, phonographs, television sets, radios, and so on—were needed to access different media forms. Now, the Internet quickly delivered all of these to any desktop computer with Internet access.

Fourth, computers, digitization, and the Internet enabled greater interactivity among media users, and between media users and media content. This allowed users to seek out a wider range of content, customize media products and delivery options, provide feedback, share and discuss with friends, and even create original media content, becoming producers as well as consumers.

Fifth, as technologies advanced, computers became smaller and more mobile. A smartphone is not really a phone in the traditional sense at all; it is a mobile computer, one of whose functions happens to be making "telephone" calls. The rise of mobile technologies has included smaller tablet computers, smartphones, and portable MP3 players—along with the emerging market of wearable computer devices in the form of glasses and wristwatches. All of these devices have made it easier to access media content, expanded the places where we can use media, and increased the amount of time we spend connected to media and communications networks.

These overlapping changes in technology have had a profound impact on media production and consumption and have transformed various media industries. But it is important to reiterate that changes in technology do not *determine* the evolution of media. Instead, as we will see, technology is only one of a number of interacting factors that shape the development and uses of media.

The rise of the Internet is a case in point. Changes in computer technology were a necessary but not sufficient condition for the existence of the Internet. It took government financing and regulation to help organize and launch the Internet system, primarily out of universities. The Internet was originally conceived as a decentralized communications network capable of functioning after a nuclear attack on central locations such as Washington, DC. Much of the funding to develop the Internet, therefore, came from public tax dollars through the Pentagon budget in the name of national defense. This is a clear example of an external social institution directly influencing the development of technology. Later, the Internet was touted as a revolutionary *information superhighway,* potentially serving as a means to educate and engage citizens in a democratic society. Over time, though, the commercial applications of the Internet became paramount with giant new media companies using the technology to advertise, sell, and deliver products in new ways, in some cases undermining the promise of democracy (McChesney 2013). The point is that, throughout the history of media, technology by itself has never led unambiguously in a specific direction; rather, broader social forces have channeled the development and application of technological capabilities.

MEDIA AND SOCIETY

Because media are such an integral part of our lives, they generate a great deal of popular interest and debate, especially regarding controversial topics. Does television have too much sex and violence? Are the news media biased? Do teens reveal too much on their

Facebook pages? Have TV talk shows and "reality" programs gone too far with their sensationalized topics? Are newspapers dead? Should the government ensure equal access to the Internet by legislating *net neutrality*? To address such questions, we need a better understanding of the mass media and their role in contemporary social life.

A sociological perspective, which underlies this book, can help us understand the media (Croteau and Hoynes 2013). For both students of mass media and citizens in the 21st century, sociology provides a set of tools to help make sense of the dizzying array of media-related issues. A sociological perspective asks us to consider the role of media in our individual lives (the micro level) in the context of social forces such as the economy, politics, and technological development (the macro level). Most of all, sociology suggests that, if we want to understand the media and their impact on our society, we must consider the relationships (both micro and macro) between media and the social world.

Mass Media in Socialization

One way in which individuals are connected to the larger social world is through socialization. Socialization is the process whereby we learn and internalize the values, beliefs, and norms of our culture and, in so doing, develop a sense of self. Americans might, for example, learn as children that the United States is a democracy whose citizens have fought valiantly in the name of freedom and have excelled in science, business, entertainment, and the arts. Such information, coupled with socializing rituals, such as Fourth of July parades, Memorial Day remembrances, pledging allegiance to the flag in school, and playing the national anthem at sporting events, encourages people to take pride in being an "American," thus helping to form one aspect of their identity.

Through the socialization process, we also learn to perform our social roles as friend, student, worker, citizen, and so forth. The process of socialization continues throughout life, but it is especially influential for children and adolescents. If socialization proceeds smoothly, we hardly notice it. The dominant values, beliefs, and norms of our society become "our" values and norms. The internalization of the lessons of socialization means that our culture becomes taken for granted. We learn to hold "appropriate" values and beliefs. We learn to behave in socially acceptable ways.

We realize the learned, taken-for-granted nature of our beliefs and values only when someone calls them into question or contradicts them. A diverse society such as the United States incorporates many different cultures, and, consequently, different groups of people are sometimes socialized into adopting distinctly different norms, beliefs, and values. These cultures can sometimes clash. It can be startling to learn, for example, that the civics book version of U.S. history that socialized proud Americans often glosses over the less noble incidents in that complex history.

We also can become aware of the learned nature of our beliefs when we travel abroad and experience a different culture or hear about other people's travels. The idea of experiencing *culture shock* suggests that we are not equipped—we were not socialized—in the ways and norms of a particular culture.

Part of the explicit responsibility of some social institutions, such as the family and schools, is to promote socialization. We expect families to pass on core values, a sense of responsibility, an appropriate work ethic, and so forth. Traditional educators often gear schools toward teaching children the necessity of submitting to authority, of being punctual and orderly, and of following instructions—skills and orientations that help produce a reliable, compliant worker for future employers.

Other socializing agents, such as adolescent peers, usually have a less intentional, though just as powerful, socializing influence. Often, however, these unofficial socializing agents can promote messages that contradict the ones being espoused by the "powers that be." When parents chastise their teenage kids for hanging around with "the wrong crowd," they are implicitly aware that the potential socializing influence of peers can work to counter parental influence. Parents and teachers might be promoting hard work and study as important values, while peers may be suggesting that partying is a more interesting way to spend one's time.

In contemporary society, the mass media serve as a powerful socializing agent. By the time an average American student graduates from high school, she or he will have spent more time in front of the television than in the classroom and will have spent even more hours consuming other forms of media. Audiences learn and internalize some of the values, beliefs, and norms presented in media products. Take the example of crime. During the 1990s, the number of crime stories on television news increased dramatically, despite the fact that violent crime declined throughout the decade. This growing incongruity led to studies examining whether media coverage of crime was needlessly promoting fear among citizens.

Some researchers say it does. In creating entertaining and emotionally engaging stories, news outlets can promote fear and *moral panic* and thereby contribute to the widespread expectation that dangers and threats are everywhere, contradicting the actual data on crime rates (Altheide 2002, 2009). Some researchers argue that we "learn" about crime even while we are watching entertainment television. For example, watching a lot of police crime shows seems to cultivate two beliefs. First, heavy viewers are more likely than light viewers to see their community as a dangerous, violent place where they are likely to become crime victims. Second, heavy viewers of crime shows tend to develop empathy for the police—even when television police are clearly violating someone's civil rights. The result of such media exposure seems to be an increased likelihood that viewers will adopt a tough law-and-order attitude supportive of authority figures such as the police (Carlson 1985, 1995).

But the relationship between media content and public attitudes is nuanced; both media forms and audience traits matter. Some research suggests that, while news coverage increases the fear of crime, fictional portrayals of crime do not (Grabe and Drew 2007). Local news seems to be especially influential in promoting fear of crime on both a personal level and as a society-wide problem, regardless of the actual local crime rates, while national news and news magazine programs do not (Escholz, Chiricos, and Gertz 2003; Romer, Jamieson, and Aday 2003). Police "reality" programs also seem to enhance fear of crime. Audience traits matter, too; one survey found that the association between television viewing and fear of crime was strongest among viewers who were female, nonvictims, low income, and younger (Escholz, Chiricos, and Gertz 2003).

Of course, the more controversial discussions of media as a socializing agent usually involve media products that seem to challenge convention and authority; music videos, song lyrics, and pornography immediately come to mind. We will explore those issues later. Media influence on socialization is not direct and unambiguous, and we will also explore some of the debates in this area of research. For now, it's enough to note that the media play a role, however qualified, in socializing us into our culture.

Mass Media in Social Relations

From a sociological perspective, the media play a crucial role in almost all aspects of daily life. However, their influence is not limited to what we know. The sociological significance of media extends beyond the content of media messages. Media also affect *how* we learn about our world and interact with one another. That is, mass media are bound up with the *process* of social relations.

This impact is most obvious when we look at the ways in which the mass media literally mediate our relationships with various social institutions. For example, we base most of our knowledge of government on news accounts rather than experience. Not only are we dependent on the media, then, for *what* we know, but the media's connection to politics also affects *how* we relate to the world of politics. Before mass media, political debates usually took place in public forums where crowds were physically present. Today, instead of attending a political event, we are more likely to read or watch the news of a political debate—followed by instant analysis and commentary—in the isolation of our homes. Rather than take part in community action, we might satisfy a desire to participate in political life by calling a radio talk show or posting on a political website. In turn, politicians rely heavily on the media to communicate their messages. Gone are the days when candidates and their campaign workers relied primarily on pounding the pavement and knocking on doors to talk with voters. When such practices take place today, they are likely to be staged by politicians for the benefit of the media. We see similar dynamics at work with televised sports, televangelist preachers, and other "mediated" aspects of social life.

Source: © Richard T. Nowitz/Corbis.

The pursuit of connections through social media can sometimes displace face-to-face social interaction.

In more subtle ways, media are often part of our most routine relations with our families and close friends. Couples talk over the radio at breakfast as they read the morning newspaper. Families often watch television together, huddled around the "electronic hearth." Friends text or e-mail to share links to interesting websites, and groups of young people go to the movies or spend the evening playing video games together. Time-strapped parents sometimes use the TV as a surrogate babysitter, allowing their children to watch hours of television at one sitting—often on a TV set in the child's bedroom. Strangers in public places, such as planes or coffee shops, are often more likely to relate to their media devices—iPods, cell phones, and laptops—than they are to the people who surround them. In all these cases, media products are connected to the ways we interact with other people on a daily basis. Media products provide a diversion, a source of conflict, or a unifying force.

The impact of media—both in content and in process—on all areas of society is undeniable. Talking about social life without including a discussion of the role of mass media risks missing an important element of contemporary society.

A SOCIOLOGY OF MEDIA

Sociologists are not the only ones who study the mass media. Political scientists are sometimes interested in the media's role in politics. Literary scholars might examine the media as cultural texts. Some psychologists are interested in the effect of media exposure on individual behavior. Most important, mass communication scholars explore a wide range of media issues that often emphasize the structure and practice of media institutions.

The lines between the different approaches to the media are rarely clear. Instead, the differences tend to be ones of relative emphasis. It is common to see references to sociological theories and concepts in the mass communication literature. In fact, some mass communications scholars were trained as sociologists before turning their attention exclusively to the media. In turn, sociologists draw on the work of mass communications scholars. But although they can overlap, there is a difference between the disciplines of mass communication and sociology. The field of mass communications is defined by a particular substantive area of interest, while sociology is a perspective that is applied to a wide range of substantive areas, including the media. Not all sociologists study the media, and not all mass communications researchers use a sociological perspective.

One of the best-known articulations of the sociological perspective came from C. Wright Mills, an American sociologist. Mills (1959) once argued that a sociological perspective—what he called the "sociological imagination"—enables us to see the connections between "private troubles" and "public issues." Such a perspective suggests that we can understand the condition of the individual only by situating that person in the larger context of society.

For example, students make very personal and individualized decisions about why they want to attend college. However, if you step back a moment, you can see that the individual, private choice of attending college makes sense only in the larger public context of society. We can understand this "individual" choice in the broader context of an economy in which a college education is now required for more and more occupations, or we can understand some students' choices in light of a larger culture that highly values formal education, as evidenced by their parents' (key socializing agents) pressure on them to attend school.

Thus, social structure inextricably links the private lives of college students to the public world of economics (jobs), politics (public universities, government loans), and culture (the value of learning).

In contemporary society, it is media that most often act as the bridge between people's private lives and their relation to the public world. That is, people often learn about their place in larger society through mass media. The lessons media products might be teaching and the experience of participating in a mass-mediated society, therefore, are of crucial interest to anyone who wants to understand how society functions.

Throughout this text, we will note examples of media research that implicitly or explicitly employ a sociological perspective. A sociological perspective also informs our organization of this text. This book is not a historical overview of the evolution of media, nor is it a mass communications account of how the media industry functions. Such works are important, but what we highlight in this text is a sociological approach that emphasizes social relations, especially in the form of the tension between structure and agency, which we explain below.

The Importance of Social Relations

Sociologists believe that the individual is, to varying degrees, a product of social relations. The language we use, the education we receive, and the norms and values we are taught are all part of a socialization process through which we develop and embrace a sense of self. We become who we are largely through our social relations with others. At its most basic level, this means that our sense of identity and individuality emerges from our social interaction with others.

For example, we develop an identity by routinely imagining how others see us. Imagine a self-conscious interaction such as an important job interview. We dress up for the part of "serious" applicant and play the role we think the employer wants to see. We might feel very nervous because we are trying to sense how the employer views us. We ask ourselves questions: "Am I dressed appropriately?" "Did I answer that question well?" "Did the employer like me?" We put ourselves in the shoes of the employer and imagine how we must appear to him or her. We then imagine the employer's judgment of us, and we experience a feeling—such as pride or embarrassment—as a result of this imagined judgment. One sociologist (Cooley 1902/1964) called this the "looking glass self." In social interactions, we try to see ourselves as if we were looking in a mirror. Our behavior is often affected by what we think others expect from us. Usually, our social interactions are not as tension filled as a job interview, but the process still applies to a wide range of our daily interactions.

Furthermore, our daily activities usually take place within the context of larger groups and institutions. (The job interview mentioned above might take place in the context of a corporation, which in turn exists in the context of a larger economy, and so on.) Family, friendship circles, school, teams, work, community—these are the collective contexts in which we develop our roles and identities as daughters or sons, friends, students, athletes, employees, citizens, and so forth. Each role brings with it a set of expectations about our actions; being a "good" student, employee, or friend usually involves conforming to those expectations. Sociology teaches us, therefore, that, if you want to understand people's actions, you must consider the larger social context in which they occur.

Understanding the importance of social relations lies at the heart of thinking sociologically. Sociologists often try to look at the "big picture" to see the interplay between parts of social systems. In considering the mass media, we will emphasize three types of social relations:

- Relationships *between institutions*—for example, the interactions between the media industry and the government

- Relationships *within an institution,* which involve the interaction of individuals occupying their institutional roles and positions—for example, the relationship between a screenwriter and the head of a motion picture studio

- Relationships *between institutions and individuals,* who are always part of larger social groups—for example, the use of media products by audiences or readers

Seeing the operation of social relations on different levels is also important to recognizing some of the different roles the media play in our society. One reason why the media are often controversial is that different groups expect the media to play different—and often incompatible—roles. For audiences, the media can serve as entertainment and diversion and as sources of information about the world beyond direct experience. For media workers, the media industry offers jobs, with resulting income, prestige, and satisfaction, as well as a place for the development of a professional identity. For media owners, the media are a source of profit and, perhaps, a source of political power. For society at large, the media can be a way to transmit information and values (socialization) and can serve as a check on the abuse of political and economic power. Many of the debates about the media relate to the relative prominence of each of these divergent roles.

Structural Constraint and Human Agency

Sociologists often link discussions of social relations to the concepts of structure and agency. In this context, structure suggests constraint on human action, and agency indicates independent action. Each social relationship noted above is characterized by a tension between structure and agency. Because the tension between social structure and human agency is at the heart of this book, these ideas deserve closer attention.

Structure

Structure is not something physical. In the broadest sense, social structure describes any recurring pattern of social behavior. For example, we can talk about *family structure* as a pattern of behaviors associated with the culturally defined idea of *family.* The "traditional family" is actually a quite recent, historically specific phenomenon (Coontz 1992). However, during the post–World War II years in Western countries, the "traditional family" usually meant married, heterosexual couples with children. In such relationships, the expected role of the wife was to work at home raising children, especially in white, middle-class families. The expected role of the husband was to work for a paycheck to cover the household bills.

When sociologists speak of the change in family structure, they are referring to the changes in the pattern of expected family behavior. Traditional expectations that a family include two parents, that the parents be married, that they be heterosexual, that a woman work only in the home, and so forth, have changed dramatically. Single-parent families, blended families, two-income families, unmarried couples, and gay or lesbian couples, to name a few, have supplemented the "traditional" family. The family structure—the pattern of behavior associated with families—has changed.

It's easy to see from today's perspective that the traditional family structure was an attractive one for some people. It enabled them to fit neatly into clearly defined roles that brought them significant rewards. Husbands and children were nurtured and cared for. Wives were spared the pressure of holding down a job outside the home, while often enjoying autonomy in the home. However, it is also easy to see that such a structure limited the options of many people. It constrained their behavior by encouraging or coercing them to conform to the accepted standards of family-related behavior. For example, husbands were denied the experience of participating significantly in raising children, while wives were denied the opportunity to use their skills outside the home in paid employment.

A more immediate example of social structure is the complex pattern of institutions that make up the educational system in the United States, within which students, teachers, and administrators fulfill their expected roles. This structure can be enabling to students who successfully navigate through the system and eventually receive diplomas. Schooling often helps these students achieve a better life. However, as all students know, the educational structure can also be very constraining. Required courses, assignments, deadlines, and grades are all part of a structure that limits the actions of students and teachers. It is this constraint feature that is most important when considering structure.

Agency

When sociologists discuss structure, they often pair it with agency. Agency is intentional and undetermined human action. In the education example, the structure of education constrains students, but students also have a great deal of leeway in what they study, how much time and energy they spend on schoolwork, and so forth. Indeed, some students reject the educational structure entirely and drop out. Students in fact have the capacity for independent action in schools—they have agency. However, the regulations and norms of the educational system—the *structural constraint*—limit that agency.

It is important to note that human agency reproduces social structure. The education system or the traditional family structure continues only as long as new generations of people accept the roles they are asked to fill. Daily activities within the family and school help to reproduce social structures, and they can also be a source for changing them. As long as most women saw themselves primarily as mothers and housewives and men accepted the role of primary wage earners, the traditional family structure was able to continue. However, when enough women began to demand the right to choose from a wider set of possible roles, including having a career outside the home, family structure began to change. Thus, while structure constrains agency, it is human agency that both maintains and alters social structures.

Structure and Agency in the Media

With respect to the media, the tension between structure and agency is present on at least three levels, which correspond to the three types of social relations discussed earlier. We can express these three levels of analysis as three pairs of questions about structural constraint and agency.

- *Relationships between institutions.* How do nonmedia social structures, such as government and the economy, affect the media industry? How does the media industry influence nonmedia social structures?

- *Relationships within an institution.* How does the structure of the media industry affect media personnel (and indirectly media products)? How much do media personnel influence the media products (and indirectly the media industry)?

- *Relationships between an institution and the public.* How do the mass media influence the readers (audiences) of media messages? How do readers interpret media messages and make use of media?

These basic social relations underlie our discussion throughout this book.

Relationships Between the Media and Other Social Institutions

First, our broadest level of analysis is the tension between structure and agency produced by different institutions. We cannot adequately understand the media industry without considering the social, economic, and political context in which it exists. Institutions outside the control of media personnel set certain legal and economic limits within which the media must operate. In turn, media have agency in the sense of acting on their own and perhaps influencing other social institutions. A totalitarian regime, for example, is likely to exert extreme constraint on the press in that society. There would be little room for agency by the mainstream media, although underground media may emerge to challenge the status quo. Labeling a society democratic, on the other hand, includes the suggestion that, at least in theory, the media are free of severe constraint by the government and thus have significant agency. Indeed, media in democratic societies can themselves exert a constraining influence over other institutions.

In the real world, there is always a mixture of structural constraint and independent agency. Media researchers, therefore, examine both how social structures external to the media affect the industry and how the media affect other social structures. This level of analysis includes questions such as the following: Does advertising revenue influence the content of popular magazines? Should music lyrics be rated as movies are? How have media affected the organization of political campaigns? Does it matter who owns major publishing houses or newspapers? How do search engine results affect how people use the Internet?

Relationships Within the Media Industry

Second, to understand the decisions made by journalists, writers, producers, filmmakers, media executives, and other media personnel, we must understand the context in which they labor. This means that we must be familiar with both the internal workings of mass media organizations and the processes of professional socialization. The sociological emphasis here is on social positions, roles, and practices, not on particular individuals. Relevant issues of concern include the structures of media institutions, who wields power within them, what professional norms and expectations are associated with different positions, and so forth.

Within the media industry, the tension between structure and agency is related primarily to how much autonomy media personnel have in doing their work. The amount of autonomy will vary depending on the position an individual occupies. The questions raised include the following: To what extent do standard journalistic practices shape the process of news reporting or the content of the news? How much do economic considerations enter into the decision-making process of Hollywood moviemaking? How "free" are musicians to create their music? How have independent bloggers influenced the norms and routines of commercial news media? In the language of sociology, structural considerations may significantly affect the individual agency of media personnel. At the same time, the collective agency of those who work in the media has the potential to alter the structures that constrain individual media professionals.

Relationships Between the Media and the Public

A third kind of social relationship occurs when the media deliver messages to readers. Here, the issues of interest involve how readers interact with media products and media technology. Readers are not passive sponges that soak up the many messages they come across in the media. This would imply a one-way relationship with the media determining the thoughts and behavior of listeners and viewers. Instead, readers of media products must actively interpret media messages. Increasingly, media users also have the opportunity to create their own content, manipulate existing content, and otherwise interact through various media platforms.

When we interpret the words of someone speaking with us face-to-face, we have an excellent resource at hand: the speaker. We interactively construct the conversation. We can elicit more information from the speaker by asking a question ("What do you mean?") or by using appropriate facial expressions to convey our reactions. We can comment on statements and thereby affect the course of the conversation. Such interaction between speakers helps promote mutual understanding about the messages being communicated.

Mass media messages, however, do not allow for the intimate interaction of sender and receiver that characterizes personal communication. We cannot ask a stand-up comedian on television to explain a joke. We either get it or we don't. If a television reporter mentions the National Labor Relations Board and we do not know what she is referring to, we cannot ask for a clarification. Audiences, therefore, must rely on other resources to make sense of media messages.

Relevant resources available to audiences might include knowledge and information gained from personal experience, other people, formal education, or other media products. These resources are neither randomly nor equally distributed. The interpretive skills that people bring with them to their viewing, listening, and reading are shaped by aspects of social structure, such as class and education. Thus, in constructing their own individual interpretations of the media, people constantly draw on collective resources and experiences that are shaped by social factors. Although media messages are impersonal and subject to multiple interpretations by audiences, the construction of meaning does not take place in individualized isolation.

Active audience interpretation is important, but we must also realize that the thousands of hours people spend with the media do have some influence on them. Readers are not completely immune to the impact of media content and media technology. The structure and agency framework suggests that we have to explore the dynamic tension between the power of social structure and the (always partial) autonomy of human activity. How powerful are media images in shaping how we think and feel? Do they affect how people are likely to behave? For example, does violent television programming encourage children to be more aggressive? What are the differences in the ways different people respond to these images? How does media technology affect our social relationships? Who is making use of new participatory and collaborative forms of media, and how are they using these new capabilities? Ultimately, these are complex questions that do not lend themselves to easy answers involving all-encompassing media power or complete individual freedom. The relationship between structure and agency helps illuminate the various levels at which mass media images, whose meanings are neither fixed nor arbitrary, influence but do not determine our understanding of the world.

A MODEL OF MEDIA AND THE SOCIAL WORLD

How can we begin to make sense of the complex relationships we have identified? Figure 1.5 provides a graphic representation of these relations. The model illustrates the fundamentals of a sociological perspective on the media. As noted above, we cannot understand the media without looking at them as one aspect of a larger social world. Our model represents this by showing that all components of the media, as well as the audience, exist within the broader framework of the social world (the shaded area).

Four components, each represented by a separate box in the diagram, make up the core of our model. We must understand that all four elements are simultaneously a part of the social world and surrounded by the social world. We must also remember that the graphic organization of these four elements is arbitrary. There is no "top" or "bottom" to the process; rather, it is a circular, multidimensional process. Arrowheads represent the potential relationships between these components. (Not all relationships will be relevant in all situations.) We will first describe the elements represented by the four large boxes (proceeding clockwise from the bottom) and then turn our attention to the unique status of the *social world* (represented by the shading), which is both in the center of the model and simultaneously surrounding it.

The box at the bottom of the model represents the *media industry,* by which we mean the entire organizational structure that makes up the media, including all media personnel. The media industry is affected by changes in *technology* (e.g., the invention of television) but is also instrumental in influencing the direction and application of technology (e.g., the use of computers for film animation).

The media industry is the producer of the *media message* or *product.* For example, a book is written by an author, designed, typeset, printed (or formatted as an e-book),

Figure 1.5   Simplified Model of Media and the Social World

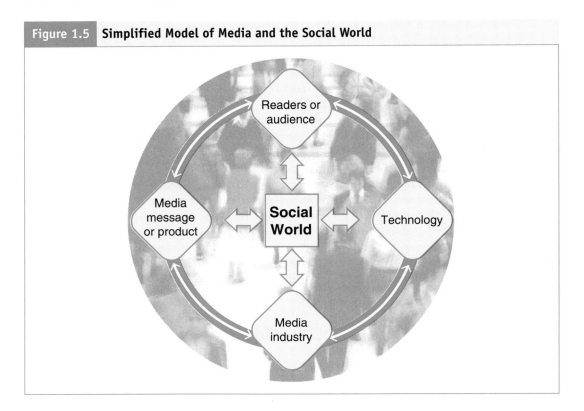

distributed by a publisher, and sold, either physically or electronically. However, the conventions of particular genres of media products also influence the creators of the products. The murder mystery genre, for example, requires the existence of a crime.

Readers or *audiences* may be influenced by the media messages they see (e.g., learning about an impending snowstorm from the weather report), but they must actively interpret and construct meaning from those messages and products (e.g., deciding whether to trust the forecast and whether to act differently as a result).

The direction and development of technology is affected by how the *readers* or *audiences* choose to use it—or not to use it. The technology for video phones has long existed but consumers have been largely resistant, perhaps for privacy reasons. In turn, technology has a potential impact on the public. For example, movie viewing usually requires close attention because the medium communicates via both sound and images. This contrasts with radio. The technology of radio makes it a very mobile medium that does not demand our full attention. Unlike movies, which we must watch in order to fully follow, radio allows us to do other things while still attending to it, such as drive a car, jog, cook dinner, or work. Books demand more attention than television. We can carry on a conversation while watching TV, but is far more difficult to read a book and carry on a conversation at the same time. Each medium, therefore, tends to produce a different experience for the readers. This is one effect of technology.

The middle, and broader context, of the model is the *social world*. We theorize this to be all the social elements not included in the four main boxes. Some of these elements are crucial for an understanding of the workings of the media and thus can be thought of as being at the center of the model. For example, in this book, we will examine the role of government and broader economic forces; these are nonmedia social factors that influence all the elements of our model.

Notice that the top and bottom elements of our model include human agents—real people—while the left and right boxes are human creations. People are the medium through which media messages and technology affect each other. Similarly, the relationship between the media industry and most members of the audience is mediated by media products, technology, and other factors in the social world. The audience has always had the capacity to respond to the media industry, for example, by writing a letter to a television network. But the change in one media element—technology—has enabled much more robust and easy-to-use feedback mechanisms whereby users can personalize media choices (therefore providing detailed feedback about likes and dislikes), leave comments and feedback instantly (with text messages, website comments, tagging, and the like), and create their own media content (via wikis, blogs, discussion forums, and other platforms).

Note, too, that any single component of the model simultaneously relates to other components. For example, the reader of a media message simultaneously experiences the impact of technology (the medium) and other social forces (including things such as race, class, and gender). Thus, readers do not interpret media messages in isolation. Similarly, media products are simultaneously influenced by the media industry that creates them, the readers who interpret them (or choose to ignore them), and other aspects of the social world, such as government regulation.

Our simplified model is meant to identify some of the key components in a sociology of media and to clarify some of the relationships among these components. Like all models, it cannot fully account for the infinite complexities of the "real" social world. However, using the model to analyze the media can help us clarify the workings and social significance of mass media.

APPLYING THE MODEL: THE CIVIL RIGHTS MOVEMENT

To illustrate briefly how the model can alert us to important real-life issues, let us consider the modern U.S. civil rights struggles of the 1950s and 1960s (Branch 1988; McAdam 1982; Morris 1984). We can think of this social movement as a part of the nonmedia social world insofar as it exists independent of our four components of the media model. For the moment, then, imagine the civil rights movement as being the element of the social world that occupies the center position in our model.

Using this premise, and moving clockwise around our model, we see that the media industry created media messages about the civil rights movement, while the genre norms of "news" coverage influenced the media personnel reporting the news. Reporters wrote stories about the movement, but because these stories constituted "news," they were supposed to be a balanced presentation of facts.

The media messages about the civil rights movement affected the viewing and reading audiences, who, in turn, were interpreting the meaning of those messages. Readers are influenced by the words and images about race-related issues that appear in a wide variety of media products, including news reports, television sitcoms, Hollywood movies, music, best-selling books, and popular magazines. In our case, some supporters in the North, for example, were moved by media accounts to make financial contributions to movement organizations in the South, while others sympathized with the forces of segregation. The media messages were having an impact, but the readers could interpret the meaning and significance of the messages.

Audiences made use of technology, especially the newly emerging television technology in the 1950s and 1960s, to access media messages. Meanwhile, technology may have indirectly influenced readers, in this case with the immediacy and impact of television pictures of police violence against demonstrators. Technology was also affecting the media industry; lighter handheld cameras allowed reporters more mobility. The industry, in turn, influenced the use of the new technology by applying it to the coverage of demonstrations.

Now, let us move to the center of the model. The civil rights movement has clearly had an impact on the media industry (and other social institutions) that, like all major industries, has changed its hiring and promotion practices to comply both with cultural changes and with laws against discrimination. The limited racial diversity that exists today in the media industry would not have come about without the influence of this social movement and the resulting changes in legislation and social norms. This is one example of how the social world influences the media industry.

However, the media industry also had an impact on the civil rights movement. Because social movements are aware of the potential effect the media may have on society at large, they have often crafted strategies that try to take advantage of potential media coverage (Ryan 1991). (They have also created their own media—from the underground press of the 1960s to the Indy Media Centers of recent years—as an alternative to corporate media.) In modern society, social movement strategies, such as marches and demonstrations, are important as much for the media coverage they generate as for the actual events themselves. Many social movements, therefore, have become media conscious in their efforts. Thus, the impact of the media industry—in the form of its personnel and its organizational routines—on such movements is evident even before the media produce any coverage of the group.

Media messages affected the civil rights movement as it tried to develop favorable media coverage and, in some cases, altered strategies that generated negative coverage. The movement did not affect media messages directly but instead did so indirectly by influencing the media industry. Thus, changes in the social world can filter through the media industry and affect media products. An industry that employs more people of color in positions of power, for example, is more likely to be sensitive to race issues in its media products.

The civil rights movement has had a direct impact on citizens who are also "readers" of media products. The presence of this movement has meant more social equality and direct material and psychological benefits for many people. At the same time, citizens have acted as social agents creating the social movement in the first place, illustrating the interaction between these two components of the model.

The technology of the 1950s that the civil rights movement relied on to communicate its messages may seem ancient by today's standards, but it was an integral part of the

Source: Sean Gallup/Getty Images.

In part because they do not have regular access to the mainstream media, many social movements must adopt tactics that will attract attention and increase their chances of gaining media exposure. A common strategy is the public demonstration, featuring eye-catching signs. Here, journalists take pictures while protestors in Berlin, Germany, demonstrate at the Chinese Embassy against press restrictions used during the 2008 Olympics in Beijing. Their banner transforms the well-known Olympic rings into handcuffs. Similar protest images were created for the 2014 Sochi Olympics.

ongoing organizing effort. Movement organizers influenced the application of the existing technology by using it for their own ends. For example, if a leaflet announcing a meeting needed to be distributed, stencils might be cut for hand-cranked mimeograph machines. Alternative newspapers were a source of movement information. Computer desktop publishing, laser printers, high-speed copiers, websites, e-mail lists, and tweets would have seemed like science fiction at the time.

Perhaps more important is the indirect manner in which technology—through the media industry—affected the movement. In the 1950s, a new generation of cameras allowed news teams to readily cover social movement events, sometimes producing dramatic images of the clashes between civil rights marchers and police. By the 1990s, this shift toward smaller cameras meant ordinary citizens could film events and pass the video along to the mainstream media for wider distribution. Video of the brutal beating of Rodney King by Los Angeles police was one example. The incongruity between these stark images and the initial acquittal of the police officers involved played an important role in the 1992 Los Angeles riot. Today, such a video could be posted online, bypassing the news media entirely.

This brief sketch of the civil rights movement illustrates the utility of a sociological approach to understanding how media interact with the social world. This interaction is always multidimensional, and each element of our model will receive closer attention in later chapters.

CONCLUSION

It is difficult to overestimate the importance of media in today's society. From the privacy of our living rooms to the public forums of presidential debates, the media serve as the informational network connecting the many elements of our society. There is no doubt that the media are significant and worth studying. A sociological approach to the media allows us to identify the key questions and reminds us to keep the "big picture" in mind when we discuss media issues.

The remainder of this book is organized into sections on media production, content, and audiences, with a concluding chapter on the future of the media in a global culture. The model of media and the social world presented in this chapter is the underlying framework for the rest of the book. At the most general level, this sociological framework helps us identify questions we should ask when we study the media. In this case, these questions concern the multidirectional relations between components of our model: the social world, the media industry, media products, audiences, and technology. Examining the relationships among these key elements is the first step toward developing a nuanced understanding of the role of mass media in our society.

DISCUSSION QUESTIONS

1. How does the influence of mass media extend beyond *what* we know to include *how* we relate to the social world?

2. How does the presence of media affect your life? How would it be different without the mass media?

3. What do you think is the most significant media development in your lifetime? Why?

4. What is meant by the terms *structure* and *agency*? What is a media-related example that shows how the two concepts are connected to each other?

Production

The Media Industry and the Social World

We begin our examination of the mass media by looking at the source of most media products: the media industry. In particular, Part II explores the social forces that influence the media industry, first highlighting relationships between institutions. In Chapter 2, we look at the economic forces that shape the industry and the consequences for media content. Chapter 3 turns to the political constraints on the media industry, exploring various debates about government regulation of mass media.

We also examine how the organization of the media industry helps shape media products. Here the concern is with relationships within the media industry. Chapter 4 analyzes the professional routines and organizational norms at work in various sectors of the media.

The emphasis in Part II is on the broad structural constraints on media production; how these economic, political, and organizational forces shape decision making and influence media content; and how actors within the media industry interpret and respond to these constraints. This "production perspective" has been the principal lens through which much contemporary sociology has looked at mass media. As we will see, it has a great deal to offer for understanding processes of decision making within the media industries.

However, as a production-oriented perspective tells us little about things such as how people use or interpret media products, it is important to remember that it is only part of our larger model of media and the social world. Issues of media content, the role of active audiences, and media influence will be addressed in Parts III and IV. Production, though, is an important piece of this larger media puzzle and a useful place to begin our exploration of the complex relationship between media and society.

BOX OFFICE

CHAPTER 2

The Economics of the Media Industry

Source: Peter Parks/Getty Images.

This chapter explores the economics of mass media and its impact on media content, focusing on media ownership, the for-profit orientation of most media, and the role of advertising. A great deal of the media content we consume is produced by media companies and most of the media in the United States and other Western democracies are for-profit businesses. Like all businesses, they are influenced by issues such as profitability, cost containment, and evolving ownership patterns. To understand the media, then, we must have some sense of the economic dimension of the media industry. (For a more in-depth treatment of the economic dynamics that shape the media industry, see Croteau and Hoynes 2006; for a focus on the global dimension of media, see Flew 2007.)

The types of questions we ask and the general orientation of this chapter build on the framework outlined in Chapter 1. We emphasize a sociological perspective that argues that social structures shape—and are in turn shaped by—human behavior. An emphasis on this tension between agency and structural constraint suggests that human activities and attitudes must be understood in relation to broader social forces. In this case, we cannot understand the media industry without understanding the forces that affect the industry. The individuals and groups that create the television we watch, the music we listen to, the websites we visit, the magazines we read, or the movies we attend are not fully autonomous actors. They do not work in isolation from the social world. Instead, they work within the constraints of an existing organization, a broader media industry, and a larger social context.

A sociological perspective suggests that we cannot look at media products in a vacuum, either. Instead, we should see media products as the result of a social process of production that occurs within an institutional framework. Some researchers call this kind of institutional approach a "production perspective" (Crane 1992; Peterson and Anand 2004) because it emphasizes the media production process rather than either specific media products or the consumption of those products. The production perspective highlights the fact most media products are the result of a complex production process shaped by a variety of social structural forces that operate on various levels, some affecting the industry as a whole, some affecting particular actors or groups of actors within the industry. Producers create media products under conditions that are always changing as economic, technological, political, and social changes occur in the broader society. Therefore, if we are to better understand media products, we must take into account the historically specific context in which people create them.

Within the explicitly sociological literature, researchers have applied the production perspective most widely to the news media. Therefore, much of this chapter explores the production of news. We also examine several non-news media examples, exploring production processes within the music industry, the film and television sector, the software industry, and new media technologies.

CHANGING PATTERNS OF OWNERSHIP

Who owns the media? This is a central question about the economic organization of media. The assumption behind the question is that owners of the media influence the content and form of media products by their decisions to hire and fire certain personnel, to fund certain projects, to give media platforms to certain speakers, and to develop or support certain technologies. In its least subtle version, such questions might imply a kind of conspiracy theory, in which a small group of powerful owners uses the media to control the thoughts of the rest of us. With its Orwellian connotations of mind control, this extreme version of the ownership question is far too simplistic and therefore not particularly illuminating. However, a substantial body of research has explored this topic in a more helpful way.

Concentration of Ownership

One of the clearest trends in media ownership is its increasing concentration in fewer hands. In his classic book, *The New Media Monopoly,* Ben Bagdikian (2004) argued that ownership of media had become so concentrated that by the mid-2000s only five global firms dominated the media industry in the United States, operating like a cartel. Bagdikian identified the five dominant companies as Time Warner, The Walt Disney Company, Viacom, News Corporation, and Bertelsmann, all multimedia entertainment conglomerates that produce and distribute newspapers, magazines, radio, television, books, and movies. According to Bagdikian, "This gives each of the five corporations and their leaders more

Most of the media products that we see, hear, and read are owned by just a handful of major media corporations.

communication power than was exercised by any despot or dictatorship in history" (Bagdikian 2004: 3).

In the years since the publication of *The New Media Monopoly*, the media landscape has changed considerably. For example, in 2006 Viacom split into the CBS Corporation and Viacom, Inc. But even in the face of such change, media ownership remains highly concentrated in the 2010s. Within each sector of the media industry, a few large companies tower above their smaller competitors. For example:

Movies. The global motion picture industry is dominated by six companies—Comcast's Universal Pictures, Viacom's Paramount Pictures, Time Warner's Warner Bros., Walt Disney Studios, the News Corporation's 20th Century Fox, and SonyPictures Entertainment. In 2012, Sony led the way with worldwide box office revenues of $4.4 billion, with less than half of its ticket sale revenue ($1.77 billion) in North America. Its top film, the James Bond movie *Skyfall,* made more than $1 billion at the global box office. Time Warner was a close second at the global box office, with $4.25 billion in 2012 ticket sales. The remaining four major motion picture companies each brought in more than $2 billion in global ticket sales in 2012: Fox ($3.7 billion), Disney ($3.6 billion), Universal ($3.13 billion), and Paramount ($2.4 billion) (McClintock 2013). In addition, some of the leading "independent" film companies are owned by the industry giants—Focus Features (Comcast), Fox Searchlight (News Corporation), Sony Pictures Classics (Sony/Columbia), Paramount Vantage (Paramount), and New Line (Time Warner).

Television. Unlike other media sectors, broadcast television has become somewhat less concentrated since the 1990s when FOX joined ABC, CBS, and NBC to expand the number of major broadcast networks to four. In 2006, Warner Bros. and CBS partnered to launch a

5th broadcast network, the CW Network, after the two partners shut down their separate fledgling networks WB and UPN. While cable television has offered the most new programming, the major cable television channels are often owned by the same companies that own the broadcast networks. For example, Time Warner (co-owner of the CW Network) owns CNN, HBO, TBS, TNT, Cartoon Network, truTV, Turner Classic Movies, and Cinemax. The News Corporation (owner of Fox) also owns FOX News, FOX Business, FX, SPEED, FUEL TV, Fox Movie Channel, Fox Soccer Channel, and National Geographic. Disney (owner of ABC) owns ESPN, Disney Channels Worldwide, ABC Family, and SOAPnet Networks; and Disney is also part-owner of several other major cable channels, including A&E, Lifetime Television, the History Channel, and the Biography Channel.

The major players in the television industry are leaders in other media sectors as well. Comcast, owner of NBCUniversal, is the nation's largest cable television company and the nation's largest Internet service provider, as well as one of the major players in television production and distribution. In addition, the broadcast television networks and the major movie studios typically share owners. Four of the five broadcast networks are owned by media conglomerates with major film studios: ABC (Disney), NBC (Universal), Fox (Twentieth Century Fox), and CW (Warner Brothers). And these major movie studios are the leading producers of prime-time programming for network television, accounting for about 90 percent of the series on the major networks (Kunz 2009). This kind of ownership structure makes it very difficult for independent producers to consistently get their programs on broadcast television.

Book Publishing. The global English-language book market is dominated by the "Big Five" publishers—Penguin Random House, HarperCollins (owned by News Corporation), Simon & Schuster (owned by CBS Corporation), Hachette Book Group, and Macmillan. Some analysts believe that additional consolidation of the book industry is on the horizon (Pfanner and Chozick 2012).

U.S. Magazines. Time Inc. (property of Time Warner, which operates, among others, the premium cable television network HBO, Warner Brothers, and CNN) towers above its competitors. Its 21 U.S. publications in print, online, and via mobile devices reach more than 138 million people (nearly half the U.S. adult population) and control a 21.5 percent share of domestic magazine advertising spending (Time Inc. 2013).

Recorded Music. Only three companies are responsible for the vast majority of U.S. music sales. Universal Music Group, Sony Music Entertainment, and Warner Music Group accounted for more than 87 percent of total U.S. music sales in 2012 (Christman 2013). (Universal purchased the number four music company, EMI, in late 2012, but European antitrust regulations required Universal to sell some of EMI's labels. In early 2013, Universal sold Parlophone—the label with rights to albums by a variety of popular artists, such as Coldplay, Radiohead, and Pink Floyd—to Warner Music Group.) Each of the big three controls a number of smaller labels and local subsidiaries.

Radio. Clear Channel, with more than 850 radio stations in 2012, is the dominant player in the U.S. radio industry. Clear Channel's radio stations and online and mobile applications reach 237 million listeners in the United States each month (Clear Channel 2013).

Live Music. A single company, Live Nation Concerts, dominates the live music scene, producing more than 22,000 shows each year for 2,300 artists. Live Nation Entertainment is the largest global live entertainment group. It includes the largest events ticketing company, Ticketmaster.com, with $6.9 billion in sales in 2011, and the world's leading artists management company, Front Line Management Group, which manages many well-known artists, including Aerosmith, John Mayer, and Miley Cyrus (Live Nation Entertainment 2013).

The major media companies own vast portfolios of products, spanning the range of media formats and delivery systems. Indeed, the media giants own such a dizzying array of entertainment and news media that the scale of their operations may surprise many readers. Because most products carry a distinct name, rather than the label of the corporate owner, most media users are unaware that a large number of media outlets are actually owned by a single corporation. In the world of newspapers, for example, chains such as Gannett and MediaNews own newspapers all over the country (see Table 2.1 and Figure 2.1). In 2013, Gannett owned more than 80 daily newspapers, including *USA Today,* the best-selling newspaper in the United States, alongside hundreds of websites and 23 television stations in the United States (Gannett 2013). MediaNews Group, the second largest newspaper publisher in the country, owns more than 60 newspapers, including the *Denver Post,* the *Detroit News,* and the *San Jose Mercury News* along with 450 websites and more than 200 specialty magazines (MediaNews Group 2013). At the newspaper chains, each paper has a different name, and it is not always apparent to readers that a paper is part of a national chain. Similarly, in book publishing, the major companies have so many different imprints that even a conscientious reader is unlikely to know the common owners of the different imprints. For example, Bertelsmann's Penguin Random House, far and away the largest English language book publisher in the world, owns more than 75 publishing imprints (see Figure 2.2).

Table 2.1	Leading U.S. Newspaper Companies, by Daily Circulation, 2011		
Newspaper Company	*Number of Newspapers*	*Total Circulation in Millions*	*Largest Circulation Daily*
Gannet	80	4.9	*USA Today*: 1,784,240
MediaNews Group	63	3.1	*San Jose Mercury News*: 575,786
News Corporation	2	2.6	*The Wall Street Journal*: 2,106,780
McClatchy Company	30	2.1	*Miami Herald*: 217,887
Advance Publications	19	1.5	*Plain Dealer*: 243,299
Lee Enterprises	52	1.3	*St. Louis Post Dispatch*: 191,631
New York Times Company	4	1.3	*New York Times*: 1,033,750
Hearst Corporation	17	1.2	*Houston Chronicle*: 369,710
Tribune Company	9	1.2	*Los Angeles Times*: 572,998
Berkshire Hathaway	27	0.9	*World Herald*: 135,282

Source: Pew Research Center 2012b, *State of the News Media: 2012.*

Figure 2.1	Daily Newspapers Owned by Gannett, 2013

National: *USA Today*

Alabama: *The Montgomery Gazette*

Arizona: *The Arizona Republic*

Arkansas: *The Baxter Bulletin* (Mountain Home)

California: *The Desert Sun* (Palm Springs), *The Salinas Californian, Tulare Advance-Register, Visalia Times-Delta*

Colorado: *The Fort Collins Coloradoan*

Delaware: *The News Journal* (Wilmington)

Florida: *Florida Today* (Brevard County), *The News-Press* (Fort Myers), *Pensacola News Journal, Tallahassee Democrat*

Indiana: *The Indianapolis Star, Journal and Courier* (Lafayette), *The Star Press* (Muncie), *Palladium-Item* (Richmond)

Iowa: *The Des Moines Register, Iowa City Press-Citizen*

Kentucky: *The Courier-Journal* (Louisville), *The Kentucky Enquirer* (Fort Mitchell)

Louisiana: *The Town Talk* (Alexandria), *The Daily Advertiser* (Lafayette), *The News-Star* (Monroe), *Daily World* (Opelousas), *The Times* (Shreveport)

Maryland: *The Daily Times* (Salisbury)

Michigan: *Battle Creek Enquirer, Detroit Free Press, Lansing State Journal, Daily Press & Argus* (Livingston County), *Times Herald* (Port Huron)

Minnesota: *St. Cloud Times*

Mississippi: *Hattiesburg American, The Clarion-Ledger* (Jackson)

Missouri: *Springfield News-Leader*

Montana: *Great Falls Tribune*

Nevada: *Reno Gazette-Journal*

New Jersey: *Asbury Park Press, Courier News* (Somerville), *Courier-Post* (Cherry Hill), *Home News Tribune* (East Brunswick), *Daily Record* (Parsippany), *The Daily Journal* (Vineland)

New York: *Press & Sun-Bulletin* (Binghamton), *Star-Gazette* (Elmira), *The Ithaca Journal, Poughkeepsie Journal, Rochester Democrat and Chronicle, The Journal News* (Westchester County)

North Carolina: *Asheville Citizen-Times*

Ohio: *Telegraph-Forum* (Bucyrus), *Chillicothe Gazette, The Cincinnati Enquirer, Coshocton Tribune, The News-Messenger* (Fremont), *Lancaster Eagle-Gazette, News Journal* (Mansfield), *The Marion Star, The Advocate* (Newark), *News Herald* (Port Clinton), *Times Recorder* (Zanesville)

Oregon: *Statesman Journal* (Salem)

South Carolina: *The Greenville News*

(Continued)

Figure 2.1	(Continued)

South Dakota: *Argus Leader* (Sioux Falls)

Tennessee: *The Leaf-Chronicle* (Clarksville), *The Jackson Sun*, *The Daily News Journal* (Murfreesboro), *The Tennessean* (Nashville)

Utah: *The Spectrum* (St. George)

Vermont: *The Burlington Free Press*

Virginia: *The Daily News Leader* (Staunton)

Wisconsin: *The Post-Crescent* (Appleton), *The Reporter* (Fond du Lac), *Green Bay Press-Gazette*, *Herald Times-Reporter* (Manitowoc), *Marshfield News-Herald*, *Oshkosh Northwestern*, *The Sheboygan Press*, *Stevens Point Journal*, *Wausau Daily Herald*, *The Daily Tribune* (Wisconsin Rapids)

Source: www.gannett.com/section/WHOWEARE06.

Figure 2.2	Book Imprints Owned by Penguin Random House, 2013

Penguin Publishers—USA

Ace Books
Alpha Books
Amy Einhorn Books/Putnam
Avery
Berkley Books
Blue Rider Press
C.A. Press
Current
Dial Books for Young Readers
Dutton Books
Dutton Children's Books
Firebird
Frederick Warne
Gotham Books
G.P. Putnam's Sons
G.P. Putnam's Sons Books for Young Readers
Grosset & Dunlap HP Books
Hudson Street Press
Jove
Nancy Paulsen Books

NAL
Pamela Dorman Books
Penguin
The Penguin Press
Perigee Books
Philomel Books
Plume
Portfolio
Prentice Hall Press
Price Stern Sloan
Puffin Books
Razorbill
Riverhead
Sentinel
Speak
Tarcher
The Viking Press
Viking Books for Young Readers

Crown Publishing Group Imprints

Amphoto Books
Back Stage Books

Billboard Books

Broadway Books

Clarkson Potter

Crown

Crown Archetype

Crown Business

Crown Forum

Doubleday Religion

Harmony Books

Image Books

Potter Craft

Potter Style

Ten Speed Press

Three Rivers Press

Waterbrook Multnomah

Watson-Guptill

Knopf Doubleday Publishing Group Imprints

Alfred A. Knopf

Anchor Books

Doubleday

Everyman's Library

Nan A. Talese

Pantheon Books

Schocken Books

Vintage

Random House Publishing Group Imprints

Ballantine Books

Bantam Dell

Delacorte

Del Rey/Lucas Books

Del Rey/Manga

The Dial Press

The Modern Library

One World

Presidio Press

Random House Trade Group

Random House Trade Paperbacks

Spectra

Spiegel & Grau

Triumph Books

Villard Books

Random House Children's Books

Golden Books

Princeton Review

Sylvan Learning

RH Digital Publishing Group

Books on Tape

Fodor's Travel

Listening Library

Living Language

Random House Audio

Random House Large Print

Sources: Company websites.

There has been much debate about the potential effect of ownership concentration on media products. We discuss these debates in some detail later in this chapter. First, though, we take note of two other trends related to media ownership: conglomeration and integration.

Conglomeration and Integration

Concentration of media ownership means that fewer corporations own the media. At the same time that concentration of ownership has been occurring, conglomeration has been taking place. That is, media companies have become part of much larger corporations, which own a collection of other companies that may operate in highly diverse business areas.

Much as in other industries, the largest media companies are growing in size and reach as they purchase or merge with their competitors. In the United States, media outlets are among the most attractive properties to both potential investors and buyers. While some high-profile mergers ultimately fail—including AOL-Time Warner (which split into two companies in 2009) and Viacom-CBS (split in 2006)—the process of conglomeration in the media industry is continuous. For example:

- Google purchased over 125 companies between 2001 and 2013, including YouTube (2006), online advertising company Doubleclick (2007), the Zagat restaurant guide (2011), and GPS navigation firm Waze (2013).

- Yahoo bought about 80 companies, including Internet radio site Broadcast.com (1999), job search engine HotJobs.com (2002), and the blogging site Tumblr (2013).

- In addition to dozens of newspapers, the News Corporation bought 20th Century Fox (1984), the Metromedia group of television stations (1986), MySpace (2005) (later sold), and Dow Jones, owner of *The Wall Street Journal* (2007).

- AOL bought early online service provider Compuserv (1997), the web browser Netscape (1998), the Moviefone data base (1999), Mapquest (1999), the online music store MusicNow (2005), and the news/entertainment site *The Huffington Post* (2011).

- The cable giant Comcast purchased a number of smaller cable companies over the years, including AT&T Broadband (2001). It partnered with Sony to buy MGM and its production studio, United Artists (2005), and NBC Universal—acquiring a controlling stake in 2011 and the remainder in 2013 (see Figure 2.3).

- Walt Disney Company acquired (and later sold) Miramax Films (1983), CapCities/ABC (1995), Marvel Entertainment (2005), Pixar animation studios (2006), and Lucasfilm (2012)—owner of the Star Wars franchise.

Media—in both news and entertainment forms—are a key segment of the American economy and are attractive to growing conglomerates. The media industry produces high visibility, substantial profits, and a major item for export to other countries.

Concentration has affected the relationships among various media organizations within a single conglomerate. Economic analysts have long used the terms *horizontal integration* and *vertical integration* to describe two types of ownership concentration in any industry. In the media industry, vertical integration refers to the process by which one owner acquires all aspects of production and distribution of a single type of media product. For example, a movie company might integrate vertically by acquiring talent agencies to acquire scripts and sign actors, production studios to create films, manufacturing plants to produce DVDs, and various venues to show the movies, such as theater chains, premium cable channels, broadcast television networks, and Internet-based streaming services. The company could then better control the entire process of creating, producing, marketing,

Figure 2.3	Anatomy of a Media Conglomerate: Comcast Corporate Holdings
Cable Television	• Largest video provider in the United States, through Comcast Cable—more than 22 million subscribers
Internet Service	• Largest residential Internet service provider in the United States—19.4 million customers
Phone Service	• 4th largest phone company in the United States—10 million customers
Broadcast Television	• NBC television network • Telemundo, Spanish language network • 10 NBC-owned local television stations • 15 Telemundo-owned local television stations
Cable Television Networks	• USA Network • Syfy • E! • CNBC • MSNBC • Bravo • Golf Channel • Oxygen • NBC Sports Network • Style • MLB Network (joint venture with Major League Baseball) • NHL Network (joint venture with National Hockey League) • 10 regional sports networks • 3 regional news networks
Film	• Universal Pictures • Focus Features
Internet Sites	• Hulu (online video) • Fandango (movie ticket sales) • Daily Candy (fashion and restaurant news) • Television Without Pity (TV fan site)
Theme Parks	• Universal Studios Florida • Universal Studios Hollywood
Sports and Entertainment	• Philadelphia Flyers, NHL Hockey Team • New Era Tickets ticketing company • Wells Fargo Center sports arena

Source: Comcast Corporate website.

and distributing movies. Similarly, a book publisher might integrate vertically by acquiring paper mills, printing facilities, book binderies, trucking firms, and Internet booksellers (see Figure 2.4).

Horizontal integration refers to the process by which one company buys different kinds of media, concentrating ownership across differing types of media rather than up and down through one industry. In horizontal integration, media conglomerates assemble large portfolios of magazines, television stations, book publishers, record labels, and so on to mutually

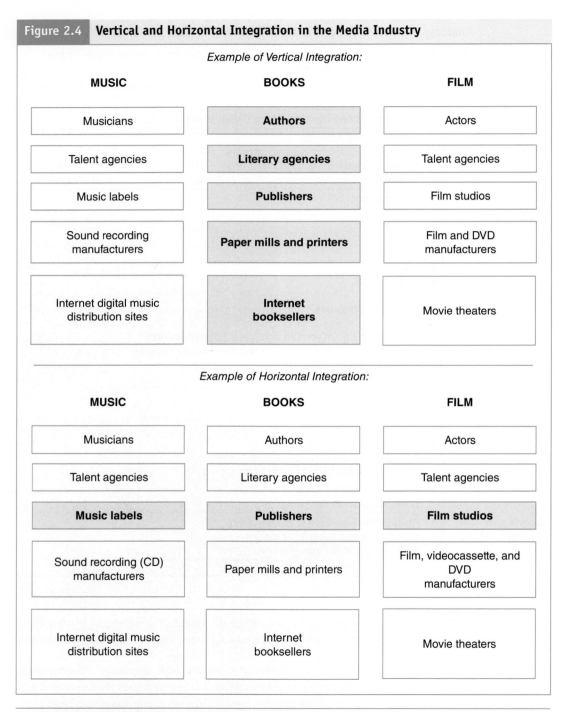

Figure 2.4   Vertical and Horizontal Integration in the Media Industry

Example of Vertical Integration:

MUSIC	BOOKS	FILM
Musicians	**Authors**	Actors
Talent agencies	**Literary agencies**	Talent agencies
Music labels	**Publishers**	Film studios
Sound recording manufacturers	**Paper mills and printers**	Film and DVD manufacturers
Internet digital music distribution sites	**Internet booksellers**	Movie theaters

Example of Horizontal Integration:

MUSIC	BOOKS	FILM
Musicians	Authors	Actors
Talent agencies	Literary agencies	Talent agencies
Music labels	**Publishers**	**Film studios**
Sound recording (CD) manufacturers	Paper mills and printers	Film, videocassette, and DVD manufacturers
Internet digital music distribution sites	Internet booksellers	Movie theaters

Note: Shaded, bold-faced companies are owned by the same corporation.

support one another's operations. In a classic example, when Warner Bros. released the 2001 film *Harry Potter and the Sorcerer's Stone,* its then-parent company AOL Time Warner pursued an elaborate multimedia strategy to cash in on the Harry Potter franchise. AOL's online services provided links to various Harry Potter web pages, including sites for purchasing the Harry Potter merchandise that AOL sold. The company's movie information site, Moviefone, promoted and sold tickets to the film, while company magazines *Time, People,* and *Entertainment Weekly* featured prominent Harry Potter stories. In addition, AOL Time Warner used its cable systems and cable networks for massive promotion of the film, and the company-owned Warner Music Group released the Harry Potter soundtrack. More recent blockbusters such as *The Avengers* (Disney 2012), *The Dark Knight Rises* (Warner Bros. 2012), and *Avatar* (Fox 2009) have employed similar strategies, taking advantage of new promotional channels, such as blogs, smartphone apps, and social networking sites.

In another example, Disney turned its sports cable franchise ESPN into a multimedia cross-promotional vehicle, developing ESPN.com, ESPN Classic, ESPN2, ESPNEWS, ESPN Deportes, ESPNU, the ESPN Radio Network, *ESPN: The Magazine*, an ESPN news service, ESPN3 (a broadband service), and ESPN Mobile, all working together to promote Disney's growing list of ESPN products. Such cross-media promotion can be a very powerful strategy. One experimental study found that a coordinated television and print ad campaign for a television program was far more effective than single-media campaigns; cross-media campaigns "resulted in higher attention from audiences, improved memory, greater perceived message credibility . . . and higher viewing intent compared to using repetitive single-source promotions" (Tang, Newton, and Wang 2007: 132). This kind of opportunity for cross-promotion is one of the driving forces behind the growth of horizontally integrated media companies.

CONSEQUENCES OF CONGLOMERATION AND INTEGRATION

While the trends in media ownership may be of interest in themselves, our prime concern is with the relationship between ownership and the media product. What are the consequences of integration, conglomeration, and concentration of ownership?

Integration and Self-Promotion

The economic factors propelling both vertical and horizontal integration are clear: Owners perceive such arrangements as both efficient and profitable. The cultural consequences are more ambiguous. However, an institutional approach suggests that such ownership patterns are likely to affect the types of media products created. In particular, integrated media conglomerates seeking the benefits of "synergy" are likely to favor products that can best be exploited by other components of the conglomerate. (Synergy refers to the dynamic where components of a company work together to produce benefits that would be impossible for a single, separately operated unit of the company.) For example, horizontal integration may well encourage the publication of books that can be made into movies and discourage the publication of those that cannot. Or it might encourage the creation of TV talent search programs because they can generate new musical acts who are contractually obligated to record for the company's music label, featured in the company's magazines, played on the company's radio stations, and showcased on their websites. More generally, promotion and marketing are likely to dominate the decision-making process within a horizontally integrated media industry.

Vertical integration becomes especially significant when the company that makes the product also controls its distribution. For example, a corporation that owns a mail-order book-of-the-month club is likely to prominently feature its own publications, limiting competitors' access to a lucrative segment of the book-buying market. Or a company with a movie studio can highlight its own films on its movie cable channel.

The possibilities for fully using horizontal and vertical integration are startling. In this era of integrated media conglomerates, media companies are capable of pursuing elaborate cross-media strategies, in which company-owned media products can be packaged, sold, and promoted across the full range of media platforms. Feature films, their accompanying soundtracks and DVD/Blu-ray Disc releases, spin-off television programs, and books, along with magazine cover stories and plenty of licensed merchandise, can all be produced and distributed by different divisions of the same conglomerate—with each piece serving to promote the broader franchise. One consequence of integration, then, is an increase in media cross-promotion and, perhaps, a decrease in media products that are not suitable for cross-promotion. It also makes it more difficult for smaller media firms to compete with the major corporations who can use their vast and diverse holdings to saturate consumers during their promotional campaigns.

The Impact of Conglomeration

What has the growth of large multimedia firms over the past few decades meant for the news, television, radio, films, music, and books we receive? In other words, to what extent does conglomeration affect the media product? The loudest warnings about the impact of conglomeration have come from within the news industry, in part because some news media had traditionally been sheltered from the full pressure of profit making. For example, for much of television history, respectable television news divisions were understood to represent a necessary public service commitment that lent prestige to the major broadcast networks. They were not expected to turn a substantial profit. However, that changed with the takeover of news operations by major corporate conglomerates during the 1980s.

Ken Auletta's *Three Blind Mice* (1991) paints a vivid picture of the clash that ensued during that time, when new corporate owners took over the major television networks and their news divisions. For those who worked at NBC News, for example, the purchase of the network by General Electric led to conflicts about the meaning and role of television news. In most of these conflicts, the new corporate owners ultimately prevailed. As Auletta tells it, when General Electric took over as the new owners of NBC, they

> emphasized a "boundaryless" company, one without walls between News, Entertainment, Sales, and other divisions. . . . At NBC's annual management retreat in 1990, many of the 160 executives questioned why Sales or Entertainment couldn't have more input into news specials, or why News tended to keep its distance from the rest of the company, as if it were somehow special. (p. 564)

General Electric chair Jack Welch even specified that *Today Show* weather reporter Willard Scott should mention GE lightbulbs on the program. According to former NBC news president Lawrence Grossman, "It was one of the perks of owning a network. . . . You get your lightbulbs mentioned on the air. . . . People want to please the owners" (Husseini 1994: 13).

Since that time, the network news programs have faced stiff competition from the 24-hour cable news channels, yet they are expected to turn a profit by attracting audiences that owners expect and advertisers demand. One result has been an increased emphasis on entertainment and celebrities on the network news—what former CBS news anchor Dan Rather called "the Hollywoodization of the news" due to the growth of "stupid celebrity stories" (*Brill's Content* 1998: 117). The changes that were seen as a threat to serious broadcast news in the 1980s and '90s are now the norm in the industry, with the broadcast networks now routinely incorporating entertainment, celebrities, human interest, and other light fare into their broadcasts. Based in a fictional cable news channel, much of the HBO series *The Newsroom* focused on how commercial pressures and celebrity trivia have undermined the quality of television news.

Conglomeration has affected print journalism as well. Some critics have long argued that corporate takeovers of print media put the emphasis on attracting and entertaining consumers rather than on informing citizens (Squires 1993). In this context, newspapers become increasingly colorful, focus attention on the lives of celebrities, and print sensationalistic stories about dramatic and bizarre happenings. One example is NewsCorp's head Rupert Murdoch—now best-known as the owner of FOX—who launched his career by buying up newspapers in Australia and England and converting them into down-market tabloids that specialized in sex, scandal, and celebrities. This was epitomized by his purchase of Britain's *The Sun,* which became notorious—and popular—for its scandalous coverage, even adopting a "Page Three" feature—a daily photo of a topless or nude model (Braid 2004). The 2011 phone-hacking scandal in England, which led to the shutdown of Murdoch's British tabloid *News of the World*, showed how far profit-focused news organizations can go in search of a story. Hundreds, and perhaps thousands, of phones were hacked by reporters at the newspaper, who sought titillating information about crime victims, their families, and celebrities. In the report on the scandal commissioned by the British government, Lord Justice Leveson concluded that "there has been a recklessness in prioritising sensational stories, almost irrespective of the harm that the stories may cause and the rights of those who would be affected (perhaps in a way that can never be remedied), all the while heedless of the public interest" (The Leveson Inquiry 2012: 10).

In addition, for today's multiplatform media companies, news becomes "content" that is increasingly expected to fit with and be usable by the other divisions of the company. As the editor of the *Chicago Tribune,* a daily newspaper that is owned by the media conglomerate the Tribune Company, admitted, "I am not the editor of a newspaper. I am the manager of a content company" (quoted in Auletta 1998: 22). Another sign of the change is the training required for top-level editorial positions at newspapers. With marketing as the focus of many local papers, MBAs with background in the business world have often replaced people with journalistic experience in executive positions (Underwood 1993). Conglomeration, therefore, has led to increased bottom-line pressure, even in areas of the media that used to be partially insulated from such pressure.

THE EFFECTS OF CONCENTRATION

As with integration and conglomeration, a key concern with the concentration of media ownership has been its impact on the media product—especially the potential homogenization of media products. A broader concern, however, to which we first turn, is the growing concentration of power and the limitation of media access.

Media Control and Political Power

Can concentrated media ownership be translated into undue political influence? Most people recognize the importance of such a question in examining the government's control of media in totalitarian nations. It is clear in such situations that state ownership and exclusive access are likely to affect media products. In the United States, most discussion about the First Amendment and free speech also focuses on the possibility of government censorship. This discussion is generally blind, however, to the impact of corporate ownership.

Source: © Ringo Chiu/ZUMA.

In 2013, as part of their effort to promote a right-wing libertarian agenda that opposes environmental and labor regulations, the billionaire industrialist Koch brothers announced an interest in buying the bankrupt Tribune Company, publishers of the *Chicago Tribune,* the *Los Angeles Times,* the *Baltimore Sun,* the *Hartford Courant*, and other papers. Protesters were concerned that media control by such ideological owners—who had earlier bankrolled Tea Party efforts—could be parlayed into problematic political power. The Koch brothers later dropped their efforts to buy the company.

In addressing this concern, Bagdikian (2004) has argued that the United States has a "private ministry of information," metaphorically referring to the type of government-led propaganda system that exists in totalitarian societies. In the case of the contemporary United States, however, private interests, not the government, largely control this information system. Bagdikian suggests that when a small number of firms with similar interests dominate the media industry, it begins to function in a way similar to a state information system. It is hard to question the underlying argument that those who own large media conglomerates have at least the potential to wield a great deal of political power.

How might ownership of media translate into political power? It is possible that those building media empires could use their media outlets to promote a very specific political agenda. Furthermore, when media barons become candidates for major office, their media holdings can be invaluable political resources. Perhaps the starkest example of this in a Western democracy is the case of Silvio Berlusconi in Italy, who managed to use ownership of private media to gain public office—which then enabled him to influence public media.

Silvio Berlusconi, a media magnate and the dominant force in Italian broadcasting and publishing, was elected prime minister three times (1994, 2001, and 2008). For Berlusconi, ownership of television and radio clearly had great political value; he owned strategic assets that were unavailable to other political actors. In the 2001 electoral campaign, he was given four times the exposure of his rival candidate on the television networks that he owns. After winning that election, he went on to effectively control 90 percent of Italian television programming (*The Economist* 2001). That's because Italian prime ministers have the right to replace the boards of directors of the three public television channels, known as RAI, and thus can influence RAI's editorial choices. In subsequent election campaigns, Berlusconi not only had his own private television networks as a political resource, but he also influenced the public channels.

Berlusconi's domination of television was so great that, after the 2001 election and again in 2004, the European Federation of Journalists called for new regulations limiting media ownership. In 2004, both the European Parliament and the Council of Europe condemned the open conflict of interest between Berlusconi's role as prime minister and that of media magnate. The corrosive effect of this arrangement on Italian democracy was so serious that Freedom House, an independent watchdog group that produces annual rankings of freedom and democracy around the world, downgraded Italian freedom of the press from "free" to "partially free" (Freedom House 2004). After Berlusconi launched a series of attacks and lawsuits against the press, Reporters Without Borders (2009) declared that Berlusconi "is on the verge of being added to our list of Predators of Press Freedom," which would be a first for a European country (Ginsborg 2005; Hine 2001). Berlusconi resigned as prime minister in 2011 in the midst of a sex scandal. In 2013, however, he was once again a prominent figure in national politics, and he lost a close election for a fourth term as prime minister.

Though the media environment is quite different largely because of the vast size of the U.S. media industry, private media ownership can be a huge political asset in the United States too. Media entrepreneur Michael Bloomberg amassed a fortune selling technology and media products to businesses. He drew on the widespread recognition of his brand-name line of Bloomberg business media products—and the enormous profits they have generated for him—in his successful campaign to become New York City mayor in 2001. In the process, he spent $69 million of his own money—more than $92 per vote. Bloomberg won reelection in 2005 then successfully had the term-limit law changed so he could run again (and win again) in 2009. There has long been speculation that Bloomberg, one of the 10 wealthiest people in the United States as of 2012 (Forbes 2012), will one day launch a presidential bid.

In some cases, owners of media companies have direct control over media products and thus are able to exert political influence by promoting ideas that enhance their interests. Conservative media magnate Rupert Murdoch, for example, has used a variety of his News Corporation's media holdings to advance his political and economic goals. In 1975, he had his Australian newspapers slant the news so blatantly in favor of his conservative choice for prime minister that Murdoch's own journalists went on strike in protest. His British papers played a crucial role in the 1979 election of British conservative Margaret Thatcher. In 1995, Murdoch financed the multimillion-dollar start-up of the high-profile conservative U.S. magazine *The Weekly Standard.* In 1996, Murdoch's News Corporation initiated a 24-hour news channel, Fox News Channel (headed by Rush Limbaugh's former executive producer and long-time Republican Party political consultant, Roger Ailes), that many have argued promotes a consistent conservative agenda (Ackerman 2001; Aday 2010; McDermott 2010). When Murdoch's News Corporation bought Dow Jones in 2007, it took over as owner of *The Wall Street Journal*, one of the most influential—and editorially conservative—papers in the country.

More recently, Charles and David Koch, the billionaire brothers who helped support the Tea Party movement and who provide major funding to the conservative movement more broadly, sought to purchase the Tribune Company, the owner of several prominent newspapers, including the *Los Angeles Times* and the *Chicago Tribune.* News of the Koch brothers' interest in the newspapers sparked concern among journalists worried that the Kochs were primarily interested in the potential political value of the newspapers. The Koch brothers later dropped their efforts to buy the company.

However, some media outlets, especially news outlets, rely on a perception of objectivity or evenhandedness to maintain their legitimacy. Journalists often see themselves as members of a sort of fourth estate, complementing the executive, legislative, and administrative branches of government. Their job is to act as watchdogs over politicians (Louw 2010; Schultz 1998). As a result, with perhaps the exception of Fox News, most major news media outlets will not consistently and blatantly promote a single political agenda. Instead, viewers are more likely to find such an approach on cable programs that focus on analysis and commentary or on the growing number of ideologically driven websites and blogs.

The process of using media to promote a political agenda is more complex than simply feeding people ideas and images that they passively accept. Owners can use media sites to disseminate a specific position on a controversial issue or to help legitimize particular institutions or behaviors. Just as important, owners can systematically exclude certain ideas from their media products. While control of information or images can never be total, owners can tilt the scales in particular directions quite dramatically.

Ownership by major corporations of vast portfolios of media gives us reason to believe that a whole range of ideas and images—those that question fundamental social arrangements, under which the media owners are doing quite well—will be visible primarily in low-profile media. This does not mean that all media images and information are uniform.

It means that some ideas will be widely available, while others will be largely absent. For example, stories critical of gridlock in the federal government are frequent; in contrast, stories critical of capitalism as an economic system that can facilitate inequality are very rare. There is no way of proving the connection, but the media's focus on the shortcomings of the government, rather than of the private sector, seems consistent with the interests of the corporate media owners.

This process is most obvious in products that directly address contemporary social and political events, but it also happens in entertainment products. Consider, for example, the depiction of gays and lesbians on prime-time television. For most of U.S. television history, there were virtually no gay or lesbian characters. As gay rights advocates made advances in the 1980s and 1990s, gay and lesbian characters began appearing, though infrequently and in often superficial depictions. Also, gay characters faced constraints that heterosexual characters did not; for example, they typically did not kiss, even as popular television continued to become more explicit in depictions of heterosexual sex. It was not until 2004 that the first television drama series to revolve around a group of lesbian, gay, bisexual, and transgendered characters appeared; *The L Word* ran from 2004 to 2009 on the premium cable channel Showtime. There is no conspiracy here. More likely, a small number of profit-making firms that rely on mass audiences and major advertisers simply avoided potential controversies that might threaten their bottom line. As network executives and major advertisers began to define such images as more acceptable to mainstream audiences, lesbian and gay characters have become more commonplace and more diverse in recent years (GLAAD 2012). We return to these issues in Chapters 5 and 6 when we explore the content of mass media.

The political impact of concentrated corporate ownership, however, is both broader and subtler than the exclusion of certain ideas in favor of others. Herbert Schiller (1989) argues that "the corporate voice" has been generalized so successfully that most of us do not even think of it as a specifically corporate voice. That is, the corporate view has become "our" view, the "American" view, even though the interests of the corporate entities that own mass media are far from universal. One example of this is the entire media-generated discourse—in newspapers, television, radio, and magazines—about the American economy, in which corporate success provides the framework for virtually all evaluations of national economic well-being. Quarterly profits, mergers and acquisitions, productivity, and fluctuations in the financial markets are so widely discussed that their relationship to the corporate voice is difficult to discern. The relationship between corporate financial health and citizen well-being, however, is rarely discussed explicitly—even in times of serious financial crisis. During the economic crises of 2008–2009, the U.S. news media were remarkably unquestioning of the message from both government and the private sector that a massive and immediate bailout of banks, Wall Street firms, and other corporate interests was absolutely essential.

A concentrated media sphere can also undermine citizens' capacity to monitor their government's war-making powers. McChesney (2008: 98) argues that "those in power, those who benefit from war and empire, see the press as arguably the most important front of war, because it is there that consent is manufactured, and dissent is marginalized. For a press system, a war is its moment of truth." The 2003 U.S.-led invasion of Iraq was justified by the alleged presence of weapons of mass destruction (WMD) in Iraq. The news media reported these WMD charges uncritically, relying on official sources and without in-depth investigation, effectively affirming the Bush administration's rationale for war. According to one study of U.S. news media coverage in the first three weeks of the Iraq war, pro-war U.S. sources outnumbered antiwar sources by 25 to 1, thus making it very difficult for citizens to access critical perspectives on the war (Rendall and Broughel 2003).

One possible political consequence of the concentration of media ownership is that, in some ways, it becomes more difficult for alternative media voices to emerge. Because mass media outlets in all sectors of the media industry are large mass-production and mass-distribution firms, ownership is restricted to those who can acquire substantial financial resources. In the age of multimillion-dollar media enterprises, freedom of the press may be left to those few who can afford to own what has become a very expensive press.

The Internet offers the possibility for small producers to create professional-looking alternative media—from websites and blogs to mobile apps and streaming video. However, without a means to effectively promote such sites, and without the budget to pay for staff to continuously produce substantive new content that continues to draw users, most online alternative media are limited to relatively small niche audiences. Television and the major daily newspapers—along with the online content associated with these major media—are still the main sources of news for most of the population.

In the end, ownership of the means of information becomes part of larger patterns of inequality in contemporary societies, and large media conglomerates can use their capacity to shape media discourse and their substantial financial resources to influence public policy. In this sense, mass media institutions are no different from other social institutions; they are linked to the patterned inequality that exists throughout our society.

Media Ownership and Content Diversity

Does a change in the pattern of media ownership change the nature or range of media products? As this question suggests, macro-level patterns and specific media products need to be understood in relation to each other. Such a link is imperative for media sociology and moves us into the realm of social relations. The key is to explain the specific nature of the relations between broad institutional forces and the everyday world of mass media.

As media ownership became more concentrated, researchers became interested in the ways such ownership patterns influence the diversity of the media in terms of both form and content. *Media pluralism* refers to the degree to which there is diversity in media content readily available to audiences. This includes the presence of different and independent voices, an array of political views and opinions, and a variety of cultures (Doyle 2002). Media pluralism is both a matter of ownership (varied media suppliers) and output (varied content).

One widely adopted argument has been that media owned by a few will lead to products that lack diversity; that is, as ownership becomes increasingly concentrated, the content of media will become increasingly uniform. This relationship is a *hypothesis,* a proposition to be studied. However, research shows that the relationship between ownership concentration and diversity is not as straightforward as we might think. We will look at how researchers have studied this relationship in the news and the popular music industries.

The Homogenization Hypothesis

Bagdikian (2004) has provided the best-known examination of the concentration of media ownership, raising questions about the relationship between ownership and diversity. His most important contribution is the way he draws connections across the various media, showing how companies that are giants in the music industry have similar positions in film, for example. The combination of ownership concentration and growing horizontal integration leads Bagdikian to conclude that the absence of competition in the media industry will lead inevitably to homogeneous media products that serve the interests of the increasingly small number of owners. While Bagdikian's homogenization hypothesis seems plausible, research on the relationship between competition and diversity reveals a more complex situation.

The Local Newspaper Monopoly

Entman (1989) looked at local newspaper competition and asked whether monopoly ownership matters. His interest was fueled by the rapid loss of the two-paper town, long the norm in major cities, which has been replaced by local newspaper monopolies. (By 2013, there were only 12 U.S. cities with more than one English-language, general-interest daily newspaper.) A variety of observers, particularly journalists, mourned the death of the two-paper town because it had provided competition between newsgathering organizations. Consistent with Bagdikian's (2004) homogenization hypothesis, it had become widely accepted that the decline in local newspaper competition was, in itself, a threat to the ideal of a free press.

Entman (1989) set out to study the issue more closely. He argues that diversity in news content can be understood in both vertical and horizontal terms (not to be confused with vertical and horizontal integration). *Vertical diversity* refers to the range of actors mentioned and the degree of disagreement *within* a single newspaper. *Horizontal diversity* refers to the differences in content *between* two newspapers. Those concerned about the consequences of the media monopoly implicitly argue that monopoly papers will be less diverse than competitive papers in terms of both the actors mentioned and the degree of disagreement. Information will be narrower—that is, less diverse—in one-paper towns.

Entman's (1989) analysis focuses on the content of 91 newspapers: 26 monopoly, 33 quasi-monopoly (where different companies jointly operated two papers in the same city), and 32 competitive. Local newspaper monopoly, then, should lead to less vertical diversity, and quasi-monopoly should lead to less horizontal diversity. In either case, the critique of monopoly suggests that genuine competition will lead to increased diversity in both vertical and horizontal terms.

However, Entman finds no consistent relationship between newspaper competition and news diversity. In fact, on measures of vertical diversity, papers in all three categories perform virtually the same, mentioning a narrow range of actors and exhibiting a small degree of disagreement. The comparison of quasi-monopoly and competitive papers shows very little difference between the two pairs of papers. Papers in competitive circumstances do not differ from each other any more or less than do papers in the same quasi-monopoly market. In both cases, the difference between the pairs of papers was minimal.

Entman's (1989) findings on the nature of local newspaper monopolies have no bearing on Bagdikian's (2004) broader claims about the concentration of power inherent in the growth of national media giants. They do, however, suggest that we need to think carefully about the way news organizations operate and about why we expect competitive papers to be somehow better than noncompetitive papers. On this front, the romanticization of newspaper competition is the central issue.

Americans tend to be suspicious of monopolies and confident about the benefits of economic competition. Especially in the post–cold war era, the superiority of the free market has taken on mythic proportions. According to this largely uncontested view, free markets and democratic political systems go hand in hand, with one being the precondition for the other. Commentators often see economic competition as a guarantor of a healthy press, which they perceive as central to democratic societies.

Entman's (1989) study suggests that there is little evidence for the argument that competition leads to either higher quality or more diverse news. Instead, the incentives built into the structure of a for-profit news industry actually have little to do with producing high-quality, diverse news. Genuine economic competition—the commonsensical protector of the news—may in fact exacerbate the problem by encouraging news organizations to minimize costs and produce a least-common-denominator product that appeals to mass-market advertisers and as broad an audience as possible. Competitive papers often try to attract the same mass audience and court the same advertisers. As a result, they may face even stiffer pressures, which contradict quality and diversity, than their noncompetitive counterparts.

It is difficult to argue with Entman's (1989) conclusion that economic competition is no panacea, especially as it is free-market economic forces that produced the local newspaper monopoly in the first place. In the news industry, ownership structure does not explain in any direct way the content of the news. However, by asking about this potential relationship, researchers have helped us see some of the underlying dynamics at work in the news industry. Entman's study reveals that concentration of ownership does not create homogenization *because all the newspapers in his study had very limited diversity!* To understand the content of the news, we must move beyond questions of ownership and explore the impact of the for-profit orientation and the role of advertisers. We will address these topics later in the chapter. Now we consider another study of how ownership patterns influence diversity and media, this time in the popular music industry.

Concentration and Diversity in the Music Industry

Between 1969 and 1990, the four largest music firms dramatically increased their share of the top 100 albums from 54.5 percent to 82 percent (Lopes 1992). What are the implications of this ownership concentration for the diversity of the music we hear?

In their analysis of the postwar music industry, Peterson and Berger (1975) argue that high market concentration leads to homogeneity, while a competitive market leads to diversity. This is, in essence, the same relationship we explored within the newspaper industry. In this case, however, Peterson and Berger provide a historical analysis that demonstrates the relationship between market concentration and several measures of music diversity.

The fundamental premise of their argument is that the late 1950s and 1960s produced a great deal of innovation and diversity in the popular music industry, representing a dramatic shift from the more homogeneous and standardized music available in the 1940s and early 1950s. The cause, they argue, was the opening of the popular music market to increased competition. Radio's shift from a national orientation to a focus on local markets helped spur this opening. Independent record companies entered the newly opened market and produced new and innovative styles of music, breaking the homogeneity-producing control of the major record companies. Peterson and Berger (1975) base their conclusion about the relationship between competition and diversity on analyses of both ownership trends within the music industry and *Billboard* magazine's singles chart from 1949 to 1972.

Peterson and Berger (1975) suggest two key components of musical diversity. First, they analyze the sheer number of different songs that made the top 10 list each year, arguing that an increase in number reflects an increase in diversity. Second, they analyze the number of new and established artists who made the top 10, from the premise that new artists are a reflection of diversity and established artists are a reflection of standardization. They found that the measures associated with increased diversity (number of songs and number of new artists) increased at times when market concentration (domination of the popular music industry by a small number of firms) decreased. They conclude that a loosening of market concentration through increased competition permits greater innovation and diversity in popular music. However, their data suggest that, in the 1970s, market concentration was again increasing. Thus, they foresaw a return to the *oligopoly* (control by a small number of firms) of the 1940s and predicted a renewed homogeneity within the popular music industry.

Sociologist Paul Lopes (1992) revisited the same question more than 15 years after Peterson and Berger (1975). Using a similar method of analysis—one that focused on the degree of concentration of the industry and the degree of diversity exhibited on the *Billboard* charts—Lopes found that the dynamics in the popular music industry had become more complex since the 1960s.

In line with Peterson and Berger's (1975) prediction, market concentration increased substantially between 1969 and 1990, with the top four record companies controlling the vast majority of hit music. However, the accompanying decrease in diversity that Peterson and Berger predicted did not follow. Instead, the number of new artists and established artists fluctuated throughout the 1970s and 1980s, reaching roughly the same number in 1990 as in 1969. Although significant market concentration occurred during this period, Lopes found little evidence that musical diversity had suffered.

The explanation, according to Lopes (1992), is that the system of production within the music industry changed from what he characterizes as a "closed" system to an "open" system. The key change is in the ratio of record labels to record firms. As in other sectors of mass media, notably the book publishing industry, the major music firms own multiple record labels and maintain links with smaller, independent labels. Among the companies producing the top 100 albums, the ratio of labels to firms changed dramatically, from less than two labels per firm in 1969 to approximately four labels per firm by 1990.

Peterson and Berger (1975) suggested that a closed system of record production dominated the industry during the 1940s and early 1950s. In this system, major companies used a limited number of familiar channels to produce and distribute the music that dominated the charts. Lopes (1992), however, argues that the substantial increase in the number of labels per firm suggests new processes at work. In this open system, the major record companies control large-scale manufacturing, distribution, and publicity but draw on semi-autonomous independent producers to maintain the vitality of the popular music market. This open system is the key to the continued diversity within the industry despite high market concentration. The open system allows for innovation and diversity, which helps the major companies maintain both their profitability and their control of the industry.

Sociologist Tim Dowd's more recent research (2004) on the music industry echoes Lopes' findings, indicating that decentralized production is the key to musical diversity, even when only a few large companies dominate the music industry. And, despite the proliferation of independent labels, websites, and music streaming services that offer independent music, the major media companies continue to dominate music distribution. While independently owned music labels accounted for 32.6 percent of U.S. music sales in 2012, *Billboard* reports that most of these sales were the result of major label distribution of indie music such that independently owned and distributed music accounted for only about 12 percent of market share. In turn, Apple's iTunes continues to dominate the music download market, accounting for almost two-thirds of paid music downloads in the United States (NPD Group 2012).

These studies of the popular music industry remind us that there is no single effect of concentrated ownership within media industries. Clearly, ownership and control within oligopolistic media industries matter. Controlling companies adopt strategies that determine, to a great degree, production and distribution systems within media industries. However, we need to explore the specific conditions under which concentration exists before we can make sense of the relationship between concentration and diversity. Still, as changes occur in the composition and tastes of the audience, the methods of distribution, the technologies of production, and the organization of media industries will likely respond in ways that enhance the bottom-line profitability of the major firms. Even when a small number of companies control media industries, increased diversity may prove to be an effective strategy in a profit-making industry.

MASS MEDIA FOR PROFIT

In a capitalist system, mass media organizations must focus on one underlying goal: the creation of products that will earn profits. This for-profit orientation provides the context within which media personnel make decisions. However, the focus on profits does not work in a uniform way across media industries or in different time periods. The example above of the popular music industry shows how the same industry responded to similar profit pressures in different ways under different conditions.

Prime-Time Profits

One of the most sensitive treatments of how profit requirements influence media production is Todd Gitlin's (2000) classic analysis of network television. In *Inside Prime Time,* Gitlin explores the decision-making processes at what were then the three major U.S. networks, suggesting that bottom-line profit pressures set the framework for programming decisions. The goal for network executives is steady profits. Executives achieve profits by broadcasting programs that will attract large audiences that will, in turn, lead to the sale of advertising time at premium rates. The problem is that there is no surefire formula for successful programming. Even the most sophisticated methods for predicting success are much better at determining which shows will not succeed than at identifying which programs will become hits.

One reason why this is the case is that failure is the norm in network television. Writers offer the networks thousands of ideas each year, but networks develop only a few hundred into scripts. Some of these scripts are made into pilots, of which a few dozen make it onto the fall schedule. Of those that make the schedule, networks renew only a handful. At each stage, executives and producers weed out another layer of programs. Only a small number of programs are ultimately successful in commercial terms. For example, of the 135 prime-time scripted series ordered by the four major broadcast networks between 2009 and 2013, two out of three (90) were not renewed for a second season (Weisman 2013).

If failure is the norm in network television, how is the system profitable? In a situation similar to that in the music, film, and book industries, the big hits—as few as 10 percent of the products, depending on the particular industry—can provide profits large enough to make up for the vast number of programs that break even or lose money. Network television has an additional advantage: Even in the age of cable television, major advertisers still perceive the networks to be the most effective medium to promote products to a national market since their audiences are much larger than cable's. For example, in the week ending June 9, 2013, the top-rated scripted program on cable was HBO's season finale of *Game of Thrones*, which attracted an audience of 5.4 million—a number that would not have put it in the top 20 programs on network television, even though many of the network offerings were reruns.

As part of the all-encompassing search for steady profits, network programmers follow a logic of safety that revolves around minimizing the risk of losing money on programs. Risky programs are those that seem unlikely to attract a mass audience or, even worse, a large advertiser. However, as we have seen, ratings hits are rare.

One consequence of the profit-driven logic of safety is the general tendency to avoid controversy, even when it might bring high ratings. The logic of safety, however, has much broader consequences than the avoidance of controversial programs. Network executives are never sure what audiences will watch or why some programs succeed and others fail. Therefore, Gitlin (2000) suggests that the corollary to the logic of safety is the notion that "nothing succeeds like success." As a result, network television constantly imitates itself, creating copies and spin-offs that can reach bizarre proportions.

Hit 1970s programs such as *The Mary Tyler Moore Show* (*Rhoda, Phyllis, Lou Grant*) and *All in the Family* (*The Jeffersons, Maude, Good Times, Gloria, Archie's Place*) produced multiple spin-offs and new programs for the stars. In the 1980s, *Cheers* led to both the short-lived sitcom *The Tortellis* and the hit program *Frasier*. The 1990s was awash in gritty police dramas—from *NYPD Blue* and *Homicide* to *Law and Order* and its various spin-offs, *Special Victims Unit, Criminal Intent, Trial By Jury,* and *Law & Order: LA*. The success of the urban 20-somethings of *Friends* spawned a rash of imitators trying to cash in on the concept, from the 2004 spin-off bust *Joey* to popular programs such as *The Big Bang Theory, How I Met Your Mother,* and *2 Broke Girls*.

In the 2000s, crime scene investigators were among the most popular television characters, led by those on the hit programs *CSI, CSI: Miami,* and *CSI: New York,* along with *NCIS* and *NCIS: Los Angeles.* Since 2000, the networks filled the airwaves with a steady stream of "reality" programs, including household-based programs like *The Real World* and *Big Brother*, dating shows such as *The Bachelor* and *Temptation Island*, workplace contests such as *America's Top Model* and *The Apprentice*, and self-improvement programs like *Extreme Makeover: Home Edition* and *The Biggest Loser.* Talent shows flourished as well, including *American Idol, The Voice, America's Got Talent*, and *Dancing With the Stars.* Perhaps the most well-known genre of reality program is the season-long adventure contest, most notably the more than 20 versions of *Survivor*, starting in 2000 with *Survivor: Pulau Tiga. Survivor* was a ratings success for more than a decade, ranking among the top 10 programs from 2000 to 2005, and remaining among the 30 most highly rated programs through the 2013 season with *Survivor: Caramoan.* The program spawned a wide array of competition shows—from *The Mole* and *Boot Camp* to *The Contender* and *Shark Tank*—all trying to capitalize on a new twist on reality-based contest programs.

Whether it is courtroom law programs, 20-something sitcoms, prime-time game shows, or reality programs, each network tries to exploit what appears to be the prevailing trend. Without any other accepted method for making programming decisions and with profit demands moving from an annual to a quarterly or weekly basis, programmers choose shows that resemble the latest hit on another network. Increasingly, they also look abroad for program ideas, or export homegrown fare for foreign audiences. *Big Brother, America's Got Talent, Dancing With the Stars, Who Wants to Be a Millionaire,* and many other programs have all been reproduced in slightly different versions, modified for local tastes, to be distributed in different countries.

Cheaper Programs for Smaller Audiences

Over the last couple of decades, network television has had to deal with declining audiences and a corresponding decline in advertising revenue. At the same time, the cost of producing quality programming has increased. To compensate for these two trends, the networks have turned to programs that are less expensive to produce, filling their schedules with programming that does not feature big budget production or expensive actors.

First, the decline in network advertising revenue was due to the loss of audience share. Broadcast network television ratings are much lower than they were in previous decades. The emergence and growth of cable and satellite television, as well as online viewing platforms such as Netflix and Hulu, have eroded the traditional network audience dramatically. Whereas 90 percent of active television sets were tuned to the three major networks during prime time in the 1970s, by 2013, fewer than 30 percent of sets were tuned to prime-time offerings on the now four major networks: ABC, CBS, NBC, and Fox. Although these networks still play an important role in the U.S. television market, the audience size for their programs is small in comparison to that of the 1970s or 1980s. Not only have TV viewers turned to cable, but many former viewers now turn to the Internet for news and entertainment, resulting in fewer television viewers overall. As a result, network executives can no longer draw audiences that match those for hit programs from previous generations, such as *M*A*S*H, Dallas,* or *The Cosby Show.* In fact, the television business has changed so much that the ratings for even the most popular programs in the 2010s, such as perennial hits like CBS's *NCIS* or Fox's *American Idol,* would probably have led to quick cancellation two decades ago.

Second, the cost of producing network television dramas and sitcoms escalated because several factors combined to allow suppliers to charge higher rates for their programs. To begin with, the existence of more channels and more competition for viewers led to more demand for program content. Next, to stand out amid the competition, networks had relied on giving their programs an often expensive look or casting high-profile celebrities. Finally, there was more leverage for actors and directors who had other options in the multichannel universe. By the 2000s, cable stations lured away talent and created some of the best-known, high-quality drama series, such as HBO's *The Sopranos, The Wire, Boardwalk Empire,* and *Game of Thrones*; AMC's *Mad Men* and *Breaking Bad;* and Showtime's *Dexter* and *Homeland.*

With lowered expectations regarding audience size and a tighter budget with which to work, television networks turned to low-cost programming that could be produced in-house. In the 1990s, this resulted in the proliferation of news magazine programs; in the 2000s, it resulted in the explosion of game shows, talent contests, and "reality" programs. Both developments followed a similar logic; these programs attract what historically would have been a small audience, but since they are so inexpensive to produce, they can still be profitable for the networks.

In 1999, NBC was broadcasting its *Dateline* newsmagazine five nights a week, ABC was running *20/20* three nights a week, and CBS developed a new edition of the newsmagazine leader *60 Minutes Two.* In subsequent years, they all continued to air newsmagazine programs (including *48 Hours* and *PrimeTime*) several nights a week. Each of the networks already had made a substantial investment in its news operations, so the newsmagazine could build on existing production, journalistic, and promotional resources. To take advantage of these resources, newsmagazines shared news gathering with the evening news programs so that short stories on the nightly news could be developed into longer magazine pieces in prime time. News stories could essentially be repackaged and reused for a magazine format, and journalists could effectively work to support both the news and the newsmagazine programs. As part of a larger news division at each network, the evening news and the newsmagazines also promoted each other routinely and built on each other's reputations and audiences. Over time, the saturation of the airwaves with newsmagazines led to declining audience numbers, and the networks found a new form of cheap programming: games shows and talent contests.

In the 2000s, ostensibly "unscripted" shows became the new cheap programming. Along with the games shows (*Who Wants to Be a Millionaire?* and *Deal or No Deal*) and talent contests (*American Idol, Dancing With the Stars, and The Voice*), networks turned heavily to various forms of "reality" programming that often combined contest elements with supposedly unscripted drama and conflict. The CBS-produced *Survivor* is probably the best known program in this genre. Its many imitators generally required very modest production budgets and were titillating enough to attract significant numbers of viewers. This combination of modest production budgets and regular viewers helped make reality contest programs a daily staple on a wide range of national cable television networks, as television schedules filled up with programs such as Lifetime's *Project Runway*, Bravo's *Top Chef*, ESPN's *Dream Job*, and Oxygen's *The Glee Project.*

Controlling Content and Distribution

The range of options for television and video viewing—both what and how to watch—continues to proliferate. You can watch a vast array of national and local broadcast and cable network programming through your cable or satellite provider. You can watch programs that you have recorded on your DVR, watch "on demand" television, and use broadband to watch the same programs on your laptop, tablet, or phone. You can stream directly from a network's website, access a growing library of television programs for streaming through subscriptions to Netflix, Hulu, and Amazon Prime, or download a program through the iTunes store. A huge amount of video content, including recognizable television programs, is available on YouTube or you can find just about anything online on websites that stream copyright protected content without permission.

This proliferation of viewing options poses challenges to the television industry. First, competition for viewers is becoming increasingly intense. We have already seen that audiences for any individual program are far smaller than in the network television era, and advertising revenue, while still the financial bedrock of television, is now divided among a growing pool of channels. Second, determining audience size has become increasingly complex, as viewers watch on the many different platforms, often at different times. Declining prime time ratings, in part, represent a shift away from traditional viewing to DVR and online viewing, rather than simply indicating a smaller overall viewership. Accurately determining ratings that include these new viewing habits is crucial, since ratings are the measures that determine advertising rates. Third, the most prominent new television viewing platforms are based, in large part, on subscriber fees, so they need to attract and hold viewers who pay a monthly or annual membership fee.

In response to these changing economic dynamics, major players in the television industry are seeking new ways to control both programming and distribution channels. This is what makes Comcast such a formidable media conglomerate. Comcast is the largest global media company, with 2012 revenues of more than $62 billion. Comcast does not own a major publishing house, magazine division, radio station group, or music label, so the range of its holdings is not as extensive as that of some of the other big media companies. However, the company is built around its linkage of programming and distribution. Comcast controls more of the wires coming into U.S. homes—for cable television, high-speed Internet, and digital phone services—than any other media company. This makes the company the nation's largest cable television company and largest broadband Internet service provider—two key channels for distribution of video content. In addition, Comcast owns a large portfolio of television networks that are a major source of programming, including NBC, Telemundo, USA Network, Bravo, E!, CNBC, Syfy, MSNBC, Oxygen, and The Weather Channel, as well as one of the major Hollywood studios, Universal Pictures, and a major producer of television programming, Universal Television. By controlling both a large amount of television and film content and distribution channels that reach into most U.S. households, Comcast has the resources to manage the uncertainty of the new media environment. It can also present hurdles to competitors, for example, by setting up tiered usage plans that charge more to customers who download large amounts of data—such as Netflix viewers.

Newer players in the television world are, similarly, seeking to control both content and distribution. Netflix helped to pioneer streaming television, offering its subscribers access to a huge library of recent and classic television series. Its service is so popular that Netflix

When the final edition of the *Rocky Mountain News* rolled off the presses in 2009, declaring, "Goodbye Colorado," it left its competitor, the *Denver Post*, with a monopoly. As of 2013, only 12 U.S. cities had more than one English-language, general-interest daily newspaper.

Source: AP Photo/David Zalubowski.

users account for one-third of all North American downstream traffic between 9 p.m. and midnight (Sandvine 2013). With new competition for streaming television, and growing awareness by copyright owners of the value of television program rights, Netflix entered the content business, producing original programming that is available only to Netflix members. Its first major original productions were the 2013 political drama *House of Cards* and the revival of the cult comedy *Arrested Development*. It also signed deals with Dreamworks Animation to create new content exclusively for Netflix. Other streaming television services moved ahead with new original programming, aiming to offer potential subscribers a specific reason to sign up. Both Amazon and Hulu rolled out new original programming in 2013 and 2014, as part of the rush to tie popular content to a specific paid distribution platform.

Profit and the News Media

How do such profit pressures influence the content of news media? News outlets, like any other company, have two ways to enhance their profits: They can either cut costs or increase revenues. In today's highly competitive news industry, both of these approaches are evident. To cut costs, news outlets rely on several or all of the following strategies:

- Decrease the number of journalists.
- Use journalistic and production staff on multiple company-owned news outlets.
- Cut back on long-term investigative reporting that produces a small number of stories.
- Use a larger percentage of wire services reports.

- At television stations, use video public relations (PR) segments (reports that have been prepared and provided free of charge by PR firms) in newscasts.

- Rely on a small number of elites (who are easy and inexpensive to reach) as regular news sources.

- Focus the news on preplanned official events (which are easy and inexpensive to cover) instead of less routine happenings.

- Focus coverage on a limited number of institutions in a handful of big cities.

All these methods allow news organizations to lower the cost of gathering and producing the news. In recent years, the number of daily newspapers shrank from 1,611 daily newspapers in 1990 to 1,382 in 2011 (Pew Research Center 2013). In addition, newspapers have cut the number of newsroom employees substantially. After increasing in the 1980s and holding stable throughout the 1990s, newspaper employment has declined steadily in the 2000s. By 2011, there were fewer newsroom employees than at any time since 1978 (see Figure 2.5). While these cost-cutting efforts save money, they are likely to make news coverage oriented more toward elites and government who provide easy-to-use information, with less coverage of events or perspectives outside the official world.

One dramatic result of cost cutting at the network news divisions was the closure of separate election night, exit-polling units at each network. Instead of sending their own teams of pollsters out to gather data on voter preferences, the television networks (ABC, CBS, CNN, NBC, Fox News) and the Associated Press created a consortium in 1990, the Voter News Service, to provide election night data for all of its members. Voter News Service centralized the exit-polling process, saving the networks millions of dollars and making elections less expensive to cover. However, this cutback contributed significantly to the confusion that reigned on election night 2000, when it was unclear whether George W. Bush or Al Gore had won the state of Florida (and therefore the presidency). Because of the cutbacks, the networks were all left relying on the same source of information, with no contrasting assessments. Following this failure, the Voter News Service was disbanded but replaced by a similar organization called National Election Pool, upon which all four television networks, CNN, and the Associated Press rely for election projections.

In addition, cost cutting led ABC, CBS, and NBC to close foreign bureaus throughout the 1990s and, more generally, to scale back their coverage of international affairs. In the wake of the September 11, 2001, attacks, the news media's cutbacks in global news gathering and international reporting left them generally ill-prepared to help Americans understand the context for the unfolding events and the attitudes outside of the United States (McChesney 2008).

At the same time, news organizations try to increase revenues by maximizing their audience and advertiser bases. The most straightforward approach for audience maximization is to create a light, entertainment-oriented news product that makes watching or reading the news fun and exciting. This helps explain why so much of our daily news focuses on the lives of celebrities and on titillating or dramatic weather or crime stories.

Profit pressures have intensified in the 2000s as a result of increased competition in the overall media sector and the demand by corporate owners for substantial returns on their

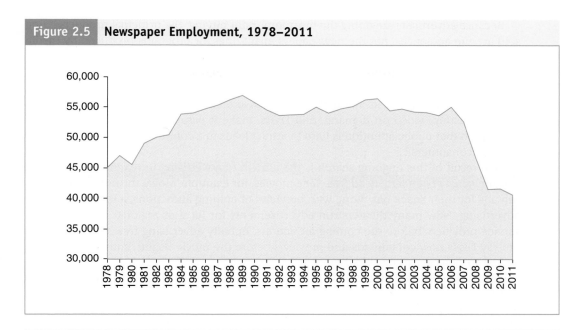

Figure 2.5   **Newspaper Employment, 1978–2011**

Source: Pew Research Center 2013, *State of the News Media: 2013*.

investments. The result is that news editors, increasingly trained in the world of business instead of news reporting, focus more on marketing and packaging the news. Profit pressures have different consequences for different media outlets. Still, the combination of cost-cutting and audience-enhancing demands is one of the key reasons why different news outlets, all responding to a comparable set of profit pressures, produce news that looks so similar.

THE IMPACT OF ADVERTISING

As we have seen, profit requirements provide incentives for the operators of media outlets to keep costs down and to create a product that will bring in sufficient revenue. We must weigh one additional factor: the specific source of revenue. In both of our previous examples, television and newspapers, the key source of revenue is advertising. This is the case with all mass-market print and commercial broadcast media. In the print world, receipts from sales account for roughly one-third of revenue, with advertising providing approximately two-thirds of operating costs. In broadcast media, advertising is the only substantial source of revenue. As a result, it should be no surprise that the magazines we read often seem more focused on the full-page glossy ads than on the articles that are buried between ad pages or that television commercials frequently seem more clever and interesting than the programs they surround. Advertising is, after all, what pays the bills for print, broadcast, and online media.

Because advertisers are doing the most important buying, the principal products being sold are the audiences, not the newspapers, magazines, or programs produced by media organizations. Advertisers are not interested in media products, except as a kind of bait to lure audiences and expose them to ads. As the phrase goes, media are in the business of "delivering audiences to advertisers." Our attention is on what is being bought and sold, and competition for that attention has intensified as technologies, such as the remote control, podcasting, video on demand, and DVRs, make it easier to avoid ads. Advertisers' perception that public attention is hard to attract leads to a continual search for new ways to reach consumers.

One result of this ongoing search is the growth of advertising in realms of media that had previously been largely ad free. Take movies, for example. Movie theaters have always run ads for their snack bar, along with previews of coming attractions, a form of industry advertising. Now many theaters run advertisements for local or regional merchants and service providers before the coming attractions. Initially advertising free, many DVD and Blu-ray Discs now contain ads and previews before the movie begins, some of which are locked so viewers cannot skip them.

Advertisements do not stop when the movie begins. Product placement within movies—whereby a character sips from a can of a well-known brand of soft drink or flies on a prominent airline—is a big business and a subtler way to promote products. The use of products on screen or the mention of brand names by star actors can bring in big money, helping to offset the rising costs of film production and marketing. For example, in the 2012 James Bond film *Skyfall,* Heineken replaced a martini as Bond's drink of

Source: AP Photo/EA Sports via *The Canadian Press.*

Advertisements are the routine backdrop to many video games, including sports simulations such as this one. Advertisers like such placements because users cannot avoid the ads while playing the game.

choice, a product placement reported to be worth $45 million courtesy of the Dutch brewing company (Child 2012). The 2013 Superman remake, *Man of Steel*, brought in more than $160 million worth of product placements from nearly 100 companies, including Nokia phones, Chrysler vehicles, and a special line of Clark Kent–inspired glasses collection by Warby Parker (Bignell and Dunne 2013).

In recent years, product placement has become increasingly sophisticated. Advertisers now think strategically about how best to build their products into the story line of a movie, television series, or video game, constructing a seemingly natural and recurring product placement that may be hard to recognize. For example, chefs on cooking shows use and talk about various brand-name cooking products; the judges on *American Idol* drink prominently displayed cans of Coca-Cola, and characters in *The Office* eat lunch at well-known chain restaurants and shop at brand-name office supply retailers—all of which are paid product promotions.

Similarly, video game developers are crafting new, innovative forms of in-game advertising to more fully integrate products into the video game environment. While billboards advertising real-world products have long appeared in a wide range of video games—on the ski slopes, on the walls of race tracks, in the urban environment—games feature more and more brand-name products for game players to drive, wear, and consume. As product placement opportunities continue to grow, advertisers now speak of a new media form, "branded entertainment," to describe media content that is closely associated with specific brand-name products (Elliott 2008).

Product placement has even made its way into the world of journalism. For example, McDonald's paid one Las Vegas television station to display its iced-coffee cups, company logo facing the camera, on the anchor desk of the morning news program, and other local television stations now see product placement as a potential revenue source to support morning news programs (Clifford 2008a, 2008b; Writers Guild of America, West 2008).

The newest trend linking products with media content are complex partnerships that advertisers call "brand integration." In some of these partnerships, companies contribute products or props that keep film production costs down, while other cases involve joint marketing campaigns to promote both a film and the brand-name products. For example, the 2013 version of *The Great Gatsby* is a prime example of how brand integration works. The film prominently featured several luxury brands, including Brooks Brothers, Prada, Tiffany, Moet champagne, and New York's Plaza Hotel. Prada and Brooks Brothers also designed and made most of the costumes, trimming nearly $2 million off of the film's budget (Armstrong 2013). Once the film was released, Gatsby's brand partners played a large role in marketing the film. Tiffany ads featured its new Gatsby collection, the Plaza Hotel started a weekly Gatsby Hour with a "speakeasy menu" and offered Gatsby products in the hotel's gift shop, and Brooks Brothers promoted its new Great Gatsby collection of men's clothing. For its part, the film promoted its brand partners on its website through a "Guide to Style" with links to its luxury product partners.

From the standpoint of advertisers, film product placement and brand integration are smart investments, in part because theatergoers cannot turn the page or flip the channel to avoid the ad. However, sophisticated approaches to branded integration may be effective precisely because the sales pitch appears less intrusive. With products integrated into a film's storyline—as they are in the party scenes in *The Great Gatsby*—the brands themselves become integral characters in the film experience. Increasingly, film producers—as well as creators of various other forms of media, from television to video games—consider potential brand integration partnerships from the earliest stages of project development, as they assess what ideas are financially viable and how they can most effectively market new content in an increasingly cluttered media landscape (Clifford 2010).

Advertisements also make their way, through various media, into unlikely places, such as the high school classroom and the doctor's office. Whittle Communications pioneered the art of producing media products, with ample room for advertisements, that reach captive audiences and ensure that other media are not available to compete for consumer attention. One example was the creation of several advertiser-friendly magazines for distribution to participating doctors. Doctors' offices received the magazines for free in exchange for an agreement to carry Whittle publications exclusively.

More controversially, schoolchildren were targeted as another captive audience. Whittle Communications developed a classroom television news program, *Channel One* (now owned by Alloy Media and Marketing, which joined CBS News in a partnership in 2009), and supplied participating schools with television and video equipment. In exchange, Channel One received a commitment to show the news program—along with advertisements—to students on a regular basis as a required part of the school day. In 2001, more than 8 million teenagers were watching Channel One each day, viewing news that was packaged to be dramatic, exciting, hip, and fun (Hoynes 1998). As Channel One was touting its educational value to teachers and parents, its corporate parent was boasting to potential advertisers about Channel One's direct pipeline to the teen market. In 2006, a study conducted by the American Academy of Pediatrics found that children watching Channel One in school tended to remember the ads more than the news. Another study found that students purchased an average of 2.5 items advertised on the program during the preceding three months (Austin et al. 2006).

More recently, Microsoft did something similar with its student-oriented products and its school initiatives. Programs like the Service & Technology Academic Resource Team (START), launched in 2010, support student leadership in the classroom, while at the same time familiarizing the students with Microsoft products. The company's recurrent donations of computers and software to impoverished schools in the United States and abroad provides Microsoft with positive publicity, while promoting brand loyalty among new computer users.

In these cases, doctors and educators exchanged the attention of those they serve—patients and students—for free media products.

Advertising and the Press in the 19th Century

Advertising is a central force in the workings of contemporary mass media, providing the bulk of the revenue for newspapers, magazines, television, and radio. In addition, as we have seen, advertising needs can generate new media products and appear in forms of media that once existed without ads. But what influence does the introduction of advertising have on the content of these media? One well-documented historical example is the impact of advertising on the British and American press in the 1800s.

The British Press

James Curran's (1977) historical account of the British press provides an important institutional analysis of the relationship between news and advertising. Traditionally, historians have argued that British newspapers gradually won their freedom from government and party control as they shifted to a financial structure that relied on advertising. In this view, newspapers achieved a kind of economic independence, permitting the press to take up its contemporary role as the fourth estate. Curran, however, argues that the simple equation of advertising with press freedom neglects the substantial influence this new economic structure had on the radical, working-class press in England. His approach is a textbook example of how the production perspective provides new insight into the workings of mass media systems by asking questions that researchers would otherwise not explore and by examining relationships that researchers had previously neglected.

During the first half of the 19th century, according to Curran (1977), a radical, working-class press thrived in England, breaking circulation records. At the same time, efforts by the government to control the press—through libel laws and press taxes—were largely ineffective. Rather than being constrained by government action, the British working-class press was undermined by the changing economics of the newspaper business, whereby the less politically inclined middle-class papers turned to advertisers, instead of readers, as a central source of revenue.

Curran (1977) argues that the growth of advertising changed the playing field and led to the decline of the British radical press. Advertising made circulation figures (the number of readers) less important than the patronage of advertisers. Radical papers did not receive the support of advertisers, even though they had large numbers of readers. More mainstream papers, meanwhile, were able to make profits with a substantially smaller readership base. Advertisers' political interests were dramatically different from the ideas espoused by the radical press. In essence, the working-class press presented a political critique of industrial capitalism, while potential advertisers were generally beneficiaries of that same system. Given a choice of which newspaper to support, advertisers elected not to support their political opponents.

In addition, advertisers had economic reasons for avoiding the radical press. Radical newspapers appealed largely to a working-class audience, and even though the papers were widely read, advertisers did not perceive the readers to be a valuable market. To advertisers, reaching smaller numbers of upper- or middle-class readers seemed to be a better sales strategy than reaching large numbers of working-class readers who did not have the necessary resources to buy many of the advertised goods and services.

Advertising changed the meaning of economic viability within the newspaper industry. With new resources coming in, the advertiser-supported papers were able to produce papers with more pages, containing both news and ads. This pushed up the cost of producing a competitive newspaper. At the same time, with advertising revenue as a base, the cover price of papers dropped dramatically, making it difficult for papers without advertising to compete.

The consequences of the rise of advertising were grave for the radical press and tell us a good deal about the broader impact of advertising on the news. Without advertising support, several high-circulation, working-class papers ceased publishing because they could be underpriced by competitors, who also had the resources to produce and distribute a more attractive product. One important consequence of advertising, then, was the end of a national radical press in Britain. Owners transformed those papers that did survive in one of two ways. Some publications became small-circulation papers, much like our alternative press today. These papers did not even try to compete with the national press. Other papers moved away from their working-class audience by focusing on items of interest to upper- and middle-class audiences. By losing their radical political commitments, these newspapers were better able to attract advertisers. Either way, from the standpoint of the working class and its radical supporters, the shift to an advertising-based press did not represent progress toward press freedom. Instead, the introduction of advertising and the subsequent decline of the radical press resulted in newspapers that provided a more limited view of events than they had before.

The U.S. Press

The move toward advertising-supported newspapers also had a significant impact on the content of the U.S. press. Until the late 1800s, U.S. newspapers had been largely funded and controlled by political parties, politicians, and partisan organizations. Then, the news shifted from a partisan, politically based press to a commercially based press. A principal consequence of this shift was a change in the definition of a newspaper's very purpose. As advertising became the key to success, news moved from the realm of politics and persuasion to the realm of business (Baldasty 1992). This was no small change. Newspapers were no longer partisan, and they no longer perceived their readers as voters or citizens. On the contrary, newspapers made an effort to avoid partisanship as much as possible and instead looked upon their readers as consumers. There is, in fact, good reason to believe that the historical roots of what we now refer to as "objectivity" in journalism lie in this process of commercialization, whereby the news industry developed a new nonpartisan framework for reporting news.

The move toward a commercial press in the United States shaped news content in two significant ways (Baldasty 1992). News purveyors began to avoid controversy, preferring instead a blander product that would be likely to attract (and not offend) large numbers of readers as well as advertisers interested in reaching those readers. This shift went beyond a nonpartisan style or voice. As advertisers' desires became intertwined with news values, political news itself—even that without any intentional partisanship—became problematic because of its inherent focus on difficult, sometimes unpleasant issues. As a result, newspapers shifted their focus away from substantive political news.

As news increasingly shied away from political issues, it turned to a variety of features— including sports, fashion, recipes, and entertainment—that existed largely to support the accompanying ads. Then, as today, such items may have been of substantial interest to readers, but they became part of the daily newspaper because these new forms of news would be both advertiser friendly and entertaining.

Commercialization led to one additional consequence of lasting significance. Newspapers became advocates for their newfound economic patrons. According to Baldasty (1992), "Early nineteenth-century newspaper editors were unabashed *advocates for political parties.* Late-nineteenth-century newspaper editors were advocates as well, *advocates for business,* for their advertisers" (p. 141). Our contemporary sensibilities suggest that news should be independent of political control. However, independence from direct political influence was achieved only by introducing a new business influence. The financial role of advertising shaped daily practices within the news industry and transformed the meaning of news for both producers and consumers.

Advertising and the Contemporary News Media

Advertising continues to exert a powerful influence on the news media (Collins 1992). Advertisers are the dominant source of revenue for print, broadcast, and online news media; journalists, editors, and producers are well aware of who pays the bills. At the same time, most journalists do not set out to intentionally produce news that is advertiser friendly. The dynamics are not so simple as either routine intervention by advertisers to protect their interests (although this does happen) or daily compliance with advertiser agendas by reporters. Rather than directly determining news content, advertising is a force that provides both incentives and constraints that influence the news in a generally predictable way.

At the most general level, news usually depicts advertisers' products and their broad interests in a favorable light. Reporters and editors may not perceive themselves as defending their advertisers' interests, but there is no doubt that they are fully aware of the economic role of their major advertisers. As a result, the dominant influence in this regard is probably more akin to self-censorship, perhaps unconscious, on the part of journalists. Self-censorship refers to the ways reporters doubt themselves, tone down their work, omit small items, or drop entire stories to avoid pressure, eliminate any perception of bias, or advance their careers.

A 2000 survey by the Pew Research Center for the People and the Press found that 41 percent of journalists had engaged in self-censorship—purposely avoiding newsworthy stories or softening the tone of their stories (Kohut 2000). Even though many critics express outrage at such a scenario, this kind of response by journalists should not be surprising. Professionals are not isolated from the social world around them, nor can they be entirely unmindful of their economic patrons. Lawyers serve their clients' interests; academics are often aware of tenure decisions and funding priorities when they are choosing their research projects; doctors respond to the financial situations of hospitals and insurance companies. Journalists are no different.

Of course, the ways journalists respond to advertiser interests are complex. Rarely is one particular advertiser important enough that journalists need to avoid any hint of criticism, and media outlets can often replace unhappy sponsors with new ones. There are other ways to protect advertisers; for example, network news producers will pull ads from an oil company on the evening that a large oil spill is in the news. More generally, though, news organizations and broadcasters need to pay attention to the interests of the entire class of advertisers, not individual sponsors. In practical terms, news personnel will tend to avoid content that is too critical of the system of consumer capitalism because this system is at the core of the interests of advertisers as a collective.

Some types of news reporting are more vulnerable to influence than others. In local newspapers, real estate and automotive coverage is notorious for its reverence of local advertisers. There are clear economic reasons for this. Local real estate agencies and local automobile dealers generally fill the bulk of these sections with their ads, often perceiving that they virtually own the pages. With other advertisers unlikely to pick up the slack, reporters writing in these two areas have little freedom to deviate from traditional, light, industry-pleasing coverage.

This dynamic works in a more affirmative way in a variety of news settings. Editors and producers create new sections in newspapers and new features on radio and television to attract new advertisers. Coverage of music, computers, food, health, and fashion, for example, is prominent in our news because it attracts advertising revenue from companies that sell products in these industries. Lifestyle coverage is an advertiser's dream, because much of it focuses on a variety of forms of consumption. Entertainment-oriented coverage meets advertisers' agendas in an additional way. News should, at the very least, maintain a tone that contributes to—and certainly does not undermine—a "buying mood" (Baker 1994). If news content is consistently negative or upsetting, audiences are not likely to be in an appropriate frame of mind to respond to the ads that accompany it. When news is in some way negative, as it often is, there is generally an attempt to brighten the picture and reassure the audience. One example is the convention of television news to end a broadcast with an upbeat story.

Finally, because news outlets need to court advertisers for financial support, there is an incentive to produce news that will appeal to an audience the advertisers want to reach: those who are well-off. As competition for sponsors increases, news outlets face increased pressure to deliver an upscale audience. One result of this pressure is that there is rarely news about the poor, except when they commit crimes, violate basic social norms, or become objects of charity. In essence, editors and producers generally restrict news about the poor to stories about how the poor affect the middle and upper classes. Much of the style and fashion coverage is geared toward people with high incomes. Of course, not all news is successful at reaching an upscale audience. Still, news outlets that we can most easily identify as upscale—the *New York Times,* PBS's *NewsHour*, the *Wall Street Journal,* the *Washington Post*—are also perceived by industry observers to be the best news in the business.

In the end, advertising does not directly determine news, but news cannot be entirely independent of advertising. Both historical and contemporary analysis indicates that the language we use to talk about news—discussions of objectivity, the meaning of "quality" or "prestige" journalism, the very categories that are defined as news—is derived, in part, from the central role of advertising in the news industry.

Marketing Online and in Niche Media

Advertisers have struggled to develop effective mechanisms for distributing promotional messages online. As users navigate the Internet, traditional ad images proved to be only marginally effective, especially because web surfers can click right past the ads. Pop up ads alienated users who found them annoying. Instead, as advertisers have sought innovative ways to focus the online attention of savvy consumers, they developed new strategies and used new forms of advertising.

Social networking sites have been gold mines for advertisers. Users often voluntarily supply a broad range of information about themselves that is of great interest to advertisers, including their sex, age, likes and dislikes, hobbies, and residence. Facebook has been especially aggressive in collecting information from its users, even while they are visiting other websites. Every time someone visits a web page and clicks Facebook's "Share" or "Like" button, data on that user is collected, producing a detailed portrait that can be sold to advertisers. However, consumer resistance to advertising continues in this new Internet environment, as well. By installing free Internet browser add-ons, such as AdBlock Plus (adblockplus.org), users are able to avoid banner ads, pop-up advertisements, and nearly all forms of advertising. Such resistance leads companies to continually innovate by delivering stealth advertising in a less intrusive way.

One approach has been the distribution of free, downloadable video games, or "advergames," which are both fun to play and full of brand-name product promotions—and can be played on a tablet or smartphone. Dr Pepper developed one of the earliest iPhone advergames in 2007, Matchcaps. In recent years, a wide range of youth-oriented products, such as soft drinks, athletic shoes, and chewing gum, have developed phone apps that build ads into games. Advergames are an example of "viral marketing," an array of ever-expanding marketing techniques aiming to use existing social networks to advertise products in fun and engaging ways. Viral marketing techniques include video clips, Facebook campaigns, tweets, and text messages. The result of advertisers' continuing efforts to develop effective promotional methods will likely play a key role in determining which new media forms become staples of our lives in the coming decades. Those that can generate revenue will continue; those that cannot will flounder.

As the media environment changes, however, the specific nature of the relationship between advertising and media is evolving as well. The most immediate social issue that will influence this relationship is the increasing fragmentation of the media audience. The concept of mass media was based on a communication structure in which a small number of senders direct messages to a large number of receivers—hence, a mass audience. Given the mass dimension of the media, advertising has encouraged the production of homogeneous, least-common-denominator media products. The Internet, the fragmentation of the media experience (through, for example, podcasting, television on demand, streaming video, and media-rich blogging platforms), and the identification of new consumer markets are changing the mass orientation of media. In its place, niche media production and distribution targets specific audience segments instead of aiming for a mass audience (see Figure 2.6). To a company that markets cookware and kitchen appliances, a cooking show with a smaller audience may be more valuable than a highly rated sitcom. With a cooking show, the advertiser is guaranteed to reach an audience that already has an interest in cooking-related products. This is not the case with a traditional network sitcom. This is the logic driving the development of digital media, where advertising is becoming increasingly personalized. As media scholar Joseph Turow puts it, "Advertisers in the digital space expect all media firms to deliver to them particular types of individuals—and, increasingly, *particular* individuals—by leveraging a detailed knowledge about them and their behaviors. . . . The new advertising strategy involves drawing as specific a picture as possible of a person based in large part on measurable physical acts such as clicks, swipes, mouseovers, and even voice commands" (2011: 4).

Advertising was long seen as a homogenizing force in the media world. It still is, in the sense that it supports only media that encourage consumption. However, as a result of new technologies and new marketing strategies, advertisers are fast becoming proponents of a very specific kind of media diversity in which different audience segments, consisting of demographically specific groups, are receiving different media to watch or read. Although the universe of available media may be more diverse, the new push toward segmented programming is likely to produce an increasingly fragmented audience. Some observers worry about the long-term consequences of this kind of segmented cultural experience. Almost two decades ago media scholar Joseph Turow (1997), for example, warned that we were entering an era "in which advertisers will work with media firms to create the electronic equivalents of gated communities" (p. 2). More recently, Italian media scholar Paolo Mancini suggests, "Media fragmentation may increase political polarization as it seems to be happening in well established democracies, especially in countries where the idea of 'common good' is not deeply rooted" (2013: 56). A more inclusive diversification of media will occur only if formerly underserved audiences are identified as growing consumer markets and new media products are directed at them. Those who are considered unimportant by advertisers, especially poor people, are likely to continue to be left out of advertiser-driven media.

Figure 2.6   Niche Media

The Arabic Channel

Aspire (African American focus, founded by Magic Johnson)

Aztec America

BabyFirstTV

Big Ten Network (college sports)

Church Channel

Cloo (mystery and crime dramas)

Destination America (U.S. travel and food)

DIY Network

Golf Channel

Gospel Music Channel

Halogen TV (social change–oriented)

Jewelry TV

The Military Channel

Outdoor Channel

Russia Today

The Science Channel

SOAPnet

Speed Channel (motor sports)

Sources: This is a small selection of cable and satellite channels available through Comcast's Xfinity, Time Warner Cable, or DirecTV.

CONCLUSION

This chapter has examined the ways in which economic versions of the production perspective help us understand the media industry. Such an approach is essential, but a focus on the economics of the production of media is a limited lens from which to view the relationship between mass media and society.

One line of argument suggests that the approach outlined in this chapter has a tendency to present an overdetermined view of the mass media; that is, it overemphasizes the ways in which economic forces determine the nature of media products. *Determine* is the key word here, for this critique suggests that the economics of the production process cannot fully define the specific nature of mass media. According to this argument, the production process involves too many additional intervening variables. Media production is directed by human beings who make judgments and interpretations at every stage. As a result, there is more variability within media than some production-oriented critics imply, and the institutional constraints on production are not all-encompassing. We accept the basic contours of this criticism but see no need to discard the insights gained from the production perspective. We cannot ignore, nor should we overstate, the impact of economic forces on media production.

The economic dimension of the media industry is certainly a critical component for analysis. However, as the next two chapters will show, more than economics is involved in understanding the contours of the media industry and the processes of media production. We must also consider political and organizational factors.

DISCUSSION QUESTIONS

1. What is the significance of ownership concentration within the media industry (film, television, music, and publishing) in a digital era?

2. How do profit pressures influence the news media? Do you think nonprofit journalism is, or can be, significantly different from for-profit journalism?

3. How responsive, if at all, are you to new advertising strategies such as product placement, brand integration, advergames, and personalized web-based ad messages? What does this suggest about the effectiveness of, and potential resistance to, various forms of stealth advertising?

4. Should we be concerned that advertiser-driven pressures lead to media audience fragmentation and contribute to political polarization? Explain why or why not.

Source: Bloomberg/Getty Images.

CHAPTER 3
Political Influence on Media

The nonprofit watchdog group Reporters Without Borders listed three democratic countries—Finland, the Netherlands, and Norway—at the top of its 2013 annual Press Freedom Index, and three countries with authoritarian governments—Turkmenistan, North Korea, and Eritrea—at the bottom of the list. (The United States ranked 32nd of the 179 countries in the report.) The index was constructed from several criteria, including the amount of violence against journalists, the nature of legislation governing media, and the degree of economic pressures on the media (Reporters Without Borders 2013).

Reporters Without Borders Secretary-General Christophe Deloire noted that the Index "does not take direct account of the kind of political system but it is clear that democracies provide better protection for the freedom to produce and circulate accurate news and information than countries where human rights are flouted." But being in a democracy does not mean the media are totally unconstrained. Deloire continued, "In dictatorships, news providers and their families are exposed to ruthless reprisals, while in democracies news providers have to cope with the media's economic crises and conflicts of interest." These various types of pressure on the media differ widely, but they all have an effect.

As the Index rankings suggest, to better understand media—news and entertainment media alike—we need to consider the political environment in which they operate. Government in all nations serves as an organizing structure that can, to varying degrees, constrain or promote the free activity (or agency) of the media (Starr 2004). This is the tension between structure and agency as it applies to media and the political world. In totalitarian systems, the structural constraint of the state largely dominates the potential agency of the media. State-owned news agencies, broadcast media, and film studios can act as propaganda arms of the state, promoting a narrow set of government-sanctioned images and messages. Authoritarian regimes hire sympathetic bloggers and tweeters to spread their messages, while using censorship and surveillance technologies to monitor potential political threats. In extreme cases, journalists can be imprisoned or killed for challenging state polices.

Democratic societies, on the other hand, pride themselves on protecting freedom of the press and freedom of expression. Such societies are usually characterized by a more diverse mix of public and privately owned media outlets offering a variety of arts, news, information, and entertainment. The media in such societies are still subject to government regulation, but they are usually given much greater latitude to operate independently. However, in some democratic societies, the media are still largely controlled by a relatively small group of powerful interests—commercial corporations. In those cases, it is corporate domination of media rather than government control that is of most concern.

The relationship between political forces and the media raises important questions about the limits of free speech, the impact of economic interests, and the appropriate role of government. These are the topics of this chapter. (Later, in Chapter 7, we will look at the media's influence on politics.) Our concern is not with the details of media legislation but rather with the general dynamics that characterize the relationship between government and media. We also address the more informal political pressure brought to bear on the media by media advocacy groups, public interest organizations, religious groups, and media critics.

THE "FIRST FREEDOM" AND THE "PUBLIC INTEREST"

In the United States, debates about media regulation—and the balancing of competing interests—go back to the founding of the country. Most Americans are familiar with the First Amendment to the U.S. Constitution, which guarantees, among other things, freedom of the press. The amendment in its entirety reads as follows: "Congress shall make no law respecting an establishment of religion, or prohibiting the free exercise thereof; or abridging the freedom of speech, or of the press; or the right of the people peaceably to assemble, and to petition the government for a redress of grievances."

Because the amendment begins with "Congress shall make no law . . ." this "first freedom" suggests that the government should take a hands-off approach toward the media. The framers of the Constitution knew all too well how European governments had persecuted authors, printers, and publishers. Throughout Europe, governments limited the right of printers through tactics such as requiring licenses, heavily taxing newsprint, censorship, and aggressively prosecuting libel (Eisenstein 1968). The U.S. legal and legislative system took a different route. It protected the freedom of the press in several key ways. First, it treated the licensing of the press as a case of illegal "prior restraint." Second, it developed a tradition of opposing special taxes on the press. Third, it greatly restricted criminal libel suits. This was the hands-off dimension of public policy embodied in the First Amendment.

But we do not have to go any further than the U.S. Constitution to see another dimension of the government's relationship with the media. Section 8 of Article I lists the powers of Congress, among which is the power "to promote the progress of science and useful arts, by securing for limited times to authors and inventors the exclusive right to their respective writings and discoveries." Here the Constitution explicitly gives Congress the right to intervene in the communications marketplace to protect the interests of authors and inventors and, in effect, to advance the public interest through the promotion of science and the arts.

Thus, the relationship between government and media in U.S. society is complex. It involves balancing the protection of free expression by *limiting* government intervention with the protection of the public interest by *using* government intervention. In many ways, these competing demands are at the heart of the debates regarding government regulation of the media.

Supporters of deregulation generally assert that the "free market" system is adequate for accommodating the needs of both media producers and media consumers. They argue that consumers have the ultimate power to choose to tune into or buy media products and that there is no need for government interference in the form of media regulation. The marketplace serves as a quasi-democratic forum in which consumers, not government agencies, get to decide the fate of media.

In its pure form, the deregulation approach is a negative prescription for policy. That is, deregulation advocates suggest what they are *against* (regulation), not what they *favor*. While they clearly support the "free market" process, there is little or no discussion about the undemocratic nature of a marketplace where more dollars mean more influence and where people are viewed as consumers rather than citizens. Nor is there much discussion of the outcome of this market process beyond the idea that media products would reflect changing market tastes. But what if explicit sex, graphic violence, and endless trivia are what market tastes demand? Should the government then involve itself in the regulation of content? And where do the needs of a democracy for news and information that may not be profitable fit in this vision? There are among the dilemmas raised by the deregulation position.

In contrast to the deregulation approach, support for media regulation is usually based on a desired outcome. The most common standard for assessing this outcome is the "public interest." The idea that media should serve the public interest was first explicitly articulated in the earliest days of radio broadcasting when the government tied serving the public interest to the granting of licenses because broadcast media were using publicly owned airwaves. But what is the "public interest"? This is a central dilemma raised by the proregulation position. (For a more detailed comparison of the "free market" versus "public interest" models, see Croteau and Hoynes 2006.)

Many of these regulation debates now involve the Federal Communications Commission (FCC), the independent U.S. government agency established in 1934. Comprised of five commissioners, appointed by the president and confirmed by the Senate for five-year terms, the

FCC regulates U.S. interstate and international communications by radio, television, wire, satellite, and cable. The FCC is also responsible for the issuance of licenses, the setting of some charges, and the enforcement of communication rules. (You can get more information on the FCC at fcc.gov.)

FCC policymakers have generally expressed agreement with the importance of serving the "public interest," and they have shared some common ground in understanding the term (Krugman and Reid 1980). For example, policymakers commonly believe that the FCC serves the public interest by attempting to balance the interests of various groups, suggesting that there is no single public interest. They also stress that the government cannot write media regulation in stone for all eternity because technological and economic changes are constantly occurring. Finally, they believe that regulation that promotes diversity in programming and services is in the public interest. However, beyond these broad parameters, much disagreement remains about what is or is not meant by the "public interest." Defining the meaning of this malleable term is one way in which different actors have influenced the construction of public policy.

REGULATION IN INTERNATIONAL PERSPECTIVE

All governments develop some policies aimed at regulating and controlling the media because they understand their political and social importance. Obviously, the method by which governments try to achieve such control varies. As noted, some nations have taken direct authoritarian control of media through state ownership of broadcast outlets, bans on opposition media, and constraints on Internet access. But most nations engage in media regulation that is nonauthoritarian in nature, combining government policies with free market forces.

The role of the U.S. government in regulating the media has always been minuscule compared to many other democratic nations (Starr 2004). The early days of radio in the United States were characterized by free market commercialism that produced considerable chaos. In contrast, European nations adopted an approach that involved government operation of the media as a technique to avoid signal interference. The result was a system that (1) emphasized public service, (2) was national in character, (3) was politicized, and (4) was noncommercial (McQuail, de Mateo, and Tapper 1992).

In many countries, this approach meant adopting a state monopoly system. The British Broadcasting Corporation (BBC), established in 1922, was the first such system. Within four years, Italy, Sweden, Ireland, Finland, and Denmark had copied the BBC model. Over time, more nations developed similar arrangements, and many variations developed as well. Most monopolies, for example, were nationwide. But in countries such as Belgium, where both Flemish and French were widely spoken, each linguistic group had a separate public broadcasting service. Also, although some countries maintained state monopolies, other nations—for example, Britain since the 1950s—adopted approaches that coupled state-run with privately owned systems.

In most European countries, the government controlled the organization and financing of broadcast services, while programming was largely run independently. Here, too, there was no single model. Producers outside the state-run system often created the actual programming. However, unlike in the United States, public broadcasting in Europe was always a central force in broadcasting. The point of government involvement was to ensure that broadcasting could deliver quality programming that served the public interest, including educational programs and news. As in the United States, the interpretation of "public interest" was debated in Europe. However, people generally considered the purpose of public service broadcasting to be to provide citizens with a diverse range of high-quality entertainment, information, and education. This in turn was generally understood to mean the production of a broad range of programs rather than only programs that were highly profitable (Donders 2011; Hills 1991). Thus, unlike in the United States, success in the purely commercial marketplace has not been the dominant model for most media in Europe. Instead, governments have invested substantially in public broadcast media, supporting the production of both news and entertainment.

Government media, however benignly run, present difficulties. In some countries, controversy regarding the political content of programs has plagued public service broadcasting. In part because of such debates, in part because of changes in technology, and in part because of shifts in the political winds, European broadcasting has undergone dramatic changes since the 1980s. Governments have significantly reduced regulations concerning the structure and financing of broadcasting. The shift has been toward more open competition between public broadcasters and commercial stations. In some countries, such as Italy, the pressure to liberalize airwaves came from private companies and business leaders, who saw the profit potential inherent in television and radio stations and challenged the state by operating illegal stations, forcing the regulators to reconsider the state monopoly principle (Ginsborg 2005; Hibberd 2008). Thus regulators have introduced advertising into many public stations (though not the BBC, which inside the UK remains advertising free) and have added new commercial stations. The results have been increases in advertising, increases in imported programming (which is often cheaper to air than original domestically produced programming), and the consolidation of media companies into ever larger corporate conglomerates that buy up formerly independent producers (Hills 1991).

Ironically, deregulation in structure and finance has been followed by increased regulation of media content, in part because free market competition has led to more violent and sexually explicit programs as a way to attract audiences. In response, some governments introduced limits on programming and regulated the amount and frequency of advertising. For example, in some European countries, governments require that news, public affairs, religious, and children's programming run for 30 minutes before a commercial break (Hirsch and Petersen 1992). Also, France, Great Britain, and Sweden (along with Canada and Australia) have restrictions against broadcasting violent programs during children's hours, with broadcasters subject to stiff fines for violations (Clark 1993). These and other policies are evolving as commercial options expand but some researchers argue that these new commercial offerings are "hardly conducive to what might be thought of as socially desirable outcomes such as range and diversity of content—including, crucially, locally produced programmes that reflect children's own communities and environment" (D'Arma and Steemers 2013: 123).

COMPETING INTERESTS AND THE REGULATION DEBATE

So far, we have presented the regulation debate in its simplest form—a free market approach versus government regulation in the public interest. But, in reality, the debate is far more complicated. Despite simple rhetoric calling for "deregulation," virtually everyone involved with the media *wants* government regulation. This includes liberal and conservative politicians, industry executives, and public interest advocates. What these groups disagree about is *what kind* of government regulation should exist.

For example, almost all calls for deregulating media are, in practice, calls for *selective* deregulation, leaving in place many of the laws and policies that benefit the media industry. Indeed, the media industry could not exist in its present form without active government regulation and control through broadcast licensing, copyright enforcement, and other provisions. That is why the media industry actively supports *some* regulations, namely, those that benefit the industry.

Meanwhile, supporters of press freedoms and increased media diversity often call for regulations that protect the interests of the public against the influence of the powerful media industry. The media industry usually cites the merits of deregulation when it is faced with such constraints. So, as we will see, the history of regulatory debates is not about *whether or not* the government should play a role in regulating the media. Instead, it is about *how* and *to what extent* government should act.

These debates reflect competing interests (Freedman 2008). Regulatory decisions create winners and losers, so it is important to ask, "Who benefits from such regulation?" as well as "Who is constrained?" This can explain a great deal about regulation debates. The media and telecommunications industry promotes its interests through a well-organized and powerful political arm that—along with individual media corporations—finances political candidates and lobbies elected officials (see Table 3.1). It is safe to assume that such efforts are aimed at promoting legislation in which the industry has an interest and at derailing efforts it deems threatening. And, of course, the media industry controls the biggest soapbox in society. One FCC official pointed out that one reason broadcasters are such a powerful Washington lobbying group is because they control the air time given to members of Congress on local stations (Hickey 1995). Politicians courting favorable media coverage for re-election are likely to be highly conscious of legislation that can affect the media industry.

Ordinary citizens, on the other hand, can try to influence regulatory debates through their own advocacy groups and social movement organizations, or by giving feedback to elected officials or the FCC when regulatory debates arise. Often, these struggles go back and forth for a long period of time. For example, in the mid-1990s the government relaxed or eliminated various regulations that the industry opposed. This led to a variety of citizen actions from across the political spectrum protesting the resulting concentration of media ownership, advocating for more diversity and more community-oriented noncommercial media, and calling for the containment of violent and sexually explicit material—all concerns that continue to this day.

Following this broad overview of the contest over media regulation, we turn to some common U.S. debates about media regulation and the public interest. We group the issues into two broad categories: the regulation of *ownership and control* and the regulation of *content and distribution.*

Table 3.1	Select Media-Related Organizations' Spending on Elections and Lobbying, 2012		
	Elections	*Lobbying*	*Total*
AT&T Inc	$6,773,161	$17,430,000	$24,203,161
Google	$3,820,612	$18,220,000	$22,040,612
National Cable & Telecommunications Association	$2,216,971	$18,890,000	$21,106,971
Comcast Corp	$5,154,400	$14,750,000	$19,904,400
Verizon Communications	$4,161,582	$15,220,000	$19,381,582
National Association of Broadcasters	$1,618,243	$14,510,000	$16,128,243
Microsoft	$5,313,086	$8,086,000	$13,399,086
National Amusements (Viacom and CBS)	$1,872,488	$7,370,000	$9,242,488
Time Warner Cable	$1,401,044	$7,770,000	$9,171,044
News Corp	$1,736,545	$6,340,000	$8,076,545
Cox Enterprises	$3,215,457	$3,140,000	$6,355,457
Deutsche Telekom (T-Mobile USA)	$832,261	$5,323,901	$6,156,162
Time Warner	$2,450,294	$3,548,000	$5,998,294
CC Media Holdings (Clear Channel Communications)	$1,025,090	$4,542,050	$5,567,140
Recording Industry Assn of America	$349,293	$5,068,387	$5,417,680
Facebook	$742,733	$3,850,000	$4,592,733
Sony Corp	$809,491	$3,258,000	$4,067,491
Sprint Nextel	$493,228	$2,745,223	$3,238,451
Motion Picture Assn of America	$871,955	$1,950,000	$2,821,955
Liberty Media (DIRECTV)	$757,719	$450,000	$1,207,719

Source: Federal Election Commission data and lobbying disclosure reports filed with the Secretary of the Senate's Office of Public Records summarized by the Center for Responsive Politics (www.opensecrets.org). Accessed June 14, 2013.

Note: Election spending includes contributions to PACs, parties, outside spending groups, and candidates in the 2012 election cycle. Lobbying spending was for the 2012 calendar year.

REGULATING OWNERSHIP AND CONTROL

In this section, we review examples of the debates over regulating media ownership and technology in the United States (Brenner and Rivers 1982; Freeman 2008; Noam 1985, 2009; Pool 1983; Tunstall 1986). We do not attempt to provide any sort of comprehensive review; rather, our primary goal is to show how debates about the relationship between politics and the media represent one kind of tension between agency and structure in the social world. We begin with a brief case study that illustrates some of the conflicts involved in regulating ownership and control.

The Case of Pirate Radio

It was 6:30 A.M., says Doug Brewer (a.k.a. Craven Moorehead), when government agents burst into his Tampa Bay, FL, home. The agents wore flak jackets and had their guns drawn. They made Brewer and his family lie on the floor while they searched the house. A police helicopter circled the neighborhood, and other officers with submachine guns stood outside. When they found what they had come for, the agents handcuffed Brewer to a chair while they removed thousands of dollars' worth of contraband (Nesbitt 1998; Shiver 1998).

Brewer was not a drug dealer. He was a "radio pirate" whose unlicensed microstation—"Tampa's Party Pirate"—broadcast "biker rock" music. The agents entering his home on that morning in November of 1997 included Federal Communications Commission (FCC) officials who were enforcing federal regulations prohibiting unlicensed radio broadcasting. The raid was part of an FCC crackdown on "radio piracy." The contraband they confiscated was electronic broadcasting equipment.

If Brewer had produced a magazine or a website, he would have been protected by the Constitution's First Amendment. But government and the courts treat broadcast media differently because they use the public airwaves to reach an audience. There is a limited spectrum of available electromagnetic frequencies, and the government regulates who can use certain frequencies. (A radio station's call number—for example, 98.6 or 101—refers to the frequency at which the station broadcasts.) The government does this by issuing licenses, which "pirate" broadcasters do not have, to stations that seek to broadcast at certain frequencies.

The argument for broadcast licenses is practical: An unlicensed radio signal can interfere with the signal of another station that is legally licensed to use the same, or a nearby, frequency. Or it may interfere with other wireless services—such as cellular phones, pagers, police walkie-talkies, digital television signals, or even air traffic control communication—all of which use the airwaves as well. The absence of government regulation of the airwaves might lead to chaos as multiple stations drowned each other out at the same frequencies and personal communications devices were interrupted. The result would be akin to a street and highway system with no lanes, signs, stoplights, or speed limits. In fact, it was precisely fear of this sort of chaos in the early days of radio that led to regulation and the practice of requiring broadcast licenses. (License requirements began in 1912, even before commercial broadcasting began, because other maritime communications traffic was interfering with the Navy's radio communications.) The government, therefore, says it uses licensing requirements to protect the "public interest."

But unlicensed "pirate" operators—who generally prefer the more neutral term *microbroadcaster*—tell a different story. They suggest it is commercial media corporations that are really behind the effort to keep them off the air. They point out that low-power stations are just that—low-power—and pose virtually no interference threat to other stations. In addition, microbroadcasters go to great lengths to ensure that their signals don't interfere with other broadcasts or communications. Even so, their efforts were illegal because the FCC simply did not grant licenses to small microstations, leaving radio to be dominated by larger, mostly commercial, interests. If the FCC is so concerned about chaos on the airwaves, radio activists asked, then why doesn't it simply allocate a section of the broad-cast spectrum for microstations and then issue licenses?

That idea ran into stiff opposition from commercial broadcasters. The National Associa-tion of Broadcasters (NAB), the industry's lobbying group, used the fear of widespread signal interference to oppose the creation of a new category of low-power FM radio sta-tions. The NAB even distributed a CD to members of Congress supposedly documenting what such interference would sound like. However, the FCC's own engineers said the audio simulation was fraudulent, and the FCC's then-chairman William E. Kennard accused the NAB of a "systematic campaign of misinformation and scare tactics" (Labaton 2000: C1). Later, an independent study commissioned by the FCC confirmed that low-power radio posed no significant interference issues (FCC 2004).

With the industry's primary argument exposed as bogus, community radio activists finally achieved some limited success in 2000 when the FCC agreed to begin licensing low-power stations. But existing broadcasters, including both the NAB and National Public Radio (NPR), successfully lobbied Congress to make licensing so restrictive as to limit the number of such stations to just a few dozen instead of the thousands originally proposed. Licensing and operation requirements were later eased somewhat and by 2010 more than 800 licenses had been granted. But community radio advocates continued to pressure for more. Finally, the Local Community Radio Act was signed into law in January 2011, giving the FCC a mandate to expand the broadcast spectrum allotted to community radio stations, marking a major victory for low-power radio advocates. The FCC began accepting applica-tions for these new low power community stations licenses in late 2013.

This pirate radio case shows that policy is a product of political activity, that different media are regulated differently, that the real debate is typically over what type of regulation should exist, and that competing interests are at stake in such media policy making. These will be recurring issues as we explore various policy debates.

Regulating Ownership of Media Outlets

When early government officials crafted the First Amendment, media ownership was largely a local, decentralized affair. As a result, the First Amendment closely links "freedom of speech or of the press" because, in colonial times, the two were very similar. Individual printers or shops employing just a couple of people created the media products of the day. The written word, therefore, was largely an extension of the spoken word.

In this context, the issue of ownership was of little concern. The equipment needed to operate a press was relatively straightforward and affordable for purchase or lease to those with modest capital. In theory, there was no limit on the potential number of different presses. Over time, however, communication media have changed in significant ways.

First, *media technology* has changed. Print was the only mass medium that existed when the First Amendment was written. Every time a new medium emerged—such as radio, broadcast television, cable, or the Internet—regulators had to create the new rules within which this medium would operate. In general, the rules regulating media have historically differed among the three basic types of communication media: print media, broadcast media, and common carriers. The latter are industries whose operators must provide equal access in their service of the public, often because they have some type of

Source: www.prometheusradio.com.

Radio activists have long worked to promote the expansion of nonprofit community-based radio. The Prometheus Radio Project in Philadelphia, whose website is pictured here, is one such group that works to demystify the media process, assist community group in creating radio stations, and promote public participation in the FCC regulatory process that oversees low-power FM (LPFM) radio.

protected monopoly. Telephone companies and the mail system, for example, are common carriers.

Broadcast media enabled producers to reach millions of people through a networked system that blanketed the country. This ability transformed the nature of the media by dramatically expanding their reach and potential influence. Also, the technologically accessible range of the electromagnetic spectrum limited the number of free broadcast stations that could operate in any market, creating the scarcity that was crucial in justifying broadcast regulation such as radio licensing. The Internet also altered the technological terrain, creating new opportunities for content providers to offer text, audio, and video to anyone with Internet access. In addition, it has enabled everyone, including nonprofessionals, to produce and post their own content—in some ways harkening back to the older model of decentralized media producers.

Second, *ownership patterns* have changed. The amount of investment capital necessary to produce and promote major state-of-the-art media products is now enormous. As the wry saying goes, freedom of the press exists only for those who can afford to own one—and the price tag keeps getting higher. With changes in technology and in the scale of production, most competitive media ownership is affordable only for those with substantial capital. Even the start-up costs for major websites now routinely run into the millions of dollars. As a result, media have moved away from their independent localism, and more and more media outlets are part of national and international corporate entities. We saw in the last chapter that large media conglomerates, for example, now own many "local" newspapers. Magazine and book publishers are now largely national, or international, enterprises. The days of free speech protecting the small publisher of pamphlets are largely over. Instead, the control of major media has become centralized in the corporate offices of giants such as Time Warner and Viacom.

These changes have led to the regulation of media ownership. For example, the FCC has regulated the number of television and radio stations a single company can own, and there have been sharp political battles over the extent of these limits. By the early 1990s, the government prohibited companies from owning more than 12 television stations or from owning stations that reached more than 25 percent of the nation's audience. Regulations also limited companies to owning a total of 20 AM and 20 FM radio stations, with no more than 2 AM and 2 FM stations in any one city. The aim was to limit the potential monopolistic power of a media conglomerate and to encourage diverse media ownership.

However, changes introduced in the 1996 Telecommunications Act and subsequent updates eased restrictions on both television and radio station ownership, leading to more concentrated ownership patterns. For example, less than two years after the elimination of limits on radio ownership in 1996, there was a 12 percent decline in the number of radio station owners, even while the total number of stations increased by 3 percent. The FCC acknowledged that the regulatory changes had led to "consolidations of radio ownership [that] have reshaped the radio industry" (FCC 1998). Ironically, this consolidation provided fuel for radio pirates to argue for the licensing of microbroadcasters.

The FCC has also restricted certain types of cross-ownership, although it sometimes gives waivers that override such restrictions. A single company usually cannot own both a daily newspaper and a broadcast outlet (radio or TV) in a single city—except in the 20 largest markets, where there remain at least 8 independent media outlets. Also, common ownership of a television broadcast station and a cable system in a single market is prohibited. The aim is to prevent monopolistic control of media in a local market. But such restrictions are constantly under revision, and media companies work to have such limits relaxed. They have plenty of opportunity to influence the rules: The 1996 Telecommunications Act requires that, every four years, the FCC reviews all of its broadcast ownership rules with an eye toward eliminating or modifying any that are no longer in the public interest due to increased media competition. As noted, revisions of the 1996 act led to further relaxation of ownership rules, and more are likely to come.

In fact, there has been a long pattern of easing regulation on media owners. For example, prompted by the merger of Viacom and CBS, which resulted in one company owning controlling interest in both the CBS and the former UPN networks, the FCC allowed the ownership of two broadcast networks by the same company, something that had long been illegal.

However, the so-called dual network rule prohibits a merger between any of the four major television networks (ABC, CBS, Fox, and NBC). In addition, court rulings in 2001 overturned, first, regulations that prevented a single company from owning an interest in cable systems that reach more than 30 percent of the country's cable homes and, second, rules prohibiting a cable company from owning more than 40 percent of the programming shown on its system. This continuing deregulation allows for the growth of larger and more concentrated media companies.

One clear way in which government can intervene in the media industry, then, is by regulating ownership of media outlets. By preventing monopoly ownership of media, the government attempts to act in the public interest because control of media information by a few companies may well be detrimental to the free flow of ideas. Through such regulations, the government prevents media giants from acquiring control of the media market.

Media companies have been so successful in rolling back ownership restrictions that some observers see an unprecedented threat emerging from the consolidation of media ownership into fewer and fewer hands. As far back as 1995, Reuven Frank, former president of NBC News, suggested that

> it is daily becoming more obvious that the biggest threat to a free press and the circulation of ideas is the steady absorption of newspapers, television networks and other vehicles of information into enormous corporations that know how to turn knowledge into profit—but are not equally committed to inquiry or debate or to the First Amendment. (quoted in Shales 1995: C1)

Since that statement was made, media consolidation has continued unabated.

Regulating Content Ownership: Copyright and the Case of Music Sampling

Rap music fans know Public Enemy's 1990 album, *Fear of a Black Planet*, as a classic in the genre. The album epitomized the group's "wall of noise" approach that layered sound fragments cut from other recordings into a new and unique composition. Though Public Enemy's use of nearly a hundred samples on the album was extreme, frequent sampling was a common practice during the "golden age of hip hop" in the late 1980s. But that age was over in 1991 when a U.S. District Court ruled in *Grand Upright Music Ltd. v. Warner Bros. Records Inc.* that artists were breaking copyright laws if they sampled sounds from other people's work without first obtaining permission from the copyright owners. The ruling changed music forever since bands could not afford to pay the permissions fees for so many different samples. Instead, contemporary recordings that use the technique typically sample only a couple of sounds to keep costs down.

In 2010, Benjamin Franzen directed a documentary film about music sampling and copyright law. In it, he used over 400 unlicensed music samples. But despite the title of his film, he and his collaborators were not *Copyright Criminals*. That's because their work is protected under the "fair use" provision of copyright law that allows creators to quote from copyrighted works without permission for the purposes of education, commentary, criticism, and other transformative uses (McLeod 2010). Ironically, the film is available for sale in a copyrighted DVD version.

Figure 3.1	**Select Ownership Rules Changes in the 1996 Telecommunications Act and Subsequent Amendments**

The 1996 Telecommunications Act eased restrictions on media ownership, leading to more concentrated ownership patterns.

Previous Rules	*New Rule Changes*
National Television	
A single entity: Can own up to 12 stations nationwide or Can own stations reaching up to 25% of U.S. TV households	No limit on number of stations Station reach increased to 35% of U.S. TV households (the limit was increased to 39% in 2004)
Local Television	
A single entity: Can own only one station in a market	Can own up to two television stations in the same local market, as long as one of the stations is not among the top four in the area, and there are at least eight independent television stations
National Radio	
A single entity: Can own up to 20 FM and 20 AM stations	No limit on station ownership
Local Radio	
A single entity: Cannot own, operate, or control more than 2 AM and 2 FM stations in a market Audience share of co-owned stations cannot exceed 25%	Ownership adjusted by market size: In markets with 45+ stations, a single entity cannot own more than 8 stations total and cannot own more than 5 in the same service (AM or FM) With 30–44 stations; 7 total, 5 same service With 15–29 stations; 6 total, 4 in the same service With 14 or fewer; 5 total, 3 same service (but no more than 50% of the stations in the market) Limits may be waived if the FCC rules it will increase the total number of stations in operation
Newspaper/Broadcast Cross-Ownership Rule	
Absolute ban on newspaper/broadcast cross-ownership	Newspaper/broadcast cross-ownership is allowed in the largest markets where there exists competition and numerous voices (2008)

The case of music sampling and the "fair use" exemptions illustrate the complicated world of copyright laws that have developed since the copyright clause of the Constitution and the original 1790 Copyright Act. Those laws protect the sale and distribution of this book. If you flip to the beginning of this book, you will find a copyright page that includes the publication date of the book, the name and address of the publisher, and a statement of copyright. This copyright statement reads, "All rights reserved. No part of this book may be reproduced or utilized in any form or by any means, electronic or mechanical, including photocopying, recording, or by any information storage and retrieval system, without permission in writing from the publisher." This statement, enforced by government laws and regulations, makes it illegal for someone to simply copy and sell this book without permission from the publisher. The language of copyright statements has evolved over time to address new technologies such as photocopying, sound recording, electronic scanning devices, and file-sharing systems. All such forms of reproduction for sale are illegal. Such regulations exist to protect both the publisher, who collects income from the sale of books, and the authors, who receive royalty payments from publishers for each copy of the book that is sold. Because they have invested the time and money necessary to create the book you are holding, the law says that they should control the right to

The FBI's anti-piracy warning label can be used to accompany copyrighted content, including films, audio recordings, electronic media, software, books, and photographs. The language that accompanies the warning notes that "The unauthorized reproduction or distribution of a copyrighted work is . . . punishable by up to five years in prison and a fine of $250,000."

sell, distribute, and profit from such sales. If the copyright laws didn't exist, there would be no way for publishers to earn a return on their investment.

While originally intended to provide incentives for people to invest the time, effort, and resources necessary to produce new creations, copyright law has changed dramatically. In the original 1790 Copyright Act, authors were given exclusive rights to their work for 14 years, renewable one time if they were still alive. Since then, media companies have successfully lobbied Congress to repeatedly extend the period covered by copyright. With the "Copyright Term Extension Act" of 1998, sometimes known as the "Mickey Mouse Protection Act" because of Disney's key role in lobbying for its passage, copyright now covers an individual creator's lifetime plus 70 years or, in the case of corporate authorship, 120 years after creation or 95 years after publication, whichever is shorter. Advocates argue this allows creators to pass on the benefits of lucrative work to their heirs or profit reasonably from their creation. Critics argue this undermines the entire purpose of copyright law to both incentivize creativity and also support a robust public domain.

Over the years, the government and the courts have extended copyright laws to include a wide variety of visual, sound, and computer software products under the rubric of *intellectual property rights*. Peer-to-peer (P2P) networks have posed distinctive challenges to companies (who fear loss of profit), legislators (who have to develop appropriate policies for the new digital platforms), and enforcement agents (who face considerable difficulties in tracking down violators). P2P networks allow Internet users to share digital files—including copyrighted music, movies, and games—with other users for free. By connecting to a site's servers using specialized software, users are able to search each other's hard drives for files and then download them for free.

Early P2P sites hoped to avoid enforcement of copyright laws because the illegally shared copyrighted material did not reside on their central servers. Instead, the P2P sites acted only as go-betweens, linking the hard drives of users. This logic, though, failed to convince the courts, who shut down one of the earliest successful P2P sites, the Napster music-sharing site, ruling that P2P file sharing was an infringement of copyright laws. (Naptser later emerged as a legal music downloading site, charging an access fee.) In subsequent years, other P2P sites, including Pirate Bay and Limewire, have been shut down—temporarily or permanently—for violation of copyright laws.

Other sorts of sites can violate copyright laws, too, including the popular YouTube video sharing site. Despite YouTube's policy that explicitly prevents users from posting creative content protected by copyright licenses registered in the United States, a great deal of copyrighted content continues to be uploaded to the site. YouTube has a system that allows users to flag a copyright violation, and they have accommodated many requests to remove such material, as courts in the United States and abroad usually hold the service provider responsible for the content posted on its site. In 2007, for example, Viacom asked YouTube to remove more than 200,000 videos because of copyright infringement.

More broadly, it is illegal to copy and sell music CDs, digital music files such as MP3s, movies, and computer software. Likewise, it is illegal to use a copyrighted photograph in a commercial publication. We had to acquire permission to use all the photographs you see in this book. (We were unable to include some photos we wanted in the book, either because the copyright holders would not grant us permission to use them or because the fees they requested were too high.) The media industry may not want government regulation in some matters but, in this case, it certainly *does* want government intervention. The government's protection of copyright is crucial to the continued functioning of the media industry. Without government enforcement of copyright laws, the for-profit media industry would be unable to survive.

In recent year, critics seeking to enrich the public domain have developed alternative approaches to copyright, such as Creative Commons licenses. Creative Commons is a non-profit organization that offers free legal tools to protect the use of creative work while maximizing the amount of material that is available for free and legal sharing, use, repurposing, and remixing (Creative Commons 2010). Unlike traditional copyright, Creative Commons licenses allow creators to give users specific rights to use their work while giving the creators the option of having "some rights reserved" (see Lessig 2005). (See Figure 3.2.)

Regulating Ownership of Programming: The Case of "Fin-Syn" Rules

While the government is concerned with protecting the rights of the owners of media property through copyright law, it has also been concerned with avoiding monopolistic

Figure 3.2	**Creative Commons Copyright Alternatives**

Creators who use a Creative Commons copyright can choose different license options, placing varying degrees of restrictions on the use of their work.

Attribution by	Share Alike sa	Non-Commercial nc	No Derivative Works nd
You let others copy, distribute, display, and perform your copyrighted work — and derivative works based upon it — but only if they give credit the way you request.	You allow others to distribute derivative works only under a license identical to the license that governs your work.	You let others copy, distribute, display, and perform your work — and derivative works based upon it — but for non-commercial purposes only.	You let others copy, distribute, display, and perform only verbatim copies of your work, not derivative works based upon it.

Source: http://creativecommons.org/about/licenses.

ownership of that property. One example of this concern was the FCC's regulation of ownership and control of television programming through "fin-syn" (financial interest and syndication) rules (Crawford 1993; Flint 1993; Freeman 1994a, 1994b; Jessell 1993). Through much of television history, the TV networks generally did not own the programs they broadcast. They merely bought the rights to broadcast programs produced by others. The fin-syn rules, established in 1970, limited the ability of the three major TV networks (ABC, CBS, NBC) to acquire financial interests or syndication rights in television programming. (In syndication, a producer sells the rights to rebroadcast a program.) In its words, the FCC "imposed these constraints to limit network control over television programming and thereby encourage the development of a diversity of programs through diverse sources of program services" (FCC 1995). The fear was that the three networks—which shared an oligopoly in television broadcasting in 1970—could also dominate programming industry-wide if they were able to own and control the creation and syndication of programming. Regulators theorized that they could encourage the emergence of a more competitive marketplace of program producers by forcing the networks to buy programming from independent producers.

For more than two decades, the fin-syn rules were the law of the land. During that period, though, the landscape of American television broadcasting changed dramatically. Many new independent television stations, cable stations, and even new television networks emerged. The audience share controlled by the three networks declined, and fear of a network monopoly subsided. Finally, in 1993, a U.S. district court ruled that networks were not subject to many of the FCC's fin-syn regulations because competing cable stations and the emergence of new networks and independent stations precluded them from monopolizing production and syndication. In that case, changes in technology were a factor in changing how government regulates media.

The changed FCC rules meant that, among other things, networks could now acquire financial interests in and syndication rights to all network programming. This encouraged vertical integration, as networks turned to studios owned by their corporate parents to produce more of their programming. Before the new regulations, network production was limited to a maximum of 20 percent of a network's prime-time programming. One year after the changes in regulation, the "Big 3" networks either produced in-house or had financial interests in about half of all prime-time programming. In the 2004–2005 season, for example, Viacom (then owner of CBS) had a financial interest in more than 90 percent of the new programs on the CBS schedule. By the 2007–2008 season, in-house production accounted for two thirds of prime-time programs on the four major networks. The major studios that own networks—Disney (ABC), Universal (NBC), Twentieth Century Fox (Fox), and Warner Brothers (CW)—produced about 90 percent of the series on the major networks (Kunz 2009). Independent producers were largely left out of this closed system of production.

But the new rules were a very lucrative opportunity for networks to generate more revenue, at no additional cost, by licensing long-running programs they produced to appear in reruns on other stations. For example, NBC generated $130 million by selling syndication rights to its popular comedy *The Office* (Dempsey and Adalian 2007).

The fin-syn debates, in all their inside details, illustrate some of the basic tensions that exist in the media industry. The unbridled growth of major media conglomerates threatens small media producers. In turn, major conglomerates argue that monopolistic control is no longer possible because we live in a diverse media world with many options. The question for policy makers is whether the government needs to use any regulatory constraint to control the actions of the growing media corporations.

These debates are yet another illustration of the tension between structure and agency. In this case, the same regulatory structure that protects the media industry's copyright claims constrained its ability to produce and resell its products. However, the agency of the media industry is seen in its ability to promote changes that favored the major networks. Meanwhile, relaxing old regulations ended up harming the viability of smaller media producers. Once again, regulations constrain some and benefit others.

Regulating Ownership and Control of Technology

For over 20 years, the growth of digital media has been seen by some observers as a revolutionary change in media development (Negroponte 1995). Digital information—the 0s and 1s that make up binary code—is now the common underlying basis for storing audio, video, and print media in many different formats, including MP3 or CD (music), DVD or Blu-ray (video), and GIF or JPG (graphics and photographs). This common digital foundation is what enables your computer, television set, or cell phone to access text, images, video, and sound and to "talk" with other digital devices.

The impact of digitization was enhanced by other technological developments that increased the amount of data that could be easily stored or transmitted. Flash drives enable you to carry hundreds of songs or other data on an iPod shuffle the size of a matchbook. Fiber optics allow a vast amount of information to travel by way of light over a tiny, pure glass fiber. Digital broadcasting via traditional transmission towers or by satellite has also increased communication options and enabled wireless devices to access all this data.

Over a remarkable short period of time, digitization has transformed the social lives of those with access to it. Computer networking through the Internet, to take just one example, links individuals to commercial sites, community organizations, government agencies, and other individuals. From a home computer or mobile device individuals can shop, pay bills, take an online course, check want ads, listen to music, engage in political discussion, register their child for the local Little League, watch a video or television program, e-mail a government official, stay in touch with friends through a social network website, Skype relatives, and check a map before travelling. All of this seems quite obvious and normal to us now, but it simply didn't exist just a few years ago.

Digitization led to a convergence of mass media formats. The lines between cable television, broadcast television, telephone, computer, and so on have become less and less identifiable. The result is the emergence of more integrated multimedia services. We will examine the implications of such technology in more detail in Chapter 9, but it is important to note here that such changes raise critical issues for the regulation of technology.

The Internet and "Net Neutrality"

Formerly, the government protected against monopolies by regulating the ownership and control of some technologies. Telephone companies, for example, could not enter the cable TV business and vice versa. In the 1990s, however, all this changed because of the merging of different media forms. In 1996, Congress revised federal laws limiting ownership of cable television. The government allowed the seven regional local telephone companies— the "Baby Bells"—to enter the cable television business. In turn, deregulation opened local phone service to competition from cable providers who wanted to carry phone service over their cables. Some hailed this change as a step toward more competitive, integrated media. Others worried that phone companies would have a substantial advantage in funding new cable ventures, given their steady stream of income from phone services. Many critics were concerned about the specter of a "single-wire" monopoly, that is, a single company providing a wire that could bring cable television, telephone, and Internet access to a home. With various media company mergers, such a bundled package is now routinely offered by providers such as Time Warner, Verizon, Cox, and Comcast.

The changes created a quandary for the FCC. In 1998, faced with convergence in Internet, cable TV, and telephone service, the FCC sought public comment on the question of whether Internet service via cable should be considered a cable service, a telecommunication service, or an information service. Each legal designation brings with it different types of regulation. As one FCC official put it at the time, "When you have the capability that the Internet provides—now you can do almost anything over one medium—you have to start thinking which rules are applicable, or whether any of our rules are applicable at all" (quoted in Simons 1998: B8). Such rethinking of the basic regulatory ground rules will continue as new technologies develop.

Early Internet dial-up via telephone modem operated as an *open access* forum, meaning that all users and content providers were treated the same. Regulations covering telephone lines require this equal treatment because telephone companies are common carriers. However, such regulations do not exist for cable. So broadband access to the Internet via cable opens up the possibility of unequal access to the Internet. A cable company, for example, might structure access so that users visiting company-owned sites (or sites that license with the cable company) are able to download material at top speed, while other sites load more slowly or are blocked entirely. Or it might be able to charge users more for access to data-heavy sites, such as Netflix and YouTube.

The possibility of some Internet content receiving preferential treatment, while other content is slowed or blocked, has raised concern among policy makers and public interest advocates. In response, they have promoted legislation to ensure *net neutrality,* preserving open access to the Internet and a level playing field for all websites, whereby all content would be treated equally. In 2009, the FCC began considering whether or not to add a non-discrimination principle to its Internet Policy Statement, mandating that service providers may not discriminate against any content or application. Many of the major telecommunications and cable providers—those companies that provide access to the Internet through their high-speed cables wired into homes and workplaces—oppose net neutrality. Instead, they have proposed various plans for a two-tiered Internet with an expensive high-speed network that major content providers will pay to access, along with a much slower lane for everyone else.

In December 2010, in a split vote, the FCC passed regulations that fell far short of true net neutrality, giving the major telecommunications firms much of what they wanted. The new rules stipulate that service providers cannot deny access to websites, but they allow cable and phone companies to charge customers more based on the amount of data they download or for access to data-heavy websites. In addition, the regulations exempt wireless service providers, so that access to certain sites via telephone or other mobile device can be blocked by the Internet service provider. For the first time, this would create a two-tier Internet where access is limited by a user's ability to pay and would allow wireless service providers to discriminate against any site they choose (Karr 2010; Stelter 2010). As of this writing, the new regulations are being challenged in court, and net neutrality remains among the most important unresolved media policy issues.

Internet Browsers

As media forms converged, companies involved in related industries became intertwined with the delivery of media content. Microsoft Corporation, best known for its software applications, is one such example. In 1998, the Justice Department and 20 state attorneys general filed an antitrust lawsuit against Microsoft Corporation. With its Windows products used on more than 90 percent of personal computers, Microsoft dominates the operating system software market. Among the allegations in this suit was that Microsoft engaged in illegal anticompetitive practices by using its operating system monopoly to attempt to control the Internet browser market as well. It did so by bundling its Internet browser (Explorer) with its operating system software and pressuring computer manufacturers to include this package on their computers. This would make it much more likely that users of the Microsoft operating system software would opt to use Microsoft's Internet browser, perhaps leading to Microsoft's monopoly control of that market as well. Microsoft was found guilty of monopolistic practices, but the suit ended with a settlement that required relatively minor changes in Microsoft practices (Auletta 2001).

In 2004, the European Commission—the executive body of the European Union—found that Microsoft had abused its dominant position in the operating system software market by its bundling of the Windows Media Player with Windows. It also criticized Microsoft's bundling of the Explorer Internet browser with the Windows operating system. The Commission ordered Microsoft to release a version of Windows without its Media Player, so consumers would have a choice, and it hit Microsoft with a US $655 million fine. When Microsoft repeatedly failed to comply, the Commission fined it again, for $370 million in 2006, and $1.18 billion in 2008. In 2010, European customers were finally able to choose their default browser from a browser choice screen (European Commission 2010).

These examples are just a few of the many similar changes occurring in media technology and subsequent media regulation. Some changes have international implications. With the advent of satellite-based television and the Internet, media products now easily cross national boundaries. In an attempt to control the social implications of such information, the Chinese government has pressured Western media companies to limit the content of some news broadcast via satellite in China. In 1996, the Chinese government announced that all Internet users would have to register with the government and that all Internet service providers would be subject to close supervision by various government agencies. Internet search engine company Google, which entered the Chinese market in 2005, was no exception. In order to enter the lucrative Chinese market, it adopted a self-censorship strategy that blocked access to certain sites, including some promoting democratic reform and human rights in China (BBC 2006). Still, on several occasions, China restricted access to Google's content. After vocal criticism from human rights advocates for its acceptance of the government restrictions, Google announced in 2010 that it would no longer comply with censorship requirements and started redirecting queries to its Hong Kong website, thus bypassing Chinese censorship (Helft and Barboza 2010). Shortly afterward, China temporarily blocked access to Google, forcing the company to stop the automatic redirect to its Hong Kong site if it was to maintain its Internet provider license in China. Such back-and-forth confrontation between media companies and governments in both democratic and authoritarian countries is likely to recur in the coming years. The dust from technological changes and their regulation has not yet settled.

REGULATING MEDIA CONTENT AND DISTRIBUTION

While the regulation of the ownership and control of media outlets, content, programming, and technology raises basic questions about the relationship between government and media, a different set of issues is raised with respect to the regulation of media content itself. However, the basic dynamic of structure and agency remains.

Regulating the Media Left and Right: Diversity Versus Property Rights

In the everyday political world, calls for media regulation come from both liberals and conservatives. However, the intended target of the regulation differs based on political orientation. The sides do not always line up neatly, but conservatives and liberals generally tend to approach the topic of regulation differently.

Liberals and the left usually see the government's role in media regulation as one of protecting the public against the domination of the private sector. (Conservatives see this as government meddling in the free market.) As we have seen, this view manifests itself in liberal support for regulating media ownership of outlets, programming, and technology, with the aim of protecting the public interest against monopolistic corporate practices. Inherent in this approach is the belief that the marketplace is not adequately self-regulating and that commercial interests can acquire undue power and influence.

Liberals and the left also tend to support regulation that encourages diversity in media content, such as the Fairness Doctrine (discussed below). Finally, liberals also support publicly owned media such as the Public Broadcasting Service (PBS) and NPR because such outlets can sometimes support important programming that may not be commercially viable. A central theme for liberals and the left is the need for diversity in all facets of the media.

Conservatives and the right tend to respond to such arguments with staunch support for property rights and the free market system. (Liberals see this as protecting corporate interests at the expense of the public interest.) When it comes to regulating ownership and control of media, conservatives tend to advocate a laissez-faire approach by government. They caution against the dangers of bureaucratic government intervention and the tyranny of "politically correct" calls for diversity. They are often enthusiasts for the ability of the profit motive to lead to positive media developments for all. Conservatives generally see the marketplace as the great equalizer, a place where ideas and products stand or fall based on the extent of their popularity. They often portray ideas like the Fairness Doctrine or public television as illegitimate attempts by those outside the American mainstream to gain access to the media.

Although conservatives abhor the idea of limiting, restricting, or regulating private property rights, they are often quite comfortable with restricting the content of media products, especially in the name of morality. The problem with a pure free market system for the media is that it leads to things such as graphic violence and pornography. Media images of sex and violence are popular and profitable (Dines 2010). However, nearly all observers agree that some restrictions on the content of media are necessary, especially to protect children and minors. In fact, it is conservatives who have often led the call to regulate material they deem unfit for minors. So while conservatives oppose government regulation that requires additional content for the sake of diversity, they are generally comfortable with regulations that restrict or prohibit the dissemination of material they deem unsuitable. The result has been both voluntary and mandatory regulation of media content. We turn now to some of the more common forms of content regulation.

Regulating for Diversity: The Fairness Doctrine

While media have tremendous potential to inform citizens about events and issues in their world, they also have unparalleled potential for abuse by political partisans and commercial interests. One way in which the government attempted to protect against potentially abusive media domination was the establishment of the Fairness Doctrine (Cronauer 1994; Frank 1993; Jost 1994b; Simmons 1978; Wiley 1994). The goal of the doctrine was to promote serious coverage of public issues and to ensure diversity by preventing any single viewpoint from dominating coverage. The Fairness Doctrine provides an interesting example of the rise and fall of a government attempt to regulate media content in the public interest.

In 1949, the FCC adopted a policy that reaffirmed the congressional precedent that "radio be maintained as a medium of free speech for the general public as a whole rather than as an outlet for the purely personal or private interests of the licensee." To achieve this goal, the FCC required, first, that licensees "devote a reasonable percentage of their broadcasting time to the discussion of public issues of interest in the community served by their stations" and, second, "that such programs be designed so that the public has a reasonable opportunity to hear different opposing positions on the public issues of interest and importance in the community" (13 FCC 1246 [1949] in Kahn 1978: 230). While the specific dimensions of the Fairness Doctrine evolved over time, the two basic provisions—requiring broadcasters both to cover public issues and to provide opportunity for the presentation of contrasting points of view—remained intact.

The goal in the application of the doctrine was to ensure diversity of views within the program schedule of a station. The Fairness Doctrine, for example, did not interfere with conservative radio talk shows but rather required the station to provide other programming that included differing points of view. Thus, the Fairness Doctrine never suppressed views, but it sometimes required additional speech for balance. The goal was not to stifle criticism but instead to ensure the airing of vigorous debate and dissent. FCC involvement in any Fairness Doctrine case came only after someone filed a complaint.

Over time, competing actors tried to use and, in some cases, abuse the Fairness Doctrine. The Kennedy, Johnson, and Nixon administrations, for example, harassed unsympathetic journalists by filing complaints under the Fairness Doctrine (Simmons 1978). But in many cases, the doctrine enabled the airing of opposing views that the public would not otherwise have heard. That was the intent of the regulation.

The broadcast industry challenged the legality of the Fairness Doctrine but, in 1969, the Supreme Court unanimously upheld the policy. The Court based its decision, however, on the scarcity of broadcast frequencies, agreeing with the FCC that, because the airwaves were a scarce public resource, broadcasters should use them to serve the public interest. Regardless, as part of the Reagan-era push for government deregulation, the FCC voted in 1987 to revoke the Fairness Doctrine (though technically leaving it on the books until it was deleted in 2011). Failed attempts to revive the Fairness Doctrine have occurred periodically ever since.

The key argument used against the Fairness Doctrine is that the premise of broadcast frequency scarcity on which it was built is no longer an issue. Critics note that, when the government introduced the Fairness Doctrine in 1949, there were only 51 television stations and 2,600 radio stations in the United States. By 2013, there were more than 2,235 broadcast television stations and more than 15,256 radio stations, not counting low-power stations (FCC 2013).

However, the scarcity discussed in the 1969 Supreme Court decision referred to the availability of frequencies, not to the number of media outlets. While the number of media outlets has exploded over the years, the demand has kept pace. As "radio piracy" vividly illustrated, there is still more demand for prime frequency use than space allows. Some new technologies, such as personal communications equipment, require more space on the limited waveband. So, despite the technological changes, a kind of scarcity still exists in broadcast media.

The debate over the Fairness Doctrine highlights an important issue that is easy for us to forget: The airwaves are a public resource, not private property. By applying for a license, broadcasters, much like automobile drivers, agree to adhere to the rules of the road. (Cable providers, too, rely on a public resource since they use public rights-of-way to string their cable lines.) Supporters of the Fairness Doctrine believe that one of those rules should be the requirement that stations air differing points of view. Opponents argue that government regulation inherently inhibits the free expression of ideas. At this writing, opponents of the Fairness Doctrine have prevailed.

Relying on the scarcity argument to support the Fairness Doctrine ignores a more fundamental issue. Allowing the marketplace to exclusively determine the content of media can mean that only popular—and thus profitable—ideas are regularly heard and seen in commercial media. With some niche market exceptions, the commercial marketplace typically operates on the basis of providing what is most popular to the greatest number. This approach may work reasonably well with consumer products, but when the "commodity" at hand is ideas, democracy is not likely to be well served by paying attention only to the popular and fashionable.

Since the abandonment of the Fairness Doctrine, the FCC no longer requires stations to seriously address issues of public interest. If stations do address public issues, they can create entire program schedules that communicate a single viewpoint without ever seriously considering alternative opinions, as was done with the rise of "right wing radio." Some argue that as partisans tune into stations that reflect only their point of view and ignore the possible merits of differing opinions, one possible result is the further entrenchment of political division. We must also remember that commercial interests drive almost all mass media. It is likely, therefore, that corporate owners of media outlets, unfettered by balance constraints, will feel no need to air the views of consumer advocates and business critics.

Regulating for Morality

In May 1995, then presidential candidate Bob Dole made a speech in Los Angeles—the capital of the U.S. entertainment industry—on the "evil" in popular culture. According to Dole, "[O]ne of the greatest threats to American family values is the way our popular culture ridicules them. Our music, movies, television and advertising regularly push the limits of decency, bombarding our children with destructive messages of casual violence and even more casual sex." Dole scolded "the corporate executives who hide behind the lofty language of free speech in order to profit from the debasing of America." He argued that "we must hold Hollywood and the entire entertainment industry accountable for putting profit ahead of common decency" (Peters and Wooley 1999).

One particular target of Dole's criticism was media giant Time Warner. He asserted that some of the company's products, especially "gangsta rap" music, "debase our nation and threaten our children for the sake of corporate profits." Such criticism spurred Time Warner to sell its 50 percent interest in Interscope Records, the producers of the rap music in question. However, there is an important footnote to Dole's apparent hostility toward Time

Warner. His "shaming" of Time Warner came despite the fact, which Dole later revealed, that the company had contributed $23,000 to his campaigns. More important, less than two weeks after his harsh speech, Dole led the battle for passage of sweeping deregulation of the telecommunications industry—a bill of enormous benefit to Time Warner.

The incident reflects some of the peculiarities in the debate over controlling media. On one hand, in the conservative tradition, Dole invoked citizen pressure—not government action—in shaming the media industry into changing its practices. On the other hand, he helped pass legislation that led to a larger, more centralized media industry that is increasingly immune from citizen pressure. Dole's actions are in line with a long tradition of conservative thought. While supporting a hands-off approach to regulating media ownership, conservatives are often at the forefront of calls to control media content.

Ratings and Warnings

One way content is regulated is by industry self-regulation rather than formal government involvement. The rating and warning systems devised for different media fall into this category (Cronauer 1994; Frank 1993; Jost 1994b; Simmons 1978; Wiley 1994). One well-known example of these self-regulation systems is that used for the motion picture industry. Before the 1960s, the movie industry, in the form of the Motion Picture Association of America (MPAA), used an internal system of self-regulation that essentially prevented the making or release of any film the MPAA considered indecent. All that changed in the 1960s when directors and studio executives began challenging the authority of the MPAA president more forcefully. More films emerged that challenged public standards by including nudity and explicit language.

This new generation of Hollywood films explicitly dealing with mature themes led to public concern and increasing calls for control. Congress seemed poised to require a rating system. To ward off government regulation, the MPAA in 1968 collaborated with theater owners and film distributors to develop a rating system that filmmakers would adopt voluntarily. An anonymous panel of citizens representing a national cross section of parents would implement the new rating system by a process of majority vote.

For years, the rating system used G to indicate material appropriate for general audiences, PG to suggest parental guidance because some material might not be suitable for young children, PG-13 to caution that some material might be inappropriate for preteenagers, R to restrict access to adults or to those under 17 accompanied by a parent or guardian, and X to indicate a film intended only for adults.

This system presented some problems. First, theaters were notoriously lax in enforcing the supposedly restricted access of R-rated films, a rating given to about half of all movies. This problem continues today. One Gallup Poll found that more than one-third of all minors ages 12 to 17 had attended an R-rated film without being accompanied by a parent or guardian (Sandler 1994). The Federal Trade Commission (FTC) even found that 80 percent of the R-rated movies it studied were being marketed to children under the age of 17. In 64 percent of the cases, the industry's own marketing plans explicitly stated that the target audience included children under 17 (FTC 2000).

More significantly, the public came to associate the X rating not with adult-oriented themes but with hard-core pornography. Part of the problem was that the MPAA applied the X rating only to about 4 percent of all films and, in most of these cases, used the rating for films that consisted almost entirely of graphic sex scenes. There was no way for the public to distinguish between these X-rated movies and the few mainstream films that also received an X rating because of mature subject matter. (For example, the MPAA gave *Midnight Cowboy* an X rating because of its adult-oriented subject matter, but the film won the 1969 Academy Award for best picture.) The X rating could mean the kiss of death for a mainstream film because many newspapers would not carry advertising for X-rated films, and many theater owners refused to show such films.

Pornographers exacerbated the problem of the public associating X-rated films with hard-core pornography by informally adopting the rating of XXX as a selling point in their advertising. This self-labeling had no connection with the MPAA's rating system, although much of the public did not know this. However, since the MPAA had failed to acquire trademark protection for their rating system, the problem persisted.

In 1990, the MPAA replaced the X rating with a new NC-17 rating, indicating that theater owners would not admit children under the age of 17. It also made sure to acquire a trademark for this new system. The development pleased artists and producers, who hoped it would lead to the possibility of more viable adult-oriented films. Some religious and conservative groups, though, denounced the move as an attempt to acquire mainstream legitimacy for sexually explicit material.

The story of movie ratings is one example in which the perceived threat of government regulation was enough to spark industry self-regulation. TV ratings are an example where government-imposed requirements were coupled with industry self-regulation, this time taking advantage of new technology. The Telecommunications Act of 1996 required development of a rating system for television programming along with the establishment of standards for blocking programming based on those ratings. In 1997, the NAB, the National Cable Television Association (NCTA), and the MPAA collaborated in producing the ratings system. It designated programs aimed at a general audience as either TVG (general audience), TVPG (parental guidance suggested), TV14 (unsuitable for children under 14), or TVMA (intended for mature audiences). In addition, children's programming was divided into TVY (suitable for all children) or TVY7 (intended for children 7 and above). (The system exempted news, sports, and unedited motion pictures on premium cable channels.)

Parents' groups complained that these broad ratings were too vague so, in 1998, additional ratings were added to create the current "age-plus-content" system (see Figure 3.3). These guidelines add the designation FV (fantasy violence) in the TVY7 category and S (sexual situations), V (violence), L (coarse language), and D (suggestive dialogue) in the remaining categories. In addition, the FCC required that, as of January 1, 2000, all new television sets must be equipped with the V-chip, capable of blocking programming based on the ratings system.

The labeling of music lyrics is yet another example of industry self-regulation (Clark 1991a; Harrington 1995). Responding to the increasingly graphic sexual language in popular music lyrics, a group of Washington, DC, parents formed the Parents' Music Resource Center (PMRC) in 1985. These weren't just any parents, however. Their founding ranks included the spouses of 6 U.S. Representatives and 10 U.S. Senators (most notably, Tipper Gore, wife of

Figure 3.3   **Content Ratings and Warnings**

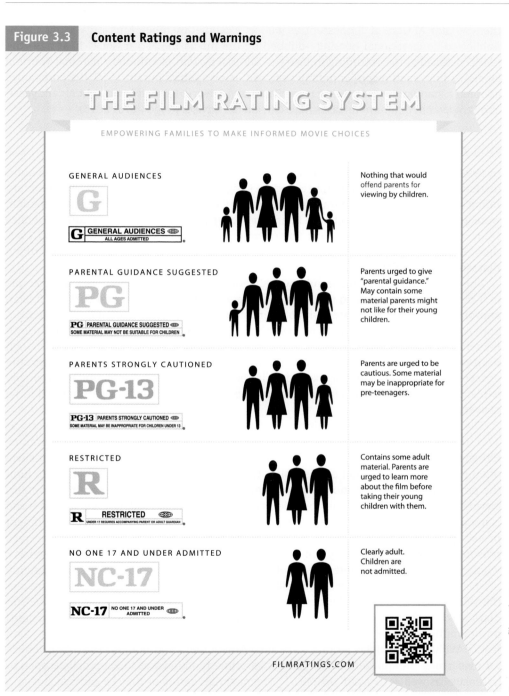

THE FILM RATING SYSTEM

EMPOWERING FAMILIES TO MAKE INFORMED MOVIE CHOICES

GENERAL AUDIENCES

G

G GENERAL AUDIENCES
ALL AGES ADMITTED

Nothing that would offend parents for viewing by children.

PARENTAL GUIDANCE SUGGESTED

PG

PG PARENTAL GUIDANCE SUGGESTED
SOME MATERIAL MAY NOT BE SUITABLE FOR CHILDREN

Parents urged to give "parental guidance." May contain some material parents might not like for their young children.

PARENTS STRONGLY CAUTIONED

PG-13

PG-13 PARENTS STRONGLY CAUTIONED
SOME MATERIAL MAY BE INAPPROPRIATE FOR CHILDREN UNDER 13

Parents are urged to be cautious. Some material may be inappropriate for pre-teenagers.

RESTRICTED

R

R RESTRICTED
UNDER 17 REQUIRES ACCOMPANYING PARENT OR ADULT GUARDIAN

Contains some adult material. Parents are urged to learn more about the film before taking their young children with them.

NO ONE 17 AND UNDER ADMITTED

NC-17

NC-17 NO ONE 17 AND UNDER
ADMITTED

Clearly adult. Children are not admitted.

FILMRATINGS.COM

Source: www.filmratings.com.

The film rating system is an example of industry self-regulation. Established by the Motion Picture Association of America (MPAA), the ratings are meant primarily to help parents decide whether or not a film is appropriate for their family. Television later adopted similar ratings (see tvguidelines.org).

then-Senator Al Gore of Tennessee), as well as 1 cabinet member. After organizing a well-publicized congressional hearing—dubbed by the media the "Porn Rock" hearings—the PMRC persuaded the recording industry to adopt a system of voluntary parental-warning labels. At first, each record company designed its own labels but, in 1990, the companies adopted a standardized label that read "Parental Advisory: Explicit Lyrics." In recent years, about 5 percent of album releases have carried the advisory logo (RIAA 2013).

Outlawing and Controlling Distribution

In 1994, in response to government pressure, the video game industry set up its own body, the Entertainment Software Rating Board, to assign ratings to video games. This voluntary rating system followed in the tradition of films and television. Video game ratings, though, were widely ignored, and California later enacted legislation aimed at preventing juveniles from renting or purchasing violent video games such as *Mortal Kombat* and *Grand Theft Auto*. However, in 2011, the Supreme Court struck down the California legislation, ruling that video games were a form of art protected by the First Amendment.

The suggestion that stores should not sell violent video games to minors is an example of a more active approach to regulating the media industry for its moral content. It is an approach most often associated with obscene material. Obscene material is different from both *pornography,* sexually arousing material, and *indecent material,* material morally unfit for general distribution or broadcast. Pornography and indecent material are legal, although the government may regulate their broadcast or distribution. The government outlaws only obscene material. (The major exception is that the government also outlaws sexually explicit materials involving children, regardless of whether it judges such material to be obscene.)

The United States has a long history of regulating sexually explicit material. As early as 1711, the "government of Massachusetts prohibited publication of 'wicked, profane, impure, filthy and obscene material'" (Clark 1991b: 977). The debates that have ensued ever since often focus on the definition of obscenity. The courts have used these definitions to limit the production and distribution of printed materials, films, and most recently, computer-based material. A 1973 Supreme Court decision set the standard for determining what is and is not obscene. For material to be considered obscene—and thus beyond First Amendment protection—it had to fail a three-prong obscenity test that asked (1) "whether the average person, applying contemporary community standards, would find that the work, taken as a whole, appeals to prurient interest; (2) whether the work depicts or describes, in a patently offensive way, sexual conduct specifically defined by applicable state law; and (3) whether the work, taken as a whole, lacks serious literary, artistic, political or scientific value" (in Clark 1991b: 981). The court intended to limit the label of obscenity to only "hard-core" pornography. However, four justices dissented from even that limited application, with Justice William O. Douglas writing, "The First Amendment was not fashioned as a vehicle for dispensing tranquilizers to the people. Its prime function was to keep debate open to 'offensive' as well as to 'staid' people. . . . The materials before us may be garbage. But so is much of what is said in political campaigns, in the daily press, on TV or over the radio" (in Clark 1991b: 981).

Various laws also regulate materials that are sexually explicit but not obscene. For example, merchants cannot legally sell pornographic magazines and videos to minors. Laws also restrict what broadcasters can air on radio and television. The FCC has set times—for example, 10:00 P.M. to 6:00 A.M. during much of the 1970s and 1980s—during which broadcasters may air indecent programming. The idea in this situation was to protect children from being exposed to material that may be too mature for them. Periodic attempts have been made to remove all indecent programming from the airwaves, but the courts have generally supported the position that the First Amendment protects indecent material. In the 1990s, radio "shock jock" Howard Stern propelled his career by pushing the boundaries of radio decency standards. The station where his program originated was hit with an FCC fine for these violations. In 2006, he moved his show to subscription satellite radio, where FCC decency regulations do not apply.

The computer and Internet have raised new questions about the need to limit sexually graphic material. Minors with access to a computer can easily obtain sexually explicit written or visual materials from online sites, which would be illegal for them to acquire in their print or video versions. They can also take part in online discussion groups that involve sexually explicit material. Should the government ban such online material because it is available to minors? Should public libraries offering Internet terminals install filtering software to prevent access to objectionable sites?

Producers of sexually explicit material argue that the Internet should be treated like the print media and thus remain unregulated. Internet producers do not use the public airwaves and are not distributing or broadcasting the material; minors must take the initiative to access sexually explicit online sites. In addition, Internet filter software, such as Net Nanny and Cyber Patrol, is available if parents want to restrict their children's access to some types of Internet sites and protect them from predators. Opponents argue that the Internet should be treated more like a broadcast medium and thus that its content should be subject to government regulation. Accessing an Internet site, they argue, is no different from tuning in to a particular television channel.

The legal and political pendulums on the issue are still in swing. An initial proregulatory position was supported by the enactment of the Communications Decency Act (CDA)—a part of the 1996 Telecommunications Act—that outlawed the transmission of sexually explicit and other indecent material on the Internet. However, before the year was up, free speech activists had sued, and the courts ruled the CDA to be unconstitutional.

In 1998, President Clinton resurrected the possibility of regulation by signing into law the Child Online Protection Act (COPA 1998), also popularly referred to as CDA II. This legislation was narrower than the original CDA in that it was limited to creating criminal penalties for any commercial distribution of material deemed "harmful to minors." After years of court battles, the law was definitively struck down in 2009.

One of the problems with COPA was that it relied on the "community standards" clause of the legal obscenity definition to determine which material was inappropriate. Because material on the Internet may originate in one place but be accessible worldwide, which community is supposed to set the standard? The notion of a self-contained community implicit in the Supreme Court's 1973 obscenity decision is not applicable to the growth in global communications and media.

The Challenges of Web 2.0

Web 2.0 refers to Internet applications that facilitate user interaction, collaboration, and information sharing. Examples of Web 2.0 applications include blogging platforms such as Wordpress, microblogging services like Twitter, collaborative online projects such as Wikipedia, and community-building sites like LinkedIn. The advent of user-generated content platforms and social networking, through Twitter, Instagram, YouTube, Facebook, Tumblr, and other services, raised an entire set of new regulatory questions focused on regulating online interaction. The primary regulatory challenges concern the protection of minors from cyberstalking and cyberbullying.

For example, in 2009, a U.K. teenager was kidnapped and murdered by a man who posed as a teenager on his Facebook profile—the murderer, who had previously been convicted of rape, became known as the "Facebook killer." The incident prompted authorities in the United Kingdom and United States to look into ways to alert other users when a convicted sex offender goes online. However, anonymity and the ability of users to create false online identities make it extremely difficult to enact such proactive policies to prevent cyberstalking.

Cyberbullying has received even more attention. In 2006, 13-year-old Megan Taylor Meier committed suicide, likely triggered by cyberbullying perpetrated by individuals who befriended her on MySpace. According to the American Cyberbullying Research Center, 44 states now have some form of laws regarding bullying, 30 of which include some reference to electronic forms of harassment. New Hampshire, for example, ruled that school boards must develop written policies on cyberbullying in collaboration with parents, students, and teachers. At the federal level, the Megan Meier Cyberbullying Prevention Act (H.R. 1966) was introduced in Congress in 2009 but was never acted upon. The proposed legislation would have imposed fines or up to two years of imprisonment on anyone who "transmits in interstate or foreign commerce any communication, with the intent to coerce, intimidate, harass, or cause substantial emotional distress to a person, using electronic means to support severe, repeated, and hostile behavior."

Who should regulate and enforce privacy protection and the safety of minors on social networking sites is still an open question. The European Union has adopted a self-regulation approach. In 2005, the European Commission launched a Safer Internet Program targeting children, parents, and teachers in order to promote a secure online environment for minors and raise public awareness of online risks. The most recent version of the program (2009–2013) includes statements of support by social networking sites and mobile communication operators. The "Safer Social Networking Rules for the EU" were voluntarily adopted by the industry (including Facebook, MySpace, Yahoo!, and Google) in 2009. Such principles include the provision of easy-to-use tools to report prohibited content and of privacy setting options to enable users to make informed decisions about what they post online.

The Issue of Violence

Violence in the media is another area of content regulation that has received a great deal of attention (Anderson and Bushman 2002; Clark 1993; Kirsh 2012; Lazar 1994; Potter

2003). Along with violence in video games, violence on television is usually at the center of this debate because it is so accessible to children. For example, the American Academy of Child and Adolescent Psychiatry notes that an average American child will see 16,000 murders on television before he or she turns 18 (Beresin 2010).

An enormous amount of research has explored the effects of media violence. Some researchers contend that, for some children, violent programming can lead to more violent behavior (aggressor effect), increased fearfulness about violence (victim effect), or increased callousness about violence directed at others (bystander effect). While such findings still inspire debate, there is growing consensus that prolonged exposure to violent programming affects some people. One classic study reanalyzed more than 200 existing major studies on television violence (Paik and Comstock 1994: 516). It concluded that, although the various studies showed different degrees of influence, there is "a positive and significant correlation between television violence and aggressive behavior."

Producers of violent media products often argue that they are merely reflecting the violence that already exists in society. However, polls repeatedly show that most Americans believe violence in the mass media contributes to violence in society. As a result, there has been fairly widespread popular support for the regulation of violent programming, especially on television.

Source: AP Photo/Activision.

The influence on young people of video games that depict violence realistically is a topic of considerable debate. The video game industry responded to the controversy by implementing a rating system, somewhat similar to that used for films and television. The Entertainment Software Rating Board (ESRB.org) uses six ratings categories: EC (early childhood), E (everyone), E 10+ (everyone 10 and older), T (teen), M (mature; 17 and up), and AO (adults only).

There are four basic approaches to responding to television violence. First, some argue that the marketplace should determine programming and, therefore, no government regulation is needed. Second, a few critics argue for a total ban on television violence, calling it a threat to public health. Third, and perhaps most common, is support for limiting violent programming to certain times of the day when young children are less likely to be watching, say, 10 P.M. to 6 A.M. Finally, ratings and the V-chip, discussed above, are other responses to violence on television.

Support for regulation of violent programming is not new. Concerns about violence on television date back almost to its introduction. The level of concern grew dramatically in the 1960s, though, as more programming regularly included violence. Movies, too, came under attack for depicting increasingly explicit violence. In 1972, the Surgeon General released a major five-volume report on the impact of television violence, concluding that, for children predisposed to aggression, there was a causal effect from television violence. However, the 1970s saw increases in the level of explicit violence on television, and the FCC took no significant action to stem the media violence.

Meanwhile, citizen and professional organizations were demanding action. In 1976, the American Medical Association passed a resolution proclaiming TV violence to be a threat to "the health and welfare of young Americans" (in Clark 1993: 278). The National Parent–Teacher Association (PTA) passed a resolution demanding that networks reduce the amount of violence on television, especially between 2 P.M. and 10 P.M. A 1982 report from the National Institute of Mental Health found that TV violence affects all children, not just those predisposed to aggressive behavior.

The 1980s, however, were an era of deregulation, and Congress did not enact restrictions on children's television. Instead, the government deregulated children's television and relaxed or eliminated many existing rules, such as those controlling the amount of advertising on children's television. One result was the development by toy manufacturers of children's cartoons that served as program-length commercials for their toys. The first of these was the He-Man cartoon, which promoted action figures and accessories of the same name. Over time, program-length commercials were selling children everything from GI Joe to Teenage Mutant Ninja Turtles. Many of these programs were violent and war related. Between 1983 and 1986, just after deregulation, war toy sales increased by 600 percent (Lazar 1994).

Violence is universal and easily understood in any culture. Producers conscious of the increasingly important international market, therefore, are likely to continue to produce violence-filled programming. The creation of such shows will no doubt generate more concern among people worried about the effects of media violence. Here, too, we see the relationship between elements of the media and the social world.

As noted above, video game violence has also drawn special attention in recent years, especially because users are active participants in perpetrating simulated violent acts rather than simply watching others do so, as with television. Concern has grown as the games have become more sophisticated and realistic and as some games have involved depictions of blatantly antisocial violence rather than fantasy violence. Though widely seen by users as a satiric commentary on American culture, the Grand Theft Auto franchise has attracted considerable attention (some of it stoked by the game makers for publicity) because it allows players to kill police officers, hire prostitutes and then rob or murder them, and engage in a wide variety of other criminal and antisocial behavior. Similar to the study of violence in other media, some studies have found playing such games desensitizes players to real-world violence and can increase aggressive behavior (Bartholow, Sestir, and Davis 2005; Carnagey, Anderson, and Bushman 2007), but other researchers argue that the concern is overstated (Ferguson 2007; Kutner and Olson 2008). Regulation of video games has so far been limited to the voluntary rating system discussed earlier—comparable to films or television.

Regulating for Accuracy: Advertising

Another area of content regulation worth noting is regulation that affects advertising (Clark 1991a). A number of different agencies regulate the advertising industry because of its broad and varied commercial dimensions, which encompass all forms of mass communication. For example, the FTC handles most cases of deceptive or fraudulent advertising practices. The Securities and Exchange Commission is responsible for the advertising of stocks and bonds, while the Transportation Department oversees airline advertising. The Treasury Department's Bureau of Alcohol, Tobacco, and Firearms regulates most tobacco and alcohol advertising, and the FCC is responsible for overseeing children's television ads.

This collection of regulatory agencies addresses two basic concerns. First, the agencies protect the public against fraudulent or deceptive advertising. Segments of the advertising industry have a reputation for hucksterism that involves, at best, the distortion of fact. The most egregious violators are usually small companies that advertise—for everything from miracle cures to bust enhancers—in the classified ads in the backs of magazines. The promises made in such deceptive ads sometimes echo turn-of-the-century patent medicine claims. But misleading ads can also come in the form of television infomercials and can come from major corporations as well.

The anonymity provided by the Internet enables advertisers to deceive consumers in ways beyond the well-known spam frauds delivered via e-mails. Some firms hire agents to post product recommendations or customer reviews on websites. Other companies provide free products to bloggers in exchange for a favorable mention in a post. But in 2009, the FTC issued new guidelines making such deals illegal. Now, the FTC says that anyone paid in cash or with free products to provide an online endorsement of a product must disclose this arrangement to readers. Though difficult to enforce, the FTC began cracking down in a series of highly visible cases, including charging one PR firm with having their employees pose as satisfied customers posting video game reviews at the iTunes store (Sachdev 2010).

The second major area in which government regulations affect advertising involves ads featuring potentially dangerous products, especially when the ads are targeted at children and minors. Thus, the government regulates advertising for products such as alcohol and tobacco. Cigarettes, for example, cannot be advertised on television. In 1995, a new government initiative to further limit tobacco advertising even banned the use of tobacco company ads at sporting events that were televised. This meant a ban on everything from cigarette billboards at baseball games to tobacco company logos on professional race cars.

The government has also acted at times to limit the total amount of advertising aimed at children. For example, the 1990 Children's Television Act limited advertising during children's programs to 12 minutes per hour on weekdays and 10.5 minutes per hour on the weekend. The advertising industry opposes these limits, arguing that the free market should determine the appropriate amount of advertising for children.

Deregulation in the 1980s eliminated FCC limits on the overall amount of time radio and television stations can devote to advertising. This has contributed to a dramatic increase in the amount of money spent on advertising overall. In 1980, total television and radio advertising expenditures in the United States were about $40 billion (in adjusted 2010 dollars). By 2006, they had risen to more than $99 billion before declining during the recession to about $90 billion in 2008 (Statistical Abstract of the United States 1990, 2010). At the same time, the amount of air time devoted to commercials was rising, and "infomercials"—30-minute commercials that look very much like programs—blurred the line between advertising and programming. While most people know that the government controls and regulates advertising in the media, they are less likely to be familiar with laws that help business and the advertising industry. Most important is the fact that most advertising is a tax-deductible business expense, saving businesses millions of dollars annually and helping to support the advertising industry. Other ways government laws help advertisers include government financing of election campaigns, much of which is spent on commercial advertising; Department of Agriculture subsidies for advertising particular commodities; and postage rate subsidies for magazines and newspapers that are filled with advertisements. Finally, the government is a direct purchaser of advertising, spending more than $945 million on advertiser services in 2010, including $545 million on military recruiting advertisements (Kosar 2012).

In this area, too, fundamental issues of constraint and agency emerge as government seeks to protect the public from misleading sales pitches; and advertisers, in turn, seek to protect the benefits they receive from government.

Regulating in the "National Interest"

What constitutes the "national interest" is a debatable topic, but governments sometimes regulate media to protect or advance what they define as the national interest—the goals and ambitions of a nation. Two important cases of such regulation involve protecting military operations and monitoring people's online behavior in the name of combating terrorism.

Media and the Military

During the Civil War, Union generals regularly read Southern newspapers to gain information about troop strength and movement. Ever since then, a tension has existed between the media's right to provide information to the public and the government's need to protect sensitive information during times of war.

The nature of this tension has varied at different points in history. During World War II, for example, the media voluntarily complied with military restrictions on information and in many ways helped promote the Allied war effort. A dramatic change in this cordial relationship occurred during the Vietnam War, when television, in particular, eventually began reporting information the military did not wish to make public. After the media followed the military's lead in the early years of the war, they later began reporting more independently in ways that the military sometimes felt were irresponsible. Some reports were even said to have endangered the safety of troops.

From the media's perspective, the military's publicity apparatus had lost credibility with the press and a significant portion of the U.S. public. Well-publicized incidents of the Pentagon lying to the press and the public contributed to a highly skeptical tone in the media. As the war in Vietnam dragged on, the press corps so distrusted the information being provided by the Pentagon that they dubbed the afternoon military press briefings the "Five O'clock Follies." The Vietnam War was also the first to be given extensive television coverage. While the government repeatedly claimed that victory was near, network television images of dying American soldiers and dissenting American demonstrators revealed a different reality.

The experience in Vietnam led the military to take the offensive on two separate fronts. First, it developed a massive PR machine to project a more positive image of the military. Ironically, part of this effort involved the hiring of press personnel (at officer status) to provide expertise on how to handle the media. The military became very adept at promoting information it wanted publicized in the media. From the military's perspective, its effort was an attempt to educate journalists and sensitize them to issues of military concern.

Second, the military began developing a strategy for controlling the dissemination of information through the media to the public. The central element of this strategy was the press pool (see Cheney 1992 and critical views in Bennett and Paletz 1994; Denton 1993; Jeffords and Rabinovitz 1994; Mowlana, Gerbner, and Schiller 1992; Taylor 1992). Tested in the invasions of Panama and Grenada and fully implemented during the Persian Gulf War, the press pool system was the Pentagon's attempt to control the information that journalists would report during a conflict by limiting the access of media personnel. The military argued that limiting access was necessary to protect journalists in the field and to curb the ever-growing number of media personnel seeking access to areas of conflict. To fight effectively, they argued, they needed to restrict the movement of journalists.

By choosing which media personnel would be included in the press pool, controlling their means of transportation in the field, and permitting access only to predetermined locations, the military was able to effectively control information about military operations. Military press personnel even monitored interviews with soldiers and screened media dispatches before publication. Journalists bristled at the new restrictions, but the major media complied. Some Americans were startled during the Gulf War to find a notice on the front page of their newspapers stating that U.S. military censors had approved all information about the war. Many critics thought the military had gone too far in restricting the press, but the majority of the public supported the restrictions.

Public support for press restrictions continued as George W. Bush launched a "war on terrorism" in the wake of the September 11, 2001, attacks on the World Trade Center and the Pentagon. In this case, however, the Pentagon simply banned press personnel from covering the fighting, citing the need for secrecy for special operations forces. The press was given limited access to U.S. military personnel on aircraft carriers and in other staging areas, but they were prevented from accompanying troops in battle zones. Once again, the Pentagon had largely succeeded in providing a sanitized version of the war and in avoiding the full coverage that characterized the Vietnam era.

In the past half century, the basic tension between an active press and a constraining military has centered on the definition of "sensitive information," which the military wishes to control. The military considered information sensitive if it might endanger U.S. troops or affect troop morale. The press had no problem with the first criterion and willingly complied with restrictions on information that might endanger U.S. troops. However, many journalists objected to the censoring of information that might indirectly and adversely affect troop morale. The military would likely consider "sensitive" anything that might undermine public support for the war effort because reduced public support might undermine troop morale.

For example, during the Gulf War, President George H.W. Bush introduced a ban on pictures of coffins of war dead: Media were not allowed to film the flag-draped coffins of U.S. soldiers being unloaded from planes that had returned to the United States. These images clearly did not threaten the safety of U.S. troops, but they did threaten public support for the war. (This ban was lifted in 2009 by President Barack Obama.) Such blatant censorship was a startling development in the government's effort to ensure public support and raised profound questions about the role of government restriction on a free press, even in times of conflict. As a result of the restrictions, much information about the war that might have been controversial—such as the high civilian death toll or the fact that the U.S. military used huge bulldozers to bury Iraqi troops alive in their trenches—did not reach the public until well after the end of the war.

During the 2003 invasion of Iraq, the U.S. military sought a more cooperative relationship with journalists. The centerpiece of the military's media management approach in the Iraq War (as well as the ongoing war in Afghanistan) was a program of embedding reporters with active duty troops in the field, which gave journalists access to the front lines of the war. The Department of Defense defines an embedded reporter as "a media representative remaining with a unit on an extended basis—perhaps a period of weeks or even months [who] will live, work, and travel as part of the units with which they are embedded to facilitate maximum, in-depth coverage of U.S. forces in combat and related operations" (quoted in Cortell, Eisinger, and Althaus 2009). The Pentagon established clear ground rules for embeds: reporters could not have their own vehicles or weapons; the military would provide basic protective gear for journalists; reporters needed consent from individual soldiers to include their names or hometowns in their reports; information on strategic issues, such as troop movements, specific locations, or future combat plans, could not be included in reports.

Rather than formally reviewing and censoring news coverage, the embedded reporter program sought to build relationships between war correspondents and troops that they relied upon for protection and with whom they shared regular meals and conversation. Pentagon officials saw the embed program as an opportunity to shape public perception of the war by emphasizing the stories and experiences of U.S. soldiers on the battlefield. Critics have argued that embedded reporters lose their independence, becoming too reliant on military sources with whom they come to identify and thus framing news reports from the perspective of U.S. soldiers rather than neutral observers (Goodman and Goodman 2004).

Research indicates that reporters who were embedded with U.S. troops believed the program was largely successful. One survey of embedded reporters found "the majority claimed their reporting was accurate, trustworthy, and fair, and did not jeopardize the safety of the troops" (Fahmy and Johnson 2005: 310). Research on the content of news coverage of the Iraq War found that there was little difference in the tone of reports by embedded reporters and "unilaterals"—reporters who were not affiliated with the U.S. or British military. Embedded reporters (embeds) did cover different stories than their unilateral counterparts. Embeds were far more likely than unilaterals to cover battles and to focus on U.S. troops, including quotes from and visual images of U.S. soldiers. Embeds were also far less likely than unilaterals to produce stories about the reconstruction of Iraq or civilian casualties and presented far fewer images of wounded or dead Iraqis in their reporting (Aday, Livingston, and Hebert 2005).

In recent years, activists, including those associated with the Wikileaks website (wikileaks.org), have challenged control of information by the military. In 2010, the site released a classified video showing a 2007 U.S. airstrike in Baghdad, Iraq, in which U.S. troops killed two Reuters employees whose cameras were mistaken for weapons. The video had been leaked by U.S. Army Private Bradley (now Chelsea) Manning, along with more than a quarter million diplomatic cables. Wikileaks later released over 90,000 of the documents Manning had leaked, providing considerable insight into the workings of the U.S. government and its diplomatic corps.

Electronic Surveillance

The U.S. government has responded to the threat of terrorism by vastly expanding its secret intelligence-gathering and surveillance capacity to include telecommunications and Internet channels Americans use every day. The programs are part of what one journalistic investigation calls a massive growth in a "Top Secret America" (Washington Post, 2013b). In turn, such operations have spawned protest actions by critics who argue they are threats to civil liberties. This is another example of how the government has come to influence both old and new media.

In the aftermath of the September 11, 2001, terrorist attacks, the U.S. Congress passed the USA PATRIOT Act. Among other provisions, the act increased the ability of law enforcement agencies to search e-mail and telephone communications and to obtain information on Internet users' personal data, including session times and durations and IP addresses (a unique address that identifies the location of a computer connected to the Internet). When these domestic surveillance programs spawned media scrutiny and lawsuits, the Administration turned to Congress for further authorization of its actions. The result was the 2007 Protect America Act and the FISA (Foreign Intelligence Surveillance Act) Amendments Act of 2008, which enabled continued surveillance and immunized private telecommunications and media companies that cooperated with government intelligence-gathering efforts.

The new legislation set the stage for the PRISM program, a government surveillance effort run primarily by the National Security Agency. The program was exposed in 2013 when an NSA whistleblower, Edward Snowden, revealed some of the details to a British newspaper. Among the revelations was the fact that a secret court order instructed the three major phone networks (Verizon, AT&T, and Sprint Nextel) to provide the NSA with daily information on the phone calls of its tens of millions of U.S. customers (Gorman, Perez, and

A protester holds a sign supporting Edward Snowden, the former National Security Agency (NSA) contractor who revealed documents naming several well-known media companies as part of a massive Internet surveillance and data collection program, code-named PRISM. ***Authors' note to the reader:*** *We originally planned to use an image here from the NSA presentation about PRISM that was leaked by Snowden, but opted not to print the image as it remains classified. At the time of publication, the slide was available for viewing at the following news websites: theguardian.com/world/2013/jun/06/us-tech-giants-nsa-data and washingtonpost.com/wp-srv/special/politics/prism-collection-documents.*

Hook 2013). In addition, the NSA had the cooperation of many well-known Internet companies, including Facebook and Google, in providing the Agency with user content, including e-mails, chat logs, videos, and other data (Black 2013).

Government monitoring of electronic communications, believed to be the main vehicle for terrorists to organize and share expertise, has become the rule in many countries. Right after the July 7, 2005, London bombing (four bombs exploded in the London public transport system, leaving 52 people dead and 700 injured), the Italian government passed an antiterrorism bill requiring public Internet access sites to identify all users by photocopying their passports or ID cards. In 2006, the European Commission, inspired by the Italian legislation, passed the Data Retention Directive (2006/24/EC), which required member states to put in place legislation to guarantee that electronic communication providers retain the communication metadata of their clients (Fuchs 2009). *Metadata* include information about source and destination of an electronic communication exchange. Data must be stored for at least six months. This directive, which proved to be very controversial, forces Internet providers to collect and store enormous amounts of data, with potential risks for individual privacy and potential political implications (such as the surveillance of political activists and dissidents).

The outbreak of international terrorism brought along new challenges for those in charge of watching the national interest. However, even in such a context, abuses of online and electronic surveillance are a serious hazard, potentially undermining people's freedom of expression and right to information.

INFORMAL POLITICAL, SOCIAL, AND ECONOMIC PRESSURE

This chapter has focused primarily on formal government regulation and informal government pressure on the media. However, it is important to remember the political role played by other actors in either directly influencing the media or prompting the government to act in relation to the media.

The most obvious players in the debates over the media are media critics and media-related think tanks, who produce much of the information that forms the basis of popular media criticism. Some of these critics are academics whose area of specialty is the mass media. Others are affiliated with privately funded think tanks that produce analyses and policy recommendations relating to the media. Such critics span the political spectrum, and knowing a little about their funding sources can provide insight into their perspectives on the issues at hand.

More important than media critics are the citizen activists from across the political spectrum who write, educate, lobby, and agitate about the media. These groups need not focus exclusively on

Source: David McNew/Getty Images.

The FCC's role in regulating the media attracts scrutiny from the industry as well as citizen activists who sometimes protest the actions—or lack thereof—of the Commission.

media issues. For example, among their many varied activities, religious groups sometimes pressure the media on moral grounds. In some cases, they have organized boycotts of advertisers who sponsor certain controversial programs or of stores that carry controversial books and magazines. There are hundreds of local, regional, and national organizations that are exclusively devoted to media-related issues, ranging from violence in Hollywood films or political diversity in the news to children's television or public access to the Internet. These groups, too, span a wide spectrum of political orientation (see Figure 3.4). For example, based in Vancouver, BC, the Media Foundation challenges the commercialism at the heart of most mass media. It produces *Adbusters,* an advertising-free magazine about the media. It also creates "uncommercials" and spoof ads that appear in Canadian media, as well as coordinates various campaigns, such as "Buy Nothing Day," that challenge consumerist values.

In the United States, citizens' groups have legal status when it comes to renewing broadcast licenses. In the early years of broadcasting, the government allowed only those with an economic stake in the outcome to significantly participate in FCC proceedings regarding radio and television licenses. This changed in the mid-1960s when the Office of Communication of the United Church of Christ won a court case allowing it to challenge the granting of a television license to a station in Jackson, MS. The Church of Christ contended that the station discriminated against black viewers. The U.S. Court of Appeals for the District of Columbia Circuit ruled that responsible community organizations, including civic associations, professional groups, unions, churches, and educational institutions, have a right to contest license renewals. While ensuing challenges rarely succeeded, activists discovered that some broadcasters were willing to negotiate with community groups to avoid challenges to their license renewals (Longley, Terry, and Krasnow 1983). They also recognized that such challenges could sometimes spark public debate about the nature of the media.

In 2003, when the FCC, in response to a request from media firms who wanted media ownership rules abolished, tried to lift the remaining barriers against media consolidation, public interest groups organized to defend the policies that limit the size and reach of the major media companies. The Philadelphia-based Prometheus Radio Project sued the FCC in federal court. In the 2004 case, *Prometheus Radio Project v. FCC,* the court ruled in favor of Prometheus, deeming the FCC's *diversity index* (a measure to weigh media cross-ownership) inconsistent.

The action repertoire of citizen groups is diverse. Some, which have access and accept the institution as legitimate, adopt a cooperative attitude, such as lobbying the FCC in order to promote reform from the inside. When citizen groups have no access or do not consider the institution as legitimate, they can be confrontational, such as protesting the NAB for its opposition to low-power broadcast licenses, discussed earlier in this chapter. Finally, rather than trying to change mainstream media, some groups promote reform from the grassroots, creating alternative media (Downing 2001; Lievrouw 2011; Milan and Hintz 2010). In practice, such strategies have translated into groups that have studied their local media and issued reports; testified before Congress on media matters; advised parents on teaching their children "media literacy" skills; organized consumers to communicate their concerns to media outlets; protested the FCC or major media headquarters using direct action and civil disobedience tactics; or developed alternative media.

While various forms of activism have ebbed and flowed with the changing media issues, citizen group pressures from both liberals and conservatives have been a constant in the media debate. They can constitute an important informal political pressure on the media industry.

| Figure 3.4 | **Examples of Media Advocacy Organizations** |

About-Face. Combats negative and distorted images of women. *about-face.org*

Accuracy in Media. Conservative/right media criticism. *aim.org*

Adbusters/Media Foundation. Liberal/left activism aimed at advertising and consumer culture. *adbusters.org*

Alliance for Community Media. Works to broaden access to electronic media. *allcommunitymedia.org*

Campaign for Commercial-Free Childhood. "Works to reclaim childhood from corporate marketers" and limit the impact of commercialism. *commercialfreechildhood.org*

Center for Democracy and Technology. A nonprofit public policy organization that focuses on "public policies that will keep the Internet open, innovative, and free." *cdt.org*

Center for Digital Democracy. Promotes open broadband networks, free universal Internet access, and diverse ownership of new media outlets. *democraticmedia.org*

Center for Media and Public Affairs. Conservative/right studies media. *cmpa.com*

Center for Media Democracy. Focuses on the public relations (PR) industry, "exposing corporate spin and government propaganda." *prwatch.org*

Center for Media Literacy. Resources "to help citizens, especially the young, develop critical thinking and media production skills." *medialit.org*

Commercial Alert. Helps people defend themselves against harmful, immoral, or intrusive advertising and marketing and the excesses of commercialism. *commercialalert.org*

Committee to Protect Journalists. Monitors restrictions on press freedom worldwide. *cpj.org*

Electronic Frontier Foundation. Works to protect free speech, privacy, innovation, and consumer rights on the Internet. *eff.org*

Fairness & Accuracy In Reporting. Liberal/left media watch group. *fair.org*

Free Press. Promotes media reform, independent media ownership, and universal access to communication. *freepress.net*

GLAAD. Monitors and works directly with media to ensure that the stories of LGBT community are heard. *glaad.org*

Media Action Network for Asian Americans. Works for accurate, balanced, and sensitive Asian American images. *manaa.org*

Media Alliance. Media resource and advocacy center for media workers, nonprofit organizations, and social justice activists. *media-alliance.org*

Media and Democracy Coalition. Coalition of telecommunications policy reform groups. *media-democracy.net*

Media Research Center. Conservative/right group that aims to "expose and neutralize the propaganda arm of the Left: the national news media." *mrc.org*

Morality in Media. Conservative, interfaith group that combats obscenity in media. *moralityin media.org*

Parents Television Council. Conservative group advocating more family-friendly programming. *parentstv.org*

Progressive Media Project. Helps diverse communities who have been shut out of the mainstream media get op-eds published. *progressivemediaproject.org*

Prometheus Radio Project. Helps grassroots organizations to build community radio stations and advocates for more low-power radio. *prometheusradio.org*

Note: More educational and advocacy groups can be found on the website for this book, http://www.sagepub.com/croteau5e.

CONCLUSION

Government regulation is important because it sets the ground rules within which media must operate. As this survey of regulatory types makes clear, forces outside the media have had significant impact on the development and direction of the media industry. When we consider the role of media in the social world, we must take into account the influence of these outside forces. The purpose, form, and content of the media are all socially determined, as are the rules that regulate them. As a consequence, they vary over time and across cultures. The particular form our media system takes at any time is the result of a series of social processes reflecting competing interests.

Media organizations operate within a context that is shaped by economic and political forces at least partially beyond their control, but the production of media is not simply dictated by these structural constraints.

Media professionals develop strategies for navigating through these economic and political forces, and media outlets have their own sets of norms and rules. In Chapter 4, we examine these media organizations and professionals.

DISCUSSION QUESTIONS

1. Deregulation advocates generally suggest what they are *against* (regulation) but not what they *favor*. What are some of the potential problems with this position?

2. Advocates of regulation generally argue that government must intervene on behalf of the "public interest" to counter the influence of powerful media conglomerates. What are some of the potential problems with this position? How would you define the "public interest" in this context?

3. In what situations do you think the government has the right to regulate media content? Explain why you believe what you do.

4. Are you concerned about the expansion of governments' electronic surveillance in the name of national security? Why or why not?

CHAPTER 4

Media Organizations and Professionals

Source: Bloomberg/Getty Images.

Chapters 2 and 3 highlighted the ways in which economic and political forces constrain the media industry. However, we must keep in mind that action does not follow inevitably and directly from structural constraint. At most, broad structural constraints will influence behavior by making some choices more attractive, some more risky, and some almost unthinkable. Despite working within certain constraints, professionals who help create media products make a series of choices about what to make and how to produce and distribute the final result. People—Hollywood directors, network television executives, book editors, news reporters, and so on—are not simply mindless cogs in a media machine. They do not churn out products precisely in accord with what our understanding of social structure tells us they should.

Our task, then, is to make sense of the dynamic tension between the forces of structure, which shape but do not determine behavior, and the actions of human beings, who make choices but are not fully autonomous. To adapt an often cited comment by Marx: Media professionals make their own products, but they do not make them just as they please; they do not make them under circumstances chosen by themselves but under circumstances directly found, given, and transmitted from the past.

This chapter focuses on the structure–agency dynamic within media organizations. We explore how professionals create media products, the ways in which media work is organized, the norms and practices of several media professions, the social and personal networks that media professionals cultivate, and the ways the organizational structure of media outlets shape the methods of media work. We also consider the growing volume of user-generated content—media products created by nonprofessionals.

THE LIMITS OF ECONOMIC AND POLITICAL CONSTRAINTS

As we have seen in earlier chapters, economic and political forces can be powerful constraints. As we examine below, media personnel actively respond to these constraints when making decisions, often limiting their impact.

Working Within Economic Constraints

Let's briefly return to our discussion in Chapter 2 of the commercial logic of prime-time television. Recall that profit demands shape programming decisions in network television. Profits result from high ratings and desirable demographics, which lead to strong advertising sales. Network executives, facing severe pressure to schedule programs that will attract large audiences, select programs that are safe, trying not to offend any significant constituency. It is the commercial logic of network television then that leads to the fact that programs on different networks look so much alike.

In Chapter 2, we emphasized the constraining power of the commercial organization of network television. However, Gitlin's (2000) classic study provides a nuanced analysis of the tension between these economic constraints and the agency of network programmers, producers, and writers. The people who actually create and select television programs work in an environment in which the decisions they make carry real costs. If you write too many scripts that are considered to be commercially unviable, your future as a television writer may be in jeopardy. Likewise, if you choose unorthodox programs for your network's prime-time lineup, and they are ratings flops, you will be looking for a new job in short order. The economics of prime-time television, then, may shape the decision-making environment, but decisions are still made at various stages by various players. And because audience tastes are both dynamic and unpredictable, these decisions cannot use any one simple formula to determine which programs will be profitable and which will not. As a result, people who work in the world of television must try to interpret both the current mood of the audience and the appeal of particular programs if they are to create and select shows that will meet profit requirements.

Here the structure–agency dynamic is quite clear: Economic forces identify the goals and shape the terrain of the decision-making process, but human actors must assess both program and audience in their effort to deliver the "correct" product. The fact that the vast majority of programs do not succeed tells us that this is not easy terrain to master. Despite the difficulty of the field, however, players within the television world still try to navigate it safely; along the way, they adopt certain rules or conventions to smooth out and routinize the decision-making process. Imitation, for example, has been routinized in the television world. One basic rule of thumb is to create programs that look like those that are currently popular. Throughout this chapter, we will give attention to the conventions that media professionals adopt, because they provide an insightful window on production processes within media industries.

Responding to Political Constraints

Political forces, particularly government regulations, also play a significant role in shaping the environment within which media organizations operate. Even here, where federal laws require or prohibit specific actions, the constraints of government regulation do not determine what media organizations will do. Sometimes media organizations comply with government regulations, but sometimes the media preempt, ignore, reinterpret, or challenge regulations.

Compliance is the easiest strategy for media organizations because it avoids conflict with regulators, thereby enabling them to shape the actions of media organizations. As we saw in the previous chapter, since Vietnam, the Pentagon has been quite adept at influencing the content of news reports using various strategies. During the 1991 Persian Gulf War, the government regulated access to information through a press pool system and required journalists to submit their battle coverage stories for approval by military censors. During the Iraq War that began in 2003, the government took a different approach, cultivating favorable coverage by embedding reporters with troops with whom they built relationships. In both cases, the Pentagon was largely successful in achieving press compliance. The popular belief in supporting troops during war, coupled with widespread public skepticism about the media, likely made press criticism of Pentagon restrictions difficult.

A second strategy used by the media in dealing with government regulation is preemption. Media industries can preempt external regulation by engaging in a public form of self-regulation. As we saw in the previous chapter, this is the strategy that the motion picture, television, music, and video gaming industries used in their voluntary adoption of age-appropriate content ratings and warning labels for their products to stave off more direct government regulation.

A third often-used strategy is rooted in the fact that government regulations are almost always subject to interpretation, giving media organizations the power to read regulations in ways that match their broader agendas. In a classic example, the 1990 Children's Television Act required stations to include educational television in their Saturday morning lineups but left a good deal of room for interpretation of the meaning of "educational" programming. As a result, broadcasters were willing to define almost anything as educational, including old cartoons such as *The Flintstones* and *The Jetsons*. While regulations were on the books, broadcasters found innovative ways to respond, demonstrating that regulation is, at best, only a partial constraint.

Fourth, media industries can simply ignore regulations. Passing laws is one thing, but enforcing regulations is another. The FCC historically has been reluctant to be a firm enforcer, in large part because of the complexities of its relationship to the U.S. Congress and to the media industries it is supposed to regulate. As a result, communications regulations can often simply be ignored with few consequences.

Finally, if they have the resources, media organizations can challenge regulations to try to alter them or rescind them altogether. Media organizations can adopt legal strategies, challenging the constitutionality of specific regulations, or they can use political strategies, lobbying potentially supportive politicians and threatening opponents in an effort to win new legislation more to the liking of the industry. The relaxation of ownership rules, described in Chapter 3, was one example where this tactic was successful.

Ultimately, just as economic forces do not fully determine the actions of media professionals, media organizations are not passively compliant in the face of political constraints. In both cases, media personnel are active agents, making decisions and pursuing strategies within particular economic and political frameworks. Their actions sustain, and sometimes help change, the basic structural constraints, but they are not determined by them.

So far, we have focused our attention primarily on the broad environment within which media producers and consumers exist. We now move more directly into the world of those who produce media to examine the processes involved in their decision making and how their work is organized.

DECISION MAKING FOR PROFIT: IMITATION, HITS, AND STARS

The broader political and economic environment sets the stage for the work of media personnel. In the United States and other democratic societies, political pressures on most types of media workers are modest. However, commercial mainstream media workers within these societies face enormous economic pressures to make decisions that will translate into profits for company owners. While the details of these decision-making processes are different across media industries, individuals working in media fields almost all have to contend with two basic problems: the high cost of producing media and the unpredictability of audience tastes.

High Costs and Unpredictable Tastes

Deciding to turn a manuscript into a book or a pitch into a movie is a difficult and risky financial decision. The upfront cost to create and promote media is usually quite high, and there is no guarantee that this investment will be recouped. A television studio must spend millions of dollars to create a pilot before they know if anybody will be interested in watching their new TV show. A book manuscript has to be written, edited, and published before the publishing house knows if enough people are willing to spend money to read it. Even media products that are relatively inexpensive to create—such as a basic music recording—must then be packaged and promoted if they stand any chance of finding a broad mainstream audience. Such promotion is expensive.

The high cost of creating and promoting media products is accompanied by a second problem: the unpredictability of audience tastes. We tend to assume that "good" media have an intrinsic value that makes them so popular. We think best-selling songs sell so well because they are the catchiest or that a best-selling novelist achieves fortune and fame because his or her writing is the most interesting and engaging. But research suggests that success is more complex than we often assume.

For example, Salganik, Dodds, and Watts (2006) created multiple music websites on which more than 14,000 participants were allowed to listen to and download songs from the same unknown bands. If songs have an inherent quality that makes them widely popular, then the same songs should become popular on each website. Instead, the researchers found that songs that were highly rated by the earlier listeners on a particular site would go on to become increasingly popular on that site—but not necessarily on the other sites. The study showed that listener decisions about what was good and worth downloading were influenced by the judgments of earlier visitors to the site. Those early judgments were more important than any intrinsic value in the individual songs.

Because popularity is not necessarily based on the intrinsic quality of a media product, predicting success can be extremely difficult. However, media producers don't just give up. Instead, they rely on a different set of techniques to try to predict and create popular hits, including imitating success and relying on stars.

Art Imitating Art

Perhaps the most common strategy mainstream commercial media companies use to increase the odds of success is to imitate products that have already been successful. Variations on this strategy include copying the sound of current hit bands, remaking hit movies, making sequels to previous film hits, and signing producers of recent hits. The underlying assumption in these cases is that hits and their makers beget more hits.

We saw in Chapter 2 how the commercial dynamic of network television helps create the conditions for rampant imitation on the small screen. We can see this dynamic in other media industries. The commercial success of New Edition and New Kids on the Block in the 1980s and Backstreet Boys, Boyz II Men, and 'N Sync in the 1990s prompted the big music labels to look for other "boy bands" that might ride the same wave. A stream of imitators saturated the market. Heavily promoted on the Disney Channel, the Jonas Brothers achieved success in the 2000s but most later boy band efforts resulted in failure. In the absence of any other major boy band hits in recent years, a group of young men wanting to sing together today would have considerable difficulty in getting a major record deal.

In book publishing, authors of popular mass-market books, such as Stephen King, J. K. Rowling, Anne Rice, Nora Roberts, and James Patterson, are paid huge sums of money for the rights to their future works. Virtually every hit movie seems to produce a sequel, and when a new hit television program emerges, each network rushes to develop its own version—or extension—of the latest hit. For example, following the success of *The Osbournes* and *The Anna Nicole Show* in 2002, television producers developed a remarkable number of new "reality" programs throughout the rest of the decade that focused on the lives of marginal and former celebrities, from *Living Lohan* to *The Celebrity Apprentice*. The cable channel VH1 even organized most of its prime-time programming schedule around its "celebreality" series of shows.

Even when using formulas for hits, however, there is no guarantee for popularity or economic success. Many products that were supposed to be popular failed to meet expectations. Witness the remarkable failure of Will Ferrell's 2009 film, *Land of the Lost,* a movie that was designed to be a blockbuster hit. A movie remake of a cult-classic TV show, starring a proven box office draw, ended up being a multimillion-dollar dud. In 2004 and 2005, two would-be blockbusters failed to capitalize on previously successful formulas. Despite heavy promotion, *The Alamo* and *Sahara*—vehicles for star Mathew McConaughey—were two of the biggest box office disappointments in the history of the film industry, with the films each losing over $130 million for their respective studios. In 2006, *Basic Instinct 2,* a long-awaited sequel to the 1992 blockbuster *Basic Instinct,* opened in 10th place at the box office and made back only $6 million of its $70 million production budget during its short run in U.S. theaters. Thus, imitation does not guarantee economic success; but as a kind of informal operating assumption, it is one way for media organizations to try to maximize the likelihood of success.

Stars and the "Hit System"

Another strategic asset in the media industry's pursuit of success is fame or stardom. Stardom is such an important resource that the media industry relies on marketing research firms to measure it. The best known of these measures is the "Q Score" (Q for *quotient*), developed by Marketing Evaluations, Inc. (qscores.com), which indicates the familiarity and appeal of anything from a Hollywood actor to a fast-food chain. The more people know about and like something, the higher its Q Score. In early 2010, for example, the performers with the highest Q Scores were well-known, long-time favorites Tom Hanks and Morgan Freeman along with Pauley Perrette (of television's *NCIS* program), who was much less well-known but who scored exceptionally high on likeability measures, suggesting her star was on the rise.

In its initial stages, fame is fleeting. The public's attention shifts often and minor celebrities come and go frequently. But this initial attention can take on a "snowball" quality for some; a modest incident of notoriety is parlayed into more fame that, in turn, grows cumulatively (Cowan 2000). Only a small percentage of celebrities who obtain some initial fame are able to build that notoriety into major stardom. However, once major stardom has been achieved, fame tends to endure and is relatively stable (van de Rijt et al. 2013). This small group of major stars is crucial to the hit system.

In a media-saturated society, popular and well-liked stars can seem almost omnipresent because a large celebrity-producing apparatus promotes them incessantly. We can see them on TV talk shows advertising their latest projects, we know about their personal lives through magazines and gossip blogs, and we can follow their daily musings on Twitter accounts.

The principal reason why stars are so visible and seem to dominate our mass media is that they are the physical embodiment of hits. Just as producers imitate already successful movies, television programs, and books in an effort to produce new successes, producers seek out stars and promote them heavily to increase the odds of successful projects. The presence of stars is a significant inducement in the public's selection of films to attend, television programs to view, music to buy, magazines to read, and so on. In turn, stars can draw higher salaries because the odds of producers recouping those expenses are greater than they would be with a relatively unknown artist. Therefore, it is in the interest of aspiring stars to maximize their exposure to the public—to become well-known and well-liked—as this translates into financial clout in signing new project deals. At the same time, it is in the interest of the producers to ensure that the stars they use remain in the public limelight, attracting attention to their projects. The result is a popular media system infused with star power.

Stars increase the chances of producing hits. Publishers want best sellers; record labels are looking for top 40 songs and platinum albums; movie studios seek blockbuster films. But most movies, songs, and books lose money. That makes hits all the more important because they more than compensate for the losses incurred by other projects. In short, the hit system is the underlying operating principle of most major media companies. And if hits are the goal, then producers see a star who can attract audiences as one of the keys to success.

This star principle is so widely adopted as a basic norm of the media world that we see its manifestation in unlikely places. Broadcast journalism, with its heavy promotion of network anchors, such as Brian Williams, Scott Pelley, and Diane Sawyer, vies for the news audience by selling the appeal of the big names. These anchors and a handful of other network reporters are full-fledged celebrities who make appearances on talk shows, are the subjects of high-stakes bidding wars, and have programs created for the purpose of giving them even more exposure. The college textbook industry also adopts the star system, seeking well-known professors as authors of high-volume introductory texts, even when unknown coauthors do most of the writing. Given a market that is dominated by a small number of standard-bearing texts—the equivalent of the hit song or blockbuster film—it is no surprise that textbook publishers seek the prestige and visibility that come with academic stars.

Because acquiring already existing stars is both expensive and difficult, most media organizations will try to create their own. One popular approach in recent years has been through talent search shows like Fox's *America Idol* or NBC's *America's Got Talent*. The vast majority of the shows' contestants quickly return to obscurity, but a few survive to create hits and become stars, including *American Idol*'s Kelly Clarkson, Carrie Underwood, and Chris Daughtry.

Creating Hits and Producing Stars

We might think that all new media products have equal chances to be hits and that their main players have equal chances at stardom—especially in the age of instant Internet access. After all, audiences are the only true judges; they make hits and stars. This view suggests that hits succeed and stars rise to the top because audiences love them, but this is a misleading view.

All media products do not have the same chance for hit status, nor do all media personalities have the same chance at stardom. Hits and stars are rare, and the resources to produce them are limited. So before audiences ever get to see them, media organizations make advance decisions about which products and people have the best chance of success. It is virtually impossible to be a star if the firm that produces and distributes your work has already decided that you do not have what it takes to be a huge hit. On the other hand, you have a chance—though no guarantee—of stardom if media professionals deem you a possessor of star quality. Thus, media professionals, rather than audiences, make the initial judgments crucial for achieving success.

Films that are seen as potential hits, for example, are slotted for heavy promotion. This might include full-page newspaper ads, frequent television commercials, talk show appearances by the stars-to-be, cross-promotional campaigns with fast-food restaurants and other outlets, and release of the film to theaters all over the country. Movies not seen as potential hits will receive much less promotion and will be released to a much smaller number of theaters, virtually guaranteeing they will not reach hit status. The next time you browse Netflix or Amazon Instant Video, take note of the large number of films that you have never heard of; many come and go from the theaters so fast, with so little advertising, that only true film enthusiasts know they exist. Some never even make it to the theater but instead are released directly to DVD. As a result, only those films that the movie studios identify as potential hits will ever get the visibility to have a chance to become blockbusters.

The same dynamic is at work in the music industry. Acts are split into potential earning divisions, with some being classified as big time and others as possessing only minor or specialized appeal (Frith 1981). The first hurdle for musicians, then, is to get through the initial classification process, which occurs before the first album is even released. Those who are identified as potential big timers will have much more opportunity, and many more resources, than those who are categorized as minor players. Such support, though, comes at a cost; artists who receive heavy promotional support must typically conform to standardized formulas that have been identified for "success." A band with a hit record is likely to be pressured by their label to produce something very similar for their next record rather than branching out to embrace new sounds or styles.

We can see a similar process in the book industry, where publicity and marketing resources are concentrated on the most likely best sellers, while mid-list authors frequently see their books disappear from the shelves relatively unnoticed. Publishers decide how to package a book, how many copies to print, what to price the book at, how to promote it, and where to distribute it based on advance judgments of sales capability. These judgments are often made before the final draft is completed. Likewise, the key decision for television programs, once they are selected for the prime-time lineup, is where they will be scheduled. Will the program be slated to pick up the tailwind of an already successful show or be dropped into a Friday night time slot where ratings are low and fewer viewers are at home? What will the competition be on the other networks during the time slot chosen for broadcast? Some time slots are more favorable than others, and programs that are predicted unlikely to attract top-level ratings are generally scheduled in a way that practically guarantees they will fail to find an audience and be canceled in short order.

Using Stars to Combat Uncertainty

Media organizations are attempting to produce popular and profitable hits, and they see stars as one key way to do this. In a media world in which uncertainty is a constant, executives seek rules to make their decisions less arbitrary. The deep commitment to stars and to the importance of reputation more generally is one of the principal ways that the fluidity and ambiguity of the media industry are brought under control.

Moviemaking, for example, is a very uncertain business. Without any method for ensuring commercial success and with so many players involved in the production and distribution of a film, the presence of a star helps reduce the perception of risk. Stars make people more comfortable with the risks they are taking, even if they are not demonstrably less risky. The presence of a star, in essence, rationalizes the entire process by providing an agreed-on currency for assessing potential projects. The star system is a useful coping mechanism in such an uncertain industry (Prindle 1993).

The dynamic in television is similar. Programmers rely on producers of prior hits as a strategy for legitimizing their decisions (Bielby and Bielby 1994). In much the same manner as the film industry, network programmers operate in a situation in which hits are hard to come by and even harder to predict. Programmers have to satisfy various constituencies—advertisers, local station managers, and network executives—and they have to demonstrate that their programming decisions are not arbitrary. In this case, reputation—the result of the prior production of a hit—is the key currency. The various players within the television industry agree that past hit production is a legitimate criterion for selecting programs. They even try to sell viewers on this notion when promotional commercials emphasize that a new series is brought to you by the producers of a previous hit.

However, the *stars* = *hits* = *success* formula is not as accurate a description of media products as industry common sense would suggest. For example, pretend you were the head of a movie studio during the 2000s and wanted to rely on the star power of Eddie

Source: Disney, http://disney.go.com/the-lone-ranger/?cmp=wdsmp_lonerngr_url_dcomloneranger_Extl.

A major star like Johnny Depp playing a well-known role from a classic hit should have added up to success. However, it's never certain that employing stars can reduce risk; 2013's *The Lone Ranger* was a massive failure at the box office.

Murphy to sell a family-friendly comedy. You could look at *Daddy Day Care* (U.S. box office: $104.3 million) in 2003 or *Norbit* ($95.7 million) in 2007 and feel reasonably safe moving forward with your new movie. Then again, you could also look at *The Adventures of Pluto Nash* (U.S. box office: $4.4 million) in 2002 or *Meet Dave* ($11.8 million) in 2008 and have substantial reasons for concern. What's the best decision to make when you know that a family-friendly comedy starring Eddie Murphy might make anywhere between 4 and 104 million dollars in the theaters? Of course, there are other sources of revenue for major motion pictures—in particular, DVD sales, TV broadcast rights, and foreign markets—and some genres of films that do not break even at the domestic box office tend to find substantial revenue elsewhere. These factors, however, create a whole additional set of variables to manage and consider.

Television networks regularly try to attract and keep celebrities on the small screen, but building a program around a star personality is also no guarantee of success. Perhaps you want to create a spin-off with a character from a wildly popular show, as was the case with the *Cheers* spin-off *Frasier* (episode run: 264), but also the case with the *Friends* spin-off *Joey* (episode run: 46). You could also try to lure a less popular movie star into a role on TV, like Kiefer Sutherland in *24* (episode run: 192) or Jerry O'Connell in a show by the creators of *Ugly Betty* and *The Office,* as was the case with *Do Not Disturb* (episode run: 2). These examples suggest that the stars = hits = success formula is far from reliable. But the organization of production in the film and television industries and the ambiguities of these creative businesses help explain why the hit–star relationship continues to shape decision making—even in the face of conflicting evidence.

Beyond Stars to a Universe of Products

Compared to Pixar Animation's other wildly popular films, the 2006 children's movie *Cars* received the worst reviews and was among the company's poorest performers at the box office. But that didn't stop a sequel, *Cars 2*, from being released in 2011. That's because *Cars* was a huge merchandising hit, generating nearly $10 billion in product sales over five years. Its anthropomorphic automobiles—sold as toys and emblazoned on an endless variety of products—were so successful that *Cars 2* was developed to do the same, only this time with planes, trains, and boats, too. In fact, *Cars 2* spawned over 300 toys and countless other merchandising products from children's clothes and backpacks to bedding and Spaghetti-O's. Coupled with video games, a 12-acre *Cars*-land attraction at the Disney theme park in California, and TV programs, *Cars* was developed to be a massive commercial franchise, not just a movie. To maximize the appeal abroad of both the film and its spin-off products, the lead character, Lightning McQueen, competes in a World Grand Prix in Japan, France, England, and Italy (Chmielewski and Keegan 2011).

Cars represents the emergence of a type of media product that is not limited to a single form. Henry Jenkins defines *convergence culture* as a "flow of content across multiple media platforms, the cooperation between multiple media industries, and the migratory behavior of media audiences who will go almost anywhere in search of the kinds of entertainment experiences they want" (Jenkins 2006: 2–3). While, in the past, media organizations tended to rely only on the power of a good story (say, a novel or a single movie) or the power of a celebrity (say, a hit novelist or blockbuster star), they now work to create entire fictional universes that can be extended and sold across a range of media platforms—films, television shows, video games, comic books, websites, and more.

For example, think of the six hit movies in the *Star Wars* film franchise (with three more on the way). While these movies have all been huge economic successes, they make up only a small portion of the media content that constitutes the vast universe of *Star Wars* products. To truly grasp the impact of *Star Wars,* we must also consider the five different animated *Star Wars* television programs, the 15 licensed *Star Wars* cell phone games, over 75 additional *Star Wars* video games, hundreds of serialized *Star Wars* novels, hundreds of serialized *Star Wars* comic books, multiple lines of *Star Wars* toys, Halloween costumes, and so on. We can see similar developments in Marvel's expansion of a multiple-platform fictional universe of superheroes and the Warchowskis' multiple-platform fictional universe of *The Matrix.* Of course, developing an entire universe of fictional characters that are compelling enough for viewers to follow across multiple media platforms is no small feat; but if a media organization is able to do so, it provides good security against the largely unpredictable success or failure of a specific media product.

Media professionals are not only constrained by continued uncertainty in the quest for producing hits or by finding a fictional universe that will connect over time with consumers out in the marketplace. Media workers must also navigate through the long-standing roles and conventions that exist within the media industries themselves. While they have some agency in choosing which media to bring to market, they face the structural constraints of their industry traditions, to which we now turn.

THE ORGANIZATION OF MEDIA WORK

In a classic study, sociologist Howard Becker (1982) observes that "producing art requires elaborate cooperation among specialized personnel" (p. 28). We can make the same statement about the production of media content. Whether we are talking about films, books, music, radio, magazines, newspapers, or television, the production and distribution of the message become the work of many people. Even the most apparently individualistic media presentation—a solo album by a singer–songwriter—still requires many other actors, including the music producer, the representatives of the music label, the designer of the album cover, the publicists who promote the music, and so on. One line of research, therefore, has been studying the organization of media work, examining how media workers collaborate to produce media products.

Conventions

Becker (1982) asks an important question about the many people who do media work: "How do they arrive at the terms on which they cooperate?" Some researchers have argued that the behavior of media personnel is shaped by the "needs" of an organization (Epstein 1973). In other words, maintaining the existence of the organization points different individuals within that organization in the same direction. In its strongest application, this approach is usually too constraining to account for the independent action of media personnel. Another way we might account for the collaboration of media workers is to suggest that they must negotiate the terms of their cooperation before each new endeavor. This approach emphasizes the capacity for independent action, but it ignores the constraints under which media personnel labor.

In contrast to these approaches and consistent with what sociologists who study occupations have found, Becker (1982) focuses on the tension between structure and agency. He tells us that "people who cooperate to produce a work of art usually do not decide things afresh. Instead, they rely on earlier agreements now become customary, agreements that have become part of the conventional ways of doing things" (p. 29).

A *convention* is a practice or technique that is widely used in a field. It is much easier to identify something as conventional than it is to explain the source and meaning of the convention. All of us could likely identify some of the conventions that govern news reporting, pop music, or advertising. For example, the sound of top 40 music rarely surprises us since it follows broad conventions regarding what instruments are used, the length of the song, the verse/chorus structure, and so on. We could ask how radio programmers learn to follow these conventions and how they know which songs will fit their stations. The answer is that radio programmers see themselves as middlemen between record producers and listeners, develop an understanding of the genres their stations represent, and establish a set of repertoires for action to ensure that both listeners and record companies feel supported and understood. Without these conventions, radio programmers couldn't do their jobs (Ahlkvist and Faulkner 2002).

Hollywood agents must also learn to casually perform the social conventions of their industry in order to be taken seriously as players. These conventions include hosting meetings in and around Beverly Hills in modernist buildings; coming off as confident, casual, and hip; and giving creative gifts with a personal touch (Zafirau 2008). Industry conventions also take forms that are more easily recognizable to consumers. You don't need to be a graphic designer to know that magazine covers have the publication's name in large letters at the top and will almost always feature a large, dominating graphic, or that an evening news broadcast will take place in a studio with a broadcaster behind a desk. Even "fake" news programs like *The Daily Show* and "Weekend Update" on *Saturday Night Live* follow these conventions. If Jon Stewart told jokes about the day's politics while standing up, we might assume *The Daily Show* was just another late-night comedy show and not actually a comedic re-creation of a news broadcast. Even media products that break from convention appear striking and innovative only because both producers and audiences are accustomed to conventional forms.

Conventions are not arbitrary, even though they may often seem to be. They are the result of the routinization of work by media professionals and partially a consequence of professional education and job training. To understand media content on the basis of its conventions, we need to consider where conventions originate, how they are followed in the work process, and how they lead to the production of media that we perceive as conventional.

News Routines and Their Consequences

News production is one type of media work that has been studied extensively, not only for its reliance on conventions but also for the distinctive dynamics associated with the field that illustrate the interaction of structure and agency. A series of classic studies from the 1970s and 1980s laid the groundwork for our understanding of news production that is still applicable today (Epstein 1973; Fishman 1980; Gans [1979] 2004; Sigal 1973; Tuchman 1978; and, for a review, see Cottle 2007). This work has since been supplemented by more recent studies that examine some changes in newsrooms, including those brought on by technological innovation and economic pressures (see Powers 2011 for a review). Together, they illustrate some of the dynamics involved in the organization of media work.

These studies help us consider a simple question: What is news? At first, the answer seems self-evident: News is information about recent important events beyond our direct experience. But how do we know what makes an event important? How do we know what information about an important event is relevant? We leave it to professional journalists to handle these questions. As a result, we rely on journalists to act as "gatekeepers" (White 1950)—to make judgments about what is or is not important, or *newsworthy*—and to provide us with factual accounts about these newsworthy events. Ultimately, if we are to understand what news really is, we need to understand how journalists form their judgments and construct their accounts. In other words, we need to examine the day-to-day work of the professional journalist because this is where news is defined and news stories are written.

Let's look at the process from the perspective of people within a news organization. A news staff must generate content for a website, broadcast, or newspaper regardless of what did or did not happen that day. This means that editors and reporters must find news. At the same time, literally thousands of things are happening: People eat meals, walk their dogs, buy and sell goods, commit crimes, announce new policies, argue court cases, participate in sporting contests, lie on the beach, fight wars, campaign for elected office, and so on. The list is virtually endless. News outlets, however, cannot report on all the things that happen; only some happenings are defined as important enough to be news. For reporters, the difficulty is determining which events are newsworthy and gathering enough information to cover these newsworthy events.

On the face of it, news reporting may seem to be an impossible job. How can journalists know which events to report and which to ignore? They cannot go to dozens of different events before deciding which one to cover; they would never meet their deadlines. How do reporters find out about relevant happenings in the first place?

Two classic sociological studies (Fishman 1980; Tuchman 1978) argue that we can find answers to these questions in the routine practices of journalism. Because news organizations cannot constantly reinvent the wheel, the processes of news gathering and news reporting must be rationalized. In other words, news organizations must be able to anticipate where news will happen—before it happens—and structure their reporters' assignments accordingly. Within news organizations, reporters follow routines that tell them where to look for news and how to gather it efficiently. When the same basic routines are adopted as professional norms, as they are in contemporary American journalism, different news outlets will make similar judgments about newsworthiness. This state of affairs makes it difficult to see that any judgments are being made at all.

What are these journalistic routines? Tuchman (1978) adopts the metaphor of the "news net" to explain the standard practice for gathering news. News organizations cast a net—made up of wire services, full-time reporters, and stringers—to catch newsworthy happenings. The net, however, does not catch everything; like all nets, it is full of holes and catches only the "big fish." This serves as an initial filter, sorting out those happenings that do not meet the standard criteria for news.

The organization of news gathering shows which criteria determine how the news net is constructed. News organizations will have staff or bureaus in places they define as important. For example, news outlets typically have bureaus in Washington, DC, and London, England, but not Houston, Texas, and Nairobi, Kenya. As a result, happenings in and around these predefined important places are more likely to become news, while happenings outside of these areas are more likely to be ignored.

News organizations also establish "beats" at prominent organizations where news can be expected to occur. In practice, this means that a series of official locations—police stations, courthouses, city halls, state houses, Capitol Hill, the White House—become sites where reporters are stationed. Each day, the reporter on the city hall beat will be responsible for providing one or more stories about the happenings there. It is likely that the city government will have a media relations staff who will be more than happy to provide the beat reporter with daily doses of news in the form of press releases, public announcements, press conferences, and so forth. Finally, areas such as sports, business, and the arts are topical beats that are expected to produce news each day, so reporters establish relationships with key players in these areas to guarantee a regular supply of news.

Beats are central to how reporters "detect" events, but each beat covers so much potential territory that reporters have to develop strategies for detecting the newsworthy events. Fishman (1980) uses the example of a local paper's "justice" beat, which included, among other things, "three law enforcement agencies: city police, county sheriffs, and an FBI office; four penal institutions . . . two juvenile facilities; two entire court systems; an extensive drug subculture" (p. 33). With such a vast terrain to cover, Fishman notes, reporters develop complex work routines that he calls "rounds."

The round structures the workday and defines what events the reporter will be exposed to in the first place. In essence, the round is a process by which beat reporters develop schedules for visiting locations and talking to sources that are likely to produce news. Such work routines are built around the bureaucratic organization of the institutions that make up the beat. For example, a justice reporter will build a work routine around the schedules of the courthouse, police department, and district attorney's office to be on hand for meetings, press conferences, and prescheduled events and to gain access to official records. The reporter may also check in on a regular basis—perhaps hourly—with a range of sites to see if anything is "happening." For example, a beat reporter might call each prison, juvenile facility, law enforcement agency, and courthouse to make sure that important events do not go undetected.

The definition of what is a relevant beat and whether what happens there deserves coverage is not universal. Rather, it changes according to a given media outlet's target audience and, more generally, its mission. For example, TMZ, a celebrity gossip–based website and television program owned by Time Warner, covers "news" that traditional news outlets typically do not consider to be newsworthy. TMZ stands for Thirty Mile Zone, and their beat encompasses the 30-mile radius around the intersection of West Beverly and North La Cienega in Los Angeles, in which all of the major U.S. production studios are headquartered. Sometimes tipped off by celebrities and their publicists seeking media attention, reporters and celebrity photographers prowl luxury stores, restaurants, and other locations seeking candid pictures and brief interviews with stars. The result is very different from a daily newspaper, but the process involved in creating the content is similar.

Because reporters on deadline must produce a news story for their employers, we should not be surprised that news work is routinized in this way. How else could reporters gather news in an efficient, consistent manner while meeting the needs of their news organizations? The problem, however, is that we rarely talk about the news in these terms, nor do we take note of the consequences.

For example, when we consider news beats, we can see that, before anything even happens on a given day, news organizations have already made decisions about where they intend to look for news. The flip side, of course, is also true: The routine practices associated with news gathering virtually ensure that certain happenings will be excluded from the news. News from Africa and South America, for example, is notoriously scarce in the U.S. media, in large part because reporters are less likely to be assigned there. The example of news beats shows that, rather than being an inherent characteristic of events, newsworthiness is typically constructed each day by professional journalists and news organizations.

Another consequence of routine journalistic practices is a reliance on official sources to feed journalists a steady diet of information to use in their stories. This dependence upon official sources for "news" means that these sources have routine access to media coverage, while outsiders or critics have a more difficult time gaining entrée to the news. The result is that news tends to reflect the views and opinions of those already in power.

Finally, routine journalistic practices result in an emphasis on events at the expense of processes. Reporters look out for what is new in the world around them (the event) and often have few resources (time, money, and expertise) to spotlight the long-term developments that may have been at the origin of the event. As a consequence, news coverage is often fleeting, shining a momentary spotlight on some event and then moving on to a new and unrelated event. This focus on events at the expense of processes likely has an impact on whether and how people understand complicated issues, such as wars, financial crises, crime trends, and budget decisions.

Technology and the New News Routines

As a result of industry changes and new technology, journalists have altered their routines significantly since the classic studies of newsrooms were done. As Powers (2011: 12) summarizes, "Compared to the time of the classic studies, today there exist more outlets, more formats, more interactions across both, and more uncertainty over who and what counts as a journalist and as journalism, respectively." Many of the basic insights about the social construction of news remain valid today, but the specifics of how this process works have changed as the structural context within which journalists' work has changed.

The rise of media conglomerates described in Chapter 2 has meant increased economic pressure on news organizations, with dubious consequences for the quality of news (Klinenberg 2007; McChesney 1999, 2004). Economic pressures in the field have led to downsizing and increased competition for jobs, less secure employment, and management demands that journalists be more efficient and productive in their work as news organizations seek to cut costs (Deuze 2007; Majoribanks 2000). At the same time,

Source: AP Photo/Mark Lennihan.

Technology has changed the look and substance of the contemporary newspaper newsroom, as with *The Wall Street Journal*'s, pictured here. Flanked by always-on television screens, journalists at newspapers create web content that is frequently updated and produce video reports as a routine part of their work.

increased pressures to attract audiences to sell to advertisers have meant that ratings and readership numbers (easily measured on news websites) have grown in importance. Taking the audience into account is a growing part of determining what does or does not become news, resulting in more content that is entertaining or oriented toward broad "lifestyle" topics (Boczkowski 2010).

Technological changes have also facilitated dramatic changes in how journalists do their work. Journalism is now often a multimedia enterprise, incorporating print, video, and graphics, changing how journalists tell their stories (Boczkowski 2004). The need for print outlets to also produce video and other content for their corresponding websites influences what is identified as newsworthy.

The expansion of news to cable and the Internet has dramatically altered the volume of news-related material that is available. Instead of a need to whittle down content to fit the space available in a daily newspaper or half-hour television news broadcast, news organizations today must produce an almost endless amount of "content" to fill 24-hour cable news channels and websites that have no limits. This need to fill a vastly expanded news hole led to the growth of cable news talk programming, featuring pundits, commentators, and advocates. It has also led to the expansion of what is treated as legitimate news sources. One study of content from the *New York Times* and the *Washington Post* found that traditional news organizations increasingly use blogs as source material, especially in covering politics.

In turn, the study found that blogs depend heavily upon traditional news outlets as sources, thereby creating a "news source cycle" (Messner and DiStaso 2008).

The era of newspapers, newsmagazines, and broadcast evening news—the subject of the classic newsroom studies—was characterized by a daily news cycle with a single deadline. In the era of 24-hour cable news and news websites, this predictable news cycle has been replaced by an unending and erratic "news cyclone" (Klinenberg 2005) in which journalists must constantly rewrite and update news stories. The need to constantly update websites has meant the time frame for making decisions about news is tightly compressed, compared to earlier times. Journalists often complain this leads to more stress and less time to make informed news judgments.

Ever since the rise of CNN, newsrooms constantly monitor 24-hour cable news organizations to follow what stories are being covered. Newspapers preview the next day's content on their websites, and editors and reporters at competing new organizations scrutinize these sites closely. If one outlet covers a story, others are likely to follow quickly. This has contributed to further homogenization of mainstream news. Imitation of other news outlets means journalists don't have to consider newsworthiness as closely (Boczkowski 2009, 2010). If a competing news outlet is covering a story, then it is automatically deemed newsworthy.

In fact, some news stories are simply rewritten versions of news from other outlets. As Philips (2010: 96) notes, "There is now a widespread practice across the news media, of reporters being asked to rewrite stories appearing elsewhere, in some cases without a single additional telephone call, and to lift quotes and case histories without any attribution." As a consequence of such practices, news from different outlets tends to be more similar today than it was in the past, even though there are many more outlets available today (Boczkowski 2010; Schudson 2011).

The authority of journalists to make judgment calls about newsworthiness has also been challenged by the rise of new types of news outlets on the Internet that vary by the degree to which they are moderated by professionals and by the extent to which they focus on editorial content versus commentary and debate from the public (Deuze 2003). Not only do websites offers alternatives to professional news production but the ability of nonjournalists to gather information, take pictures, and capture videos has often meant that coverage of breaking news in mainstream news outlets includes content created by nonprofessionals.

Whether classic studies or contemporary updates, a sociology of news work gives us insight into the making of news by demonstrating the significance of the ways in which journalists respond to the demands of news organizations. The standard practices for gathering news, the shared definition of where news is likely to happen, and the increasing likelihood that cash-strapped news organizations imitate other outlets help explain why so much of our daily news across so many news outlets looks so similar and focuses on the activities of official institutions. The news we get is the end result of professional routines, which generally focus on the activities of legitimate, bureaucratic institutions.

News Wire Services

While news gathering is done by journalists, only major newspapers and television networks can afford a significant staff to gather original news stories on a full range of topics. As we have seen, imitation and recycling of news from other outlets has become common.

But even more important, most news organizations subscribe to news agency services that supply a steady stream of stories (Fenby 1986). (News agencies originally delivered their news via telegraph and are still sometimes referred to as newswires or wire services.) These agencies have correspondents in many locations, varying according to their reach and linguistic, geographic, and thematic specialization. They prepare news, feature stories, pictures, and videos that can be republished by the subscribing media outlet with little or no modification. The world news in your local newspaper is likely to come from a news agency.

The first news agency was created in France in 1835, and still exists: *Agence France-Presse* (AFP) has 200 bureaus in 150 countries and, on a typical day, produces about 5,000 stories, 3,000 photographs, 200 videos, and 100 graphics in six different languages (AFP.com). Together with Reuters (United Kingdom) and Associated Press (AP, United States), AFP is one of the three largest wire services in the world. Most news agencies are private corporations (Reuters). Others are government-chartered public corporations, such as AFP, and are directly owned by the government (Canadian Press, China's Central News Agency), whereas others are cooperatives of smaller contributing media organizations (Associated Press, Australian Associated Press).

However they are structured, news agencies can be considered the backbone of modern journalism. They scout and produce the news that we read daily in newspapers and watch on television. They are the fundamental source of reporting on national and international news for the large majority of local and regional media outlets, which largely reproduce or rebroadcast news agency products. As a result, news agencies have a significant impact on the selection of what constitutes relevant news. But like all newsgathering organizations, news agencies themselves follow standardized news routines and staff-recognized beats that ensure they produce sufficient material to supply to subscribing news outlets.

Objectivity

We have seen that the specific definitions of *news* and *newsworthiness* are, in large measure, the result of the ways reporters organize their work. However, there is more to be learned by exploring the profession of journalism. Consider the concept of *objectivity.* Most contemporary evaluations of the performance of the American mainstream news media begin or end with claims about their adherence (or lack thereof) to the standard of objectivity and related notions of impartiality, balance, and fairness. Politicians and other public figures routinely criticize the press for its supposed lack of objectivity, charging journalists with taking sides, being too opinionated, or having a routine bias. Even popular discussions of news media often focus on the question of objectivity. The central position of objectivity in American journalism is something we take for granted. We all seem to "know" that the news is supposed to be objective; the problem is that the news often does not live up to this widely shared expectation.

But where did the value of objectivity come from? Why are we so concerned with it? How does the ideal of objectivity affect the daily practice of journalism? Michael Schudson's (1978) important study, *Discovering the News,* treats the ideal of objectivity as something to be explained rather than something to be taken for granted. It is a perfect example of how studying professional norms and practices can help us better understand the media.

The Origins of Objectivity

What do we mean by *objectivity*? Schudson (1978) provides a useful definition: "The belief in objectivity is a faith in 'facts,' a distrust of 'values,' and a commitment to their segregation" (p. 6). Objectivity is a doctrine that perceives the separation of fact and value as a messy business that requires the use of a method, or set of practices, to ensure their separation. This method is objective journalism. According to Schudson, the concept of objective journalism is a relatively recent development. Only in the years after World War I did objectivity become the dominant value in American journalism.

Prior to World War I, reporters did not subscribe to a belief in what we now term *objectivity*. The AP—one of the first wire services—tried to present news in a way that would be acceptable to many different papers, and the *New York Times* used an "information" model of reporting to attract an elite audience. But journalists did not think about the separation of facts and values, nor did they believe that facts themselves were at all problematic. Rather, to journalists before World War I, the facts spoke for themselves. The goal of fact-based journalism was simply to uncover these facts, and doing so did not require a method of objective reporting. The task was straightforward: Find and report the truth. In this era, journalists were confident of their ability to identify the relevant facts and to report them accurately.

This faith in facts held by American journalists was thrown into doubt in the 1920s. Many American reporters had participated in wartime propaganda efforts during World War I. The success of such efforts made them uncomfortable with any simple understanding of "facts." Having seen how easily facts could be manipulated, journalists became more cynical. They began to mistrust facts, realizing that facts could be made to serve illusion as well as the truth.

At the same time, the field of public relations (PR) emerged, and professional publicists became early "spin doctors." They fed information to reporters, carefully controlling access to their powerful clients, and they staged events such as the press conference or photo opportunity expressly for the media. With PR professionals spinning the facts, dispensing information strategically, and shaping a good deal of news content through the use of official handouts or press releases, journalists' emerging cynicism became even more pronounced.

The recognition that information could be manipulated and the rise of a profession—PR—expressly dedicated to the shaping of public attitudes left journalists with a crisis of confidence about their own ability to report the "facts" in a neutral way. In Schudson's (1978) account, objectivity emerged as a "scientific" solution to this crisis of confidence—in other words, "a method designed for a world in which even facts could not be trusted" (p. 122). By training would-be reporters in the "scientific" method of objectivity, journalists transformed their fact-based craft into a profession with a particular method. Objectivity, therefore, can be seen as a set of practices or conventions that the professional journalist is trained to follow.

What practices make up this method? W. Lance Bennett (2009), synthesizing the research on the professional norms of journalism, identifies six key practices: (1) maintaining political neutrality; (2) observing prevailing standards of decency and good taste; (3) using documentary reporting practices, which rely on physical evidence; (4) using standardized formats to package the news; (5) training reporters as generalists instead of specialists; and (6) using editorial review to enforce these methods. The practical implication of belief in the ideal of objectivity is adherence to these basic practices.

Objectivity as Routine Practices and Their Political Consequences

The day-to-day routine practices of journalism, more than some abstract conception of objectivity, are key to understanding the news media. News accounts have a tendency to look similar because reporters all follow the same basic routines. They talk to the same people, use the same formats, observe the same basic dos and don'ts, and watch one another closely to make sure that they are not out of step with the rest of the profession. If we understand objectivity to be a set of routine journalistic practices, we can see why all news coverage is pretty much the same. Journalists adhere to the same methods and monitor each other's work so they produce similar news. In fact, if news differed substantially from outlet to outlet, questions would be raised about the method of objective reporting, likely signaling a new crisis for the profession.

However, following a common set of practices does not ensure the achievement of the ideal of objectivity, that is, the separation of values from facts. Indeed, it can be argued that adherence to the practices associated with objectivity directly benefits particular political interests.

As we have seen, things that happen in and around established institutions, especially official agencies, are defined as news. Happenings outside of these boundaries are likely never to be detected by professional journalists. Even if they are detected, they are not likely to be defined as newsworthy by the established definitions of importance. This is one of the principal reasons why so much news is about the world of officialdom, even when such stories are often routine and predictable. Journalists and news organizations rely on and build their work around the routine and predictability of these established institutions. Newsworthiness, then, is socially constructed. It is not a property inherent in events but is instead something that is attached to happenings by journalists. Once we realize this, the traditional ways we talk about news begin to seem inappropriate. In particular, the metaphor of news as a "mirror"—a simple reflection of events—no longer works. Even a mirror cannot reflect the whole world. It must be facing a particular direction, including some subjects in its reflection and excluding others. Thus, the image propagated by the media is far from complete. At best, it reflects only a small part of society.

In addition, the objects being reflected in the media are not passive. Instead, people holding different interests, wielding different amounts of power and enjoying different relationships to those producing the news, actively attempt to influence the content of the news. Thus, the resulting images often reflect the relative power of actors in our society rather than some "objective" reality.

News, therefore, is the product of a social process through which media personnel make decisions about what is newsworthy and what is not, about who is important and who is not, about what views are to be included and what views can be dismissed. None of these decisions can be entirely objective. The ideal of objectivity—separating values from facts—is ultimately unobtainable, although some would argue it is a valuable goal. Furthermore, the practices associated with objectivity are tilted in one direction; they give those in power enormous visibility in the media, while those outside the centers of power are largely ignored. The reliance on "appropriate," available, and preferably authoritative sources means journalists talk mostly to government and corporate officials and end up reproducing their view of the world. Thus, "objective" journalism, by highlighting the views and activities of officials, can be seen on balance to favor those in power.

Rejecting Objectivity: Alternative Journalism

As we have seen, objectivity as a standard of U.S. journalism is a fairly recent phenomenon. When the nation's founders protected the freedom of the press, they were referring to publishers of what were mostly highly partisan pamphlets and periodicals. Through the 19th century, newspapers were often affiliated with political parties, openly arguing from a particular perspective rather than trying to retain a neutral stance on the issues. While "objective" journalism has displaced this older tradition, "advocacy" or "alternative" journalism has survived and can be found in many forms today.

Atton and Hamilton (2008) argue that alternative media "seek to challenge objectivity and impartiality from both an ethical and a political standpoint." They challenge the very notion that "it is possible in the first place to separate facts from values and that it is morally and politically preferable to do" (Atton and Hamilton 2008: 84). Alternative journalists not only reject the idea of not getting involved in the story, they seek to play an active role in advancing their causes.

Alternative journalism projects span a wide range of media, including newspapers, magazines, websites, radio programs, and television shows. In recent years, the Internet has made alternative journalism more easily accessible and more visible while enabling its unprecedented global expansion (Lievrouw 2011).

There is a broad range of work that might be called alternative journalism. Some of it is in the muckraking tradition—fact-based reporting aimed at exposing a social ill or wrongdoing that is being ignored by mainstream media—that dates back to the 19th century. For example, founded in 1976, the nonprofit magazine (and now website) *Mother Jones* is named after an early labor movement leader and bills itself as "a nonprofit news organization that specializes in investigative, political, and social justice reporting" (Motherjones. com 2011). It has won numerous awards for its investigative reporting.

Other efforts are aimed at broadening the range of perspectives available in the news. *Democracy Now!* is a syndicated radio program that features "people and perspectives rarely heard in the U.S. corporate-sponsored media, including independent and international journalists, ordinary people from around the world who are directly affected by U.S. foreign policy, grassroots leaders and peace activists, artists, academics and independent analysts" (Democracynow.org 2011).

Some efforts take advantage of the Internet to build international links. For example, the global network Indymedia offers what it bills as "grassroots, non-corporate coverage . . . a democratic media outlet for the creation of radical, accurate, and passionate tellings of truth" (Indymedia.org 2001). Indymedia activists do not aim at being objective; they take sides, presenting a typically left or progressive view on issues of the day.

Conservative activists have also created their own media forms that blend news and opinion. Websites like Townhall—a commercially owned operation—assemble what it describes as "political commentary and analysis from over 100 leading columnists and opinion leaders, research from 100 partner organizations, conservative talk-radio and a community of millions of grassroots conservatives" (Townhall.com 2011). The site links to hundreds of conservative bloggers. Conservative media activist Brent Bozell and his Media Research Center argue for a liberal bias in mainstream media and have created the Cybercast News Service (CNS) (cnsnews.com), which presents a distinctly right-wing spin on the news or, as the site's slogan puts it, "The Right News. Right Now."

At their best, efforts that—through well-reasoned, fact-based reporting—broaden the range of perspectives or tackle issues overlooked by mainstream commercial media can make a substantial contribution to keeping people informed and engaged, even when they clearly approach the issues from a particular political viewpoint. But at their worst, some partisan media—whether bitter cable talk shows on mainstream media or alternative websites—can also contribute to political polarization and the propagation of falsehoods. If people immerse themselves only in media that confirm their preexisting beliefs and play to their prejudices, it is unlikely that they will understand the arguments of opponents, be able to productively discuss issues with people who hold different opinions, or find the kind of common ground necessary for a healthy functioning democracy. Instead, relying solely on such media may contribute to the entrenched and bitterly divisive politics of recent years.

As we have seen, news media production is the result of a series of conventions and routines that enable professionals collectively to do their jobs and meet the demands of the organizations for which they work. These conventions incorporate fundamental professional norms (e.g., objectivity) and basic organizational goals (e.g., gathering news). Routine media practices shape, to a great degree, the final media products.

We have also seen that some media reject some of these conventions—most notably the idea of objectivity—to create new forms of reporting and opinion. Another alternative to traditional mainstream commercial news can be seen in the growing number of experiments involving user-generated content, some of which bypass traditional journalists, while others involve collaboration with them.

THE RISE OF USER-GENERATED CONTENT

With the exception of alternative journalism, most of our discussion so far has focused on mainstream professional journalism. However, the Internet has enabled the creation of a growing number of news sites that use amateur producers and user-generated content rather than professional journalists. User-generated content is produced by the end user. It has become increasingly popular, thanks to the availability of broadband Internet access, multifunction smartphones, easy-to-use blogging platforms, and wiki software. (Wiki software allows users to collectively create and edit web pages such as those at Wikipedia.)

Various forms of user-generated media overlap and often go by different names, but we can loosely group user-generated journalism into four different types, each with a different degree of amateur participation and control over content. First, some traditional news sites invite audiences to submit content in various forms; second, "pro-am" efforts involve the pairing of traditional professional journalists with input from amateurs to create news content; third, some all-amateur sites make use of collaborative wiki platforms; and fourth, some amateur sites involve the submission of "citizen journalism" projects.

Users and Mainstream Media: iReport

The first category of user-generated content piggybacks on existing traditional news websites. For example, in 2006, CNN launched iReport, its platform for user-generated content, with the aim of "paint[ing] a more complete picture of the news" (iReport.cnn.com 2011). Users can "take part in the news" by producing and uploading their own stories, which are published on the website. In doing so, contributors give CNN the right to edit and use their work in any way without payment. A small number of stories that are vetted by the CNN staff are marked with a special badge, and may be used in other CNN platforms. Otherwise, as the CNN site warns, iReport stories are "not edited, fact-checked, or screened." Similar initiatives include Fox's UReport and MSNBC's FirstPerson.

The "comments" section on news websites provide another way for users to contribute by commenting on the facts reported in an article. Unlike a traditional letter to the editor, these comments appear instantaneously, unscreened, sometimes moments after a story appears. According to Robert Quigley, the social media editor at the *Austin American-Statesman,* comments on stories are a "living, breathing thing with people jumping into a breaking story with live updates and thoughts" (quoted in Lavrusik 2009).

Traditional news outlets often encourage the use of platforms that enable audience feedback, a sign of the convergence of these various media forms (Quandt and Singer

Source: ireport.cnn.com.

CNN's iReport feature invites readers to submit material for publication on their website and, possibly, for use on air. Those who contribute are not compensated in any way. Here, CNN asks for reactions to everyday racism following the 2013 acquittal of George Zimmerman, charged with murdering Trayvon Martin.

2008). Often anchors on news broadcasts suggest that you also follow their Twitter feed, or they show some of the tweets or e-mails from their viewers about the topics covered during the evening's broadcast. In such cases, audience perspectives are more visible in the news, but professional journalists still select and approve the contributions.

Professionals and Amateurs Together: Pro-Am Efforts

A number of mainstream news organizations have launched efforts to enlist the assistance of amateurs in creating news stories while maintaining control and employing professional journalistic standards of fact-checking. These can involve professional journalists soliciting information from readers about a topic they are investigating. For example, the Florida *Fort Myers News-Press* newspaper announced an investigation into the high cost home buyers were being charged for simple water- and sewer-line connections, asking readers to supply stories and information about their experiences. Bids, contracts, blueprints, and other documents were submitted by readers and posted on the paper's website for examination and discussion. The paper learned of cases where home owners were charged up to $30,000 for a simple hookup; eventually, it exposed illegal price-fixing in some bids. The paper now has a "Team Watchdog" feature, which regularly solicits input from readers and uses volunteers to "serve as consultants, research data, work side by side with the professional reporting staff and interact with readers" (News-press.com/watchdog 2011).

Another pro-am approach is to enlist the help of nonjournalists to sort through mountains of information, a process sometimes referred to as "crowd-sourcing." In the United Kingdom, *The Guardian* newspaper asked readers to help them review over 700,000 expense reports from members of Parliament. Over 20,000 readers took part, tagging reports in a range of categories from "not interesting" (involving routine documents and cover sheets) to "investigate this!" (involving suspicious, high-ticket items). Many other crowd-sourcing experiments, using various formats, have followed (Anderson 2009).

Collaborative Content Creation: Wikinews

A third form of user-generated content involves all-amateur collaborative creations. Wikipedia is a well-known collaborative online encyclopedia. Wikinews is its spin-off project, where stories are written as news articles as opposed to encyclopedia entries. Unlike mainstream news sources and the professional journalists who work for them, anyone with Internet access can write or edit a Wikinews article.

So what have Wikinews users done in a totally new media platform? Ironically, they have largely re-created the conventions of traditional news media. Most notably, in defining "what is news," Wikinews—like Wikipedia (Wales 2001)—insists that articles be written from a "neutral point of view." This foundational operating principle guides much of the decision making on the site. In addition, like traditional news, Wikinews separates fact from opinion, noting in its guidelines that "news is factual. Opinions should be sourced from qualified sources." Without using the term, the site even lists criteria for newsworthiness, noting that "news is relevant. . . . Stories should appeal to a large number of people" (Wikinews.org 2011). In fact, Wikinews users have adopted an elaborate set of official policies regarding both content and style that serve as the conventions for one of the latest news platforms—but which echo the conventions of traditional news media.

For example, Wikinews explicitly emulates mainstream media, defining news as "stories like those you read in the newspaper, or see on the television news." Its policies encourage writers to cite sources, avoid copyright infringement, and follow standard grammatical rules—policies familiar to any professional journalist. Wikinews relies on many volunteer contributors to crowd-source its content—including checking facts and correcting errors—and provides a nonprofit service to Internet users, but it does not employ professional journalists to enforce these rules.

Citizen Journalists: OhmyNews

A fourth form of user-generated news content can be broadly labeled "citizen journalism" and includes examples such as OhmyNews. OhmyNews is a South Korean online news outlet with the motto "Every Citizen Is a Reporter." Founded in 2000 (with an English version appearing in 2004), it was the first in the world to publish articles by its readers, which account for about 80 percent of the total content that goes online. Its declared aim is to "help correct the imbalance in the Korean media environment" (OhmyNews 2010). Unlike CNN's iReport, stories are fact-checked by the site's editorial team before publication.

Some observers worry that some forms of citizen journalism serve as cheap labor for the benefit of profit-making multinationals (Deuze 2008). Demotix (demotix.com), a user-generated content website and 15,000-strong online community, seeks to address this by collecting news content to sell to commercial media. As such, it seeks to bridge the gulf between amateurism and professionalism.

These various user-generated news efforts have produced a variety of models, none of which have yet proven their long-term viability. It seems certain, however, that user-generated news—in one form or another—is here to stay. Taking a broader perspective on media organizations and conventions, we can see that these new efforts are, in some ways, a return to older types of media that were neither centrally owned nor produced by commercial media conglomerates. In fact, to a large extent, citizen journalism has emerged out of dissatisfaction with the existing commercial news media.

As these new forms of media continue to evolve, they will follow in the footsteps of older media in developing conventions and routines that enable people to work together—whether in amateur journalism or in professional-amateur collaborations.

OCCUPATIONAL ROLES AND PROFESSIONAL SOCIALIZATION

Journalists are not the only media professionals who follow routine practices. Analyzing work practices and professional norms can help us understand other media as well. Let's turn to two additional examples—photographers and book editors—and place them in the context of roles.

Roles

The concept of *role* has a long history in sociological theory and research. It has helped clarify the relationship between society and individuals, and the relationship between the forces of structure and agency. We also use the term in everyday conversation: We know that actors play specific roles, we might refer to a member of a basketball team as a role player, and on learning of a recent dispute at the local bar, we might ask our friends what role they played in the squabble. Sociologically, roles can be thought of as the bundles of expectations that are associated with different social positions. For example, students know the basic requirements of their role: attend class, complete assignments, show a certain measure of respect for teachers, and so on. We rarely think about the specific content of roles because we have largely internalized them. In fact, roles become part of our sense of self. You would say, "I am a student," not "I play the role of a student."

However, sometimes the socially constructed nature of roles becomes apparent, for example, when role expectations are obviously breached. Take the classroom as an example. If a student were to fall into a deep sleep in class, begin snoring loudly, and perhaps even slide onto the carpeted floor to get a bit more comfortable, others in the class would feel a bit uneasy because the snoring student had rather blatantly violated a key component of the student role. Students are expected not only to attend class but to show some interest—even if feigned—in what goes on there. These kinds of situations clarify role norms; seeing what we shouldn't be doing reaffirms what we should be doing.

Another time when we become aware of roles is when we have to learn a new one. Think about starting a new job that involves a kind of work you have never done. During the first few days, the bundle of expectations associated with this new role—whether it be waitress, teacher, or stockbroker—is likely to be a bit unclear, even confusing. Eventually, though, you must learn the ropes to be successful in your new job. You do this by following instructions, watching others do the work, and getting feedback on your own efforts.

The process by which we learn the basic ground rules of a role is called *socialization*. Every media occupation that we will encounter in this book—journalist, photographer, writer, filmmaker, musician, and so on—requires a kind of socialization into that role. We tend to think of this kind of work as *creative,* done by people who have a special talent. However, we need to keep in mind that even these creative media jobs are performed by people who must fulfill the expectations of their role and must fit into the expectations of the organizations with which they work.

On one hand, the concept of role highlights the significance of external social controls. Specific roles, we might say, serve as a social control mechanism by clarifying what is expected of us. Because other members of a social group also know the norms of the role, the expectations are enforced by our interaction with others. We generally do not consider role expectations oppressive because the social control is not simply imposed on us. We internalize, to varying degrees, the components of the role, often so thoroughly that we hardly acknowledge any social control. The role concept, then, explains how individual behavior is both patterned by and influenced by broader social forces.

This is, however, only half of the story. Roles are not rigid; they do not dictate specific behaviors. On the contrary, individuals often have a good deal of room for negotiation within the framework of the roles they occupy. Parents, for example, can relate to their children in a variety of ways—as friend, strict disciplinarian, or hands-off monitor—without violating the norms of the parent role. However, there are limits. Certain actions will be widely perceived as violating basic norms, and some actions may even lead to the removal of children from the home, an effective termination of the parent role.

Roles also are not static. The parent example illustrates the dynamic nature of roles. What is expected of parents today is different from what was expected 50 years ago. Nor are roles permanent. Changing social conditions both create and eliminate the need for particular roles. In the following sections, we explore how roles and socialization apply to media professionals and how changing social conditions have affected these roles.

Photography

We see photographs everywhere, and to most people they are not much of a mystery. Digital cameras are our companions at outings with friends, family gatherings, or on vacations. We can use our cell phone to take pictures, Instagram to share our images, and Photoshop for more elaborate manipulations. Amateur photographers use these pictures to tell stories, remember distant friends or places, or display their artistic talent. So what separates those of us who take photos from someone who is a professional photographer?

The easiest answer is to note that photographers get paid for their pictures, but many of us know people whose amateur photographs rival anything that is published, making this distinction a mere technicality. Another answer to this question is talent. Professional photographers have a vision for their pictures that the rest of us typically lack. There is undoubtedly something to this distinction, but we would be hard-pressed to put it to practical use. Who should define this talent or vision? How do we decide who is worthy of the status of photographer, and who is just a weekend picture taker?

Instead, it is more useful to think about photographers as people who take on the role of photographer and behave according to the norms of that role. Indeed, Battani (1999) demonstrates how a specific occupational role of the photographer emerged in the mid-19th century, as early photographers sought to institutionalize their emerging field as a legitimate profession. To enhance their reputations, attract wealthy customers for portraits, and build favorable relationships with the suppliers of photographic materials, the early photographers worked to promote "an image of their studios and practices as places of refined culture" (p. 622).

Of course, there are different types of photography and, therefore, different versions of this role. For example, the photojournalist and the advertising photographer may use similar basic equipment, but each has a different role—with different sets of tasks, expectations, and norms. Rosenblum's (1978) classic study *Photographers at Work* shows that role expectations and organizational demands are central to explaining the different styles of photography in newspapers and advertising as well as the different conceptions of creativity held by photographers in the two settings.

News photos and advertising photos draw on distinct stylistic conventions that make the images quite different from each other in ways that are readily apparent even to the untrained eye. Photo images selling jeans or perfume in *Vanity Fair,* for example, are usually easily distinguishable from a front-page photo illustrating the lead story in the *New York Times*. If the photo styles and their associated conventions are different, the sources of these differences can be found in the socialization of photographers, their work roles, and the organizational goals the pictures need to meet.

Socialization of Photographers

Socialization refers to the process by which people learn the expectations of a particular role. It is likely that young news and ad photographers begin with similar sets of skills. Each knows the basic technical requirements of taking pictures. Socialization allows the beginner to move beyond the technical aspects of the work and learn how to conceptually see images in ways that are distinct to the professional photojournalist or the ad photographer. This distinct vision must be learned in order for each photographer to produce suitable pictures. One underlying assumption here is that ways of seeing images are socially constructed. Photojournalists and ad photographers must learn to see images in ways that are in line with their professional and organizational roles.

Entry-level photographers have to learn and internalize the basic norms of the organizations they work for and, at the same time, learn the culture of their profession. A beginning photojournalist learns the kind of news that the paper and its website feature and, more important, becomes acquainted with the picture selection process at that news organization. If you have ever seen photojournalists on assignment, you have probably noticed that they are likely to take a large number of pictures of various aspects of the scene. When you pick up the paper in the morning, however, only one of these shots will have made it into print, and even the paper's website is likely to feature only a few of the many pictures taken. The photo editor is responsible for selecting which pictures to use. Part of the process of socialization, then, is learning the norms of the selection process to be able to produce the kind of pictures that the photo editor will select. After all, one of the principal goals of photojournalists is getting their pictures published.

It is one thing to know what your editors expect; it is another to be able to produce it. The beginner must learn the role of the press photographer. To produce suitable news photos, press photographers usually believe that they should not behave in such a way that

Both of these photos show people eating. Which is from the news and which is the sort used in an advertisement? The obvious differences illustrate the different level of control that news and ad photographers have over their pictures.

Sources: Left photo: U.S. Navy photo by Chief Mass Communication Specialist Steve Johnson; right photo: iStockphoto.com/vm.

their presence changes the unfolding of events. This is one of the fundamental professional norms of photojournalism: Pictures should document happenings, not transform them. While pictures inevitably provide selective snapshots of complex phenomena, the commitment to unobtrusiveness is central to the ideology of photojournalism. News photographers, then, have to learn techniques to stay out of the way yet still get good pictures.

Taking pictures that are suitable for publication while remaining unobtrusive is no easy task. Because the events that photographers cover are almost all either prescheduled (e.g., press conferences, parades, sporting events) or fit into standard story formats (e.g., fires, accidents, crimes), photographers learn that they will be successful if they can anticipate what they will see to plan the kinds of shots they will take. This anticipation allows photographers to locate themselves in strategic spots, use the appropriate lenses, focus on the setting or people that are central to the event, and produce the kinds of pictures that will be acceptable to their editors. Thus, the socialization of the photojournalist involves learning how to anticipate action and plan shots in advance.

Advertising photographers must learn a set of organizational and professional norms that are different from those of photojournalism. One difference is that advertising photographers learn to leave nothing to chance; every aspect of each photo is the responsibility of the photographer. We are exposed to so many ad images each day that we can easily forget that everything about an ad photo has been staged. This staging is most obvious in respect to lighting and setting, but it extends to every last detail: the hairstyles, clothing, and jewelry of the models; items that sit in the background of the picture; and the specific nature of any key props for the shot. Should the woman in the lingerie ad wear a wedding ring? If so, how will she hold her hand to both look natural and display the ring? The ad photographer must learn how to exert precise control and develop the technical skills required to accomplish it.

Advertising photographers learn that ad photography is a collective process; managing relationships with art directors and representatives of the advertiser is a key part of the job. The ad photographer learns that success requires not only vision or skill in creating compelling images but also the ability to negotiate with—even please—those who have creative control over the advertisements. In practice, this means that photographers learn that there is little room for individualists who perceive themselves as pure artists. The profession requires that ad photographers see their role as just one part of a collective process driven by the logic of commerce.

Photographers' Work Roles and Organizational Goals

The division of labor within newsrooms shapes the kinds of pictures that photojournalists take. Newspaper photography involves various people in coordinated activities: the person who decides on the assignment, the photographer, the photo editor who selects the pictures, the printer, the editor who decides which stories to run, and the webmaster who manages the paper's site. News organizations are highly developed bureaucracies that rely on clearly defined rules and classification systems. This kind of organization leads photographers to take standard pictures, the kinds of photos that we would be likely to recognize as news photos. The key is the system of classification, in which events are grouped into types: the disaster, the war, the political campaign, the court case. In producing news coverage, news organizations impose a standard script—including images—on these basic types of stories. Photographers are expected to produce images that fit the standard scripts. When images that do not fit the script are routinely weeded out by the photo editors, photographers soon learn not to take these kinds of pictures in the first place.

Role expectations also provide the framework for definitions of creativity. Editors expect photographers to have good news judgment, to be willing to use initiative to get good pictures, and to produce pictures that can tell various aspects of the story. Moreover, photographers are expected to regularly provide the kind of standard pictures that can accompany standardized stories, which both editors and readers come to expect. This expectation does not leave much room for the independent creativity of the photojournalist. The subject matter is assigned, and the organizational norms suggest the kinds of pictures that are appropriate. As a result, photojournalists generally see themselves not as creative artists but as reporters who take pictures.

Ad photographers, in contrast, take on the role of merchants as they must sell their services to an ad agency and an advertiser, follow the lead of the art director, and produce pictures that are generally prescripted. Thus, much ad photography is reduced to technical work. The photographer must have the knowledge and skills to effectively carry out the wishes of those making the creative decisions. Much of the day-to-day work of the ad photographer involves creating scripted images and adding small variations—in angle or lighting, for example—so that art directors have several different versions of the picture from which to choose.

For the vast majority of ad photographers, creativity is not in the conception of the images but in the ability to capture the desired image. They often achieve this by devising solutions to technical problems in the photographic process. Creativity in ad photography, then, is being innovative enough to figure out how to get the image the art director wants when standard techniques do not work. The creativity of ad photography is not in the vision but in a kind of technical mastery (Rosenblum 1978). In the digital age, this technical mastery increasingly involves the skillful use of software to manipulate images to meet client needs.

Photographers, then, are not all the same. They work in different kinds of organizations that place different demands on them. They are socialized into different professional roles and take different kinds of pictures. Organizational and professional norms provide the context for understanding the pictures photographers take, the daily routines in the workplace, and the ways photographers evaluate their own work. One of the central lessons to be learned from our focus on photographers is that authority relations within the workplace can tell us a good deal about the kind of work that media professionals do. Photographers, in both news and advertising, have specific superiors whom they must satisfy by producing appropriate pictures. Most of the time, they carry out the creative wishes of others rather than conceptualizing on their own. What about media professionals who are higher in the organizational hierarchy? What norms or social forces affect how they organize their work? A look at the work of book editors will help us answer these questions.

Editorial Decision Making

Book publishing is a dynamic, multifaceted industry. Books are published on a wide range of subjects, packaged in various formats, sold in many different settings, and bought by many types of readers. In addition, there are several different kinds of publishing companies, from large commercial houses that sign prominent authors to seven-figure, advance-payment contracts to small presses that publish scholarly monographs.

In all publishing firms, the key decision is which manuscripts to publish. Regardless of whether the house is aiming for the best-seller list, with sales in the millions, or for adoption by college professors as a classroom text, where success might mean only a few thousand copies sold, all publishers have to sift through many submissions and proposals and select the few that will become books. These selection processes take place in other media industries as well. Record labels sign a small number of musicians, Hollywood studios produce a limited number of films, and the television networks add only a handful of new programs to their prime-time schedules each year. In each of these industries, decision makers need to make a large number of choices for projects about which they have only partial knowledge. These decisions, of course, have substantial consequences—they dictate the books, music, films, and television programs that will be available.

Different industries and the various sectors within each industry have different rules that govern the decision-making process. The search for steady profits by commercial media companies makes evaluations of the potential for economic success a central feature of the decision-making process. Those in decision-making roles need to develop strategies for evaluating the potential profitability of a particular movie or book.

The Work of the Book Editor

In most publishing houses, the people who solicit, evaluate, and sign manuscripts are called acquisitions editors. It is their job to get high-quality books for the press, to weed out titles that do not fit, and to work with authors to produce books that will meet organizational goals. Acquisitions editors have varying degrees of autonomy and different editorial mandates at different presses, but they are ordinarily the principal filter through which the decision to publish is made.

One study of publishing (Coser, Kadushin, and Powell 1982) found that a key factor in whether a manuscript is published is the channel that brings a potential author to a publisher's attention. Abstract measures of the quality or significance of a book manuscript are far less important—at least in determining whether a book is published—than the way the manuscript comes in the door. There are different "lines" of authors (perhaps a better image is piles of manuscripts) awaiting the eyes of editors. These different piles are organized according to how they were received. The longest, and by far least successful, line is made up of authors who send their unsolicited manuscript to a publishing house, hoping that it will be impressive enough to be accepted for publication. Unfortunately for aspiring authors, there is very little likelihood that this route will pay off. One large publisher estimated that only 1 out of 15,000 unsolicited manuscripts is published each year (Anand, Barnett, and Carpenter 2004).

Other avenues are more likely to lead to publication. Unsolicited manuscripts that are addressed to the appropriate editor by name are more likely to be considered seriously than those not directed at an individual. More important, personal contacts are what really facilitate the publication of a book. Manuscripts that come through informal networks—other authors, friends, or professional meetings—go into a much smaller pile that is taken more seriously. And authors who have agents are placed in yet another pile.

These piles are not likely to exist in any concrete form (although the volume of unsolicited manuscripts is so high that it is hard to believe they sit anywhere except in piles on an editorial assistant's desk); the pile metaphor suggests that publishing houses organize work, even if unconsciously, along these lines. Organizationally, this system operates like a kind of obstacle course with different entry points. Depending on where each manuscript starts the course, it will face different hurdles, opportunities, time frames, and perhaps even personnel until it completes the course or is rejected. The specific nature of the obstacle course depends on the particularities of the organization of the publishing house.

While the basic factors influencing acquisition editors discussed by Coser and colleagues (1982) still hold true, more recent studies have found additional dynamics at play in today's publishing industry. For example, acquisition editors today often feel increasing pressure to sign only books with blockbuster potential. Likewise, they struggle with reading submissions, as more of their time is dedicated to the marketing and publicity of books, and specialized marketing and publicity staff have an increasing say in which books are published (Greco, Rodriguez, and Wharton 2007). Publishing houses often resort to working with authors who have their own ability to get their names out and cross-promote their books—through popular blogs they write, shows they host or appear on, or through newspapers and magazines to which they regularly contribute.

With an increased emphasis on potential blockbuster books—and the lucrative movie rights often associated with them—the growth of famous authors who command a loyal readership, and the rise of "super-agents" who advocate for their author/clients, the balance of power in this portion of the publishing industry has shifted in recent years away from the publishing houses to the celebrity authors and their agents. In his study of the trade book industry in the United States and Britain, John Thompson (2010) notes that these new super-agents

> thought of themselves less as intermediaries, mediating between author and publisher, and more as dedicated advocates of their client's interests. They conceived of their task primarily in legal and financial terms, and they displaced the centrality of the publisher by asserting control over the rights of their client's work and deciding which rights to allocate to which publisher and on what terms. In their eyes, the publisher was not the central player in the field but simply a means to get what they wanted to achieve on their clients' behalf, which was to get their work in to the marketplace as effectively and successfully as possible. (p. 66)

Thompson stresses that this portion of the publishing world is unique and does not represent the vast number of smaller publishers who handle the work of authors without agents.

With some 250,000 titles published by U.S. houses each year, editors and publicity staff feel great strain in competing for the public's attention—and new competition has appeared, as self-publishing has exploded in recent years. While firm numbers are difficult to determine, some estimates are that more than 600,000 new titles are now self-published each year in the United States (Morgan 2013). Most of these self-published books have tiny sales figures; but some have had moderate success, and a few have become best-sellers. The massive best-selling erotic romance novel, *Fifty Shades of Grey*, for example, began as a self-published title before being bought by a traditional publisher. Publishing houses have taken notice, and some have even responded by launching their own self-publishing brands, such as Simon & Schuster's Archway Publishing.

As you can see, there are far too many books published each year for any one bookstore to place on its shelves. Just as publishers follow a set of conventions as they determine which books to publish, brick-and-mortar bookstores adopt their own conventions to help them decide which books to sell. Advance reviews and publishers' catalog descriptions help booksellers make selection decisions. As on the front pages of newspapers, publishers put their most promising books toward the front of the catalog and dedicate more space to their displays. In addition to these catalogs, according to Miller (2006), the buyers for booksellers (those who decide which books a bookstore will carry) consider past sales of the author's previous work; the current popularity of the book's genre; the publisher's promotional budget and plans; whether the author will be touring or making any media appearances; the sales rep's or editor's enthusiasm and recommendations; the ease of ordering and receiving from the book's supplier; the terms at which the book is being made available (discount, shipping costs, payment, and return policies); the book's list price, production quality, and cover design; the book's topicality; the buyer's understanding of local tastes and habits; and the buyer's personal tastes. Miller argues that both the independents and the chains employ routine conventions to sift through the vast array of potential books, but the independents give much more weight to local interest in their decisions.

Online sellers like Amazon don't have to worry as much about which books to stock, as their store exists only in virtual space, with physical books stocked in relatively inexpensive, unadorned warehouses. While this gives them an advantage over bookstores who have to pay high prices for rent in foot-trafficked areas and who have to contend with not having an in-store copy of a book that a reader may want, online sellers face additional difficulties in allowing users to browse their selections. In response to this problem, online sellers use pictures of book covers on their websites, show similar and recommended books on the webpage of a book that a user has searched, and provide options like the "Look Inside!" feature on Amazon to try to give buyers the experience of browsing in a physical bookstore (Weedon 2007). The quickly growing popularity of e-books gives online retailers the additional competitive advantage of being able to provide books instantly—without the cost of storing and shipping a physical product. E-books made up about 20 percent of book sales in 2012 (Milliot 2013).

Scholarly Publishing

Walter Powell (1985) studied the operating procedures that govern the process of manuscript selection in two scholarly publishing houses. Scholarly publishing is a segment of the book industry that is not so clearly oriented to profitability. As a general rule, books need to be able to sell enough copies to pay for the costs of production and meet the house's criteria for scholarly quality. However, editors do not have to focus their attention on signing best sellers. As a result, acquisitions editors at scholarly publishing houses have a more ambiguous goal than their counterparts at the large commercial houses, where sales potential is the dominant goal.

As is the case at commercial houses, scholarly editors follow a set of routines, governed by standard operating assumptions, that help them make decisions about what to publish. The volume of manuscripts is so high that it is impossible to attend to each project. Manuscripts from unknown authors who have never had contact with the publishing house do not receive much editorial attention and are, therefore, unlikely to be published. Manuscripts from an author with previous connections to the house or those solicited by an editor receive much more thorough and quicker attention. In addition, editors make use of prominent academics who serve as series editors to help attract new authors or evaluate manuscripts. In this way, editors can farm out evaluations to a stable, trusted group of scholars who may be more expert in the particular field. Most scholarly houses also use outside reviewers—people the editor selects to anonymously assess the quality of the manuscript. Editors use all these practices to manage their workload in ways that are consistent with their editorial goals and their obligations to their authors, colleagues, and friends. All of this suggests a good deal of autonomy for editors; they can draw upon series editors when they choose to, send manuscripts to an outside reviewer who is likely to be supportive (or not), and give closer attention to projects that involve scholars they already know.

In his study, Powell (1985) first accepted editors' explanations that they had wide discretion in acquiring books. However, he later noticed several things that made him skeptical: Editors had a clear sense of which authors deserved priority service and which could be put off for long periods; editors never proposed atypical books, demonstrating their sense of boundaries; and there was a high turnover rate among editors, yet stability in the kinds of decisions that were made. In addition, Powell found that his observation at the houses had made him an expert in predicting which manuscripts would be signed and which would be rejected. In essence, he had learned the informal rules so well that the decision-making process was no longer a mystery.

Scholarly publishing is similar to photography. Through a process of socialization, acquisitions editors learn the values and preferences of their publishing houses. This socialization process is one of the mechanisms by which organizations assert a kind of unobtrusive control. The key to the socialization of editors is learning about the types of books the press publishes. As part of their socialization, editors learn about the history and traditions of the house; they may already be familiar with the prominent books and authors that the house has published. In short, successful editors must understand the house's "list"—its currently available books, including new releases and the backlist of older titles. New books must complement other titles. Editors understand this constraint and adopt it as a norm in their own editorial decisions. In this way, choices about new books are shaped in important ways by the types of books that a house has previously published. In addition, most outside reviewers are authors who have published with the house, thus reinforcing a similar set of norms for each new year's crop of books.

Powell (1985) attributes his finding that editors rarely had their selections rejected by their superiors to their internalization of the basic norms of the publishing house. Editors do not have their projects rejected because they have already weeded out those that did not fit. The manuscripts that they send on for approval by superiors fit with the house list. This is what makes them good editors. They enjoy a good deal of autonomy in their work because they do not think too independently while doing it.

A focus on the practices that editors use to organize their work and on the organizational premises that guide these decisions shows the dynamic relationship between human agency and structural constraint in media production. While organizational premises—structure—may make change more difficult, small changes in routine practices may help alter these premises, leading to the publication of new types of books. The backlist is the concrete embodiment of the relationship between agency and structure. It represents the accumulation of decisions made by prior editors, a tradition that shapes current decisions. But those current decisions will alter the backlist and, in turn, affect the framework for future decisions. In this example, we see both the stability and the potential dynamism of the socialization process.

NORMS ON THE INTERNET, NEW MEDIA, AND NEW ORGANIZATIONS

The three occupations we have explored—journalism, photography, and editorial work—are well-established professions with lengthy traditions. But what about more recent forms of media and online interaction? How does work in these media differ from—and in what ways does it resemble—the occupations and organizations found in traditional media?

The highly decentralized nature of the Internet makes it tempting for us to think that social activity in cyberspace is totally autonomous, free from the kinds of conventions that guide the production of traditional media forms. But while cyberspace permits new forms of interaction and challenges our assumptions about the nature of mass-mediated communication, anyone who has spent time surfing the Internet is likely to have a sense of a clear set of norms that govern behavior in cyberspace, as well as a set of potential consequences for violators. These norms and conventions are generated by both the creators of websites and the users who contribute to them.

The creators of many Internet websites are part of larger media organizations and are governed by the occupational norms and standards that predominate in their fields. For example, professional web developer associations promote norms and conventions regarding user-friendly web design, universal access standards, and other issues. These groups operate much like other traditional media professionals. Those who have constructed and are expanding the platforms and networks that connect us to one another—through discussion groups, instant messaging, microblogging, social networking sites, e-mail, and websites—are technological innovators who both draw on and create conventions that help structure our interaction within these networks.

For example, a search engine such as Google operates within a set of conventions that were created—and sometimes change—based on its design. The rankings of search results are produced by Google's calculation of the number and importance of pages that link to each site, thereby steering users toward the sites with more links to them. As Vaidhyanathan (2011: 14) notes, "Through its power to determine which sites get noticed, and thus trafficked, Google has molded certain standards into the web." For example, Google downplays the importance of porn sites to reduce the likelihood of unintentionally stumbling across such sites when posing ambiguous search terms. Placing the word "define:" before a word in a Google search produces definitions of that word. "Time" plus a name of a city produces the local time there. These and many other features of a site are the structural conventions produced by its creators. Every form of media has similar conventions, such as Twitter's 140-character limit or Facebook's use of *friends, likes,* and *pokes.*

However, as noted earlier, one of the defining characteristics of the Internet as a medium is that *users* are often the source of content. These users are not professionals, nor is content creation their occupation. As a result, different and more informal mechanisms have developed to teach the conventions of the medium and guide appropriate behavior.

For example, over time, we have developed language that helps users understand the technology. This language also imposes a kind of logic onto cyberspace by formalizing conventional ways of perceiving, even behaving on, the Internet. Terms used to describe behaviors in cyberspace—such as *trolling, spamming, morphing,* and *lurking*—characterize some of the ways our virtual behavior is both predictable and patterned. Some cyberspace terms, such as *newbie/noob* and *moderator,* even explicitly describe particular cyber roles with accompanying expectations.

Another example of a common set of conventions involves the use of "emoticons" (a composite of the words emotion and icon). Created in the 1980s, emoticons—such as the smiley face :o) or wink ;o)—have become the most common way of supplementing e-mail or text messages with facial cues that simulate the inflection of face-to-face talk. We use emoticons to express emotion, to strengthen a message, and to express humor, usually in informal communication and in a positive context rather than in a negative one (Derks, Bos, and von Grumbkow 2008). Another linguistic convention of cyberspace is the use of acronyms in chat conversations. Examples include LOL (Laughing Out Loud), ROFL (Rolling on the Floor Laughing), BTW (By the Way), AFK (Away From Keyboard), BAK (Back at Keyboard), and WYSIWYG (What You See Is What You Get). Such terms can seem perplexing at first until a user is socialized into learning their meaning.

As we saw in our earlier discussion of user-generated news content, often the norms that develop on new media platforms closely emulate the conventions that already exist in traditional media. But new media forms also require new conventions. In one early study of conventions on the Internet, McLaughlin, Osborne, and Smith (1995) explored the "standards of conduct" in online discussion groups, or newsgroups. In effect, they examined the expectations associated with the role of the online newsgroup participant. In particular, they argue that there are specific types of "reproachable" network behavior, that is, actions that violate the basic norms of the Internet, commonly referred to as "netiquette."

What are the behaviors that elicit reproaches from other network users? One involves the incorrect use of the technological apparatus and is generally associated with novices who have not mastered the format. An example is a user who accidentally posts a message to an entire newsgroup that was intended only for a single recipient. A second norm is not to write messages in capital letters (which is equivalent to SHOUTING). A third is the violation of a basic network convention, such as failing to include your electronic signature with your message or neglecting to include a previous message about which you are commenting ("quoting"). Users who behave in these reproachable ways are likely to be admonished online by fellow users who are committed to the orderly functioning of the group. Such admonishment may be, at least initially, gentle and intended to be educational in nature. But admonishment can become rather venomous, referred to as "flaming." Many violators likely will learn from their mistakes, seek out help with the technology, and learn the conventions.

Those who persist in their reproachable behavior may be threatened with loss of access to the group, and repeat offenders will ultimately be expelled from the newsgroup.

Online norms are powerful shapers of virtual behavior. Perhaps that is why the vast majority of newsgroup subscribers are perpetual lurkers, reading messages but not posting their own. One widely held newsgroup norm, in fact, is to follow a group for some time before posting a message. This allows newcomers to become socialized into the ways of the group, to learn about the group's history and traditions, and to see the kinds of issues that are generally on the group's agenda. Additional practices help socialize new members of newsgroups. Upon subscribing, members receive an electronic how-to manual for participation in the group, which includes both technical advice on the workings of the system and instructions on appropriate conduct. Archives of previous group discussions are often available, and new group members are encouraged to read through them. In addition, a file of frequently asked questions (FAQs) is sent to new members so that they do not clutter up the network with the same questions.

Why do such standards of conduct develop in the first place? One answer is that they provide a foundation for the maintenance of the identity of the newsgroup. This identity is passed along to new members through socialization into the norms of the electronic community and is enforced when new members are admonished for not adhering to the ground rules. Where do these standards come from? Many are practical responses to the needs of the medium. For example, regular users are aware that certain conventions, such as using an appropriate subject line on a posting, enable users to follow threads over time or search and find them later on. Those who use subject lines inappropriately or leave the line blank make participation in the virtual community both more confusing and more time-consuming.

Technological conventions may seem trivial, and notes of reproach for violations may seem nasty, but the requirement of maintaining some kind of order in cyberspace is their driving force. Perhaps most important, McLaughlin and her colleagues (1995) argue that there are underlying social roots to cyber conventions. These conventions reinforce and protect the collective identities of the electronic communities and can be used to ward off newcomers who pose a threat to these identities or to the stability of the group. Like other producers of media, users of the Internet are part of a social world in which tradition, organizational history, group identity, and the routinization of daily activities help shape the norms and practices that pattern even our virtual behavior.

The lessons from these early Internet newsgroups apply to more recent media platforms. Large media sites—such as Facebook, YouTube, and Twitter—each have their own official policies on acceptable behavior: Facebook's Statement of Rights and Responsibilities, YouTube's Community Guidelines, and the Twitter Rules. These policies define appropriate (and inappropriate) uses of these social media services, specifying rules on, for example, privacy, copyright, spam, pornography, and hate speech. These policies establish a framework for conduct on social networking sites, and provide guidelines for how to respond to those who violate established policies. However, such official policies are only a starting point. Regular users of social media are socialized into the conventions of these online spaces and are familiar with a wide range of norms that go beyond corporate policies, including the dos and don'ts of posting on friends' Facebook walls or how to respond (or not) to Facebook friend requests.

CONCLUSION

This chapter has rounded out our discussion of media production by showing how professional norms, institutional premises, and organizational structures shape the day-to-day work of media producers—whether professionals or amateurs. We have seen that human agents—reporters, photographers, book editors, and Internet users—are active participants in the construction and reconstruction of production routines. These routines serve as conventions that help organize the collective work of media production.

Routines and conventions are shaped by economic, political, and organizational forces, as well as technological constraints, in each sector of the media industry. Conventions can change, although this change is likely to be slow. Ultimately, conventions become a form of structural constraint, producing guidelines for action and decision making by future media professionals.

A production perspective helps us understand the media messages that are part of our lives. In Part III, we turn to the content of mass media, focusing on questions of inequality and ideology.

DISCUSSION QUESTIONS

1. How do media producers respond to economic and political constraints? In what ways do these constraints shape media work? To what degree do media professionals have autonomy in the face of these constraints? Use examples to illustrate your analysis.

2. What are "conventions," and how does this concept help us to understand the work of media professionals? Why do media professionals make use of conventions? Use examples to illustrate your discussion.

3. What is the relationship between news routines and the organization of newsgathering? Why do reporters and news organizations develop such news routines?

4. Explain how recent forms of media have developed conventions similar to those of more traditional media. What might this suggest about the "newness" of such media and the continuity found across different forms of media?

PART III

Content

Media Representations of the Social World

Part II emphasized processes of production within the media industry and among media users. However, outside of user-generated content, most of us never actually see these processes taking place. What we are exposed to—what we watch, read, and listen to—are media products, the movies, music, television shows, Internet sites, and print publications that result from this production process. These media products are the most common way that most of us experience the mass media.

In Part III, we turn our attention to the content of these media products, exploring the ways in which mass media represent the social world. Chapter 5 introduces the question of ideology, exploring the values, beliefs, and norms that mass media products routinely display. The chapter looks at the underlying perspectives in the images that confront us every day, as well as the potential contradictions and ambiguities that are built into mass media texts. Chapter 6 examines how media portray central social cleavages in contemporary society, focusing on issues of race, class, gender, and sexual orientation. The chapter looks at how various groups are depicted in mass media, how such depictions have changed over time, and how these representations relate to social reality.

Source: Screen Gems/Getty Images.

CHAPTER 5

Media and Ideology

Most media scholars believe that media texts articulate coherent, if shifting, ways of seeing the world. These texts help to define our world and provide models for appropriate behavior and attitudes. How, for example, do media products depict the "appropriate" roles of men and women, parents and children, immigrants and local communities, or bosses and workers? What defines success, and how is it achieved? What qualifies as criminal activity, and what are the sources of crime and social disorder? What are the underlying messages in media content, and whose interests do these messages serve? These are, fundamentally, questions about media and ideology.

Most ideological analyses of mass media products focus on the content of the messages—the stories they tell about the past and the present—rather than the effects of such stories. In this chapter, then, we focus primarily on media messages. Part IV of this book will turn to the relationship between media messages and their audiences.

WHAT IS IDEOLOGY?

An ideology is basically a system of meaning that helps define and explain the world and that makes value judgments about that world. Ideology is related to concepts such as *worldview, belief system,* and *values,* but it is broader than those terms. It refers not only to the beliefs held about the world but also to the basic ways in which the world is defined. Ideology, then, is not just about politics; it has a broader and more fundamental connotation.

Ideology and the "Real" World

Ideologies do not necessarily reflect reality accurately; in fact, they can often present a distorted version of the world. In everyday language, it can be an insult to charge someone with being ideological, precisely because this label suggests rigidly adhering to one's beliefs in the face of overwhelming contradictory evidence. When Marxists speak of *ideology,* they often mean belief systems that help justify the actions of those in power by distorting and misrepresenting reality.

As we will explore in the next chapter, media scholars are often interested in assessing how media content compares to the "real" world. But analysts of ideology generally perceive the definition of the *real* as, itself, an ideological construction. Which aspects of whose "reality" do we define as the most real? Those that are the most visible? The most common? The most powerful? Instead of assessing images and making some judgment about levels of realness, ideological analysis asks what these messages tell us about ourselves and our society.

We can often be unaware of the ideological position of contemporary media because it reflects our own taken-for-granted views of the world. It is easier to recognize ideological content of media images by looking at older media. Old movies or television programs, for example, can seem unusual to us because they present an understanding of society that is at odds with our contemporary assumptions. For example, most U.S. television programs made in the 1950s and early 1960s featured almost entirely white casts; African Americans and other racial and ethnic minorities were virtually nonexistent. These same programs typically assumed that sharply defined, divergent, and unequal gender roles were appropriate and desirable, usually with men as breadwinners and women as stay-at-home moms. Old Western movies of the era typically took for granted the right of European Americans to conquer the land of native peoples, who were often portrayed as violent savages, rather than as indigenous people trying to defend against invaders.

In discussing ideology, the primary question about such images is not whether they were realistic reflections of society; they clearly were not. (At best they were distorted and selective representations of a narrow slice of white, middle-class life; at worst they were highly prejudicial stereotypes that are offensive to today's sensibilities.) Instead, an examination of ideology is concerned with what messages these images send about the nature of the world, how it operates, and how it should be. Media portrayals from this period reflect an ideology—beliefs about who is and isn't worthy of inclusion, what roles are appropriate for different groups, and what is just. The images in today's television and movies often suggest a different ideology than the one portrayed in this earlier era.

When scholars examine media products to uncover their ideologies, they are interested in the underlying images of society they provide. Therefore, they tend to be interested in the recurring patterns that are found in the media rather than in a specific example of media content—things depicted in a single newspaper, website, movie, or hit song. For ideological analysis, the key is the fit between the images and words in a specific media text and broader ways of thinking about, even defining, social and cultural issues.

Dominant Ideology Versus Cultural Contradictions

One key debate regarding the ideology of media is between those who argue that media promote the worldview of the powerful—the "dominant ideology"—and those who argue that mass media texts include more contradictory messages, both expressing the dominant ideology and at least partially challenging worldviews.

We prefer to think of media texts as sites where cultural contests over meaning are waged rather than as providers of some univocal articulation of ideology. In other words, different ideological perspectives, representing different interests with unequal power, engage in a kind of struggle within the media. But it is not an even battlefield. Some ideas will have the advantage—because, for example, they are perceived as popular or they build on familiar media images—and others will be barely visible or difficult to communicate in certain forms because they are unfamiliar.

For example, a political analyst who says, "We need a strong military to fight terrorism," is tapping into a popular sentiment in the United States, which requires no explanation; it is a widely taken-for-granted assumption about the world—an ideological position. Another analyst who says, "Perhaps the presence of our troops around the world is one factor provoking terrorism," is likely to generate puzzled looks or even anger. Such an argument will require much more explanation to be understood because it runs counter to the dominant ideology in the United States—though it would be much more familiar in some other societies.

Different actors try to use media to communicate their interpretation of the world to a broader audience. But there is no guarantee that audiences will understand or interpret the meaning of this content in any uniform way—a topic we explore more fully in Chapter 8 on audiences. For example, the 2009 film *Precious* is a fictional story about a poor, obese, physically and emotionally abused, African American girl named Claireece Precious Jones, who eventually finds a faint glimmer of hope for the future with the encouragement and support of a teacher at an alternative school. What is the ideological content of such a movie? Some critics argued that the stark film sent a negative message about the black community. *New York Press* film critic Armond White (2009) criticized the film for its use of "brazenly racist clichés," including a scene in which the title character steals and eats a bucket of fried chicken. Other critics thought the film—produced with the backing of Oprah Winfrey and Tyler Perry—was a realistically desolate, disturbing, and ultimately positive story that portrayed a damaged young woman struggling against overwhelming odds to save herself. A *Washington Post* critic called it "the most painful, poetic, and improbably beautiful film of the year" (Hornaday 2009). Clearly, the meaning and significance of this single media product were interpreted very differently by different critics.

In addition, broader trends in media content—and their ideological significance—are often the focus of controversy and debate. For example, some Christian conservatives and Islamic fundamentalists find themselves in agreement when they point to the U.S. media as a prime example of a decadent and sinful society, while most Americans take the presence of sex, violence, and consumerism in the media as a simple fact of life. Time and time again, the media are simultaneously criticized by some for the messages they supposedly send while being applauded by others. These media battles often become quite fierce, with some voices calling for outright censorship, others defending free speech, and still others worrying about the consequences of cultural struggles that seem to represent a war of absolutes with no possibility of compromise.

The "Culture War" Battles Over Ideology

For those engaged in the promotion of particular ideas, including diverse groups such as politicians, corporations, citizen activists, and religious groups, media are among the primary contemporary battlegrounds. Media, in fact, are at the center of what James Davison Hunter (1991; Hunter and Wolfe 2006) has called the "culture wars" in contemporary American society, in which fundamental issues of morality are being fought. Hunter stresses the ways in which media—advertising, news, letters to the editor, and opinion commentary—provide the principal forms of public discourse by which cultural warfare is waged. The morality of abortion, homosexuality, immigration, or capital punishment is debated, often in very polarized terms, in the mass media, as cultural conservatives and cultural progressives alike use various media technologies to promote their positions— including blogs, user-generated content platforms such as YouTube, and social networking sites like Facebook.

One of the principal reasons why media images often become so controversial is that they are believed to promote ideas that are objectionable. In short, few critics are concerned about media texts that promote perspectives they support. Ideological analysis, then, often goes hand in hand with political advocacy, as critics use their detection of distorted messages to make their own ideological points. As a result, exploring the ideologies of mass media can be very tricky.

The most sophisticated ideological analysis examines the stories the media tell as well as the potential contradictions within media texts, that is, the places where alternative perspectives might reside or where ideological conflict is built into the text. Ideological analysis, therefore, is not simply reduced to political criticism, whereby the critic loudly denounces the "bad" ideas in the media. Nor, in our view, is analysis particularly useful if it focuses on the ideology of one specific media text without making links to broader sets of media images. It may be interesting to ruminate over the underlying ideology of a popular movie such as *Forrest Gump*. (Is it a nostalgic valorization of white men in the days before multiculturalism or a populist story of the feats of an underdog?) However, this inquiry will move from party conversation to serious analysis only if we think more carefully about the patterns of images in media texts rather than analyzing one film in isolation. At its best, ideological analysis provides a window onto the broader ideological debates going on in society. It allows us to see what kinds of ideas circulate through media texts, how they are constructed, how they change over time, and when they are being challenged.

Ideology as Normalization

In October 2009, U.S. First Lady Michelle Obama gave an interview to the magazine *Glamour,* whose readers had voted her one of the most important women of the year. The interview was reported in a Danish newspaper, whose journalists decided to focus on Obama's love tips. The underlying idea was that, having attracted and married the U.S. President, Ms. Obama could give some good advice to other women on how to catch powerful men. The description of Ms. Obama concentrated on her appearance ("brilliantly white smile," "bare upper arms"), ignoring her law school education and her successful career prior to becoming the First Lady. Ms. Obama was pictured as a devoted wife who does everything to please her husband, including dressing and smiling appropriately. According to the Global Media Monitoring Project (GMMP), a research project focusing on gender representation in the news media, the story "reinforces the stereotype that a woman's goal is to attract, attain and keep a man. The underlying message is that dressing and smiling like Michelle Obama, can enable women to attract and keep powerful men" (GMMP 2010).

What are the stakes in the battles over the ideology of media? As the Obama example highlights, media texts can be seen as key sites where basic social norms are articulated. The media give us pictures of social interaction and social institutions that, by their sheer repetition, on a daily basis, can play important roles in shaping broad social definitions. In essence, the accumulation of media images suggests what is "normal" (e.g., women must be preoccupied with their appearance if they want to be successful) and what is "deviant." This articulation is accomplished, in large part, by the fact that popular media, particularly television and mass advertising, have a tendency to display a remarkably narrow range of behaviors and lifestyles, marginalizing or neglecting people who are different from the mass-mediated norm. When difference is highlighted by, for example, television talk shows that routinely include people who are otherwise invisible in the mass media—cross-dressers, squatters, or strippers—the media can become part of a spectacle of the bizarre.

The key in understanding such messages is to see the overall pattern rather than any single story. For example, the 2010 GMMP found that more than half—52 percent—of news stories in the United States reinforce traditional gender stereotypes through "generalized, simplistic and often exaggerated assumptions of masculinity and femininity" (p. 32). In contrast, only 13 percent of the news stories in the United States challenged traditional gender stereotypes. Traditional gender stereotypes were prevalent in news media around the world. The GMMP analysis found that 46 percent of the news stories in Europe reinforce traditional gender stereotypes; the figure jumps to 81 percent in news media in the Middle East.

Despite the likelihood of their having very different political stances, those who are concerned about media depictions of, say, premarital sex have the same underlying concern as those who criticize the prominence of stereotypical gender images. In both cases, the fear is that media images normalize specific social relations, making certain ways of behaving seem unexceptional. If media texts can normalize behaviors, they can also set limits on the range of acceptable ideas. The ideological work lies in the patterns within media texts. Ideas and attitudes that are routinely included in media become part of the legitimate public debate about issues. Ideas that are excluded from the popular media or appear in the media only to be ridiculed have little legitimacy. They are outside the range of acceptable ideas. Therefore, the ideological influence of media can be seen in the absences and exclusions just as much as in the content of the messages.

Media professionals generally have little patience with the argument that the media are purveyors of ideology. Instead of seeing media as places where behaviors are normalized and boundaries are created, those in the industry tend to argue that the images they produce and distribute simply reflect the norms and ideas of the public. This is not ideology but simply a mirror that reflects the basic consensus about how things are.

To be sure, ideologies do not usually appear in media texts because writers and producers consciously want to impose their value systems on audiences. Rather, they are the result of the intersection of a variety of structural forces, including the producers' ideas of who the target audience is and what viewers would like to see, industry culture, genre conventions, the producers' own knowledge of human relationships, and more general cultural standards in a given social context (Levine 2001). In fact, as we saw in Chapter 2, most mass media are commercially organized to attract audiences for profit, so there is good reason to believe that popularity will be more important to media producers than a commitment to any specific ideology, beyond the promotion of consumerism. So our investigation of the ideology of media does not mean that producers are consciously trying to sell certain ways of thinking and being. Ideology is produced not only by committed ideologues. As we will see, we can find ideology in our everyday lives, in our definition of common sense, and in the construction of a consensus.

THEORETICAL ROOTS OF IDEOLOGICAL ANALYSIS

The analysis of ideology can be traced back to the works of Karl Marx and, especially, to 20th-century European Marxism. The analysis has evolved over time, maintaining some elements of its Marxist origin while developing more complexity and nuance. In what follows, we take a look at the evolution of ideological analysis, starting with its Marxists origins. This work is relevant insofar as it helps uncover a specific view of how society functions—that privilege and power are connected to one's position in the economy and class structure.

Early Marxist Origins

For early Marxists, the discussion of ideology was connected to the concept of "false consciousness." Ideology was seen as a powerful mechanism of social control whereby members of the ruling class imposed their worldview, which represented their interests, on members of subordinate classes. In such a system, the subordinate classes who accepted the basic ideology of the ruling class were said to have false consciousness because their worldview served the interests of others. For Marx and early Marxists, social revolution depended on the working class breaking free of the ideas of the ruling class—moving beyond their false consciousness—and developing a "revolutionary" consciousness that represented their material interests as workers. This new way of thinking would then stand in opposition to the ruling ideology, which promoted the economic interests of the capitalist class. (Later, scholars looked beyond the economy and the class structure in order to analyze how privilege and power are distributed according to other identity factors, such as race, gender, and sexual identity.)

In this context, ideology was understood to involve having ideas that were "false" because they did not match one's objective class interests. One of the ways capitalists ruled industrial society was by imposing on the working class a worldview that served the interests of capitalists yet pretended to describe the experiences of all humankind. For example, owners often used a divide-and-conquer strategy in stoking conflict among workers by promoting resentment and hatred toward racial minorities and recent immigrants. In the United States, white workers often came to believe that their biggest problem was minorities or immigrants taking away their jobs. As long as this belief was dominant, employers knew that internal divisions among workers would prevent effective organizing for better pay and working conditions. For workers, holding such beliefs actually worked against their own economic interests.

Ideology, then, was about mystification, the masking of interests, and the conflation of the particular and the universal. Moreover, ideology could be understood in straightforward economic-class terms. Capitalists had a class interest in the accumulation of capital through the exploitation of labor. Their ideology, which celebrated individualism and the free market, was a result of their economic interests. Workers had a class interest in fundamentally changing the conditions of their work and restructuring the social relations of production; this could be accomplished by a social revolution—a collective response and a regulation of markets. Any system of ideas that did not recognize these economic realities, according to an early school of Marxism, was the result of the ideological power of capitalists. Ideological analysis, from this perspective, meant identifying the ways working people's ideas failed to reflect their class interests; in essence, it was about pointing out how consciousness was "false" and in need of correction.

The critique of ideology has evolved a great deal from its connections to the concept of false consciousness, but it still maintains some of the basic outlines of the early Marxist model. Ideological analysis is still concerned about questions of power and the ways in which systems of meaning—ideologies—are part of the process of wielding power. And ideological analysis continues to focus on the question of domination and the ways certain groups fight to have their specific interests accepted as the general interests of a society. But the contemporary study of ideology is more theoretically sophisticated, paying attention to the ongoing nature of ideological struggles and to how people negotiate with, and even oppose, the ideologies of the powerful. Ideas are not simply false, and the connection between ideas and economic interest is not necessarily straightforward. In fact, much of the contemporary study of ideology has moved away from a focus on economic-class relations toward a more dynamic conceptualization of the terrain of culture.

Hegemony

The key theoretical concept that animates much of the contemporary study of the ideology of media is *hegemony*. Drawn from the work of Antonio Gramsci (1971), an Italian Marxist who wrote in the 1920s and 1930s, the notion of hegemony connects questions of culture, power, and ideology. Gramsci argued that ruling groups can maintain their power through force, consent, or a combination of the two. Ruling by way of force requires the use of institutions such as the military and the police in an effort to physically coerce—or threaten coercion—so that people will remain obedient. There is no shortage of historical examples of societies in which the use of force and the threat of even more severe forms of coercion have been the principal strategy of ruling. The military dictatorship is the most obvious example.

Gramsci (1971) noted, however, that power can be wielded at the level of culture or ideology, not just through the use of force. In liberal democratic societies, such as the United States, force is not the primary means by which the powerful rule. Certainly there are important examples of the use of force—turn-of-the-century efforts to crush the labor movement, the incarceration of members of the Communist Party in the 1950s, the violence directed at the Black Panther Party in the 1960s. But these examples stand out because the use of physical force is not the routine strategy for maintaining social order. Instead, Gramsci's work suggests that power is wielded in a different arena—that of culture in the realm of everyday life—where people essentially agree to current social arrangements.

Consent, then, is the key to understanding Gramsci's use of hegemony, which is exercised through a kind of cultural leadership. Consent is something that is won; ruling groups in a society actively seek to have their worldview accepted by all members of society as the universal way of thinking. Institutions such as schools, religion, and the media help the powerful exercise this cultural leadership because they are the sites where we produce and reproduce ways of thinking about society.

Hegemony, though, is not simply about ideological domination, whereby the ideas of one group are imposed on another. Instead, the process is far subtler. Hegemony operates at the level of common sense in the assumptions we make about social life and on the terrain of things that we accept as "natural" or "the way things are." After all, what is common sense except for those things we think are so obvious that we need not critically evaluate them? Common sense is the way we describe things that "everybody knows," or at least should know, because such knowledge represents deeply held cultural beliefs. In fact, when we employ the rhetoric of common sense, it is usually to dismiss alternative approaches that go against our basic assumptions about how things work. Gramsci (1971) reminds us that one of the most effective ways of ruling is through the shaping of commonsense assumptions. What we take for granted exists in a realm that is uncontested, where there is neither need nor room for questioning assumptions (Gamson et al. 1992).

Hegemony theorists remind us that commonsense assumptions, the taken for granted, are social constructions. They imply a particular understanding of the social world, and such visions have consequences. It is common sense, for example, that "you can't fight city hall" or that women are better nurturers than men or that "moderate" positions are more reasonable than "extreme" positions. When people adopt commonsense assumptions—as they do with a wide range of ideas—they are also accepting a certain set of beliefs, or ideology, about social relations.

A similar dynamic applies to what we think of as "natural." Nature is something that we define in opposition to culture because nature is perceived to be beyond human control. We generally think that the "natural" is not a social construction; nature is more enduring and stable than the creations of human societies. Thus, if social structures and social relationships are defined as natural, they take on a kind of permanency and legitimacy that elevates them to the realm of the uncontested. Think about the social relationships we call "natural" (or "unnatural"). Is it natural that some people are rich and some are poor, that people will not care about politics, or that people of different racial and ethnic backgrounds will prefer to live with their own groups? If these conditions are simply natural, then there is little reason to be concerned about economic inequality, political apathy, or residential segregation because they are not social problems but the natural order of things.

Source: http://www.aljazeera.com/programmes/empire.

The U.S. media's assumptions about the world are discernible when we consider the perspectives used in foreign media. For example, the English-language version of Qatar-based *Al Jazeera* (available in the United States) features a regular investigative series on "People and Power," which examines abuse of power by those in control of governments and corporations, and "Empire," which analyzes the "global powers and their agendas." Such programs often present a distinctly different, bottom-up approach to news.

Let's look at some more controversial claims about the natural. One of the principal underpinnings of racist ideology is the belief that one race is naturally superior to others. Sexism rests on the assumption that men and women, by nature, are suited to different and unequal tasks. And contemporary discussions of sexuality are filled with claims about the "natural" status of heterosexual relationships and the "unnatural" status of gay and lesbian relationships. These examples illustrate how claims about nature work in the service of ideology. If such claims are widely accepted—if they are seen as the outcome of nature instead of culture—then there may be legitimate reason for racial inequality, sexual discrimination, and the demonization of gays and lesbians as these relationships are the result of the natural order of things. What we think of as natural and normal, then, is a central part of the terrain of hegemony.

Hegemony, however, is neither permanent nor unalterable. Gramsci (1971) understood it as a process that was always in the making. To effectively wield power through consent, ideological work through cultural leadership is an ongoing necessity. The terrain of common sense and the natural must be continually reinforced because people's actual experiences will lead them to question dominant ideological assumptions. People are active agents, and modern society is full of contradictions; therefore, hegemony can never be complete or final. Some people will not accept the basic hegemonic worldview, some people may resist it, and changing historical conditions will make certain aspects of hegemonic ideology untenable. Ultimately, Gramsci saw hegemony as a daily struggle about our underlying conceptions of the world, a struggle always subject to revision and opposition. Rulers who try to maintain their power by defining the assumptions on which the society rests work to bring stability and legitimacy and to incorporate potentially opposing forces into the basic ideological framework. In a striking example, images of rebellion from the 1960s have become incorporated into our democratic story and now are used to sell cars and clothing.

Sociologist Stuart Hall, the leading voice of British cultural studies, has provided a sophisticated analysis of how mass media institutions fit into this conception of hegemony. He argues that mass media are one of the principal sites where the cultural leadership, the work of hegemony, is exercised. Media are involved in what Hall calls "the politics of signification," in which the media produce images of the world that give events particular meanings. Media images do not simply reflect the world, they *re-present* it; instead of reproducing the "reality" of the world "out there," the media engage in practices that define reality. As Hall (1982) puts it, "Representation is a very different notion from that of reflection. It implies the active work of selecting and presenting, of structuring and shaping; not merely the transmitting of an already-existing meaning, but the more active labour of *making things mean*" (p. 64).

Media representations are intertwined with questions of power and ideology because the process of giving meaning to events suggests that, potentially, there are multiple definitions of reality. For example, a workers' strike can be represented in several competing ways. The personal stories of the workers or an interview with a union leader can give a positive picture of the strikers. Reports highlighting statements from the company's management may shed negative light on the strike. A story that focuses on the inconvenience caused to the general public can make the issues involved in the conflict seem irrelevant. In *Prime Time Activism*, media sociologist Charlotte Ryan (1991) recalls her early activity as a union organizer in a public hospital. Every evening, after leaving the picket line, union activists would run home to watch the news on television to see how their efforts had been represented on the local news: Was the workers' or the company's perspective emphasized? How were the workers on strike represented?

Media have, as Hall (1982) says, "the power to signify events in a particular way." The question, then, is, "What are the patterns by which events are represented?" This is fundamentally a question about ideology because it suggests that media are places where certain ideas are circulated as the truth, effectively marginalizing or dismissing competing truth claims. Many scholars argue that media generally adopt the dominant assumptions and draw on the commonsensical views of the world that everyone knows. As a result, media representations, while not fully closed, have the tendency to reproduce the basic stories and values that are the underpinnings of this hegemony. For example, according to Becker (2006), when reality television shows like ABC's *Supernanny* or Fox's *Nanny 911* focused on heterosexual middle-class families, these programs helped to "naturalize" certain ideologies of parenting and the family, marginalizing alternative family forms, particularly single-parent households and families with same-sex parents. In this way, the ideology of the nuclear family presented in these kinds of programs participates in broader cultural conflicts about the family and emphasizes a particular perspective in, for example, the ongoing debate about gay marriage.

Media are, without doubt, not simple agents of the powerful—such as political leaders, major corporate actors, or cultural and religious authorities. As we will explore further in Chapter 8, the ideas of the powerful are not simply imposed on readers or viewers. Media are cultural sites where the ideas of the powerful are circulated and where they can be contested. Social change activists and social movements, for example, regularly seek to challenge the ideas of the powerful in the mass media (Ryan 1991). As we move from a theoretical discussion of media, ideology, and hegemony to specific cases that illustrate the ideology of mass media products, we will see the complex ways in which media products are a part of larger ideological debates.

NEWS MEDIA AND THE LIMITS OF DEBATE

For decades, Americans have debated the politics of the news media, with criticisms of the news coming with equal vigor from both sides of the political spectrum. The underlying assumption in this debate is that news media are, in fact, ideological; the selection of issues, stories, and sources is inescapably value laden. While media outlets fend off attacks from the political right that they are too liberal and attacks from the left that they are too conservative, journalists find themselves precisely where they want to be: in the middle. This middle ground serves as a haven for reporters, a place that is perceived as being without ideology. After all, if ideological criticism comes from both sides, then the news must not be ideological at all. Attacks from both sides make the center a defensible place.

Because we generally associate ideology with ideas that are perceived to be extreme, those in the middle are viewed as pragmatic rather than as ideological. And as ideology is something to be avoided, the journalistic middle ground becomes safe. There is good reason for journalists to want to occupy this territory. It insulates them from criticism and gives the news legitimacy with a wide range of readers and viewers who see themselves as occupying some version of a middle ground.

However, the notion that the news reflects the "consensus" is itself ideological because news does the active work of defining that consensus. Once that consensus is defined, the claim that reporting is a mere reflection of an already existing consensus is blind to the ways such definitions work to solidify it. We might say the same thing about the journalistic center. The news does not so much occupy the middle ground as define what the middle ground is. In the process, news reporting effectively defends the legitimacy of this worldview, which is oriented to the reproduction of current social arrangements. In short, the middle ground is ideological precisely because it is a cultural site where commonsense assumptions are produced, reproduced, and circulated.

Elites and Insiders

A large body of scholarly literature has explored the ways in which news media produce ideological visions of the nation and the world. One of the principal findings of this research is that news focuses on powerful people and institutions and generally reflects established interests. Whether this makes news "liberal" or "conservative" is another matter; some claim "the establishment" is liberal, while others argue that it is conservative. In either case, our reading of the research literature suggests that news reaffirms the basic social order and the values and assumptions it is based on.

In his classic work *Deciding What's News,* sociologist Herbert Gans (2004) found that two of the most prominent enduring values in the news are *social order* and *national leadership.* This focus on order and leadership gives the news a view of society that is both moderate and supportive of the established hierarchy. As Gans notes,

> [W]ith some oversimplification, it would be fair to say that the news supports the social order of public, business and professional, upper-middle-class, middle-aged, and white male sectors of society. . . . In short, when all other things are equal, the news pays most attention to and upholds the actions of elite individuals and elite institutions. (p. 61)

With its focus on elites, news presents images of the world that are significantly lacking in diversity. This has substantial consequences for the way the news depicts the political world. Politics, according to most major news media, is not about broad questions of power—who wields it, in what arenas, under what circumstances, with what consequences—nor is it a forum for wide-ranging debate and controversy about current events. Instead, politics is framed as an insider's debate, with only a privileged few invited to the table.

The "insider" nature of political news means that a small group of analysts are regular commentators and news sources, regardless of the wisdom of their previous commentary or of their prior actions when they occupied positions of power. To be—or to have been—an insider, with access to powerful circles, makes one a de facto "expert" as far as the news is concerned. As a result, individuals are qualified to comment on and analyze current events to the extent to which they are or have been insiders. The "debates" we see in the news, therefore, are often between insiders who share a common commitment to traditional politics to the exclusion of those outside the constructed consensus.

The range of insiders invited to discuss issues is often so narrow that a host of unaddressed assumptions are implicit in their approach. For example, debating the effectiveness of drone attacks in Pakistan and Afghanistan in the war against Al-Qaeda in 2010 ignores a variety of assumptions about the consequences of this kind of military action in the first place. Debating President Obama's 2009 approach to health care reform versus Republican attempts to limit reform neglects other possible alternatives, such as a single-payer system. The result is that contrasting perspectives in the news frequently represent the differences—generally quite narrow—between establishment insiders. This approach to the news does little to inform the public of positions outside this limited range of opinion. More important, it implicitly denies that other positions should be taken seriously. Ultimately, one principal way the news is ideological is in drawing boundaries between what is acceptable—the conventional ideas of insiders—and what is not.

Economic News as Ideological Construct

News coverage of economic issues is remarkable in the way it reproduces a profoundly ideological view of the world. Most news coverage of the economy is by and about the business community (Croteau and Hoynes 1994). While individuals can play a range of roles in economic life—worker, consumer, citizen, or investor—economic news focuses overwhelmingly on the activities and interests of investors. One of the most striking examples of this phenomenon is the fact that virtually every newspaper has a Business section, while almost none has a Consumer or Labor section. As a result, economic news is largely business news, and business news is directed at corporate actors and investors.

In this kind of news, the ups and downs of the stock market are often the centerpiece, serving as an indicator of the economic health of the country. But, in fact, about half of American households own no stock whatsoever, and over 80 percent of stocks in the United States are owned by just the wealthiest 10 percent of households (Wolf 2012). By equating economic health with the fortunes of investors, news tips its ideological hand. Such definitions fail to recognize that different groups of people can have different economic interests. Although a rise in the stock market is depicted as positive economic news for the country as a whole, there are clearly losers even when the market soars. For example, a rise in corporate profitability may be the result of an increase in productivity, which in turn may be accompanied by extensive layoffs. When business news programs cover corporate layoffs, stories often focus on the implications of such layoffs for stock performance. Or, as we have seen in the last few years, soaring stock prices can be fueled by growing consumer debt. Focusing primarily on the health of companies who sell goods and services neglects the long-term effects of this growing debt burden on ordinary Americans.

The government bailout and recession that followed the economic crisis of 2008 is another striking example of the top-down view and preoccupation with investors that dominates economic news reporting. In a comprehensive study of media coverage from February to August 2009, the Project for Excellence in Journalism (PEJ 2009: 1) found that "the gravest economic crisis since the Great Depression has been covered in the media largely from the top down, told primarily from the perspective of the Obama Administration and big business, and reflected the voices and ideas of people in institutions more than those of everyday Americans." The study found that corporate voices were the most common source in news stories, appearing in about 40 percent of the coverage, while representatives of labor unions were "virtually shut out of the coverage entirely" (p. 8), appearing in just 2 percent of the stories. Further, the study found that when the interests of investors were threatened—as indicated by stock market declines—the media dramatically increased its economic coverage. Once that threat to investors had receded and the stock market rose, economic coverage—as a percentage of the "newshole" or amount of time and space devoted to news—declined accordingly (see Figure 5.1). Meanwhile, though, millions of ordinary Americans faced continuing economic uncertainty and unemployment.

The U.S. media were not alone in presenting narrow economic coverage during the economic crisis. One study of British news outlets concluded that, despite the massive meltdown of the global capitalist economy, "the range of stories and the form of reporting presented a fairly homogeneous array of messages which, with only a few exceptions, promoted or at least did not question the dominant free-market ideology" (Robertson 2010).

Let's hypothetically turn the tables on this traditional way of viewing economic news. What if coverage of the economy focused predominantly on the experiences and interests of workers, evaluating economic health from the standpoint of working conditions and highlighting the economic analysis of labor union officials? It would likely be labeled "anti-business" or "pro-labor" and be targeted by critics for its "biased" reporting. It would, in short, be identified as providing a fundamentally ideological view of the economy. It is striking, however, that the news media's emphasis on the corporate and investor perspective is

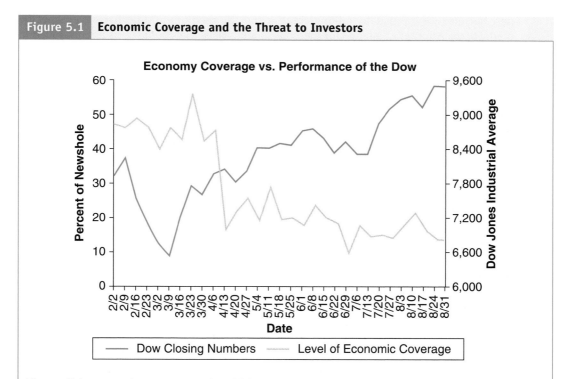

Figure 5.1 | **Economic Coverage and the Threat to Investors**

The media's economic coverage tends to highlight a top-down, investor perspective, neglecting ordinary working Americans. The economic crisis of 2008 threatened investors by producing a plunge in the stock market and elevated levels of economic coverage in the media. After government bailouts of Wall Street firms led to rising stock prices and the threat to investors was reduced, the media's coverage of the economic crisis declined dramatically, despite the fact that ordinary Americans saw little or no improvement in their economic fortunes.

Source: Project for Excellence in Journalism (2009).

generally accepted as the appropriate way to cover the economy. Indeed, the dominance of the business worldview in economic news coverage is so complete that it seems natural. We take it for granted, assuming that the economy equals corporate America and that economic health is equivalent to investor satisfaction. No conscious effort at manipulation is being made here, but it is a clear example of the ways media products draw on and reproduce a hegemonic ideology.

MOVIES, THE MILITARY, AND MASCULINITY

One of the difficulties of ideological analysis of media products is that there is no singular mass media. The term *mass media,* we should reiterate, is plural, signifying the multiple organizations and technologies that make up our media environment. As a result, we have to be careful when we make generalizations about the ideological content of media, in large part because we are usually talking about a specific medium and perhaps even specific media texts. Another challenge for ideological analysis is that media texts are produced in specific historical contexts, responding to and helping frame the cultural currents of the day. Mass-mediated images are not static; they change in form and content in ways that are observable. Ideological analysis, therefore, needs to pay attention to the shifts in media images—sometimes subtle and sometimes quite dramatic—to allow for the dynamic nature of mass media.

If the study of media and ideology needs to be both historically specific and wary of overgeneralizing from single texts, what analytic strategies have proved useful? One of the most common approaches is to focus on specific types or genres of media, such as the television sitcom, the Hollywood horror film, or the romance novel. Because texts within the same genre adopt the same basic conventions, analysts can examine the underlying themes and ideas embedded within these conventional formats without worrying that any contradictions they might uncover are the result of the distinct modes of storytelling of different genres. The result is that most scholarly studies of media ideology are both quite specific about their subject matter and narrow in their claims, focusing on issues such as the messages about gender in the soap opera (Modleski 1984), the ideology of the American Dream in talk radio (Levin 1987), or notions of romance in film and television (Ingraham 2008).

In addition, scholarly studies of media texts generally either focus on a specific historical period—for example, foreign policy news in the Reagan era (Herman and Chomsky 2002)—or provide comparisons of one genre of media across several time periods—for example, best-selling books from the 1940s through the 1970s (Long 1985). These analyses provide, on one hand, an understanding of how a specific medium displays a particular worldview or ideological conflict and, on the other hand, an understanding of how such stories about society change over time in different historical contexts.

Two film genres in a particular historical period—action-adventure and military/war films from the 1980s and early 1990s—are worth exploring for their underlying ideological orientation because of their popularity. With action-adventure movies, such as *Raiders of the Lost Ark* and *Romancing the Stone,* and military movies, such as *Rambo* and *Top Gun,* attracting large audiences—and inspiring sequels and seemingly endless imitators—scholars have used an ideological framework to understand the underlying messages in these films. What are these movies about, and why were they so attractive to American audiences of this period? In other words, what are the ideologies of these films, and how do these ways of seeing the world fit within broader ideological currents? These questions help both to interpret the films and to locate their meanings in a social context.

Action-Adventure Films

Action-adventure films were among the most popular movies of the 1980s. The three Indiana Jones films, starring Harrison Ford, are the archetype of this genre, in which the male hero performs remarkable feats that require bravery and skill throughout a fast-paced 90-minute struggle with an evil villain. The hero ultimately emerges triumphant after several close calls, defeating the villain, saving the day, and usually winning the affection of the female lead. One version of this genre places the hero in faraway, exotic lands, making the villains and the action more unpredictable. But the basic story line can be found in films set in the United States, such as *Die Hard, Speed, Rush Hour,* and *Mission Impossible.* On one level, these kinds of movies can be thrilling, suspenseful (even though we know, deep down, that the hero will triumph), and even romantic as we watch the hero overcome new challenges and seemingly impossible odds on the road to an exciting and satisfying finish. However, if we dig below the surface of the action, we can explore the kinds of stories these movies tell and how the stories resonate with our contemporary social dilemmas.

Gina Marchetti (1989) has argued that the key to the ideology of this genre is the typical construction of the main characters, the hero and the villain, which leads to specific stories about the nature of good and evil, strength and weakness, and courage and cowardice. One underlying theme of the action-adventure genre is the drawing of rigid lines between "us" and "them," with the villain representing the dangers of difference. There are, of course, many different versions of the central determinant of the in-group and the out-group. Nationality and ethnicity are frequent boundary markers, with white Americans (Michael Douglas, Bruce Willis) defeating dangerous foreigners. In other versions, civilized people triumph over the "primitive" (*Indiana Jones and the Temple of Doom*), or representatives of law and order defeat the deranged (*Speed*).

Ultimately, the hero effectively eliminates the danger represented by "the other"—the difference embodied by the villain—usually by killing the villain in a sensational climactic scene. Metaphorically speaking, social order is restored by the reassertion of the boundaries between what is acceptable and what is not, with the unacceptable doomed to a well-deserved death. The films go beyond xenophobic demonization of difference, however, by demonstrating the terms on which people who are different can become part of mainstream society. The hero's local accomplices—such as Indiana Jones's child sidekick, Short Round, in *Temple of Doom*—demonstrate that it is possible to be incorporated into mainstream society. This is the flip side of the violent death of the villain: The difference represented by the friend or buddy can be tamed and made acceptable (Marchetti 1989). Difference, then, must be either destroyed or domesticated by integrating the other into the hierarchical social relations of contemporary society, where the newly tamed other will likely reside near the bottom of the hierarchy. Ultimately, the action-adventure genre, with its focus on the personal triumph of the hero, is a tale about the power of the rugged male individual, a mythic figure in the ideology of the American Dream.

Vietnam Films and War Films Today

One particular 1980s version of the action-adventure genre was the return-to-Vietnam film, symbolized most clearly by the hit movie *Rambo*. In these films—which also include the *Missing in Action* trilogy and *Uncommon Valor*—the hero, a Vietnam veteran, returns to Vietnam a decade after the war to rescue American prisoners of war that the U.S. government has long since abandoned. In the process, the Vietnamese are demonized as brutal enemies who deserve the deaths that the heroes—most notably Sylvester Stallone and Chuck Norris—inflict on the captors as they liberate the prisoners.

The ideological work of these films is not very subtle, and given that they were popular during the presidency of conservative Ronald Reagan, their ideological resonance should not be surprising. In essence, these films provide a mass-mediated refighting of the war, in which Americans are both the good guys and the victors. The films serve as a kind of redemption for a country unable to accept defeat in Vietnam and still struggling with the shame of loss. If the United States did not win the Vietnam War on the battlefield, the movies allow its citizens to return in the world of film fantasy to alter the end of the story. In these stories, there is no longer shame or defeat but instead pride, triumph, and a reaffirmation of national strength. This outlook was, to be sure, part of the appeal of Ronald Reagan, whose campaign for president in 1980 called for a return to a sense of national pride, strength, and purpose that would move the nation beyond "the Vietnam syndrome."

The back-to-Vietnam films were, perhaps most fundamentally, part of the ideological project to overcome the Vietnam syndrome by providing a substitute victory. Susan Jeffords (1989) has argued that these films are about more than our national pride and the reinterpretation of defeat in Vietnam. She makes a persuasive case that the return-to-Vietnam films are part of a larger process of "remasculinization" of American society, another key component of the ideology of the Reagan years, in which a masculinity defined by its toughness is reasserted in the face of the twin threats of the defeat in Vietnam and the growth of feminism.

These Vietnam films are, to Jeffords (1989), fundamentally about the definition of American "manhood" at a time when the traditional tough image had been challenged by the social movements of the 1960s and the defeat in Southeast Asia. The Sylvester Stallone and Chuck Norris characters—Rambo and Braddock—return to Vietnam in order to recapture their strength and power, all the while resisting and chastising the government for being too weak (read: "feminine") to undertake such courageous missions. The return is as much about returning to a mythical past in which a strong America ruled the world and strong American men ruled their households as it is about rescuing POWs. Rambo and Braddock symbolize the desires of, and provide a mass-mediated and ideologically specific solution for, American men struggling with the changing social landscape of the 1980s.

Such popular media images are not simply innocent fantasies for our viewing entertainment. If we read these films in ideological terms, both the film texts themselves and their popularity tell us something about American culture and society in the 1980s. The masculine/military films of the time both reflected the fears and desires of American men and helped reproduce a new brand of toughness that became prevalent in the 1990s. The films were part of a political culture that created the conditions for the popular 1989 invasion of Panama and the even more popular 1991 war in the Persian Gulf, where TV news images did not differ much from those in the 1986 hit film *Top Gun*. Americans did overcome the Vietnam syndrome in the late 1980s, as symbolized by the willingness of the population to support military action in Panama, Iraq, and later in the "war against terrorism." Part of the ideological work necessary for that transformation was performed by popular Hollywood films.

By the turn of the century, though, real world events once again made the simple Hollywood vision of war problematic. The vulnerability of the United States to a powerfully symbolic terrorist attack on 9/11, the failure to find weapons of mass destruction during the invasion and protracted occupation of Iraq, and the ambiguous—at best—outcome of the war in Afghanistan were reflected in a new generation of movies. Some films, such as *Three Kings* (1999) and *Syriana* (2005), still privileged the perspectives of the American characters and, despite a potentially critical lens, ultimately defined as "abnormal, unacceptable, or impossible" alternative visions of U.S. foreign policy (Fritsch-El Alaoui 2009/2010: 131). The Academy Award–winning film *The Hurt Locker* (2008) glorified the work of explosive ordnance disposal (EOD) teams in a way that simply updated the war films from the '80s and '90s. But other films, such as *Jarhead* (2005) and *Stop-Loss* (2008), focused on the growing cynicism and despair of U.S. soldiers caught in the seemingly endless cycle of war. In one unique approach, Clint Eastwood's World War II drama *Flags of our Fathers* (2006) exposed the mythology behind the iconic raising of the U.S. flag at

Source: Universum Film/dapd.

Promoting a brand of tough masculinity common in war films, the 2012 film *Act of Valor* featured plenty of military helicopters, amphibious assault ships, submarines, drones, and other taxpayer-financed equipment and personnel—including active duty Navy SEALS. That's because the very idea for the film, which depicted an elite Naval Special Warfare squad's attack on a terrorist compound, originated with the Pentagon as a recruitment project. The Pentagon commonly provides valuable assistance in the production of films whose content it approves, and denies such assistance when it objects to script content.

Iwo Jima, while his accompanying *Letters from Iwo Jima* (2007) presented the horrors of that battle from a Japanese perspective. These more recent war films suggest a broader range of approaches than has been common in the past.

TELEVISION, POPULARITY, AND IDEOLOGY

While certain genres of popular films have been the subject of ideological analysis, it would be fair to say that the whole range of television programming has been studied for its ideological content. In fact, ideological analysis of media is sometimes reduced to the study of television, just as claims about "the media" are often claims about televised images. That's because television has been the dominant form of media. For the moment, this continues to be true even as new forms of online media grow in popularity and even as television viewing habits are changing with DVRs and the streaming of TV programs to computers and mobile devices. In 2014, a top-rated network television program could still be viewed by upwards of 15 million people. From presidential elections to championship sporting events, from natural disasters to mass shootings, ideas and images still circulate most widely through television.

Television is more than just the most popular medium in terms of audience size. It also regularly comments on popular media. In fact, an astounding number of television programs have been, at least in part, about the media (see Figure 5.2). In addition, talk shows and entertainment-oriented programs focus on the lives of media celebrities and the ins and outs of the television, film, and music worlds. With popular media as the subject and setting for so much programming, television is a virtual running commentary on the media world. Television is often so self-referential—or at least media centered—that the programs assume that viewers are deeply engaged with the culture of media, and the humor often requires knowledge of the specific media reference. Our exposure to television and its self-referential "winking" about popular culture have made most of us rather skilled viewers who catch the references and know what they are all about.

Television and Reality

If television is as central to our mass-mediated culture as a broad range of scholars maintain, then the underlying ideas that television programs disseminate are of substantial social significance. What stories does television tell us about contemporary society? How does television define key social categories, depict major institutions, or portray different types of people? What is "normal" in the world of television, and what is "deviant"?

One reason why television is often considered to be so ideologically charged is that it relies, almost exclusively, on conventional, "realist" forms of image construction that mask the workings of the camera. As a result, the family sitcom invites us to drop in at the home of our electronic neighbors, and the courtroom drama allows us to sit in on a trial. Most of us do not consciously mistake such families and courtrooms for "real life"; we would not confuse these televised images with our real neighbors, for example. Still, part of the allure of television is that it seems real; we routinely suspend disbelief while we are watching.

Figure 5.2	Select Television Programs About the Media	
Program	*Network (Dates)*	*Featured Media Setting or Occupation*
The Newsroom	HBO (2012–)	Cable news station
My Dad Says	CBS (2010–2011)	Writer/blogger
Free Radio	VH1 (2008–2009)	Radio station
Flight of the Conchords	HBO (2007–2009)	Musicians
30 Rock	NBC (2006–2013)	Sketch comedy program/corporate world
Brothers and Sisters	ABC (2006–2011)	Radio and TV talk show host
Extras	HBO (2005–2007)	Movie industry
How I Met Your Mother	NBC (2005–2014)	TV reporter
Entourage	HBO (2004–2011)	Hollywood film star/business world
Talk to Me	ABC (2000–2001)	Radio talk show
Curb Your Enthusiasm	HBO (2000–)	Television writer
Sports Night	ABC (1998–2000)	Sports news TV show
Just Shoot Me	NBC (1997–2003)	Fashion magazine
Everybody Loves Raymond	CBS (1996–2005)	Newspaper sports writer
News Radio	NBC (1995–1999)	All-news radio station
Frasier	NBC (1993–2004)	Radio call-in program
The Larry Sanders Show	HBO (1992–1998)	Late-night talk show
Mad About You	NBC (1992–1999)	Documentary film maker
Home Improvement	ABC (1991–1999)	Home improvement TV show
Murphy Brown	CBS (1988–1998)	Network newsmagazine
Family Ties	NBC (1982–1989)	Public television station
WKRP in Cincinnati	CBS (1978–1982)	Radio station
Lou Grant	CBS (1977–1982)	Major newspaper office
The Mary Tyler Moore Show	CBS (1970–1977)	Local TV station
The Partridge Family	ABC (1970–1974)	Musicians
The Dick Van Dyke Show	CBS (1961–1966)	Writer for a comedy/variety TV show

The pleasures of television are a result of our ability to temporarily ignore our knowledge that there is no *NCIS* investigator named Ziva David, no film star named Vincent Chase with an entourage, and the counter-terrorism unit (CTU) depicted in *24* does not exist.

The ideological work of television, then, lies in the ways it defines and orders its pictures of "reality"—in its claims to reflect the humor and hardships of family life, the dangers of police work, the fun and confusion of 20-something single life, or the drama of the courtroom. This reality is created and packaged by writers and producers with the goal of attracting a mass audience. The images are not simple reflections of an unproblematic reality but representations of a world that is not as orderly as a 30- or 60-minute program.

In striving for popularity, the television producers have often adopted the strategy of least objectionable programming, whereby programs are intended to avoid controversy and remain politically bland. This approach is, itself, ideological; blandness favors certain images and stories and pushes others to the margins or off the air entirely. This is one reason why, for example, television programs typically avoid dealing with topics like abortion or religious beliefs—both of which could be seen as controversial.

It is difficult, however, to make broad generalizations about the ideology of television programming beyond the observation that network executives want popularity without controversy. This formula for programs reaffirms the dominant norms of contemporary society. For a more nuanced understanding of how television programs are ideological and how they respond to the often volatile social and political world, we need to look more carefully at a particular genre of programming. Ella Taylor's (1989) study of the changing image of the family on prime-time television from the 1950s through the 1980s provides a clear example of the ideological twists and turns of network television.

Television and the Changing American Family

Beginning in the 1950s and 1960s, domestic life as represented by programs such as *Leave It to Beaver, Ozzie and Harriet,* and *Father Knows Best,* along with zanier fare such as *Bewitched* and *I Dream of Jeannie,* was predominantly white, middle class, happy, and secure. Network television presented the suburban family as the core of the modern, postscarcity society—a kind of suburban utopia where social problems were easily solved (or nonexistent); consensus ruled; and signs of racial, ethnic, or class differences or conflict were difficult to find. Taylor (1989) suggests that if, indeed, such families existed, they were precisely the people whom network advertisers sought. Still, this image of the postwar family—and the not-so-subtle suggestion that this was what a "normal" family looked like—was a particular story masked as a universal one. Certainly, these families were not typical American families, no matter how often they were served up as such.

The television family did not remain static, however; changing social conditions and new marketing strategies in the television industry helped create competing domestic images. The biggest change came in the 1970s with what Taylor (1989) calls the "turn to relevance," when the television family became a site where contemporary social and political issues were explored. The program that epitomized the new breed was Norman Lear's *All in the Family,* which was expected to flop yet became one of the most popular and profitable shows of the decade. The program revolved around the ongoing tension among a cast of diverse characters in their Queens, New York, home. These included Archie Bunker, a stereotypical white, working-class bigot; his strong but decidedly unliberated wife, Edith; their feminist daughter, Gloria; and her husband, Michael, a sociology graduate student with leftist political views. From week to week, Archie and Michael argued over race relations, the proper role of women in society, American foreign policy, and even what kind of food to eat. Throughout the political debates, the main characters traded insults and vented their anger at each other, while Archie waxed nostalgic over the good old days of the 1950s and Gloria and Michael looked nervously at their futures. Programs such as *The Jeffersons* and *Maude,* both *All in the Family* spin-offs, as well as *Sanford and Son* and *Good*

Source: Bob D'Amico/Getty Images.

Television's early days featured "traditional," white, two-parent, heterosexual families exclusively, while today's programs feature a wider variety of families. The popular program *Modern Family* featured several family types, including a same-sex couple who adopted a child—something that would have been unthinkable on U.S. television in an earlier era.

Times—among the most popular programs of the mid-1970s—may have been less acerbic than *All in the Family,* but they were all a far cry from the previous generation of conflict-free, white, middle-class family images.

By the middle of the 1970s, the image of the family was neither all white nor all middle class, and domestic life was no longer a utopia; instead, the family was depicted as a source of conflict and struggle as well as comfort and love. In short, social problems made their way into the television family. Taylor (1989) argues that the key to this change was the networks' desire, particularly at CBS, to target young, urban, highly educated viewers—an audience that was highly coveted by advertisers. The new image of the family, self-consciously "relevant" instead of bland and nostalgic, was perceived to be attractive to the youthful consumers who had lived through the social turbulence of the 1960s. But television's ideological change was slow and in many respects subtle. Nostalgic programs that presented the ideal middle-class family were also popular in the 1970s—*Happy Days* is a classic example.

At the same time that the television family was losing its blissful image in the 1970s, a new version of family appeared in the world of work. In programs such as *M*A*S*H, The Mary Tyler Moore Show, Taxi,* and *Barney Miller,* the setting was not the home; instead, the programs revolved around the relationships among coworkers that Taylor (1989) calls a "work-family." In these programs, the workplace became a place where people found support, community, and loyalty and served as an often warm and fuzzy kind of family for people who were much more connected to their work than to their home lives. Taylor argues that the image of the work-family was popular precisely because of broad cultural anxiety about the changing boundaries between private life and public life in the 1970s, particularly for young professionals seeking prestige and success. Work-families, in essence, provided a picture of a safe haven from domestic conflicts in both the world of television and the experiences of viewers.

Given the growing rationalization of the American workplace in the 1970s, when more men and women came to work in large, bureaucratic organizations, finding images of the family in the workplace is surprising. Taylor (1989) argues that the popularity of the work-family programs tells us a great deal about the social role of television:

> If we understand the television narrative as a commentary on, and resolution of, our troubles rather than a reflection of the real conditions of our lives, it becomes possible to read the television work-family as a critique of the alienating modern corporate world and an affirmation of the possibility of community and cooperation amid the loose and fragmentary ties of association. (p. 153)

Of course, the neat and orderly resolution of social dilemmas is precisely the area in which television is ideological. In this case, network television presented images of domestic conflict but resolved them in the workplace through a professional, career-oriented ideology that reassured us that, despite change, everything would be OK. In the end, even as it incorporated conflict and relevance into its field of vision, television still gave viewers satisfying families and happy endings that affirmed the basic outlines of the American Dream.

The last few decades have presented television viewers with conflicting visions of family life. In the 1990s, popular programs included everything from the nostalgic *Wonder Years* and the idyllic *Cosby Show* to the cynical *Married With Children* and the sober *Grace Under Fire*. In the 2000s, the dysfunctional animated families of *The Simpsons* and *Family Guy,* the secret-filled lives of well-off suburbanites in *Desperate Housewives*, and the sober two-career family of *Friday Night Lights* were among the programs that vied for viewer attention. Programs with a variety of family structures have also become common, including *The New Normal* (single mother), *Two and a Half Men* (single father), *Modern Family* (same-sex parents, multiethnic parents), and *Parenthood* (single mother and extended multigenerational family). Single-parent families, two-career families, same-sex parents, and blended families are all part of the universe of television families today.

The ever-changing family images show that television programs and the ideology they circulate are far from static. In the midst of cultural conflict over the meaning of family today, network television images are, themselves, part of the ongoing ideological contest to shape the definition of a proper family.

Revising Tradition: The New Momism

Amid the newly diverse images of American families that now populate the media, some traditional ideas remain prominent. In particular, the perfect mother who featured notably in 1950s television has been resurrected, revised, and distributed across media platforms in what Douglas and Michaels (2004) call the "new momism." Ads, movies, and magazines show mothers changing diapers, taking care of their children, and looking after the house, but now they also show mothers going to the gym, pursuing careers, and looking sexy. Usually media show "perfect" mothers, such as when glossy magazines celebrate celebrity moms, highlighting both their accomplishments and their splendid bodies while distributing advice on how to be a "good" mother. Douglas and Michaels (2004) argue that the "new momism" involves a "set of ideas, norms, and practices, most frequently and powerfully represented in the media, that seem on the surface to celebrate motherhood, but which in reality promulgate standards of perfection that are beyond our reach" (pp. 4–5). According to Douglas and Michaels, this "new momism," grounded in the feminist belief that women have autonomy and can make choices about their lives, actually contradicts feminism by implying that the only enlightened choice for a woman is to become a mother.

More broadly, argue Douglas and Michaels, motherhood has been under the media spotlight across media platforms. An ideology of motherhood that romanticizes and commercializes the figure of mothers can be found in magazines such as *Parents* and *Working Mother,* television shows like *Supernanny* and *In the Motherhood,* talk radio programs like *Dr. Laura,* as well as advertising images and news segments. These media images perform classic ideological functions by setting standards of perfection and prescribing what a "good mother" should do. In addition, media representations of mothers instill a sense of threat in contemporary mothers: Being compared to "perfect" models, many are likely to end up feeling inadequate and constantly under surveillance. According to Douglas and Michaels, this relatively recent media obsession with motherhood is fueled by specific media dynamics, most notably the interest of producers and advertisers in reaching a target audience of working women.

RAP MUSIC AS IDEOLOGICAL CRITIQUE?

We have seen that mass media can be analyzed in ideological terms, but media products are not ideologically uniform. They are both contradictory and subject to change. In short, there is no single ideology embedded within mass media texts. Even so, most mass media can be seen as sites where facets of the dominant version of the American story—an ideology that essentially sustains the current social order of our capitalist and democratic society—are displayed, reworked, and sometimes contested. At the same time, conventional norms and mainstream values are generally reaffirmed, even if in slightly modified form, by those mass media texts—news, popular films, and network television—that seek large audiences. Thus, hegemony is constructed, perhaps challenged, and reasserted on a daily basis through the products of our mass media. But is it possible for widely circulating mass media texts to be oppositional or counterhegemonic? Can mass media provide challenges to the dominant ways of understanding the social world?

Tricia Rose (1994), in her study of the meanings of early rap music, argues that rap should be understood as a mass-mediated critique of the underlying ideology of mainstream American society. Rap presents an alternative interpretation—a different story—of the ways power and authority are structured in contemporary society. Robin D. G. Kelley (1994) argues that some rap lyrics are "intended to convey a sense of social realism" that "loosely resembles a sort of street ethnography of racist institutions and social practices, but told more often than not in the first person" (p. 190).

Much of early rap music was a critique of institutions such as the criminal justice system, the police, and the educational system, all of which are reinterpreted as sites that both exhibit and reproduce racial inequality. These alternative interpretations are not always explicit; often they are subtle, requiring a form of insider knowledge to fully understand what they are about. Rose (1994) suggests that rap

> uses cloaked speech and disguised cultural codes to comment on and challenge aspects of current power inequalities. . . . Often rendering a nagging critique of various manifestations of power via jokes, stories, gestures, and song, rap's social commentary enacts ideological insubordination. (p. 100)

While public attention once focused on the anger of "gangsta rap," Rose (1994) points out that a much larger body of rap music acts in subtle and indirect ways to refuse dominant ideological assumptions about black youth, urban life, and racial inequality by articulating opposing interpretations of current social relations.

Rap's ideological displacement of the conventional story with new stories is rooted in the inequalities of the social world. Rose (1994) argues that rap's stories—its ways of understanding society in alternative, even oppositional ways—come from the life experiences of black urban youth. In essence, rap presents an ideological critique from below; it is a musical form that criticizes social institutions from the perspective of those who have comparatively little power in contemporary society.

At the same time, rap is full of ideological contradictions. While some politically radical male rappers critique the institutions of society as being racist, the lyrics and imagery of their music are often sexist and homophobic. They often depict women in degrading ways, including references to violence against women. So even as they are challenging the dominant ideology about race, some black male rappers generally accept and reinforce traditional ideological assumptions about gender roles and sexuality. The discourses within rap music, then, are not unambiguously oppositional in ideological terms.

Rose (1994) notes, however, that the alternative interpretations of social reality in rap lyrics, while partial and contradictory, only partly explain why rap can be understood as a form of ideological critique. Rap music, even that not expressly political in its lyrical content, is part of a broader struggle over the meaning of, and access to, public space. In short, the dominant discourse about rap—one frequently encountered in news media coverage of the rap scene—is connected to a broader discourse about the "spatial control of black people." In the case of rap, the focus is on ways in which the culture of rap, particularly the gathering of large groups of black youth at concerts, is a threat to social order. Rose contends that the very existence of public rap events, at which black youth make claims to their right to occupy public space, is part of an ideological struggle in which the rap community refuses to accept the dominant interpretation of its "threat" to society. It is in such large gatherings, already politicized by the kind of resistance implied by the use of public space, that new forms of expression and new ideas have the potential to emerge. This fight for public space is at the center of what Rose calls rap's "hidden politics."

Rap, of course, is much more than a form of political expression, however contradictory, that circulates within the black community. It is also a highly profitable commercial industry. In fact, rap's commercial success is due, in large part, to the fact that the music is popular among white suburban youth. Whites actually buy more rap and hip-hop music than blacks. This complicates the ideology of rap, making it difficult to simply accept the argument that rap can be "counterhegemonic," a form of resistance to dominant ideological constructions. Such media messages are unlikely to be attractive to upper-middle-class white suburbanites or corporate record companies. Central to Rose's (1994) argument is that the ideology of rap is often masked and is most accessible to those who know the black urban culture that forms its roots. Therefore, black youth may interpret the meaning of rap in ways very different from white youth, even though both may enjoy the music. As we will explore in Part IV, there is good reason to believe that the meanings of rap are multiple and contested. Even so, we are still stuck with the dilemma posed by commercialization.

Is it possible for corporate-produced, commercial mass media products to be fundamentally oppositional in ideological terms? Even rap music—with its critique of the police, schools, and mainstream media—is part of the corporate sector and, as such, is subject to the rules that govern the culture industry. In particular, this means that rap is a commercial product that is packaged and marketed to be sold to demographically specific sets of buyers. To the extent that the music does not sell, it will not be available in the mass market for very long; the musical packages and marketing strategies that do work will lure record companies into strategies of imitation until profits dry up. In short, rap is as much a commercial commodity as it is an intervention in ideological contests.

As it did with the commercialized images of rebellion from the 1960s—Janis Joplin's tongue-in-cheek prayer for a Mercedes was used in ads for Mercedes-Benz cars, and an image of John Lennon and Yoko Ono helped to market Apple computers—the culture industry is capable of incorporating potentially oppositional forms of expression into the mainstream by turning them into commercial products subject to the rules of the market. By becoming a prominent commercial product that is now routinely used in national advertising campaigns, rap may have lost a good deal of its critical impact. Rap music is now about selling records and products as much as it is a forum for potentially oppositional expression. Still, incorporation into the marketplace is not likely to entirely empty a cultural form, such as rap, of its potential to provide ideological critique, particularly if that critique is disguised in the ways Rose (1994) suggests.

Furthermore, the adoption and adaptation of rap—and the broader hip-hop culture of which it's a part—to reflect local circumstances worldwide has often revived rap's more critical ideological edge (Morgan and Bennett 2011). One example is the work of Tunisian rapper Hamada Ben Amor, known by his MC name, El Général, whose work had long been banned by his government. Just before the Arab Spring uprisings in 2010, El Général released a song on YouTube called "Rais Lebled" ("Head of State") that chronicled the complaints against the repressive government and became what *TIME* magazine called "the rap anthem of the Mideast Revolution." The song and a subsequent one that praised the growing protest movement in Tunisia brought the wrath of the Tunisian government, which arrested El Général, only to release him a week later after political protestors rallied to his cause. After the Tunisian government was overthrown, El Général was invited to perform his anthem live for thousands of young demonstrators.

Ultimately, the example of rap music at home and abroad demonstrates the workings of hegemony. Mass media texts are contradictory; they can be oppositional, presenting ideological alternatives, even as they reproduce specific dominant ideological assumptions. But maintaining even this limited form of critique is difficult. Commercialization is part of the process through which the ideological struggle is waged; even critical media products have a tendency to be (at least partially) incorporated into mass, commercial products that accept the boundaries of mainstream definitions of social reality. This is, of course, an ongoing process, and incorporation is never total. But the media industry has proved to be remarkably resilient and innovative—it seems that virtually any form of expression can be tamed enough to be sold to a mass market. But the rise of platforms like YouTube also suggests that, under the right circumstances, rap music can now be distributed in a way that bypasses the taming influences of the commercial marketplace to play a role in vibrant movements for political change.

ADVERTISING AND CONSUMER CULTURE

Each day, we are bombarded with advertisements in our homes, cars, workplaces, online, and on the street. As businesses seek new places to advertise their goods and services, ads can be found just about everywhere. Buses and subways have long been prime advertising spaces, catching the eyes of riders and passersby alike. Airlines sometimes sell ad space on the outsides of planes. Television and radio have long been chock-full of ads. When you log onto the Internet, you find that colorful advertisements are also part of the cyberspace experience: pop-up windows in online newspapers, banner ads at the bottom of e-mails sent through "free" e-mail services, in "free" blogging platforms and websites, and also on Google and Facebook. Ads surround sporting events, both on television and in sports arenas. They arrive in the mail and via cell phone. We wear advertising logos on our clothes and hum advertising jingles in the shower. In short, ads are so deeply embedded in our environment that we are likely to see, hear, and even smell them (in the form of magazine perfume ads) without thinking twice.

What kinds of stories do advertisements tell about ourselves and our society? Certainly, on one level, ads are specific to their product or service. They tell us that if we drink a particular brand of beer, we will meet attractive women or that if we wear the right makeup, we will meet handsome men; if we purchase a certain automobile, we will gain prestige; if we use specific cleansers, we will save time; and if we wear certain clothes, we will find adventure. Ads may also tell us that a particular item will save us money, that a specific service will make us healthier, or that a new product will make a great gift for a loved one. There is a wide range of specific messages in these ads, suggesting connections between products and lifestyles and between services and states of mind and presenting a host of information about prices, availability, and the like. We are not

Advertisements occupy increasingly large amounts of public space. This photo shows a particularly striking example of ads towering over an urban setting. Ads also populate our daily landscape in less dramatic ways. In addition to the regular media, T-shirts, bumper stickers, grocery bags, junk mail, and many other sites all carry ads. Where have you seen advertisements today?

simply passive participants in all of this. We recognize advertising conventions and don't expect the connections depicted in ads—cosmetics and love, suits and success, for example—to be taken literally.

Despite the diversity of advertising messages and their frequent use of irony and humor, there is an underlying commonality to almost all advertisements: They are fundamentally about selling. They address their audiences as consumers and celebrate and take for granted the consumer–capitalist organization of society. This perspective is, of course, decidedly ideological. Ads tell us that happiness and satisfaction can be purchased, that each of us is first and foremost an individual consumption unit, and that market relations of buying and selling are the appropriate—perhaps the only—form of social relations outside the intimacy of the family. Sometimes even the intimacy of the family is seemingly up for sale. One recent commercial implied that a father could spend more quality time with his son if he bought a DirecTV satellite dish! Advertising presumes and promotes a culture of consumption, normalizing middle- or even upper-middle-class lifestyles and making buying power a measure of both virtue and freedom.

In the process, advertising elevates certain values—specifically, those associated with acquiring wealth and consuming goods—to an almost religious status. Moreover, advertising promotes a worldview that stresses the individual and the realm of private life, ignoring collective values and the terrain of the public world (Schudson 1984). The values that advertising celebrates do not come out of thin air, but this does not make them any less ideological. Whether or not ads are successful at selling particular products—some ad campaigns succeed, and others fail—the underlying message in advertising, which permeates our media culture, is the importance of the values of consumerism.

Selling Consumerism in the Early 20th Century

Stuart Ewen (1976) has explored the historical roots of what we now call consumer culture, tracing the role of early 20th-century advertising in its creation. Turn-of-the-century capitalists, captains of industry, saw mass advertising as a means of shaping the consciousness of the American population in a way that would give legitimacy and stability to the rapidly industrializing society. The key to this new consciousness was the creation of a new way of life based on the pleasures of consumption. Mass advertising emerged in the 1920s, when leaders of the business community began to see the need for a coordinated ideological effort to complement their control of the workplace. Advertising would become the centerpiece of a program to sell not only products but also a new, American way of life in which consumption erased differences, integrated immigrants into the mainstream of American life, and made buying the equivalent of voting as a form of commitment to the democratic process.

From the start, then, advertising was more about creating consumers than selling individual products. If a mass production economy was to be profitable and if those who worked for long hours under difficult conditions in the factory were to be pacified, new needs and habits had to be stimulated. This was the job of advertising. Its early practitioners built on people's insecurities about their lives and their appearances to shape desires for new consumer products. Solutions to personal problems were to be found in the world of consumption, an early version of the currently prevalent attitude that views a day of shopping as a way to cheer up oneself. Ads suggested that new products, such as mouthwash, hand lotion, and deodorant, would protect people from embarrassment and give them tickets to the modern world. Old habits and folkways—the traditions that recent immigrants brought to the United States—were to be discarded in favor of the new "American way," participation in a consumer society. Ads sold consumerism as a gateway to social integration in 20th-century America and as an ideology that would smooth over social conflicts—especially class conflict—and serve as a form of social cement.

One way advertising tried to sell a cross-class ideology of consumerism was through its focus on the realm of consumption and its neglect of production. The industrial workplace might be unsatisfying, even degrading, but advertising offered a world that was far removed from the drudgery of work, emphasizing the wonders of the consumer lifestyle. It was, after all, that lifestyle and associated worldview that ads were selling, regardless of whether people had the means to really live it. As Ewen (1976) puts it, while the ideology of consumerism

> served to stimulate consumption among those who had the wherewithal and desire to consume, it also tried to provide a conception of the good life for those who did not. . . . In the broader context of a burgeoning commercial culture, the foremost political imperative was *what to dream*. (p. 108)

Such dreams could be realized only by consuming goods, and even this was only a temporary realization, requiring continuous consumption in search of the lifestyle promoted by advertising. Our culture of consumption, then, is intimately connected to advertising, which helped create it and continues, in new forms, to sustain consumerism as a central part of contemporary American ideology.

Women's Magazines as Advertisements

The "women's magazine" is one medium that is particularly advertising oriented and consistently promotes the ideology of consumerism. Its emphasis on ads—which often seem to make up the bulk of the content—has led one critic to label this genre the "women's advertising magazine" (McCracken 1993). Publications such as *Vogue, Glamour, Redbook, Cosmopolitan,* and *Modern Bride* include page after page of glossy ads featuring products targeted specifically at women.

Source: AP Photo/Hearst.

So-called women's magazines are loaded with advertisements and editorial content, nearly all of which promote an ideology that celebrates consumption associated with beauty, fitness, attracting men, and the "good life."

More generally, the magazines promote the consumer lifestyle by showing how beauty, sexuality, career success, culinary skill, and social status can be bought in the consumer marketplace. Social problems, from the standpoint of consumer ideology, are redefined as personal problems that can be solved by purchasing the appropriate product. Women's magazines, in addressing a specific social group, identify women as a consumption category with special product needs. The magazines link an identity as a woman with a set of specific consumer behaviors, making the latter the prerequisite for the former. To be a "woman," then, is to know what to buy; the ad content in women's magazines both displays the specific products and celebrates the pleasures and needs of consumption.

But there is more to women's magazines than just the ads, even though a common reading strategy is to casually leaf through the pages, glancing at the ads and headlines. Ellen McCracken (1993) argues that the editorial content—the nonadvertising articles—is itself a form of "covert advertising" that promotes the same kind of consumer-oriented ideology. The most visible ad is the cover of the magazine. The standard image of the ideal woman on the cover suggests that purchase of the magazine will provide clues to how and what to buy in order to become the ideal woman. In addition, covers are often reproduced inside the magazine along with information about the products displayed, suggesting that the image depicted is one that can be purchased.

Even the "editorial advice" provided by women's magazines is a form of covert advertisement, selling the consumer ideology. Beauty advice, for example, routinely suggests the consumption of various forms of makeup as a way to achieve beauty. Such advice often identifies brand names that are most effective—brands frequently promoted in ads in the same magazine. The regular makeover feature, in which an "average" woman is turned into a glamorous model look-alike, is, in essence, an endorsement of the beauty products advertised elsewhere in the magazine. Advice, then, really concerns appropriate consumption habits. Just as early ads identified newfound needs, the women's magazine suggests what women need. In the end, women's magazines use both direct and covert advertising to sell magazines and promote an ideology that celebrates the consumption of gender-specific products as a means to identity formation and personal satisfaction—the dream of the "good life."

ADVERTISING AND THE GLOBALIZATION OF CULTURE

The dreams that advertisements sell within the United States are also exported all around the globe. American-made ads for American brands—from Coca-Cola to Nike—circulate through the growing global media culture. More generally, American media products, from television programming to Hollywood films, are consumed by a vast international audience. Both the ads and the programming serve as a kind of international promotional vehicle for the American way of life by focusing on the material abundance and consumer opportunities available in the United States.

While different products use different sales pitches and the entertainment media explore a range of themes set in various locations, most American media—especially those that are exported—share an underlying frame of reference that defines America by its combination of consumer capitalism and political freedom. Because media are owned and operated by profit-making companies, it should not be surprising that the cornucopia of images converges in the promotion of the benefits of a consumer society. Given the rapidly growing global economy, American-based companies see the international market as one of the keys to 21st-century success.

If advertisements and exported entertainment promote the American way of life, what exactly are they selling? After all, it is difficult to reduce the United States, a diverse and fragmented culture, to simple, unambiguous themes. The images on global display, like much domestic advertising, are about dreams. America is portrayed as a kind of dreamland where individuals can fulfill (or buy?) their desires. The images of the dreamland do not require a rigid uniformity, because central to the ideology on display are the notions of individuality and freedom, which merge into the concept of *consumer choice*. Dreams are fulfilled by individual consumers who make choices about what to buy: Coke, Pepsi, or 7Up; Calvin Klein, The Gap, or Ralph Lauren; Nike or Reebok; Macintosh or IBM; Avis or Hertz. The route to happiness in this electronic dreamworld is consuming the "right" product. Think about how happy the diners are in McDonald's commercials or how peaceful the world is in the Ralph Lauren magazine ads.

The world portrayed in television programs, such as *Modern Family* or *Brothers and Sisters,* similarly displays images of attractive people living comfortable lives surrounded by contemporary consumer goods. Both advertisements and entertainment media promote a commitment to the latest styles—for example, in clothes, cars, leisure activities, and food—that requires not just consumption but continuous consumption to keep up with stylistic changes. The focus on style is directed particularly at youth, who are increasingly the most coveted market and who are particularly avid media users. The international advertising, television, and music scenes have helped generate an emerging cross-national, global youth culture in which teens and young adults in different countries adopt similar styles in clothes and appearance and select the same brands; consume the same soda, cigarettes, and fast food; and listen to and play the same kinds of music. The international teen market may cross national boundaries; but, with the help of American media products, youth style is based to a great degree on American images and consumer goods.

American media products may be the most prominent in global circulation, but they are not the only media images out there. Various European and Japanese companies also produce media and advertising for an international market, often in concert with U.S.-based companies. Herbert Schiller (1992), one of the early critics of the export of American mass media, argues that globally circulating media images all promote a similar ideology, regardless of their national origin. While the use of mass media as a tool for marketing lifestyles may have had its origins in the United States, it has become a global phenomenon. Although global media images may display national cultural differences as part of the sales pitch, they highlight difference as part of the promotion of the value of consuming and acquiring things. Ironically, cultural differences in global media images—such as multicultural images in American media—attract audiences for the promotion of a consumerist ideology that most fundamentally aims to bring different cultures together into an increasingly homogeneous, international consumer culture. If "we are the world," as the 1980s hit song for famine relief asserted, it is because we all buy, or dream about buying, the same things.

Culture has become increasingly global, with media images circulating across national boundaries. At the same time, U.S. media images display more difference than they did a generation ago. But what messages do U.S. media images present about the status of Americans and the status of foreigners in this global culture? This question fundamentally addresses ideology.

In his study of advertising images of foreigners, William O'Barr (1994) argues that the ideological analysis of ads requires us to look at what he calls the "secondary discourses" within the advertisements. As opposed to the primary discourse, which concerns the specific qualities of the advertised product, secondary discourses are those ideas about social relationships that are embedded within the ads. The ideology of advertising images, from this perspective, is to be found in the ways the images convey messages about social life at the same time they try to promote a specific product. Context, setting, characteristics of the principal actors, and the interaction between actors within the ad are central to these secondary discourses.

In contemporary print ads, according to O'Barr (1994), there are three main categories of ads that feature images of foreigners: travel ads, product endorsements, and international business ads. The foreigners within travel ads are depicted as the "other"—different from the "us" that the ad is targeting—and the ads suggest that these others are available for the entertainment of American tourists. Implicit both within the images of local people dancing, painting, and smiling with American tourists and within the ad copy that invites tourists as "honored guests" or offers to "open both our homes and hearts" to visitors is a message that foreign lands are in the business of serving American visitors. Such images, by offering satisfaction from local people who aim to please, suggest that the needs and desires of Americans are the key to the potential relationship. The pattern in travel ads is unambiguous; the American tourist dominates the relationship with foreign cultures, particularly when the ads promote travel to Third World countries.

Product advertisements that draw on images of foreigners make connections between the advertised commodity and associations we have with foreign lands. O'Barr (1994) suggests images that, for example, link lingerie to Africa through the use of black models in apparently "primitive" clothing or that connect perfume to China or India by associating the product with Chinese art and characters or the Taj Mahal tell us stories about these foreign societies. The irony is that the products—in this case the lingerie or perfume—have nothing to do with societies in Africa, China, or India; the images of "others" are used to promote products made and used in the West.

Why, then, do ads draw on such images? O'Barr (1994) argues that the images of foreign lands are intended to suggest that the products are exotic or romantic. In so doing, they suggest that Africans, Chinese, or Indians are different from Americans, often depicting them as more primitive and, particularly, more sexual. These associations are intended to make the products attractive while simultaneously reaffirming that foreigners are fundamentally different.

Images of foreigners in ads for travel and products highlight difference, depicting an "other" who is subordinate to, but a source of pleasure for, American tourists and consumers. The ideology underlying these images about the place of the United States in the contemporary global order differs little from the messages in earlier ad images of foreigners. But the globalization of the economy has produced a new ad image of the foreigner: the potential business partner.

When the issue is international business, ad images no longer suggest difference, which might be an obstacle to conducting business. Instead, images of foreigners in international business ads emphasize that Americans and foreigners share a perspective and have a common set of goals. Foreign businesspeople are depicted not as "others"—as an exotic or threatening "them"—but as people just like us. These ads are directed at a much more limited audience—international businesspeople—than are the travel or product ads. Business ads, however, do suggest that there is an alternative to the depiction of foreigners as others, even if it is now limited to the global corporate community.

The most widely circulating images of "otherness" in advertising convey messages about foreigners from a distinctly American point of view and suggest that there are fundamental differences between "us" and "them"; that we have power in our relationships with "them"; and that "they" are available to stimulate, entertain, and serve "us." Media in a global culture may provide more images of foreign people and lands—and international business ads suggest that new kinds of images are emerging—but the underlying message in advertisements about who we are and who they are draws on age-old assumptions about the relationship between powerful Americans and subordinate foreigners.

CONCLUSION

This chapter has looked at the content of mass media by adopting an ideological approach. We have reviewed the underlying theoretical frameworks of ideological analysis and examined several specific cases to detect ideology at work in mass media. As our examples suggest, there is no singular ideology that is promoted by popular media. Researchers who study the ideology of media are interested in the underlying stories about society that the media tell, the range of values that the media legitimize, and the kinds of behaviors that are deemed "normal." Most popular media promote, often in subtle and even contradictory ways, perspectives that support our basic social arrangements and endorse the legitimacy of social institutions, marginalizing attitudes and behaviors that are considered to be out of the "mainstream."

Media images can and sometimes do challenge this mainstream, status quo–oriented ideology by providing a critique of contemporary social organization and norms, but commercialization makes it difficult for media to maintain a critical voice. The search for popularity, wider distribution, and profitability tends to dull the critical edges of media imagery, pushing media back toward more mainstream (and marketable) ideologies. There are, to be sure, media that consistently promote alternative ideological perspectives. Local weekly newspapers, journals of opinion, public access television, and independent films are often quite self-conscious about providing perspectives that differ from the dominant popular media. These alternatives, however, remain on the margins of the media scene, reaching small audiences and lacking the capital to mount a serious challenge to the dominant media.

In this chapter, we have explored the ideology of various media texts, examining the underlying perspectives within the images that confront us every day. As we examine media content, we need to look even more specifically at the ways that mass media represent the social world. In Chapter 6, we turn our attention to the relationship between media images and social inequality.

DISCUSSION QUESTIONS

1. What is ideology and how are media images central to the contemporary "culture wars" in the United States? Use examples to illustrate your analysis.

2. How and why is the concept "hegemony" significant for ideological analysis of media? How does it differ from analyses of "false consciousness"? Where does the concept suggest we look for evidence of ideology at work?

3. How have television images played a role in the cultural conflict about the definition of the family? What is the relationship between changes in images of the family and changes in family structure?

4. Can rap music be seen as a critique of mainstream norms and values, even when popular rap songs are used as advertising jingles? Why or why not?

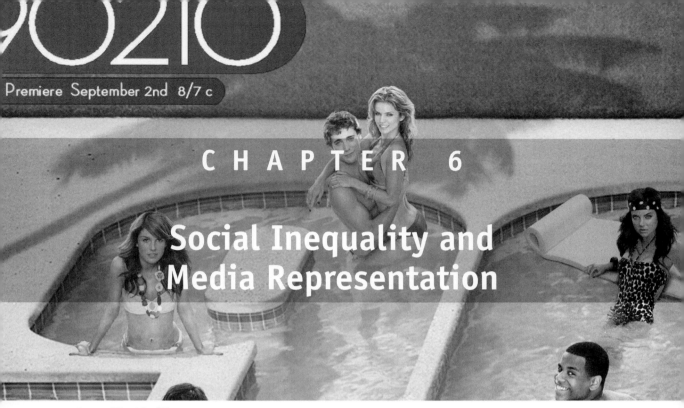

Source: AF archive/Alamy.

The examination of media content traditionally has been the most common type of media analysis, perhaps because of the easy accessibility of media products. The production process takes place in the relative remoteness of movie lots, recording studios, and editors' offices. In contrast, media products surround us and are within easy reach of the researcher.

Whatever the reason, there is an enormous volume of research and commentary on the nature of media content. Rather than try to review this vast literature, we have organized this chapter on media content around the single theme of representation. We explore the question, "How do media representations of the social world compare to the external 'real' world?" As we discuss below, this is not the only possible line of investigation related to media content. However, given our sociological interest in the relationship between the media and the social world, it is a central one.

Furthermore, our discussion focuses on the issue of social inequality. We argue that the creators of media content have often reproduced the inequalities that exist in society based on race, class, gender, and sexual orientation. This is not to say that the media have acted as a mirror, passively reflecting the inequalities of society. Rather, white, middle- and upper-class men have historically controlled the media industry, and media content has largely reflected their perspectives on the world. Therefore, the inequalities in the social world have affected the organization of the media industry that produces media products.

In turn, activists have challenged the media to broaden their narrow perspectives. Some have developed alternative media and told their own stories through words and pictures. Over the years, progressive social change movements have succeeded in altering some facets of social inequality in society at large. This human agency has created changes in the social world, which, in turn, have affected the organization of the media industry. Increasingly diverse contemporary media content reflects these changes to varying degrees.

COMPARING MEDIA CONTENT AND THE "REAL" WORLD

Does media content reflect the realities of the social world? Based on the accumulated volume of media research, the answer is an emphatic no. Content analyses of media products have repeatedly shown them to be quite different from key measurable characteristics of the social world. This gap between the "real" world and media representations of the social world is the subject of this chapter.

"How do media representations of the social world compare to the external 'real' world?" is an important question because we conventionally organize media according to how closely they represent reality. We talk, for example, about fiction versus nonfiction, news or public affairs versus entertainment, documentaries versus feature films, "reality" programs, and so on. The impact of media, as we will see in Part IV, can actually become more significant if media products diverge dramatically from the real world. We tend to become more concerned, for example, when media content lacks diversity or overemphasizes violence, sex, or other limited aspects of the real world.

The question of how media representations of the social world compare to the external "real" world also raises several issues. First, the literature in media and cultural studies reminds us that representations are not reality, even if media readers or audiences may sometimes be tempted to judge them as such. Representations—even those that attempt to reproduce reality, such as the documentary film—are the result of processes of selection that invariably mean that certain aspects of reality are highlighted and others neglected. Even though we often use the "realness" of the images as a basis for evaluating whether we like or dislike particular representations, all representations *re-present* the social world in ways that are both incomplete and narrow.

Second, the media usually do not try to reflect the "real" world. Most of us would like news programs, history books, and documentary films to represent happenings in the social world as fairly and accurately as possible. (After examining the production process, we now know how difficult it is to achieve this, if only because of limited time and resources.) But by its very nature, a science fiction film, for example, will diverge significantly from contemporary social life. Without that gap between reality and media image, the genre would cease to exist.

We cannot push this point too far, however, because even fantasy products such as science fiction films hold the potential for teaching us something about our society. Often, this is the attraction of the genre. When Captain Kirk and Lieutenant Uhura of *Star Trek* kissed on prime-time television in the 1960s, it was the first interracial kiss on a U.S. television series. This media content, though clearly embedded in a fantasy science fiction about the future, just as surely was making a statement about race relations in contemporary America. Social commentary continued in later *Star Trek* spin-offs when producers cast an African American as the commander of *Deep Space Nine* and a woman as captain of *Voyager*. Both of these programs were science fiction, yet clearly both were commenting on social conditions at the time of their creation.

The point is that there is potential social significance in all media products—even those that are clearly make-believe fantasies. Creators of media products are often aware of this fact and use entertainment media to comment on the real social world. In turn, readers and audiences develop at least some sense of the social world through their exposure to both entertainment media and news media. It behooves us, therefore, to attend to what these media messages might be. That includes looking at media forms—including science fiction, soap operas, music videos, and romance novels—that clearly do not claim to accurately reflect society.

A third issue raised by the question of how media representations of the social world compare to the "real" world concerns the troublesome term *real*. In an age in which sociologists teach about the social construction of reality and postmodernists challenge the very existence of a knowable reality, the concept of a "real" world may seem like a quaint artifact from the past. We generally agree with the social constructionist perspective, which suggests that no representation of reality can ever be totally "true" or "real" because it must inevitably frame an issue and choose to include and exclude certain components of a multifaceted reality. However, some social facts seem solid enough to be used as a measure of reality. To give a simple example, we have a pretty good idea of the age distribution in the United States. In 2012, for example, the Census Bureau estimated that about 23 percent of the U.S. population was younger than age 18 (census.gov). Imagine that, for some unknown reason, television situation comedies became inundated with children who made up, say, half of all characters. We could then reliably state that, compared to the real world, such programs featured twice as many children. Such a claim is possible only because we have a reasonably accurate way of measuring age distribution in the population as a whole.

The legitimacy of the question becomes much more dubious, however, with other examples. Is media content more liberal than society at large, as some contend? That depends on how you go about defining *liberal* and how you attempt to measure it in both the media and the "real" world. Such a concept is much more ambiguous than age and, therefore, we have to be careful about claims of "bias" leveled at the media. In the end, we can make some useful comparisons between the content of media and society, but our limited ability to measure the social world necessarily limits such claims.

Finally, the question of how media representations of the social world compare to the "real" world seems to imply that the media *should* reflect society. This premise is not agreed on. For many people, media are an escape from the realities of daily life. Therefore, how "real" media products are is irrelevant to many people. However, it is not necessary to believe that the media should accurately reflect society in order to compare media representations with the social world. Gaps between media content and social reality raise interesting questions that warrant our attention.

THE SIGNIFICANCE OF CONTENT

While this chapter focuses on the content of media, it is important to realize that many researchers study media content to make inferences about other social processes. In other words, they study media content to assess the significance of that content. There are at least five ways in which researchers can assess the significance of media content. They involve linking content (1) to producers, (2) to audience interests, (3) to society in general, (4) to audience effects, or (5) examining content independent of context.

To illustrate, let's return to our hypothetical example about children and situation comedies. If researchers found that child characters appeared on situation comedies twice as often as children do in the real world, then several lines of interpretation would be possible. Each of these different approaches tries to explain the source and significance of media content.

Content as Reflection of Producers

First, it would be possible to infer that this child-centered content reflected the intent of the program writers and producers. This line of interpretation—linking content to producers—encourages us to investigate the social characteristics of situation-comedy writers and producers. We might find that such creative personnel are disproportionately 30-somethings with children of their own, who draw on their own family lives for story inspiration. As a result, a disproportionate percentage of programs feature children. Or perhaps corporate advertisers have expressed strong interest in sponsoring child-related programs, influencing producers to create more such programs. Determining this connection would require research that moved beyond media content and studied media personnel and the production process more generally (exactly the kind of research we examined in Part II). Content analysis would alert us to this issue but by itself could not provide an adequate explanation for the heavy population of children on such programs.

Content as Reflection of Audience Preference

Second, we might infer that perhaps the high number of child characters reflects the audience for situation comedies. This does not necessarily suggest that children constitute a large percentage of the audience. It may simply mean, for example, that many viewers are parents who enjoy watching the antics of young children on situation comedies. Here the implication is that media personnel are merely responding to the interests of their likely audience, not to their own interests or to the influence of the production process. This approach suggests that content is a reflection of audience preference. The idea that media producers are only "giving the people what they want" also implies that people want what they get. To test such claims, researchers must explore more than media content. They must move into the area of audience research.

Content as Reflection of Society in General

Third, some researchers investigate media content as a gauge of social norms, values, and the interests of society in general—not just the audience. Some analysts might suggest that child-dominated situation comedies reflect a high level of social concern for children. They might reflect the fact that we live in a child-centered society where people value children highly. The difficulty in firmly making such sweeping assessments should be clear. To support such claims, research would need to extend well beyond the boundaries of media content.

Content as an Influence on Audiences

Fourth, researchers sometimes examine media content for potential effects on audiences. Perhaps the preponderance of children on television will encourage couples to have children or to have more children. Here, too, the researcher would have to link content analysis with research on audience interpretations—a topic examined in Part IV. The influence of media is so diffuse, however, that a direct link is usually very difficult to establish. The emphasis in this case—in contrast to the first three—is not on content as a reflection of the production process, audiences, or society. Instead, it is on content as a social influence on audiences.

Content as Self-Enclosed Text

Finally, a substantial body of work addresses media content on its own terms. That is, it usually makes no attempt to link content to producers, audiences, or society but instead examines media as a self-enclosed text whose meaning is to be "decoded." For example, in the 2007 thriller *The Brave One,* Jodie Foster plays a New York City radio host whose fiancé is murdered while they are walking through Central Park. In response, Foster's character takes the law into her own hands and kills several people who have committed crimes. One analysis of this film suggests it is a metaphor for the trauma faced by the United States in the wake of the 9/11 attacks, concluding that the film

> is constituted by and constitutive of cultural trauma. Its confrontation with personal trauma functions as a trope for not only recoding the vigilante film but also figuring the nation as posttraumatic. While [*The Brave One*] posits the damaging effects of traumatic loss, it does so in order to mitigate such harms; and, while this film insists that its female hero walk in a man's shoes, it does so while carefully mapping the boundaries of gendered and national identity. (King 2010: 128)

This tradition has many variations associated more with the structuralism and semiology found in literary studies and linguistics than with the content analysis found in the social sciences. However, researchers sometimes combine this approach with studies of production and audience reception under the rubric of cultural studies. It is often difficult or impossible to assess the validity of the claims of such analyses because no standard methods exist in this field. Still, such work can be useful for those whose concerns lie with issues such as the relationship between elements of a text or the language, grammar, and vocabulary of image production.

Having sketched out the different ways in which researchers assess the significance of media content, we now turn to the content itself. As you will note, it is impossible to examine content without touching on the role of producers, audiences, or larger social norms. However, we will focus primarily on media content per se. We will also limit our discussion to a few basic characteristics—race, class, gender, and sexual orientation—that are illustrative of a sociological approach to content analysis and that relate to our theme of inequality.

RACE, ETHNICITY, AND MEDIA CONTENT: INCLUSION, ROLES, AND CONTROL

Sociologists and anthropologists recognize that *race* is a socially constructed concept whose meaning has evolved over time and varies across cultures. There is no biologically valid difference in the genetic makeup of different races. In fact, different blood types might be more biologically significant than different racial classifications. However, racial distinctions have powerful social meaning with profound real-world consequences. Social scientists chart the development and implications of these socially constructed distinctions, especially as they influence discriminatory structures and practices. *Ethnicity*, which refers to shared cultural heritage that often derives from a common ancestry and homeland, is also a cultural creation.

Given their significance in social life, it is not surprising that there has been much interest in content analysis that examines how media messages treat the issue of race and ethnicity. Historically, the U.S. media have taken "whites" to be the norm against which all other racial groups are measured. The taken-for-granted nature of "whiteness" means that it need not be explicitly identified. For example, we generally do not talk about "white culture," "the white community," "the white vote," and so forth. We do, however, often hear reference to "black culture," "the Latino community," and so on. The absence of a racial signifier in this country usually signifies "whiteness." The pervasiveness of white perspectives in media is perhaps its most powerful characteristic.

With whiteness as the unspoken backdrop, the study of race and ethnicity in the U.S. media tends to focus on the portrayal of minorities. To understand how racial difference is portrayed in the mass media, we must recall the earlier roots of racial stereotyping in American culture. Throughout much of U.S. mass media history, blacks, Native Americans, Asians, Latinos, and other racial and ethnic minorities have been, at best, of little consideration to the media industry. Because such minorities comprised a relatively small part of the population, mainstream media did not see them as an important segment of the mass audience. When it came to media content, racial minorities were either ignored or stereotyped in such roles as the Black Mammy, the Indian Maiden, the Latin Lover, or the sinister Asian Warlord. Such stereotypical images were the product of white media producers and bore little resemblance to the realities of the different racial and ethnic groups (Wilson, Gutierrez, and Chao 2012).

When we consider how racial and ethnic differences have been portrayed in the media, three crucial issues emerge. First is the simple issue of *inclusion*. Do media producers include the images, views, and cultures of different racial and ethnic groups in media content? The second issue of concern is the nature of media *roles*. When producers do include members of racial and ethnic minorities in media content, how do they portray them? Here the history of racial and ethnic stereotypes takes center stage. Finally, the *control* of production is crucial. Do people from different racial and ethnic groups have control over the creation and production of media images that feature different groups? This last issue is more about the production process and the nature of the media industry than about media content in itself. However, the history of media suggests that content very often reflects the views of those in control.

Racial and Ethnic Diversity in Media Content

A sample of some research findings on racial and ethnic inclusion in the modern media will help provide historical context and alert us to the changes that have occurred over time. In general, the inclusion of different racial and ethnic groups in the media has changed dramatically, with the media becoming much more diverse today than it was in the past. However, the progress has been uneven and incomplete.

Film. In early Hollywood films of the 1920s and 1930s, blacks were largely absent or were relegated to two roles: entertainer or servant. Not until after World War II did more African Americans begin appearing on the screen and, even then, there were a limited number of available roles (Bogle 2001; Cripps 1993). Since then, the trend has clearly been toward more racial diversity in films, and black roles have been roughly proportional to the black population in the United States. For example, while blacks made up 12.6 percent of the U.S. population, one study found that African American actors had a similar percentage of speaking roles in the 100 top grossing box office films of 2008 (13.2%) (Smith and Choueiti 2011). Asians were overrepresented, accounting for 7.1 percent of speaking roles compared to 4.8 percent of the population. Hispanics (who can be of any race), though, were underrepresented significantly, holding just 4.9 percent of speaking roles in 2008 films even though they were 16.3 percent of the population.

Television. On television through the 1940s and 1950s, the presence of blacks was limited largely to their traditional, stereotypical roles as entertainers and comedians. There were virtually no serious dramatic roles for blacks in this period. Instead, comedies and variety shows were the only regular forum for black talent (Dates 1993). In the 1960s and 1970s, this began to change as television programs featured more blacks and, to a lesser extent, other racial and ethnic groups. By the 1969–1970 season, half of all dramatic television programs had a black character. Surveys conducted from this period through the early 1980s show that, whereas roughly 11 percent of the population was black at that time, 6 percent to 9 percent of all television characters were black (Seggar, Hafen, and Hannonen-Gladden 1981).

During the 1990s, African American representation on television increased and was nearly proportional to their presence in the population as a whole (Greenberg and Brand 1994). By the 2003–2004 season, African Americans accounted for 16 percent of the characters on prime-time television programs—a figure that is larger than their percentage of the U.S. population (Children Now 2004). But this period also reflected significant racial segregation on television. Many programs had all- or nearly all-white casts (Signorielli 2009). Many of the African American characters appeared on programs that

Source: © Bettmann/CORBIS.

From 1968 to 1971, Diahann Carroll portrayed the title character on the sit-com *Julia*. A widowed single mother (her husband was killed in Vietnam), Julia was a nurse and lived a middle-class life. Criticized at the time for being apolitical and distant from the concerns of poor and working-class African Americans, Julia was also one of the earliest nonstereotypical roles for a black woman on network television.

featured mostly minority casts, which were more likely to appear on the smaller television networks (UPN and WB, which merged and became CW) than on the major networks (ABC, CBS, NBC, Fox).

Few other racial or ethnic groups were regularly portrayed on prime-time TV. In the 1970s, only two situation comedies, *Chico and the Man* and the short-lived *Viva Valdez,* centered on Latino characters. The 1980s saw a few major roles for Latino characters on programs such as *Miami Vice* and *L.A. Law.* However, by 1997, only 2.6 percent of characters on prime-time television were Latino (*Reuters* 1998). In more recent years, Latino characters have become increasingly visible but are still badly underrepresented compared to their share of the population as a whole. The Screen Actors Guild (2008) reported that, in 2008, Latino actors accounted for more than 6 percent of film and television roles that year, representing a significant increase from the 1990s but a serious underrepresentation of some 15 percent of the population.

Asian characters, too, were few and far between. It was only in 1994 that an Asian family was used as the premise for a situation comedy, *All-American Girl* (Wilson, Gutierrez, and Chao 2012). More recently, though, the Screen Actors Guild's casting data report found that Asian-Pacific actors accounted for 3.8 percent of film and television roles in 2008, almost double the 2.1 percent reported in 1998, but still slightly below the 4.5 percent of the U.S. population represented by Asian Pacific Americans.

In recent years, racial and ethnic diversity has become a staple of most prime-time television programs. However, whites are still somewhat overrepresented as regular prime-time characters, while blacks, Asians, and, especially, Latinos are all underrepresented—a situation that has been stable for several years. (See Figure 6.1.) In addition, nearly all minority

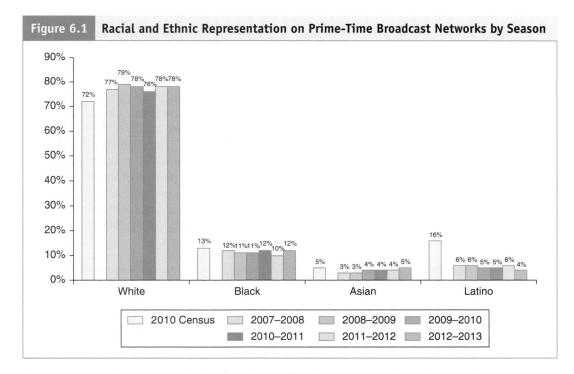

Figure 6.1 | **Racial and Ethnic Representation on Prime-Time Broadcast Networks by Season**

One tabulation of the race and ethnicity of recurring characters on prime time broadcast television finds that whites are overrepresented and Latinos are the most underrepresented, compared to their presence in the population as a whole.

Source: GLAAD 2011, 2012.

actors in recent years played supporting roles for white lead characters. In the 2010s, a few programs have bucked this trend, suggesting more change may be coming. Fox's sitcom, *The Mindy Project*, starred a South Asian American actress—a first for network TV; ABC's political drama *Scandal* starred an African American woman—the first black female lead in a network series in nearly 40 years; and NBC's short-lived, prime-time soap opera *Deception* starred two black actors in the lead roles.

Advertising. Studies of advertising have repeatedly found underrepresentation of minorities. A study of *Cosmopolitan, Glamour,* and *Vogue* in the late 1980s found that only 2.4 percent of ads featured black women (Jackson and Ervin 1991). However, changes in these areas of the media have been significant as well and advertisements are now far more diverse. One study found that models in a 2004 sample of major magazines exhibited significant racial and ethnic diversity: 19.2 percent were black, 14.5 percent Hispanic, and 7.2 percent Asian (Peterson 2007). In addition, a study of ads on prime-time television in 2003 and 2004 found that 43 percent of ads included at least one African American character—although they spoke far less, an average of one second, in comparison to white actors, who speak for an average of five seconds (Hollerbach 2009).

Video Games. As video games have become an increasingly large component of the media landscape, new research on representations within gaming worlds has emerged (Dill et al. 2005; Nakamura 2009). One effort to describe the demographic landscape of the video game universe—a "virtual census" of all the characters in the 150 most popular games on Xbox, Playstation, and Nintendo platforms—found that 80 percent of all video game characters are white, while 11 percent are black, and 5 percent are Asian—figures that closely mimic the U.S. population (Williams et al. 2009). Hispanics, however, are significantly underrepresented in video game worlds, constituting fewer than 3 percent of all characters—about one fifth of their percentage in the U.S. population. The racial and ethnic makeup of primary game characters is less diverse, with whites accounting for 85 percent of the primary roles in video games. In contrast, blacks constitute fewer than 10 percent, and Asians fewer than 2 percent, of primary characters. None of the games studied had Hispanics or Native Americans as a primary character; they were present solely as secondary characters (Williams et al. 2009).

Even this cursory overview shows that most media have begun to include more minorities, though Latinos remain underrepresented. There are simple economic reasons for this development. Increasing racial diversity in the population as a whole means that people of color make up larger segments of the audience than in the past. Many advertisers have become interested in reaching this growing minority market.

This trend has been facilitated by the growth in media outlets—especially cable television and new forms of digital media. In the late 1980s, for example, the new Fox network created a significant number of programs aimed at black audiences because the other networks were largely ignoring this market niche. As the Fox network gained prominence in the 1990s, though, it began competing with the "Big 3" networks for more lucrative white audiences, and its programs, too, became whiter. The process then repeated itself in the late 1990s as the WB and UPN networks (which later merged to become the CW

Network) tried to establish themselves, in part, by appealing to minority audiences. Today, the CW Network has the highest percentage of white recurring characters of all the broadcast networks (GLAAD 2012).

Another result of media outlet growth is that audiences are fragmenting and many Americans are not seeing the growing diversity in mass media. Instead, television programming became more segregated, leaving white audiences watching white programs while black households tuned in to black programs. For example, during the week of July 19–25, 2010, only one program—CBS's *The Mentalist*—was among the 10 highest rated programs in both black and white households (Target Market News 2010).

The segmentation of media audiences has stirred concern that the media are losing their role as a common socializing agent. Media companies compete for advertising dollars by developing products that are targeted at the narrow, demographically specific audiences advertisers want to reach. As targeting becomes more sophisticated, audiences increasingly pay attention to media products that are designed specifically for their demographic, or lifestyle group, and ignore media designed for others. Turow (1997) warns that this process "may accelerate an erosion of the tolerance and mutual dependence between diverse groups that enable a society to work" (p. 7).

Race, Ethnicity, and Media Roles

For much of U.S. history, most white-produced images of other racial groups have been unambiguously racist. As early as the late 1700s, the "comic Negro" stereotype of "Sambo" appeared in novels and plays. On the stage, Dates and Barlow (1993) note, this racist character "was cast in a familiar mold: always singing nonsense songs and dancing around the stage. His dress was gaudy, his manners pretentious, his speech riddled with malapropisms, and he was played by white actors in blackface" (p. 6). Such images in popular culture are the precursor of racist stereotypes in later mass media.

Early Images of Race

Racist stereotypes were peppered throughout popular culture in the 19th century. In the novel *The Spy*, James Fenimore Cooper introduced the stereotypical image of the loyal, devoted, and content house slave who doubled as comic relief because of his superstitious beliefs and fear of ghosts. This image reappeared in many later books and films. Whites in blackface performed racist stage acts, portraying blacks as clownish buffoons. In the 1830s, a white actor named Thomas Dartmouth Rice copied a song-and-dance routine he saw performed on a street corner by a young slave boy. Rice used burnt cork to blacken his face, dressed in tattered clothes, and popularized the Jump Jim Crow routine. Early minstrel shows consisted of whites in blackface copying black music and dance traditions. Native Americans, too, were ridiculed in stage performances. One popular play was titled *The Original, Aboriginal, Erratic, Operatic, Semi-Civilized and Demi-Savage Extravaganza of Pocahontas* (Wilson, Gutierrez, and Chao 2012). Popular songs, sung on the stage and printed in sheet music, also featured many racist stereotypes. Even well-intentioned works, such as Harriet Beecher Stowe's antislavery novel, *Uncle Tom's Cabin,* perpetuated a "positive" image of blacks as gentle, suffering victims with childlike innocence.

The end of slavery brought different but equally racist images. The "contented slave was taken over by the faithful servant: the female side of this stereotype became the domestic mammy caricature, while the male side matured into elderly Uncle Toms" (Dates and Barlow 1993: 11). The folksy character of Uncle Remus, speaking in stereotypical black dialect, became the prototypical apologist for postbellum plantation life. Free black men began appearing as angry, brutal, and beastlike characters in novels. When D. W. Griffith's 1915 film glorifying the Ku Klux Klan, *Birth of a Nation,* featured similar characters, it was an indication that producers would fill the new film medium, as well, with racist images.

By 1920, the United States had fought in World War I "to make the world safe for democracy," according to President Wilson. However, early U.S. films were routinely presenting racist images of white supremacy. Blacks were viciously attacked in films such as *The Wooing and Wedding of a Coon* (1905) and *The Nigger* (1915). The Mexican government banned films such as 1914's *The Greaser's Revenge,* which portrayed Mexicans as bandits, rapists, and murderers. Movies portrayed Asians as a threat to American values, as in the film *The*

Source: Photos 12/Alamy.

Early films often portrayed Asians as an exotic threat. Here the white actor, Boris Karloff, plays an Asian evil criminal menace, Dr. Fu Manchu, in the 1932 film, *The Mask of Fu Manchu.* Based on earlier novels and short stories, a series of Fu Manchu movies were made, all of which featured the title character as a diabolical killer bent on vengeful murder of whites. In one 2007 *AsianWeek* article, Fu Manchu was chosen as the "most infamous yellow face film performance" ever for representing "pure evil, the very embodiment of the 'yellow peril' menace" (Chung 2007).

are now more subtle, and stereotyped thinking is reinforced at levels likely to remain below conscious awareness" (p. 345). Is this modern racism found in the news media? Entman argues that it is; but, at first, some of his claims can seem counterintuitive.

One of his findings was that the local news prominently covered the activities of politically active African Americans. We could easily see the exclusion of such activities as racially motivated but, here, Entman (1992) says that the form of their *inclusion* suggests a racist image. Entman found that "black activists often appeared pleading the interests of the black community, while white leaders were much more frequently depicted as representing the entire community" (p. 355). Thus, Entman argues, it is possible for viewers to get the impression that blacks are pursuing a politics of "special interests" rather than one of public interest. The cycle of racial stereotypes becomes difficult to break. Political marginalization, as a result of years of racism, may spur black leaders to agitate on behalf of the "black community." The news media duly cover this activism. Such coverage unintentionally conveys a message that blacks are seeking special treatment, thus fostering white resentment and perpetuating the political marginalization of African Americans.

Wilson and his colleagues (2012) note other problems in the media coverage of minority issues in general. They argue that in recent years, "the media coverage of people of color has often focused inordinate attention on the more bizarre or unusual elements of minority communities, such as youth gangs, illegal immigration, and interracial violence" (p. 29). While these are legitimate issues, the near-exclusive emphasis on such negative stories "resulted in a new stereotype of racial minorities as 'problem people,' groups either beset by problems or causing them for the larger society" (p. 26).

Figure 6.2	**Fighting Media Stereotypes**

There are numerous organizations that fight stereotyping by the media. The Media Action Network for Asian Americans (MANAA) is one such group. It is a media-monitoring and advocacy organization whose goals include "to educate the public and the media about what persons of Asian Pacific descent find racially offensive, stereotypical, and/or inaccurate and why it is harmful," and "to advocate and provide reinforcement for fair, accurate, sensitive, and balanced depictions of persons of Asian Pacific descent in all facets of media."

MANAA produced an open memo to Hollywood titled "Restrictive Portrayals of Asians in the Media and How to Balance Them." The following is excerpted and adapted from that memo.

"Despite the good intentions of individual producers and filmmakers, limited and unbalanced portrayals of Asians have traditionally been the norm in the entertainment industry. . . . Hollywood typically restricts its portrayals of Asians to a limited range of clichéd stock characters. And this has affected how Asian Americans are perceived and treated in the broader society. . . . Below is a list of restrictive Asian portrayals that are constantly repeated in the mainstream media and an explanation of why each is objectionable. . . . Each description is followed by a 'Stereotype-Buster' that can combat the inaccuracies of such portrayals.

"This list . . . is designed to encourage Hollywood's creative minds to think in new directions—to help our storytellers create more interesting roles for actors by avoiding old, stale images."

(Continued)

Figure 6.2   (Continued)

Stereotype	Stereotype-Buster
"Asian Americans as foreigners who cannot be assimilated."	"Portraying Asians as an integral part of the United States. More portrayals of acculturated Asian Americans speaking without foreign accents."
"Asian cultures as inherently predatory."	"Asians as positive contributors to American society."
"Asian Americans restricted to clichéd occupations."	"Asian Americans in diverse, mainstream occupations: doctors, lawyers, therapists, educators, U.S. soldiers, etc."
"Asians relegated to supporting roles in projects with Asian or Asian American content."	"More Asian and Asian American lead roles."
"Asian male sexuality as negative or non-existent."	"More Asian men as positive romantic leads."
"Unmotivated white-Asian romance."	"Interracial romances should be as well-motivated and well-developed as same-race romances."
"Asian women as 'China dolls'."	"Asian women as self-confident and self-respecting, pleasing themselves as well as their loved ones."
"Asian women as 'dragon ladies'."	"Whenever villains are Asian, it's important that their villainy not be attributed to their ethnicity."
"Asians who prove how good they are by sacrificing their lives."	"Positive Asian characters who are still alive at the end of the story."
"Asian Americans as the 'model minority'."	"The audience empathizing with an Asian character's flaws and foibles."
"Asianness as an 'explanation' for the magical or supernatural."	"Asian cultures as no more or less magical than other cultures."
"Anti-Asian racial slurs going unchallenged."	"If absolutely necessary for a film or TV project, anti-Asian racial slurs should be contextualized as negative and insulting."
"Asian arts as negative when practiced by Asians but positive when practiced by whites."	"Culturally distinct Asian skills positively and realistically employed by Asian people."
"Lead Asian roles labeled 'Amerasian' or 'Eurasian' solely to accommodate white actors."	"Until the proverbial playing field is truly level, Asian roles—especially lead roles—should be reserved for Asian actors."

Source: Adapted from Media Action Network for Asian Americans, http://www.manaa.org/asian_stereotypes.html.

In his study, Entman (1992) criticizes the portrayal of politically active African Americans as being inadvertently racist. However, he also criticizes the regular use of blacks who "did not talk in angry or demanding tones" (p. 357). He is referring to black newscasters, who are generally "unemotional, friendly but businesslike" (p. 357). Station managers often use a black newscaster as a coanchor, with a white newscaster, for the local news. While this practice may be seen as a very positive step, Entman suggests that "[s]howing attractive, articulate Blacks in such a prestigious public role implies that Blacks are not inherently inferior or socially undesirable—and that racism is no longer a serious impediment to black progress" (p. 358).

Entman's analysis suggests that we have to understand race and the media in a holistic fashion. Racially diverse news anchors really do not indicate much progress if, at the same time, the content of news remains racially skewed. Real change will come when all aspects of the media—including media content—more accurately reflect the racial diversity of society.

Entman (1992) suggests that we must pay closer attention to how the process of media production influences the content of the media. Entman believes that the production norms of news are linked with the perpetuation of stereotypical images. To create dramatic stories, for example, reporters will often choose sound bites from black leaders that are emotional and suggestive of conflict. Such dramatic quotes, though sometimes misleading, follow media conventions for "good television." The unintended result is that such norms and practices contribute to stereotypical images of African Americans.

These stereotypical images are often subtle, as Entman and Rojecki (2000) found in their survey of various forms of media. On local television news, for example, they found that crime stories tend to overrepresent both black perpetrators and white victims. Compared to whites, blacks were more likely to be shown in mug shots and were twice as likely to be shown under the physical custody of police. Thus, the authors contend, blacks tend to be portrayed in ways that make them more threatening and less sympathetic than whites.

Much of the news coverage of Hurricane Katrina in New Orleans in 2005 took a similar approach. By depicting African Americans as either helpless victims or looters, in contrast to depictions of whites as rescuers and protectors, news media undermined their compassionate tone by reinforcing negative stereotypes. One study of new photographs in Katrina coverage in the most widely circulating daily newspapers in the United States concludes that photojournalism of events in New Orleans built upon and reproduced the kind of modern racism that Entman and others have described: "The overwhelming representation of White military and social service personnel 'saving' the African-American 'refugees' may be one of the most significant themes in images of people in the coverage" (Kahle, Yu, and Whiteside 2007: 86).

Race and Class

Entman's (1992) study hints at—but does not explore—the intervening issue of class in the portrayal of African Americans. He is, in effect, contrasting black anchors who exude upper-middle-class manners and confidence with the poor and working-class blacks featured in many news accounts. To understand contemporary media images of different racial groups, therefore, it is important to consider their class (and, as we will see, their gender). There is no longer any single image of African Americans in the mainstream media.

The intervention of class in the portrayal of blacks on television has resulted in a bifurcated set of images (Gray 1989, 2004). On one hand, even though audiences are more fragmented now, middle-class blacks have become mainstream in prime-time entertainment programs. Epitomized by *The Cosby Show* of the 1980s, these programs portray African American families who have succeeded in attaining a piece of the traditional American Dream. On the other hand, news coverage and documentaries about blacks tend to focus on poor African Americans in the so-called underclass, mired in drugs, crime, and violence. One implicit message in these contrasting images may be that, because some blacks have clearly succeeded, the failure of other blacks is their own fault.

In their conclusion to a sweeping review of black images in television, radio, music, films, advertising, and PR, Dates and Barlow (1993) suggest that the tension between white-produced images of blacks and black cultural resistance "has become increasingly entangled in more complex social conflicts and concerns. In effect, the primacy of the 'color line' is being challenged by generational, gender, and class differences" (p. 527). We have moved beyond the point where we can say that a single set of media images represents African Americans—or any other racial or ethnic group.

Controlling Media Images of Race

The absence or stereotyping of different racial groups in the media highlights a fact often taken for granted: Affluent, white men have historically controlled the mainstream mass media. But although whites have often propagated racist images, it is important to note that, historically, African Americans and other minorities have responded by producing a culture of resistance. From the slave chronicles of Frederick Douglass to the poetry of Langston Hughes, from the blues of Bessie Smith to the rap of Public Enemy, from the diverse work of Paul Robeson to the films of Spike Lee—to name just a few of the better-known personalities—black activists and artists have created a counterculture that opposes the racist stereotypes being propagated in white-owned media and culture. *Freedom's Journal* was the first African American newspaper in the United States. Its editors wrote in the first 1827 edition, "We wish to plead our own cause. Too long have others spoken for us. Too long has the publick been deceived by misrepresentations" (in Rhodes 1993: 186). The importance of presenting a distinct "black perspective" continues to this day, as Jacobs (2000) chronicles in his study of the black press's coverage of major events such as the Watts and Rodney King uprisings.

These sentiments also underlie efforts by other racial groups to create alternatives to mainstream media. In journalism, for example, the first Latino paper, *El Misisipi,* was published in 1808 (by a white publisher) in New Orleans. The first Native American newspaper, *Cherokee Phoenix,* was published in 1828. What was probably the first Asian American newspaper, *The Golden Hills' News,* first appeared in San Francisco around 1851. All three publications were bilingual, and ever since, bilingual publications have served Latino, Asian, and Native American communities in many areas (Wilson, Gutierrez, and Chao 2012).

People of color, as well as women and people promoting the interests of the working class and poor, have had to confront a basic dilemma: They have had to choose between developing alternative media and struggling to change mainstream media from within. The first strategy—developing alternative media—has the advantages of being feasible with more limited financial resources and of promising control for the producers. The Internet, for example, has enabled the creation of a vast array of websites that provide news, entertainment, and political discussion specifically aimed at different racial and ethnic groups. However, this approach usually means sacrificing the chance of reaching a mass and broad audience in favor of a smaller, narrower one, in part because media operations working on a shoestring budget cannot hope to match the slick, seductive production quality and staffing levels of the mainstream media.

The second strategy—changing the mainstream media from within—offers an opposite set of advantages and challenges. Mainstream success can result in access to major financial resources that allow a product to reach millions of people. However, ownership and control of mainstream media are still predominantly in the hands of wealthy, white men. While some people of color and some women have worked their way into positions of authority and influence, they are still vastly underrepresented.

The example of newspapers illustrates this. In the more than 30 years between 1978 and 2012, the percentage of racial and ethnic minorities at U.S. newspapers tripled from 4 percent to 12.4 percent. Although this was progress, it was far slower progress than news editors had anticipated, and it still woefully underrepresented minorities, who actually make up about 37 percent of the U.S. population. Minorities are also concentrated at lower levels of the newsroom hierarchy, making up 26 percent of newsroom interns, 16 percent of photographers and videographers, 13 percent of reporters and bloggers, and only 10 percent of supervisors (ASNE 2013). One way minority journalists have worked for change in their field is by organizing a variety of associations that often collaborate on efforts to promote diversity in the newsroom. These include the National Association of Hispanic Journalists, the Asian American Journalists Association, the National Association of Black Journalists, and the Native American Journalists Association.

Minority underrepresentation exists in other media fields as well. In 2009 films, minorities were just 5 percent of writers (Writers Guild of America, West 2011). On broadcast and cable television in the 2011–2012 season, minorities made up 15.6 percent of the writers (an increase from 7.5% 12 years earlier) and 7.8 percent of executive producers (Hunt 2013).

GENDER AND MEDIA CONTENT

In some ways, the media's history of portraying women parallels its history of portraying people of color. Women were often marginalized in all types of media. Simple, blatantly stereotypical images dominated the earlier years of mass media. As media audiences and the media industry felt the influence of movements struggling for women's rights, these stereotypical images gave way to a wider diversity of images and roles for women. Here too, then, we see a history of injustice, inequality, and change.

Women: Presence and Control in the Media

Family and heterosexual relationships are central to the plots of many films, music videos, and television programs, ensuring that women (unlike racial minorities) are regularly included in these media. However, reviews of the extensive literature on gender and the media reveal a fundamental inequality in the frequency of appearance of women and men. Prime-time television, for example, has long featured more portrayals of men than women, and men appear more often in lead roles (Fejes 1992; Greenberg and Worrell 2007; Signorielli 2009). Though the gap has been closing over the years, in the 2012–2013 season, men were still a majority of recurring characters on prime-time broadcast TV—55 percent, compared to women's 45 percent (GLAAD 2012). Similarly, characters in animated television programs and in video games are disproportionately male (Klein and Shiffman 2009; Robinson et al. 2009).

Control of the creation and production of media images is also in male hands—though women have made substantial gains over the past two decades. In the top 250 domestic grossing films in 2012, women were just 9 percent of directors, 15 percent of writers, 17 percent of executive producers, 20 percent of editors, and 2 percent of cinematographers (Lauzen 2013). On broadcast and cable television programs in the 2011–2012 season, women were just 18.6 percent of executive producers and 30.5 percent of writers. One out of ten television programs had no women writers on staff at all (Hunt 2013). In local broadcast news, women made up 40 percent of the workforce in 2009 but only 28.4 percent of news directors. Similarly, in local radio news, women made up 29.2 percent of the workforce but only 18.1 percent of news directors (Papper 2010). At daily newspapers in 2012, women made up 34.6 percent of supervisors, 39.9 percent of copy/layout editors and online producers, 37.8 percent of reporters, and 24.9 percent of photographers and videographers (ASNE 2013).

Indeed, the dynamics relating to gender are similar to those found in the discussion of race and ethnicity. Women are generally not in positions of control and, perhaps as a result, are less likely than men to be prominently featured in media products. Summarizing the status of women and minorities in television—in words that apply to other media forms as well—sociologist Darnell Hunt (2013: 1) concludes that "despite a few pockets of promise— much more work must be done on the television diversity front before the corps of writers telling our stories looks significantly more like us as a nation."

Changing Media Roles for Women . . . and Men

The media images of women and men reflect and reproduce a whole set of stereotypical but changing gender roles. On prime-time television, men are more likely than women to be cast as main characters, and men typically speak more than women. In addition, we are likely to see women focused on family, friends, and romance, while men are more likely to be portrayed in work-related activities (Lauzen, Dozier, and Horan 2008). Men are also more likely than women to be portrayed as having high-status jobs—in traditionally male occupations— and are less likely to be shown in the home (Glascock 2001). Female television characters are, on average, younger than male characters; and middle-aged male characters are more likely than their female counterparts to "play leadership roles, wield occupational power, and have goals" (Lauzen and Dozier 2005: 253).

In a summary of television roles that remains an accurate overall assessment, Fejes (1992) concluded that "men, as portrayed on adult television, do not deviate much from the traditional patriarchal notion of men and masculinity" (p. 12). They are generally portrayed in the media as powerful and successful. They "occupy high-status positions, initiate action and act from the basis of rational mind as opposed to emotions, are found more in the world of things as opposed to family and relationships, and organize their lives around problem solving" (p. 12). Alerting us to the intersection of different identities, Fejes points out that "the masculinity portrayed on television is a white, middle-class heterosexual masculinity" (p. 12). While important distinctions exist, we can make similar observations about advertising, film, music, and other media.

Women's roles have often reflected similar stereotypes about femininity. Over the years, the dominant roles for women have been as mother, homemaker, or sexual object. The media industry, though, responded to feminists organizing for social change. As with racial stereotypes, the industry has muted the blatant simplicity of stereotypical gender images in more recent years. There is certainly a wider palette of roles and media images of women in the 2010s than there was a few decades ago. However, the inequality that women still face in society as a whole is clearly reflected in the unequal treatment women receive in the media. Some of this unequal treatment, such as that in sexist advertising and degrading pornography, is straightforward and easy to spot, as are some of the stereotypical roles writers still create for women on television situation comedies and dramas. However, like racist stereotypes, sexist stereotypes have often taken subtler forms, as in the coverage of women's sports.

The Case of Women's Sports

For more than a quarter century, researchers have studied both the quantity of coverage women's sports receive as well as the quality of that coverage. They have found that the amount of coverage women's sports receive is minuscule compared to men's sports, and they have also noted that the quality of this limited coverage has remained stereotypical, though less blatantly so.

In one early study, Tuggle (1997) found that ESPN's *Sports Center* and CNN's *Sports Tonight* devoted less than 5 percent of their coverage to women's sports, concluding that "in nearly every measurable way, the two programs portrayed women's sports as less important than men's athletic competition." More than a decade later, Messner and Cooky (2010) found that less than 2 percent of local television sports coverage focused on women's sports; similarly, ESPN's *Sports Center* devoted less than 2 percent of its coverage to women's sports. Messner and Cooky conclude that the coverage of women's sports is just as marginal as it had been in 1990, when they first began studying sports news on television. In fact, they note that "the gap between TV news and highlights shows' coverage of women's and men's sports has not narrowed, it has widened" (p. 22). Kian, Mondello, and Vincent (2009) summarize the past decade of research on media and women's sports, noting that, "despite the vast increase in the number of women and girls who actively participate or once played organized sports, research has consistently shown sport media generally provide far more coverage of men's sports than women's sports. This holds true in nearly all levels of competition and in the vast majority of sports" (p. 447).

Source: Doug Pensinger/Getty Images.

Research shows that women's sports receive less coverage than men's sports and that the nature of that coverage often has been stereotypically sexist—though less blatantly so in recent years.

Concern about women's sports coverage extends beyond quantity to include the quality of the coverage that does exist. Early, blatant stereotypical images of women in sports have given way to coverage that is still stereotypical but less obviously so. Studies conducted in the 1970s and 1980s found that, on the rare occasions when women athletes were covered on television, they "were likely to be overtly trivialized, infantilized, and sexualized" (Messner, Duncan, and Jensen 1993: 123). According to Schell (1999), women were often portrayed as "sexual objects available for male consumption rather than as competitive athletes."

When Messner and his associates (1993) studied television coverage of the 1989 men's and women's National Collegiate Athletic Association (NCAA) and various matches in the 1989 U.S. Open tennis tournament, they found the commentary framed women's and men's sports differently. Gender was constantly "marked" in women's basketball coverage, as in "NCAA *Women's* National Championship Game" or "*women's* basketball." In contrast, television coverage referred to men's competition in a universal way, without mentioning gender at all: "The Final Four," "The NCAA National Championship Game," and so on. The naming of athletes also differed by gender. The announcers called women "girls," "young ladies," and "women." They never called men "boys," only "men," "young men," or "young fellas." Commentators covering tennis matches referred to female athletes by first name seven times as often as they did male athletes. In basketball, the ratio was about two to one. Messner and his associates reminded readers that "dominants generally have license to refer to subordinates (younger people, employees, lower-class people, ethnic minorities, women, etc.) by their first names" (p. 128). Finally, an array of differences appeared in the language used to describe athletes. Male coaches "yelled," while female coaches "screamed." While an excellent shot by a female player was "lucky," excellent play from a male player showed that he was "imposing his will all over this court."

However, coverage has since improved somewhat. In a 2010 report, Messner and Cooky examined ESPN's *SportsCenter* as well as television sports news on the local network affiliates in Los Angeles. They found that stories that trivialize women's sports and sexualize female athletes were now rare, noting that the disparaging portrayals and sexualized humor have largely disappeared from sports news. Instead of sexualized humor and images, which aim to make women's sports attractive to male viewers, one new wrinkle in recent coverage is the focus on women athletes as family members, emphasizing their roles as mothers, wives, or girlfriends—another strategy for attracting male audiences. In general, however, sports reporters have not developed a new approach to covering women's sports. Instead, as Messner and Cooky point out, when sports news programs stopped portraying women athletes in trivial and sexualized ways, the overall amount of coverage of women's sports on television declined. Ultimately, as these studies demonstrate, coverage of women's sports is symptomatic of the subtle ways in which media both reflect and re-create gender inequality.

It is possible that the Internet may provide new opportunities for more in-depth and substantive coverage of women's sports. One recent study (Kian, Mondello, and Vincent 2009) found that ESPN.com focused substantial attention on the 2006 NCAA women's basketball tournament. In the coverage of March Madness that year, 38 percent of the stories on ESPN.com focused on the women's tournament. This stood in sharp contrast to CBSSportsline.com, where only 6 percent of the stories focused on the women's tournament. Because ESPN was broadcasting the complete women's tournament, regular online coverage of women's basketball may have served a valuable promotional role for ESPN. Perhaps more important, Kian and his colleagues report that online coverage did not feature the common gender stereotypes described in studies of television coverage. In particular, they note that "there was a significantly higher proportion of descriptors about the positive skill level/accomplishments and psychological/emotional strengths in women's basketball articles than those on men's basketball" (p. 491). Whether online media will provide a regular forum for more robust coverage of women's sports remains an open question.

CLASS AND THE MEDIA

Interestingly, researchers have not given a great deal of attention to class in media content. There are fewer studies about class in television, for example, than about either race or gender. Yet class permeates media content, and it is useful to examine both the class distribution of people in the media and the roles given to characters of different class status. It is also important to keep in mind the relationship between class and the media industry.

For Advertisers, "Some People Are More Valuable Than Others"

Class underlies the media industry in a distinctive way. Class considerations connect advertisers, producers, content, and audiences. The for-profit, advertiser-driven nature of all commercial media means that advertisers are keenly interested in the economic status of media consumers. They want to reach people with enough disposable income to buy their products. You can guess which class a media product reaches by examining the ads that accompany it. Everybody has to buy toothpaste and breakfast cereal, but when a program or publication features ads for jewelry, expensive cars, and investment services, you know it is aimed at an affluent audience. (Take a look at the Sunday morning talk shows, for example. Whom do you think advertisers are trying to reach?) Media outlets, in turn, want to attract affluent consumers and often gear their content to a more affluent reader or viewer.

The influence of class can sometimes take on strange dimensions. For example, one of the lesser-known strategies sometimes employed in the newspaper business is to *reduce* circulation to increase profits. While at first this may seem to be an impossible strategy, here is how publishers make it work. Newspapers receive about two thirds of their revenue from advertisers, not readers; therefore, they must be sensitive to advertiser needs to stay in business. In turn, as noted above, advertisers want to reach only readers with enough disposable income to buy their products. In the information that major newspapers send to potential advertisers, they usually tout the affluence of the consumers who read their paper because these are the readers advertisers want to reach. To sell advertising space at a premium, newspapers want to improve the demographic profile (in terms of average household income) of their readership. They can do this in two ways: Attract more affluent readers and/or get rid of poorer readers.

The first approach is reflected in media content that is clearly aimed at more affluent households. This content includes major business sections with extensive stock market reports and "Style" sections with articles that highlight fashion, culture, restaurants, and other upscale consumer activities. The second strategy is more direct. Some papers have made it difficult for poor people to buy their product. Publishers sometimes limit the paper's distribution in poor neighborhoods and in some cases even raise the price of the paper in these areas while reducing it in wealthier areas! In the 1990s, the *Los Angeles Times,* for example, raised its daily sales price in inner-city neighborhoods from 35 cents to 50 cents. At the same time, it reduced the price to 25 cents in affluent surrounding counties (Cole 1995).

Newspaper publishers are not the only ones who recognize that affluent people are more important for the media industry than poor or working-class people. In the 1970s, ABC issued a profile of its viewing audience, highlighting its desirable demographics. The network titled the profile "Some People Are More Valuable Than Others" (Wilson, Gutierrez, and Chao 2012: 25). It is important, therefore, to keep in mind the underlying profit-oriented nature of the media when we examine class in media content.

Class and Media Content

Overwhelmingly, the American society portrayed in the media is wealthier than it is in the real world. The real world is predominantly working or lower-middle class, with the vast majority of Americans working in service, clerical, or production jobs. Media, however, portray the social world as one heavily populated by the middle class—especially

CBS's legal and political drama, *The Good Wife*, is one of many programs that is set in an upper-middle-class environment, with an affluent home and furnishings. There is a gourmet kitchen in the background, elegant dining room furniture, stylish wall sconces, and tastefully framed artwork.

Source: CBS Photo Archive/Getty Images.

In contrast to the usual middle-class fare, the set of CBS's comedy, *2 Broke Girls*, suggests something closer to reality for working-class Americans of more modest means. While quite large for a Brooklyn apartment, the kitchen features an aging refrigerator, old-fashioned linoleum flooring, a utility sink, and rough shelving—certainly not an upper-middle-class gourmet kitchen.

Source: AF archive/Alamy.

Social Class in Prime-Time Programs. The class status of television characters is communicated to viewers in various ways, one of which is the set used to represent home life, as seen here in two contrasting programs.

middle-class professionals. Images showing the comfortable, middle-class life fill magazines, films, and television programs. These images are most obvious in advertising. Simply put, advertisements aimed at selling products do not feature poor people and rarely feature working-class people. Instead, comfortable middle-class and affluent upper-class images reign in ads.

Family-Based Situation Comedies

Entertainment is little different from advertising. Butsch (2003) examined 315 family-based situation comedies that aired from 1946 to 2000. Because programs based in a workplace—such as police shows—would dictate the occupation of the main characters, he intentionally excluded these. The focus of domestic-based situation comedies is home life away from work. Thus, creators of such programs are free to give their characters a wide range of potential occupations. Butsch found that only 14 percent of such programs featured blue-collar, clerical, or service workers as heads of the household. More than two thirds (68%) of home-based situation comedies featured middle-class families. And the adults in these television families weren't your run-of-the-mill professionals, either. The elite professions were vastly overrepresented. Doctors outnumbered nurses 9 to 1, professors outnumbered schoolteachers 4 to 1, and lawyers outnumbered less glamorous accountants 10 to 1. All these high-paying jobs for television characters meant lots of disposable income, and families in these situation comedies overwhelmingly lived in beautiful middle-class homes equipped with all the amenities.

There is an exception to the relative scarcity of working-class characters on sitcoms: animated programs. Ever since Fred in *The Flintstones* was written as a rock quarry "crane" operator, prime-time animated comedies have highlighted working-class characters: Peter Griffin of *Family Guy* was a blue-collar worker; Cleveland Brown in *The Cleveland Show* was a cable installer; *King of the Hill* featured a propane salesman; and Homer in the long-running program *The Simpsons* was a woefully underqualified technician in a nuclear power plant. The prominence of the working class in cartoon portrayals contrasts sharply with its scarcity in live-action programs.

In recent years, *2 Broke Girls* and *The Middle* have each dealt with working-class life in different ways, but few other prime-time broadcast programs have. The exceptions to the relative absence of prominent, working-class characters are notable precisely because there have been so few of them. Doug Heffernan in *King of Queens* (1998–2007) was a deliveryman, and his wife was a secretary. The main character in *Roseanne* (1988–1997) held various jobs, including a factory worker, waitress, and shampooer in a beauty salon, while her husband struggled as a construction worker and mechanic. Al Bundy, the father in the highly dysfunctional family on *Married With Children* (1987–1997), was a shoe salesman. Harriet Winslow, the mother on *Family Matters* (1989–1997), worked various jobs in a department store while her husband, Carl, was a police officer. Archie Bunker from *All in the Family* (1971–1979) was a bigoted dock worker. *Good Times* (1974–1979) featured a working-poor family in Chicago's housing projects; Florida was a former maid and her husband, James, fought unemployment, sometimes working two low-paying jobs when he could find them. Ralph in *The Honeymooners* (1955–1956) was a bus driver. Interestingly, such working-class programs often highlighted their characters' aspirations for middle-class life through the launching of small businesses. For example, Archie Bunker became a bar owner in the later program, *Archie's Place* (1979–1983). Both parents on *Roseanne* opened up businesses of their own: an unsuccessful motorcycle shop and a diner. The title characters in *2 Broke Girls* are trying to save enough money to start their own business.

In contrast to the relatively few portrayals of working-class families, there are a large number of domestic-based situation comedies in which the head of the household had a middle-class job. The list of lawyers, doctors, architects, advertising executives, journalists, and businesspeople on such programs is a long one. Butsch (2003) argues that the predominance of middle-class characters in these television situation comedies conveys a subtle but significant message. The few working-class characters who do populate some programs are the deviant exception to the norm, and therefore, it must be their own fault that they are less economically successful. (This observation is quite similar to the one Gray [1989] made when examining the portrayal of blacks in the media. As you may remember, Gray argued that middle-class blacks on entertainment programs were the "norm" against which real-life blacks in the news were contrasted.)

The message that people in the working class are responsible for their fate is a quintessential middle-class idea that ignores the structural conditions that shape social class. It is also an idea reinforced by another tendency identified by Butsch (2003). In contrast to most middle-class television families, the father in working-class families is usually ridiculed as an incompetent, though sometimes lovable, buffoon. Ralph Kramden, Fred Flintstone, Cleveland Brown, Peter Griffin, Doug Heffernan, Al Bundy, and Homer Simpson are perhaps the most obvious cases. All, to varying degrees, were simpletons who pursued foolish get-rich schemes and wound up in trouble because they simply weren't very smart. Each of these shows portrayed the female main character as more levelheaded and in control. Often, these programs even portrayed the children of working-class men as smarter and more competent than their fathers. In fact, Butsch (2005) argues that television representations of working-class men have followed a relatively standard script for five decades.

> While there have been variations and exceptions, the stock character of the ineffectual, even buffoonish, working-class man has persisted as the dominant image. In the prime-time tapestry he is contrasted with consistently competent working-class wives and children and manly middle-class fathers—a composite image in which working-class men are demasculinized and their class status justified. (p. 133)

Butsch (2003) acknowledges that this kind of program sometimes also ridiculed middle-class fathers but not nearly as often as working-class fathers. Instead, the norm in comedies with middle-class families—from *Father Knows Best* and *Leave It to Beaver* to *Bewitched* and the *Brady Bunch* to the *Cosby Show* and *The Wonder Years*—is for middle-class fathers to be competent at their jobs and often to be wise and capable parents. The implication, argues Butsch, is that working-class families struggle because of incompetence and lack of intelligence, while middle-class families succeed because of competence and intelligence. Such images help reinforce the idea that class-based inequality is just and functional.

Tabloid Talk Shows and Hollywood Films

Daytime television talk shows and Hollywood movies are two other media genres where class issues are evident. In very distinct ways, each tends to help reinforce myths about class.

Daytime talk shows featuring ordinary citizens first began appearing in the United States in the 1970s but reached their peak of popularity in the 1980s and 1990s. Early daytime talk show pioneer Phil Donahue often featured serious discussion about contested issues such as abortion, women's rights, and new cultural trends. Defenders of daytime talk shows saw them as providing a unique space for the inclusion of voices that were otherwise ignored. In his study of these programs, Gamson (1998) notes, "Talk shows, defenders claim, give voice to common folks and visibility to invisible folks. . . . Indeed, Donahue and others assert, the talk show genre was and is a 'revolutionary' one. 'It's called democracy,' Donahue argues, 'but [before my program] there were no shows that—every day, let just folks stand up and say what-for. I'm proud of the democracy of the show'" (p. 14).

Such democratization had it benefits. Gamson (1998) credits these talk shows with increasing the visibility of gays, lesbians, bisexuals, and transgender people in American households. However, especially as the genre evolved over time, the format and structure of these programs presented a wildly distorted take on "common folks." They highlighted tawdry subjects, encouraged conflict, and orchestrated bizarre spectacles, becoming known as "tabloid talk shows" or "trash TV."

As a consequence, one of the only television forums where working-class and poor people were routinely spotlighted ended up perpetuating the myth that such people were undisciplined, violent, lazy, sex-crazed, and generally dysfunctional. Sensationalistic talk shows, such as those hosted by Jerry Springer and Maury Povich, often highlighted particularly extreme lifestyles of people from poor or working-class backgrounds. Sought out precisely for their wild behaviors—and often coached by producers to exaggerate such antics to create dramatic and entertaining television—guests were treated as freak shows to entertain audiences.

Television is not alone in its relative dismissal and distorted representation of working-class people. With some notable exceptions (Zaniello 2003), especially in the early years of filmmaking (Ross 1999), movies have highlighted a myth of classlessness in America, emphasizing opportunities for individual mobility in the form of the classic American Dream rather than seriously addressing structural sources of inequality and the value of working people uniting to promote social change (Bodnar 2006). In fact, this focus on individualism, as opposed to collective action, is another key feature of media content.

The Union Taboo

If media rarely show working-class folks, they are even less likely to show working people in labor unions, despite the fact that more than 14 million Americans belong to a union. And as Puette (1992) has shown, the media's portrayal of unions has been anything but sympathetic. Like the stereotypical images of racial groups and women, the media stereotypes of unions have evolved over the years. After examining the image of labor unions in Hollywood movies, television dramas, TV news, and editorial cartoons, Puette argues that there are some basic "lenses" that color and distort media portrayals of organized labor and its leaders. Among these media images are the stereotypes that unions protect and encourage unproductive, lazy, and insubordinate workers; that unions undermine America's ability to compete internationally; that union leaders, because they do not come from the educated or cultured (privileged) classes, are more likely to be corrupted by power than are business or political leaders; and that unions are no longer necessary. Certainly, unions are far from perfect organizations, and they are fair game for media criticism. However, with very few exceptions, Puette's analysis points to a systematic and relentless disparagement of the most visible effort at collective empowerment by working Americans.

A decade later Martin (2003) added to the study of media coverage of unions, examining the reasons why the coverage is so poor. His analysis focuses on the idea that media outlets relate to their audiences almost exclusively as consumers, rather than as workers. By focusing on consumer issues, commercial media manage to sidestep the actual questions involved in labor disputes. For example, the news media spends more time highlighting travel delays for passengers than they do on why airline employees have gone on strike. News media conventions also rely on simply reporting "both sides" of the story, rarely informing viewers or readers about the veracity of the conflicting claims. Such coverage is uninformative and tends to portray labor disputes as bickering that is of little relevance to the audience.

The idea of a positive—or at least balanced—portrayal of a labor union is so rare on U.S. television that when one does occur it becomes notable. When the police drama *The Bridge* first appeared on CBS, the *Los Angeles Times* television critic noted that the program would appear foreign to viewers not because it was set in Canada but because of its major storyline. "Americans will know they're viewing an import the moment the uber narrative makes itself clear. 'The Bridge' is about a street cop attempting to rid the force of corruption through . . . wait for it . . . its union" (McNamara 2010). In addition to a rare positive portrayal of a union, the program also highlighted class issues. The show's title refers to a bridge that separates a wealthy Toronto neighborhood from a poor one. The program was canceled after just three episodes aired in the United States but was renewed for another season in more union-friendly Canada.

News Media

Class enters directly into news media content as well. News tends to highlight issues of concern to middle- and upper-class readers and viewers. Take the example of stock market reports. Fewer than half of American families own any stock at all—directly or indirectly (such as through mutual funds, pensions, or retirement accounts). In fact, over 80 percent of the nation's stocks (whether owned directly or indirectly) are owned by just the wealthiest 10 percent of the nation's families (Wolf 2012). Thus, the vast majority of the public is unlikely to be interested in stock reports. Most Americans do not even understand stock listings and reports. Yet stock market reports are a prominent feature of news programs and newspapers. Now think for a moment. When was the last time you saw a news story explaining how to apply for welfare benefits or an extension on unemployment insurance, or reviewing the legal rights of workers to form a union, or to learn about health and safety hazards in the workplace? Even suggesting such stories might seem odd because it contradicts our taken-for-granted notion of what news is "supposed" to be.

On the whole, the news reflects a middle- and upper-class view of the world. In this world, newspaper business pages flourish, but labor reporters are almost an extinct breed. News may address "regular" people as consumers, but it almost never addresses them as workers. Even consumer-oriented stories are scarce because they have the potential to offend advertisers. For example, the *San Jose Mercury News* once published an innocuous feature story advising consumers on how to buy a new car. The prospect of well-informed customers apparently concerned a group of 47 local auto dealers. They retaliated by collaborating and canceling 52 pages of advertising in the paper's weekly "Drive" section—a loss of $1 million for the paper. While pressure from local car dealers is infamous in the newspaper industry, this time the paper went to the Federal Trade Commission (FTC), which ruled that the auto dealers had illegally conspired. The dealers reached an agreement with the FTC and agreed not to boycott the newspaper in the future (Chiuy 1995). This episode is a dramatic illustration of how advertisers can influence media content—directly or indirectly. Advertisers do not want media content to interfere with the "buying mood" of the public.

The people who populate news and public affairs programs also represent a skewed sample of American life. "Hard news" usually features people in positions of power, especially politicians, professionals, and corporate executives. We might argue that, for many journalists, the very working definition of news is what those in power say and do. As we saw in Chapter 4, the organizational structure of journalism also favors coverage of the wealthy and powerful. The industry organizes its news beats around powerful political institutions, such as the city hall, the state house, and federal offices. People with substantial resources and influence can also command attention from the media by supplying journalists with packaged information, such as press releases, press conferences, and pseudo-events. The only regular features on working-class and poor people are likely to come from the reporter on the crime beat.

Unlike straight news broadcasts, public affairs programs offer a great deal of flexibility in the list of guests who are invited by producers to comment on and analyze current issues. Yet the class characteristics of the guests on such programs are also heavily skewed toward professionals. On prestigious public affairs programs, politicians and professionals have long dominated the guest lists (Croteau and Hoynes 1994). Representatives of organizations speaking on behalf of working people are almost nonexistent on such programs. Public television in general is skewed toward professional sources, usually leaving the public out of the picture (Croteau, Hoynes, and Carragee 1996).

Finally, there is often a racial dimension to class images. The term *working class* often conjures up images of whites, even though people of color are disproportionately working class. Barbara Ehrenreich (1995) notes, "The most intractable stereotype is of the working class (which is, in imagination, only White) as a collection of reactionaries and bigots—reflected, for example, in the use of the terms 'hard hat' or 'redneck' as class slurs" (p. 41). She also observes, "It is possible for a middle-class person today to read the papers, watch television, even go to college, without suspecting that America has any inhabitants other than white-collar people—and, of course, the annoyingly persistent 'black underclass'" (p. 40).

That last phrase is important. In the media, the "poor" tend to be equated with blacks—even though only about 27 percent of people living below the poverty line in the United States are black; about two thirds of poor people are white; and over 40 percent are white non-Hispanic. One study of the major newsmagazines and the three major networks (Gilens 1996) examined images used to accompany stories about poverty. It found that, although blacks made up less than 30 percent of the poor in real life at the time, 62 percent of poor people pictured in newsmagazines and 65 percent of those on television were black. Such gross misrepresentation of class and race can easily contribute to misperceptions on the part of the public. Indeed, polls have shown that Americans—of all races—tend to vastly overestimate the percentage of poor people who are black.

Sociologist Diana Kendall (2005) reminds us that class stereotypes in news and entertainment media can play a vital role in our collective understanding of inequality. Media images and narratives that represent the poor as the "other"—as genuinely different from mainstream citizens—and those that "play on the idea that the clothing, manners, and speech patterns of the working class are not as good as those of the middle or upper classes" (p. 234) help to sustain a view that the middle and upper classes are superior and deserving of their wealth and privilege. At the same time, such representations reveal little about the increasing inequality in American society and do little to illuminate the complexity of the contemporary stratification system.

SEXUAL ORIENTATION: OUT OF THE CLOSET AND INTO THE MEDIA

The LGBT (lesbian, gay, bisexual, and transgender) community is another group in society that historically has been underrepresented and distorted in media coverage. For decades, lesbians and gays have been either ignored or ridiculed in nearly all media accounts. Like the movements for racial equality, women's rights, and organized labor, the LGBT movement has both developed alternative media and worked for more positive portrayals in the mainstream media. It has also had a dramatic impact on U.S. society, changing social norms and laws, and thereby serving as a catalyst for changing media content. (See Figure 6.3 for highlights.)

Reviewing the literature on the topic, Fejes and Petrich (1993) argue that, until the early 1930s, film portrayals of homosexuals were used either as "comic devices," as "a form of erotic titillation," or "to depict deviance, perversion and decadence" (p. 397). From the mid-1930s to the early 1960s, more conservative norms reigned in Hollywood, and producers severely restricted and censored images of gays and lesbians. When they reemerged in the 1960s, lesbian and gay images were usually quite negative in tone. Fejes and Petrich note that, during this period, "homosexuality was portrayed at best as unhappiness, sickness, or marginality and at worst perversion and an evil to be destroyed" (p. 398). They cite one review of all the films made between 1961 and 1976 that featured a major homosexual character. Thirty-two such films appeared in this period. Eighteen of these films featured a homosexual character who ends up being killed by another character, 13 featured a homosexual character who commits suicide, and the one remaining film featured a gay man who lives—but only after being castrated. The portrayal of gays and lesbians in mainstream films has improved since then—there was no place to go but up. Over time, the number of realistic and positive portrayals slowly increased. For example, *Brokeback Mountain* (2005), about two modern cowboys struggling with their sexuality, and *Milk* (2008), the bio-pic of Harvey Milk starring Sean Penn as the first gay man to be elected to public office in California, were two mainstream films that dealt sensitively with issues of homosexuality. Transgender portraits have appeared as well, with 1999's *Boys Don't Cry* and 2005's *Transamerica* marking major Hollywood successes. While Hollywood was catching up, independent films by lesbians and gays long provided a broader range of images of the LGBT community.

Figure 6.3	Out of the Closet . . . A Select Timeline of Milestones in LGBT Portrayals in Film and Television
1970	The fictionalized biographical film, *The Christine Jorgensen Story*, is released about real-life transsexual Christine Jorgensen.
1971	On CBS's *All in the Family*, Archie Bunker learns his macho drinking buddy, Steve, is gay. While viewers may have suspected that characters on earlier programs were gay, this is the first clear identification of a gay character on a television sit-com.
1972	ABC's *The Corner Bar*, a short-lived sit-com, features television's first major recurring gay character, a flamboyant set designer named Peter Panama.
1972	ABC's *That Certain Summer* is the first television movie to deal sympathetically with homosexuality.
1977	On *All in the Family*, the Bunkers attend the funeral of Edith Bunker's cousin, Liz, and learn that she had been the lover of her longtime female "roommate." Archie is outraged.
1977	ABC's *Soap* premiers. A madcap parody of day-time soap operas features Billy Crystal in the recurring role of a gay man.
1978	*A Question of Love* is a television movie in which a lesbian couple fights for custody of their son when challenged by one partner's ex-husband.
1983	ABC's *All My Children* features the first gay story line on a daytime soap opera.
1984	After being rejected by the networks, *Brothers* airs on cable's Showtime channel, featuring both homosexual and heterosexual characters discussing sexuality, homophobia, and AIDS.
1985	NBC's *An Early Frost* is the first major movie to deal with AIDS.
1988	ABC's *Roseanne* premieres. Eventually, the title character has a lesbian buddy, a mother with a girlfriend, gay employers, and, in one episode, is kissed by a lesbian in a gay bar.
1989	On ABC's *thirtysomething*, two male characters are shown in bed after having spent the night together. Though they do not touch on camera, advertisers pull $1 million worth of commercials and the episode is not shown again during the summer rerun season.
1990	CBS's comedy *Northern Exposure* premiers, featuring two recurring gay male characters who run a bed and breakfast and have a wedding ceremony in one episode. In another episode, the show's fictional town of Cicely, Alaska, is revealed to have been founded by 19th-century lesbian pioneers.
1991	*Angels in America*, a two-part play by Tony Kushner about gay life and AIDS, opens, winning the Pulitzer Prize for Drama and Tony Award for best play. HBO converts it into an award-winning miniseries in 2003.
1992+	Supporting gay characters become more common on television programs, including *Melrose Place* (1992), *Frasier* (1994), *Ellen* (1995), *Relativity* (1996), *Profiler* (1996), *Chicago Hope* (1996), and *Spin City* (1996).
1993	Tom Hanks portrays a gay man with AIDS in *Philadelphia*. Bruce Springsteen writes the movie's title song.
1994	On MTV's *Real World: San Francisco*, a male couple exchanges rings shortly before one of the men dies of AIDS-related complications.
1994	PBS airs the U.K.-produced miniseries drama, *Tales of the City*, set in '70s San Francisco featuring portrayals of gay and lesbian relationships.

Figure 6.3	(Continued)
1994	On ABC's *My So-Called Life*, a teenage character's parents throw him out of the house after he reveals he's gay.
1996	On the sit-com *Friends*, Ross' ex-wife marries her lesbian lover in a ceremony officiated by Candace Gingrich, the sister of conservative Republican Congressman Newt Gingrich.
1997	Ellen DeGeneres comes out, as does her character on the ABC sit-com *Ellen*, creating the first gay title character on network television.
1997	ABC's *Relativity* features TV's first full lesbian kiss.
1998	*Will and Grace* premieres, featuring a gay lawyer as one of the title characters.
1999	The film drama *Boys Don't Cry* is released, based on the real-life story of a transsexual man who was raped and murdered by his friends when they discovered his secret.
2000	Showtime's *Queer as Folk* premieres as the first program whose main characters are gay and includes first graphic depictions of gay sex on TV.
2003	Gay parents become more common. On HBO's *The Wire* a gay detective, Kima Greggs, adopts a child with her partner. A major character on the hit medical drama *E.R.*, Dr. Kerry Weaver, comes out and raises a son with her female partner, a firefighter.
2003	Bravo's *Queer Eye for the Straight Guy* premieres joining the increasingly popular "reality" TV genre.
2004	Showtime's *The L Word* is the first to focus on a group of lesbian, bisexual, and transgender characters.
2005	*Brokeback Mountain* is released and wins several Oscars. It is a romantic drama about two male cowboys—both married to women—who develop a sexual and emotional relationship.
2005	*Transamerica* is released with a transgender woman as the lead character.
2005	LOGO TV—owned by Viacom—premiers as the first cable channel devoted to LGBT programming.
2007	*Dirty Sexy Money* premieres on ABC, featuring broadcast television's first recurring transgender character.
2007	Soap opera *As the World Turns* airs first-ever kiss between two men on daytime TV.
2008	Sean Penn portrays gay-rights activist Harvey Milk in the film *Milk* and wins an Academy Award.
2009	Soap opera *All My Children* airs first day-time same-sex legal marriage.
2009	Fox's *Glee* premieres, featuring one of broadcast TV's most inclusive casts.
2009	ABC's *Modern Family* premiers, featuring a committed gay couple who go on to adopt a daughter. President Barack Obama says it's his family's favorite TV program.

Through the last few decades of the twentieth century, LGBT portrayals in the mainstream media were rare and often controversial. By 2009, though, LGBT characters were commonplace; and one prominent program with a gay family became the First Family's favorite show, indicating broad mainstream acceptance.

Sources: Compiled by authors from Jacobs (2013), Sparta (2002), Thompson (2013), and other sources.

Television has followed much the same route as Hollywood. From comic drag queens to threatening villains, television routinely disparaged homosexuals. In a 1967 CBS documentary the host, Mike Wallace, concluded, "The average homosexual, if there be such, is promiscuous. He's not interested in, nor capable of a lasting relationship like that of a heterosexual marriage"—a claim that now seems especially ironic given the recent push to legally recognize gay marriage (Fejes and Petrich 1993: 400). As the gay and lesbian movement gained strength in the 1970s and 1980s, it more actively sought fairer television portrayals of homosexuals. A 1974 episode of the medical drama *Marcus Welby* featured a homosexual child molester and suggested that homosexuality was a treatable disease. The program angered gay activists, who responded by organizing media watch efforts that challenged the negative media portrayals of gays and lesbians. Because of such efforts, gay and lesbian characters began to appear on prime-time programs, especially in episodes that revolved around homosexuality. Such programs, though, almost always framed these images as a "heterosexual view of homosexuality. Dramatic programming portrayed homosexuality as a problem disrupting heterosexuals' lives and expectations" (Fejes and Petrich 1993: 401). In the 1980s and 1990s, gay and lesbian characters began appearing in more serious and realistic portrayals, especially in roles highlighting the issue of AIDS. This time, it was conservative and religious fundamentalist groups who organized to challenge the media images. They objected to the positive portrayals of lesbians and gays and organized boycotts against advertisers on such programs.

A milestone was reached in 1997 when the lead character of the situation comedy *Ellen*—and the actress that played her, Ellen DeGeneres—"came out" in a highly publicized and anticipated episode. To commemorate television's first openly gay lead character, the Gay and Lesbian Alliance Against Defamation (GLAAD) sponsored "Coming Out With Ellen" benefits, and the Human Rights Campaign developed a party kit for the thousands of hosts celebrating the event across the country (Rosenfeld 1997).

Lesbian and gay characters have since become more prominent on television, especially on cable. *Queer as Folk* aired on Showtime from 2000 to 2005 and was the first series to focus on gay characters, including their sexuality. *The L Word,* which ran from 2004 to 2009, was the first series to focus on the lives of lesbian, bisexual, and transgender people. David Fisher of the HBO series *Six Feet Under* is considered to be among the first complex gay male characters on television. His eventual 2005 marriage to a police officer was the first ever gay wedding depicted in an American television series. Together, the couple later adopted two children. Positive portrayals of gay people have also made their way to broadcast television. ABC's *Modern Family,* which premiered in 2009, featured a gay couple who adopted a child.

While there are disparities among the networks, television is becoming more inclusive. In the 2012–2013 season, 31 series regulars on broadcast prime-time scripted television were lesbian, gay, bisexual, or transgender characters—4.4 percent of regular characters. This was a four-fold increase over the number just five years earlier (GLAAD 2012). Fox's, *Glee* alone had six LBGT characters—the highest of any program. Of all 49 lesbian, gay, and bisexual characters on broadcast TV—regulars or not—61 percent were gay men, 20 percent were lesbian, and 18 percent were bisexual (7 women, 2 men).

Cable's scripted programs, too, have been increasingly inclusive. In the 2012–2013 season, 35 LGBT characters were included, with HBO's *True Blood* featuring six gay, lesbian, and bisexual characters—the highest on cable. The sexual orientation of characters on cable was more diverse than it was on broadcast TV. Of all 59 lesbian, gay, and bisexual characters—regulars or not—49 percent were gay men, 27 percent were lesbian, and 23 percent were bisexual (9 women, 5 men).

As GLAAD's president Herndon Graddick noted, the increase in LGBT characters on television "reflects a cultural change in the way gay and lesbian people are seen in our society. More and more Americans have come to accept their LGBT family members, friends, coworkers, and peers, and as audiences tune into their favorite programs, they expect to see the same diversity of people they encounter in their daily lives" (GLAAD 2012: 3–4).

News coverage of lesbians and gays has also changed over the years. Rarely mentioned before the 1960s, homosexuality entered the news as a result of gay and lesbian activism (Gross 2001). The AIDS epidemic in the 1980s prodded the news media to address issues related to the gay community more directly. In the 21st century, debates about lesbians and gays serving in the military and gay marriage have been front-page stories. The move toward more positive coverage of lesbians and gays has taken place primarily in larger metropolitan areas with large, active, and visible gay and lesbian organizations. Smaller, more conservative communities have often lagged behind in their coverage of gay and lesbian issues.

Over two decades ago, Fejes and Petrich (1993) noted that change in mass media images of gays and lesbians did not occur spontaneously. Such changes "were not brought about by more enlightened social attitudes. Rather, the activism of gays and lesbians in confronting and challenging negative stereotypes played a decisive role in the change" (p. 412). The same holds true in the ensuing years. Nardi (1997) observed that changing images are also partially the result of "an increase in the production of media by gays and lesbians themselves, such as the lesbian and gay film festivals regularly held in many major cities, gay newspapers and magazines that increasingly attract mainstream advertisers, and gay public access television" (p. 438). These important points apply to all the groups we have examined. Women's organizations and civil rights groups, as well as lesbian and gay organizations, were significant social factors, in the form of collective human agency, in influencing the media industry to change the nature of media content. Labor unions and other organizations representing working-class and poor people have not had the same impact on media coverage of their constituents.

CONCLUSION

Entertainment and news media do not reflect the diversity of the real world. However, by its lack of diversity, media content does reflect the inequality that exists in the social world—and in the media industry.

The dynamic relationship between media content and the social world is complicated. Is media content cause or effect? A sociological approach would suggest that it is both. The social world affects media producers and media products. For example, we have seen how the efforts of social-movement organizations have influenced changes in media content. In this case, human agency has altered the operations of a major institutional structure. In turn, media content certainly influences our understanding of the social world. However, to fully assess the potential impact of media content, we must look at the meanings actual audiences attach to the media they read, watch, and listen to. We also need to explore the ways in which media are a part of the political world and our everyday social interaction. Having examined media production and media content, we turn in Part IV to the ways the media influence contemporary social and political life.

DISCUSSION QUESTIONS

1. Should media strive to be "realistic" in their portrayal of diversity in the social world? Why or why not? Are there different circumstances when it is more or less important to be "realistic"?

2. Do you think that college students are portrayed realistically in the mass media? Why or why not? If there is a gap between media image and reality, how do you account for this difference?

3. Explain why middle- and upper-middle-class people are vastly overrepresented in mass media content.

4. How do you explain the significant improvement in the portrayal of the LGBT community in mainstream media?

PART IV

Audiences

Meaning and Influence

$\mathbf{P}$art IV focuses on the relationship between audiences and the mass media. Building on our previous discussion of media production and media content, we round out our socio-logical analysis of media by examining both how they influence the social world and how human activity shapes the interpretation and use of media.

Chapter 7 explores the indirect influence of mass media on our political lives, focusing on how news media coverage has helped transform elections and on how various political actors use the media as a strategic resource. Chapter 8 turns directly to mass media audiences—people like us—who ultimately view, read, and listen to mass media. The chapter explores the ways audiences actively construct meaning from media messages rather than passively receiving prefabricated messages. Chapter 9 shifts the focus to the role of media technologies and examines the different kinds of interaction that are facilitated by the different forms of media. The chapter explores how media technologies shape social communication as well as how people influence the development of media technologies.

CHAPTER 7

Media Influence and the Political World

Source: Charles Ommanney/Getty Images.

For more than a half century, the mass media have helped to fundamentally alter the nature of American politics. Among the most important political events in each of the past six decades were the McCarthy hearings in the 1950s, the Vietnam War in the 1960s, Watergate in the 1970s, the election of Ronald Reagan in the 1980s, the Persian Gulf War and the Clinton impeachment in the 1990s, and 9/11 and the election of Barack Obama in the 2000s. Each of these developments was profoundly influenced by mass media exposure. Through nationally televised congressional hearings and press conferences, Senator Joe McCarthy used the media's soapbox to peddle his extreme and often unsubstantiated brand of anticommunism. The conflict in Vietnam was America's first "television war"; the media brought the brutal realities of modern warfare—and the widespread opposition to it—into American living rooms. The print media, especially the *Washington Post,* played the central role in exposing the Watergate scandal. The Reagan era set the standard for mediated politics as a former Hollywood actor and his staff skillfully manipulated news coverage. The Gulf War featured a massive government effort to manage the media by strictly controlling the flow of information and images available to them. The Clinton–Lewinsky scandal—and eventual impeachment of the president—was accompanied by a flood of media coverage that included not only traditional media but also several all-news cable stations and a vast number of Internet websites. When the second plane hit the World Trade Center's South

Tower on September 11 and the towers subsequently collapsed, the television networks broadcast the dramatic images live to tens of millions of viewers. Finally, the 2008 and 2012 elections saw a master image maker successfully use the Internet, as well as traditional media, to become the nation's first African American president.

As we saw in Part I, media are affected by the constraints of legal and informal political pressures, as well as by the economic forces that shape the media industry. However, the media's impact on the political world is real and undeniable. The media are formidable actors who, within the structural constraints already examined, influence the political world in a variety of ways. This influence reaches not only presidents and political elites but also ordinary citizens.

The media industry, most directly, is a powerful lobbyist for its interests. As noted in Chapter 3, media corporations are major contributors to political campaigns. They have also organized themselves into specialized lobbying groups that represent the interests of different segments of the media industry. The Motion Picture Association of America, the Association of Magazine Media, the National Association of Broadcasters (NAB), the National Cable & Telecommunications Association, the American Newspaper Publishing Association, and the Internet Alliance are but a few examples of these groups. When legislation that might affect a particular segment of the industry is being discussed in Congress, the media's political lobbyists spring into action—and sometimes even draft sections of proposed legislation.

The media industry has long lobbied for the elimination of regulations that constrain its activities. During the 2012 election cycle, the media industry (television, movies, and music) contributed $69.8 million to political campaigns—most of these contributions came from individuals associated with the entertainment industry. Media giants Comcast Corporation ($6 million) and Time Warner ($2.5 million) were both major campaign contributors. The media industry spends even more money on lobbying the federal government in an effort to influence legislation. In 2012, the television, movie, and music industry spent more than $117 million on lobbying—more than double the $58 million in media industry lobbying in 2005. The National Cable & Telecommunications Association ($18.9 million) and Comcast Corporation ($14.8 million) were the leading media industry lobbyists in 2012 (Center for Responsive Politics 2013). With such ongoing contributions, it was no accident that media deregulation was a key legislative priority in the 1990s and 2000s, including the Telecommunications Act of 1996 and a series of policy decisions that weakened public interest rules associated with cable and telephone companies' Internet infrastructure (Kovacs 2010). Such is the power of the industry's direct lobbying.

This chapter, however, focuses on the media's more *indirect* influence on political life. The bulk of the chapter is devoted to the role of print, broadcast, and online news media in the electoral process. We look at both how media involvement has changed the behavior of politicians and how media coverage has affected voters. In turn, we consider how political actors have adapted by incorporating media into their repertoire of political strategies. Like other social relationships, that between the media and the political world involves both structural constraint and human agency.

However, politics is more than just voting, and the political impact of the media emanates from more than just the news media. Therefore, we also consider the media's impact on social movement efforts and look briefly at the political implications of film, entertainment television, music, and the Internet. Again, we highlight the structure–agency dynamic. This time we explore how media can be active agents in affecting the political structure while at the same time serving as an institutional structure used by political actors to achieve success.

MEDIA AND POLITICAL ELITES

Too often, commentators discuss media influence solely in terms of the potential impact on regular citizens. For example, the question of whether the news media affect voting behavior is a perennial favorite among researchers. However, the most profound and direct influence of the media on the political world probably takes place at the level of political elites. The media's influence on a hundred politicians has much more significant and pronounced implications than their influence on a hundred regular voters. It is insiders—politicians, lobbyists, campaign managers, financial contributors, political consultants, and so forth—who pay closest attention to and are most likely to be influenced by the media. Nowhere is this more evident than in the changes in political campaigns in response to media coverage.

Politicians have long understood the potential power of the mass media. The print media, for a time, were directly associated with political parties. When broadcast media emerged, politicians quickly saw their possibilities for influence. Herbert Hoover launched a successful presidential bid over the radio. Franklin Roosevelt used radio "fireside chats" to communicate with the public during the Depression. Dwight Eisenhower used television campaign commercials in 1952, and the Kennedy campaign in 1960 solidified the influence of television on American politics that has continued to this day. The Internet has been widely used in electoral campaigning ever since the 1996 election (Bimber 1998). The 2008 Obama campaign relied heavily on the Internet to mobilize supporters and raise campaign funds. With nonstop 24-hour cable news and a vast amount of election coverage and political commentary online, we can hardly overestimate the media's influence on election campaigns and the running of government.

A Politics of Image

Media considerations are perhaps the single most important factor around which candidates organize electoral campaigns. This is especially true for presidential and congressional elections, but many of the following observations apply to state and local elections as well.

The Importance of Appearance

At its simplest level, we see the importance of media in the fact that a camera-friendly style and appearance greatly enhance a candidate's chance of success. Looking and acting comfortable on camera can aid a candidate's cause. All major campaigns have media "handlers," consultants who coach candidates on improving their appearance in the media. An early indication of the importance of appearance was the infamous presidential debate between Kennedy and Nixon in 1960. The debate was televised, but Nixon declined to wear

Source: Paul Schutzer/Getty Images.

The first Kennedy-Nixon debate of 1960 has come to symbolize the influence of television on politics. Looking fit, tanned, and confident, the underdog Kennedy was widely seen as having defeated the underweight, pale, and sweaty Nixon, still recovering from a recent hospitalization. The event raised the importance of appearances in political campaigns.

the heavy makeup that aides recommended. On camera, he appeared haggard and in need of a shave, while Kennedy's youthful and vibrant appearance was supported by the layer of television makeup he wore. The significance of this difference in appearance became apparent after the debate. Polls showed that a slim majority of those who heard the debate on the radio thought Nixon had won, while an equally slim majority of those who watched the debate on television gave the edge to Kennedy. After this dramatic event, the fear of not performing well in televised debates so intimidated presidential hopefuls that it was 16 years before another debate was televised.

Ever since then, the lesson has been clear: Appearance matters. Charismatic individuals who have experience in dealing with the media are at a decided advantage in the political realm. Media coverage of elections, especially on television, tends to highlight images. News accounts of elections emphasize personal stories, personalities, and preplanned campaign events and are less likely to explain the background and implications of substantive issues and policy debates (Graber 2009a). In this way, as political scientist Doris Graber (2001) puts it, media seek to "please audiences who do not care very much about serious political news" (p. 111).The result of expanded media coverage has, in many ways, been a loss of substance in favor of appearance.

A number of celebrities have used their media skills, status, and experience to pursue political careers. The best known example of celebrity-turned-politician is Ronald Reagan, whose reputation as the "great communicator" was surely in part the result of the training he received as actor, radio personality, and ad salesman. His oratorical skills were largely limited to scripted events. He was notorious for misstating facts and for rambling, sometimes incoherently, when faced with spontaneous speaking situations. On occasion, he even confused his movie roles with real-life experiences. The ability of his staff to maintain the president's polished public image was central to his success. After the first two years of poor showings in the polls, the Reagan presidency was marked by high public popularity—even though polls showed most Americans disagreeing with many of Reagan's key policy positions. Some took this result to be the ultimate triumph of image over substance. As Reagan's own chief of staff, Donald Regan (1988), admitted,

> Every moment of every public appearance was scheduled, every word was scripted, every place where Reagan was expected to stand was chalked with toe marks. The President was always being prepared for a performance, and this had the inevitable effect of preserving him from confrontation and the genuine interplay of opinion, question, and argument that form the basis of decision. (p. 248)

More recent presidential elections again highlighted the importance of being telegenic in contemporary politics. In 1996, youthful and publicly affable Democrat Bill Clinton had a distinct advantage over the older and more sullen Bob Dole, who often appeared uncomfortable in the media spotlight. In 2000 and 2004 campaigns, it was Republican George Bush whose friendly demeanor seemed to play better in the media spotlight in comparison to the stiffer Democratic candidates John Kerry and Al Gore. In 2008 and 2012, a youthful and media-savvy Barack Obama was far more comfortable on camera and in front of crowds than his opponents John McCain—who could come across as gruff and old-fashioned—and Mitt Romney—who sometimes seemed stiff and disconnected from audiences.

Being comfortable in the media spotlight has helped dozens of media celebrities to successfully pursue political careers. Professional football quarterback Jack Kemp was elected to Congress in 1970, while New York Knicks basketball star Bill Bradley was elected New Jersey senator in 1978. Sonny Bono, known for his pop singing act with wife Cher, was elected to Congress in 1994. Fred Thompson is an actor who became a Tennessee senator in 1994 and then returned to acting, playing a district attorney on television's *Law & Order.* Pro wrestler and Hollywood actor Jesse Ventura parlayed his fame into a successful third-party campaign for governor of Minnesota in 1998. Arnold Schwarzenegger, former bodybuilder and *Terminator* actor, was elected governor of California in 2003. Sarah Palin competed in beauty pageants and began her career as a sportscaster before being elected Alaska's governor. Comedian Al Franken, best known for his *Saturday Night Live* appearances, was elected Minnesota senator in 2008.

In fact, politicians with media connections are common. Among the members of Congress in 2013 were five radio talk show hosts, six television or radio broadcasters, seven reporters or journalists, a radio station manager, a public television producer, a comedian, a screen writer, and a documentary filmmaker (Manning 2013).

Setting the Stage

The significance of media images goes well beyond the specific appearance of the candidate to include the more general visual context in which a candidate appears. In this regard, too, observers generally point to Ronald Reagan's campaign and presidency as the epitome of the masterful use of visuals to enhance a candidate's image. Both during the campaign and after the election victory, the Reagan team showed remarkable skill at manipulating media coverage by providing television with an irresistible visual to support the "line of the day"—the message the White House wanted the media to emphasize in that day's reporting. In this way, they could direct media coverage—at least in visual terms—by making it efficient for the news media to use the visual settings they had orchestrated. The administration even coordinated the 1986 U.S. bombing of Libya to coincide with the start of the evening news (Kellner 1990). Michael Deaver, the Reagan White House media specialist, later pointed out that he and his staff found television reporters quite "manageable" because he gave "the nightly news good theater, a good visual every evening, and pretty much did their job for them" (*Nightline,* September 27, 1989).

Former President Bill Clinton's media team lifted a page or two from the Reagan playbook. Clinton was well known for his tireless campaigning and his choreographed events. As one journalist noted later, "Every stump speech, every debate appearance, and every interview was scripted—right down to what appeared to be ad lib remarks, delivered with a thoughtful expression and a contemplative biting of the lower lip" (Flint 1997: 1190).

In one of the more elaborate publicity efforts of the 1996 campaign, the Clinton team hired a Hollywood producer to orchestrate a train trip leading up to the Democratic national convention. In the absence of any real news coming out of the convention—the president faced no serious challengers for the Democratic Party nomination—the Clinton campaign put its candidate on a train traveling through small towns in the Midwest. The train's stops were choreographed to provide nostalgic background images evoking Harry Truman's whistle-stop campaigning nearly a half century earlier. But this train was different. It was equipped with state-of-the-art communications equipment, including a satellite dish that enabled the invited local press corps to broadcast live interviews from the train. The local media loved it and, even though there was no real news emanating from the trip, the train received extensive regional coverage—just as the campaign had planned.

The September 11, 2001, terrorist attack and subsequent U.S. war effort once again provided ample opportunity for politicians to carefully script public appearances that benefited from the country's outpouring of patriotism. Visits to ground zero in New York, photo opportunities with that fall's World Series participants, and visits with U.S. military personnel were just some of the photogenic backdrops for image-conscious public officials. Through skillful use of the media, President Bush successfully transformed his image from a president with limited foreign policy knowledge and questionable standing in the international community to become a strong and respected leader of the "war on terrorism."

In early 2003, he took the cockpit of a Navy jet to theatrically land on the aircraft carrier *Abraham Lincoln* returning from the war in Iraq. A "Mission Accomplished" banner hung behind the president as he announced the end of combat operations in Iraq. The event, carefully staged by the Bush team, dominated the newscasts for the following days. According to *Washington Post* media critic Tom Shales (2003),

> this was not just a speech but a patriotic spectacular, with the ship and its crew serving as crucial backdrops for Bush's remarks, something to cheer the viewing nation and to make Bush look dramatically commander in chief. . . . There were several eloquent turns of phrase in the address . . . but they were overwhelmed by the visual impact. (p. C1)

The "mission accomplished" image, though, came to haunt Bush, as the war and the occupation of Iraq dragged on past the end of his presidency.

During the 2008 and 2012 campaigns, Barack Obama's campaign was widely credited as having been much more adept at shaping positive media portrayals of the candidate than his opponents were. In 2008, John McCain was often portrayed at a podium, in static poses, while Obama was depicted as a world leader, speaking to crowds during trips to Europe and the Middle East. In 2012, Obama's performance was more uneven; but at his best, he still seemed to develop a rapport with crowds that played well on television and that eluded his opponent, Mitt Romney.

The Influence of Images

Political media events are staged to produce press coverage and influence public opinion. The various types of staged media events include speeches, "spontaneous events" (which, as the name ironically suggests, are supposed to look spur of the moment), state visits, foreign trips, and arts or culture-related events. Such events allow candidates to control the agenda, construct favorable political images providing audiences with visual cues, help authenticate a leader's image, "tell a story" and thus dramatize policy, and give the audience an emotional experience by using powerful symbols such as the flag or military personnel (Schill 2009). The effect of media events, however, is cumulative: A single event rarely produces a decisive shift in voting behavior, but a series of events is more likely to have significant impact (Scott, Nardulli, and Shaw 2002).

The careful construction of photo opportunities has become a routine part of presidential politics. Most of the pictures we see of the president are likely to have been scripted ahead of time by collaborative "advance teams" of reporters and political aides who scout out the best angles for photo opportunities at upcoming events. Using stand-ins for the president and his entourage, these advance teams often stage practice photos that they later distribute to the media. These photos, along with notes about the camera lenses likely to produce the best results, are then used by photojournalists in planning their coverage of the "real" event.

Postmodernist theorists, especially Baudrillard (1983), have argued that the rising importance of images signals a new kind of "reality." In postmodern society, they argue, the image has come to replace the "real" as a new form of *hyperreality*. As a result, the public is often unable to distinguish between image and reality. The practical application of postmodernist theory to the political world suggests that substantive policy debates will continue to take a backseat to polished, telegenic candidates and scripted photo opportunities.

The most artificial of all political media is the campaign commercial, over which candidates have complete control. Television and, increasingly, Internet-based advertising are a central part of electoral campaigns, and evidence has long suggested that voters receive more information about candidates from campaign advertisements than from news coverage (McClure and Patterson 1976). Increasingly, campaign ads have relied on negative "attack" formats to achieve maximum effect. According to the Campaign Media Analysis Group, more than half of all commercials aired for the 2010 midterm elections were attack ads, and almost 70 percent of all commercials in U.S. Senate campaigns were negative (Steinhauser 2010).

The Decline of Political Parties and Mediating Institutions

As the media have become more important in political campaigns, political party organizations have become less important (Negrine 2008; Negrine et al. 2007). In American politics, political parties used to maintain a grassroots organization that contacted voters, educated them about candidates, and encouraged them to vote. This system resulted in an intricate infrastructure of party workers, often organized down to the urban "block captain." For the most part, such organizational structures have ceased to exist. Also in decline are a range of other "mediating institutions" (Greider 1992)—especially labor unions—that used to serve as structures to organize and mobilize groups of ordinary citizens. These institutions served as links between the public and the political process.

Now, media serve as the vehicles for conveying political messages and mobilizing voters (Louw 2010). Candidates spend the vast bulk of campaign finances on producing and airing campaign commercials. Rather than being active participants in dialogues about issues and

Source: Rockthevote.org.

Popular media campaigns such as MTV's "Rock the Vote" can help encourage people to vote but they do not contribute to a lasting political structure the way political parties used to organize.

candidates, citizens increasingly are an audience for televised debates and political commercials that sell the latest candidate. Public service campaigns to encourage voting (as seen on MTV, for example) do nothing to create any lasting political structure. Instead, such endeavors promote voting as an individual act devoid of any long-term political commitment. Ads sell candidates/products to voters/consumers in a way that blurs the line between politics and commerce. The way public affairs are currently covered in the mass media contributes to civic disengagement and political apathy (Norris 2000).

The decline of party structures has been accompanied by a decline in party allegiance. In the 1940s, when researchers conducted early studies of voters, the most important determinant of a person's vote was party affiliation, followed by group allegiance, perception of the candidate's personality, and consideration of issues. After a half century of media coverage, the order of importance has changed. Now, in presidential campaigns, the candidate's personality is of greatest importance to voters, followed by the issues, party membership, and group membership (Bartels 2002; Graber 2009a; Prysby and Holian 2008). The media, which communicate a great deal about personality and issues, have taken on an increasingly significant political role, while the influence of other institutions has declined. As a result, the role of professional political communications specialists has grown as well.

The Professionalization of Political Communication

On August 26, 2002, Vice President Dick Cheney declared, "Simply stated, there is no doubt that Saddam Hussein now has weapons of mass destruction." On February 5, 2003, Senator Hillary Clinton (D-NY) accused Iraq of "actively seeking a nuclear weapons capability, and supporting and harboring terrorist organizations." Many similar charges appeared in newspapers and on television news in late 2002 and early 2003. The U.S. invasion of Iraq was launched on March 20, 2003. A few days later, U.S. Army Gen. Tommy Franks said: "As this operation continues, those weapons will be identified, found, along with the people who have produced them and who guard them" (Counterpunch Wire 2003).

The alleged presence of weapons of mass destruction (WMD) in Iraq and the supposed connections between Saddam Hussein and Al-Qaeda were centerpieces of the Bush Administration's effort to sell the war to the American public. The WMD story is a prime example of "spin," the strategic manipulation of news media presentations of events and issues in an effort to shape public opinion. While WMD were never found in Iraq, media reports of their prewar existence helped to legitimize the air assault and subsequent invasion of Iraq.

"Spin" is a form of propaganda that involves the creation and diffusion of a specific interpretation of an event, a campaign, or a policy, with the aim of creating consensus and public support. Public relations (PR) experts who employ such news management tactics are sometimes called "spin doctors," even by the reporters they are trying to manipulate. The importance of PR consultants is partly a consequence of the central role of television in daily life (Louw 2010). Television plays to the advantage of politicians because it can easily provoke emotional responses. Spin doctors use television to try to build indignation or generate enthusiastic support. But how does this kind of news management actually work? And why do politicians need spin doctors?

Politicians seek to generate consent: In other words, they want to prevent citizens from disrupting the decision-making process. In addition, they need to keep citizens involved, giving ordinary people the impression that they are actually participating in policy making (Louw 2010).

Effective political leadership requires a basic level of public consent. In order to achieve their political objectives, politicians employ media-savvy professionals who use political marketing techniques to mold and steer public opinion (Louw 2010). Spin is effective because of the symbiotic relationship among PR teams, politicians, and journalists. Spin doctors need the news media to disseminate stories that serve their clients' agendas, and journalists need access to powerful politicians to effectively report on government. As a result, journalists are vulnerable to well-crafted spin, which has become increasingly sophisticated in recent years. However, because reporters do not like to be openly manipulated by PR professionals, there is often tension between spin doctors and journalists.

Spin tactics include leaking stories to journalists and providing them with selective "off-the-record" information, scripting speeches in a way that makes sound editing and quote retrieval easy, orchestrating strategic photo opportunities, but also organizing smear campaigns against opponents and planting stories on the Internet, for example, by posting videos on YouTube (Louw 2010). By deploying these techniques, spin doctors seek to set the agenda for the media and of their audiences by defining what's important and offering easily digestible interpretations of events. They may also attempt to change the way ordinary citizens think about a policy problem, either to discourage citizens from getting involved or to try to mobilize them to support a specific policy. In fact, news media is full of spin. News on television, radio, and online regularly includes political pundits who offer decidedly different interpretations of the same events. Even the "No Spin Zone" on Fox News' popular program *The O'Reilly Factor* is notable for the host's highly partisan perspective on political events (Conway, Grabe, and Grieves 2007).

The growth of the PR machine and the permanent campaign that characterizes contemporary politics have dramatically increased the cost of elections (Louw 2010). Consider this: During the 2008 presidential campaign, Barack Obama had eight dedicated video production units located in the key swing states. Each unit produced a weekly video, which helped visually promote the campaign's themes of hope and change.

Spin, however, does not always work. In some cases, spin can backfire and become a problem for politicians and PR handlers. In a political world where a candidate's image is a valuable currency, the appearance of deception or dishonesty can be very damaging. Whether or not spin succeeds can depend, in large part, on the presence of an independent press that has the resources to rigorously scrutinize politicians' claims. However, investigative journalism generally has a limited impact. According to Peter Teeley, press secretary to then Vice President George H.W. Bush, "You can say anything you want during a debate, and 80 million people hear it. If anything turns out to be false and journalists correct it, so what. Maybe 200 people read it, or 2,000 or 20,000" (quoted in MacArthur 2003).

Politics as Spectator Sport

The decline of political party organizations and the increasing importance of PR in political campaigns have been accompanied by media coverage that treats political life as a spectator sport. The American news media are notorious for their "horse race" coverage of elections that highlights campaign strategy rather than candidate substance. Too often, critics contend, the media are less interested in where candidates stand on the issues than in their electability as measured by polls. For example, one study of the early months of the presidential primary campaign in 2007 found that news coverage focused on the horse race far more than any other topic, with "strategy and polls" accounting for half of all the coverage. While this study found that horse race coverage was the dominant framework in all sectors of the news media—newspapers, network and cable television, commercial and public radio, the Internet—coverage of strategy and polls was highest at the online news outlets (PEJ 2007).

Highly publicized poll results have potential implications for knowledge about, interest in, and support for candidates; but definitive empirical evidence of these effects does not yet exist. The impact of media polls can be especially important to campaign consultants, staff, journalists, and especially financial contributors. Candidates who can demonstrate their electability by doing well in early polls are much more likely to attract the campaign contributions—before any votes are cast—that are essential to run an effective campaign. Thus, poll results may represent a self-fulfilling prophecy.

The effect on regular voters, though, is less clear. The danger is that, especially for those with little involvement with or knowledge about candidates, poll results can signal how people *ought* to vote instead of reflecting existing voter preference. This would make it extremely difficult for third-party candidates and other "dark horses" to be successful. Some studies provide evidence that voter judgment of what others believe does affect candidate preference and that polls showing a clear front-runner depress voter turnout (Traugott 1992). Both of these findings suggest that publicized polls may have a potentially significant impact on voters.

The media's emphasis on winners and losers continues even after the campaigns are over. Journalists and pundits on public affairs programs often interpret political news through a lens that highlights the ups and downs of political careers rather than the substantive content of policy proposals (Fallows 1996). The sports metaphor of "winning" and "losing" dominates political life. When journalists ask, "Who won the week?" they inevitably give their interpretation of events. According to critic Jay Rosen (1993),

> the question . . . permits the media to play timekeeper, umpire, and finally, judge. The question would not occur to an ordinary citizen, but it remains a favorite of pundits and reporters because it appears to place the press on the outside of a process—the shaping of perceptions—that is profoundly affected by what the press itself does. (p. 9)

The negative impact of such media coverage permeates political life. "By now even the denizens of the White House think they've achieved something by 'winning the week.' They fret and fuss when the week, according to the pundits, has been lost." These comments by Rosen (1993: 9) highlight the dual impact of media coverage—it potentially affects voters and political elites alike.

Another symptom of the transformation of politics into a spectator sport is the increasing importance of celebrity in political life. In some cases, politicians employ celebrity-making publicity strategies to capture public attention (Louw 2010). Consider, for example, Sarah Palin's appearance on *Saturday Night Live* or Barack Obama's appearance on the *Tonight Show* with Jay Leno. Media scholar Eric Louw describes this kind of political activity as "televisualized populism" (p. 83), strategic media appearances that allow politicians to connect with citizens by extending their media presence beyond everyday government-related activities.

In other cases, entertainment industry celebrities take advantage of their popularity to speak for a cause or a candidate. For example, Oprah Winfrey, George Clooney, and Jay-Z were prominent endorsers of Barack Obama in 2012, while Kid Rock, Jeff Foxworthy, and Clint Eastwood made their pitch for Mitt Romney. Celebrity status can also be used by non-politicians to make political statements (Street 2002, 2004). For example, U2 front man Bono used his popularity to speak in favor of reducing the debt of developing countries. He met President George W. Bush and Pope John Paul II; and, in 2002, he toured Africa with the U.S. Treasury Secretary Paul O'Neill. Together with fellow musician Bob Geldof, Bono organized the charity Live 8 concerts in Scotland in 2005, which helped focus media attention on poverty in Africa.

In all these situations, media are crucial actors in the construction of such celebrity status because celebrity derives from media exposure. Manufacturing a politically useful celebrity requires careful work in scripting, staging, and performing to create a specific image in the media.

MEDIA AND INDIVIDUAL CITIZENS

We usually cannot, or do not, experience firsthand the goings-on of public life. Consequently, as citizens, we are partially reliant on the news media for an informative and accurate account of what is happening in the world around us. That is why the media are such an important element of the democratic process. Citizens in a democracy need adequate information to make informed decisions and to take appropriate political action.

Media Effects: From Influence to Interaction

Given the media's central role in the political process, it is no wonder that researchers have repeatedly asked questions about how the media affect that process. The answers that have emerged over the decades range from simple models emphasizing direct media influence to more sophisticated analyses highlighting the interaction of media and audience.

The Hypodermic Model

The earliest speculation about media effects suggested a direct and powerful influence on the public. Some commentators wrote of a "hypodermic" (or "silver bullet") model, with the media injecting a message directly into the "bloodstream" of the public. The anecdotal evidence for this belief dates at least as far back as the Spanish-American War in 1898 when, as one historical account (Palmer and Colton 1978) puts it, "The newspapers, especially the new 'yellow' press, roused the American public to a fury of moral indignation and imperial self-assertion" (p. 612).

The introduction of broadcast technology only raised further concern about the media's influence. Everything from government propaganda efforts during the two world wars to the famous panic caused by Orson Welles's 1939 radio broadcast of *War of the Worlds* suggested that the media could directly manipulate a passive and gullible public. In the 1990s, when some popular critics warned against violent rap lyrics causing antisocial behavior or against portrayals of lesbians and gays promoting homosexuality, they hearkened back to this vision of all-powerful media.

Mass Society Theory

Mass society theory of the post–World War II years was a broader current of sociological theory that also suggested the potential for dramatic media influence (e.g., Kornhauser 1959; Reisman 1953). Although it existed in various forms, at the core of the theory was the argument that then-contemporary society was characterized by growing homogenization of the population and a decline in interpersonal and group relations. At its base, the theory suggested the decline of more traditional personal bonds. The traditional extended family was giving way to smaller (and, later, fragmented) nuclear families whose members, because of work and school, spent less time with one another. Strong religious ties gave way to more perfunctory religious, or even secular, identities. A "melting pot" culture discouraged ethnic group identity. Cohesive neighborhoods and community participation declined with the rise of dispersed and isolated suburbs. Work in large, corporate-owned organizations became more and more alienating.

While mass society theorists saw trends toward isolation and depersonalization in postwar America, they also noticed the rise in mass media, especially television. They argued that these mass media played a crucial role in uniting (and homogenizing) a disparate and atomized population. Stripped of significant personal ties, the mass population was especially susceptible to the influence of media messages. The language of mass society was perhaps best suited to totalitarian regimes. Indeed, it was concern over the use of propaganda in Nazi Germany and the Soviet Union that motivated much of the early research. However, the notion of an alienated public tuned in to mass media to gain some semblance of collective identity may not seem far-fetched in today's media-saturated society. Although mass society theory per se has not continued as a vibrant thread of thought, many of the concerns raised by the original theory have lived on in other research traditions.

The Minimal Effects Model

Belief in an all-powerful media did not hold up under the scrutiny of early empirical research. In a classic study of voters, *The People's Choice,* Lazarsfeld, Berelson, and Gaudet (1948) argued that the media's impact on individuals was weak and short-lived. This "minimal effects" model suggested that media messages acted to reinforce existing belief rather than to change opinion. The authors suggested that social characteristics such as class and religion were more important than the media in explaining voter behavior. In part, this is because people who pay close attention to the news media tend to already have strong political beliefs, and thus media messages are less likely to affect them. People who are more likely to be undecided and uninterested are less likely to pay attention to media coverage.

Whatever effect the media did have, Lazarsfeld and colleagues (1948) argued, was often achieved through a "two-step flow of influence." The media transmitted information to opinion leaders who tended to pay close attention to the news media. These leaders, in turn, could influence those with whom they had personal contact. Some theorists also argued that interpersonal contact was more influential than the media in affecting a change in belief because it involved the desire for social acceptance that is part of all direct human interaction.

The problem with the earlier hypodermic model was that it left out the active agency of the reader of media messages. Taken literally, that early model ignored the preexisting ideas and orientation of the reader. The minimal effects model gave more weight to the ability of the reader to select, screen, and judge media information. The reader, after all, is not a passive sponge soaking up media messages but an active, thinking individual capable of ignoring or resisting media messages.

Agenda Setting and Priming

The minimal effects approach to the media reigned until the late 1960s, when researchers increasingly accepted the "agenda-setting" role of the media. In a classic phrasing of the argument, Bernard Cohen (1963) claimed that the news "may not be successful in telling people what to think, but it is stunningly successful in telling its readers what to think about" (p. 13). This ability to direct people's attention toward certain issues became known as agenda setting. Agenda setting highlighted the important role that journalists play in selecting and shaping the news.

Researchers empirically examined Cohen's claim by studying undecided voters in the 1968 presidential election (McCombs and Shaw 1972, 1977). They found a remarkable similarity between the media's issue focus and the issue agenda of undecided voters. While this finding showed a correlation between the media's agenda and the agenda of voters, the study's design did not allow for determining a causal relationship.

Funkhouser (1973) tackled the issue by looking at three sources of data: (1) public opinion polls regarding the most important issues facing the nation, (2) media coverage in the nation's top three weekly newsmagazines, and (3) statistical indicators measuring the "reality" of key issue areas. Confirming earlier findings, Funkhouser found substantial correlation between public opinion and media coverage. More important, he found that neither public opinion nor media coverage correlated well with statistical indicators of the "real" world. For example, media coverage and public concern regarding the Vietnam War peaked *before* the greatest number of U.S. troops were sent there. Media coverage and public concern about unrest on college campuses and in urban areas also peaked *before* the period in which the greatest number of campus demonstrations and urban riots took place. This suggested that the media's coverage of issues affected public opinion more than the issues' objective prominence in the "real" world. It also showed that media coverage did not necessarily reflect real-world trends.

Simple experimental work examining this agenda-setting function of the media later confirmed a causal relationship between media coverage and the issue agenda of the audience. Iyengar and Kinder (2010) showed test participants different videotapes of edited television news broadcasts. The different versions of the broadcasts were the same, with one exception. The researchers added stories to the tapes so that some participants saw pieces either on the environment, on national defense, or on inflation. Tests before and after viewing showed that those issues the researchers had highlighted in each of the doctored broadcasts were more likely to be chosen by participants as important. Researchers found some agenda-setting effects after the viewing of only a single broadcast. However, most effects took place only after participants had watched several of the altered newscasts.

While the agenda-setting function of the media is now firmly established, it is neither simple nor complete (McCombs 2004). Some work added nuance to the agenda-setting model. *Priming* is a related phenomenon that involves mass media attending to certain issues or aspects of an issue, thereby increasing the sensitivity of audiences to the significance of such information (Scheufele and Tewksbury 2007). For example, a focus by the media on economic issues can "prime" audiences to pay special attention to the economic qualifications of a candidate.

Some work has tempered claims about the media's ability to set the agenda. Brosius and Kepplinger (1990) coupled a yearlong content analysis of German television news programs with weekly public opinion polls on the most important issues of the day. They found strong agenda-setting effects on some issues. However, on other issues, either public concern largely *preceded* media coverage, or the two simply did not correlate well. This kind of finding suggests the necessity for caution in assessing the media's role in setting the public agenda. Perhaps agenda setting is most pronounced when individuals have no direct contact with an issue and thus are dependent on the media for information. Perception of issues that directly affect an individual's life may be more resistant to media influence.

The agenda-setting approach has traditionally looked at who sets the public agenda. Evidence points convincingly to the news media. However, this begs the question of who sets the news media's agenda. As we have shown, a number of important influences affect the functioning of the media, including the demands imposed by corporate owners to ensure profitability; the role of sources, PR agencies, and other powerful players in initiating stories; and the "gatekeeping" and professional norms of journalism. In fact, there is a large body of literature showing the importance of multiple influences on news media.

For example, one political economy approach to this topic is dubbed the "propaganda model" (Herman and Chomsky 2002). It argues that the media's agenda is set by a combination of government and corporate forces intent on protecting the interests of the rich and powerful. This model "traces the routes by which money and power are able to filter out the news fit to print, marginalize dissent, and allow the government and dominant private interests to get their messages across to the public" (p. 2). News content is influenced by the facts that (1) media corporations have a profit orientation, and their ownership is heavily concentrated; (2) the media depend on advertising as their primary income source; (3) the media rely on officially approved sources and experts; and (4) powerful players are able to deliver "flak" about media content of which they disapprove.

The Gap Between Theory and Popular Perception

For some time, many researchers accepted the idea that media could influence the public's agenda while having little impact on what people believed—in essence, a move from "minimal effects" to "limited effects." This idea contrasted sharply with the public's general perception that media play a very influential role in society. There are three major reasons for this gap in perceptions (Graber 2009a).

First, most research has looked only at a narrow range of media effects issues. For example, researchers looked at the most convenient unit of analysis: voters. If voters did not change their minds as a result of media exposure, the argument went, then there was no media influence. Because researchers conducted these influential early studies at a time when party loyalty was strong, they found little change in voter preference based on media influence. However, this research did not gauge the range of possible media effects in other, less predetermined situations.

Second, research sometimes mistakenly equated the absence of factual learning from the media with the absence of media influence, in essence ignoring more complex or unintended effects. For example, a study of a media campaign to promote awareness of environmental pollution found that people learned very few of the facts highlighted in the campaign. However, there was an unintended effect. After the campaign, people were more likely to blame big business for most pollution (Graber 2009a). By overemphasizing the transmission of factual information, researchers may be missing some of the evidence of media influence.

Finally, researchers have had great difficulty clearly measuring media effects because media stimuli routinely interact with other social stimuli. Disentangling these multiple influences is extremely difficult; and, as a result, clear evidence of direct media influence is difficult to obtain. Still, more recent trends in media research seem to point toward a dual concern with the power of audiences to interpret media and with the subtler influences of media.

Media–Reader Interaction

As we will highlight in Chapter 8, recent trends in media research have paid more attention to how the audience actively uses information. This focus shines the light of inquiry on the dynamic interaction between media and reader.

Various studies, using a range of methods, have also shown that media information is but one element that citizens use in developing political beliefs. Over the course of a year, Doris Graber (1988) monitored the media while at the same time conducting intensive interviews with 21 participants. Her interviews revealed that, while people used media information to make sense of public issues, what they knew about these issues was not limited to the information the media supplied. Silvo Lenart (1994) used experimental data to argue that media information and interpersonal communication "are complementary halves of the total information whole." William Gamson (1992) showed how regular working people in his focus group study constructed meaning by combining media-based information with popular wisdom and experiential knowledge. His study treated the media as a tool or resource that people can use, to varying degrees, to help them make sense of current events. While accepting the potential influence of the media, this approach balances media power with the creative agency of readers.

Political Socialization Theory

We must understand media effects in subtler terms than simply their ability to change the mind of a potential voter. The long-term, cumulative effect of exposure to mass media needs to be considered as well.

Media influence may be especially strong in the early political socialization of adolescents, who are old enough to seriously consider political issues but have not yet fully developed a political orientation. For example, high school students say they rely on the mass media more than on families, friends, or teachers in developing attitudes about current events, such as economic or race issues (Graber 2009a). This runs counter to the "two-step" model of influence, which sees personal interaction as more influential than media exposure. We can speculate that the influence of the media may have increased in recent years as children and adolescents have spent more and more time with the mass media. Exposure to the media is now a central means by which young people learn and internalize the values, beliefs, and norms of our political system, a socialization that lays the foundation for much of later political life. As we will see below, the lessons of such socialization sometimes emanate from entertainment television as well as news and public affairs media. Research suggests that children's early support for the political system usually gives way to growing disillusionment in the teen years, but this skepticism often dissipates as teens become young adults (Graber 2009a).

Cultivation Theory

Another brand of theory that addresses the cumulative impact of media on the public is cultivation theory. This theory is based on a project by George Gerbner and his associates (2002; Morgan 2009) that, for more than 20 years, examined the impact of growing up and living with television. They argue that, through its regular and almost ritualistic use by viewers, television plays a homogenizing role for otherwise heterogeneous populations. Influence occurs because of continued and lengthy exposure to television in general, not just exposure to individual programs or genres.

They suggest that immersion in television culture produces a "mainstreaming" effect, whereby differences based on cultural, social, and political characteristics are muted in heavy viewers of television. The result is that heavy television viewers internalize many of the distorted views of the social and political world presented by television (such as those discussed in Chapter 5). For example, compared to the real world, television programs drastically underrepresent older people, and heavy viewers tend to similarly underestimate the number of older people in society. Television portrays crime and violence much more frequently than it occurs in real life, and these television portrayals seem to influence heavy viewers in this area as well. Heavy viewers are more likely than moderate or light viewers to believe that most people cannot be trusted and that most people are selfishly looking out for themselves (Gerbner et al. 1984, 1993).

The impact of television cultivation on political belief seems to be in a conservative direction (Gerbner et al. 1982, 1984). A journalistic pose of an "objective" balancing of views seems to encourage heavy viewers to avoid calling themselves either "conservatives" or "liberals." However, self-described "moderates" who are heavy television viewers actually hold beliefs that are closer to those of conservatives than to those of liberals on a whole range of social issues, such as race, abortion, and homosexuality. On economic issues, heavy viewers are more likely than moderate or light viewers to adopt the conservative call for lower taxes, but they are also more likely to support a populist call for more social services.

Lessons From the Research

Research on the media's impact on citizens highlights the tension between media influence and reader agency. Media messages are negotiated by readers, but these messages can have an impact. Media influence what people think about and, to a lesser extent, how they understand the world.

For example, one of the most talked about issues in the last two decades has been the growth of cynicism and alienation in the American electorate. For some time, observers have argued that media coverage of the political world has contributed to this rise in cynicism, undermining the democratic process (Entman 1989; Goldfarb 1991; Robinson 1976; Rosen 1993). Among the arguments is the claim that the press promotes cynicism and undermines its credibility when it focuses superficially on the ups and downs of individual politicians. Cappella and Jamieson (1997) argue that the news helps to drive a "spiral of cynicism," in which coverage of political strategy erodes public trust and fuels disengagement from politics. Too often, critics argue, the media suggest that

> yet another president is a bumbling clown, that government is a hopeless mess, that politics repays no serious effort to attend to it. Mindlessly, the press contributes to these perceptions and then stands back to survey the damage as if it were some naturally occurring disaster. (Rosen 1993: 9)

However, the influence of the media is neither blatant nor unqualified. Perhaps the most significant effects of media exposure come about after long-term, heavy use. As we will see in Chapter 8, readers approach media products with a preexisting set of beliefs and experiences through which they filter media messages. Readers also occupy specific social positions that affect how they interpret the media. To understand the impact of media, therefore, we must remember that media consumption is often an active processing of information, not just a passive reception of media words and images.

MEDIA AND SOCIAL MOVEMENTS

We have highlighted media effects on political elites and individual citizens. We now turn our attention to the media's coverage of social movements—groups of citizens who have banded together to promote a social or political cause. Social movements are an especially important part of the political landscape because they can mediate between individual citizens and political elites.

We can think of the relationship between media and social movements as a transaction between two complex systems, each trying to accomplish a particular goal. Movements ask the media to communicate their messages to the public, while the media look to movements as one potential source of "news." However, the media hold the upper hand in their relationship with social movements. Movements usually need the mass media to widely publicize their activities. Such coverage helps social movements mobilize support, achieve validation as a significant political player, and expand the scope of conflict to attract potential allies or mediators. The media, on the other hand, have many alternatives to social movements as news sources (Gamson and Wolfsfeld 1993).

The task that faces social movements, therefore, is twofold. First, they must convince media gatekeepers that they are worthy of coverage; that is, they represent an interesting story angle or are significant "players" in the issues at hand. This task involves the direct issue of media access. Social movement activists often find that they need to conform to media expectations to gain this access. As the author of a media handbook for activists colorfully puts it, "An effective media strategy requires—at least to some extent—a willingness to cater to the often warped priorities and short attention span of the news media" (Salzman 1998: 3). Small grassroots organizations that do not achieve what the media consider to be "player" status may even have to resort to dramatic actions, such as demonstrations and protests, to attract the media's attention.

Second, social movements must work to influence the nature of the media coverage they receive. This task involves the struggle over "framing" messages (Gamson and Modigliani 1989; Gitlin 1980; Snow et al. 1986; Snow, Vliegenthart, and Corrigall-Brown 2007; Tuchman 1978). A *frame* generally refers to the context into which the media place facts. Frames organize information and help make it intelligible. For example, imagine the case of an environmental group suing a corporation to prevent the construction of a new facility that it believes will harm the local environment. The news reports about this issue might frame it as a story of David versus Goliath—the little local environmental group versus the big multinational corporation. However, the news reports could also frame the story as a handful of unreasonable extremists trying to stop rational progress. The first frame might help the movement mobilize support. The second frame would probably hurt their efforts. Movements, then, try to influence the coverage they receive in the media.

Gaining access to media coverage by staging dramatic actions can be counterproductive for a movement if the media use a discrediting frame in their coverage. Discrediting techniques used by the media include downplaying content in favor of emphasizing the spectacle of an event, painting demonstrators as deviant and unrepresentative of the population, granting comparable coverage and thus "false balance" to a tiny number of counterdemonstrators, and undercounting the attendance at demonstrations (Parenti 1986). For example, the Occupy movement that began in 2011 successfully brought national attention to the neglected issue of economic inequality. However, over time, the tactic that attracted media attention—long-term encampments on Wall Street and other locations—was not only difficult to maintain but was used by critics to suggest that the protesters did not represent average Americans.

As with electoral politics, the media's desire for succinct sound bites and interesting visuals has a significant impact on social movement efforts. Mass media will usually ignore movements that are unable to accommodate journalists' needs. Although pandering to media desires for dramatic visuals risks undermining the effective communication of a movement's message, proactive planning is a necessity if movements are to do all they can to develop favorable media coverage (Ryan 1991). Grassroots citizens' organizations with few resources for PR and media strategizing are at a distinct disadvantage when they face off against well-funded government agencies, corporations, and other organizations, especially when these movements are challenging mainstream norms.

The media have also been central to an extreme form of political movement: terrorism. Al-Qaeda and other movements that use terrorist tactics have fully incorporated mainstream media into their overall strategy. Media attention to terrorist acts is their main tool for publicizing their cause and triggering responses from their targets in the West, their own governments, their allies and supporters, and a broader mass audience. As media scholars Barnett and Reynolds (2009) note, acts of terrorism are primarily efforts to attract "the attention of the news media, the public, and the government. As coverage of September 11 showed, media are delivering the terrorist's message in nearly every conceivable way" (p. 3). In this sense, some critics argue that mainstream news media often indirectly assist terrorists in publicizing both their grievances and their capabilities.

The hurdles social movements face when they attempt to cultivate positive media attention from the mainstream media have often led to their use of "alternative" or "independent" media to promote their messages (Downing, 2001, 2011; Langlois and Dubois 2005). For example, in the late 19th and early 20th century, the labor movement produced a diverse array of labor newspapers, often catering to different immigrant groups (Hoerder and Harzig 1987; Pizzigati and Solowey 1992). In the politically vibrant environment of 1960s social activism, a thriving "underground" press emerged, made up of local newspapers and even alternative wire services reflecting the views and concerns of political activists and countercultural participants (Armstrong 1981). In the 1970s and 1980s, the do-it-yourself politics and sensibility of the punk and hardcore scenes resulted in a wide variety of "zines" that combined political and cultural analysis and commentary. These alternative magazines ranged from tiny efforts that were little more than photocopies to larger, nationally distributed publications with slicker production and substantial print runs. The zine format was adopted by many subcultures; for example, "girl zines" emphasized feminist themes, and music and "queercore" zines focused on gay rights issues and gay and lesbian punk music. Later, some of these zine efforts went online in the form of e-zines. Today, the Internet serves as the "printing press" of many social movement organizations, providing visitors with information and analysis that is rarely found in mainstream media. That is just one of the ways digital media has changed the world of politics.

THE INTERNET AND POLITICAL NEWS

Television remains the most common source of news in the United States by a large margin. But the news landscape is rapidly changing, as a growing portion of the population now goes online for news from a dizzying array of new media options. For example, during the 2012 election cycle, 67 percent of voters cited television as a major source of elections news—far more than those who cited newspapers (27%). However, the percentage of voters citing the Internet as a major source of election news has grown from just 11 percent in 2000 to 47 percent in 2012. Voters under 30 years old use the Internet for election information at an even higher rate (64%), suggesting that its importance will only continue to grow (Pew Research Center 2012a).

Political Campaigns and the Internet

Increasingly, political actors have incorporated the Internet into their electoral political strategies. Among the advantages of online campaigning is that candidates can control their messages as well as defend themselves from attacks—they do not have to rely on journalists to communicate to the public. The 1996 campaign was the first to extensively use the Internet to post press releases and position papers online and to quickly respond to developing stories. In 2004, the Howard Dean campaign pioneered the use of the Internet as a way to parlay many small contributions into substantial fundraising. Some of the staff from that campaign led a similar effort for Obama's 2008 campaign and pushed Internet use further. Obama's campaign team posted over 1,800 videos on YouTube, perhaps most notably a celebrity-studded "Yes We Can" music video by Will.i.am. Thanks to the campaign's interactive site, each supporter could create her or his own network, organize events, and even phone undecided voters in his or her neighborhood, thereby taking on many of the functions that political parties used to serve. By 2012, though, the Obama campaign was using state-of-the-art techniques that one analysis noted made Obama's "much-heralded 2008 social media juggernaut—which raised half billion dollars and revolutionized politics—look like cavemen with stone tablets" (Romano 2012).

For example, if you Googled the phrase "immigration reform" during the 2012 campaign, your results would likely have been accompanied by an ad from the Obama campaign, which courted supporters of immigration reform. Clicking on that ad to visit the Obama site would have loaded cookies onto your computer that not only tracked what you viewed on the campaign website, but also tracked your movements across the web to see where you shop and what other interests you have—a technique often used by commercial advertisers. If you opened your Facebook page, the campaign could gather more information on your circle of friends and your "likes," among other things. On a subsequent visit to the Obama website, content customized to your data profile—including your interest in immigration reform—would be highlighted. If you supplied the campaign with your e-mail address, it might also make pitches for financial contributions by highlighting the issue they knew you were already interested in, customized to your likely demographic based on the data they gathered on you. It would also likely encourage you to join with other voters in your area to help with the campaign. In this way, candidates use the Internet to reach voters with their message, gather information about them, solicit financial support, mobilize them to volunteer for the campaign, and encourage them to turn out to vote. These sorts of tactics were quickly copied by other campaigns.

With the Internet, campaigns are not constrained by the high cost and limited format of the 30-second campaign commercial. Candidates can use online advertising creatively to post videos on YouTube, encourage the spread of information via Facebook, and stay in touch with supporters through Twitter. Despite the much heralded interactivity of Web 2.0, though, campaigns rarely respond to supporter messages or "retweet" messages from citizens. Instead, they use the Internet to push their messages to voters in a largely one-way flow of information (Project for Excellence in Journalism 2012).

Mainstream news organizations and media companies also have adapted to the Internet, experimenting with new formats and offerings. For example, Google offered 2010 Election Ratings, an interactive map that allowed users to access candidate information and track poll data for each house, senate, and governor's election. Campaign Tracker, a news aggregator for smartphones, allowed paid subscribers to keep updated on campaign news, election data, and even tweets from their preferred candidates. The *St. Petersburg*

Times introduced PolitiFact, where journalists fact-checked statements by politicians, lobbyists, and interest groups, and rated them on a Truth-O-Meter. Newer innovations taking advantage of Internet capacities will certainly continue.

Social Movements and the Internet

Social movements also rely heavily on new technologies (Kahn and Kellner 2004). Because movements have often been shut out of mainstream media, they have used the Internet extensively to post information and videos, promote their causes, and solicit new members. Thousands of websites from across the political spectrum, along with numerous politically oriented discussion groups, populate the Internet. Human rights groups, environmental groups, and labor organizations have used the Internet to help organize across national borders. Tea Party organizers and gun rights advocates have used the Internet to post analyses and organize members.

The relatively unregulated cyberworld has also been a boon for hate groups—supporting everything from white supremacy to violent homophobia—to put out their messages and recruit new members. The Internet also affords terrorist groups and their supporters with new opportunities to communicate through their own websites, which include discussion groups, videos, political articles, and leaders' speeches (Seib and Janbek 2011). For example, the various branches of Al-Qaeda produce their own videos, which are available on YouTube and other video-sharing sites, and are regularly broadcast on regional and international television. They also produce an English-language online magazine, *Inspire*, to promote their cause.

Many more conventional alternative information projects have emerged, hastened by the availability of smartphones, digital video cameras, user-friendly editing software, laptop and tablet computers, and inexpensive Internet connections—all of which have facilitated the growth of media that is independent of the corporate-owned mainstream media. Thanks in part to the development of new forms of digital media, social movement media projects have dramatically expanded their production capacity; activist media projects across the political spectrum now involve many nonexperts and operate on larger scales than ever before.

One of the earliest examples of social movements using new media in a sophisticated way originated during the 1999 World Trade Organization protests in Seattle, Washington. Concerned that mainstream media would not adequately cover the issues raised in those demonstrations, activists created an independent media center, Indymedia.

> The center acted as a clearinghouse of information for journalists, and provided up-to-the-minute reports, photos, audio and video footage through its website. Using the collected footage, the Seattle Independent Media Center (seattle.indymedia.org) produced a series of five documentaries, uplinked every day to satellite and distributed throughout the United States to public access stations. The center also produced its own newspaper, distributed throughout Seattle and to other cities via the internet, as well as hundreds of audio segments, transmitted through the web and Studio X, a 24-hour micro and internet radio station based in Seattle. (Indymedia.org 2001)

The Indymedia effort in Seattle was replicated to varying degrees at subsequent demonstrations protesting the International Monetary Fund, World Bank, the Group of Eight, and other global economy meetings. More local Indymedia sites emerged, networked together to provide significant information, analysis, and commentary, all outside of the mainstream media system.

Since then, however, many of the functions pioneered by Indymedia had been replicated elsewhere. A variety of new commercial media outlets offered individual activists and social movements new options for distributing independent media. For example, YouTube makes it easy for users to post videos, while commercial blogging platforms such as Wordpress and Blogger permit anyone to publish their own news or commentary.

Digital Technologies and the Future of Politics

The future impact of the Internet and mobile digital platforms on political life is being intensely debated. The full effect of these new technologies may not be seen for some time, as people develop media consumption habits at young ages, and some of these technologies are relatively new (Chadwick 2006; Lee and Delli Carpini 2010; Shah, Kwak, and Holbert 2001). The changes we face are not only technological, but they involve socioeconomic, political, and cultural issues as well (Fenton 2010; Washbourne 2010). Some observers see great hope for new technologies to revitalize the democratic process, while others warn about potential dangers. All agree that the effects of new technologies on news and information in a democratic society raise important questions.

For example, will new technologies crowd out more traditional forms of media? So far, the answer is no. In 2010, just 12 percent of Americans relied on the Internet and mobile devices exclusively for their news. The percentage of Americans who watch news on television remained almost unchanged from the mid-1990s to 2012. (See Figure 7.1.) Newspaper readership and radio news listenership, however, has declined steadily for two decades. Meanwhile, the use of the Internet as a news source has increased and now surpasses that of traditional newspapers and radio, though it still lags behind television. But many of these Internet news sources are, in fact, produced by news organizations involved in traditional media. Yahoo News and Google News were the two most popular ways to get news online; both link to traditional news sources online (Pew Research Center 2012c). However, one of the great questions facing news organizations is how can mainstream news remain economically viable in an era when users expect news to be available online for free? One answer has been for major news outlets such as the *New York Times* and the *Washington Post* to set up "pay walls" to charge regular readers for online content.

Will new technologies increase the audience for news? So far, the answer to this is also no. While Internet news sources are increasing the overall amount of time people spend with news, they are not expanding the size of the news audience. The percentage of people who report getting no news the day before has remained almost unchanged over the last two decades, at 17 percent in 2010. Age is not a major factor here; young people are the most likely to make use of digital platforms, but they are not doing so for news at any higher rate than older Americans are. For all age groups, about half of Americans say they get some news from a digital source (Pew Research Center for the People & the Press 2010).

| Figure 7.1 | **Where People Got News Yesterday** |

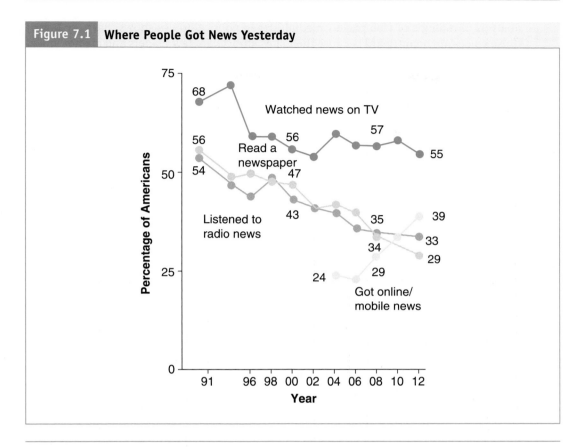

Source: Pew Research Center 2012c.

Relatedly, will the Internet expand the pool of people involved in politics? Here, too, the tentative answer seems to be no. Internet use does seem to increase the political knowledge of people who are already interested and active in political life, but does not increase interest among those who have been inactive (Prior 2007). Instead, for example, campaign websites tend to be visited by partisans and are used by campaigns to raise funds and mobilize volunteers rather than attract new voters or sway those who are undecided (Foot and Schneider 2006; Howard 2005).

Will the Internet provide a democratic platform for influential new voices to be heard in political life? There is no doubt that the Internet has enabled new forms of political organizing, but it is not clear whether those involved in such efforts are new to the world of politics. Nor does it seem that any significant quantity of new voices are being heard via the Internet. Hindman (2009) highlights the important distinction between speaking and being heard. The Internet has certainly made it easier for many more people to speak about politics or any other issue, especially through the use of blogs. But Hindman's analysis of millions of web pages on a half dozen political topics shows that very few of those voices are being heard because their sites attract very few readers and are not linked by other sites. Instead, Hindman finds that online audiences are actually *more* concentrated at a few major sites than audiences for traditional media. He points out that "despite—or rather because of—the enormity of the content available online, citizens seem to cluster strongly around the top few information sources in a given category" (p. 18). This clustering creates a hierarchy that is "structural, woven in to the hyperlinks that make up the web; it is economic, in the dominance of companies like Google, Yahoo! And Microsoft; and it is social, in the small group of white, highly educated, male professionals who are vastly overrepresented in online opinion" (pp. 18–19). So while the Internet may be very useful in giving people access to information, it may not be so helpful in giving them a political voice.

As the number of information sources grows dramatically, will enclaves of "news" and opinion presented from a distinctly partisan perspective further contribute to the political divide in the country? That remains to be seen, but there is some cause for concern that new media forms are doing just that (Sunstein 2002). The Internet allows much greater news customization to occur automatically. News feeds can be set up to present information only on stories in which a reader has already expressed an interest, closing out the chance of learning something on a new and unrelated topic. Receiving baseball scores, but not golf or tennis results, on your news feed may not be particularly significant, but excluding global news in favor of celebrity features, for example, fundamentally changes the experience of consulting news sources. The danger is that specialized news and opinion sources lead to isolated topical and ideological encampments where citizens receive only news about their narrow interests and hear only views with which they already agree.

Since its earliest years, most media scholars have been cautious about the long-term impact of online media. When Neuman (1996) asked, "Will the evolution of C-SPAN, CNN, and the Internet political discussion groups have a measurable impact beyond those policy wonks and news junkies already addicted to the intricacies of political life," his answer was, "probably not" (p. 14). Although new media outlets make more information readily available than ever, citizens must first feel the need to investigate such sources.

The political media landscape is certainly changing, but more information and new technologies, by themselves, are unlikely to overcome a high level of political disengagement. Barnett's (1997) early observation remains relevant: "The real challenge—to change the dominant political culture from one of alienation, cynicism and detachment to one of concerned involvement—cannot be left simply to new communicative devices" (p. 213).

POLITICS AND ENTERTAINMENT MEDIA

Our discussion about the media's impact on political life has emphasized the most obvious and immediately relevant form of media: the news. Such "serious" media were long the focus of academic research. Until the 1980s, the academic community did not take popular culture or entertainment media very seriously. That situation, however, has changed. Recent work on nonnews media suggests that they have a profound importance in shaping (and often distorting) our understanding of the world. This section briefly considers a few examples of the political significance of nonnews media.

Television and Film

We usually associate prime-time television with a variety of entertainment programs ranging from dramas and situation comedies to game shows, sports, and "reality" programs. Such programs attract much larger audiences than news broadcasts. Most people usually think of such shows as "only entertainment," but they feature characters and story lines that directly or indirectly have political significance. All TV, in fact, is political. Certainly, not all writers and producers of television fare have an explicit political agenda, but we can interpret all media content from a political viewpoint. Most obviously open to political interpretation is programming that directly tackles social issues. Dramas, sitcoms, and animated programs have addressed a wide range of social issues such as sexual abuse, racism, terrorism, and homelessness (Gournelos 2009; Holtzman 2000; Lichter, Lichter, and Rothman 1994).

However, political implications lie behind every type of cultural product, including entertainment television that is not explicitly political. Television programs were just as political when they avoided issues such as sexism and corporate corruption. Even situation comedies featuring characters who have nothing to do overtly with political issues make normative political statements by their avoidance of politics. Refusing to take a stand is, in fact, taking one. Indeed, "nonpolitical" programs may be making the strongest political statements of all. In not questioning the status quo, such programs reinforce it by contributing to its taken-for-granted nature. Sometimes, by disparaging all politics or efforts at change, these shows may foster a cynicism and a fatalism that are dismissive of real efforts to promote change. Therefore, we can find much of the political implication of prime-time television in unstated assumptions.

A word of caution is in order when we are discussing the political role of entertainment television. There is no conspiracy at work to indoctrinate prime-time viewers. Instead, as we have seen, programming decisions are usually made on the basis of trying to satisfy the tastes of the viewing public—whatever the popular sentiment happens to be at the time—while meeting the needs of advertisers (Gitlin 2000). Commercial television, remember, is a for-profit enterprise in the business of delivering audiences to advertisers. Creating entertainment that does not contradict this capitalist agenda is television's major form of political proselytizing. Ratings and profits are the bottom line (Meehan 2005).

When researchers study viewers and not just the content of prime-time programming, they find the political impact of television to be complicated. The content of media does matter; however, audiences play an important role in interpreting what they see. For example, in the 1970s sitcom *All in the Family,* heated arguments between the two main characters covered political ground such as the Vietnam War, race relations, and the status of women. How did such a program affect viewers? According to one study (Vidmar and Rokeach 1974), the effects depended on the preconceptions of the viewer. On race, for example, the views of both liberals and the prejudiced were reinforced by watching the program.

All in the Family may have been unusual in the degree to which it routinely articulated clashing views. Most shows do not regularly feature views that are such polar opposites.

However, even when they suggest a more singular worldview, entertainment programs are open to interpretation. Such was the case with the late-1980s hit *The Cosby Show*. The program was a traditional professional-class family situation comedy, with one major exception: All the leading characters were black. Many critics hailed the program as a positive portrayal of African Americans rarely found on television. However, Jhally and Lewis (1992) found in their interviews with viewers that many of them were interpreting the show in a quite different light. White viewers interpreted the location of black characters within the elite world of the professional class (the mother was a lawyer, and the father was a doctor) as a sign that racial barriers no longer existed. The authors argue that, ironically, the program contributed to a new "enlightened racism" among these viewers. Black viewers, on the other hand, tended to welcome the positive portrayal of a sensitive, intelligent, and most of all, successful black family. Jhally and Lewis, though, suggest that this reaction reinforces the stereotype that a positive image must equal a prosperous image.

Anecdotal evidence suggests that widely divergent interpretations of media content are common. For example, the comedy show *M*A*S*H* was a hit on CBS for 11 years. As it chronicled the trials and tribulations of a surgical unit during the Korean War, it presented antiauthoritarian and antiwar humor. The show's original writer, Larry Gelbart, wanted the program's message to be that war was futile. However, he left the show after four years because he feared that the original intent of the series had been defeated. Ironically, he felt that the show's long-term success routinized the characters' fatalistic acceptance of war. He may have been right.

One of the series' main actors, Mike Farrell, learned from his fan mail that audiences could interpret the same material in a multitude of ways. As he recounted, he received some letters that said, "'Boy, you guys make war look like fun,' and/or, 'After watching your show I've decided I'm going to sign up'." Farrell commented, "I read those and I kind of shake my head, and I've written back and said, 'I don't quite understand how you can watch our show and come to that conclusion'." But Farrell reported that he "also got a wonderful letter from a kid who said that he had intended to be a professional soldier, and after watching our show over the years he had seen that that's not what he wants to do, and as a matter of fact he's decided to become a priest" (in Gitlin 2000: 217). One lesson is that, perhaps more so than with news coverage, viewers can interpret the ambiguous political messages of entertainment television in many different ways. We explore this topic in more depth in the next chapter.

As with television programs, the political content of popular films takes a backseat to their ability to turn a profit. Big-budget Hollywood films, especially, must appeal to a broad and diverse audience to be profitable. The political content of such films is often left ambiguous so as not to offend potential moviegoers (Christensen and Hass 2005; Prince 1992). As a result, many of the biggest box office hits—blockbusters such as *Titanic, Jurassic Park,* and *The Avengers,* along with various incarnations of *Iron Man, Transformers, Lord of the Rings, Star Wars, Indiana Jones, Batman, Pirates of the Caribbean,* and *Harry Potter* movies—are upbeat, feel-good, action-adventure films with cartoon-like characters and little serious content, political or otherwise.

Even this kind of light entertainment fare can be politically meaningful. Research suggests that entertainment media are an important agent of political socialization, especially among young people. One study found that watching entertainment television may, in fact, discourage people from participating in political conversation. As Jackson (2009) puts it, "The dying art of intelligent political conversation is being hurried to its grave by increased use of entertainment television" (p. 160). Entertainment media can have a significant global political impact. For example, Graber (2009b) found that public perceptions of life in the United States among citizens in the Middle East are more consistent with the content of globally circulating reruns of once-popular television programs such as *The West Wing, Friends,* and *That '70s Show* than with the stories of American life that appear in U.S. government public diplomacy campaigns directed at the Arab world. More generally, entertainment television can have a powerful influence on how we understand issues and events with which we have no direct experience.

Music

The world of music and music video has its own set of political implications. Like television and film, music is generally a commercial product sold for profit. As such, producers must be cautious about promoting messages that alienate too many in the audience. Mainstream radio hits, therefore, are full of platitudes about love and—well—little else. It might be argued that, as a diversion from the problems of the day, such music helps maintain the status quo, though it does not contain overt political messages. Some forms of music, however, attract an audience precisely because they promote politically charged, controversial, or alternative views. Such music is especially significant because it tends to be much more meaningful to people who listen to it.

We can use the example of music to highlight a point about the construction of meaning in media (which we explore more fully in the next chapter). An ongoing interactive process is involved in the production and consumption of media products (Gottdiener 1985). The producers of music (the corporate owners, not necessarily the bands) are usually interested in the creation of profit. In more theoretical terms, what is important to producers is the *exchange value* of the product (what it can be sold for). People who buy—or otherwise download—music have a totally different motivation. They want to enjoy the music on their MP3 players. What is important to consumers is the *use value* of the product (the function it serves).

The process does not stop there. Those buying the music infuse the product with symbolic meaning (or *sign value*). Saying that you regularly listen to pop idol Lady Gaga, the rock band The Black Keys, country music performer Taylor Swift, rapper Lil Wayne, the electronic band The Chemical Brothers, or cellist Esperanza Spalding often suggests something significant that goes beyond a difference in musical tastes. Music fans often infuse the music they like with meaning. They associate music they cherish with an outlook on life, with friends and lovers, or with important memories in their lives. Musical taste—especially a taste for music that is outside of the mainstream—can also signal a political orientation or a set of values. That is why alternative music is often associated with a broader subculture marked, for example, by fashion and style. Heavy metal's leather and chains, punk rock's dyed hair and body piercing, psychedelic music's tie-dyed T-shirts, rap's hip-hop clothes, and grunge's flannel shirts were all examples of this. They originated as meaningful expressions of values and orientations associated with music. As these styles became commercialized, they often lost their original meaning and were reduced to mere commodities.

Producers—in the form of the corporations that sell music—do not attach the same kind of meaning to the products as consumers do. Many people have had the unpleasant shock of hearing a song that had special meaning for them transformed into supermarket Muzak. A media product with meaning to a consumer has been repackaged and stripped of meaning by producers.

Often, the meaning that is attached to music has political significance. But even in this case, the music industry has learned how to adeptly manipulate articulations of dissent into viable, profitable commercial products. In some cases, these products may maintain the veneer of a rebellious alternative lifestyle but, in fact, they have become well-controlled sources of corporate profit. For example, music that at one time may have represented anger toward and rejection of authority figures and the status quo—we are thinking here, especially, of rock, punk, and rap music—has been absorbed by corporate America and transformed into a commodity stripped of its political significance.

In the 1980s, punk rock, which thumbed its nose at the commercial slickness of mainstream music, was smoothed around the edges and repackaged as new wave music. Not long after rap's appearance as a powerful music of resistance, it was incorporated into corporate advertising strategies (the Pillsbury Doughboy even began rapping to sell cookie dough!) or mass-marketed as controversial—and very saleable—"gangsta rap." The "grunge" movement of the early 1990s was grounded in local music scenes; featured low-cost, used-clothing fashions; and was seen by many of its fans as a rejection of corporate-dominated rock and fashion. However, grunge quickly became a major profit maker for multinational corporations. By the mid-1990s, the grunge sensibility had been repackaged under labels such as "alternative" and "buzz" and represented a mainstream trend in the rock music industry. In the late 1990s, the angry politics of some rage rock bands, such as Rage Against the Machine, were supplanted by a heavy dose of misogynous and homophobic lyrics by performers such as Limp Bizkit. The resulting controversies were effectively packaged and marketed.

On a smaller scale, world music fusion has also been co-opted. The multiracial band Mano Negra inaugurated in the 1990s a rhythm called *patchanka:* a mix of punk rock, Latin and African rhythms, ska, and reggae, with lyrics often inspired by political and social issues. Later the Mano Negra front man, Manu Chao, started a solo career; and many of his songs, charged with political content but packaged in a hip sound, became commercial hits. Many bands worldwide were inspired by the sound of Mano Negra, but their music is often devoid of political content.

In all these cases, the music industry transformed voices of rebellion into highly marketable commodities in just a few short years, usually divested of political significance. By the time you read this, there is likely to be a newly emerging music trend that, once again, attempts to resist the corporate pressures of commercialization. The active resistance of audiences to being co-opted by the mainstream may well be one of the prime forces behind creativity in the music industry.

Drawing on an even earlier period of time, the media industry has enlisted the rock and roll of the 1960s and 1970s to enhance sales. Corporate advertising has appropriated music that once represented a countercultural critique of contemporary society. Bob Dylan's political anthem "The Times They Are A-Changing" sold financial services. While keeping the catchy tune, a seafood chain turned the Allman Brothers' countercultural refrain "love is in the air" into "lobster everywhere." The Beatles' "Revolution" sold sneakers. Steppenwolf's "Born to Be Wild" sold cars. (You can't help but wonder which meaningful songs of today will be the commercials of tomorrow.)

In recent years, more musicians have embraced commercials as a venue for their work, fusing music with consumerism. In an industry first, Moby licensed all 18 songs on his 1999 album, *Play,* for use in commercials. Today, the list of contemporary artists whose songs end up in commercials is seemingly endless. Nissan cars alone were sold with songs by Seal, the Smiths, Smash Mouth, The Breeders, Lenny Kravitz, Stevie Ray Vaughan, The Who, Black Sabbath, and Stone Temple Pilots. Meanwhile, Fatboy Slim sold Oldsmobiles, Oasis promoted AT&T, The Dandy Warhols sold Pontiac, and The Temper Trap sold Chrysler.

While profit-seeking corporations largely use mainstream commercial music for their own purposes, there is a long, rich history of music associated with different political causes. The labor and civil rights movements, for example, each developed a distinct repertoire of political music that was a cornerstone of each movement. Conservative religious movements also draw on a wide range of "Christian" music aimed at promoting a biblically inspired political message. Some forms of rap and hip-hop music continue to be a forum for the expression of political views. Over the past several decades, there have been a series of music-based charity and political projects, including Live Aid for famine relief in Ethiopia, Farm Aid for U.S. farmers facing foreclosure, Live Earth to raise awareness about climate change, Live 8 to "make poverty history," Mandela Day Concerts that raise funds for the fight against HIV/AIDS, and several Amnesty International tours for human rights worldwide. To varying degrees, each of these efforts has made a political statement out of music.

It is important to remember that audiences appropriate music for their own purposes, regardless of how it is marketed. The sale of some music can profit a corporation while simultaneously serving a different function for the consumers of that music. In many cases, the social and political commentary in the music of classic and contemporary bands, such as Gang of Four, Chumbawumba, Public Enemy, The Clash, Paris, Rage Against the Machine, or Tracy Chapman, has significant meaning for those who listen—regardless of the corporate label for which the music is recorded. This demonstrates another aspect of the complex tensions involved in the social process of media creation and consumption.

The fragmentation of popular music has been the story of recent decades. The music scene is fractured into rap, rock, pop, country, techno, blues, folk, jazz, Latin, new age, reggae, and many others. In turn, each of these genres is fractured into many different subcategories, making it impossible to speak of a single version of any of these musical types. Each genre consists of many different, sometimes contradictory, tendencies. For example, as we have seen, some forms of rap are well known for their angry and progressive political sentiments regarding racism, economic inequality, and police brutality. Other rap artists have incorporated messages of misogyny and anti-Semitism and seem to glorify violence. Still other rap music is concerned with personal themes of love and relationships, not with political issues. Thus, there is no single political message promoted by rap or any other genre of music.

Whatever the genre, the political impact of music is mixed. Musicians and fans endlessly struggle to claim their music as something different and, in some cases, as a political statement of alternative views. The music industry, however, is less interested in *why* music sells than in *how well* it sells. The result is oppositional cultures that are endlessly being absorbed into the commercial marketplace, which transforms what were once vibrant political statements into product jingles, movie soundtracks, and elevator Muzak. At the same time, enclaves of local and noncommercial ventures—college radio stations, small alternative clubs, and independent record labels—continuously nurture newly emerging alternatives.

GLOBAL MEDIA, GLOBAL POLITICS

The global dimension of the media's political impact has become all the more significant in recent years as the media industry itself has taken on global proportions. We can divide the growing body of transnational research into studies of the Western (especially U.S.) media's impact on other societies and, more recently, studies of indigenous media. Critics have often examined Western media in the context of *cultural imperialism,* an approach with which we begin this discussion.

The Cultural Imperialism Thesis

For a number of years, the discussion of global media was influenced by the argument that media products of the West, especially of the United States, so dominated the rest of the world that they amounted to a form of cultural imperialism. The basic argument of the cultural imperialism thesis was that Western media products introduced into other countries, especially "developing" countries, contributed to a decline in local traditional values and promoted, instead, values associated with capitalism. In addition, ownership and control over media were maintained in U.S. hands, and other nations became more dependent on the United States for cultural production. Early articulations of this position emphasized the role of television (Schiller 1971) and were an important antidote to ethnocentric and sometimes racist thinking about the superiority of American culture.

However, the argument that U.S.-owned media hardware and programs were part of a plan to culturally subjugate the world now seems overdrawn. Evidence suggests that the imperialism thesis is problematic on at least two counts (Tunstall 1977). First, researchers questioned the early claims of powerful effects, pointing out that the media capacities of other nations quickly allowed them to produce their own programming, reducing their reliance on U.S. shows. For example, a 25-year longitudinal study of South Korean television found that the proportion of imported programming that aired was reduced by about half, to less than 8 percent. However, the feature films that aired continued to be overwhelmingly foreign, probably due to the higher production costs associated with such projects (Lee 2007). Also, as we examine in Chapter 8, research has shown that media audiences in different countries make local interpretations of U.S. media products. The program might be the same, but the local meaning of the program in two countries could be quite different. Over time, researchers made cultural imperialism theory more subtle by recognizing such variation in impact. Theorists recognized that the type of society into which media products were introduced, the forms and volume of media products, and many other variables affected the strength and particular characteristics of the media's impact.

Second, interest shifted away from a focus on television toward a broader, more generalized understanding of the influence of different media—including everything from radio to comic books. For some capital-intensive media products, especially film, American dominance truly did reach global dimensions. However, in less expensive and more easily produced formats, such as television and music (Laing 1986), local indigenous programming grew, and regional export centers developed.

In this century, the situation has become quite complex. U.S. media still have a significant impact on foreign nations, and some TV programs have become popular worldwide. American television programs are still widely popular abroad. American film is also very popular, with action-adventure films making the biggest splash. Sex and violence, especially, seem to cross cultures easily, whereas comedy and some forms of drama have a more difficult time. As American producers and film studios become increasingly reliant

Source: Mark Ralston/Getty Images.

The U.S. film *White House Down* is advertised outside a Beijing theater in 2013. Despite massive growth in the number of movie theaters there, China limits the number of foreign films that can be shown to just 34 per year.

on overseas distribution to make a profit on expensive blockbusters, the ease with which a film crosses cultural barriers becomes a relevant factor. Thus, violence-packed action-adventure films are still hits with Hollywood producers even though they are often less successful in the U.S. market than more family-oriented fare.

Meanwhile, in the area of pop music, American artists are sometimes heavily influenced by other cultures. Western musicians such as Paul Simon, David Byrne (formerly of the Talking Heads), and Sting (formerly of The Police) are among the best-known mainstream artists who early on incorporated African and South American sounds and musicians into their work. Observers have sometimes criticized the process of Western musicians drawing on indigenous cultures as being exploitative because it represents a raiding of local culture for the profit of Western artists and record conglomerates. Critics have also accused musicians of creating a watered-down or homogenized musical sound. However, others argue that the increased exposure of indigenous music has led to a greater appreciation of it by a wide variety of audiences. In fact, "world music" has grown in popularity to become a recognizable music category that represents both music produced in particular parts of the world and an amalgam of varied instruments and rhythms resulting in a generic "global" sound ungrounded in any single tradition.

The meeting of Western and international music can be complicated. For example, various elements of South African "township jive," *mbaqanga, kwela,* and Zulu choral music dominated the sound on Paul Simon's hit album *Graceland.* Simon's interest in South African popular music was sparked in part by the fact that the sound reminded him of 1950s American rock and roll. In fact, American rock music and other African American musical styles of the 1950s and 1960s were distributed in South Africa (Garofalo 1992). Thus, local cultures had absorbed the infusion of 1950s American rock and roll and had produced new sounds that, in turn, were the inspiration for popular American music in the 1980s and 1990s. A simple model of cultural imperialism cannot account for the complicated interconnections that have become world music.

The Politics of Media in Other Nations

Recent decades have been a time of enormous global change. The growth in communication technologies has been a major element of this change. In one early assessment of the global political significance of new forms of media, O'Neil (1993) argued that factors such as the increased "range of public knowledge across the barriers of space, illiteracy, and national sovereignty" have helped promote mass-based "people power" politics. Such politics is not inevitably democratic, but it does tend to restrict the license of rulers while opening the way for potentially democratic action. O'Neil also noted that global media have changed the nature of leadership by making strong visual and emotional appeal more important than knowledge or experience.

Communications media have clearly become central to political action. However, we need to take care in assessing their impact. Consider one famous image from the 1989 student uprising in China's Tiananmen Square. In grainy footage, a single unknown youth stood defiantly in front of an oncoming tank. The tank stopped, turned, and tried to go around the youth. He moved over, again blocking the tank. The standoff continued in this manner until bystanders dragged the youth to safety. The image became an inspirational one in the West.

However, the film was also shown—repeatedly—on state-sponsored Chinese television. Why? Because the government wanted to show how cautious it had been in putting down the rebellion. In the eyes of the Chinese government, the film showed foolish defiance by a youth and restrained response by government officials.

Clearly, however, modern communication technologies have become a central part of political activity for at least a quarter century. For example, when leaders of a 1991 coup against Soviet President Gorbachev knocked out the transmission capabilities of some media outlets in Moscow, some Russians were able to receive news of developing events by way of satellite dish, courtesy of CNN. When government officials essentially blacked out coverage of the events in Tiananmen Square, Chinese students studying abroad faxed newspaper stories to the student leaders in China. In January 1995, the Iranian parliament approved a ban on satellite dishes in an attempt to control reception of popular Western television programs that Islamic clerics claimed were promoting moral decay. After Afghanistan's Taliban forces gained power in 1996 and tried to enforce a strict version of Islamic rule, they banned television sets, VCRs, videotapes, satellite dishes, movie theaters, nonreligious music, and all print material from outside the country (Abdullah 1998).

When the United States launched the air war against Iraq in March 2003, the U.S. military bombed television broadcasting facilities, seeking to undermine Saddam Hussein's capacity to communicate with the military and the civilian population. Expecting that broadcasting facilities would be targeted, the Iraqi government employed mobile television facilities and continued to broadcast for more than two weeks, finally ceasing their television transmission the day before the U.S. military entered Baghdad (Human Rights Watch 2003).

The impact of social media in the Middle East and northern Africa has received considerable attention. In 2009, demonstrators protesting a disputed presidential election in Tehran, Iran, posted regular updates on Twitter for outside observers. The U.S. State Department even asked Twitter to delay scheduled maintenance to avoid disrupting communication among activists. Social media also played a role in the various Arab Spring protests, including the Egyptian revolution (Howard and Hussain 2013; Saleh 2012). Demonstrators used the Internet to help organize their protests and to send video of their actions to the outside world; but the protests were also organized through existing traditional networks and organizations, especially labor unions (Lee and Weinthal 2011). In fact, the impact and significance of social media should not be overstated. For example, while the Iranian demonstrations were widely touted in Western media as the "Twitter revolution," later analysis suggested that most of the Twitter chatter originated from outside Iran, and the messages that originated from within the country were largely aimed at outside audiences, not local citizens (Esfandiari 2010). Those messages frequently perpetuated wild, unsubstantiated rumors that often confused the situation. Within Iran, such high-tech communications played a much less significant role than old-fashioned word of mouth. Western observers seemed to overlook the fact that Twitter did not support Farsi, the language most used in Iran. As Mehdi Yahyanejad, the Los Angeles manager of a Farsi-language news site, commented at the time: "Twitter's impact inside Iran is zero. . . . Here [in the United States], there is lots of buzz, but once you look . . . you see most of it are Americans tweeting among themselves" (Musgrove 2009). Such observations suggest that we need to be cautious when assessing the role of these new media in political life.

Source: CNN/Getty Images.

The same media content may be understood quite differently in different cultural contexts. The well-known photo above was taken during the 1989 Tiananmen Square political demonstrations in Beijing, China. It shows a lone demonstrator briefly preventing a tank from proceeding on its way. As the tank tried to go around the demonstrator, he moved and again blocked the tank's progress. Friends pulled the demonstrator away shortly after this photo was taken.

In the West, the incident came to symbolize heroic individual defiance in the face of overwhelming power. In China, though, the video of the incident was shown repeatedly on state-controlled television to illustrate the great restraint used by the military in dealing with demonstrators. The meaning of the same image was quite different for people of different cultural sensibilities.

CONCLUSION

The media's influence on the political process has utterly transformed the way politics is conducted in many countries. It reaches beyond the content of political coverage in the news and entertainment media, extending into the social process of political deliberation and transforming the physical, social act of conducting politics. The media have facilitated the development of a mass audience for political spectacles. This audience usually has no serious affiliation with political parties, labor unions, or other political organizations. It learns about candidates through the media lens.

The structure of the mass media enables politicians to reach a broad audience. However, to do so, politicians must play by the ground rules set by the media. Parties and platforms matter less in glossy, mediated politics, while personality and image matter more. Politicians, acutely aware of this fact, tailor their activities accordingly. They often steer away from substantive policy to a politics of sound bites and photo opportunities.

Mass media and new digital media that host user-generated content have the potential to facilitate information sharing and political discussion. However, the potential role of the media in promoting a more vibrant political process remains unrealized.

As should now be clear, discussion of the role of media in political life must be tempered by the realization that audiences are not passive receptors of media messages. As we explore in Chapter 8, audiences are active participants in the construction of meaning.

DISCUSSION QUESTIONS

1. How does the presence of media affect political life? How does it impact political elites and ordinary citizens?

2. What are the key arguments of each of the following theoretical models? Which seem more plausible to you? Why?
   a. hypodermic model
   b. minimal effects model
   c. agenda setting
   d. cultivation theory

3. How has the Internet affected politics, both at home and abroad? Do you think digital media have promoted democracy (if so, how?) or are they largely reproducing traditional political life? Explain.

CHAPTER 8

Active Audiences and the Construction of Meaning

Source: Maciej Dakowicz/Alamy.

With the emergence of the Internet and the continuing growth in digital and interactive media, the boundary between media producer and media audience is sometimes blurry. However, even in the digital environment, most of us spend far more time as audience members—watching, reading, and listening to content created by others—than we do as media producers. Understanding media audiences, and how they make meaning of the various media products they consume, remains an essential task for media scholars.

For a long time, however, scholars and critics did not take media audiences very seriously. Concern about the potentially manipulative nature of media led researchers to focus on the messages themselves, which were subjected to rigorous scrutiny. Some research and debate focused on the ways media messages "cause" specific behaviors. Do violent movies make people use violence in their lives? Does heavy metal music cause listeners to commit suicide? Does television viewing lead teenagers to have sex at early ages? Audiences, from this perspective, were the recipients of forms of external stimulus—a movie, song, or television program—that elicited an observable response.

Certainly, researchers who focused on media effects were asking significant questions. Perhaps you can recall seeing a particularly violent movie or TV show that was so graphic that it made you wonder how it might affect other viewers. What the effects research highlighted, and what virtually all observers now accept, is that media messages matter.

They are not somehow separate from our "real" lives, picked up for fun and discarded when we turn real world pursuits. On the contrary, media messages are central to our everyday lives. This is, indeed, one of the basic premises of this book.

But there is a crucial difference between this position and one that focuses on the direct effects of media on audiences. Often, the discussion of media effects ignores living, breathing human beings. People exist only as receptacles for media messages, passive individuals whose behaviors and attitudes are the result of a powerful external force: the media. The implicit assumption is that, to understand the media's effect on people, all we need to know is what the messages say. Certainly, this image is a bit exaggerated. Few researchers would now explicitly take this position. But it does point out the underlying problem of the *effects* framework. By focusing on the effects of media, this perspective largely strips members of the audience of any human agency.

In many respects, *audience* is a problematic term. It evokes the image of a mass of passive receivers ingesting their daily dose of media products. Not surprisingly, this is the traditional media-industry image of audiences, who need do nothing except go to a movie, listen to a song, or turn on the right channel. What audiences actually think or do is irrelevant as long as they show up.

For our purposes, however, this view of audiences is insufficient. We prefer to think of audiences as active "readers" rather than passive recipients. We see the meaning of media texts as something that these active audiences construct rather than something that is delivered prefabricated by media producers. There are two good reasons for conceptualizing the audience in this way. First, it fits with our own experiences as media consumers and as members of various audiences. Second, a large body of research demonstrates that media audiences are active interpreters of media. Real people with lives, histories, and social networks are the audiences—readers, viewers, listeners, fans, and players—for media products. The notion of the active audience brings these real people into our model of media and the social world. This chapter examines the ways audiences actively interpret media, and explores new forms of activity that challenge the foundations of the idea that media audiences are passive.

THE ACTIVE AUDIENCE

A long line of media research has argued that mass media serve primarily to transmit the ideas of the dominant groups in society to the population. In this view, people are indoctrinated by media in ways that are often so thorough that they do not even realize they are being dominated. The idea that the audience is active arose in opposition to the notion of this kind of all-encompassing ideological domination. It is driven by a kind of populism that views people, not only media institutions, as wielders of power in their relationships with media messages. Proponents of the active audience theory argue that media cannot tell people what to think or how to behave in any direct way because people are not nearly as stupid, gullible, or easy to dominate as the media indoctrination perspective would have us believe.

The notion of an *active audience* appeals to our belief in the intelligence and autonomy of individuals. The term is both a critique of cynicism about the power of media and an expression of faith in the power of people. For those who do not want to simply dismiss people—especially those who enjoy devalued forms of media, such as talk shows, celebrity-oriented websites, and romance novels—the concept of the active audience is a significant step forward.

While the idea of an active audience fits with our sensibilities by granting people some power and agency in their use of media, we still have not explained what kind of activity audiences engage in. We need to move beyond the general label to define what we mean by an "active audience." There are four basic ways in which media audiences have been seen as active: through individual interpretation of media products, through collective interpretation of media, through collective political action, and through producing their own audience-centered media. We examine each of these areas of audience activity below.

Interpretation

The first kind of audience activity is *interpretive*. The meanings of media messages are not fixed; they are constructed by audience members. This construction comes from a kind of engagement with media texts, generally through routine acts of interpretation. Interpretive activity does not require a special set of skills. It is part of the process whereby media messages come to mean something to us; it is how we derive pleasure, comfort, excitement, or a wide range of intellectual or emotional stimulation. We engage in interpretive activity, to various degrees, each time we turn on the television, read a blog, listen to a song, or go to the movies.

Source: Richard Levine/Alamy.

Audiences from all perspectives can engage in a wide variety of actions to express their criticisms of the media. Here, conservative activists stand in front of the *New York Times* building to protest the "liberal media."

This interpretive activity is crucial because it is in the process of audience reception that media texts take on meaning. Producers construct complex media texts, often with a very clear idea of what they intend to say, but this intended message is not simply dumped into the minds of passive audiences. Instead, audiences interpret the message, assigning meanings to its various components. Sometimes there will be a very close correspondence between the intended meaning and the ways a particular audience interprets the message. This correlation may be the result of fine craftsmanship on the part of the producer, the use by producer and audience of a shared interpretive framework, or just plain luck. But there is no guarantee that producers will get their message across in the ways they want. Audiences may not know the implicit references, they may draw on a different interpretive framework, or they may focus on different components of the message than the producer had planned. Audiences, then, may not construct the meaning intended by the producer, nor will all audience members construct the same meaning from the same media text.

The Social Context of Interpretation

The second kind of audience activity grounds us firmly in daily life. Audiences are active in the sense that they interpret media messages socially. That is, audiences do not simply watch, read, or listen to a media text; develop independent interpretations of what it means; and stick to them. On the contrary, media are part of our social lives, and we engage with media in social settings. Sometimes we partake of media in groups; we go to the movies with a date, watch television with our family, or go to a concert with friends. Other times our media use is initially an individual activity but later becomes part of our broader social relationships. We talk with friends, roommates, or coworkers about the book we have just finished, the songs we have recently downloaded, or the news article we have just read. You might pass along a book, post an article on your Facebook page, retweet a link, or post a comment on a blog in order to pursue the discussion further. Audiences can also bridge the gap between watching television alone, while simultaneously using a "second screen"—smartphone, tablet, or laptop—to discuss the program with others online. If you stop to think about it, you might be surprised at how much of your everyday conversation is related to media.

Many people even engage with media that focus on other media: Book and film reviews in newspapers and magazines, blogs about new music, television programs that evaluate news media, and websites that provide commentary on virtually every form of mass media are all widely available. Twitter is full of real-time commentary about what's live on television, and some new stations scroll a running stream of audience tweets across the bottom of the screen. The cynic might say that this abundance of media commentary is all about marketing; in a clever move, the media industry has created a whole sector of media that is geared principally to selling other media. This is certainly part of the story, but it misses the ways audiences use these media-about-media in the social act of interpreting and evaluating media texts. In both kinds of activity—the ways audiences construct meaning and the ways audiences engage with others as they interpret media texts—we can see that audiences are far from passive.

Collective Action

A third way in which audiences can be active, as we saw in Chapter 7, is when they organize collectively to make formal demands on media producers or regulators. Whether they are outraged by the images they see in a popular film, distressed by the exclusion of their points of view from the news, or concerned about the online advertising directed at their children, audiences can engage in collective action to try to change media texts or media policies. Such collective action can include public protest, boycotts of specific media products, publicity campaigns to broaden audience indignation, online petitions, pressure on advertisers to withdraw financial support, mass letter writing to highlight audience outrage, and lobbying of Congress for government action. Citizens can also monitor the media to identify recurrent stereotypical representations and promote campaigns for change. For example, Project Censored (projectcensored.org), a media research program founded in 1976, analyzes news stories that are underreported or ignored by the U.S. corporate media and publishes an annual list of the top 25 censored stories. A growing body of research (Hackett and Carroll 2006, Jansen, Pooley, and Taub-Pervizpour 2011; McChesney, Newman, and Scott 2005; Mueller, Kuerbis, and Pagé 2004; Napoli 2007; Wible 2004) describes how organized political activity has helped to define certain media products as controversial, often mobilizing audiences to try to shape (and sometimes censor) media offerings. A number of organizations from a variety of political perspectives—such as the progressive Free Press (freepress.net) and Fairness and Accuracy In Reporting (FAIR) (fair.org), or the conservative Accuracy in Media (aim.org) and Media Research Center (mrc.org)—monitor the U.S. media on a daily basis and support citizen efforts to organize for change.

Audiences as Media Producers

In addition, audience members can produce and distribute their own media, both to criticize the major media and to provide alternative perspectives that are rarely available from national media outlets. Media activists from across the political spectrum produce, post, and publish a wide range of media that evaluates, criticizes, and sometimes praises major news and entertainment media; and much of this activist media hosts online forums for audience comments and responses. In the digital age, however, the possibilities for audiences to also be media producers has expanded well beyond the realm of independent or alternative media. Just about anyone with a smartphone or a laptop can now create and distribute media in a wide variety of formats. Audiences whose activity was, until recently, generally limited to acts of individual meaning making, social interpretation, and collective action now can make their own media, often with limited technological know-how and at a relatively low cost. For example, media audiences commonly blog, tweet, contribute to wikis, and post photos and video online—often in response to the major media products they experience. In this way, the range of audience activity has expanded as the audience-producer boundary becomes increasingly blurry. Still, even with the increased opportunities for citizen-produced media, it remains difficult for most user-generated media to reach a broad public; and most audience members continue to focus on professionally produced media content. (We explore the possibilities and limits of user-generated content further in Chapter 9.)

MEANINGS: AGENCY AND STRUCTURE

The notion of active audiences does more than throw into question the traditions that identify meaning as something imposed on audiences by media texts. It undermines the very idea that each media text has a singular meaning. If audiences are active interpreters of media and if different audiences have different backgrounds, social networks, and defining experiences, then it is likely that there will be multiple interpretations of the same media text. This certainly complicates any analysis of media texts and their potential power because it destabilizes the meaning of media. No longer is it enough to ask media creators what they had in mind in making a film, developing a video game, or composing a song. Nor is it enough to use the skills of the literary critic to uncover the hidden meaning of texts. Understanding media requires that we explore the interpretive strategies of real people as they encounter various forms of media.

Agency and Polysemy

In the field of cultural studies, scholars use the term *polysemy* to describe the notion of multiple meanings in media texts. Media are said to be polysemic—to have multiple meanings. But where do these meanings come from? Is polysemy the result of audience activity, or is it the result of the properties of the media themselves? In other words, are multiple meanings simply the result of different audience members constructing different interpretations, or do they exist because the texts themselves are "open"—that is, structured in such a way as to allow for multiple readings?

One cultural studies scholar, John Fiske (1986), has argued that media texts contain an "excess" of meaning within them. Many of the components of a television program, for example, will fit together into one relatively consistent interpretation that is likely to be the dominant interpretation. But lots of bits and pieces around the edges of the program do not quite fit, and the dominant interpretation cannot completely contain them. Humor and irony are particularly tricky because they are full of the kind of ambiguity that can be interpreted in different ways. Media, from this perspective, contain the raw materials for multiple interpretations; the texts are structured in ways that facilitate, even if they do not encourage, people's "reading against the grain."

Movies, websites, music, television, and all kinds of advertisements are packed with potentially meaningful images, words, and sounds. It is no wonder, then, that each and every piece of a media text does not fit perfectly into a coherent whole. We are not talking about a simple jigsaw puzzle; a better metaphor would be a jigsaw puzzle with far too many pieces. You need only some of the pieces to create a picture, but choosing different pieces will result in different pictures. The same can be said of media texts.

Let's look at an example: What makes a movie an "antiwar" film? The most straightforward response is that a movie is antiwar if its message is critical of or in opposition to warfare. But as we saw in the previous chapter, the makers of the television series *M*A*S*H* were astounded to find that some viewers saw their antiwar messages as actually making the military attractive. So who is to determine that the message in a film is critical of warfare? The filmmaker? The leading film critics? The trained media scholar? All of these people may have quite sophisticated analyses of why a specific film should or should not be considered antiwar. In fact, we might even be comfortable relying on such prominent analysts to decide whether we should label the film "antiwar." But even a film that seems to have all the qualities of an antiwar film and leads us to question the morality of organized warfare (for example, films about the Iraq War such as *Green Zone, The Hurt Locker, Redacted,* or *Act of Valor*) will likely contain elements that can be used as the basis for very different interpretations. Perhaps a film depicts soldiers brutally and indiscriminately killing a group of defenseless noncombatants. Is there more than one way to interpret this scene? Although many, perhaps even most, people would likely find this scene horrific, it is likely to provide the seeds of an alternate interpretation, suggesting, for example, the necessity of war, the commitment of soldiers, or the evil of our enemies. Perhaps the victims did not speak the same language as the soldiers, or the soldiers expressed fear or confusion, or the battle is proclaimed a victory later in the film. Any of these circumstances can be the key to different readings of even an apparently straightforward text.

Is one interpretation of the film "correct" and another just plain "wrong"? Can we say that the film is really an antiwar film and those who see otherwise just don't get it? Of course we can and, in fact, we regularly do when we talk—perhaps argue—with friends and family about a movie we have just seen. Did *Zero Dark Thirty*, the 2012 Academy Award nominated film about the search for and ultimate killing of Osama Bin Laden, depict the effectiveness of harsh interrogation techniques, including torture? Or did the film portray the brutality and moral complexity of torture? Upon its release, *Zero Dark Thirty* sparked widespread debate about what, indeed, the filmmakers were saying about torture, and how the film's narrative squared with the historical record. Even if we are sure our interpretations are correct, these convictions are ultimately of little consequence if the film means something else to others. It is likely, then, that media texts do have some degree of openness in their very structure, making widely divergent readings possible—even though difficult.

Given the substantial competition for the attention of audiences, this kind of openness is a highly desirable feature for mass-market media. The most successful media often have components that appeal to different audiences. Take, for example, the pioneering HBO drama series *The Sopranos*. The show revolved around Italian-American mob boss Tony Soprano and his effort to manage his family and private life, as well as his criminal activity and the extended family around it. Tony Soprano is clearly an antihero; he kills and exploits, yet the audience is called to identify with him and must—at some level—find him likeable (Carroll 2004). Many of the characters in *The Sopranos* were portrayed as morally ambiguous, busy with eating and killing; as a result, some Italian Americans expressed frustration at the representations of Italian Americans offered in the series. Congresswoman Marge Roskema (R-New Jersey) brought the question to Congress, introducing a resolution condemning HBO and the series creator David Chase for propagating offensive stereotypes (Lavery 2002). The entire series is built on contrasting meanings and spurs ambiguous feelings in the audience—and this is one of the keys to its success. As David Chase explained, "We all have the freedom to let the audience figure out what's going on rather than telling them what's going on" (quoted in Lavery 2006: 5).

In one classic study, Jhally and Lewis (1992) explored the ambiguity of media texts in their study of audiences for the hit sitcom, *The Cosby Show*. As we saw in the previous chapter, white audiences either interpreted the Huxtable family to be, for all intents and purposes, "white" because they were upper-middle class or saw the Huxtable family's success as an indication of the end of racism in the United States, providing evidence that black families can be just like white families. Black audiences expressed pride in the portrayal of a successful black family on national television, and many were pleased to see such a positive representation of blacks. For black audiences, this positive image did not mean that the Huxtables were "white," nor did it signify the end of racial discrimination. In short, black and white audiences drew very different lessons about race relations from *The Cosby Show*. From the standpoint of the producers of the program, however, this ambiguity was its very beauty. It may be that popularity in a diverse society requires ambiguity; in the case of *Cosby*, both blacks and whites could enjoy the program even though they interpreted it in very different ways.

Perks (2012) found a similar dynamic among viewers of *Chappelle's Show*. While a diverse array of viewers found *Chappelle's Show* funny and enjoyable to watch, audiences from different racial backgrounds decoded the program differently. Describing her focus group discussions with viewers, Perks notes that some viewers enjoyed Dave Chappelle's "truth telling" approach to comedy, but they defined the truth in more than one way: "the voices of many African American participants indicated that the show presented a unique and realistic African American perspective, whereas non-African American participants commonly found the show's stereotypes to be realistic" (p. 302). Differently located audiences may indeed be laughing for quite different reasons.

You can see how the ideas of an active audience and a polysemic text open up the meaning of media. Does that mean that audiences are interpretive "free agents," that they can derive any meaning they want, or that the meaning of texts is limited only by the number of audience members? There is a tendency in some branches of media studies to really push the boundaries, arguing that ways of making meaning are so diverse that we cannot fully understand them and that, in fact, audience members have the ultimate power in their interactions with media because they can make the media texts mean whatever they like. In this view, social structure is almost completely erased, and audiences are no longer constrained at all. The texts themselves matter very little. They are not simply open; they are wide open to be interpreted in a limitless number of ways.

This view replaces one oversimplified perspective (meaning is given) with an alternative (meaning is entirely open) that suffers from the same basic flaw. In essence, this latter view is all agency and no structure. In disputing the notion that media texts have any meaning prior to their interpretation, this view makes the texts themselves irrelevant. And in arguing that interpretations are virtually limitless, this position neglects the social context in which we experience and interpret media, the often familiar conventions that media representations use, and the underlying patterns these interpretations have.

Structure and Interpretive Constraint

We are not simply "free" of constraints when we experience media; we do not live in some electronic netherworld. We experience media as part of daily life, not separate from it, and our lives unfold in specific social locations. Our ages, occupations, marital and parental status, races, genders, neighborhoods, educational backgrounds, and the like help structure our daily lives and our media experiences. Media texts are not a random hodgepodge; those that seek a mass audience are built around familiar images and traditional themes that regular media users are likely to have experience interpreting. Media messages matter, but so do our locations in various social groups. Social location matters because it shapes whom we talk to about different media, what we perceive to be our own best interests and most important concerns, and what kinds of interpretive frameworks we bring to our media experiences.

The task, then, is to be mindful of how meaning is constructed by socially located audiences under specific historical circumstances. This means that we have to understand both the role of agency—audiences constructing meaning—and the role of structure—the patterns of interpretation and the social locations that shape them. Who we are does not determine how we will interpret media texts, but neither are our social identities irrelevant. At the same time, media texts do not have singular meanings to be detected by audiences, but neither do they have limitless meanings.

Some meanings will be easier to construct because they draw on widely shared cultural values and sets of assumptions about the way the world works. Other meanings will be less commonly derived because they require substantial rethinking or depend on the use of alternative informational resources. As a result, meaning may be actively constructed by audiences, but in most cases, one interpretation is likely to be most common and fit with the underlying values of the culture. We can think of this as the "preferred" reading, in that the text itself is most amenable to this interpretation. Of course, the possibility still exists for alternative readings, and one's "interpretive community," or web of social networks, is one of the keys to whether people interpret media in line with the "preferred" reading or with some divergent reading.

DECODING MEDIA AND SOCIAL POSITION

Our discussions with friends and family about the meaning of media messages provide strong evidence that audiences indeed interpret media in diverse ways. At the same time, as we explored in Chapter 6, media products are often ideological in the sense that they consistently promote certain messages over others. These ideological representations are most powerful when they pervade the realm of "common sense," such that competing meanings are no longer even entertained. This is an apparent contradiction. How can we negotiate the terrain between the active audience and the ideological nature of many media texts? By pointing to the role of social structure, several classic studies helped reconcile the forces of ideological constraint and audience agency in the interpretation of media.

Class, *Nationwide*, and the Encoding–Decoding Model

As we have seen, the notion of the active audience raised serious questions for the study of media. It was no longer enough, for example, to study the content of media messages because such messages are at least partially open to different interpretations. But where do these different interpretations come from? One answer is in the relationship of meaning to social position. In pioneering research, David Morley (1980) tackled this question in his study of the British television "magazine" program *Nationwide*. In short, Morley analyzed the text of the *Nationwide* broadcast to determine the "preferred" meaning of the messages, and he interviewed groups of people from different social backgrounds who had viewed the program to see if and how social position and meaning making are related.

If we are to understand the relationship between media and society, Morley's question is a profound one. A focus on the individual act of interpretation may be preferable to the notion of a passive audience, but it tells us little about what media messages will mean to different audiences. It is tempting to believe that people are simply free to construct their own interpretations because this radically individualist position assigns great power to each of us. However, research on audiences suggests that social position influences interpretation. It acts as a central mediator of the interpretive process—not as a determinant of meaning but as a key provider of the resources we use to decode media messages.

Morley (1980) explores this terrain, paying particular attention to the role of social class. In his study of *Nationwide,* he makes use of Stuart Hall's ([1973] 1980) "encoding–decoding" model, a method that highlights both messages and their interpretations by audiences. One of the key contributions of this model is the way it conceptualizes media—borrowing from linguistics—as messages that are constructed according to certain "codes." Understanding or "decoding" these messages requires knowledge of the conventions of the medium and the workings of the culture. Because we are all connected in various ways to our media-saturated culture, much of this competence is so taken for granted that we do not even think about it.

Even though our competence may seem "natural" when we watch television, browse the Internet, scan our Twitter feed, or pick up a fashion magazine, our abilities to interpret these media depend on our familiarity with the basic codes of each medium. (We saw this in our discussion of photography in Chapter 4.) We know about beginnings and endings of programs and articles, about the relationship between pictures and words, about the presence (or absence) of the author, about the difference between advertisements and the articles or programs, about banner ads and pop-up windows, about retweets and news feeds, and so on. Imagine what television viewing would be like if we did not understand the ad–program relationship. It would seem like a random jumble of images. Or what if we had no idea about the codes of supermarket tabloids? We might be shocked by the newest "revelations" instead of being entertained by them. Think about what *The Daily Show* or *The Colbert Report* would look like to someone who is not familiar with the codes of "fake news." Without some implicit knowledge about the codes of satire and comedy, it is likely that the newcomer would be confused by the way the audience laughs and Jon Stewart and Stephen Colbert poke fun at politicians.

Media messages also draw on broader sets of cultural codes about how the world works. These codes build on assumptions that do not have to be articulated. In other words, the meaning of media texts depends, to a great degree, on the taken for granted. News stories about the president's day do not have to explain why he is important, magazine images assume certain definitions of beauty or success, and films and television programs draw on layers of assumptions about relationships between men and women, parents and children, the rich and the poor. Decoding, then, is the process whereby audiences use their implicit knowledge of both medium-specific and broader cultural codes to interpret the meaning of a media text.

The encoding–decoding model focuses on the relationship between the media message, as it is constructed or "encoded" by a media producer, and the ways that message is interpreted or "decoded" by audiences. Encoding and decoding are connected because they are processes that focus on the same media text, but a particular decoding does not necessarily follow from a specific encoded meaning. According to this model, producers create media texts in ways that encode a preferred or "dominant" meaning—the interpretation that will most likely follow from a decoding based on the codes of the medium and the dominant assumptions that underpin our social lives. Morley (1980) suggests a very simple approach: People can read the preferred meaning, they can develop a "negotiated" reading, or they can draw on extratextual resources to construct an "oppositional" reading. The question for Morley, then, focuses on which groups decode messages in line with the preferred meaning and which groups produce negotiated or oppositional meanings.

The *Nationwide* study indicated that there was a tendency for people from different socioeconomic classes to interpret the meaning of the television program in different ways. There was no direct correlation between class and interpretation, and Morley was reluctant to draw definitive conclusions from this study. Still, the general pattern is worthy of our attention. In decoding *Nationwide* coverage of economic issues, workers and managers constructed very different interpretations. The bank managers whom Morley interviewed read the preferred meaning. They saw so little controversy in the presentation of the economy that they focused their attention on the program's style rather than its content. Morley argues that the *Nationwide* framework was a perfect fit with the commonsense views of the bank managers. The group of trade unionists he interviewed saw the economic coverage as entirely favoring management. At the same time, younger management trainees also saw the coverage as ideological, but they saw it as favoring the unions. Morley reports that these distinctions between the interpretations of the bank managers, management trainees, and trade unionists are rather sharp. He concludes that

> these examples of the totally contradictory readings of the same programme item, made by managers and trade unionists, do provide us with the clearest examples of the way in which the "meaning" of a programme or "message" depends upon the interpretive code which the audience brings to the decoding situation. (Morley 1992: 112)

Students from different social classes also derived different meanings from the items in *Nationwide*. Groups of middle-class students criticized the program for failing to include enough detail in its coverage of issues. They viewed it as lacking the seriousness that would make an informational program worthwhile. It was, in their view, a trivial program. The mainly black, working-class students used an entirely different evaluative scheme. They suggested that the program was too detailed and, ultimately, boring. For these students, the program was also viewed as largely worthless, not for its trivial nature but because it lacked the entertainment value that makes television worthwhile. In short, the groups of students from different classes approached *Nationwide* with distinct interpretive frameworks—one group focused on information, the other on entertainment—and thus viewed the program in dramatically different ways.

In evaluating the meaning of this study, Morley (1980) makes an important qualification about his results to which we should pay careful attention. Social class, Morley argues, does not determine how people interpret media messages. Meaning is class stratified but not in ways that are constant or entirely predictable. If we reduce meaning making to some simple formula focused on social class, we deny audiences the agency that the active audience theory has so usefully brought to our attention.

How, then, does class influence interpretation? Social class—and we would add age, race, ethnicity, gender, and other central markers of identity—plays a key role in providing us with cultural "tools" for decoding. Some class-based tools are useful for navigating the world of politics (Croteau 1995). Others are helpful for decoding media. Among the media-related cultural tools are what we might call *discursive resources,* for example, the language, concepts, and assumptions associated with a particular subculture or a political perspective. Different groups of people will have access to different discursive resources for decoding media messages. The distinction between "negotiated" and "oppositional" readings is significant in this context because oppositional readings require that audiences have access to discursive resources that allow them to make meanings opposing the preferred one. For example, trade union activists bring a discourse of union politics—involving "the introduction of a new model, outside the terms of reference provided by the programme" (Morley 1992: 117)—to bear on their interpretation of messages about the economy. This allowed them, in Morley's study, to produce readings critical of the economic organization of society. We can easily imagine oppositional readings among other groups with sufficient discursive resources. Perhaps a feminist perspective—again, a set of discursive resources—provides some women with the tools to make oppositional readings of the images in popular women's magazines.

It should not be surprising that people occupying different social positions possess different kinds of discursive resources. Our social positions provide the frames through which we view the world, making some things visible and others more difficult to see. If, indeed, social position shapes the tools we have available for interpreting media images, then the meanings we assign to different media products will ultimately be related to social position. Audiences are still active in this view; they still have to do the decoding work, and access to particular tools does not guarantee a particular interpretation. But the same cultural tools are not available to everyone. Our social positions provide us with differential access to an array of cultural tools, which we use to construct meaning in more or less patterned ways. The result is a model of humans as active agents constrained by specific structural conditions.

Gender, Class, and Television

Morley's study of *Nationwide* was, of course, only a start; the study raised some enduring questions and provided tentative answers. Most important, it provided an example of audience research that was both cognizant of the interpretive activity of audiences and grounded in the social world. Other researchers followed this fruitful path, examining the ways different audiences interpreted similar media texts. Andrea Press's (1991) study, *Women Watching Television,* is one of the well-known studies that have focused on the relationship between social structure and audience interpretation. Press interviewed middle-class and working-class women, focusing on their backgrounds, their attitudes toward gender issues, and their television viewing histories and preferences.

Press suggests that middle-class women watch television differently from working-class women in that they use a different set of criteria for evaluating programs and identifying with television characters. The first difference is in assessing the degree of "realism" of television programs. Women from different classes view this issue in widely disparate terms. Working-class women place a high value on images they believe to be realistic, while middle-class women do not expect television to be realistic. Working-class women are likely to view televised depictions of middle-class life as realistic, especially in comparison to what they see as the "unreal" (and uncommon) depictions of working-class life. Middle-class women are much less likely to think about whether the programs are realistic as, for the most part, they assume (and accept) that they are not.

The results of these differences, Press (1991) argues, are substantial. In short, the combination of a focus on realism and a sense that common television images of the middle-class household are realistic portrayals leads working-class women to an interpretation that devalues their own class position. In other words, as Press puts it, "Working-class women are particularly vulnerable to television's presentation of the material accouterments of middle-class life as the definition of what is normal in society" (p. 138).

While middle-class women may be cynical about the realistic nature of television depictions, they are much more receptive to depictions of women on television than their working-class counterparts. Working-class women were consistently critical of the image of both the independent working woman and the stereotypically sexy woman—two stock images for television characters—in large part because they perceive them to be unrealistic. Working-class women belittled and even dismissed popular images of women because these images bear little resemblance to their sense of what it means to be a woman in American society. Middle-class women, however, were much more likely to focus on the positive nature of these images, either defending such televised characters or indicating a sense of identification with them. The result is that middle-class women's interpretations of televised images of women are part of their own definitions of womanhood, whereas working-class women show a tendency to resist these interpretations.

We can see that class plays a central role in how audiences make sense of television images. We can use Press's (1991) research to suggest a broader speculative connection between social class, production, content, and audience interpretation—all elements of our media/society model. Because of their lived experience, working-class women know that most television programs present a distorted, unrealistic picture of working-class life in general and working-class women in particular. However, without extensive lived experience of middle-class life, working-class women are more likely to accept the media's portrayal of the middle class as plausibly realistic. Middle-class women, on the other hand, are more likely to have a background similar to that of middle-class media producers, including having a shared and taken-for-granted understanding of class. Middle-class women, therefore, largely ignore questions of class and find the media's depiction of women's roles as "normal" because the images more closely reflect their own middle-class perspective. Thus, we have more evidence that social position and meaning making are connected, albeit in complex and indirect ways.

Race, News, and Meaning Making

Morley's (1980) and Press's (1991) studies are representative of a larger body of work on media audiences, their interpretive strategies, their cultural tools, and their relationships to the media industry. Scholars have used a similar approach to study the meaning of a broad array of media texts.

For example, Darnell Hunt (1997) examined the ways that differently "raced" groups interpreted television news coverage of the 1992 Los Angeles riots. The riots erupted after the announcement of the not guilty verdict for the police officers who had severely beaten black motorist Rodney King in an incident that was captured on videotape and aired repeatedly on television news. Hunt noted that attitudes about the riots differed dramatically by race. Much like the subsequent racial divide in views about the O. J. Simpson murder trial, public opinion surveys showed that black and white Americans had very different understandings of the roots, significance, and consequences of the events in Los Angeles in April 1992.

In an effort to make sense of the relationship between media power and audience power, Hunt showed a 17-minute news report from the first night of the riots to 15 groups from the Los Angeles area, equally divided among white, African American, and Latino groups, and asked each group to discuss what they would say to a 12-year-old child about what they just saw. Hunt's analysis of these group discussions showed that responses to this news segment did not vary much by gender or class but that there were significant racial differences in how viewers interpreted the news. Given the differences in attitudes toward the riots, it comes as no surprise that race was a significant factor here.

Because Hunt (1997) "was interested in analyzing how the social locations of informants may have influenced" (p. 172) their interpretation of the news coverage, he did more than just take note of the racially stratified perspectives. He showed some of the ways that these differences unfold as viewers actively make sense of television news. For example, Hunt found that black viewers were much more likely than either Latino or white viewers to use solidarity (we, us, our) or distance (they, them, their) pronouns in the group discussion. As black viewers discussed the news coverage of the riots, they identified themselves and the larger issues in racial terms, something that was absent in the white groups' discussions and far less common in the Latino discussions. In addition, the African American and Latino groups were more visibly active than the white groups as they watched the news segment. Whereas the Latino and especially the black groups talked, laughed, and were generally animated during the screening of the news, the white groups were quiet and motionless as they watched. The ongoing talk among the black viewers was not idle banter but was full of commentary about the news and its credibility. In fact, Hunt found that the black viewers "seemed predisposed to questioning many of the assumptions embedded" (p. 143) in the news coverage, challenging both the accuracy of and the terminology used in the newscast. In contrast, Hunt argued that the white viewers were much more comfortable with the way the newscast covered the events.

Drawing on Morley's (1980) framework, Hunt (1997) argued that the viewers in his study constructed "negotiated" readings of the news, with different groups bringing different resources to their decoding. Black viewers were far more likely to decode the news in ways that suggested an alternative or oppositional interpretation of the riots, whereas the white and Latino viewers were likely to interpret the news in line with the text's preferred meaning. Hunt suggested that this racial difference in decoding media was, in large part, the result of differences in social networks and the sense of group solidarity among the different groups. In this particular case, the discursive resources associated with racial identity shaped both how viewers watched the news and how they decoded the news text. At the same time, differential interpretations helped to reaffirm a sense of racial identity among viewers. Such "raced ways of seeing," as Hunt termed them, both shape and are constituted by the social process of decoding.

International Readings of American Television

If you have traveled outside the United States, you probably know that American television programs are very popular in other countries. Dozens of countries broadcast either reruns of classic programs or current prime time hits. Because, as we have seen, meanings are multiple and are constructed by socially located audiences, we should consider what these popular television programs actually mean to viewers outside the United States. How do audiences in France or Saudi Arabia, for example, interpret programs such as *NCIS, Grey's Anatomy, Desperate Housewives,* or *Jersey Shore*? What do these programs mean to audiences who have little or no experience with Washington, Seattle, Orange County, and the New Jersey coast or the cultural context within which these programs are viewed by people in the United States? What about situation comedies? Are *The Big Bang Theory, Modern Family,* or *Two and a Half Men* seen as humorous by people in Singapore, Argentina, or Poland? If so, how do audiences interpret the programs in ways that make them laugh? What does it mean that *The Mentalist* was the most watched TV show in the world in 2012, having drawn an audience of 58.1 million worldwide? The 1990s action drama series *Baywatch,* about Los Angeles County lifeguards, is still the most popular program in the history of international television: At its peak of popularity in 1996, the series was watched by an estimated 1.1 billion viewers in 148 countries and translated into 44 different languages (Guinness 2008). What lessons about life in the United States do international audiences draw from these popular television programs?

These are classic sociological questions about the relationship between culture and meaning—what do popular media images mean in different cultural contexts?—and researchers still have much to learn about this relationship. It is too easy to assert that American television images simply indoctrinate global viewers to support American consumer capitalism or to argue that international audiences easily adapt these foreign images to their own social situations. It is more difficult and ultimately more rewarding to explore the complex ways in which active audiences make use of images that often are heavily laden with ideological messages (McMillin 2002).

Dallas *Abroad*

The most sophisticated effort to study this terrain is Liebes and Katz's classic (1993) study of the 1980s television program *Dallas,* which was popular with audiences in dozens of countries. This evening drama—which returned in 2012, with some of the original cast members, on TNT—chronicled the lives of a wealthy Texas oil family named Ewing and its lead character/villain J. R. Ewing. The program followed family members through ups and downs, with a regular focus on secret love affairs, backroom business deals, and an almost constant tension between loyalty and betrayal. What was the underlying message in the program? Was it ultimately about the corrupting influence of wealth or the power of money? Was it about the control of women by the men in their lives or the prevalence of self-interest in all social relationships? These are difficult questions, but they become even more complicated when we recall that the program was watched vigilantly by people all over the world.

Liebes and Katz (1993) compared the "decodings" of six different ethnic groups from three different countries: Americans from Los Angeles, Japanese, and four different communities in Israel—recent Russian immigrants, Moroccan Jews, Arab citizens of Israel, and kibbutz members. The study was based on several focus group discussions within each ethnic group; groups of friends watched the program together at one viewer's home and participated in a guided discussion about the program on its completion. Liebes and Katz found substantial differences among the ethnic communities both in how they watched the program and how they interpreted it. In each focus group, viewers were asked to "retell" the story of the just-completed program as if they were explaining it to a friend who had missed the episode. The different ethnic communities used very different storytelling approaches. Both Arabs and Moroccan Jews were most likely to retell the episode on a scene-by-scene basis, often in great detail. The Americans and kibbutzniks were more likely to focus on the characters instead of the plotline. And the Russians explained the message of the program instead of either the action or the characters. Of course, not all members of each ethnic group fit neatly into a box, with all using the same interpretive strategy, but the interpretive patterns were very clear.

Where do these different approaches come from? This is a much more difficult question to answer. Liebes and Katz (1993) suggest that the distinct strategies can be explained by the cultural position of the different groups. Arabs and Moroccan Jews are the most "traditional" groups in the study, and their linear storytelling draws connections between their own cultures and the perceived reality of the lives of the extended family living in Dallas. Russians, on the other hand, draw on their skill at reading between the lines for the underlying message, a skill that was well developed in the former Soviet Union. And the American and kibbutznik groups build on their cultures' interest in psychology and group dynamics to explore the attitudes and actions of the characters. In each case, the retelling approach is anchored in underlying cultural dynamics that provide the different audiences with culturally specific resources.

Viewers from all ethnic groups talked about the connections between the program and real life much more frequently than they subjected the program to critical analysis. Even here, however, significant differences were evident. The Russian, American, and kibbutz groups were three times as likely to use "critical," or analytical, statements as the Arab or Moroccan Jewish groups. Discussions focused on a consistent set of themes—human motivations, family relations, moral dilemmas, and business relations—in all the groups. Although the groups discussed similar themes, they talked about them in very different terms. For example, the Americans and kibbutzniks employed a "playful" approach, relating the story to imagined situations or trying on the characters much more frequently than the other groups, who almost always discussed the story in straightforward ways, relating the story more directly to life.

In addition, the Arab groups were much more engaged with the program than the other groups. In fact, the Arab groups were the only ones to make regular use of a normative interpretive framework, making moral judgments about the activities depicted in the program. Liebes and Katz (1993) suggest that the more frequent use of an analytical framework by the Western audience members is likely a result of their greater experience with television as a medium and their greater familiarity with the society portrayed in *Dallas*. In short, the American, Russian, and kibbutz groups had different resources for analyzing the images in *Dallas* than do their Arab and Moroccan counterparts.

The distinctive retellings of the program indicate that, while the different ethnic groups may have watched the same program, they did not see the same thing. For example, the Americans were playful and detached in their reading of the program, while the Arabs were emotionally engaged, asserting their opposition to the program's values. As a result, the Arabs were most likely to read the meaning of the program as "Americans are immoral," while the Americans were most likely to assert that the programs meant little beyond entertainment. Ultimately, the broad depiction of family relations—their triumphs and tragedies—made *Dallas* widely popular, even if people used different cultural resources to interpret what these images said about people, society, or the United States.

Although it was an international hit, *Dallas* was not popular everywhere. In Japan, where *Dallas* was a bust, viewers made more "critical" statements about the program than any other ethnic group and made very few comments that connected *Dallas* to their own lives. This might help explain why *Dallas* never caught on in Japan; viewers were never able to really engage with the program. Instead, *Dallas* was perceived as full of inconsistencies that the Japanese could not accept—inconsistencies with the genre of the evening drama, with the viewers' perceptions of American society, with their sense of their own society, and even with their view of the characters' motivations.

The Japanese viewers focused on very different aspects of the program than did other groups, interpreting *Dallas* in ways that led viewers to prefer other programs. They did not exhibit the playfulness of the Americans, the detective work of the Russians, or the moral disapproval of the Arab viewers. The program, in short, had very little meaning to the Japanese beyond its utter inconsistency. While its openness to diverse interpretations might help explain why the program was popular in so many different countries, with the text itself allowing very different viewers to engage with it, the possibilities were not limitless. In a Japanese cultural context, *Dallas* evidently had very little to offer viewers.

Other International Studies

More recently, a variety of studies have built upon the classic work of Liebes and Katz by continuing to explore how international audiences interpret and make use of various media products.

For example, Chitnis and his colleagues (2006) compared the reception of the sitcom *Friends* in the United States and India. They wanted to explore whether or not young Indians and young Americans interpret *Friends* the same way. Respondents were asked to watch an episode of the series, which promoted safe sex and the use of condoms. The authors found that American respondents developed a virtual relationship with more characters in *Friends* than their Indian counterparts. (Indian viewers identified themselves with Joey and Phoebe but not with Rachel and Ross, for example.) However, Indian youth felt generally more included in the plot than Americans did, as they were more likely to perceive the depiction of close relationships among friends as similar to their own experiences of friendship. The two groups differed greatly in their assessment of the truth value of the program. Indian viewers assessed the coherence of the story in relation to their own lived experiences. They found the open discussion about sex among friends to be culturally inappropriate and saw it as inconsistent with Indian attitudes. In other words, the behavior of the series characters with respect to discussions of safe sex and condom use did not resonate with the Indian viewers' worldview. In contrast, the safe sex message was generally well received by young American viewers, who were more likely to see the storyline as realistic. While *Friends* was popular among both American and Indian audiences, viewers' interpretations of the program's meaning were mediated by their respective cultural experiences.

In a subsequent study, Tan (2011) found that viewers of *Friends* in South China did not recognize the safe sex message in the same *Friends* episode, interpreting the emphasis on condom use as commentary on birth control, missing the broader health-related message about the importance of practicing safe sex. In contrast to U.S. and Indian audiences, Tan notes that Chinese viewers did not decode the program's "preferred reading" in this case, pointing to different experiences and cultural understandings as the source of this differential decoding. In general, Tan argues that viewers in South China enjoyed *Friends*, even as they sometime struggled to make sense of the program's story lines and the characters' motivations, noting that cross cultural decoding of Friends was "not a smooth sail, frequently interrupted by diverse audiences' dissimilar readings that vacillated between amazement and embarrassment, between incomprehension and illumination" (p. 222).

In addition, Chitnis and his colleagues (2006) found that the purposeful placement of pro-social messages such as condom use in a television show was more effective among U.S. viewers than among the Indian audience. This confirms the important role played by the viewers' value systems in filtering global media texts. Similarly, Rogers, Singhal, and Thombre's (2004) research on the reception by Indian viewers of discussions about HIV/AIDS in the American soap opera *The Bold and the Beautiful* suggests that HIV/AIDS messages embedded in popular media do not lead directly to a change in perceptions of health behavior in India. However, the authors note that long-running programs like *The Bold and the Beautiful* may gradually influence the perception of the disease, at least among the urban and elite audience.

In their research, Rogers and colleagues (2004) analyzed how a series of health-related episodes of *The Bold and the Beautiful,* then broadcast in more than 110 countries, was interpreted by Indian viewers. This Hollywood soap opera occasionally featured episodes about issues such as abortion, alcoholism, and teenage pregnancy. The authors wanted to know how these themes, widely discussed in the United States, were interpreted by an audience in countries where these issues are not on the public agenda. In a number of episodes broadcast between 2001 and 2002, series character Tony suspects and subsequently discovers that he is HIV positive. His girlfriend Kirsten decides to stay with him nonetheless; they marry and adopt a child from an African orphanage. The researchers found that Indian viewers believed that Tony's HIV story showed an ideal situation regarding HIV/AIDS, but one that was far removed from Indian reality, where HIV/AIDS is still highly stigmatized. Furthermore, Indian audiences seemed to be "shocked" at the sexual openness of the soap opera: Some admittedly watched the series only in private or with close friends. Indeed, the series spurred discussion of issues of sexuality and morality, which are otherwise taboo in much of Indian society; however, many respondents commented that the show provided negative role models for Indian viewers.

Some research suggests that international television can be interpreted in such a way as to be an empowering resource for audiences. For example, Kim (2005) found that young Korean women reflect on their own experiences while considering the worlds they see depicted on global television, which "opens up a rare space in which Korean women can make sense of their life conditions in highly critical ways" (p. 460). And Espiritu (2011) found that young women in the Philippines enjoyed Korean television dramas, which they defined as more "refined and wholesome" than locally produced programs or those imported from the United States and Mexico. Espiritu argues that the women's critique of U.S. television and their expressions of a preference for Korean television can be seen as "an act of resistance to the American cultural hegemony in the Philippines" (p. 369).

THE SOCIAL CONTEXT OF MEDIA USE

When and where do people watch television, listen to music, read magazines, or browse the Internet? How do people experience the routine activity of reading, watching, listening, or browsing? If we are interested in the media experience of audiences, we need to think about both the active interpretation of media messages and the act of media use itself.

Romance Novels and the Act of Reading

One of the most influential studies of media audiences is Janice Radway's (1991) classic field-defining book, *Reading the Romance*. One of the principal reasons why Radway's work has been so influential is that it challenged many of our basic assumptions about "lowbrow" mass media, such as romance novels. Radway's work helps clarify the basic tension between structure and agency that we have emphasized in this book, and it serves as an exemplar of what it means to study the active yet socially located media audience.

Romance novels may seem an odd topic for a serious study of media. They are widely denigrated by academics, who are not likely to read them. They are culturally devalued, like soap operas, in part because they are seen as the exclusive domain of women. Moreover, the romance genre is widely associated with traditional, sexist visions of society: the damsel in distress, the woman who is incomplete without her heroic man, even the woman who finds love with the man who has sexually assaulted her. All this makes it easy to dismiss the romance novel as frivolous trash with straightforward, sexist messages that serve only to oppress women.

However, it is worth exploring if this common assessment of the medium as traditional, sexist, and even dangerous is a reasonable description of the meaning of the romance novel to those who regularly read them. Radway turned to a group of white, middle-class romance novel readers to do just that. Instead of assuming that her skillful interpretation of the texts revealed their "true" meaning, she compared her formal analysis of the texts with the interpretations of women readers of the romance novels. Her findings suggest that the question of meaning is rather complex: Readers are certainly active, but they are also responding to their fundamental social situations.

One of Radway's principal findings is that women answer her questions about why they read romance novels by focusing on the *act of reading* instead of on the content of the stories. These readers, who do not work outside of the home but are busy with the demands of the full-time roles of wives and mothers, suggest that the activity itself is meaningful as an escape from the demands of their daily lives. In essence, reading romance novels gives women time to themselves, peace and quiet, and a break from the emotional work of nurturing others. It provides what Radway calls a "free space," away from the social world that the women occupy.

But why romance novels? Radway argues that the romance novel allows the women to "escape" from the constraints of their social existence by taking time each day to do their own thing and enter the fairy-tale world of the romance heroine, who has all of her emotional needs satisfied. It is both a literal escape, through the act of reading, and a figurative escape, through the fantasy of the romantic plots. The romance novel, then, represents a kind of freedom for these women, a place where they can assert their independence and vicariously experience the kind of nurturance they seek in their own lives.

Source: www.cleanromances.com.

While romance novels are often derided as sexist fluff, a classic study of white middle-class women who read them found that the act of reading can be a way women assert their independence, by providing an escape from the demands of daily life. At the same time, the romantic content offers a way for these women to experience the kind of nurturance they seek in their own lives.

We can see the meaning of the romance novel for these women only if we understand their social roles as wives and mothers. The lives of Radway's romance readers are tightly circumscribed by traditional cultural norms that specify what it means to be a good wife and mother. While the women largely accept these norms, their own emotional needs are not satisfied by their daily existence, precisely because of cultural restrictions on the activity of women. Reading romance novels, then, is a way for women to refuse, if only temporarily, to accept these norms. The romance novel "compensates" women by helping them meet their own need for nurturance and by allowing them to focus on themselves instead of others. According to the readers, romance reading also makes the women more assertive in their domestic relationships, in part because they have to defend their reading time. Some even mention that they are inspired to become romance writers themselves.

Ultimately, Radway finds that reading romance novels is both a small protest against the social conditions of women and participation in a "ritual of hope" that men can meet the needs of women and traditional relationships can provide the blissful existence of the romantic heroine. Romance novels, then, are not simply sexist trash that reaffirms cultural restrictions on female behavior. Indeed, Radway finds that her readers attach a much different meaning to these texts, one that is a kind of critique of their own social conditions. The act of reading is based on dissatisfaction. It implicitly suggests that heterosexual marriage cannot meet all of the women's needs even as the romance stories provide a vision of how women can be fulfilled. At the same time, this protest is both subtle and partial; it does not become outright rebellion against the wife/mother role. In fact, the protest is bound by a basic acceptance of gender roles within the traditional family. Romance reading does not challenge these roles but instead provides vicarious pleasures that help satisfy needs not met by these highly circumscribed roles.

Romance novels, then, do not mean only one thing. The women Radway interviewed—white, middle-class, Midwestern women—interpret romance novels in ways that help explain their own social world and compensate for its shortcomings. This is likely to be a very different reading from the interpretation of trained academic literary critics or even of potential male readers, who inhabit different social worlds. Of course, the content of the novels themselves is significant. Radway's readers actively seek out books that allow them to escape and to hold onto the hope that men can satisfy women's needs, that the heroine and hero will live happily ever after, and that the woman's commitment to the relationship will prevail over the traditionally male commitment to public achievement. As a result, the women make rigid distinctions between romance novels they like and those they dislike. They are not so free to interpret the texts that any romance novel will meet their needs. Because the books provide the raw materials for the women's interpretations, making some more likely and others next to impossible, part of the art of romance novel reading is to be able to find, or at least quickly determine, those novels worth reading.

Radway's study of romance readers is a good example of how audiences make meaning out of media texts under conditions not of their own choosing. Audiences may be active, but they exist within particular social worlds and are interpreting media texts with specific properties. The nurturance and hope that the women get from the romance novel may surprise some of us, but we should be able to see that Radway's readers draw on their own experiences, their assumptions about the social world, and the messages in the books to reach their understanding of what these novels mean.

Similarly, Puri's (1997) study of romance readers in India further demonstrates the ways that social context shapes the process of interpretation. Puri found that for young, middle-class Indian women, U.S. and British romance novels serve as "relatively progressive, liberal 'Western' representations, as alternatives to the structural inequalities and uncertainties experienced in their own lives" (p. 449). Studies such as Radway's and Puri's should make us sensitive to the conditions under which people consume mass media. The very act of reading the romance novel is central to the meaning of the text.

Watching Television With the Family

In a work subsequent to the *Nationwide* project, David Morley adopted Radway's focus on the act of media use. Morley's (1986) *Family Television* explores the domestic context of viewing television and shows how television use is embedded within the social relations of the household. If we are to understand what television messages mean, we have to focus on the social experience of watching television. Although television viewing options continue to proliferate, many of us watch television in a domestic setting with members of our families or with household partners. These domestic relations help shape what we watch, how we watch, and what meanings we assign to the programs. The social practice of watching television—often in a collective setting—is, like the act of reading a romance novel, central to what its text means to audiences.

According to Morley (1986), gender is one of the keys to understanding how people experience television. If we focus our attention on the use of television in a family context, this statement should not surprise us. After all, roles in the family are structured, to a great degree, by gender, and Morley's study focused on relatively traditional British families, in which gender roles are likely to be clearly defined. Since men have a tendency to control the program selection process, television is a potential site for domestic power struggles.

One result of gender roles within the family is that adult men and women watch television very differently. Men indicate that either they are very attentive when they watch or they don't watch at all. Women, on the other hand, see television viewing as a social act that is

Source: George Frey/Getty Images.

Television viewing can be a family affair. However, studies suggest that women and men view television differently. Men tend to watch attentively. Women are more likely to engage in casual conversation while they watch or simultaneously carry out household tasks.

accompanied by conversation and other household activities. For women, just sitting down to watch television without doing anything else seems like a waste of time. In addition, men and women generally view the same programs because they watch television together in the evening, but they do not view them with the same attentiveness. In short, our interpretations of television programs are connected to our engagement with the program. We may tune in to get information, to relax, to find excitement, to tune out the noises of the highway next to our house, or to gather the family for a rare moment of togetherness. These different approaches to television will help shape the meaning we attach to different programs.

Television is a great conversation generator. Because it is so widely viewed, television is the subject of much small talk. When we talk about television or other forms of media with our friends and families, we engage in a kind of collective interpretive activity. We recount what happened, why it happened, what it means, and what is likely to happen next. All of this is part of a process by which we construct meanings for television programs—or movies, songs, blog posts, and so on. After watching a particularly interesting or funny television program, attending a provocative movie, or reading a humorous series of tweets, we tend to seek out others to talk with, hoping that they have seen or read the same item. Perhaps this is why people go to the movies or a concert with others; even though the viewing or listening in these settings allows for little conversation, you can talk with your friends about the event on the way home.

According to Morley (1986), talking about television, while common among women, is rarely admitted by men. Men either do not talk with friends about television or are unwilling to admit that they engage in a behavior they define as feminine. Morley suggests that this has real consequences:

> Given that meanings are made not simply in the moment of individual viewing, but also in subsequent social processes of discussion and "digestion" of material viewed, the men's much greater reluctance to talk about (part of) their viewing will mean that their consumption of television material is of a quite different kind from that of their wives. (p. 158)

Interaction with media and discussions about media products are important parts of the process of meaning making. Here again, we can see how meanings are generated in social settings by active audiences. Radway and others have adopted the term *interpretive community* to suggest both the social structural forces at work—our membership in communities—and the forces of human agency—the act of interpretation. When we think about audiences, then, we need to remember that the meanings people make of apparently omnipresent media products are connected to experiences and social structures outside the world of media. Media are, in essence, part of our lives and must be understood in the context of the relationships that constitute our lives.

ACTIVE AUDIENCES AND INTERPRETIVE RESISTANCE

The meaning of media messages, as we have seen, cannot be reduced to the "encoded" or "preferred" or even most common reading of a particular media text. Audiences, drawing on specific sets of cultural resources and located in specific social settings, actively interpret media products. The distribution of social and cultural power remains significant, for it structures the discursive resources at our command, the context in which we use media, and the production of media texts. But this power is not absolute or uncontested. The power to define social reality, of which the media are a part, is not something that is simply imposed on unwitting audiences. If media messages circulate versions of a "dominant" ideology, these messages are only the raw materials of meaning; they require construction and are subject to revision.

It is clear that the relationship among media messages, audiences, and meaning is a complex one. We cannot treat the media as some simple vehicle for brainwashing people. This realization has led many scholars to investigate the possibility that some audiences interpret media texts in an "oppositional" way or engage in a kind of interpretive "resistance." Some critics argue that a political struggle is occurring at the level of individual interpretation, thereby rescuing "the people" from a perception that they consent to current social and political arrangements. In other words, audiences "resist" the imposition of preferred meanings, actively reinterpreting media messages in contrary, even subversive, ways.

These claims of interpretive resistance employ an image of audiences as "semiological guerillas," fighting a daily war against the symbolic power of the media industry (Carragee 1990). Rather than small arms and sneak attacks, the weapons these guerillas use are their own interpretive skills, which they deploy against the purveyors of ideological conformity. The war is waged each day in small, virtually invisible ways in the very act of reading the newspaper or going to the movies. However, with its focus on the almost unlimited agency of audiences, the resistance thesis has a tendency to be far too casual in its dismissal of social structure.

Instead of simply assuming that media audiences consistently behave as symbolic resistance fighters, we need to examine more specifically the ways particular audiences produce from media texts meanings that can be characterized as oppositional. Theorists have argued that individuals resist the definitional power of authorities by reinterpreting media messages, but research has demonstrated neither the process by which such interpretations become oppositional nor the conditions under which such resistance occurs. Instead, the argument for the possibilities of resistance is largely the result of faith in the power of citizens to think and behave as active subjects rather than passive objects of history. Such faith and optimism, while admirable political qualities, do not adequately explain the relationship between active audiences and a powerful culture industry, nor do they provide the basis for understanding the possibilities for and conditions conducive to actual resistance.

If audiences do engage in interpretive resistance by constructing oppositional meanings from media products, we should be able to look at specific examples of these practices. Indeed, several important cases touch on these issues; as we have seen, Morley's (1980) study of *Nationwide* and Radway's (1991) study of romance readers certainly suggest that audiences have the capacity to produce meanings that are at least partially oppositional. Hunt (1997) concluded his study of news about the Los Angeles riots by suggesting that viewer opposition to the assumptions embedded in the news can be seen "either as constituting meaningful acts of resistance in their own right, or contributing to a consciousness necessary for meaningful social action at some later point in time" (p. 162).

In addition, Naomi Klein (2000) has explored the ways that "culture jamming"—for example, when activists remake billboards to create counter-advertisements with messages that parody or criticize the original ad—is creating "a climate of semiotic Robin Hoodism" (p. 280). The main strategy employed by culture jammers is known as "pranking" (Harold 2004). Typical pranks include sabotage and appropriation of company symbols and products in order to communicate a different message than originally intended by the producer. The *Yes Men* duo and *Adbusters* magazine are probably the most well-known examples of "culture jamming." Adbusters (adbusters.org) engages with the creation of "subvertizements" (ads mimicking mainstream brands) and "uncommercials" (subversive TV and radio spots) (Liacas 2005). Andy Bichlbaum and Mike Bonanno, a.k.a. the *Yes Men* (theyesmen.org), use parody to expose deception perpetrated by multinational corporations, governments, and transnational organizations. For example, the Yes Men created a spoof of the World Trade Organization's (WTO) website, which looked so real that they received invitations to address various groups on behalf of the WTO, where they offered stinging critiques of international economic institutions. The 2009 documentary *The Yes Men Fix the World* chronicles the group's culture jamming activities. One media scholar (Strauss 2011) suggests that the film can be an effective tool for teaching public relations students about corporate social responsibility and professional ethics. Just as important, Strauss argues that the film—and culture jamming, more generally—may offer students and teachers a sense of possibility:

> The "Yes Men" movie's final segment invokes the power of individual and collective action and encourages the watcher to do as the Yes Men do: identify injustice in the world, point it out to others, and work to remedy it. In this way, it can be a valuable motivator for students who may have become jaded or feel powerless to address the problems and injustice in society. Perhaps just as importantly, it can also have a similar effect on the instructor by rejuvenating the belief that our chosen profession, and the students we teach, can make a positive impact on our world. (Strauss 2011: 547)

Interpretive Resistance and Feminist Politics

Resistance can be said to occur when people read media messages in ways that oppose their preferred or commonsensical meaning, articulating a kind of refusal to accept dominant meanings. That is, audiences resist the imposition of meaning and construct new readings that stand in political opposition to the preferred meanings. Linda Steiner's (1988) study of the "No Comment" feature of the original *Ms.* magazine provides a good example of oppositional decoding among a community of readers. *Ms.* was a glossy feminist monthly founded in 1972 and subsequently reincarnated as an advertising-free, less slick bimonthly in 1990. It published "No Comment" each month as a compilation of reader-submitted items—mostly advertisements—that were offered as evidence of sexism in American society. The submissions came from a wide range of sources, including large and small newspapers, magazines, catalogs, and billboards, and often several people submitted the same item.

"No Comment" was a space where readers of *Ms.* could identify images from mainstream media and "expose" their underlying sexism. One common set of images depicted women as the property of men; an insurance ad, for example, suggested that wives were "possessions," and a news article identified a female politician simply by citing her husband's name. Other themes included images that dismissed feminism, advertising that blatantly exploited women's bodies, images that implied that women enjoy sexual violence, and items that trivialized women's accomplishments. One of the more popular items—submitted to *Ms.* by more than 40 people—was a 1977 quote from a prominent U.S. Army general that appeared in *Parade* magazine; it criticized women for entering West Point because this deprived men of their positions.

Ms. readers likely either gasped in outrage or had a good laugh, or perhaps both, when they read the items in "No Comment." But what does this have to do with resistance? Steiner (1988) argues that the point of "No Comment" was precisely for the community of feminists around *Ms.* to collectively resist media messages that reinforced a sexist image of the world. The items were put on display in "No Comment" and decoded in ways that opposed their dominant meaning precisely so that the traditional definitions of what it means to be a woman could be resisted by *Ms.* readers.

No doubt, in this case, those who submitted the items were interpreting the messages in ways contrary to their intended meanings. And as *Ms.* is a feminist publication, it is likely that readers of "No Comment" drew on a set of cultural tools that would lead to a widely shared oppositional reading of the images as "sexist." Readers may give themselves a pat on the back for their critical interpretive skills and wink knowingly at others who read such texts in opposition. But does exposing images as sexist provide a means for readers to actually "resist" the culture and society they define as sexist?

There is good reason to see this action as more than just "oppositional decoding" of media images and to define the public presentation of these interpretations in "No Comment" as a kind of resistance. While such resistance may not change social structures, it helps create a feminist group identity. Collective refusal to accept traditional interpretations of femininity gives strength to such an oppositional identity, with real potential consequences. In this case, when mass media images of women were read in oppositional ways by the feminist community, the decodings helped solidify a feminist identity opposing the traditional norms and roles that are the underpinnings of the media images being exposed.

These decodings were not, however, solitary acts of interpretation; they were both public and collective. When readers submitted items to the "No Comment" section as a way of sharing their oppositional decodings with like-minded feminists, they helped build a shared meaning system that could serve as a basis for social solidarity within the feminist community. In so doing, they drew on and helped reproduce a feminist discourse that served as a key resource for such oppositional readings. If there is resistance here, it is not just at the level of individual interpretation. We need to locate the oppositional decodings in the context of a feminist community that provided the cultural resources for such interpretations and served as a site where meaning making became a more explicitly political act.

Resistance and Identity

Other feminist scholars have explored the ways women respond to and resist media images. In her discussion of the relationship between media images of dancing and the activity itself,

Angela McRobbie (1984) argues that teenage girls construct interpretations of dance films, such as *Flashdance,* in ways that oppose the dominant meaning of the film. Rather than reading the film as a story about a woman who marries her boss's son, using her sexuality to please men in the process of becoming a successful dancer, the girls in McRobbie's study decoded the film in ways that highlighted their own autonomy and sexuality. Dancing, in this interpretation, is not about pleasing or displaying one's body for men; it is about enjoying one's own body and is an expression of sexuality. This reading opposes the dominant interpretation of female sexuality by asserting a sexual identity that does not require the approval of men. The girls drew on their own experiences of dancing in clubs to reinterpret *Flashdance* in ways that supported their own identities as strong, independent, and sexual females.

Teenage fans of performers such as Madonna and Cyndi Lauper, according to Lisa Lewis (1990), engaged in a similar kind of interpretive resistance. Performances that built on apparently traditional images of female sexuality and male pleasure—and styles of dress that drew on the same images—were interpreted by teenage fans as expressions of their own desires. For female teenage fans, the sexuality of these videos—which differed dramatically from the traditional MTV video—was a sign of female power because women were the subjects, not the objects. Female fans who imitated the style of these female performers, rather than adorning themselves for men, were asserting their demands for fame, power, and control without giving up their identity as girls. This was the core of their interpretations of the music video texts—texts routinely dismissed in the broader culture as negative portrayals of women.

What connection do these examples have to resistance? Both suggest that there is a relationship between oppositional forms of decoding and social action. These oppositional decodings are part of the construction of a subcultural identity that embodies a resistance to traditional norms and roles. The female fans, in the case of MTV, were principal players in the struggle over music video images—their demands on the music industry helped open the door for female musicians. Also, in both cases, the oppositional decoding is not free-floating; it is part of the collective activities of audiences in specific social settings. Still, the media industry has shown a remarkable capacity for finding ways to package resistance as a new style. In *The Conquest of Cool,* Thomas Frank (1997) shows how the advertising industry co-opted a rebellious youth culture, developing new marketing campaigns that build on the discourse of rebellion and liberation to promote new forms of "hip consumerism."

Ultimately, the key question about the possibility of resistance concerns the social consequences. How are these interpretations linked to social action? We have seen three examples that provide a clear analysis of the relationships among oppositional decoding, human activity, cultural tools, and social setting. Such examples suggest that oppositional decoding and resistance are useful concepts, but they need to be used with care (Condit 1989). Instead of admiring the almost unlimited capability of people to resist domination, we need to take the notion of resistance seriously by looking at the conditions under which concrete audiences engage in such resistance and what consequences follow.

THE PLEASURES OF MEDIA

Perhaps the principal reason we spend so much time with media is that it is fun. We listen to our favorite music, go to the movies, browse through a popular magazine, or spend the evening online or in front of the television because these activities are enjoyable or relaxing. The media world is, in large part, a world of entertainment, offering us a wide range of choices for how to entertain ourselves. We spend a large portion of our lives having fun and seeking pleasure from the media. But making a rigid distinction between entertainment ("it's only entertainment") and the serious stuff that "really matters" would be a mistake. We need to take fun seriously and explore what it is that makes media a source of pleasure.

Media scholars historically have tended to be suspicious of the pleasures of media. On one hand, media research through the 1970s paid almost exclusive attention to "serious" forms of media, particularly news. On the other hand, pleasure itself was seen as the problem: Media entertained people as a means of distracting them from the more important arenas in life. After all, how can people challenge the social order if they are busy each evening watching *American Idol* or updating their Facebook pages?

Instead of dismissing fun or assuming that it makes people content with the status quo, more recent work has examined the specific sources of media pleasure and the conditions under which people derive fun from media. Feminists, in particular, have focused their attention on the realm of pleasure, arguing that the pleasures associated with mass media can be liberating for women (Walters 1995). Feminist media scholar Ien Ang, in a now classic study of *Dallas* (1985), points to fantasy as the key to explaining the pleasures of media, noting that fantasy allows us to imagine that we are different, that social problems can be solved, or that we can live in a utopia. The meanings of such media pleasures cannot be perceived simply by analyzing a media text; media audiences can incorporate media into complex fantasies that can make daily life much more enjoyable.

We began to see this in Radway's (1991) romance novel study, in which the pleasures of the act of reading are taken seriously. The enjoyment that the romances provide and the reasons for seeking such pleasure are connected to the social position of the women readers. Romance novels are enjoyable because reading provides a free space and vicarious fulfillment of the women's romantic fantasies. Indeed, Radway suggests that such mass-mediated pleasures may obviate any need to change the social world. Even so, some women use romance reading as a means of asserting their right to pleasure in a social situation where pleasure is routinely neglected.

Celebrity Games

The world of entertainment celebrity is also connected to questions of pleasure. Who are these famous people, where do they come from, and why are they worthy of our attention? If we look around at contemporary American society, there can be little doubt that these are important questions. How can we explain the national (and international) fascination with the personal lives of the Kardashian sisters, Paris Hilton, or Lindsay Lohan? Why do so many of us pay attention to the details of the lives of actors, musicians, and other media personalities, keeping up with their relationships, weight changes, and hairstyles? What keeps audiences watching ABC's *Dancing With the Stars* where a minor celebrity is paired with a professional dancer, or CBS's *I Get That a Lot*, in which celebrities hide their identities and pull pranks on ordinary Americans, all for a good laugh?

Serious scholars might be inclined to dismiss the celebrity world as meaningless trivia or, worse yet, to sound an alarm about the dangerous distraction that captivates the

American public. This doesn't tell us much about either celebrity or its meaning to audiences. Let's face it—celebrity watching is not confined to a small number of obsessed fanatics. Many people pay some attention to the celebrity scene, whether by reading a newspaper interview with a favorite movie star, watching *Entertainment Tonight*, picking up a copy of *People*, or clicking through TMZ.com. In fact, for the vast majority of Americans who engage, in various ways, with media, the world of entertainment celebrity is likely to be a regular feature.

Joshua Gamson (1994) suggests that celebrity watching is a complex act and that audiences use a range of interpretive strategies in these mass-mediated interactions with the celebrity world. Some audiences essentially believe what they see, take the celebrities at face value, and focus on their great gifts or talents. Others see celebrity as an artificial creation and enjoy the challenge of seeing behind the images, unmasking these celebrity "fictions." Other audiences are what Gamson calls the "game players," who neither embrace the reality of celebrity nor see it as simple artifice but who adopt a playful attitude toward the celebrity world.

This playfulness revolves around two kinds of activities: gossip and detective work. For some, the fun of celebrity comes from the game of gossip. In this game, it does not matter whether celebrities are authentic people or manufactured creations or whether they deserve their fame or not. The fun lies in the playing of the game, and the game is sharing information about celebrity lives. This game of gossip is fun because the truth of each comment is irrelevant; friends can laugh about the bizarre or enjoy evaluating celebrity relationships with the knowledge that there are no consequences.

Other game players focus their energy on detecting the truth about celebrities. This game is animated by the ever-present question of what is real in this world of images, even though the game players are not certain whether they can ever detect the reality. As a result, the fun lies in the collective detective work, not in any final determination of truth or reality. The game itself is the source of pleasure, as players scrutinize celebrity appearances and entertainment magazines, sharing their knowledge with one another as they peel away the never-ending layers of the proverbial onion. Each performance or news item adds to the story, and the detective game continues. The pleasure comes with the speculation, the moments of "aha," and the search for additional information—which the celebrity system produces almost endlessly.

Ultimately, the world of celebrity is a place where the real and the unreal intermingle and where the boundaries between the two are blurred. Game-playing audiences know that the game is located in a "semifictional" world, which makes it both fun and free. Moreover, the pleasure of these games comes from the very triviality of the celebrities themselves. According to Gamson (1994),

> it is the fact that the game-playing celebrity watchers don't really care about the celebrities—contrary to the stereotypical image of the fan who cares so much and so deeply—that makes the games possible and enjoyable. . . . [Celebrities] literally have no power of any kind over audiences. If they did, the "freedom" of the games would be dampened. What matters to celebrity-watching play is that celebrities do not matter. (p. 184)

We see that mass-mediated pleasure can come from a recognition by audiences of media's trivial nature, which makes them perfect sites for fun and games.

Pleasure and Resistance

We have seen that audiences derive pleasure from their use of various forms of mass media. But is there a relationship between the interpretive activity of audiences and their enjoyment? The research in this area has produced a healthy debate but certainly no consensus on the matter. Here we return to the notion of the active audience, which is a requirement for the mediated pleasures we have been discussing. The pleasure of media use comes precisely from interpretive engagement with media texts; media are fun because we actively participate in the making of meaning, not because we simply turn off our brains.

Even if we accept the argument that it is interpretive activity itself that is a source of pleasure, we still need to ask whether all interpretations are equally enjoyable. Does it matter whether we accept the "preferred" meaning or "resist" it? Do both kinds of interpretive strategies result in our having fun? In his study of television, John Fiske (1987) argues that the act of interpretive resistance itself produces pleasure. In this view, the fun of media use and the "popularity" of popular culture are the result of assertions of independence by audiences; the media allow audiences a kind of freedom to understand the world on their own terms. Resistance is fun, we might say, because it empowers those who do not wield power in their daily lives.

While this "pleasure of resistance" view is a provocative hypothesis, we in fact know very little about how widespread such pleasurable resistance actually is. The studies we have identified in this chapter certainly suggest that pleasure and resistance are not necessarily connected. Media use can be fun in situations where audiences are not resisting dominant meanings. Some critics argue that it requires more work to produce oppositional interpretations (Condit 1989). Such interpretations may be a source of great pleasure because of the hard work involved, but this interpretive work may be an obstacle that will prevent many audience members from making oppositional meanings. Interpretive resistance may be fun, but it may also be comparatively rare. Still, the digital media landscape may offer new ways for audiences to enjoy the pleasures of resistance, extending beyond making oppositional interpretations (Ott 2004). It can be amusing to express one's resistance by creating media that makes fun of or criticizes popular media texts—including everything from writing television reviews on a blog and posting comments on celebrity websites to reversioning film scenes by adding a humorous voiceover and making your own music mashup.

We do know that media can be fun, that audiences are active, and that meanings can be variable. If the social positions of audiences and a corresponding set of cultural tools help explain the patterns of interpretation, they may also help clarify the nature of mass-mediated pleasure. Media can be fun because reading or watching offers a space away from the demands of daily life. Feminist media theorists have argued that this is a particularly significant issue for women, whose social roles give them little space. Pleasure can come from entrance into a world of fantasy; here, again, social position shapes the kinds of fantasy worlds that are attractive and the ways audiences engage with fantasy images. Pleasure can also come from asserting autonomy in the face of conformity and from seeing through media in ways that are empowering. More generally, media can be fun because they are a forum for play in a society that values work far above leisure.

Media Fans

One particularly active subset of the media audience consists of those who identify as fans of a particular genre, text, or author. Over the past two decades, scholars have explored the activities and experiences of a wide range of media fans—the practices of "fandom"—developing a specialized subfield within media scholarship of fan studies (Gray, Sandvoss, and Harrington 2007; Jenkins 2012).

Fan studies emerged in the 1990s as a challenge to the popular stereotype of the fan as a "fanatic," an eccentric or extremist whose obsession makes them different from most media audiences. Rather than dismiss fans for their avid interest, fan studies scholarship has explored the various forms of fan activity, offering a helpful window onto each of the four forms of audience activity we enumerated earlier in this chapter.

First, fans are undoubtedly active interpreters of media, often paying careful attention to the nuances of plot development, character traits, and narrative techniques. Fans typically accumulate substantial knowledge about their favorite media texts, paying attention, for example, to a director's background, a musician's travel experiences, or narrative loose ends from a prequel. In fact, learning background information about a television program, film, musical group, or comic book series is a defining feature of the fan experience—and the depth of knowledge and intensity of commitment is part of what differentiates fans from casual audiences. Fans use their knowledge as an interpretive resource, helping them to make sense of a plot twist, a new sound, or the return of a familiar character. Participating in this interpretive activity, the process of decoding, is often a source of pleasure for media fans, and is often a central part of what makes media fandom fun.

Second, fandom is a social activity. Many fans are active participants in fan communities, which typically offer fans regular opportunities to share their media interests with like-minded others. They can share information about their favorite programs, artists, or film genres, debating the meaning of recent developments and building collective interpretations of the media texts. Fan communities offer a variety of ways for fans to connect, from online discussion forums and Facebook pages to fan newsletters and annual conferences. For example, *Lost* was one of many popular television programs whose fans created a Facebook page to network with each other to share commentary on the program and links to other *Lost*-related websites. SoapOperaFan.com hosts online discussion forums dedicated to each of the major daytime soaps; the *Days of Our Lives* forum has more than 150,000 posts. The Star Wars Chicks website, created by female fans in 1999, includes a detailed timeline of the Star Wars Universe, various Star Wars games, electronic greeting cards, and plenty of fan fiction. Harry Potter enthusiasts can attend any number of conventions—commonly referred to as Cons—hosted by organizations such as The Leaky Cauldron and The Group That Shall Not Be Named. For many fans, some kind of ongoing interaction with other fans is the core activity of the media fan experience.

Third, some fans become activists, participating in collective action aimed at promoting, saving, or changing a particular media form or text. Fans are typically passionate about their chosen media, and they are often connected through shared participation in fan communities. As a result, fans are often already organized and are ready to mobilize in the face of a perceived injustice. Fans have organized campaigns to save television programs slated for cancellation, including an unsuccessful 1999 fan effort to continue the 35-year run of the daytime soap opera *Another World* (Scardaville 2005) and the 2012 campaign that brought the NBC comedy *Community* back for another season. Fans of Nickelodeon's cartoon *Avatar: The Last Airbender* organized a 2009 campaign demanding that the film adaptation include Asian actors. While these fan-activists failed, and the film was made with white actors, the campaign continued as an ongoing effort to promote the casting of Asian Americans and other underrepresented groups in Hollywood films (Lopez 2011). Sometimes fans participate in activist efforts that have no specific connection to their media interests; for example, Lady Gaga has mobilized her fan community in support of marriage equality for gay and lesbian couples. Fan activism has grown more common in recent years, and much of it is not connected to broader efforts promoting political change (Earl and Kimport 2009), but mobilized fans employ a wide range of activist tactics and offer an interesting example of activism rooted in the experiences and preferences of consumers, rather than citizens.

Fourth, fans have long been producers of their own media, and these often serve as valuable resources for building and maintaining connections within fan communities. In the predigital era, fans produced and distributed their own, often photocopied, publications—dubbed fanzines, or just zines—that were full of fan commentary about a specific media form. Many of the most popular zines focused on music, with a rich variety of early zines focused on punk rock in the 1970s and 1980s. Fans of *Star Trek,* one of the first organized fan communities, were pioneers in the development of fan fiction—stories written by fans that extended the story lines of the television programs, often imagining new experiences and challenges for the major characters. Fan fiction has become increasingly popular in the digital age, with online platforms making it easier to produce and distribute fan-authored stories. The website fanfiction.net archives fan fiction associated with anime, movies, comics, television shows, and other media, with a vast library of stories, including more than 300,000 stories about the Japanese anime series *Naruto* and more than 96,000 *Glee* stories. Fan-produced media typically circulate within fan communities, offering dedicated fans an opportunity to express themselves, hone their skills, and build media-based connections with similarly interested fans.

Fans are certainly active audiences. While the intensity of their activity may exceed that of more casual media audiences, they engage in the same forms of audience activity. As new digital media expand the opportunities for audiences to produce their own media, fans are among the most avid creators of amateur media. In this context, it will be helpful to consider briefly how audience experiences are changing with the continuing growth of user-generated media.

From Audience to User

We have seen the diverse forms of audience activity, emphasizing how the active audience challenges long-standing assumptions about passive media consumption. At the same time, we need to recognize that audiences are not static; audience experiences evolve in response to the changing media environment. Amid the continuing growth in user-generated media—everything from videos posted on YouTube and photos shared on Instagram to the vast blogosphere and a diverse array of wiki-based collaborative media—some scholars argue that we need new terminology, other than "audience," to describe the hybrid experience of being simultaneously consumer and producer of media (Bruns 2008; Bruns and Schmidt 2011). The language to describe our relationship to media is likely to be in flux in the coming years—after all, verbs such as "browse," "friend," and "like" now describe everyday media-related activities in ways that would not be recognizable to an earlier generation of media consumers—but the term "user" is emerging as one common term that describes our contemporary media activity.

How, if at all, users are different from audiences is a complex question, and contemporary media research and theory has done little to specify the contours of the user experience, or how and why the activity of media users is substantively different from the activity of audiences. Still, the term "user" implies an activity that involves both media making and meaning making. Users are amateurs, not media professionals. They create media content, which they share with other users, typically for free. As the forms of digital media and technologies for sharing content continue to proliferate, we may all be in the process of becoming media users, routinely creating and consuming, circulating and interpreting media to and from a variety of professional and amateur sources.

Sometimes you may be literally producing and consuming media at the same time, creating and circulating your own small bits of content in response to the media you are experiencing. Popular television programs typically generate a steady stream of Twitter traffic throughout the program, the "second screen" phenomenon (Highland, Harrington, and Bruns 2013). In doing so, audience members create and contribute to a real-time, user-generated media landscape that exists alongside, and in response to, traditional mass circulation television. This second screen experience has become increasingly common (McClelland 2012), as a growing segment of television viewers engage in media activity that extends well beyond the boundaries of traditional audience.

The second screen phenomenon highlights the ways the audience experience is shifting in the digital media era. Audiences may be distracted by their second screen, and they may be even more involved with other users than they are with the program they are ostensibly watching. At the same time, we should not neglect the significance of that "first screen," the media content that engages audience interest and provokes users to post their own comments and content. As scholars continue to study the various forms of media audience activity, it will be helpful to examine specific everyday media practices, paying careful attention to the ways new media users are similar to, and different from, traditional media audiences.

CONCLUSION

This chapter has examined the ways in which audiences are active interpreters of media messages. The central contribution of much audience research lies in its interest in individual and collective forms of human agency. The active audience tradition brings real people into focus in media research by exploring the interaction between people and media texts and locating meaning in those interactions.

Although audiences are active, their activity is still subject to a variety of structural constraints. The media messages themselves matter—even if they can have multiple meanings—because they make some interpretations more likely than others. The cultural tools that audiences bring to the interpretation of media are not uniform; different people from different social locations will not have the same resources at their command. By ordering the distribution of cultural tools, social structure serves as a constraint on the process of meaning making.

Audiences, then, are active, but they are not fully autonomous; a sociology of the media needs to be sensitive to both the interpretive agency and the constraints of social structure. Audience research is particularly useful when it clarifies the intersection of agency and structure in the analysis of what media messages mean. Research that compares the interpretive work of audiences from different social locations has been particularly helpful in this regard. But what about the different kinds of media? Do the specific properties of a medium affect this interpretive work? And how substantially do new media disrupt long-standing producer-audience relations? We turn, in Chapter 9, to a consideration of media technology.

DISCUSSION QUESTIONS

1. How, if at all, do you consider yourself as "active" when you watch television, listen to music, read a book, or browse the web? Are the forms of activity different for different types of media?

2. Do you think social context influences your experience of movie viewing? Why or why not? Consider the similarities and difference in watching a film in a theater, the classroom, on a television screen in a family living room, and on a laptop with headphones.

3. What resources are necessary for individuals to decode media in an oppositional way? Do you think you have ever interpreted media in ways that challenged the preferred reading? Why or why not?

4. In what ways are media fans similar to, or different from, broader media audiences? How, if at all, does the term "user" signify a way of experiencing media that is different from being part of a media audience? What term would you use to describe your own media use?

CHAPTER 9

Media Technology

In previous chapters, we have explored the industries and organizations that produce our mass media, the content of the media images that circulate widely, and the meaning of these media images for both audiences and the broader political system. In this chapter, we pay closer attention to the specific communication medium on which the various media industries rely. Because we cannot have traditional newspapers without printing presses, television programming without equipment to transmit and receive visual images, or an Internet without the computer networks on which data travel, we need to examine media technologies themselves if we are to understand how media work. What kinds of information do the different forms of media communicate? What makes "new" media new? How do different media forms influence the ways we think or help shape the character of our social relationships? These questions focus specifically on media's technological apparatus—the medium itself.

The importance of media technology is widely recognized. In fact, a body of work has focused almost exclusively on technology as a driving force of social change. While technology certainly has consequences for society, a more sociological perspective examines the broader context in which technology exists. Thus, in this chapter, we consider the different properties of the various media. Then we go further and examine how the development and application of media technology are socially constructed. This discussion takes into account the dynamic tension between media technologies and the various social forces that have shaped their evolution and use. Finally, we survey some of the ways that technology matters, helping to shape aspects of social life, and we conclude by focusing on select new media issues.

THE NATURE OF MEDIA TECHNOLOGY

If we stop and think about them, the technologies that form the basis of our media can seem remarkable to those of us who are not engineers. How, exactly, is a book composed and printed? How do radio and television really work? How does a text message get from here to there? Most of us will not be able to answer such questions, at least not in technical terms. We know very little about the technological aspects of printing presses, broadcast technology, computers, and mobile devices. And, in many ways, it doesn't matter. We are still able to read a book, watch TV, surf the Internet, and use our smartphones. One important characteristic of media technology, then, is that it is so user-friendly that we often take it for granted. And by taking it for granted, we often overlook how technology helps shape our media experience.

Differing Technological Capabilities

Each medium has its own technological capabilities that affect the delivery of text, sound, and visual images (see Figure 9.1). For example, a music concert performed by one of your favorite artists could be broadcast live by a radio station; you would hear the sound but not be able to see the performers. A magazine could print a story about the concert and provide photographs to show you what the event looked like, but only after the fact and without sound. A television program could deliver live sound and video, but any text delivery would be awkward, perhaps limited to a scrolling "crawl" at the bottom of the screen. A DVD would also have sound and video, but it would be available only well after the original concert date. The Internet is unique in its ability to serve as a digital platform that enables all of these features—print, sound, still photos, and video—and do it live. In addition, those watching the streamed concert online could communicate with other music fans through instant messaging or tweets, introducing a form of interactivity that is not possible with radio, magazine, television, or DVD versions of the concert.

Because of their capacities and limitations, the various media technologies provide different ways of communicating the concert experience, both in the kinds of information they present and in the ways we access and experience them. So technology clearly matters; it places limitations on what a medium can be used for and makes some types of media more suitable for some purposes than others. As media technologies evolve, they provide opportunities for different forms of communication.

Mediating Communication: Traditional Versus "New" Media

Media technologies are structural constraints. Like all structures, they have been developed by humans and, subsequently, both enable and limit human action. How they do this is at the center of a sociological understanding of media technology.

Figure 9.1	Select Characteristics of Different Media					
	Live?	*Text?*	*Sound?*	*Picture?*	*Video?*	*Interactive?*[a]
Print	No	Yes	No	Yes	No	No
Radio	Yes	No[b]	Yes	No	No	No
Film	No	No[b]	Yes	Yes	Yes	No
Television	Yes	No[b]	Yes	Yes	Yes	No
Sound recording	No	No	Yes	No	No	No
DVD	No	No[b]	Yes	Yes	Yes	No
Internet	Yes	Yes	Yes	Yes	Yes	Yes

The technological limitations of each medium set the parameters for their use. With digitization, though, different media converge toward a single digital multimedia, making some distinctions less clear. The Internet—whether accessed via computer, mobile device, or game console—is, in effect, a generic platform of computer networks that allows for the delivery of all forms of media.

Notes: [a]We are using *interactive* here to mean a medium that enables two-way communication between producer and receiver.

[b]While film, television, DVDs, and digital radio can show text on the screen, they are not primarily textual media.

As we noted in Chapter 1, *media* is derived from the Latin word for *middle*. This signifies that the media are in the middle of a communication process, specifically, in between the sender and the receiver of a message. The early use of the term *media* was as part of the phrase *mass media of communication*. We long ago dropped the explicit reference to communication in everyday language and talked of the *mass media*—and, increasingly, simply the *media*. But it is useful to remember that media technologies of all sorts have social significance because they enable and affect forms of human communication. As a result, they raise unique sociological issues.

Beyond their common role as a mechanism of communication, however, media technologies vary. Two important phases of media development are what we might call traditional mass media versus "new" media.

Media, before the rise of the Internet, can be thought of as belonging to the era of traditional mass media, which typically involved:

- one-to-many communication,

- with anonymous receivers,

- through one-way communication channels,

- with a clear distinction between producers and receivers.

Let's consider these features more closely.

Some forms of media, such as the traditional landline telephone, connect one individual with another single individual; they have a one-to-one orientation. *Mass media,* however, enable communication to be sent from one source and be received by a large audience elsewhere; they have a one-to-many orientation. A newspaper, for example, is produced by a particular news organization and is sold to a large group of readers. There is one sender, the news organization, and there are many receivers, all of the readers. Films, television, and music are similarly centrally produced, and they are distributed through various channels to often large audiences.

Another property of mass communication is that it involves a known sender and generally anonymous receivers. Readers typically know the author of the book they are reading, but authors clearly cannot know who, exactly, is reading their books. When we watch a television program or go to the movies, the names of the producer, director, and actors are prominently displayed, while the moviegoers and television audiences are anonymous and often spread around the world.

Third, traditional forms of mass media typically enable one-way communication that does not allow direct feedback from receivers of the messages. That is, these media are not interactive. When we read a book or a magazine, listen to the new CD we just bought, or turn on the television, there is no way to use those media to directly respond to the messages we have received. We could, if we wanted, take the time to write or call the distributor, producer, or author to let them know how much we liked or disliked their book, music, or television program; but that would be using another media form.

Finally, these one-way communication channels create a clear distinction between producers and receivers of media content. With traditional mass media, the producers of nearly all content are commercial companies, nonprofit media organizations, and governments, while ordinary people are limited to being audience members.

Digitization and the rise of the Internet have blurred the boundaries between types of media and changed the broad parameters that used to be associated with all mass media. As a result, it makes more sense to speak of "new" media as breaking significantly with many of the features that characterize traditional mass media. We place the term *new* in double quotes because the "new" media, of course, are no longer new; the Internet is well into its third decade. However, no other single umbrella term has yet emerged to encompass the variety of media that now exist and to flag their distinctiveness from traditional mass media. For now, we're stuck with the awkward term: "new" media.

"New" Media: Digitization, the Internet, and Mobile Devices

Any media content that is digital can be stored as the 1s and 0s of computer code, including text, audio, pictures, and video. This digital content can be delivered via different media, such as a compact disk (CD), digital video disk (DVD), or digital radio or television broadcast signal. By itself, the shift from analog (nondigital) to digital media content was significant. A music CD, for example, has different properties than a phonograph record; CDs typically have lower audio quality, but they are immune from the accumulation of scratches and pops that eventually plague vinyl records. And identical copies of a CD's content can be made easily on a computer. However, much more significant changes developed when digital media content was united with the Internet.

The Internet is the communications platform on which digital media content can be delivered to a wide variety of devices, including desktop computers, wireless laptops, smartphones, and other mobile devices. Over the past few decades, the growth of digital media, the rise of the Internet, and the proliferation of mobile devices have combined to burst open the very meaning of mass media in several ways (Bolter and Grusin 2000; Lister et al. 2009).

First, the Internet blurs the distinction between individual and mass audiences, and replaces the one-to-many model of traditional mass media with the possibility of a many-to-many web of communication. This can be seen as people use the Internet and digital content for individual communication with single known recipients (e-mail, instant messaging), small group communication with a limited number of recipients (forums, social-networking sites), and mass communication with an unlimited number of unknown recipients (websites, blogs, streaming video). This blurring of the boundaries between communication to individuals and communication to a large audience has led observers to often replace the language of *mass media* with that simply of *media* (though we will see later that there is still good reason to pay attention to distinctions in audience size).

Second, the notion of known senders and anonymous receivers becomes problematic on the Internet. The producer of media content may remain anonymous to the typical reader, listener, or viewer, such as when no identifying information is provided on a website or blog. This opens the door to mischief, as with spam e-mail and false information or rumormongering through blogs or anonymous websites. On the other hand, with the Internet, the audience is sometimes known by the producer, as when registration is required to access a website, join an online community, post comments on a site, or receive an electronic mailing. Even when we do not supply personal information to websites—or use fictitious identities—we still leave our digital footprint (in the form of our computers' IP addresses). This changes the relationship between users and producers because, as we will see, advertisers on the Internet can know a good deal more about the identities and behaviors of those they seek to reach than they ever could with traditional mass media.

Third, with "new" media, communication is often potentially interactive, rather than being one way. For example, readers of newspaper websites can provide instant feedback on a story, shoppers can post their own product reviews at online retail sites such as Amazon.com, and viewers can comment or vote to "like" or "dislike" a video on YouTube. Interactivity can also mean that users are able to employ these media to communicate with each other.

Finally, the interactive capacities of "new" media blur the distinction between producers and receivers. Not only can audiences comment on or respond to media content created by others, but the widespread availability of digital media tools means that people with relatively modest financial resources and basic technological literacy can create their own media content and contribute to or alter content on other media platforms. The requirements for such a task are still insurmountable hurdles for the world's impoverished and illiterate—and indeed the majority of the world's population—but the creation of media content is within the grasp of more people than ever, especially in more affluent countries. People can create blogs and websites, upload videos, post their photographs, and engage in a host of other activities. They can also contribute content to existing sites by, for example, using a television station's website to submit photos and video that might be broadcast. In some cases, the traditional terms *audience* and even *readers* no longer accurately reflect the active role of what can be called more appropriately *users* of the "new" media.

TECHNOLOGICAL DETERMINISM AND ITS LIMITS

Given the technological sophistication of our media, its importance in communications, and its widespread utilization by broad segments of the population, we should not be surprised that discussions of media technology often emphasize the awesome power of the newest media to affect society. But it is easy to overstate the influence of media technologies by claiming that they dictate processes of social change; this is referred to as *technological determinism*. As we will see below, the arguments of technological determinists can raise important questions about the social impact of new technologies, but they fail to recognize that technology is only one element of the media process in the social world.

Technological Determinism

We can think of technological determinism as an approach that identifies technology, or technological developments, as the central causal element in processes of social change. In other words, technological determinists emphasize the "overwhelming and inevitable" effects of technologies on users, organizations, and societies (Lievrouw and Livingstone 2006: 21).

Sociologist Claude Fischer (1992) characterizes the most prominent forms of technological determinism as "billiard ball" approaches, in which technology is seen as an external force introduced into a social situation, producing a series of ricochet effects. From this perspective, technology causes things to happen, albeit often through a series of intermediary steps. For example, the invention of the automobile might be said to cause a reduction in food prices because the automobile "reduced the demand for horses, which reduced the demand for feed grain, which increased the land available for planting edible grains," making food less expensive (Fischer 1992: 8). The problem, however, is that there is no human agency in this type of analysis. The technological determinist's view is all structural constraint and no human action. It argues that technological properties demand certain results and that actual people do not use technologies so much as people are used by them. In this view, society is transformed according to a technical, rather than a human, agenda.

The Influence of Social Forces

Contrary to technological determinists' views, many scholars argue that technologies are determined by social forces. These analyses acknowledge that technology matters, but social forces, such as cultural norms, economic pressures, and legal regulations, shape the ways in which technologies develop and are used.

For example, British cultural studies scholar Raymond Williams (1974, 1983) argued that technology cannot determine cultural or social outcomes, as technology is merely the extension of human capacity. In such an approach, human agency takes center stage, and technology is what we do with it. Similarly, in his social history of the telephone, Fischer (1992) argues that we should not even ask what "impact" a technology has had on a particular society, for this question implies from the outset that the technologies do something to us. Instead, Fischer suggests that we focus our attention on the people who use the technologies, sometimes in surprising ways.

Before the creation of broadcasting, for example, early developers envisioned telephone technology as a way to bring news and entertainment into the home, not as a device for personal communication. Many early radio enthusiasts thought that its principal use would be point-to-point communication—a kind of wireless telephone—rather than broadcasting. The early Internet was born as a military communications system, was adapted by a myriad of academic researchers and computer enthusiasts, and then was commercialized by major telecommunications and media companies. In each of these cases, as we will see in more detail next, social forces determined how a technology developed and was ultimately used.

THE SOCIAL CONSTRUCTION OF MEDIA TECHNOLOGIES

Sociological approaches to technology don't ignore the inherent capacities of different media. As we have seen, the technical properties of each medium place constraints on the ways people can use it by providing parameters within which human agents must operate and by more readily lending itself to particular applications.

But humans have agency—they can act—and they have a range of options with respect to how they use media technology. As a result, the development and application of new media technologies is neither fixed nor fully predictable (Douglas 1987). Instead, a sociological approach emphasizes that media technologies are embedded in ongoing social processes that affect their evolution. For example, the Internet is subject to social forces that help to shape how it functions and how it is used. These forces include legal regulations, social norms, and market pressures, as well as the medium's inherent technical properties (Lessig 1999, 2006). Together these forces—law, social norms, market pressures, and technological architecture—have shaped the Internet, just as they have shaped every other communications medium. Thus, looking sociologically at the development of media technologies entails thinking simultaneously about the technological and the social (Bijker and Law 1992). To understand the relationship between media and society, the most important question is not, "What does a new technology do to people?" but, instead, "How do people use the new technology?"

Scholars have documented the importance of these forces to the introduction and evolution of various new media technologies. By looking back at studies of earlier technologies, as well as the rise of today's Internet, we can see how human agency shaped the technologies we now take for granted.

The Early Years of Radio

In its earliest years, people knew radio by a different name and understood it as a very different form of communication. What we now take for granted—a model of broadcasting music, news, and entertainment programming—took two decades to evolve (Douglas 1987; McChesney 1994; Schiffer 1991).

For 10 years after its invention by Marconi in 1895, people called radio the *wireless*. Early radio was essentially the same technology we know today; it used the electromagnetic spectrum to transmit audio signals from sender to receiver. However, the social forces that later shaped the direction of radio technology had not yet coalesced, so the meaning of the technology was different. Corporate consolidation of the radio industry had not yet occurred, the government had not yet regulated the use of the electromagnetic spectrum, and investors had not yet recognized the profitability of producing household radio receiving devices. The wireless had not yet become radio.

When Marconi first demonstrated his wireless in 1899 at the America's Cup in New York City, he thought of the technology as a telegraph without wires. In the eyes of its inventor, then, the wireless was an improvement of an existing point-to-point communication technology; it had nothing to do with broadcasting music or other entertainment. Consequently, Marconi's business acumen directed his attention to those institutions that had come to rely on the telegraph in their routine business practices, particularly newspapers and steamships. Perhaps his wireless could serve as a substitute, or an upgrade, providing a less cumbersome means for long-distance communication.

The primary users, in Marconi's vision, would be large commercial interests with a regular need for transmitting information to and receiving information from a distance. There was little sense that individuals would use wireless and, therefore, little reason to produce equipment for individual use. In addition, early developers conceived of wireless as a two-way communication device—wireless users would both send and receive messages. At the beginning of the 20th century, the notion that receive-only devices—what we call radios—would be the core of the technology was still far off. In fact, the uncertainty in the future of wireless can be seen in its eventual name changes. The wireless became *radiotelegraphy;* then, when it began to transmit voice instead of Morse code, it became *radiotelephony;* and finally just *radio* (Douglas 1987).

In the early years of the 20th century, a struggle over the control of radio—and over the definition of its proper uses—brought corporate interests, the U.S. military, and amateur operators into conflict. Corporate interests, including the American Marconi Company, sought private control of the airwaves in order to use them for profit. The Navy sought government control of the airwaves in order to use them for official purposes, particularly during wartime. And amateur radio enthusiasts, mostly young men and boys in the years between 1906 and 1920, saw the airwaves as a form of public property to be used by citizens to communicate with one another. As amateurs learned how to use the new technology and how to construct their own transmitters and receivers, a radio subculture emerged in which sending and receiving long-distance communications became an increasingly popular hobby. As listeners tuned in at night, seeking transmissions from sites hundreds of miles away, it was amateurs who planted the seeds of the broadcast model and made the act of listening a leisure activity.

It took a number of years for the new medium of radio to evolve into what we know it as today. Beginning as the "wireless," radio was first conceived of as a telegraph without wires that could improve one-to-one communication. Amateur radio enthusiasts adopted the technology to send and receive long-distance messages as a hobby. Only later did radio become primarily a way to broadcast music, news, and talk.

In the years prior to 1920, corporate and government radio operators still saw radio as a form of point-to-point communication, even as the airwaves became increasingly populated by amateurs. Because the airwaves have limited space, it was becoming increasingly clear that the government would have to organize and delimit their use. The Marconi Company complained about the use—and what it saw as abuse—of the airwaves by amateurs. The sinking of the *Titanic* enhanced public perception of the value of wireless (and made Marconi even more famous) because the survivors were rescued by a ship that had received a wireless distress signal. Both the U.S. Navy and the Marconi Company supported government regulation of the airwaves. In this context, Douglas (1987) explains, "The necessary reforms were now obvious to the press and to Congress. . . . Most importantly, the amateurs had to be purged from the most desirable portion of the broadcast spectrum. They had to be transformed from an active to a passive audience, allowed to listen but not to 'talk'" (p. 233). The result was the Radio Act of 1912, which regulated the use of the airwaves by requiring all transmitting stations to be licensed by the federal government, thereby curtailing access for amateurs. Even before the notion of broadcasting had taken hold, therefore, the institutional structure of broadcasting was in place: centralized, licensed senders and large numbers of individual listeners.

Despite these restrictions, amateurs continued to operate radios in even larger numbers. Some made use of the shortwave frequencies that the government allocated, others were granted government licenses to use the airwaves, and still others continued to operate without licenses. In 1917, when the United States declared war on Germany, the government ordered all amateur radio operators to shut down and dismantle their equipment. Douglas (1987) reports that the police closed down more than 800 stations in New York alone. In need of skilled radio operators, the Navy recruited amateurs, many of whom served in World War I. They returned home after the war even more skilled in radio technology. By 1920, amateurs were experimenting with playing music and providing information over the air to other amateurs, who were encouraging their families and friends to listen along. Several amateur transmitters built up substantial audiences for their "programming," while the corporate radio industry continued to focus on point-to-point communication.

All of this changed when, in the hope of increasing sales of their radio equipment, a Pittsburgh department store ran a local newspaper advertisement for a musical program broadcast by amateur Frank Conrad. Shortly thereafter, Westinghouse, one of the major manufacturers of radio sets, began financing Conrad's station as a means of selling its radios. Radio manufacturers AT&T and General Electric, along with department stores, quickly jumped into the business of broadcasting by setting up stations to stimulate the sale of radio sets. The market for the broadcast model was much larger than for the point-to-point model, offering the possibility of greater profits. As news coverage of radio programming increased, owning a radio set and being able to listen to the programs became highly popular. In 1922, AT&T began selling access to the airwaves as Marconi had done for private communication, but with a much larger audience. The broadcast model, with programming financed by the sale of advertising, was finally in place.

The route to radio broadcasting of music, news, and serials, all surrounded by ads, was not the straightforward result of some technological imperative. In fact, one of radio's great technological capacities—its ability to both send and receive messages—was not utilized in the final model. By including factors beyond technology in our understanding of radio, we can see that what we often take for granted as radio's natural order of things is in fact the result of a complicated social process involving commercial interests, amateur enthusiasts, and government regulators. Moreover, we can see that things could have turned out differently. Basic wireless technology might have been applied or further developed in a different direction, leading to different social consequences.

What if corporate capital had not been inclined to develop—or had been prevented from developing—a commercial radio industry? What if the government had maintained exclusive control of radio, as some urged in the post–World War I years? What if government had stayed entirely out of radio, enacting no regulations at all to control the use of the airwaves? What if amateur radio enthusiasts had prevailed in spreading the popularity of individual-to-individual radio communications? In each of these cases, the development and ultimate meaning of radio would likely have taken a distinct path, making some uses more likely than others.

We don't need to rely on pure speculation to imagine these alternatives. In other countries, radio has played a different role than in the United States. In some countries, radio has served as a more distinct form of top-down communication, providing official information (and often propaganda) from the government to its citizens. In others, listeners have much more widespread access to the airwaves, which are not used to sell products with the same zeal as in the United States. In several countries, including England, Australia, Argentina, and Uruguay, a portion of the airwaves has been earmarked for "community radio" (Gordon 2008; cf. Hintz 2011; Rennie 2006).

The evolution of radio, and the variations in how it has been adopted, illustrates the fact that we cannot understand a new medium simply by looking at its technological component because this ignores the social processes that ultimately shaped its use.

Television Finds a Home

Twenty-five years after the consolidation of the radio industry, television was available as a mass consumer item. Manufacturers marketed it as a new form of entertainment that would bring the family together to enjoy public amusement without ever having to leave home. If sales of television sets are any indication, this pitch worked quite well. Television became a household staple faster than any previous home appliance. The percentage of American households with television sets skyrocketed from just 0.02 percent in 1946 to almost 90 percent in 1960 (Spigel 1992). In relatively short order, television found a home in American life.

In its remarkable rise to prominence as a central part of American domestic life, the television industry both accommodated already existing family practices and tried to mold these practices (Spigel 1992). In this era, middle-class women were perceived as having a great deal of "free time" during the day for leisure or relaxation while also attending to housework. Therefore, producers directed most early television programming at women viewers, whom they considered to be the largest and most accessible audience. As a purely aural medium, radio could provide entertainment while women worked, as listening did not interfere with other activities. However, as a visual medium, it was more difficult to market television as something women could enjoy at the same time as they were doing housework (Spigel 1992). Leaders of the television industry feared that the new medium might not fit into women's lives and therefore might be underused or ignored altogether.

One effort to overcome this hurdle was the 1952 development of a TV-Stove, an appliance that allowed women to watch television while they cooked. By designing an apparatus that accommodated existing cultural practices and traditions, the television industry hoped to attract loyal viewers. The TV-Stove demonstrates that cultural practices can shape the development of media technology. It also shows how cultural practices can be more powerful than technological innovation: The TV-Stove was a market failure.

The television industry was more successful by designing the content of programming to accommodate the practices of 1950s middle-class women. In the formative years of television, producers designed the soap opera and the variety show as programming that would not interfere with women doing housework. Soap operas contained little action but a great deal of verbal explanation and often repeated the same themes. Viewers could listen from an adjacent room or could miss episodes without losing track of plot developments. Variety shows moved from one act to the next, making it easy for viewers to watch only parts of the program. This, too, was ideal for women working around the house.

For television to be successful, then, it had to make itself fit into the routines and cultural practices of the white, middle-class families that producers saw as the core of the consumer market. But this is only one side of the story. The television industry also tried to reshape family routines to be compatible with television viewing. As Spigel (1992) puts it, "Not merely content to fit its programming into the viewer's rhythms of reception, the network aggressively sought to change those rhythms by making the activity of television viewing into a new daily habit" (p. 85). For example, promoters billed NBC's *Today Show* as the TV equivalent of the morning newspaper; the networks routinized their schedules, previewed upcoming programs, and linked program times to the household activities of women and children, all of which encouraged viewers to adapt their daily routine to the television schedule.

In the end, commercial television became the centerpiece of U.S. consumer culture, influencing and disrupting American traditions, practices, and buying habits. Still, television was not a predetermined entity; cultural practices shaped its early development and uses, just as the medium in turn influenced these practices.

Introducing the Internet

The Internet is yet another example of a medium that has evolved substantially over the years, responding to government influence, commercial pressures, and user habits (Abbate 1999; Hafner and Lyon 1996; Naughton 2000).

In the early 1960s, MIT Professor Joseph Licklider conceived the idea of a network of information-sharing computers (Waldrop 2001). This concept was later financed by the U.S. Defense Advanced Research Projects Agency (DARPA), a body within the Defense Department dedicated to the development of new technologies for military use. The prospective decentralized computer network could allow core U.S. government agencies to communicate during a national emergency, even after a nuclear attack.

ARPANET (Advanced Research Projects Agency Network) went online in 1969, at first linking just four universities. By 1975, over 50 university and government sites were networked, and the control of ARPANET was transferred to the Defense Communication Agency (DCA), which later decided to create a separate subnetwork dedicated to military uses, MILNET. In 1983, the control of civilian sites was shifted to the National Science Foundation, which took over with a mandate to disseminate the new technology among U.S. universities for research purposes; commercial uses of the emerging Internet were forbidden. In 1991, the U.S. Congress passed the High Performance Computing and Communication Act, authored by Al Gore, which provided the funding to substantially expand the infrastructure that was becoming popularly known as the *information superhighway*.

Once the military uses of the Internet were separated from civilian uses, government financial support came with relatively few strings attached in the name of promoting academic research and information sharing. This enabled early developers to work without the pressures of commercial market forces, while acting on their "technocratic belief in the progress of humans through technology" (Castells 2001: 61; Kahn 2004). Within this context, a subculture of computer enthusiasts (sometimes known as hackers) emerged who promoted principles such as sharing, openness, decentralization, and free access to computers (Jordan 2008; Levy 2010). Their efforts were the foundation for later "open source" and "free software" movements.

Up until this point, however, using the Internet was generally limited to engineers, computer scientists, and others who possessed the necessary specialized computer skills. That changed when Tim Berners-Lee at the European Laboratory for Particle Physics (known as CERN) developed a new protocol for information distribution that created a user-friendly network interface. Launched in 1991, the new protocol was known as the World Wide Web—the familiar "www" at the beginning of web addresses—and was based on hypertext.

As the potential of the Internet to reach the wider general public became increasingly clear, private developers started to create independent network tools that would allow users to bypass the government-funded Internet infrastructure. For example, in 1993, Netscape Corp. developed the early Internet browser, Mosaic. As more private developers invested in the Internet, the National Science Foundation ended its sponsorship of the national Internet infrastructure, and the Internet became an increasingly commercially oriented system.

The excitement over the potential money to be made on the rapidly growing Internet grew frantic in the latter half of the 1990s, contributing to wild investment in new "dot-com" companies that drove the U.S. stock market to unprecedented levels. But consumers at the time were not interested in buying groceries (webvan.com), kitty litter (pets.com), or sporting goods (mvp.com) online. As a result, many much-hyped companies collapsed, and the dot-com "bubble" burst in 2000, sending the stock market plummeting.

As with other media, the Internet did not travel a straight line from introduction to mass adoption. Instead, the Internet is the result of complex social processes, involving government funding, the culture of computer enthusiasts, commercial interests, and user preferences.

Web 2.0 Versus the 1% Rule

In the years before the 2000 dot-com crash, many companies had tried to use the Internet to simply continue the delivery of traditional content (e.g., newspapers) and facilitate traditional activities (e.g., shopping)—often unsuccessfully. But as the Internet gained a greater foothold in society in the 2000s, more emphasis was placed on how this technology enabled users to customize, create, and share content, representing a sharper break from traditional media. Web 2.0, one of the popular labels given to highlight this collection of interactive capacities, suggested a technological change from the original Internet. Web 2.0 enthusiasts pointed to a wide range of examples to highlight these changes. New technologies, they argued, enabled the rise of blogs, social-networking sites, content platforms such as YouTube, collaborative wikis such as Wikipedia, virtual game worlds such as *World of Warcraft,* social bookmarking such as Diigo, and virtual worlds such as Second Life.

In fact, Web 2.0 did not reflect any substantial change in the technological capacity of the Internet. Instead, Web 2.0 was a concept coined in 2004 to indicate a shift in how software developers and users utilized the existing medium (Scholz 2010). Part of this was marketing hype; in the wake of the dot-com bust, developers had to convince investors that there was something new and fundamentally different about Web 2.0 that made it a better and safer investment than the failed dot-com era. Just as the uses to which radio and television technology were put evolved over time, Web 2.0 highlighted and developed capabilities of the Internet that had existed since its inception. The basic technology wasn't new, but the uses to which it was now put had evolved. This is another example of how changes that result from social forces have been popularly and erroneously understood as being the result of technological innovations.

With Web 2.0, software developers, commercial content providers, and ordinary citizens took greater advantage of the technological capacities of the Internet. However, while the technology enabled activity, the decision of whether or not such an activity is worth pursuing is ultimately up to users. In this regard, the enthusiasm about interactivity and content creation suggested by Web 2.0 can sometimes be overstated.

In reality, large online communities and social networks are typically made up of a relatively small number of people who generate most of the content and many more lurkers who look but don't contribute. This phenomenon is sometimes referred to as *participation inequality,* and two popular informal rules of thumb have emerged to describe it. The 1% Rule says that, for every person who creates content, there are 99 who do not (Arthur 2006). A variation, the 90–9–1 Principle, says that participation typically breaks down into 90 percent of users who are lurkers, 9 percent who occasionally provide content, and 1 percent who account for most contributions (Nielsen 2006). These are obviously inexact rules of thumb, and rates of participation vary from site to site. However, the general idea of participation inequality has been confirmed, both anecdotally and through a variety of measurements of participation rates on specific websites (Arthur 2006; McConnell 2006; Wu 2010).

The 1% Rule and 90–9–1 Principle are geared toward single websites. But what about Internet use more broadly? Perhaps a person reads Wikipedia entries without contributing, but she is active in an online forum on her favorite hobby; in one context, she is a lurker, while in another, she is a contributor. The media research firm Forrester Research surveys adults to assess their degree of participation with new media across websites and has developed overlapping categories of users to describe these various roles, including (Bernoff and Anderson 2010):

1. Creators make content that is consumed by others, such as writing blogs, and uploading videos, music, and text.

2. Conversationalists share their opinions with consumers, companies, and others, for example, through social-networking sites or Twitter.

3. Critics respond to the content of others by posting reviews, commenting on blog entries, or editing wiki articles.

4. Collectors organize content for themselves or others, using RSS (Really Simple Syndication) feeds, tags, and voting mechanisms such as Digg.

5. Joiners maintain a profile on social-networking sites.

6. Spectators consume content generated by others.

7. Inactives neither create nor consume new media content.

Table 9.1 provides examples of the data Forrester collects on these categories.

Two features stand out from this basic data. First, perhaps not surprisingly, the most common role played by those who use new media is that of spectator, just as it was with traditional mass media. The opportunity to create content afforded by the technological

Table 9.1	Social Media Participation Types, 2009 and 2011 (in percent)					
	US		EU		Japan	
	2009	*2011*	*2009*	*2011*	*2009*	*2011*
Creators	24	24	15	23	34	25
Conversationalists	n/a	36	n/a	26	n/a	18
Critics	37	36	20	33	30	24
Collectors	21	23	6	22	11	15
Joiners	51	68	30	50	26	29
Spectators	73	73	50	69	69	72
Inactives	18	14	39	21	23	24

Source: Forrester Research, Inc., n.d.

capacities of Web 2.0 is tempered by the reality of dynamics associated with the 1% Rule. Some people are simply not interested in being content creators. Creating any substantial content is time-consuming and still requires a level of technological literacy that is not universally shared. As a result, even in a new media world, most people, most of the time, will be audience members, spectators consuming the creations of others. Second, Internet use varies by region, even when data is limited to a few wealthy societies. Japan has lower rates of "conversationalists" and "joiners," for example, than does the United States or European Union (EU). In addition, Internet participation is increasing over time. For example, the percentage of "inactives" in the United States dropped from 18 percent in 2009 to 14 percent in 2011. This likely results from a larger share of the population being digital natives, born into a world where new media are a taken-for-granted part of life (Palfrey and Gasser 2008).

In this section, we have illustrated how social forces influence the development and application of media technologies, emphasizing the importance of human agency. We turn now to a variety of topics that illustrate how the use of new media has influenced social life in the past and may influence us today. The developments associated with Web 2.0 reflect the ways people choose to use new media—by developing new software applications, creating content, and the like—as well as how they limit their participation.

HOW MEDIA TECHNOLOGY MATTERS

The term *medium theory* refers to the body of literature that focuses on the technological aspects of media beyond their content (Meyrowitz 1994). Medium theorists see media as more than conduits for the transmission of messages; they argue that the very nature of the medium can be the key to its social impact. From this perspective, media technologies can be powerful social forces, affecting how we perceive and understand the world.

All medium theorists take seriously the potential impact of technology, but they differ in the degree to which they acknowledge the influence of social factors. Some analysts are technological determinists, while others see the interaction of various social forces with technological developments. They also differ in their assessment of the social changes prompted by new technologies. Some analysts have chronicled the dire effects of new media, while others have optimistically embraced new technologies.

McLuhan's Optimistic Message

One of the most widely read medium theorists is the Canadian literary scholar Marshall McLuhan (1911–1980), who was both a technological determinist and an enthusiast for the new electronic media of his day. McLuhan was mostly interested in the cultural effects introduced into society by electronic media, especially television. McLuhan is best known for his assertion that "the medium is the message" (McLuhan and Fiore 1967). Although McLuhan's technological determinism often led him to overstate his case, his ideas about the relationship between technology and culture still resonate with some contemporary technology enthusiasts.

Briefly, McLuhan (1964) argued that, if the influence of media interests us, then we should focus our attention on the ways each new medium disrupts tradition and reshapes social life. The real message, for McLuhan, was not the formal content of media but the ways the media themselves extend our senses and alter our social world. McLuhan was quite insistent about this position, colorfully arguing that "the 'content' of a medium is like the juicy piece of meat carried by the burglar to distract the watchdog of the mind" (p. 32). What changes people, he argues, is not the content of media but the experience of the medium itself.

In an early work, *The Gutenberg Galaxy,* McLuhan (1962) focused on the shift from oral to print societies, exploring the social implications of the 15th-century invention of the printing press by Johannes Gutenberg. He argued that new media technologies rework the balance of our senses, isolating and highlighting certain senses at the expense of others. Print, from this perspective, intensified the visual—we use our eyes to read—and separated it from other senses, in particular, sound.

In another work, *Understanding Media: The Extensions of Man,* McLuhan (1964) turned to the shift from print to electronic media, especially television. In it, he argued that, by delivering both images and sound, electronic media could help reconnect the senses that had been fragmented by print's exclusive focus on the visual, thereby bringing us back to a kind of preprint state of harmony. Further, McLuhan argued, by allowing us to see images and hear sounds from distant places instantaneously, electronic media are a global exten- sion of our senses. "[W]e have extended our central nervous system itself in a global embrace, abolishing both space and time" (p. 19), he wrote. This perspective led him to utopian predictions of the development of a new "global village" based on the wonders of communication technology—a claim we explore in the final chapter.

In McLuhan's technological determinism, each medium was seen to shape our senses in such a way that certain social outcomes would be almost inevitable. And as the dominant media of an era are all encompassing, McLuhan argued it is virtually impossible for people to see the ways technology influences them. Because McLuhan was an enthusiast for new technologies, this sort of stealth determinism did not alarm him. Instead, he saw electronic media as opening the door to new and more holistic ways of thinking. In the end, McLuhan's technological determinism may be limited, but it did prompt other scholars to think about the impact of media technology, including his observations about media's effect on our senses of time and space.

Media's Impact on Time and Space

We usually take it for granted, but a live television image of an event that is hundreds or thousands of miles away is an astonishing manipulation of time and space. We can "be there" without being there, and we can experience the events instantaneously, joining in what Tomlinson (2007) calls a "telemediated cultural experience" (p. 74). For example, Major League Baseball's World Series was under way in the San Francisco Bay area when the 1989 Loma Prieta earthquake occurred. Residents of Boston or Dallas who had their televisions turned on to the game received more and faster information about the size and scope of the earthquake than did local San Francisco residents, whose electricity and phone service were knocked out. Through media technology, those further away learned more than those closer to the event, and they learned it almost instantaneously.

This is just one of the ways that medium theorists say electronic media and new communications technologies have changed the way people experience time and space. And this influence extends beyond television.

The Never-Ending News Cycle

A society's dominant media help set the rhythm of social life. For a long time, the daily newspaper—and later the evening news broadcast—created a particular news cycle; essentially, news was updated once a day. The introduction of specialized cable news channels, beginning with CNN in 1980, changed all that. Founder Ted Turner's original vision for CNN was for it to be, in essence, a televised newspaper that offered more serious and in-depth news than was found on television's brief 30-minute evening news (Turner and Burke 2008: 165). However, instead of depth, cable news came to emphasize speed, spotlighting its unique ability to be the first to cover an event—often live. This led to the now-familiar, never-ending news cycle where cable news, websites, and other news sources are constantly updated throughout the day and news outlets compete to be the first to report a story. Critics charge this approach leaves little time for reflection or in-depth analysis, results in chaotic and unreliable news, and makes the news media more susceptible to manipulation by sources (Kovach and Rosenstiel 1999, 2010). So the growth of cable television technology, and cable news in particular, coupled with web-based news sites, has changed our sense of time in relation to the news. Waiting 24 hours for a news update now seems like an eternity.

Time Shifting and Binge Viewing

Media technologies have also given users more control over time. To watch or listen to a particular program, traditional broadcast media required audience members to tune in at a time determined by the broadcaster. *Time shifting* refers to the practice of recording or downloading media content to watch or listen at a later time that is more convenient for the audience. The VCR and audio cassette tape player were the first widely available technologies to enable time shifting. Later digital technologies such as the DVR and the MP3 player made time shifting much easier and more popular. Now, viewers can record television programs for later viewing or watch them from a website at times of their choosing. They can also download podcasts for later listening at their convenience. Time shifting creates problems for advertisers who often gear their ads to specific time frames—a summer clearance sale, for example. Waiting to view content at a later date makes such ads irrelevant. Portable laptops, tablets, and mobile devices such as smartphones and MP3 players also enable *place shifting*—enabling users to access media content anywhere as well as any time.

Time shifting has enabled the practice of *binge viewing,* watching many episodes of a television series in one sitting or over a few days. In the traditional broadcast model, television networks typically launched new programming schedules in the fall of each year and aired one new episode a week. Viewers saw these episodes at the same time and shared the social experience, leading to "water-cooler" discussions at work the next day about popular television programs. Binge viewing does away with this structure, making the entire concept of a "season" irrelevant, since viewers can consume an entire season at once and viewing becomes asynchronous; water-cooler discussions have been replaced by spoiler alerts. Binge viewing has helped to fuel the proliferation of serialized programs in which a

Source: Netflix.

Netflix's original *House of Cards* became the first-ever digitally distributed series to win an Emmy—collecting nine nominations and three wins in its first season. Netflix was a key player in promoting a new model of video consumption: content delivered by apps via the Internet rather than broadcast and cable channels. The flexibility of such a model means that viewers can choose from a vast library of titles and watch anytime they want, challenging the traditional advertising model of television.

story arc develops slowly over multiple episodes. In the past, studios shied away from such series, preferring those with self-contained episodes that wrapped up neatly each week. These self-contained episodes could be watched out of order in syndication.

Netflix has had success catering to binge viewers. When it created its first original series, *House of Cards*, it released an entire "season" of 13 episodes simultaneously, an industry first. Netflix even altered how programs are streamed by determining the moment at the end of the show when most viewers turn it off. Now, at that moment, Netflix minimizes the credits at that point and prompts viewers to immediately start the next episode, encouraging marathon viewing. The strategies have worked. The number of episodes of a single serialized program that the average Netflix subscriber watched each week rose from 4.9 in 2009 to 6.1 in 2012. Netflix data shows that some of the most popular binge viewing series are old television programs that completed their run years ago, including *24*, *Lost*, and *Prison Break*. Some foreign programs that never aired on U.S. television have also been surprise hits with binge viewers, including Australia's *McLeod's Daughters*, about a ranch run by women, and South Korea's Cinderella-like soap opera, *Shining Inheritance* (Jurgensen 2012).

Crossing Social Boundaries

In his classic work, Meyrowitz (1985) recognized that television compressed distances and transcended physical boundaries by allowing us to see things that were far away. However, he emphasized that television transcended social boundaries as well. Before the development of electronic media, our social roles and identities were closely tied to the physical places where we performed these roles. Because electronic media enable us to transcend physical distances, they also allow us to overcome boundaries. For example, Meyrowitz (1985) points out that, in earlier eras, children would have to know how to read—and be sophisticated enough to understand—the content of adult-oriented print media to access adult social life. But as a visual medium that does not require literacy, television allows children to see parts of the social world that were previously hidden or difficult to access, thus "blurring" childhood and adulthood. By showing children the "backstage" behaviors of adults, television permits children to be "present" at "adult interactions"—socially, if not physically. The result is that an important boundary between adults and children, which in the past was reinforced by different levels of reading skill, no longer holds. (This may have a good deal to do with the popular belief that children grow up faster today than they did in the past.) The Internet has only expanded this process, for example, contributing to the "mainstreaming" of pornography by making it easily available to Internet users of all ages (Dines 2010). In providing such access, television and the Internet compete with the socializing role of parents, schools, and other agents and provide children with ideas and images that often contradict the stories and myths handed down in the family and at school.

Localism and Virtual Communities

Media technologies have altered our sense of space and place in other ways as well. For example, traditional media tended to be rooted in a particular physical location. Newspapers were grounded in particular cities, and radio stations produced their programs locally.

Today, though, with satellites and the Internet (along with the consolidation of the media industry discussed in Chapter 2), many forms of media are placeless. *USA Today,* ungrounded in any particular city, is the nation's most-read newspaper, while the *New York Times* website is among the most popular sites anywhere in the country. Meanwhile, radio stations that are programmed remotely from corporate headquarters, satellite radio, and Internet radio streaming have largely displaced "local" radio. Rocker Bruce Springsteen bemoaned this loss of place in his aptly named song "Radio Nowhere."

By affecting our sense of place, media technologies have also altered our sense of community. Birkerts (1994) notes that new media technologies created an entirely new social space, cyberspace, which allows for new forms of interaction with little connection to the physical world. People can take on new identities in cyberspace, transcending the limits and the responsibilities of their physical environments—at least temporarily.

The concept of *virtual community* (Rheingold 2000) suggests that communities no longer need to be geographically based. People all over the globe can become "virtual" neighbors through the space-bridging technology of the Internet. By "friending" others on Facebook, joining discussions in chat rooms or online forums, and playing in virtual worlds, users can employ the Internet to connect with others. According to Rheingold (2000), the Internet can constitute a powerful antidote to the loss of traditional community values and can help reestablish social ties. However, a plethora of research suggests that online networks have a more complex relationship to geographic communities. Online networks, for example, sometimes supplement physical communities, providing new means of communication that can facilitate interaction among neighbors, but such online connections are not likely to replace the place-based bonds associated with neighborhood-based communities (Hampton and Wellman 2003; Van Dijk 1998; for an overview, see Jankowski 2006).

Finally, the loss of media rooted in distinct physical places has been accompanied by the loss of media content that is located in distinct social spaces. For example, with the Internet and mobile media, the distinction between public and private has become blurry, and this process is intensified by new forms of mobile media (Ling and Campbell 2009). Issues and topics once thought to be private—belonging to a separate, backstage personal sphere of social life—are increasingly discussed in and displayed on the public front stage of media. This shift of social space ranges from the spectacle of television talk shows that expose the intimacies of dysfunctional families to Facebook pages, tweets, and Tumblr posts through which individuals reveal the often mundane details of their daily lives.

Network Society

With the rise of the Internet, Manuel Castells (2001) provocatively claimed that "the network is the message." For Castells, the Internet is the technological basis of a new organizational form, the network. In his work, the boundaries between network as a form of social organization and network as a technological infrastructure are blurred. Castells (2000) argues that, in the Internet age, our "network society" is rooted in telecommunications and new media and has been reshaped by the flow of information that is independent of physical proximity. In addition, our perception of time is modified by the immediacy of communication technologies. Time is "dissolved," and this process has been accelerated by wireless and mobile technology (Castells et al. 2006).

But despite his invocation of McLuhan, Castells has a much more sophisticated analysis that recognizes the role of human agency in shaping media technology. In fact, the Internet, says Castells (2001), is "a particularly malleable technology, susceptible of being deeply modified by its social practice" (p. 5). Three independent processes in the last quarter of the 20th century contributed to the rise of the network as a new organizational form and its technological counterpart, the Internet: (1) pressure from the corporate sector to globalize capital, production, and trade; (2) citizen demands for individual freedom and open communication; and (3) unprecedented advances in the telecommunication and computing fields, which paved the way for the microelectronic revolution. Thus, unlike technological determinists, Castells highlights the interaction between technological capacities and human agency. According to Castells, the Internet works as a lever for the transition to a new form of society, one in which the power of information, and therefore the possibilities of participation, are potentially distributed throughout the full range of human activity.

With all these developments that have affected our sense of time and space, media technologies have enabled change to occur, but social forces ultimately have determined the specific form of these changes. Competition and market forces influenced the rise of the never-ending news cycle. Users chose to have more control over when and where they watched and listened to media content—often to the dismay of traditional media companies. A lax regulatory environment that allowed growth in media conglomerates, coupled with cost-conscious commercial media firms, helped produce the consolidation of media ownership that led to the expansion of media without local roots. And many people voluntarily gave up their privacy on Facebook pages and TV talk shows, while developers of social-networking sites, television producers, and advertisers encouraged these behaviors. Ultimately, it is how media technologies are used, rather than the technologies themselves, that helps to shape our sense of time and place.

The Rise of Television Images

While McLuhan's vision of new technologies was an optimistic one, other analysts have cast a more skeptical eye on technology, focusing on how change from one medium to another affects what we know and how we think.

For example, some critics—most notably Neil Postman (1985)—argued that the rise of television was the central cause of the decline in the seriousness of public life. The underlying premise is that what we say is, in large part, the result of the form—or technology—we use to say it. According to this view, the substance of democracy—participation by an informed citizenry—was undermined by the rise of television. The properties of television encouraged, perhaps even dictated, particular ways of talking and thinking that were antithetical to serious debate and discussion. To envision an extreme version of this, we need only think of the rapid-fire sound bites and shouting matches that often characterize television and radio programs about contemporary politics or the many "fluff" pieces that make their way onto "news" programs. In the end, according to the title of

Postman's best-known work, as a society infatuated with entertainment television that is no longer able to think seriously about social and political issues, we are *Amusing Ourselves to Death.*

This kind of critique of the television age is often a nostalgic lament for the bygone days when print was the dominant form of media in American society. Following McLuhan, Postman (1985) argued that print-based societies encourage rationality, seriousness, and coherence in both our ways of thinking and the content of public discourse. Reading creates a mind in which analytic thought, based on logic and clarity, is premium. Societies that rely on the printed word as the central means of both private and public communication, therefore, develop rational, serious populations. Postman identified 18th- and 19th-century America, which witnessed the birth and rise of U.S. democracy, as the most thoroughly print-based culture in history. Others have made similar arguments about the connection between print and rationality, suggesting that, for example, the development of the printing press played a key role in the rise of scientific thinking (Eisenstein 1979). Unlike McLuhan, though, Postman was concerned with the ways television challenges the rationality and coherence of print-based modes of thinking by holding up entertaining and trivial images.

Postman's close historical analysis connects the decline of serious substance in the media to the impact of even earlier technologies, in particular, the role of the telegraph and the photograph, in cultural change. By altering our sense of physical place—specifically, by making it possible to communicate with people who were physically distant—the telegraph, according to Postman, challenged the world defined by print in three fundamental ways. First, because they could get information from faraway places, newspapers were full of stories that were largely irrelevant to their readers. News no longer had to have any relationship to its audience, nor did information have to be functional in any way—it just had to be "new." Daily news consisted of new things, and novelty became more important than relevance. Second, because the telegraph made it easy to transmit so much information, little of which was relevant to the lives of readers, news no longer had any connection to action. People could not do anything about the things they read about in the paper. Information may have been abundant, but events were happening so far away and were so disconnected from people's lives that the news encouraged feelings of powerlessness. Third, in privileging speed and abundance of information, the telegraph sacrificed context. No longer did news have to be linked to any broader, historical framework. There was no need to connect one story to the next or one day's headlines to the next day's. The point was to keep the information flowing—to report the new things that happened—rather than to contextualize messages or events by linking them to prior messages or events. Quantity became more important than either quality or depth.

The photograph extended what Postman (1985) saw as a revolution in the ways we understand the world. Photos do not encourage logical argument or contextual knowledge. Instead, as Postman put it, "The point of photography is to isolate images from context, so as to make them visible in a different way" (p. 73). As the saying goes, a picture is worth 1,000 words. But Postman argued that, when we trade words for pictures, we lose something in the deal. The very meaning of information, of truth, is altered by a focus on the visual image of the photograph. Truth is no longer knowledge produced from logical thought, the kind of thinking that reading encourages. Instead, seeing is believing.

If seeing is believing, then those who can skillfully manipulate what we see can also influence what we believe. A generation before Postman, historian Daniel Boorstin (1961) argued that the pervasiveness of visual images was changing the very meaning of "reality." Images have become so embedded in our consciousness, in this view, that it is becoming harder to discern the difference between image and reality. It is not that we are losing our ability to think; it is that image-oriented pseudo-events blur the distinction between image and reality. *Pseudo-events* are events planned for the express purpose of producing dramatic images that can be disseminated or reported. In effect, they are events that have no independent existence; they take place only to be publicized. Pseudo-events include press conferences, televised debates between political candidates, and photo opportunities—all staged to produce dramatic images. Pseudo-events, however, are neither true nor false; they actually happen, but only to produce dramatic images. Appearance, not substance, is what matters. Indeed, pseudo-events may be more interesting than spontaneous happenings, a state of affairs that suggests that our definition of reality may be changing.

Postmodernist theorists suggest that contemporary society is increasingly characterized by this kind of "hyperreality," in which the boundary that used to separate reality from its representation has "imploded," leaving images with no real-world referents (Baudrillard 1988). One does not have to be a postmodernist, however, to see the significance of image making. In 1961, in the early years of the television age, Boorstin was exploring the relationship between the medium of communication and our ways of knowing. In a similar vein, Postman (1985) identified an image-dominated world as a "peek-a-boo" world; things come and go with little coherence, but our lives are always chock-full of entertainment. Writing in the age of television—but still relevant today—Postman saw that, in a world dominated by visual media, fast-paced entertainment may have become the model for all of society. As other realms of experience increasingly competed with and even imitated television, pretelevision ways of knowing the world were becoming more and more marginal—an argument that, as we will see, has been echoed by analysts of the Internet.

There can be little doubt that critics such as Postman and Boorstin were correct about the significance of images and visual media in American society. However, the causal claims—that inherent properties of media technology are the key determining force—are much more difficult to accept. The problem with such technological determinism is that it ignores people, except perhaps as victims of an all-powerful medium. Even though it is rarely explicit, most critics of television write about *commercial television,* not simply television technology (Hoynes 1994). The claims that television, as a technology, must be about entertainment, attractive images, and rapid movement from one idea to the next are not some technological law of nature. They are the result of a broadcast industry—driven by people and market forces—in which the need to sell products and make profits has dominated.

The commercial organization of broadcasting did not just happen naturally; it was developed—in the face of rarely mentioned opposition—by people who would profit from the commercial organization of the industry (McChesney 1994; Starr 2004). Medium theorists often fail to explore the ways human actors or public policy have shaped the uses of technology. In addition, this perspective has little room for the kind of critical, intellectual activity on the part of active audiences that, as we saw in Chapter 8, happens all the time.

New Media and the Culture of Distraction

The new media have produced an era of abundance. There are more information, more media outlets, more mobile devices, more media content, and more communication options than ever before. But what has this increase in the quantity of media technologies done to the quality of our thinking and communication? A wide variety of analysts, from different disciplines and perspectives, have addressed this question, and many have concluded that our adoption of new media technologies is producing significantly negative social consequences. Interestingly, critiques of the impact of new media on social life have come mostly from people who are at the center of developing, studying, or using such media themselves. These are not Luddites who resist new technologies; they are mostly people who have experienced the effect of new media firsthand. Their concerns involve an overlapping range of issues that—while far from definitive—suggest an often uncritical embrace of new media may be overlooking some insidious effects.

Early Cautions

One of the early analyses of new media came from Sven Birkerts (1994), who picked up the questions asked by prior medium theorists and applied them to the posttelevision, digital age. The title of his book, *The Gutenberg Elegies,* suggested that he was working in the tradition of McLuhan. If McLuhan's *Gutenberg Galaxy* was about the transition away from print culture, Birkerts began with the premise that print culture was dead. His elegies were both a celebration of a bygone era and a warning about the future digital age. Birkerts argued that new media sped up processes already begun by electronic media, in particular allowing for a much faster flow of information and breaking the spatial connection between the physical and the social. The result was an increasing commitment to the instantaneous nature of computer-mediated communication.

In this digital age, where data seem almost limitless, Birkerts (1994) argued that our ways of thinking are changing. No longer do we value unhurried deliberation; quick decisiveness rules the day. We do not need to know about the world; instead, we need to know how to access the data that will tell us about the world. The abundance of information now available electronically and the complex ways of storing and manipulating it put a premium on a new set of skills—retrieving and referencing, rather than understanding.

The development of hypertext, in this view, was the strongest signal of a change in our culture. Using hypertext is different from the experience of reading. With hypertext, readers choose from a range of links to follow in an electronic document. Each link leads to another text with even more links. Even though we are using our eyes and looking at words, Birkerts (1994) argues we are engaged in a different sort of activity. Reading involves engaging with ideas, listening to an author, and considering an argument presented in a linear fashion. In the social space created by reading, authors have a kind of cultural authority, at least while we are reading their work. Hypertext replaces the process of listening to a substantive coherent argument with a process that involves bouncing from text to text, often taking in only short snippets of an argument. Hypertext even challenges the very idea of authorship; the author no longer matters in the same way when readers are moving from one link to the next. In the world of hypertext, the experience of reading and the writer–reader relationship has changed.

Writing at the dawn of the digital age, Birkerts (1994) had the same concern as many other medium theorists before him: that new media would squeeze out prior cultural forms, including reading and rigorous thinking. Birkerts was also concerned that, as we become more and more enmeshed in new media technologies, we will lose any sense of unmediated experience, making the social world of media the only world we know or value. It's hard not to think of this sort of concern today when observing a group of people in a public space, all engrossed with their laptops and smartphones—and all ignoring each other.

Too Busy to Think: The Dangers of 24/7 Connectivity

Some of Birkerts' early concerns are echoed and developed by later analysts. Maggie Jackson (2008), a psychologist, argues that our embrace of new media has produced a sort of attention-deficit culture, expressed through the presence of constant stimulation, interruption, and multitasking. This fleeting culture of distraction, she contends, produces superficial "McThinking" that can be fun and engaging but that provides little intellectual nutritional value. Such a culture undermines our ability to focus, concentrate, and attend to the deeper and more substantive issues in life that are the bedrock of intimate social relationships, wisdom, and advances in culture.

While the ability of the Internet and mobile devices to connect people is typically celebrated as one of its greatest features, William Powers (2010), a journalist who covers technology issues, considers what he calls the "conundrum of connectivity." Yes, argues Powers, technology that allows us to connect to information and people from anyplace 24/7 is an awesome achievement. But history suggests that wisdom, insight, and perspective are gained from being *disconnected,* by creating time and space for solitude and contemplative thought. A healthy and vibrant life in the digital age, he argues, needs to involve a balance between the advantages of connectivity and the benefits of solitude.

Nicholas Carr (2008, 2010) is another critic who argues that the fragmented, transient, and hyperstimulative environment of the Internet and other new media contributes to ways of perceiving and thinking that are similarly fragmented and shallow. To make his case, Carr (2010) turns to experimental evidence from neuroscience showing that surfing the Internet indeed develops different neural pathways in the brain than does reading a book. The constant stimulus, fleeting distractions, frequent interruptions, and pervasive multitasking that characterize the contemporary media environment help produce a decline in people's ability to focus, concentrate, and engage in serious thought, he contends. The ability to concentrate, think seriously, read deeply, and follow an argument are not instinctual; they must be nurtured through training and practice that occurs when engaging for extended periods of time with complex ideas and arguments, as we do when we read a book. The world of tweets, hyperlinks, Wikipedia summaries, text messages, viral videos, and Tumblr posts, however, does not promote such skills. Such constant stimulus—and, conversely, the lack of prolonged consideration—is literally affecting how our brains develop, Carr argues. And these changes affect how we think. Sustained contemplation is being replaced by fleeting and shallow reactions.

Generation Me?

Some critics suggest that, despite a world of knowledge at their fingertips, the younger generation that has grown up with new media is less informed, less literate, more self-absorbed, and more depressed than any that has preceded it (Bauerlein 2008; Twenge 2006). They point to the popularity of social networking as one source of the problem. The immediacy and personalized nature of social networking, such critics argue, emphasizes the value of newness and facilitates an extreme focus on the self and immediate networks of friends. Information or news that isn't about this narrow world is often of little interest. The result is a worldview that promotes entitlement and self-centeredness, what Jean Twenge (2006) dubbed "Generation Me." (Such entitlement, though, meets reality soon enough; and younger people, Twenge notes, have higher levels of dissatisfaction with their jobs and lives than earlier generations.)

The Internet and its ancillary mobile devices make up a medium of interpersonal communication rather than one of wide exploration and learning. A parallel from an earlier era might be that, instead of reading a book, such users are writing notes to their friends; both involve writing and reading, but the nature of those efforts are radically different. Instant messages, chat, and microblogs are primarily insulated communication about self and friends, not broader considerations of larger cultural, social, or political issues. Further, the trend toward briefer instantaneous messages not only threatens thoughtful communication, but it even promotes the erosion of traditional spelling, grammar, and punctuation that have long served as a useful foundation for serious communication (Bauerlein 2008).

This sampling of ideas and analyses raises provocative questions and identifies changes in broad social patterns that are clearly linked to changes in media technology. At their best, they recognize the influence of users of the technologies along with the economic, organizational, and political forces that shape the development of new media.

NEW MEDIA TECHNOLOGY AND SOCIAL FORCES

In his early analysis of new media, W. Russell Neuman (1991) used the metaphor of a tug-of-war to describe the push-and-pull between the technical capabilities of new media and other social forces. We have already seen how various media, including the Internet, were affected by social forces as they were developed and deployed. In this section, we explore more closely how user habits, commercial interests, and government regulation have influenced the tug-of-war shaping the development and application of new media.

Commercial Interests and User Habits

New media give users the opportunity for more control and more choice, which can lead to increased content diversity and a shift of power from media corporations to users. However, other social forces—especially commercial interests and user habits—often pull in the opposite direction, leading to sameness and conformity.

Economic forces such as those examined in Chapter 2 help limit diversity. The earlier shift from broadcast to cable television is a good example of this dynamic. Digital cable offers hundreds of channels, but more programming has not necessarily meant diverse programming. In the days of network broadcast television, viewers could watch the weekly program *Wide World of Sports;* with cable, they can watch a number of sports channels 24/7. With network broadcast television, children's cartoons were largely limited to Saturday morning; with cable television, children can choose from several cartoon networks. In short, as a new technology, cable television typically brought larger quantities of similar content from the same producers.

Though it is touted for its diversity and many producers, the Internet, too, has often served as a channel for more content from the same providers. Most users have deeply ingrained media habits that do not change dramatically simply because of new technological capabilities. In the early years of the Internet, well-known corporations could translate their brand-name recognition into an advantage because users were already familiar and comfortable with them. These media conglomerates also had the extensive investment capital needed to launch risky online ventures and the traditional media venues (newspapers, television, etc.) to advertise and promote them. As the web matured and major media companies developed more online content and focused their marketing strategies on the online audience, people spent more time online but visited fewer websites (Harmon 2001). As a result, instead of being new or different, many of the most popular websites to this day are the online extensions of companies with roots that predate the web.

For example, in 2013, the top 50 U.S. websites (as measured by the Amazon-owned company, Alexa) included a number owned by traditional media and technology companies, such as Time Warner (CNN.com), NewsCorp (Foxnews.com), Microsoft (MSN.com, Live.com, Bing.com, Microsoft.com), Disney (ESPN.com, Go.com), Apple, *The New York Times* (nytimes.com, about.com), NBC Universal (weather.com, NBCnews.com), and Comcast (Comcast.net).

Source: Gabriel Bouys/Getty Images.

Mobile devices and related applications have made their way into virtually all aspects of social life. Even the Pope has a Twitter account (@pontifex) through which he addresses his followers.

Over time, though, new media firms entered the Internet market and became major players themselves, also appearing among the top 50 U.S. websites in 2013. These included Google (Google.com, YouTube.com, Blogger.com), Yahoo (Yahoo.com, Tumblr .com), Facebook, and Twitter. Today, the Internet's most popular sites are dominated by this combination of older companies that moved onto the web plus new Internet-based corporate giants. A miniscule number of these sites dominate web traffic. For example, despite more than a quarter of a billion websites available to users (Netcraft 2010), the 50 most popular U.S. websites account for about 40 percent of all pages viewed by Americans (Angwin 2010).

Thus, even with new technologies that enable a wider range of producers, major corporate players are the ones who continue to make the biggest splash in the new media environment. However, their route to dominance has not necessarily been an easy one, with companies searching for effective business models to use in a new technological environment.

The Business Models of New Media Companies

The most important force shaping the development and application of new media has been economic; major media players—old and new—have sought ways to profit from the capacities of the new media. This is never a simple proposition because another social force—users—have their own ideas about what they want or don't want from new media. The result has been an ongoing tug-of-war as media companies try to develop a business model that generates profits, while users often prove to be independent minded.

Managing Access: Portals and Search Engines

In the first phase of commercialization of the Internet in the 1990s, many firms looking for a successful business model focused their resources on developing *portals*—gatekeeping sites such as today's Yahoo! and MSN.com, where users start their explorations of the web—and search engines, most notably Google—which help users find what they want amid the overwhelming material on the web. In many cases, these two functions were combined on a single site.

Portals are a good example of how the Internet's technological capabilities were steered toward traditional commercial goals, as well as how complex it was for the major media companies to assert control over the new media world. Portals are, in essence, doorways to the world of online media: they classify sites, provide key word searching of Internet pages, and even give short reviews of a variety of sites. Some of these portals have been among the most widely visited pages on the Internet. Over time, these sites were transformed from simple filing systems to an advertiser's dream.

One of the earliest portal sites, Yahoo!, began as a simple catalog of Internet sites organized by topics such as computers, sports, news, and health (Robischon 1998). Yahoo! helped users find information on the rapidly growing and chaotic Internet and thus quickly became popular. As a result of its initial popularity, Yahoo! was transformed into Yahoo!, Inc., a commercial site with advertising sponsors. What began as a practical solution to a user problem—navigating the Internet—was now driven by commercial concerns.

Soon, websites could track how long a user stayed on a page, something referred to as a page's *stickiness*. This was a key factor online advertisers considered when buying ad space as sticky sites could hold the attention of users long enough for them to notice the banner ads that ran across the top of the page. (At the same time, advertisers also began employing more intrusive techniques to attract users' attention, such as pop-up window ads that were impossible to ignore and ads with eye-catching motion and video.) To increase its stickiness, Yahoo! began adding features to its pages that eventually included a search function, news, e-mail, chat groups, and Yahoo! Clubs—bulletin boards devoted to everything from sports and science to politics and hobbies. With these new features, Yahoo! visitors lingered longer and explored more linked pages, allowing Yahoo! to charge higher rates for advertising. Advertisements could also be customized for specific users. For example, if you navigated to Yahoo!'s recipe listings, a banner ad related to cooking was likely to appear.

The success of Yahoo! led to many imitators developing similar sites with more or less the same features. By the late 1990s, the handful of search engines and portal sites were generating more than a third of all advertising revenue on the Internet (Robischon 1998), and major media companies devoted substantial resources to developing and promoting these portal sites.

However, the portal strategy of the major media companies met with mixed results. The web portals employed a broadcast-oriented business model, based on attracting large audiences that could be sold for advertising revenue. But the downturn in the online advertising market in 2000—a result, in part, of the collapse of so many dot-com companies that were leading online advertisers—led to significant financial problems for many of the portals. In 2001, NBC announced that it was closing its NBCi web portal less than two years after it launched this would-be rival of Yahoo! and MSN. This followed a previous announcement by Disney that it intended to close its portal Infoseek. And AT&T's effort to build a powerful broadband Internet network was undermined by the financial problems of Excite@Home, whose Excite portal was another victim of the 2000 dot-com bust.

In contrast to Yahoo!'s strategy of promoting stickiness to its portal by adding more and more channels for content, Google maintained a simple main page design that highlighted its exclusive role as a search engine. Founded in 1998 by two Stanford students, Google today is the most successful search engine and has used this success to expand into a multifaceted media company. Google now offers a wide range of Internet-based services, such as e-mail (Gmail), a picture-sharing platform (Picasa), a scheduling app (Google Calendar), social-networking service (Google+), online maps (maps.google.com) and Google Earth, a 3-D graphic design program (SketchUp), a web browser (Chrome), virtual tours of art museums (Google Art Project), news, various newsgroups, and Google Books. In 2013, Google was the world's second most visited website (after Facebook) and was used as the primary search engine by 66 percent of U.S. users. Google's software provides the search engine built into many websites, making Google one of the foundations of the Internet. Google became so popular that the verb *to google* became synonymous with *searching the Internet* (not only in English but, similarly, in German, Italian, and other languages).

Google's success is due, in part, to its unique approach. Early search engines ranked pages mostly based on how often the search terms appeared on a page. Google based its page rankings on the principle that the highest ranked pages should be those to which the greatest number of other sites link; if others found a site valuable enough to link to, then Google search engine users would likely find it useful as well. In doing this, Google high-lighted better-known sites—giving an advantage to mainstream sources. It also achieved success by piggybacking on the efforts of large numbers of Internet users, who created the page links on which Google rankings were based. As we will see, this was an important step toward harnessing the free labor of Internet users that has become a central business model for Internet companies. Over time, Google evolved its search algorithms, intervening more in how search results are delivered (Vaidhyanathan 2011).

Instead of attracting a mass audience to a main site, Google also pioneered the strategy of selling much smaller, targeted audiences to advertisers. It did so by focusing on advertise-ments tied to search results that appeared only after results were generated. A search for "Boston Red Sox" would generate both page rankings and ads related to Red Sox tickets and products, for example. Advertisers liked the fact that their messages appeared directly to users who had already expressed interest in a related topic. Google later used the same strategy with Gmail, its popular free e-mail service. Gmail software monitors the content of your mail and inserts subject-specific ads. If you write an e-mail to your friend about traveling to Argentina, your friend might receive an e-mail that includes a few "sponsored links" to websites offering flights, hotels, restaurants, and perhaps even tango lessons. Today, virtually all commercial websites use some form of targeted advertising, including Facebook's delivering of ads based on what you have listed as your hobbies, your home-town, and other personal information.

Yahoo! had long steered users to paid sponsors by listing their sites higher up on its "channels," which organized sites by topic. Google adopted the strategy by blending its search engine results with pay-for-placement features. Advertisers pay for prominent dis-play in Google's key word search results, but—due to concerns that it might undermine the credibility of their results—the number of sponsored links are usually limited, at the top of the page, and clearly marked as such to be recognizable by users. Still, critics worry that commercial interests will make it more and more difficult for independent, nonsponsored sites to make themselves known to the average Internet user and for users to be steered toward sponsors' sites, with or without their knowledge.

The Limits of Selling Content

As we saw in Chapter 2, there were two basic revenue streams for traditional media. Media companies generated income by selling content to audiences, as with movie tickets or the price of a book, or by selling audiences to advertisers, as with radio and television com-mercials. Some media forms used a combination of the two revenue streams, as with newspapers and magazines. New media technology, however, upset this traditional media revenue world.

From their earliest years, new media technologies have made it very difficult for com-panies to sell content to users. Digitization made it simple for content to be copied, while the Internet made it easy for copied content to be shared. This combination was a disaster for traditional media companies. Users quickly developed a culture of sharing that under-cut the ability of companies to charge for content. Newspapers had hoped users would pay to access their websites, but this rarely happened. When papers tried to charge, many users simply went elsewhere to find free equivalents. Major newspapers have only recently reinstated modified pay walls out of economic necessity.

The music industry's struggle against piracy is the best-known example of this tug-of-war between commercial forces and user habits. The music recording industry did not have an advertising revenue stream. The prices consumers had paid for records, cassettes, and CDs was their primary source of income; concerts were largely promotional tours to sell more recorded music. Consequently, when new media emerged, music companies wanted users to pay for music, as they had always done in the pre-Internet world. Users, though, quickly learned it was easy to copy and share music for free. Even users with qualms about violating copyright laws could be lured into a culture of sharing that made file swapping simple and easy. In such an environment, paying for what you can get for free doesn't make obvious sense—especially to young people who had never experienced the pre-Internet media business model.

Napster was the best-known site driving this trend. The Napster site enabled users to find and share music with other users, bypassing the need to purchase music. Many music listeners rejoiced at the development of music-sharing sites, celebrating Napster and its imitators as a challenge to the highly concentrated corporate music industry. As music sharing developed, its freewheeling, collective spirit was, for some, a sign of the potentially democratizing and decentralizing tendencies of the Internet. At the same time, major music companies feared the devastating economic impact of the free distribution of songs over the Internet. And some musicians feared that online music sharing, which bypassed royalty payments, would threaten their livelihoods.

The industry turned to the legal system to limit the use of new technology, eventually winning its battle with Napster but, arguably, losing the larger war. The music industry aggressively pursued music "pirates," targeting Napster as the facilitator of millions of copyright violations. By 2001, as part of a settlement of the case, the original Napster site was shut down to reemerge later as a subscription pay site. But Napster proved to be the tip of the iceberg as a new generation of peer-to-peer (P2P) software emerged that enabled users to share files without the need for a central Napster-like site. Without a central site to target legally, it became extremely difficult to limit P2P file sharing, and such services expanded rapidly.

In addition to its legal strategy, the music industry also turned to technology itself to limit piracy, by installing various types of digital rights management (DRM) software on its products. Some DRM code limited the number of times a song could be copied, others limited the devices on which a song could be played, and some made it impossible to use a computer to rip music from a CD. DRM was wildly unpopular with users who complained of limitations on legitimate use of music they had paid for and were appalled when it was revealed that some DRM code installed itself on computers without notice and left users with major security vulnerabilities. A popular backlash against such restrictions led most music companies and music sellers to drop the effort. In a turnaround, sellers like Apple's iTunes even advertised the fact that their products were DRM free.

New media technologies and their utilization by consumers have led to significant changes in how the music industry operates. As the industry faced the reality of the file-sharing world, it lowered its prices, hoping to lure consumers back to paying for music by offering individual songs for less than a dollar. The industry hoped users would be willing to pay such a modest price for the convenience, reliability, and safety of legal music in contrast to risking virus infections and dealing with corrupted or poor-quality files that are sometimes part of file sharing. This approach found some success, with sites such as iTunes and Amazon's music download sites. However, the easy accessibility of downloading has meant a shift away from the longer album format to a renewed emphasis on singles as the standard unit of purchase for music fans, reducing revenue. As users grew accustomed to buying online, though, companies began to increase prices again, experimenting with charging more for new releases from best-selling artists. The industry also raised concert ticket prices, seeing such events as genuine revenue streams rather than just promotional vehicles to sell recorded music, and tried to license more music for use in commercials and films. Meanwhile, more musicians used the capabilities of new media to offer their music directly to listeners, setting up independent labels and websites or joining collectives of independent music artists who sold their music online.

The film industry faced many similar issues with file sharing, especially after the invention of BitTorrent software enabled faster sharing of much larger files. It, too, has turned to legal efforts and invoked DRM and other technologies to limit such sharing. It has also tried to highlight the unique experience of theatergoing by promoting 3-D films as a way to draw audiences to the theater and charge higher ticket prices.

The Wisdom of Crowds and the Use (and Abuse?) of Free Labor

Because commercial media companies have had difficulty selling media content to new media users, they have had to rely increasingly on selling users to advertisers. We have already seen how early portals and search engines depended on attracting audiences to generate revenue from advertisers. As such sites developed, they sought to entice users to stay longer on their sites (making them more valuable for advertisers) and began to target advertising more narrowly to specific users. But in more recent years, rather than giving users content that draws them to a site, many sites harness the talents of users to create content that, in turn, makes the site worth visiting.

Some observers have praised "smart mobs" (Rheingold 2002) and the "wisdom of crowds" (Surowiecki 2005) when connected via the Internet and mobile devices, especially in relation to Web 2.0 capabilities. If large groups have members with diverse opinions and experiences, who are independent of each other, decentralized, and able to collect their ideas, then large crowds can generate "wisdom" unavailable to any individual member (Surowiecki 2005). Perhaps the best known example of this approach in practice is Wikipedia, the wiki-based online encyclopedia supported by a nonprofit foundation. Wikipedia's millions of entries are written by volunteer users who also police each other's entries for accuracy and verifiability. Collectively, the group of writers and editors produce content that is consulted by millions of other users.

But what if the voluntary efforts of many users could be harnessed for private profit? Many media companies adopted exactly this approach in creating some of the Internet's most popular websites. Instead of focusing on producing content, social-networking sites (Facebook, MySpace), photo- and video-hosting sites (Flickr, Photobucket, YouTube), blog publishing and microblogging services (Blogger, Twitter, Tumblr), and others (LinkedIn, Craigslist, eBay) depend upon users to post content that draws visitors. (This even includes popular porn sites that feature live sex chat and video submissions from "amateurs.") By creating content that draws more visitors, users help make the sites attractive to advertisers and thus profitable for site owners.

Such trends concern some observers. Jaron Lanier (2010)—an early developer of virtual reality—argues that many of the applications of Web 2.0 that celebrate sharing information, collaborative efforts, and collective wisdom have come to actually facilitate something quite different. Such media applications, he contends, undermine the integrity of the individual by emphasizing a "hive" mentality in which independent thought and achievement is neglected and undervalued in favor of the faceless—and easily replaceable—microcontributions of many. In this context, commercial firms have discovered that they can harness and harvest the free labor of others to generate profits for themselves. YouTube, Facebook, Twitter, and others make money off of the fact that so many people are willing to fill their sites with content without compensation.

The harnessing of user-generated content—some of which is personal—to meet the needs of advertisers has, in turn, raised serious concerns about online privacy more generally.

THE THREAT TO PRIVACY: THE EXPANSION OF BEHAVIORAL TARGETING

In 2010, the *Wall Street Journal* published a series of articles on what it called "one of the fastest-growing businesses on the Internet . . . the business of spying on Internet users" (Angwin 2010). The extensive investigative report concluded that "the tracking of consumers has grown both far more pervasive and far more intrusive than is realized by all but a handful of people in the vanguard of the industry" (Angwin 2010). While privacy advocates had long tried to warn the public and the government of the intrusive nature of online spying and the inadequacies of current regulations (Solove 2006), the alarming report from a conservative pillar of the business community helped to spark renewed interest in the topic.

The investigative series found that the nation's top 50 websites each installed, on average, 64 different pieces of tracking technology on a visitor's computer—almost always without warning. Sites aimed at children were even more aggressive in tracking users than those aimed at adults (Stecklow 2010). This tracking technology is the foundation for *behavioral targeting,* advertising that is triggered by a user's actions.

The best-known form of online spying involves cookies. When you visit a website, many of them assign you an identifying number stored on your computer as a bit of code, known as a *cookie*. Cookies were first created in 1994 for the early web browser, Netscape Navigator, to enable online shopping by allowing a consumer to place different items in a virtual shopping cart. As a consumer browsed through a site's various pages, the cookies kept track of the items placed in the cart and remembered them when the customer was ready to check out.

The online retailer Amazon.com was a pioneer in expanding the use of cookies to connect all of your actions on its site, including the pages you visit, the products you buy, and the user information you provide. If you browse the page for a book on, say, Latino history, the site remembers this and recommends related books and DVDs. When you later return to Amazon, the site reads the cookie it installed earlier and continues to recommend items related to your interests. It also remembers personal information you might have provided on your last visit, such as your name, address, and credit card information. These features of cookies can be quite useful in learning about related products and speeding up the checkout process.

But the use of cookies soon extended beyond single-site applications. Now, cookies are mostly planted by *trackers*—companies whose business is based on spying on and recording the actions of users on the web—who plant what are known as "third-party cookies" (Angwin 2010). Trackers can get their files on your computer by paying a website to let them do it. They can also hide these files in banner ads or in free downloads, such as games, apps, ringtones, screen savers, and desktop images. For example, when you visit a site (the first party) with a banner ad for a company (the second party), you are likely to also get a cookie from the advertising firm that actually placed the banner ad—the "third-party" tracker.

Because the ad networks that place these cookies can contract with thousands of different websites, they are in the position to accumulate an enormous amount of information about you, your interests, and your online habits across the Internet. Stream videos from Netflix, post a hobby on your Facebook page, browse the stories on a conservative political website, book a flight and hotel for your Colorado vacation, check the weather forecast for your hometown, click on dozens of "like" or "don't like" buttons at many different sites, visit an Internet dating site, look at Thai restaurants in your city, buy tickets to a professional sporting event, consult a health site for information on your hyperactivity or weight loss—and all of this can become part of your data file. From this information, the tracker firm uses sophisticated statistical analyses and algorithms to develop an exhaustive profile of you that identifies—or predicts—your sex, age, income, residence, marital status, whether you have children or own a home, your likes and dislikes, your probable health issues, and a host of other characteristics. This profile is used to advertise products you are more likely to buy. Visit a bank or insurance site, and the site might steer you to a particular set of products based on an estimate of your income; visitors from different income brackets would see totally different offers.

Advertisers used to buy space on specific websites; now they mostly deal with these third-party trackers who can deliver access across many different sites to a specific group of people who fit a certain profile. One 17-year-old woman featured in a *Wall Street Journal* story had been concerned that she might be overweight and had consulted websites for advice. Later, she was inundated with weight-loss advertising whenever she went online. "I'm self-conscious about my weight," she said. "I try not to think about it. . . . Then [the ads] make me start thinking about it" (Angwin 2010). That's exactly what advertisers want: to reach audiences already predisposed to respond to their messages.

The technological capacities of the Internet are used for other privacy-invading practices, too. Often operating in a legal gray area, *scraping* involves copying online conversations and personal information from social-networking sites, résumé and job seeking sites like Monster.com and LinkedIn, and online forums where people might discuss a wide range of aspects of their lives including hobbies, health concerns, exercise regimens, relationships, politics, and school (Angwin and Stecklow 2010). Sometimes scrapers sift through this information to assemble profiles of individuals that are sold to employers, advertisers, and other websites; this can include linking people's real names to the various "screen names"—or pseudonyms—they might use on some sites. Other times, scrapers sell "listening services" to clients, reporting what people are saying about a particular product or topic. Social-networking sites, such as Facebook and MySpace, have been especially fruitful sources for information scrapers as they often include a great deal of personal information that users have voluntarily posted online. A company might pay a data scraper to assemble both snail mail and e-mail addresses of people who have discussed their products—along with similar information about their online friends.

Developers and users concerned about privacy have tried to limit the amount of information advertisers can gather. Cookies were originally designed to prevent the collection of data across more than one site, but advertisers found ways to work around these restrictions. Many users learned to reduce the invasion of privacy by regularly deleting cookies from their computers, but trackers created new types of cookies—known as *flash cookies*—that can regenerate themselves even after they have been deleted by a user. Trackers have also developed *beacons* that provide real-time data on a user's actions, including tracking what they are typing and where their mouse pointer is moving. All of these data are compiled and auctioned off with lightning speed via data exchanges to potential advertisers—often within seconds.

As the accumulation of information about Internet users becomes more and more sophisticated and detailed, consumer advocates have called for new regulations to limit the amount and type of data that can be compiled, while allowing consumers to find out what information is known about them. In 2008, Microsoft's product planners wanted its Internet Explorer browser to automatically prevent online tracking unless users opted to switch settings reducing their privacy. Company executives overruled the plan, fearing it would undermine their ability to make money from selling online advertising (Wingfield 2010). In 2010, the Federal Trade Commission (FTC) called for a "do not track" option that would allow users to opt out of tracking cookies entirely, a move advertisers vehemently oppose. In a development that echoes the film and video game industry's efforts to preempt regulation in an earlier era, in 2011, a group of online tracking companies launched a service called the Open Data Partnership to let consumers see and edit the information that has been collected on them. However, this effort does not allow users to opt out of data tracking as privacy advocates want (Steel 2010).

As alarming as such practices by advertisers are to many observers, they likely pale in comparison to what government intelligence agencies can do. Many people first became aware of this reality in 2013 when whistleblower Edward Snowden revealed that the U.S. National Security Agency (NSA) was collecting the phone records of millions of Americans; monitoring Internet usage through direct access to the servers of nine leading tech companies; extracting e-mails, audio, video, and other content; and even had the capability to monitor what a person is typing in real time (*The Guardian* 2013; *The Washington Post* 2013a). However, shrouded behind the veil of "national security," the extent and range of such data gathering capacities in the United States and other countries are still largely unknown. The little information that is available suggests that the degree of data gathering on citizens by governments around the world is vast and growing at an exponential rate. This capacity for government surveillance, too, is a major concern of privacy advocates.

The debates about privacy in the digital age will certainly continue and will ultimately be determined by social forces—market interests, user concerns, and government regulations—rather than technological ones.

IN SEARCH OF AN AUDIENCE:
THE LONG TAIL AND THE FRAGMENTATION OF MEDIA

Netflix offers tens of thousands of movie and television titles for streaming or DVD rental to its more than 38 million subscribers in 40 countries. That gives subscribers a vastly wider array of content to choose from than is traditionally available either in theaters or in video rental stores. Out of these many titles, a large number of Netflix members rent (or stream) a relatively small number of well-known new Hollywood films, the kinds of films that might have recently played at a local first-run movie theater. But Netflix also rents a huge number of different DVDs to relatively small numbers of subscribers, such as fans of classic film noir movies, nature documentaries, Japanese anime, or other niche fields. These latter titles make up a "long tail"—a large number of items sold (or in this case rented) in relatively small quantities (Anderson 2008). While the vast majority of media products—such as books, DVDs, and songs—sell in relatively small numbers, the combined total of all these small-audience media products equals a large, and potentially highly profitable, consumer market. At Netflix, for example, few subscribers are likely to rent, say, *Godzilla: King of the Monsters* or *Simply Ballet: A Master Class for Beginners,* but collectively, the availability of such eclectic titles draws a large number of subscribers and forms the company's business model. Netflix has found a substantial audience of subscribers by assembling a wide variety of content. With a huge and diverse product line, some title will be hugely popular and will be in high demand among subscribers. Most of the available titles, however, will be of interest to a relatively small segment of Netflix customers; still, a small number of rentals for each item in this vast film library provides a steady revenue stream.

The Internet similarly offers users a vast array of possible sites to visit. That's because technological change has allowed the number of media "producers" to expand dramatically. Though major websites with sophisticated original content can cost millions of dollars to develop and maintain, a simple blog, for example, can be created inexpensively and with almost no specialized technical knowledge. Consequently, there is a huge range of websites and blogs providing information and diversion that would not have found a home in the world of "old media."

However, as we have seen, most of the time, most users will gravitate to a relatively small number of major websites, mostly operated by major media corporations. These are the equivalent of the Hollywood hits that a large number of Netflix users will watch. In fact, while producers, such as blog writers, find online material easier and cheaper to produce, they still face the difficult task of finding an audience. They do not have the sorts of resources and staff that enable major sites to constantly generate new content. Even if a small site does offer unique content, it still faces an uphill battle in becoming known.

Search engines, such as Google, tend to steer users to sites that are already well-known and to which others have linked, making it difficult for a new and lesser known site to ever get noticed. Internet memes—such as viral videos that circulate broadly by being forwarded to friends—are rare (and fleeting) phenomena compared to the amount of content that is generated on the web. The overwhelming majority of Internet sites have a modest or miniscule number of visitors—if any. Most blogs, for example, are rarely read; the vast majority are unknown, and many don't survive very long. In fact, between 60 percent and 80 percent of blogs are abandoned within one month (Caslon Analytics 2009).

In this regard, new online media are the quintessential niche media, often reaching small fragmented and specialized audiences. The niche orientation of mass media, driven in large measure by advertisers who sought to reach specific audience segments, was already well under way before the Internet's arrival. But the specific organization and technological capabilities of the Internet sped up the pace of audience segmentation. This is an example of how the technological properties of new media—especially their flexibility and relatively low cost—work in concert with both social developments, such as multiculturalism, and economic forces, such as the search for new consumer markets, to produce new patterns of social communication.

The implications of niche, rather than mass, media are far from clear. Some have long seen niche advertising and media as contributing to a fragmentation of American society, a breaking of the common cultural bonds—which were once reinforced and reproduced by mass media—that formed the basis for a national identity in the United States (Turow 1997). Others see the seeds of a new cultural democracy in which alternative meanings circulate and communication patterns are as much people to people as they are top down, creating spaces for new forms of public communication and participation.

CONCLUSION

We have traveled a long way in this chapter, from the differing capacities of media technologies to the intervention of social forces in shaping the development, application, and influence of such technologies. We have seen the pitfalls of a technologically deterministic view that neglects the role of human agency while also considering how media technologies contribute to the social environment in which we live.

This overview reminds us that media technologies are always embedded in specific social, economic, and political contexts. Social change is not linear; it involves the various "tugs-of-war" described in this chapter that can sometimes lead to unexpected developments. Citizens don't always use media technologies as they are initially packaged. User habits change; Internet sites and platforms that are tremendously popular today may well fall out of favor to be replaced by new favorites. Corporate players will continue to try to shape the new technologies in ways that benefit their search for profits. And, by their action or inaction, governments will continue to influence the development and use of new media. The direction of such change is uncertain, but we know that the future of new media will be determined by the actions of people, not by any quality inherent in the technology.

DISCUSSION QUESTIONS

1. Explain the differences between technological determinism and "medium theory."

2. What do the histories of the telephone and of television teach us about the interaction of technology and human agency?

3. In what ways have the use of electronic media, especially television and the Internet, changed social life? What is different about how we live because of the presence of these media? What changes do you think might be coming in your lifetime?

4. What have been some of the most important advantages to the rise of the Internet and the expanded use of mobile devices? What are some of the potential negative consequences of these changes?

PART V

Globalization and the Future

CHAPTER 10

Media in a Changing Global Culture

Source: Raveendran/Getty Images.

In the mid-1960s, Canadian cultural scholar Marshall McLuhan (1964) wrote that, with the rise of electronic media, "we have extended our central nervous system itself in a global embrace" (p. 19). McLuhan believed that the rise of electronic media marked a new phase in human history. For the first time, physical distance was no longer a barrier, and instantaneous mass communication across the globe was possible. The result was McLuhan's notion of the "global village," in which the people of the world would be brought closer together as they made their voices heard. Such an information environment, according to McLuhan, "compels commitment and participation. We have become irrevocably involved with, and responsible for, each other" (McLuhan and Fiore 1967: 24).

In the years since McLuhan wrote, the media have moved steadily toward becoming truly global in nature. News Corporation, owner of the Fox Television Network and perhaps the most global media enterprise, has investments in five continents. Like other media conglomerates, it defines itself as "a diversified global media company"; its CEO, Rupert Murdoch, says their intent is to continue "aggressively growing our businesses across geographical borders and new global platforms" (News Corporation 2012: 9, 6). U.S. television series are distributed worldwide; *The Simpsons* is broadcast in more than 70 countries around the globe. Major sporting events are seen by hundreds of millions of viewers worldwide; television coverage of the 2012 London Olympic Games was seen by an estimated

4.8 billion people, or more than two in three people worldwide. The Internet is a global phenomenon, with over 2.4 billion people online by 2012—about a third of the world's population (Internet World Stats 2013).

However, the consequences of increasingly global media have not been as straightforward as McLuhan's (1964) work suggests. In fact, the trends in media globalization are marked by distinct ambiguity and contradiction. Some developments seem likely to produce positive changes of the sort envisioned by McLuhan; others seem cause for alarm. Some trends seem certain, others more tenuous. What is clear, though, is that whatever future direction the media take, it will have a global facet; there is no turning back. Understanding some of the basic global dimensions of media, therefore, is central to consideration of the future of all media.

This chapter explores the nature and potential consequences of media globalization. We have already addressed some global dimensions of media in earlier chapters. It is impossible to separate globalization from the issues with which we have been concerned. However, this chapter allows us to do two things. First, we discuss media globalization as a distinct social force that both contributes to social change and is influenced by global changes. Second, we reintegrate concepts that in earlier sections of this book we separated for analytic purposes. In the real world, media ownership, production, ideology, content, politics, audiences, and technology are all inextricably intertwined. We had to separate these and other concepts to discuss them coherently. In this final chapter, though, we move freely from one topic to another in a more integrated manner that more closely resembles the real—and complex—world of media.

WHAT IS GLOBALIZATION?

In broad terms, globalization involves a number of ongoing interrelated processes, including the internationalization of finance and trade, the development of international organizations such as the World Bank, the increased circulation of people, the growth of transnational nongovernmental organizations (NGOs) such as Oxfam and Amnesty International, and the diffusion of digital technologies. The idea of "global media" is tightly linked to these larger globalization processes. For example, the United Nations Conference on Trade and Development (UNCTAD) identifies five trends that have facilitated the expansion of global creative industries: (1) the deregulation of national cultural and media policy; (2) increasing global incomes that allow more spending on media and cultural products; (3) technological change and digitalization; (4) the global rise of service industries; and (5) the expansion of international trade (UNCTAD 2004: 5).

In relation to the media, we can think of globalization as having two central components. The first relates to the changing role of geography and physical distance and the growing interconnectedness and intensification of connections. As we saw in Chapter 9, with electronic media, instantaneous communication and interaction can be carried out over great distances. Globalization carries this phenomenon to its global limits, enabling almost instantaneous communications around the world. Such electronic communication has been a feature of globalization at the same time as it has facilitated other forms of globalization, such as international finance and manufacturing, which would be impossible without international communication networks.

The second dimension of globalization involves the content of this communication. With electronic media, the ideas, images, and sounds of different cultures are potentially available to vast networks of people outside the culture from which the message originated. In this sense, culture becomes more accessible to larger numbers of people, with both potentially positive outcomes (e.g., mutual understanding) and potentially negative consequences (e.g., cultural homogenization). We examine each of these components of globalization, beginning with time and space.

Crossing Limits of Time and Space

When humans began orbiting the Earth, photographs taken from space allowed people for the first time to see the planet in a single image—a tiny blue ball amid the vast darkness of space. Perhaps nothing better captures the symbolism of globalization than these now well-known pictures. In the click of a camera's shutter, the vast expanses of the Earth, which had taken humankind centuries to explore and map, suddenly seemed small and fragile. A single photographic image captured the great distance between the plains of Africa and the plains of the American Midwest, suggesting that perhaps the distance was not so great after all.

The ability to capture the entire globe in a single image was symbolic of the move toward globalization in many spheres. Space, in the form of physical distance, has come to have less practical significance. Physical transportation to all corners of the globe is now easier than ever, making immigration, international travel, and the transportation of goods commonplace. More important for our purposes, when people do move, electronic communications often enable them to stay in touch with those at home. Travelers, immigrants, and sometimes even refugees can contact friends and family via the Internet or mobile phone; they can listen to online radio stations and watch satellite television broadcasts in their native languages. By making a Skype call, typing an e-mail message, or communicating via a microblogging platform, travelers can dissolve the distance between the sender and receiver of a message. In some cases, electronic communication can make the need for physical travel obsolete: Many meetings, for example, happen by video link, and companies are increasingly encouraging their employees to work remotely ("telecommuting").

While the significance of space has been reduced, the barrier of time has also been overcome. Communication happens almost instantaneously, meaning that we are often plugged into the media world 24/7. Feeling a habitual need to check our e-mails, texts, or social networking pages is a symptom of the accelerated rate at which communication takes place. As we saw in the previous chapter, such communications can be useful and fun; they can also be overwhelming and stressful. The speed and ease with which media content can be produced, coupled with the speed and ease with which we can access information, also means that our biggest task is often sifting through it all to find what is useful to us.

Crossing Cultural Boundaries

Globalization is not just about the technological innovations used to communicate over long distances. In addition, and perhaps more important, it also refers to the exchange and intermingling of cultures from different parts of the globe. The globalization of media, especially, refers to the content—the cultural products—available globally.

Let's use music as an example. Music is one of the easiest media products to sell globally because its language is universal. Print media may be international to a degree, but the barriers of language and literacy limit their reach. Producers must translate print media to cross cultural boundaries, and a significant literate audience must be available to receive the product. Visual media, such as television and movies, are more accessible because an audience does not have to be literate to enjoy them. Usually, though, these media have dialogue that must have subtitles or be dubbed in the local language. Music, however, can sell across national and cultural borders even when the lyrics are in an incomprehensible foreign tongue. The music, not the lyrics, generates sales.

The globalization of music has resulted in at least three developments. First, music that would not normally have traveled beyond a particular culture is now more readily available to different cultures. Listeners can hear American or British music worldwide. Buyers can find recordings of anyone from Kanye West to Taylor Swift in China's prolific bootleg music scene. Fans can hear American jazz and blues around the globe. Artists around the world now accompany the distinctive rhythms of rap with lyrics in many different languages. To a lesser extent, music from other cultures is also more readily available within the United States and elsewhere. Online music sites feature a wide variety of music from different cultures. The reggae of Jamaica has been a major musical force in the United States for decades. The Latin Grammy Awards were launched in 2000 to recognize the rapidly grow-ing popularly of Spanish-language music in many different styles. A wide variety of artists from Africa and the Middle East have found a niche in Western music circles. This diversity represents the broad distribution of many different kinds of music across cultures.

A second development has been the exchange of musical elements among different cultures. For example, contemporary Afro-pop sometimes combines the electric guitars of Western rock and roll with melodies and rhythms of more traditional African music. West-ern rock drummers, on the other hand, have long used a tradition from Africa whereby the sounds of many different drums are combined. In some traditional African cultures where music performances were part of communal events, a large number of drummers would each play a single drum, allowing mobility for dance. In Western rock, with its typical small bands of only four or five musicians, a musician assembles a collection of drums in a drum kit accessible to a single drummer. In both these cases, artists have incorporated and adapted components of one culture within the context of another. Afro-pop and Western rock still have their distinct sounds, but they also share a good deal. We might say that the cultural distance between them has been compressed.

Globalization of music has also resulted in a third development, a hybrid form of music that incorporates many different cultures in its new, unique sound. By using a wide variety of instruments and incorporating melodic and rhythmic sensibilities from many cultures, musicians produce new music that is not clearly identifiable with any single culture, thus it sometimes goes by the name "world music." World music, grounded in traditional ethnic sounds, makes up a modest niche market. However, some artists have incorporated a world music approach into their mainstream music. For example, Columbian-born pop star Shakira achieved mainstream commercial success selling over 50 million albums by com-bining the Latin music of her native country, the rhythms of American and British rock and roll she listened to growing up, and sometimes, the flavor of Middle Eastern music (her father was Lebanese). One of her best-known songs, "Waka Waka (This Time for Africa)," featuring Afro-Colombian instruments and South-African guitars, was selected as the official anthem of the 2010 South African World Cup. Critics disagree as to whether this sort of synthesis represents a positive integration of different cultures or the "melting" of distinct cultures into a more homogeneous blend. Whatever the verdict, the globalization of music has resulted in the crossing of cultural boundaries in yet another way.

The Promise and Reality of Media Globalization

In McLuhan's (1964) vision of the "global village," media offer an electronic soapbox from which differing voices may speak. This multiplicity of voices, in turn, extends the range of publicly available knowledge about many different areas and aspects of the world. Finally, the airing of voices and knowledge can promote greater understanding between different nations and cultures.

There is no doubt that today's new media technologies facilitate much greater personal communication and enable users to make content available on the Internet, although the audience for such content is often quite limited. However, most of the world's population does not have access to such media; their voices are not heard. And the power to produce traditional mass media that reaches a large audience—especially movies and television—remains concentrated in relatively few hands.

As a result, the promise of the global village remains largely unfulfilled. Indeed, global media have led to a series of developments that may be more a cause for concern than a source of hope. As we have seen, the globalization of media has included the rise of centralized media conglomerates of unprecedented size and influence. Commercial interests, rather than educational concerns or altruistic motives, have almost always fueled this globalization of media. In short, the dream of a global village in which equals share information and culture does not describe the reality of today's global media. While media globalization continues to offer some promises that are worth holding onto, we must also be aware of the social impact of these enticing developments. We explore below four key areas of concern related to media globalization: ownership, content, consumption, and regulation.

THE GLOBAL MEDIA INDUSTRY

The first area we explore is that of ownership. As we saw in Part I, ownership and control of production must be understood in order to understand the overall nature of media.

Global Products, Centralized Ownership

The iTunes Store, the digital media site operated by Apple, offers more than 28 million songs categorized in 20 genres, ranging from country to electronic, from Christian/gospel to hip-hop/rap. This cornucopia of diversity, however, obscures an underlying reality: Most media content available on the site—and in the global marketplace—is produced by a handful of large media corporations. For example, just three conglomerates dominate the popular music industry, accounting for over 80 percent of all music sales worldwide. These "big three" are Sony Music Entertainment (Japan), Universal Music Group (United States), and Warner Music Group (United States). In the U.S. market, these "big three" accounted for over 88 percent of album sales and nearly 86 percent of digital tracks in the first half of 2013 (Nielsen 2013c).

Television production has also developed a global dimension. For example, the reality television show *Big Brother* has been produced in more than 40 countries worldwide, including Serbia, India, the Philippines, Nigeria, and Ecuador. The show is modified slightly to fit local tastes, but the program's many versions are owned by a single company. Other formats that have been exported worldwide include *Who Wants to Be a Millionaire, American Idol,* and *Dancing With the Stars.*

The "big three" in music, Microsoft's dominant position in the software industry, and the global spread of reality television shows like *Big Brother* illustrate one of the central ironies in the globalization of media: While the distribution of media products has spread out across the globe, the ownership and control of media production are largely centralized in a few megacorporations usually composed of dozens, if not hundreds, of different companies. Consumers, seeing a wide variety of company names on the products they buy, may not realize that these different brands are often divisions of the same multinational corporation with production and distribution facilities dispersed in many different countries. These transnational corporations can shift resources from country to country in the pursuit of higher profits, which usually makes meaningful regulation by individual countries extremely difficult.

The Case of the News Corporation

A brief look at one of the major media companies will illustrate the vast expanse of these corporations. The News Corporation is one of the largest media conglomerates in the world. In 2012, NewsCorp had more than 50,000 employees and revenues of more than $33 billion (see Figure 10.1). The vast reach of this one company include holdings in broadcast television, cable television, satellite television, film production, newspaper and book publishing, along with some online media properties and an education technology company that produces digital products for the K–12 market.

The company has its roots in the Australian newspaper business, expanded into Europe via newspapers in Britain and satellite Europe-wide, made the leap to the United States by creating the Fox Broadcasting network, and has since developed a major presence in Asia. In the United States, the company owns some of the best known media outlets, including the Fox Broadcasting company and 27 television stations; Twentieth Century Fox and Fox Searchlight Pictures film studios; the FX, National Geographic, SPEED, Fox Movie Channel, and Fox Sports regional cable channels; *The Wall Street Journal* and *New York Post* newspapers; and a portion of the Hulu video streaming site.

The example of News Corporation illustrates that, while the tentacles of global corporations extend to all sectors of the media and to all corners of the globe, the control of the corporate conglomerates remains centralized in wealthy, developed nations. Recall that

Figure 10.1   News Corporation, Select Holdings by Region, 2012

United States

Television
Fox Broadcasting Company
27 Fox television stations
MyNetworkTV

Cable
Fox News Channel
Fox Business Network
FX
Fox Movie Channel
Fox Soccer Channel
SPEED
FUEL TV
FSN
Fox College Sports
Big Ten Network (51%)
National Geographic Channel (70%)
STATS (50%)
Fox Deportes

Film
Twentieth Century Fox
Fox 2000 Pictures
Fox Searchlight Pictures
Fox Music
Blue Sky Studios
Shine Limited

Publishing
HarperCollins Publishers
Dow Jones & Company (*The Wall Street Journal,
Barron's,* Factiva, MarketWatch)
New York Post (Community Newspaper Group
The Daily)

Other
News Corp Digital Media Group (IGN
Entertainment, AskMen, Making Fun)
Wireless Generation
Hulu (32%)
Amplify

Asia

Cable
Fox
Fox Life
FX
Fox Crime
Fox Traveler
Fox Family Movies
Fox Filipino
BabyTV
Fox Movies Premium
National Geographic International (52%)
ESPN STAR Sports (50%)

- All or part of 21 channels in India, including
  STAR Plus, Fox Action Movies
- 6 channels in Hong Kong
- Zing Kong (47%) and CMC-News (47%) in
  China
- STAR Chinese Channel in Taiwan
- STAR (25%) channel in Japan
- Channel V music channels in Taiwan, Hong
  Kong, Thailand

Satellite
Tata Sky Limited (29.8%)

Publishing
HarperCollins India (40%)
The Wall Street Journal Asia

Europe

Cable
Fox
Fox Life
FX
Fox Crime
Fox Retro
Fox Next
Fox Sports
VOYAGE
BabyTV
24 Kitchen
Fox News
History Channel (license)
National Geographic International (52%)

Film
Shine Limited

Satellite
SKY Italia
British Sky Broadcasting (39%)
Sky Deutschland (49.9%)

Publishing
HarperCollins Publishers
The Times
The Sunday Times
The Sun
The Wall Street Journal Europe
eFinancialNews
The Times Literary Supplement

Other
NDS (49%)
News Corporation Stations Europe

Australia/New Zealand

Cable
Fox Sport Australia (50%)

Film
Shine Limited

Satellite
FOXTEL (25%)
Sky Network Television Limited (44%)

Publishing
HarperCollins Publishers
140 newspapers, including *The Australian, The Daily Telegraph,* and the *Herald Sun*

Other
News Digital Media
CareerOne.com.au (50%)
Realestate.com.au (62%)

Latin America

Cable
Fox
Fox Life
FX
Fox Sports
BabyTV
UTILISIMA
SPEED
LAPTV (78%)
Telecine (13%)

Middle East and Africa

Cable
Fox Retro
Fox Sports
Aquavision
Rotana (19%)
Moby (33.5%)

Source: News Corporation (2012) *Annual Report.*

Source: © Reed Saxon//AP/Corbis.

The News Corporation is one of the largest media conglomerates in the world, with more than 50,000 employees and $33 billion in 2012 revenues generated from across the globe.

the corporate home bases of the music "big three" are Japan and the United States. Globalization of the media clearly does not extend to ownership, which has not yet gone beyond a few prosperous nations. Even in the age of new media, Western media corporations continue to dominate the flow of media products around the world (Artz and Kamalipour 2003; Hamm and Smandych 2005; Harindranath 2003; Miller et al. 2008; Mosco and Schiller 2001).

The importance of centralized ownership and control is that decision making related to the purpose and content of the media, as well as the benefits that accrue from owning what are often highly profitable ventures, remains firmly in the hands of a few major corporations based in the wealthiest nations.

GLOBAL MEDIA CONTENT

In this section, we sample the global dimension of the debates over media, in particular the "cultural imperialism" thesis and the controversy over global information flow.

The Debate Over "Cultural Imperialism"

In Chapter 7, we briefly introduced the "cultural imperialism" thesis, the argument that a large volume of media products flow from the West, especially the United States, and so powerfully shape the cultures of other nations that they amount to a cultural form of domination (Boyd-Barrett 1977).

Here the link between ownership and media content is made explicit. Values and images of Western society, according to this argument, are embedded in the media products sold by Western corporations. Norms of individualism and consumerism, for example, pervade media products exported by the West and often conflict with the traditional values in the nations where such products are sold. The flow of media products, the argument continues, results in the erosion of local cultures and values.

Local elites have often cooperated with major multinational media companies in facilitating the import of Western media. In fact, Harindranath (2003) argues that, in discussing cultural imperialism, it may be more useful to think in terms of elites versus the general population rather than in terms of geographical inequalities. As a result, some of the most visible concern about the homogenization of culture has been taking place in the streets, not in government meeting rooms. Alternative globalization protests and social movements across the world have often included critiques of the global homogenization of culture in everything from media to fast-food chains. Nongovernmental organizations, such as the Communication Rights in the Information Society (CRIS) campaign, were instrumental in the adoption by the United Nations Educational, Scientific, and Cultural Organization (UNESCO) of the Convention on the Protection and Promotion of the Diversity of Cultural Expressions. The convention, ratified by more than 100 countries, aims to protect and promote cultural diversity, creating "the conditions for cultures to flourish and to freely interact in a mutually beneficial manner," encouraging dialogue among cultures, and promoting respect for the diversity of cultures (UNESCO 2005).

The fight to preserve local cultures comes in the wake of both anecdotal and more systematic evidence suggesting the widespread, varied, and pervasive influence of foreign media in many countries. The fear is that the globalization of media is resulting in the homogenization of culture. Like sand castles on a beach, local cultures are being eroded and flattened by the gradual impact of the endless tide of U.S. and other Western media products. According to UNESCO (2010),

> the dominant trends, which are noticeable, are the top-down flow of content from economically and socially powerful groups to less privileged and disadvantaged groups; from the more developed countries and media houses to the less developed countries and networks. The unprecedented impact of these media is radically changing concepts of identity and the social bonds within communities and cultures, often at the cost of local cultural expression.

The idea of cultures losing their distinctive elements is perhaps what critics fear most. If music, literature, film, and television become globally mass produced and homogenized—like so many standardized McDonald's restaurants strewn across the international cultural landscape—then the world as a whole loses.

One reason why some Western—and especially U.S.—media products have been so successful is that these projects tend to have substantial budgets, resulting in very slick and attractive production values. The Motion Picture Association of America (MPAA) calculated that the average U.S. feature film cost $106.6 million to make in 2007—the last year the MPAA released such data (Verrier 2009). This is far more than is spent in other countries. The Hollywood blockbuster, as an extreme case, typically relies on dramatically photographed scenes, advanced computer graphics, pyrotechnics, and gripping chase sequences to hold an audience's attention. All these things are very expensive to produce—more expensive than most non-U.S. production studios can afford.

For example, *Avatar* was a U.S. megaproduction that cost about $310 million to produce and $150 million to advertise (Barnes 2009). The irony is that, to finance increasingly expensive blockbuster productions, Hollywood must rely on substantial revenues from foreign markets. By the end of 2010, nearly three quarters of *Avatar*'s gross box office receipts had come from foreign markets; the film had grossed more than $760 million in the United States and Canada but more than $2 billion elsewhere (Box Office Mojo 2010).

Most nations simply do not have the resources to develop the infrastructure necessary to produce the high production values associated with this type of media product. Even for those nations that do have major production facilities available, it is almost always cheaper to buy U.S.-made media products than to produce their own. When a for-profit market model drives media-related decision making, as it does in many nations, it generally makes good short-term business sense to import U.S.-made cultural products. The impact on local cultures, critics contend, can be devastating (Hamm and Smandych 2005; Mattelart 1979; Schiller 1992).

The Fight to Preserve Local Cultures

There is no denying the overwhelming presence that U.S. culture has in other countries. American television, films, and music are ubiquitous in most societies across the globe, even in wealthy nations. In 2012, 62 percent of cinemagoers in the European Union went to see U.S. productions (European Audiovisual Observatory 2013). In contrast, European films accounted for less than 7 percent of the North American film market share in 2010 (European Audiovisual Observatory 2010). European-produced programming is virtually nonexistent on American television outside of BBC productions on public television. If the developed countries of Europe—with their relative affluence and rich media tradition—are dominated by American media products, you can just imagine the role U.S. media play in poorer countries that do not have substantial film or television production industries.

Wealthier nations, though, have the resources to produce alternatives to U.S. media fare and they have established regulations to help. Europe has been at the forefront of efforts to preserve local culture in the face of an influx of American media products. In 2005, the President of the European Commission, Jose Manuel Barroso, asserted that "on a scale of values, culture comes before the economy" (https://12826.lapetition.be/). That attitude reflected a widespread belief that a "cultural exception" is needed to protect locally produced cultural goods in an era of global free trade policies.

The "cultural exception" idea is most closely associated with France, where taxes on television channels, Internet providers, box office proceeds, and more go to subsidize French filmmakers and French television stations must air at least 40 percent French-produced content. Other European countries have similar, though less extensive, policies giving financial support to domestic artists and media companies in an effort to provide an alternative to imported foreign fare. The European Union has stipulated that 51 percent of all broadcast programming must be produced within the European Union (Little 2008).

But trade officials in the United States see these sorts

Filmmaking has long existed in nearly all parts of the globe but was limited due to the high cost of production. As the cost of film technology has declined, local creation of movies has expanded rapidly. Popular in local markets, the best of these indigenous films make their way across the globe to art houses and film festivals, such as this one in Portland, Oregon.

of policies as a barrier to "free trade" and want an end to such practices. European concerns, though, were only exacerbated in recent years as American companies Netflix, Amazon, Apple, and Google lobbied for the right to stream directly to European audiences, bypassing local laws established to help protect European film and television industries.

The elimination of laws protecting local culture was debated intensely in 2013 leading up to U.S.-EU trade talks. European Commission President Barraso seemed to back away from his earlier support for the policies, saying that French cultural laws were "reactionary." The backlash was immediate and intense. Leading figures in the European film industry responded by launching a petition arguing that "The Cultural Exception is Non-negotiable!" and that cultural and creative goods should be exempted from any free trade agreement (https://12826.lapetition.be/). The petition received over 5,000 signatures from European directors, writers, technicians and producers. German director Wim Wenders told the European Parliament in a letter, "Culture is not merchandise; you can't put it in the same category as cars, lamps, or screws and bolts" (France 24 2013). Parliament agreed, passing a resolution that kept cultural goods out of the trade negotiations—at least for now.

Some of the biggest names in Hollywood—who appreciate the unique contributions of European films—support "cultural exception" policies. During the 2013 dispute, director

Steven Spielberg argued that, "The cultural exception is the best way to defend diversity in film-making." Hollywood megaproducer Harvey Weinstein added, "The cultural exception encourages filmmakers to make films about their own culture. We need that more than ever" (France 24 2013).

European cultural policies have not excluded American films. In 2012, American films made up about 62 percent of the European market by admission, and 22 of the top 25 films in Europe were U.S. movies. But the policies have helped the French film industry compete. In 2012, the French film *The Intouchables* became the most successful non-English film ever in the international market (European Audiovisual Observatory 2013).

French director Michael Hazanavicius, whose film *The Artist* won five Oscars in 2012, noted that, "It is very complicated for us to be competitive in a deregulated market. The Americans can make a $100 million movie, because they sell all over the world. Our market is France. If we eliminate 'l'exception culturelle,' we won't die, but we will have a sclerotic cinema" (in Bohlen 2013).

The Imperialism Thesis: Some Complications

While the flood of Western media around the globe is undeniable, the signs of cultural imperialism are more mixed than might be apparent at first glance, revealing some limitations in the theory (Tomlinson 1991, 2003).

First, in its simple version, the cultural imperialism thesis often does not distinguish between different types of media. U.S. products clearly dominate some media sectors, most notably the movie industry, while other media continue to be primarily local in nature, such as much of print. As we explore below, recognizing difference, subtlety, and shades of influence is a vital part of discussing something as complex as the world's diverse cultures.

Second, the cultural imperialism thesis generally assumes a passive audience, failing to take into account the multiple interpretive strategies used by audiences in different cultures, as we discussed in Chapter 8. The meaning a particular product holds for local audiences may vary widely because of local cultural values (Butcher 2003; Liebes and Katz 1993; Sreberny-Mohammadi 1997; Strelitz 2003). Thus, we cannot assume that foreign audiences interpret U.S. media products in any single way. Some studies suggest that imported media's influence is often extremely limited, as in the case of U.S. television imports in Greece (Zaharopoulos 2003). In fact, the circulation of U.S.-produced global media products does not seem to be creating any singular Americanized consciousness, as some had feared. Nor is it creating any singular "global consciousness," as some had hoped. The early comments of Barnet and Cavanagh (1994) on this latter point still seem accurate and are worth quoting at length:

> Although hundreds of millions of children and teenagers around the world are listening to the same music and watching the same films and videos, globally distributed entertainment products are not creating a discernible global consciousness—other than a widely shared passion for more global goods and vicarious experience.

Because of the great range of personal experience consumers bring to global cultural products, the emotional impact on fans can differ widely in unpredictable ways. . . . Hearing the same music, playing the same globally distributed games, or watching the same global broadcast do not appear to change people's sense of who they are or where they belong. Serbs and Croats, Sinhalese and Tamils, listen to the same Michael Jackson songs as they take up arms against each other. The exotic imagery of music video offers the illusion of being connected to cultural currents sweeping across the world, but this has little to do with the consciousness philosophers from Kant to Marshall McLuhan have dreamed of, an identification with the whole human species and the planet itself. (p. 138)

In considering the power of global media, we need to be cautious about the belief that exposure to media products fundamentally changes people.

In addition, as Gray (2007) notes, the assumption that U.S. media exports invariably promote a chauvinistic U.S. worldview is too simple. His study points out that one of the most successful U.S. cultural exports, the long-running animated series *The Simpsons,* is often a highly critical parody of American culture and capitalist values. As such, it is part of a long tradition of U.S. television shows—popular both at home and abroad—that have shown the United States as unequal and often dysfunctional. This includes *Roseanne, Married With Children, King of the Hill, Malcolm in the Middle, South Park, Arrested Development, The Jerry Springer Show,* and others. So even if U.S. products are being exported widely and being consumed enthusiastically, there are competing messages within these popular media products.

Third, the cultural imperialism thesis likely underestimates the role played by local media. Locally produced media content, finely attuned to local culture, tends to be enormously popular. Thus, local producers have in some cases successfully competed with the global media conglomerates by providing localized alternatives that differentiate themselves from homogenized international media fare. Some signs suggest that the wave of U.S. media products flooding foreign markets may be reaching its peak as local media industries compete more effectively for national markets.

For example, the Korean film industry has expanded dramatically in recent years, representing the tip of the iceberg of a lively cultural production industry in East Asian nations. Korean film is mostly aimed at local audiences, and the share of Korean audiences watching Korean-made films more than doubled between 1996, when it was 23.1 percent, and 2004, when it reached 54.2 percent. Korean films have entered the global market, achieving a modest $58 million in international revenue in 2004, 20 percent of which came from Europe and North America (Flew 2007).

The biggest example of a vibrant film industry outside of the West is not new at all. "Bollywood," the section of the Indian film industry specializing in Hindi-language films, is based in Mumbai and dates back to the silent film era of the early 20th century. Its name comes from a fusion of Bombay (Mumbai's former name) and Hollywood. Bollywood specializes in musicals, romantic feature films, and melodramas and produces many more films than Hollywood does each year. These films are generally low budget, and 90 percent of them do not last more than a week at the box office. Bollywood films are popular in

India, where movie tickets cost about one tenth of what they do in Western countries; however, they make up only about 2 percent of the global movie market (Bose 2006).

While recognizing the heavy presence of U.S.-imported media content, observers of Latin-American context have long highlighted the attachment to locally produced material. They prefer to speak about "asymmetrical interdependence" rather than cultural imperialism, acknowledging that the presence of U.S. media in local markets is not linear but blended with some forms of localization of national broadcasting systems (Straubhaar 1991). In Brazil, Flew (2007) notes "a combination of selective incorporation of international best practice and a restless search to develop programme types that tapped into local cultural desires and dynamics, such as the *telenovela*"—a television soap opera miniseries (p. 121).

Fourth, media corporations know that there are limits to the appeal of Western—and, in particular, U.S.—culture in other nations. In response to changing circumstances, many multinational corporations have become more sophisticated in addressing local markets in foreign countries. Most media conglomerates have adopted some variation of a two-pronged approach to selling cultural products. The first prong of the strategy is the promotion and distribution of Western artists as global superstars. For example, global music stars such as Michael Jackson and Lady Gaga were able to sell albums regardless of linguistic differences. The second prong of the corporate strategy is to accommodate local cultures within an existing media form. MTV, the world's most widely distributed cable television network, took this approach by exporting the U.S. model while adapting it to local conditions. MTV now reaches approximately 600 million households—the vast majority of which are outside of the United States in more than 160 different countries (Viacom n.d.). It has done this by creating about 70 "localized" versions of MTV, including MTV Africa, MTV Asia, MTV Australia, MTV Brasil, MTV Europe, MTV Latin America, and MTV Russia. These channels often feature a mixture of international and local music acts.

Another version of this second-prong strategy is to nurture indigenous talent, which companies can then package and sell to local or regional markets, if not a global market. MTV and other music platforms, for example, can help to promote stars who are wildly popular locally and regionally but may not be well known in the West. Japan's Hikaru Utada, Russia's Valeriya, China's Wei Wei, Ghana's Samini, and a host of other artists sell millions of recordings in their regions but few in the United States. This approach, of course, is itself a double-edged sword. Even as major media conglomerates acknowledge the importance of local cultural tastes, they may be contributing to the decimation of local media companies by moving into local media markets. Sometimes, this means being in outright competition with local companies, creating a David and Goliath scenario. In some cases, this movement has taken the form of joint ventures in the coproduction of cultural products such as television programs.

The irony is that the corporate drive for profit—the very force that has fueled fears of cultural imperialism—has also forced companies to pay attention to local cultures and customs, even if only superficially. Companies have realized that locally customized media products often sell better than standardized global products.

One consequence of "local adaptation" has been that, in some parts of the world, the resistance to foreign culture has waned. The most recent wave of television and other cultural products into the region has not met with the kind of opposition that marked earlier influxes of foreign culture. In an era when more governments are adopting market capitalism and opening their markets to the import of more foreign products, and when global corporations are careful to at least superficially tailor their products to local cultural tastes, the flow of Western goods abroad is now widely considered to be inevitable.

The trends in global media, therefore, are mixed. The ability to pour massive resources into the production, promotion, and distribution of cultural products favors the global media corporations. The ability to innovate and adapt quickly to changing social and cultural tastes favors decentralized, locally produced products. It remains to be seen whether, in the long term, vibrant, locally produced media will successfully compete with global products from the major corporate conglomerates. It also remains to be seen whether some form of partnership between global and local producers will become the wave of the future.

The Politics of Information Flow

The formal political concern with media globalization dates back at least as far as 1925. In that year, the League of Nations adopted a resolution to create a committee charged with

> determining methods of contributing towards the organization of peace, especially: (a) by ensuring the more rapid and less costly transmission of Press news with a view to reducing risks of international misunderstanding; (b) And by discussing all technical problems the settlement of which would be conducive to the tranquillisation of public opinion. (in Gerbner, Mowlana, and Nordenstreng 1993: 183)

The dissemination of information worldwide through the media, therefore, was endorsed as a tool for the promotion of peace and understanding. These and subsequent discussions of global information flow were not limited to media, but that is our concern here.

The uses of propaganda during World War II once again prompted concern over the distribution of information in the media. The United States used the forum of the United Nations to promote a policy that allowed for the international collection, sale, and distribution of information worldwide. The Final Act of the 1948 UN Conference on Freedom of Information argued that "freedom of information is a fundamental right of the people, and it is the touchstone of all the freedoms to which the United Nations is dedicated without which world peace cannot well be preserved." The act further stipulated that, in order to be valid, freedom of information depended on "the availability to the people of a diversity of sources of news and opinion," and it condemned the use of "propaganda either designed or likely to provoke or encourage any threat" to peace (in Gerbner, Mowlana, and Nordenstreng 1993: 179, 181).

While the idea that information should flow freely across national boundaries sounds benign to Western ears, many developing countries came to understand it as privileging the "First World's" market-driven perspective of information flow. At the time, First World and developing nations had very different levels of infrastructure development and capital resources. As a result, the operating reality of "free" international information flow was that major advertiser-funded news organizations from developed nations dominated the collection and dissemination of information. It was as if everyone had been invited to contribute to a multicultural mural, but only some people were equipped with paint and brushes. Those with advantages in resources were able to express their visions, while those lacking resources were effectively silenced.

Western wire services such as the Associated Press (AP) and United Press International (UPI) in the United States and Reuters in the United Kingdom dominated the news accounts that traveled around the globe. They collected information and wrote news stories from what has been described as "a limited perspective reflecting the economic and cultural interests of the industrialized nations" (MacBride and Roach 1993: 6). This criticism extended to entertainment media as well as to the use of newer technologies, such as satellites, to directly transmit news and entertainment.

Developing nations, which did not have the private investment needed to support major commercial media, looked to their governments to nurture media that served public, rather than private, needs. These public needs covered a vast and varied territory. In some cases, fulfilling public needs involved the dissemination of basic information on everything from public health to agricultural practices to child education. In other cases, the concern was with more generalized access to information as a central element of a democratic society.

To many Westerners, the involvement of government in the organization and production of media immediately raises the specter of censorship and state domination—which in some cases did occur. However, in many developing nations, government involvement with local media represented the only way to ensure the existence of an alternative to Western media conglomerates. In addition, many developing nations did not want to be simply flooded by the "free flow" of information from the West. Instead, they wanted a free and more balanced flow of information. The intervention of government was needed to regulate the vast quantity of information flowing from more developed nations, an action that Westerners found antithetical to the idea of a "free" information flow.

The call by poorer nations for a "new world information and communication order" (NWICO) was taken up by UNESCO. While reaffirming the right of journalists to "have freedom to report and the fullest possible access to information," a 1978 UNESCO declaration on the mass media also suggested, among other things, that mass media contribute to peace and understanding "by giving expression to oppressed people who struggle against colonialism, neo-colonialism, foreign occupation and all forms of racial discrimination and oppression and who are unable to make their voices heard within their own territories." It went on to declare that "it is necessary that States facilitate the procurement by the mass media in the developing countries of adequate conditions and resources enabling them to gain strength and expand, and that they support cooperation by the latter both among themselves and with the mass media in developed countries" (in Gerbner, Mowlana, and Nordenstreng 1993: 176, 178). The declaration was suggesting a need to hear those voices that had not been included in the established media—a position that threatened the status quo.

In 1980, UNESCO appointed an International Commission for the Study of Communication Problems, chaired by Irish Nobel laureate Seán MacBride. The commission's task was to analyze communication in modern societies and propose policies to further human development through communication. The MacBride Commission's (1980) report, titled "Many Voices, One World," identified the "right to communicate" as a basic human right. The commission also criticized proponents of a simple "free flow" of information, arguing that critical acceptance of this doctrine reinforced Western cultural domination in developing countries.

Developing nations often saw their efforts as an attempt to balance the scales of information production and distribution that had always been tipped sharply in favor of wealthier Western nations. Many in the West saw such efforts as a form of censorship that threatened their freedom to interpret the world and to communicate their interpretation globally. Western nations, threatened by the NWICO proposals, responded with a powerful campaign aimed at discrediting the idea of a new information and communication order—and UNESCO. (The United States and the United Kingdom announced their resignation from UNESCO at the end of 1983.) Critics of the ideas being aired in UNESCO argued that these ideas were controversial, political, and opposed to freedom. The campaign was successful, stalling any progress for NWICO and paralyzing the work of UNESCO. In the late 1980s and early 1990s, the United Nations and UNESCO backed away from the promotion of NWICO.

However, the NWICO debate continued due to the emergence of nongovernmental organizations, which started to organize independently of the UN and national governments. Progressive media professionals and academics formed the MacBride Roundtable, an advocacy group that met annually from 1989 to 1999, bringing new actors into the discussion. In the 2000s, various NGOs and social movements began to emphasize communication issues, stressing the ongoing Western domination of the international flow of information.

This domination of information by the West has continued. Many developing nations have had enormous difficulty creating and supporting effective communication infrastructures that reach their populations, especially in rural areas. With digitization, the problem became even more prominent; the majority of the world's population is excluded from accessing the Internet, resulting in their isolation from cultural and information flows. Such a global imbalance in the flow of media content and information raises significant doubts about the appropriateness of McLuhan's "global village" metaphor.

GLOBAL MEDIA CONSUMPTION: LIMITS OF THE "GLOBAL VILLAGE"

In the mid-1980s, a group of mostly American pop musicians got together to record a song to raise money for famine relief in Ethiopia. The song, titled "We Are the World," was meant to suggest the interdependence and mutual responsibility of the world's populations. However, the title also is open to a more cynical interpretation. American pop artists were affirming the global nature of their efforts—sung in English—with very little participation from the rest of the world. "We Are the World" was, to say the least, an overstatement.

We can make a similar point about media "globalization." For example, if the world's major media conglomerates are all from North America, Europe, and Japan—wealthy, industrial nations—can such a media system truly be called "global"? If the dominant ownership and control of the "global media" remain firmly in the hands of media conglomerates based in a few wealthy nations, wouldn't it be more accurate to describe the process as the international export of media from wealthy nations? When was the last time you saw a television program produced in Asia, watched a movie made in Africa, or read a book written by a South American author? Asking someone from Asia, Africa, or South America about the last time they saw, read, or heard a U.S. media product would elicit a quite different response.

Without belaboring the point, the term *global media* is misleading insofar as it obscures the fact that ownership and control of the "global" media industry are not really spread out globally but instead are centralized and concentrated in a few wealthier nations. We must remember that global communications are highly stratified. Those with substantial resources—the corporations of the wealthy nations of the world—are able to benefit most from the globalized media culture. McLuhan's (1964) "global village" suggested an even playing field occupied by equally influential actors. That image certainly does not describe the state of affairs that exists today in media production.

One could argue, however, that ownership and production are not necessarily the focus of the term *global media*. Even though major corporations in a few wealthier nations still disproportionately control media production, these media products are being distributed and consumed worldwide. That universal consumption, one could argue, is the essence of "global media." We would agree that the application of the label *global* to the consumption of media products is more justified than its application to the production of media. However, here, too, we must be careful not to overgeneralize.

Media are not equally accessible around the globe. The consumption of media requires money, whether for the purchase of equipment, such as computers, radios, and television sets, to receive media (hardware) or for the purchase of actual media products, such as books and music recordings (software). Globally, patterns of media consumption follow the same pattern as economic inequality. The richer nations that disproportionately own and produce media also disproportionately consume media. The egalitarian image of a "global village" once again obscures reality.

For example, the "global digital divide" refers to the gap in access to information and communication technologies between the wealthy and poor regions of the world. Figure 10.2 shows the massively skewed distribution of Internet access around the world; while more than three quarters of people in North America are Internet users, only about 16 percent of the population in Africa has access to the Internet.

Such vast disparities indicate that we cannot analyze the consumption of media in any uniform global manner. Only the middle- and upper-class segments of many countries are able to afford regular access to global media products. Writing about South America, one early commentator noted, "In a continent where so many are still poor, the mass culture tends to accentuate differences. . . . It makes a student in Buenos Aires much closer to a counterpart in New York than to someone in a poor province 300 miles away" (Escobar and Swardson 1995: 1, A18). The people in many poorer nations who are tuned in to the global media are the relative elites of those nations. However, these are the very people who are most able to influence the future direction of their societies. Through their consumption by the middle and upper classes, mediated words, images, and sounds are likely to have an impact that, in the future, will reverberate ever more widely in ways we cannot predict.

Despite rhetoric to the contrary, consumption of media is still limited by the staggering degree of economic inequality that exists globally. With all the talk of global media and instantaneous communication, it is easy to forget that the basic struggle for survival still marks daily life for significant segments of the Earth's population.

The digital divide—and the difficulty in bridging it—can be seen in the case of the affordable laptop. In 2002, MIT professor Nicholas Negroponte launched a campaign called

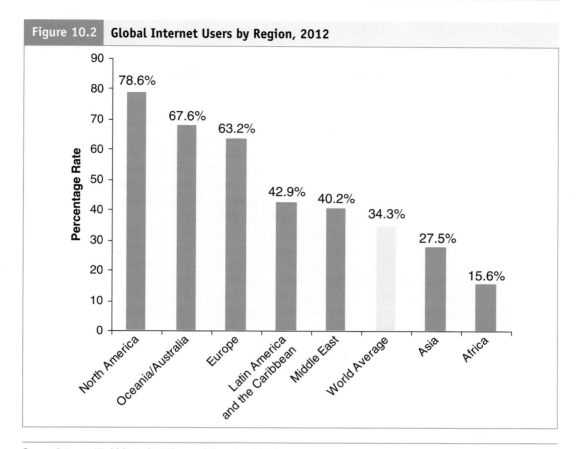

Figure 10.2 **Global Internet Users by Region, 2012**

Source: Internet World Stats (2013), www.internetworldstats.com.

"One laptop per child," with the aim of providing school children in developing countries with their own specially designed $100 laptop. But the program directors' faith in technology and the device's top-down design overlooked the social dimension of technological adoption. The people in poor countries struggling with basic subsistence issues often had little use for laptops. The original design for the computers to be powered by hand cranks, so as to be useable in areas without electricity, proved unfeasible and was abandoned. Instead, people in developing countries found cell phones to be much more useful for both Internet access and personal communications. Despite its noble intentions and considerable achievements, the laptop program proved to be controversial and, in the eyes of many observers, a failure (Nussbaum 2007; Rawsthorn 2009). Faith that technology designed by Westerners and brought to the developing world would help change the dynamics of global inequality proved to be naïve. The enormous disparities between wealthy and poor nations were too big to bridge with just laptops.

REGULATING GLOBAL MEDIA

Who governs McLuhan's global village? That question becomes complicated when national governments and regulatory agencies must address the boundary-crossing nature of communication and information. They face the problem of having to regulate the borderless arena of cyberspace and immaterial resources, such as digital technologies and software, that are rapidly changing and difficult to capture. In the age of terrorist threats, governments are increasingly monitoring who goes online and for what purposes. Governments and companies are also interested in enforcing intellectual property rights. Meanwhile, citizens and social movements are concerned with the developments associated with media globalization and in particular with questions of access, diversity, pluralism, and equality. In this section, we briefly discuss how global media are regulated and look at how citizens' groups sometimes try to influence media globalization.

We saw in Chapter 3 that regulation of the media constitutes a major social force influencing the media. But with media ownership and programming extending beyond national borders (Sreberny 2005), governments face new challenges in regulating media markets, media content, and communication flows (Calabrese 1999; Price 2002).

In particular, three structural changes are weakening the capacity of national governments to regulate the media. First, national governments and international organizations are feeling increased pressure from global media conglomerates and transnational private capital. For example, the International Chamber of Commerce is very vocal in promoting corporate interests (Flew 2007). Second, global agreements on trade and investment increasingly circumvent the influence and control of national governments, insofar as they set many of the rules and standards governments and companies are obliged to follow (Chakravartty and Sarikakis 2006). Examples include the World Trade Organization's Trade Related Aspects of Intellectual Property Rights (TRIPS), which regulate the rights of performers, broadcasters, and music producers; and multilateral governance institutions, such as the International Telecommunication Union (ITU) and the World Intellectual Property Organization (WIPO) (Ó Siochrú and Girard 2002). Third, the borderless nature of the Internet makes it, by definition, impossible to constrain within national boundaries. The development of the Internet is currently supervised by a nonprofit U.S. private corporation called the International Corporation for Assigned Names and Numbers (ICANN), which has been widely criticized for an absence of transparency and accountability and for its proximity to the U.S. Department of Commerce, upon which it depends (DeNardis 2010; Mueller 2002, 2010).

In addition, the Internet is an extremely valuable infrastructure that is of great interest to private companies who may want to exert control over Internet exchanges as if they were regulating access to a toll road. Debates continue in the United States concerning the net neutrality principle, according to which "all like Internet content must be treated alike and move at the same speed over the network" (Lessig and McChesney 2006). While the net neutrality principle states that every byte is equal, some private companies would like to speed up certain content (such as the content users pay for) and leave other content in the slow lane. These dramatic changes are generating tensions between national governments and global media companies.

The ICANN remains the only governing body with effective control over the Internet, including power, for example, to withdraw top-level domain names, such as .com and .us or .uk, if deemed necessary in times of war, or to create new top-level domain names. However, other venues have emerged in which control of the Internet is being debated. One of them is the Internet Governance Forum (IGF), an international forum for policy dialogue created in 2006 under the auspices of the United Nations Secretary-General. Governments, regulatory bodies, supranational agencies, and representatives of nongovernmental organizations gather once a year to discuss emerging issues—but the IGF has no power to implement its recommendations. Global institutions, such as the UNESCO, are also active in promoting the protection of culture and access to digital technologies. The Convention on the Protection and Promotion of the Diversity of Cultural Expressions, adopted by the UNESCO in 2005, encourages governments to take into account cultural diversity when developing other policies.

In response to media globalization, some citizens' groups are advocating for more democratic media and creating their own independent media "from below." In the United States and abroad, a network of media reform organizations is challenging media concentration. In the United States, the media reform agenda includes issues of media consolidation, the quality of journalism, support for public service broadcasting, criticism of the disconnection between media regulators (the FCC) and citizens, net neutrality, and the portrayal in the media of men and women of color. A wide range of organizations are involved in the media reform movement.

For example, the Media Alliance (media-alliance.org), created in 1976, strives for "excellence, ethics, diversity, and accountability in all aspects of the media in the interests of peace, justice, and social responsibility" (Media Alliance n.d.). It functions as an advocacy network for media professionals, nongovernmental organizations, and grassroots activists. It emphasizes media monitoring, organizing public forums on media issues, and training nonprofit staff in communication skills, as well as the development and dissemination of critical knowledge about the U.S. media environment (Hackett and Carroll 2006).

The media reform organization Free Press (freepress.net) was founded in 2002 by media scholar Robert W. McChesney with the aim of promoting diverse and independent media ownership, quality journalism, and strong public media. Today, Free Press has a 30-person staff and has built a network of nearly 500,000 members. Its "Save the Internet" campaign mobilized citizens to pressure the FCC for net neutrality. The campaign "Save the News" advocates public policies to promote serious journalism in the United States, because "democracy depends on quality reporting."

In addition, citizens can create their own media to counteract the increasing media concentration and the limited access to commercial media platforms. The Independent Media Center (IMC) network, or Indymedia, was born in Seattle in 1999 as an open publishing platform, which rapidly spread across the globe—by 2002, three years after its founding, there were already 89 IMCs on six continents (Kidd 2002). Across the United States, the Prometheus Radio Group holds "radio barn raisings" to build low-power radio stations in the spirit of the Amish barn raisings, where neighbors work together to erect a community infrastructure. Radio Free Nashville in Pasquo, Tennessee; Radio Free Urbana in Champaign-Urbana, Illinois; and Valley Free Radio in Northampton, Massachusetts, were each built in the course of a weekend by community activists who, with the help of facilitators, built the studio, raised an antenna, and put the station on the air. Other examples of "alternative media" in the digital age include self-organized local news websites and blogs, grassroots video production, and culture jamming (Atton 2002; Coyer, Dowmunt, and Fountain 2007; Downing 2001; Lievrouw 2011).

AFTERWORD: THE UBIQUITY OF CHANGE AND THE FUTURE OF MEDIA

Change is one of the great constants of human history. The discipline of sociology emerged, in large measure, in response to the political, economic, and intellectual changes that marked 19th-century Europe. Social thinkers of the day were trying to make sense of the revolutionary changes that were taking place around them, as modern industrial societies replaced traditional agrarian societies.

With industrialization, urban centers replaced rural farming communities. Population densities grew, as did the social problems now associated with urban life. The emergence of factory wage laborers, who replaced farmers and artisans, brought fundamental changes in family life and child-rearing practices. No longer did children learn basic work skills alongside their parents in the home or the field. Parents now left the home to work in shops and factories. The bustling diversity of city life replaced the relative homogeneity and isolation of rural life. Different ethnic, religious, and racial groups intermingled as never before. The haphazard rise of industrial centers brought incredible wealth to a few people in the emerging capitalist class and laid the foundations for a mass production economy. The price paid for this dramatic transformation included poverty, urban slums, exploitative child labor practices, dangerous and underpaid work, and a host of other social problems.

In the 21st century, the economic and social changes that provided the impetus for early sociological thinkers have largely run their course. In American society, industrialism has, in many ways, given way to a new and perhaps equally fundamental change. Just as the rise of industrial society rested on technological innovations that made factory production viable, new technological developments are part of contemporary processes of profound social, economic, and political change. The rise in electronic communications and computerization has enabled the emergence of a U.S. economy rooted less in manufacturing and more in services and information. We are living, as some label it, in a "postindustrial" or "information-based" society.

With the continued evolution of computers and mobile devices, the changes that will come this century are likely to be as profound as those that marked the dawning of industrialization. But as with all technological change, the direction taken by future media will depend on the decisions made by members of society. There is nothing inevitable about the march of technology or of the media. Perhaps you have a role to play in helping direct that change.

Our argument for a sociological analysis of media began in Chapter 1 with a sketch of a model for approaching the study of media and the social world. We have tried to show that understanding the media involves understanding a series of social relationships. By now, it should be clear that looking only at media content—the most common way to talk about "the media"—provides us with an incomplete picture of the media and their significance for society. Instead, we must be alert to the relationships that exist within our model, relationships that involve the media industry, media messages or products, technology, active audiences and users, and the social world beyond the media. Even in the years to come, regardless of the changes that occur, understanding the media will mean understanding these social relations in all their complexity.

DISCUSSION QUESTIONS

1. Marshall McLuhan envisioned an electronic "global village" in which people would become "irrevocably involved with, and responsible for, each other." In what ways has McLuhan's vision proven to be correct? In what ways was he wrong?

2. Why is it so difficult for developing nations to compete with media products produced in wealthier developed countries?

3. What are some of the ways that countries have responded to the influx of foreign media products in their attempt to protect local culture?

4. What is the evidence supporting and contradicting the "cultural imperialism" thesis?

References

Abbate, Janet. 1999. *Inventing the Internet*. Cambridge, MA: MIT Press.

Abdullah, Zaheeruddin. 1998. "Fading Entertainment Options." *Richmond Times-Dispatch,* July 13, p. A4.

Ackerman, Seth. 2001. "The Most Biased Name in News: Fox News Channel's Extraordinary Right-Wing Tilt." *Extra!*. July/August. Retrieved March 7, 2011 (http://www.fair.org/index.php?page = 1067).

Aday, Sean. 2010. "Chasing the Bad News: An Analysis of 2005 Iraq and Afghanistan War Coverage on NBC and Fox News Channel." *Journal of Communication* 60 (1): 144–164.

Aday, Sean, Steven Livingston, and Maeve Hebert. 2005. "Embedding the Truth: A Cross-Cultural Analysis of Objectivity and Television Coverage of the Iraq War." *Harvard International Journal of Press/Politics* 10 (1): 3–21.

Ahlkvist, Jarl A. and Robert Faulkner. 2002. "Will This Record Work for Us? Managing Music Formats in Commercial Radio." *Qualitative Sociology* 25 (2): 189–215.

Al Jazeera. n.d. (http://english.aljazeera.net).

Altheide, David L. 2002. *Creating Fear: News and the Construction of Crisis*. Piscataway, NJ: Aldine Transaction.

____. 2009. "Moral Panic: From Sociological Concept to Public Discourse." *Crime, Media, Culture* 5 (1): 79–99.

Anand, Bharat N., Kyle Barnett, and Elizabeth Carpenter. 2004. *Random House Case Study*. Boston, MA: Harvard Business School.

Anderson, Chris. 2008. *The Long Tail*. New York: Hyperion.

Anderson, Craig A. and Brad J. Bushman. 2002. "The Effects of Media Violence on Society." *Science* 295 (March): 2377–2378.

Anderson, Michael. 2009. "Four Crowdsourcing Lessons From the Guardian's (Spectacular) Expenses–Scandal Experiment." *Nieman Journalism Lab*. June 23. Retrieved November 29, 2010 (http://www.niemanlab.org/2009/06/four-crowdsourcing-lessons-from-the-guardians-spectacular-expenses- scandal-experiment/).

Ang, Ien. 1985. *Watching Dallas*. London, UK: Methuen.

Angwin, Julia. 2010. "The Web's New Gold Mine: Your Secrets." *Wall Street Journal*. July 30. Retrieved December 8, 2010 (http://online.wsj.com/article/SB10001424052748703940904575 3950735129 89404.html).

Angwin, Julia and Steve Stecklow. 2010. "'Scrapers' Dig Deep for Data on the Web." *Wall Street Journal*. October 12. Retrieved December 8, 2010 (http://online.wsj.com/article/SB1000142405 27487033 58504575544381288117888.html).

Armstrong, David. 1981. *A Trumpet to Arms*. Boston, MA: South End Press.

Armstrong, Stephen. 2013. "The Great Gatsby Gamble." *The Evening Standard* (London). May 17 (http://www.standard.co.uk/lifestyle/esmagazine/the-great-gatsby-gamble-8619334 .html).

Arthur, Charles. 2006. "What is the 1% Rule?" *The Guardian*. July 20. Retrieved December 8, 2010 (http://www.guardian.co.uk/technology/2006/jul/20/guardianweeklytechnologysection2).

Artz, Lee and Yahya R. Kamalipour, eds. 2003. *The Globalization of Corporate Media Hegemony*. Albany, NY: SUNY Press.

Atton, Chris. 2002. *Alternative Media*. Thousand Oaks, CA: Sage.

Atton, Chris and James F. Hamilton. 2008. *Alternative Journalism*. London, UK: Sage.

Auletta, Ken. 1991. *Three Blind Mice: How the TV Networks Lost Their Way*. New York: Random House.

____. 1998. "Synergy City." *American Journalism Review* (May): 18–35.

_____. 2001. *World War 3.0: Microsoft and Its Enemies.* New York: Random House.

Austin, Erica Weintraub, Yi-Chun "Yvonnes" Chen, Bruce E. Pinkleton, and Jessie Quintero Johnson. 2006. "Benefits and Costs of Channel One in a Middle School Setting and the Role of Media-Literacy Training." *Pediatrics* 117 (3): 423–433.

Bagdikian, Ben. 2004. *The New Media Monopoly.* Boston, MA: Beacon Press.

Baker, C. Edwin. 1994. *Advertising and a Democratic Press.* Princeton, NJ: Princeton University Press.

Baldasty, Gerald J. 1992. *The Commercialization of News in the Nineteenth Century.* Madison, WI: University of Wisconsin Press.

Barnes, Brookes. 2009. "Avatar Is No. 1 but Without a Record." *New York Times.* December 20. Retrieved December 9, 2010 (http://www.nytimes.com/2009/12/21/movies/21box.html).

Barnet, Richard J. and John Cavanagh. 1994. *Global Dreams: Imperial Corporations and the New World Order.* New York: Simon & Schuster.

Barnett, Brooke and Amy Reynolds. 2009. *Terrorism and the Press.* New York: Peter Lang.

Barnett, Steven. 1997. "New Media, Old Problems: New Technology and the Political Process." *European Journal of Communication* 12 (2): 193–218.

Bartels, Larry. 2002. "The Impact of Candidate Traits in American Presidential Elections." Pp. 44–69 in *Leaders' Personalities and the Outcomes of Democratic Elections,* edited by Anthony King. New York: Oxford University Press.

Bartholow, Bruce D., Marc A. Sestir, and Edward B. Davis. 2005. "Correlates and Consequences of Exposure to Video Game Violence: Hostile Personality, Empathy, and Aggressive Behavior." *Personality and Social Psychology Bulletin* 31 (11): 1573–1586.

Battani, Marshall. 1999. "Organizational Fields, Cultural Fields, and Art Worlds: The Early Effort to Make Photographs and Make Photographers in the Nineteenth Century." *Media, Culture, and Society* 21 (5): 601–626.

Baudrillard, Jean. 1983. *Simulations.* New York: Semiotext(e).

_____. 1988. *Selected Writings.* Mark Poster, ed. Stanford, CA: Stanford University Press.

Bauerlein, Mark. 2008. *The Dumbest Generation: How the Digital Age Stupefies Young Americans and Threatens Our Future.* New York: Penguin.

BBC (British Broadcasting Corporation). 2006. "Google Censors Itself for China." Retrieved February 16, 2011 (http://news.bbc.co.uk/2/hi/technology/4645596.stm).

Becker, Howard S. 1982. *Art Worlds.* Berkeley, CA: University of California Press.

Becker, Ron. 2006. "Help is On the Way! *Supernanny, Nanny 911,* and the Neoliberal Politics of the Family." Pp. 175–191 in *The Great American Makeover; Television, History, Nation,* edited by Dana Heller. New York: Palgrave Macmillan.

Bennett, W. Lance. 2009. *News: The Politics of Illusion.* 8th ed. New York: Longman.

Bennett, W. Lance and David Paletz, eds. 1994. *Taken by Storm: The Media, Public Opinion, and U.S. Foreign Policy in the Gulf War.* Chicago, IL: University of Chicago Press.

Beresin, Eugene V. 2010. "The Impact of Violence on Children and Adolescents: Opportunities for Clinical Interventions." American Academy of Child and Adolescent Psychiatry. Retrieved November 29, 2010 (http://www.aacap.org/cs/root/developmentor/the_impact_of_violence_on_ children_and_adolescents_opportunities_for_clinical_interventions).

Bernoff, Josh and Jacqueline Anderson. 2010. "Social Technographics Defined." Forrester. Retrieved December 8, 2010 (http://www.forrester.com/empowered/ladder2010).

Bielby, William T. and Denise D. Bielby. 1994. "All Hits Are Flukes: Institutionalized Decision Making and the Rhetoric of Network Prime-Time Program Development." *American Journal of Sociology* 99: 1287–1313.

Bignell, Paul and Lauren Dunne. 2013. "Superman Is Already a $170m Brand Superhero as Man of Steel Tops the Product Placement Charts." *The Independent.* June 10. Retrieved (http://www.independent.co.uk/arts-entertainment/films/news/superman-is-already-a-170m-brand-superhero-as-man-of-steel-tops-the-product-placement-charts-8651215.html).

Bijker, Wiebe and John Law, eds. 1992. *Shaping Technology/Building Society: Studies in Sociotechnical Change.* Cambridge, MA: MIT Press.

Bimber, Bruce. 1998. "The Internet and Political Mobilization. Research Note on the 1996 Election Season." *Social Science Computer Review* 16 (4): 391–401.

Birkerts, Sven. 1994. *The Gutenberg Elegies*. Boston, MA: Faber & Faber.

Black, Ian. 2013. "NSA spying scandal: What we have learned." *Guardian*. June 10 (http://www.guardian.co.uk/world/2013/jun/10/nsa-spying-scandal-what-we-have-learned).

Boczkowski, Pablo. 2004. *Digitizing the News: Innovation in Online Newspapers*. Cambridge, MA: MIT Press.

____. 2009. "Technology, Monitoring and Imitation in Contemporary News Work." *Communication, Culture & Critique* 2 (1): 39–58.

____. 2010. *News at Work: Imitation in an Age of Information Abundance*. Chicago, IL: University of Chicago Press.

Bodnar, John. 2006. *Blue Collar Hollywood: Liberalism, Democracy, and Working People in American Film*. Baltimore, MD: Johns Hopkins University Press.

Bogle, Donald. 2001. *Toms, Coons, Mulattoes, Mammies, and Bucks: An Interpretive History of Blacks in American Film*. New York: Continuum International Publishing Group.

Bohlen, Celestine. 2013. "Protecting European Cinema." June 21. *New York Times*. Retrieved July 24, 2013 (http://www.nytimes.com/2013/06/22/world/europe/22iht-letter22.html).

Bolter, Jay David and Richard Grusin. 2000. *Remediation: Understanding New Media*. Cambridge, MA: MIT Press.

Bonilla Silva, Eduardo. 2009. *Race Without Racists*. Lanham, MD: Rowman & Littlefield.

Boorstin, Daniel. 1961. *The Image*. New York: Atheneum.

Bose, Derek. 2006. *Brand Bollywood: A New Global Entertainment Order*. Thousand Oaks, CA: Sage.

Box Office Mojo. 2010. "Worldwide Grosses." Retrieved December 9, 2010 (http://boxoffice mojo.com/alltime/world/).

Boyd-Barrett, Oliver. 1977. "Media Imperialism: Towards an International Framework for an Analysis of Media Systems." Pp. 116–135 in *Mass Communication and Society*, edited by James Curran, Michael Gurevitch, and Janet Woollacott. London, UK: Edward Arnold.

Braid, Mary. 2004. "Page Three Girls—The Naked Truth." *BBC News Online*. September 14. Retrieved November 29, 2010 (http://news.bbc.co.uk/2/hi/uk_news/magazine/3651850.stm).

Branch, Taylor. 1988. *Parting the Waters: America in the King Years 1954–1963*. New York: Simon & Schuster.

Brenner, Daniel and William L. Rivers. 1982. *Free but Regulated: Conflicting Traditions in Media Law*. Ames, IA: Iowa State University Press.

Brill's Content. 1998. "Dan Rather on Fear, Money, and the News." October: 116–121.

Brooks, Brian S., Daryl R. Moen, Don Ranly, and George Kennedy. 2012. *Telling the Story: The Convergence of Print, Broadcast, and Online Media*. New York: Bedford/St. Martin's.

Brosius, Hans-Bernd and Hans Mathias Kepplinger. 1990. "The Agenda Setting Function of Television News: Static and Dynamic Views." *Communication Research* 17 (2): 183–211.

Bruns, Axel. 2008. *Blogs, Wikipedia, Second Life, and Beyond: From Production to Produsage*. New York: Peter Lang.

Bruns, Axel and Jan-Hinrik Schmidt. 2011. "Produsage: A Closer Look at Continuing Developments." *New Review of Hypermedia and Multimedia* 17 (1): 3–7.

Butcher, Melissa. 2003. *Transnational Television, Cultural Identity and Change: When STAR Came to India*. Thousand Oaks, CA: Sage.

Butsch, Richard. 2003. "A Half Century of Class and Gender in American TV Domestic Sitcoms." *Cercles* 8: 16–34.

____. 2005. "Five Decades and Three Hundred Sitcoms About Class and Gender." Pp. 111–135 in *Thinking Outside the Box: A Contemporary Television Genre Reader*, edited by Gary R. Edgerton and Brian G. Rose. Lexington, KY: University Press of Kentucky.

Calabrese, Andrew. 1999. "Communication and the End of Sovereignty?" *Info: Journal of Policy, Regulation and Strategy for Telecommunications, Information and Media* 1 (4): 313–326.

Cappella, Joseph N. and Kathleen Hall Jamieson. 1997. *Spiral of Cynicism: The Press and the Public Good*. New York: Oxford University Press.

Carlson, James M. 1985. *Prime Time Law Enforcement: Crime Show Viewing and Attitudes*

Towards the Criminal Justice System. New York: Praeger.

____. 1995. "Political Socialization Through Media." Pp. 47–54 in *"Media" Res: Readings in Mass Media and American Politics,* edited by Jan P. Vermeer. New York: McGraw-Hill.

Carnagey, Nicholas L., Craig A. Anderson, and Brad J. Bushman. 2007. "The Effect of Video Game Violence on Physiological Desensitization to Real-Life Violence." *Journal of Experimental Social Psychology* 43 (3): 489–496.

Carr, Nicholas. 2008. "Is Google Making Us Stupid?" *The Atlantic.* July/August. Retrieved December 8, 2010 (http://www.theatlantic.com/magazine/archive/2008/07/is-google-making-us-stupid/6868/).

____. 2010. *The Shallows: What the Internet Is Doing to Our Brains.* New York: W. W. Norton.

Carragee, Kevin M. 1990. "Interpretive Media Study and Interpretive Social Science." *Critical Studies in Mass Communication* 7 (2): 81–96.

Carroll, Noël. 2004. "Sympathy for the Devil." Pp. 121–136 in *The Sopranos and Philosophy,* edited by Richard Greene and Peter Vernezze. LaSalle, IL: Open Court.

Caslon Analytics. 2009. "Blog Statistics and Demographics." Retrieved November 22, 2010 (http://www.caslon.com.au/weblogprofile1.htm#ephemerality).

Castells, Manuel. 2000. *The Rise of the Network Society.* 2nd ed. Malden, MA: Blackwell.

____. 2001. *The Internet Galaxy. Reflections on the Internet, Business, and Society.* New York: Oxford University Press.

Castells, Manuel, Mireia Fernandez-Ardevol, Jack Linchuan Qiu, and Araba Sey. 2006. *Mobile Communication and Society: A Global Perspective.* Cambridge, MA: MIT Press.

Center for Responsive Politics. 2013. Various databases at opensecrets.org.

Chadwick, Andrew. 2006. *Internet Politics: States, Citizens, and New Communication Technologies.* New York: Oxford University Press.

Chakravartty, Paula and Katharine Sarikakis. 2006. *Media Policy and Globalization.* Edinburgh, UK: Edinburgh University Press.

Cheney, Richard. 1992. "Media Conduct in the Persian Gulf War: Report to Congress." Washington, DC: Department of Defense, Public Affairs Office.

Child, Ben. 2012. "Bond Causes a Stir With Taste for Beer in Skyfall." *The Guardian.* April 17 (http://www.guardian.co.uk/film/2012/apr/17/bond-taste-for-beer-skyfall).

Child Online Protection Act, 47 U.S.C. §231 (1998).

Children Now. 2004. *Fall Colors: 2003–04 Prime Time Diversity Report.* Oakland, CA.

Chitnis, Ketan S., Avinash Thombre, Everett M. Rogers, Arvind Singhal, and Ami Sengupta. 2006. "(Dis)Similar Readings: Indian and American Audiences' Interpretation of *Friends.*" *The International Communication Gazette* 68 (2): 131–145.

Chiuy, Yvonne. 1995. "FTC Settles Car Ad Boycott Case." *Washington Post.* August 2, p. F3.

Chmielewski, Dawn C. and Rebecca Keegan. 2011. "Merchandise Sales Drive Pixar's 'Cars' Franchise." *Los Angeles Times.* June 21. Retrieved July 8, 2013 (http://articles.latimes.com/2011/jun/21/business/la-fi-ct-cars2-20110621).

Christensen, Terry and Peter J. Haas. 2005. *Projecting Politics: Political Messages in American Films.* Armonk, NY: M. E. Sharpe.

Christman, Ed. 2013. "Universal Music Still Market Top Dog in 2013." *Billboard.biz.* January 3. Retrieved January 17, 2013 (http://www.billboard.biz/bbbiz/industry/record-labels/universal-music-still-market-top-dog-in-1008068352.story).

Chung, Philip W. 2007. "The 25 Most Notorious Yellow Face Film Performances." *AsianWeek.* November, 28. Retrieved August 7, 2013 (http://www.asianweek.com/2007/11/28/the-25-most-infamous-yellow-face-film-performances-part-1/).

Clark, Charles S. 1991a. "Advertising Under Attack." *CQ Researcher* 1: 659–679.

____. 1991b. "The Obscenity Debate." *CQ Researcher* 1: 971–991.

____. 1993. "TV Violence." *CQ Researcher* 3: 267–284.

Clear Channel. 2013. About Us. www.clearchannel.com/Corporate/. Retrieved January 11, 2013.

Clifford, Stephanie. 2008a. "A Product's Place Is on the Set." *New York Times.* July 22, p. C1.

____. 2008b. "Product Placements Acquire a Life of Their Own on Shows." *New York Times.* July 14, p. C1.

____. 2010. "Before Hiring Actors, Filmmakers Cast Products." *New York Times.* April 5, p. A1.

Cohen, Bernard. 1963. *The Press and Foreign Policy.* Princeton, NJ: Princeton University Press.

Cole, Williams. 1995. "Readers for Sale! What Newspapers Tell Advertisers About Their Audience." *Extra!* 8 (3): 6–7.

Collins, Ronald K. L. 1992. *Dictating Content: How Advertising Pressure Can Corrupt a Free Press.* Washington, DC: Center for the Study of Commercialism.

Condit, Celeste M. 1989. "The Rhetorical Limits of Polysemy." *Critical Studies in Mass Communication* 6 (2): 103–122.

Conway, Mike, Maria Elizabeth Grabe, and Kevin Grieves. 2007. "Villains, Victims and the Virtuous in Bill O'Reilly's 'No-Spin Zone.'" *Journalism Studies* 8 (2): 197–223.

Cooley, Charles Horton. 1902/1964. *Human Nature and the Social Order.* New York: Scribner's.

Coontz, Stephanie. 1992. *The Way We Never Were: American Families and the Nostalgia Trap.* New York: Basic Books.

Cortell, Andrew P., Robert M. Eisinger, and Scott L. Althaus. 2009. "Why Embed? Explaining the Bush Administration's Decision to Embed Reporters in the 2003 Invasion of Iraq." *American Behavioral Scientist* 52 (5): 657–677.

Coser, Lewis A., Charles Kadushin, and Walter W. Powell. 1982. *Books: The Culture and Commerce of Publishing.* New York: Basic Books.

Cottle, Simon. 2007. "Ethnography and news production: New(s) developments in the field." *Sociology Compass* 1(1): 1–16.

Counterpunch Wire. 2003. "Weapons of Mass Destruction: Who Said What When." Retrieved September 9, 2013 (http://www.counterpunch.org/2003/05/29/weapons-of-mass-destruction-who-said-what-when/).

Cowan, Tyler. 2000. *What Price Fame?* Cambridge, MA: Harvard University Press.

Coyer, Kate, Tony Dowmunt, and Alan Fountain, eds. 2007. *Alternative Media Handbook.* London, UK: Routledge.

Crane, Diana. 1992. *The Production of Culture.* Newbury Park, CA: Sage.

Crawford, Alan Pell. 1993. "Finis to Fin-Syn." *Mediaweek* (April 12): 15.

Creative Commons. 2010. "What is CC?" Retrieved November 29, 2010 (http://creativecommons.org/about/what-is-cc).

Cripps, Thomas. 1993. "Film." Pp. 131–185 in *Split Image: African Americans in the Mass Media,* 2nd ed., edited by Jannette L. Dates and William Barlow. Washington, DC: Howard University Press.

Cronauer, Adrian. 1994. "The Fairness Doctrine: A Solution in Search of a Problem." *Federal Communications Law Journal* 47 (1): 51–77.

Croteau, David. 1995. *Politics and the Class Divide: Working People and the Middle Class Left.* Philadelphia, PA: Temple University Press.

Croteau, David and William Hoynes. 1994. *By Invitation Only: How the Media Limit Political Debate.* Monroe, ME: Common Courage Press.

_____. 2006. *The Business of Media: Corporate Media and the Public Interest.* 2nd ed. Thousand Oaks, CA: Pine Forge/Sage.

_____. 2013. *Experience Sociology.* New York, NY: McGraw-Hill.

Croteau, David, William Hoynes, and Kevin M. Carragee. 1996. "The Political Diversity of Public Television: Polysemy, the Public Sphere, and the Conservative Critique of PBS." *Journalism and Mass Communication Monographs* 157: 1–55.

Crowley, David and Paul Heyer. 1991. *Communication in History.* New York: Longman.

Curran, James. 1977. "Capitalism and Control of the Press, 1800–1975." Pp. 195–230 in *Mass Communication and Society,* edited by James Curran, Michael Gurevitch, and Janet Woollacott. London, UK: Edward Arnold.

D'Arma, Alessandro and Jeanette Steemers. 2013. "Children's Television: Markets and Regulations." Pp. 123–135 in *Private Television in Western Europe: Content, Markets, Policies*, edited by Karen Donders, Caroline Pauwels, and Jan Loisen. New York: Palgrave McMillan.

Dates, Jannette L. 1993. "Commercial Television." Pp. 267–327 in *Split Image: African Americans in the Mass Media,* 2nd ed., edited by Jannette L. Dates and William Barlow. Washington, DC: Howard University Press.

Dates, Jannette L. and William Barlow, eds. 1993. *Split Image: African Americans in the Mass Media.* 2nd ed. Washington, DC: Howard University Press.

DeFleur, Melvin L. and Margaret DeFleur. 2009. *Mass Communication Theories.* Boston, MA: Allyn & Bacon.

Democracy Corps. 2008. "Third Presidential Debate: McCain Digs Himself a Deeper Hole." Retrieved November 11, 2010 (http://www.democracy corps.com/focus/2008/10/third-presidential-debate/).

Democracynow.org. 2011. "About Democracy Now." Retrieved February 21, 2011 (http://www .democracynow.org/about).

Dempsey, John and Josef Adalian. 2007. "'Office,' 'Earl' Land at TBS." *Variety.* June 21. Retrieved November 29, 2010 (http://www.variety.com/article/VR1117967376?refCatId=14).

DeNardis, Laura. 2010. "The Emerging Field of Internet Governance." *Yale Information Society Project Working Paper Series.* Retrieved December 9, 2010 (http://ssrn.com/abstract=1678343).

Denton, Robert, ed. 1993. *The Media and the Persian Gulf War.* Westport, CT: Praeger.

Derks, Daantje, Arjan E. R. Bos, and Jasper von Grumbkow. 2008. "Emoticons and Online Message Interpretation." *Social Science Computer Review* 26 (3): 379–388.

Deuze, Mark. 2003. "The Web and Its Journalisms: Considering the Consequences of Different Types of News Online." *New Media and Society* 5: 203–226.

____. 2007. *Media Work.* Malden, MA: Polity Press.

____. 2008. "The People Formerly Known as the Employers." Retrieved November 29, 2010 (http://deuze.blogspot.com/2008/10/people-formerly-known-as-employers.html).

Dill, Karen E., Douglas A. Gentile, William A. Richter, and Jody C. Dill. 2005. "Violence, Sex, Race and Age in Popular Videogames." Pp. 115–130 in *Featuring Females: Feminist Analysis of the Media,* edited by Ellen Cole and Jessica Henderson Daniel. Washington, DC: American Psychological Association.

Dines, Gail. 2010. *Pornland: How Porn Has Hijacked Our Sexuality.* Boston, MA: Beacon Press.

Donders, Karen. 2011. *Public Service Media and Policy in Europe.* New York: Palgrave McMillan.

Douglas, Susan J. 1987. *Inventing American Broadcasting, 1899–1922.* Baltimore, MD: Johns Hopkins University Press.

Douglas, Susan and Meredith W. Michaels. 2004. *The Mommy Myth: The Idealization of Motherhood and How It Has Undermined Women.* New York: Free Press.

Dowd, Timothy J. 2004. "Concentration and Diversity Revisited: Production Logics and the U.S. Mainstream Recording Market, 1940 to 1990." *Social Forces* 82 (4): 1411–1455.

Downing, John D. H. 2001. *Radical Media: Rebellious Communication and Social Movements.* Thousand Oaks, CA: Sage.

Downing, John D. H., ed. 2011. *Encyclopedia of Social Movement Media.* Thousand Oaks, CA: Sage.

Doyle, Gillian. 2002. *Media Ownership: The Economics and Politics of Convergence and Concentration in the UK and European Media.* London, UK/Thousand Oaks, CA: Sage.

Earl, Jennifer and Katrina Kimport. 2009. "Movement Societies and Digital Protest: Fan Activism and Other Nonpolitical Protest Online." *Sociological Theory* 27 (3): 220–243.

Ehrenreich, Barbara. 1995. "The Silenced Majority." Pp. 40–43 in *Gender, Race, and Class in Media,* edited by Gail Dines and Jean M. Humez. Thousand Oaks, CA: Sage.

Eisenstein, Elizabeth. 1968. "Some Conjectures About the Impact of Printing on Western Society and Thought." *Journal of Modern History* 40 (1): 1–56.

____. 1979. *The Printing Press as an Agent of Change.* Cambridge, UK: Cambridge University Press.

Elliott, Stuart. 2008. "Up News, a Show From our Sponsor." *New York Times.* July 12, p. C5.

Entman, Robert. 1989. *Democracy Without Citizens.* New York: Oxford University Press.

____. 1992. "Blacks in the News: Television, Modern Racism, and Cultural Change." *Journalism Quarterly* 69: 341–361.

Entman, Robert and Andrew Rojecki. 2000. *The Black Image in the White Mind.* Chicago, IL: University of Chicago Press.

Epstein, Edward J. 1973. *News From Nowhere.* New York: Vintage.

Escholz, Sarah, Ted Chiricos, and Marc Gertz. 2003. "Television and Fear of Crime: Program Types, Audience Traits, and the Mediating Effect of Perceived Neighborhood Racial Composition." *Social Problems* 50 (3): 395–415.

Escobar, Gabriel and Anne Swardson. 1995. "From Language to Literature, a New Guiding Lite." *Washington Post.* September 5, pp. 1, A18.

Esfandiari, Golnaz. 2010. "The Twitter Devolution." *Foreign Policy.* June 10. Retrieved November 30,

2010 (http://www.foreignpolicy.com/articles/2010/06/07/the_twitter_revolution_that_wasnt).

Espiritu, Belinda Flores. 2011. "Transnational Audience Reception as a Theater of Struggle: Young Filipino Women's Reception of Korean Television Dramas." *Asian Journal of Communication* 21 (4): 355–372.

European Audiovisual Observatory. 2010. "Focus: World Film Market Trends." Retrieved December 9, 2010 (http://www.obs.coe.int/oea_publ/market/focus.html).

_____. 2013. "Decline in admissions in the European Union in 2012 but European films' market share on the up." May 7. Retrieved July 24, 2013 (http://www.obs.coe.int/about/oea/pr/mif2013_cinema.html).

European Commission. 2010. "Microsoft Case." Accessed February 16, 2011 (http://ec.europa.eu/competition/sectors/ICT/microsoft/index.html).

Ewen, Stuart. 1976. *Captains of Consciousness.* New York: McGraw-Hill.

Fahmy, Shahira and Thomas Johnson. 2005. "How We Performed: Embedded Journalists' Attitudes and Perceptions Towards Covering the Iraq War." *Journalism & Mass Communication Quarterly* 82 (2): 301–317.

Fallows, James. 1996. "Why Americans Hate the Media." *Atlantic Monthly.* February, pp. 45–64.

FCC (Federal Communications Commission). 1995. "Comments Sought on November 1995 Expiration of Fin-Syn Rules." *News Report No. DC 95–54.* April 5. Retrieved March 7, 2011 (http://www.fcc.gov/Bureaus/Mass_Media/News_Releases/1995/nrmm5050.txt).

_____. 1998. "FCC Explores Idea of Creating Low Power FM Radio Service for Local Communities." Retrieved December 23, 1998 (www.fcc.gov/mmb/prd/lpfm).

_____. 2004. "Report to the Congress on the Low Power FM Interference Testing Program." Retrieved February 16, 2011 (http://fjallfoss.fcc.gov/edocs_public/attachmatch/DOC-244128A1.pdf).

_____. 2013. "Broadcast Station Totals as of March 31, 2013" (http://www.fcc.gov/document/broadcast-station-totals-march-31-2013).

Fejes, Fred. 1992. "Masculinity as Fact: A Review of Empirical Mass Communication Research on Masculinity." Pp. 9–22 in *Men, Masculinity, and the Media,* edited by Steve Craig. Newbury Park, CA: Sage.

Fejes, Fred and Kevin Petrich. 1993. "Invisibility, Homophobia and Heterosexism: Lesbians, Gays and the Media." *Critical Studies in Mass Communication* 20: 396–422.

Fenby, Jonathan. 1986. *The International News Agencies.* New York: Schocken Books.

Fenton, Natalie. 2010. *New Media, Old News. Journalism & Democracy in the Digital Age.* Thousand Oaks, CA: Sage.

Ferguson, Christopher John. 2007. "The Good, the Bad and the Ugly: A Meta-Analytic Review of Positive and Negative Effects of Violent Video Games." *Psychiatric Quarterly* 78: 309–316.

Fischer, Claude. 1992. *America's Calling.* Berkeley, CA: University of California Press.

Fishman, Mark. 1980. *Manufacturing the News.* Austin, TX: University of Texas Press.

Fiske, John. 1986. "Television: Polysemy and Popularity." *Critical Studies in Mass Communication* 3: 391–408.

_____. 1987. *Television Culture.* London, UK: Routledge Kegan Paul.

Flew, Terry. 2007. *Understanding Global Media.* New York: Palgrave.

Flint, Anthony. 1997. "The Culture of Spin: Just Part of the Landscape Now." *American Behavioral Scientist* 40 (8): 1190–1192.

Flint, Joe. 1993. "Networks Win, Hollywood Winces as Fin-Syn Barriers Fall." *Broadcasting & Cable.* November 22, pp. 6, 16.

Foot, Kirstin and Steven Schneider. 2006. *Web Campaigning.* Cambridge, MA: The MIT Press.

Forbes. 2012. "The Forbes 400: The Richest People in America." Retrieved January 15, 2013 (http://www.forbes.com/forbes-400/).

Forrester Research. n.d. "What's the Social Technographics Profile of Your Customers?" Retrieved April 14, 2011 (http://www.forrester.com/empowered/tool_consumer.html).

France 24. 2013. "Film world leaps to defence of French 'cultural exception.'" June 14. Retrieved July 24, 2013 (http://www.france24.com/en/20130614-french-cultural-exception-spielberg-weinstein-berenice-bejo-cannes-france).

Frank, Reuven. 1993. "Fairness in the Eye of the Beholder." *New Leader.* November 15–29, pp. 20–21.

Frank, Thomas. 1997. *The Conquest of Cool.* Chicago, IL: University of Chicago Press.

Freedman, Des. 2008. *The Politics of Media Policy.* Malden, MA: Polity Press.

Freedom House. 2004. *Freedom of the Press 2004: A Global Survey of Media Independence.* Lanham, MD: Rowman & Littlefield Publishers, Inc.

Freeman, Des. 2008. *The Politics of Media Policy.* Oxford, UK: Polity Press.

Freeman, Michael. 1994a. "A Last Gasp for Fin-Syn?" *Mediaweek.* November 28, p. 5.

——. 1994b. "Producers Fight for Fin-Syn." *Mediaweek.* December 5, pp. 10, 12.

Frith, Simon. 1981. *Sound Effects.* New York: Pantheon.

Fritsch-El Alaoui, Khadija. 2009/2010. "Teaching the Meter of the Impossible in a Classroom: On Liberal Hollywood's Mission Impossible." *Transformations* 20 (2): 129–137.

FTC (Federal Trade Commission). 2000. "Marketing Violent Entertainment to Children." Retrieved July 19, 2001 (www.ftc.gov/reports/violence/vioreport.pdf).

Fuchs, Christian. 2009. "Social Networking Sites and the Surveillance Society: A Critical Case Study of the Usage of StudiVZ, Facebook, and MySpace by Students in Salzburg in the Context of Electronic Surveillance." Salzburg/Vienna: Research Group UTI. Retrieved November 29, 2010 (http://fuchs.icts.sbg.ac.at/SNS_Surveillance_Fuchs.pdf).

Fuller, Linda. 1995. "Hollywood Holding Us Hostage: Or, Why Are Terrorists in the Movies Middle Easterners?" Pp. 187–198 in *The U.S. Media and the Middle East: Image and Perception,* edited by Yahya R. Kamalipour. Westport, CT: Greenwood Press.

Funkhouser, G. Ray. 1973. "The Issues of the Sixties: An Exploratory Study in the Dynamics of Public Opinion." *Public Opinion Quarterly* 66: 942–948, 959.

Gamson, Joshua. 1994. *Claims to Fame.* Berkeley, CA: University of California Press.

——. 1998. *Freaks Talk Back: Tabloid Talk Shows and Sexual Nonconformity.* Chicago, IL: University of Chicago Press.

Gamson, William. 1992. *Talking Politics.* New York: Cambridge University Press.

Gamson, William, David Croteau, William Hoynes, and Theodore Sasson. 1992. "Media Images and the Social Construction of Reality." *Annual Review of Sociology* 18: 373–393.

Gamson, William and Andre Modigliani. 1989. "Media Discourse and Public Opinion on Nuclear Power." *American Journal of Sociology* 95: 1–37.

Gamson, William and Gadi Wolfsfeld. 1993. "Movements and Media as Interacting Systems." *Annals of the American Academy of Political and Social Science* 528 (July): 114–125.

Gannett. 2013. Our Brands (http://www.gannett.com/section/BRANDS&template=cover).

Gans, Herbert. 2004. *Deciding What's News,* 25th anniversary ed. Chicago, IL: Northwestern University Press. (Original work published 1979)

Garofalo, Reebee, ed. 1992. *Rockin' the Boat: Mass Music and Mass Movements.* Boston, MA: South End.

Gerbner, George, Larry Gross, Michael Morgan, and Nancy Signorielli. 1982. "Charting the Mainstream: Television's Contributions to Political Orientations." *Journal of Communication* 32 (2): 100–127.

——. 1984. "Political Correlates of Television Viewing." *Public Opinion Quarterly* 48 (1): 283–300.

Gerbner, George, Larry Gross, Michael Morgan, Nancy Signorielli, and James Shanahan. 2002. "Growing up With Television: Cultivation Processes." Pp. 43–68 in *Media Effects: Advances in Theory and Research,* edited by Jennings Bryant and Dolf Zillmann. Mahwah, NJ: Lawrence Erlbaum Associates.

Gerbner, George, Hamid Mowlana, and Kaarle Nordenstreng, eds. 1993. *The Global Media Debate: Its Rise, Fall, and Renewal.* Norwood, NJ: Ablex.

Gilens, Martin. 1996. "Race and Poverty in America: Public Misperceptions and the American News Media." *Public Opinion Quarterly* 60 (4): 515–541.

Ginsborg, Paul. 2005. *Silvio Berlusconi: Television, Power and Patrimony.* London, UK: Verso.

Gitlin, Todd. 1980. *The Whole World Is Watching: Mass Media in the Making and Unmaking of the New Left.* Berkeley, CA: University of California.

——. 2000. *Inside Prime Time.* Berkeley, CA: University of California Press.

GLAAD. 2011. *Where We Are On TV: 2011–2012 Season.* Retrieved July 18, 2013 (http://www.glaad.org/publications/whereweareontv11).

____. 2012. *Where We Are On TV: 2012–2013 Season.* Retrieved July 18, 2013 (http://www.glaad.org/publications/whereweareontv12).

Glascock, Jack. 2001. Gender Roles on Prime-Time Network Television: Demographics and Behaviors. *Journal of Broadcasting & Electronic Media* 45 (4): 656–669.

GMMP (Global Media Monitoring Project). 2010. *Who Makes the News?* World Association for Christian Communication. Retrieved November 6, 2010 (http://www.whomakesthenews.org/gmmp-2010-reports.html).

Goldfarb, Jeffrey. 1991. *The Cynical Society.* Chicago, IL: University of Chicago Press.

Goodman, Amy with David Goodman. 2004. *The Exception to the Rulers.* New York: Hyperion.

Gordon, Janey. 2008. "Community Radio, Funding and Ethics. The UK and Australian Models, in Gordon." Pp. 59–79 in *Notions of Community. A Collection of Community Media Debates and Dilemmas,* edited by Gordon Janey. New York: Peter Lang.

Gorman, Siobhan, Evan Perez, and Janet Hook. 2013. "U.S. Collects Vast Data Trove." Wall Street Journal. June 7 (http://online.wsj.com/article/SB10001424127887324299104578529112289298922.html?mod=WSJ_hpp_LEFTTop Stories).

Gottdiener, Mark. 1985. "Hegemony and Mass Culture: A Semiotic Approach." *American Journal of Sociology* 90: 979–1001.

Gournelos, Ted. 2009. *Popular Culture and the Future of Politics.* Lanham, MD: Lexington Books.

Grabe, Maria E. and Dan Drew. 2007. "Crime Cultivation: Comparisons Across Media Genres and Channels." *Journal of Broadcasting & Electronic Media* 51 (1): 147–171.

Graber, Doris A. 1988. *Processing the News: How People Tame the Information Tide.* New York: Longman.

____. 2001. *Processing Politics: Learning From Television in the Internet Age.* Chicago, IL: University of Chicago Press.

____. 2009a. *Mass Media and American Politics.* 8th ed. Washington, DC: Congressional Quarterly Press.

____. 2009b. "Looking at the United States Through Distorted Lenses: Entertainment Television Versus Public Diplomacy Themes." *American Behavioral Scientist* 52 (5): 735–754.

Gramsci, Antonio. 1971. *Selections From the Prison Notebooks.* New York: International Publishers.

Gray, Herman. 1989. "Television, Black Americans, and the American Dream." *Critical Studies in Mass Communication* 16 (6): 376–386.

____. 2004. *Watching Race: Television and the Struggle for Blackness.* University of Minnesota Press.

Gray, Jonathan. 2007. "Imagining America: The Simpsons Go Global." *Popular Communication* 5 (2): 129–148.

Gray, Jonathan, Cornel Sandvoss, and C. Lee Harington, eds. 2007. *Fandom: Identities and Communities in a Mediated World.* New York: NYU Press.

Greco, Albert N., Clara E. Rodriguez, and Robert M. Wharton. 2007. *The Culture and Commerce of Publishing in the 21st Century.* Stanford, CA: Stanford University Press.

Greenberg, Bradley S. and Jeffrey E. Brand. 1994. "Minorities and the Mass Media: 1970s to 1990s." Pp. 273–314 in *Media Effects: Advances in Theory and Research,* edited by Jennings Bryant and Dolf Zillman. Hillsdale, NJ: Lawrence Erlbaum.

Greenberg, Bradley S. and Tracy R. Worrell. 2007. "New Faces on Television: A 12-Season Replication." *The Howard Journal of Communications* 18: 277–290.

Greider, William. 1992. *Who Will Tell the People: The Betrayal of American Democracy.* New York: Simon & Schuster.

Gross, Larry. 2001. *Up From Invisibility.* New York: Columbia University Press.

Guinness World Records. 2008. "Largest TV Audience—Series." Retrieved November 30, 2010 (http://www.guinnessworldrecords.com/news/2008/02/080228.aspx). H. R. 1966, 111th Cong. (2009).

Hackett, Robert A. and William K. Carroll. 2006. *Remaking Media. The Struggle to Democratize Public Communication.* New York: Routledge.

Hafner, Katie and Matthew Lyon. 1996. *Where Wizards Stay Up Late: The Origins of the Internet.* New York: Simon & Schuster.

Hall, Stuart. (1973) 1980. "Encoding/Decoding." Pp. 128–38 in *Culture, Media, Language: Working Papers in Cultural Studies, 1972–79,* edited by Centre for Contemporary Cultural Studies. London, UK: Hutchinson.

____. 1982. "The Rediscovery of 'Ideology': Return of the Repressed in Media Studies." Pp. 56–90 in *Culture, Society, and the Media,* edited by Michael Gurevitch, Tony Bennett, James Curran, and Janet Woollacott. London, UK: Routledge Kegan Paul.

Hamm, Bernd and Russell Smandych, eds. 2005. *Cultural Imperialism.* Toronto, ON: University of Toronto Press.

Hampton, Keith and Barry Wellman. 2003. "Neighboring in Netville: How the Internet Supports Community and Social Capital in a Wired Suburb." *City and Community* 2 (4): 277–311.

Harindranath, Ramaswami. 2003. "Reviving 'Cultural Imperialism': International Audiences, Global Capitalism, and the Transnational Elite." Pp. 155–168 in *Planet TV: A Global Television Reader,* edited by Lisa Parks and Shanti Kumar. New York: New York University Press.

Harmon, Amy. 2001. "Exploration of World Wide Web Tilts From Eclectic to Mundane." *New York Times.* August 26, pp. 1, 22.

Harold, Christine. 2004. "Pranking Rhetoric: Culture Jamming as Media Activism." *Critical Studies in Media Communication* 21 (3): 189–211.

Harrington, Richard. 1995. "Reviving the Label Movement." *Washington Post.* June 14, p. C7.

Helft, Miguel and David Barboza. 2010. "Google Shuts China Site in Dispute Over Censorship." *New York Times.* Retrieved February 16, 2011 (http://www.nytimes.com/2010/03/23/technology/23google.html).

Herman, Edward and Noam Chomsky. 2002. *Manufacturing Consent: The Political Economy of Mass Media.* New York: Pantheon.

Hibberd, Matthew. 2008. *The Media in Italy: Press, Cinema and Broadcasting From Unification to Digital.* New York: Open University Press.

Hickey, Neil. 1995. "Revolution in Cyberia." *Columbia Journalism Review* (July/August): 40–47.

Highland, Tim, Stephen Harrington, and Axel Bruns. 2013. "Twitter as a Technology or Audiencing and Fandom: The #Eurovision Phenomenon." *Information, Communication & Society* 16 (3): 315–339.

Hills, Jill. 1991. *The Democracy Gap: The Politics of Information and Communication Technologies in the United States and Europe.* New York: Greenwood.

Hindman, Matthew. 2009. *The Myth of Digital Democracy.* Princeton, NJ: Princeton University Press.

Hine, David. 2001. "Silvio Berlusconi, the Media and the Conflict of Interest Issue." *Italian Politics: A Review* 17: 261–276.

Hintz, Arne. 2011. "From Media Niche to Policy Spotlight: Mapping Community Media Policy in Latin America." *Canadian Journal of Communication* 36: 147–159.

Hirsch, Mario and Vibeke G. Petersen. 1992. "Regulation of Media at the European Level." Pp. 42–56 in *Dynamics of Media Politics: Broadcast and Electronic Media in Western Europe,* edited by Kareen Siune and Wolfgang Truetzschler. London, UK: Sage.

Hoerder, Dirk and Christiane Harzig. 1987. *The Immigrant Labor Press in North America, 1840s–1970s.* Westport, CT: Greenwood Press.

Hollerbach, Karie L. 2009. "The Impact of Market Segmentation on African American Frequency, Centrality, and Status in Television Advertising." *Journal of Broadcasting & Electronic Media* 53 (4): 599–614.

Holtzman, Linda. 2000. *Media Messages: What Film, Television, and Popular Music Teach Us About Race, Class, Gender, and Sexual Orientation.* Armonk, NY: M. E. Sharpe.

Hornaday, Ann. 2009. "'Precious' Mettle." *Washington Post.* November 13, P. C1.

Howard, Philip. 2005. *New Media Campaigns and the Managed Citizen.* New York: Cambridge University Press.

Howard, Philip and Muzammi Hussain. 2013. *Democracy's Fourth Wave? Digital Media and the Arab Spring.* New York: Oxford University Press.

Hoynes, William. 1994. *Public Television for Sale: Media, the Market, and the Public Sphere.* Boulder, CO: Westview.

———. 1998. "News for a Teen Market: The Lessons of Channel One." *Journal of Curriculum and Supervision* 13 (4): 339–356.

Human Rights Watch. 2003. "Off Target: The Conduct of the War and Civilian Casualties in Iraq." December 11. Retrieved November 12, 2010 (http://www.hrw.org/en/reports/2003/12/11/target).

Hunt, Darnell M. 1997. *Screening the Los Angeles "Riots": Race, Seeing and Resistance.* New York: Cambridge University Press.

Hunt, Darnell. 2013. "Writers Guild of America—West 2013 Staff Briefing." Retrieved July 19,

2013 (http://www.wga.org/uploadedFiles/who_we_are/tvstaffingbrief2013.pdf).

Hunter, James Davison. 1991. *Culture Wars.* New York: Basic Books.

Hunter, James Davison and Alan Wolfe. 2006. *Is There a Culture War?* Washington, DC: Brookings Institution Press.

Husseini, Sam. 1994. "NBC Brings Good Things to GE." *Extra!* November/December, p. 13.

Indymedia.org. 2001. "About Indymedia." Retrieved December 1, 2001 (www.indymedia.org/about.php3).

Ingraham, Chrys. 2008. *White Weddings: Romancing Heterosexuality in Popular Culture.* 2nd ed. New York: Routledge.

Internet World Stats. 2013. "Internet User Statistics." Retrieved July 23, 2013 (http://www.internetworldstats.com/stats.htm).

iReport.cnn.com. 2011. "About CNN iReport." Retrieved February 21, 2011 (http://ireport.cnn.com/about.jspa).

Iyengar, Shanto and Donald R. Kinder. 2010. *News That Matters: Television and American Opinion.* Updated ed. Chicago, IL: University of Chicago Press.

Jackson, David J. 2009. *Entertainment & Politics: The Influence of Pop Culture on Young Adult Political Socialization.* 2nd ed. New York: Peter Lang.

Jackson, Linda A. and Kelly S. Ervin. 1991. "The Frequency and Portrayal of Black Families in Fashion Advertisement." *Journal of Black Psychology* 18 (1): 67–70.

Jackson, Maggie. 2008. *Distracted: The Erosion of Attention and the Coming Dark Age.* Amherst, NY: Prometheus Books.

Jacobs, Matthew. 2013. "LGBT Milestones In Pop Culture: The Watershed Moments That Got Us Where We Are Today." Huffington Post. Retrieved July 20, 2013 (http://www.huffingtonpost.com/2013/06/13/lgbt-milestones-in-pop-culture_n_3429832.html).

Jacobs, Ronald. 2000. *Race, Media, and the Crisis of Civil Society.* New York: Cambridge University Press.

Jankowski, Nicholas W. 2006. "Creating Community With Media: History, Theories and Scientific Investigations." Pp. 55–74 in *Handbook of New Media. Social Shaping and Social Consequences of ICTs,* edited by Leah A. Lievrouw and Sonia Livingstone. London, UK: Sage.

Jansen, Sue Curry, Jefferson Pooley, and Lora Taub-Pervizpour. 2011. *Media and Social Justice.* New York: Palgrave Macmillan.

Jeffords, Susan. 1989. *The Remasculinization of America.* Bloomington, IN: Indiana University Press.

Jeffords, Susan and Lauren Rabinovitz, eds. 1994. *Seeing Through the Media: The Persian Gulf War.* New Brunswick, NJ: Rutgers University Press.

Jenkins, Henry. 2006. *Convergence Culture.* New York: New York University Press.

____. 2012. *Textual Poachers: Television Fans and Participatory Culture,* 2nd edition. New York: Routledge.

Jessell, Harry A. 1993. "Networks Victorious in Fin-Syn Fight." *Broadcasting and Cable,* April 5, pp. 7, 10.

Jhally, Sut and Justin Lewis. 1992. *Enlightened Racism.* Boulder, CO: Westview.

Jordan, Tim. 2008. *Hacking.* Malden, MA: Polity Press.

Jost, Kenneth. 1994a. "The Future of Television." *CQ Researcher* 4: 1131–1148.

____. 1994b. "Talk Show Democracy." *CQ Researcher* 4: 363–375.

Jurgensen, John. 2012. "Binge Viewing: TV's Lost Weekends." July 13. *The Wall Street Journal.* Retrieved January 14, 2013 (http://online.wsj.com/article/SB10001424052702303740704577521300806686174.html).

Kahle, Shannon, Nan Yu, and Erin Whiteside. 2007. "Another Disaster: An Examination of Portrayals of Race in Hurricane Katrina Coverage." *Visual Communication Quarterly* 14 (Spring): 75–89.

Kahn, Frank J., ed. 1978. *Documents of American Broadcasting.* 3rd ed. Englewood Cliffs, NJ: Prentice Hall.

Kahn, R. E. 2004. "Working Code and Rough Consensus: The Internet as Social Evolution." Pp. 16–21 in *Internet Governance: A Grand Collaboration,* edited by Don MacLean. New York: United Nations ICT Task Force.

Kahn, Richard and Douglas Kellner. 2004. "New Media and Internet Activism: From the 'Battle of Seattle' to Blogging." *New Media & Society* 6 (1): 87–95.

Karr, Tim. 2010. "FCC Caves on Net Neutrality." Retrieved February 16, 2011 (http://www.savetheinternet.com/blog/10/12/21/fcc-caves-net-neutrality).

Kelley, Robin D. G. 1994. *Race Rebels.* New York: Free Press.

Kellner, Douglas. 1990. *Television and the Crisis of Democracy.* Boulder, CO: Westview.

Kendall, Diana. 2005. *Framing Class.* Lanham, MD: Rowman & Littlefield.

Kian, Edward M., Michael Mondello, and John Vincent. 2009. "ESPN—The Women's Sports Network? A Content Analysis of Internet Coverage of March Madness." *Journal of Broadcasting & Electronic Media* 53 (3): 477–495.

Kidd, Dorothy. 2002. "Indymedia.org: A New Communications Commons." Pp. 47–70 in *Cyberactivism: Online Activism in Theory and Practice,* edited by Marta McCaughey and Michael Dayers. New York: Routledge.

Kim, Youna. 2005. "Experiencing Globalization: Global TV, Reflexivity and the Lives of Young People." *International Journal of Cultural Studies.* 8 (4): 445–463.

King, Claire Sisco. 2010. "The Man Inside: Trauma, Gender, and the Nation in the Brave One." *Critical Studies in Media Communication* 27 (2): 111–130.

Kirsch, Steven J. 2012. *Children, Adolescents, and Media Violence: A Critical Look at the Research.* Thousand Oaks, CA: SAGE.

Klein, Hugh and Kenneth S. Shiffman. 2009. "Underrepresentation and Symbolic Annihilation of Socially Disenfranchised Groups ('Out Groups') in Animated Cartoons." *The Howard Journal of Communications* 20: 55–72.

Klein, Naomi. 2000. *No Logo.* New York: Picador.

Klinenberg, Eric. 2005 "Convergence: News Production in a Digital Age." *Annals of the American Academy of Political and Social Science* 597 (Jan.): 48–64.

____. 2007. *Fighting for Air: The Battle to Control America's Media.* New York: Metropolitan Books.

Kohut, Andrew. 2000. "Self Censorship: Counting the Ways." *Columbia Journalism Review,* May/June, p. 42.

Kornhauser, William. 1959. *The Politics of Mass Society.* New York: Free Press.

Kosar, Kevin R. 2012. "Congressional Oversight of Agency Public Communications: Implications of Agency New Media Use." Washington, DC: Congressional Research Service (http://www.fas.org/sgp/crs/misc/R42406.pdf).

Kovach, Bill and Tom Rosenstiel. 1999. *Warp Speed: America in the Age of Mixed Media.* New York: The Century Foundation Press.

____. 2010. *Blur: How to Know What's True in the Age of Information Overload.* New York: Bloomsbury.

Kovacs, Kamilla. 2010. "The 2000s: A History of the FCC's Internet Policy Deregulation." Media Access Project. August 27. Retrieved November 8, 2010 (http://www.mediaaccess.org/2010/08/the-2000s-a-history-of-the-fcc%E2%80%99s-internet-policy-deregulation/).

Krugman, Dean M. and Leonard N. Reid. 1980. "The 'Public Interest' as Defined by FCC PolicyMakers." *Journal of Broadcasting* 24: 311–323.

Kunz, William M. 2009. "Prime-Time Television Program Ownership in a Post-Fin/Syn World." *Journal of Broadcasting & Electronic Media* 53 (4): 636–651.

Kutner, Lawrence and Cheryl Olson. 2008. *Grand Theft Childhood: The Surprising Truth About Violent Video Games and What Parents Can Do.* New York: Simon & Schuster.

Labaton, Stephen. 2000. "F. C .C. Heads for Showdown With Congress Over Radio Plan." *New York Times.* March 26, p. C1.

Laing, David. 1986. "The Music Industry and the 'Cultural Imperialism' Thesis." *Popular Music and Society* 8: 331–41.

Langlois, Andrea and Frédéric Dubois, eds. 2005. *Autonomous Media: Activating Resistance & Dissent.* Montréal, QB: Cumulus Press.

Lanier, Jaron. 2010. *You Are Not a Gadget: A Manifesto.* New York: Alfred A. Knopf.

Lauzen, Martha M. 2013. "The Celluloid Ceiling: Behind-the-Scenes Employment of Women on the Top 250 Films of 2012." San Diego State University. Retrieved July 19, 2013 (http://womenintvfilm.sdsu.edu/files/2012_Celluloid_Ceiling_Exec_Summ.pdf).

Lauzen, Martha M. and David M. Dozier. 2005. "Recognition and Respect Revisited: Portrayals of Age and Gender in Prime-Time Television." *Mass Communication and Society* 8 (3): 241–256.

Lauzen, Martha M., David M. Dozier, and Nora Horan. 2008. "Constructing Gender Stereotypes Through Social Roles in Prime-Time Television." *Journal of Broadcasting & Electronic Media* 52 (2): 200–214.

Lavery, David, 2006. "Introduction: Can This Be the End of Tony Soprano?" Pp. 1–14 in *Reading the Sopranos: Hit TV from HBO,* edited by David Lavery. London, UK: I.B. Tauris.

Lavery, David, ed. 2002. *This Thing of Ours: Investigating the Sopranos.* New York: Columbia University Press.

Lavrusik, Vadim. 2009. "7 Ways News Media Are Becoming More Collaborative." *Mashable.* Retrieved November 29, 2010 (http://mashable .com/2009/12/29/7-ways-news-media-are-becoming-more-collaborative/).

Lazar, Bonnie A. 1994. "Under the Influence: An Analysis of Children's Television Regulation." *Social Work* 39 (1): 67–74.

Lazarsfeld, Paul, Bernard Berelson, and Hazel Gaudet. 1948. *The People's Choice: How the Voter Makes up His Mind in a Presidential Campaign.* New York: Columbia University Press.

Lee, Angela M. and Michael X. Delli Carpini. 2010. "News Consumption Revisited: Examining the Power of Habits in the 21st Century." Paper presented at the 11th International Symposium on Online Journalism, Austin, TX, April 23–24, 2010.

Lee, Eric and Benjamin Weinthal. 2011. "Trade unions: The Revolutionary Social Network at Play in Egypt and Tunisia." *Guardian.* February 10. Retrieved February 24, 2011 (http://www .guardian. co.uk/commentisfree/2011/feb/10/ trade-unions-egypt-tunisia).

Lee, Sangoak. 2007. "A Longitudinal Analysis of Foreign Program Imports on South Korean Television, 1978–2002: A Case of Rising Indigenous Capacity in Program Supply." *Journal of Broadcasting & Electronic Media* 51(1): 172–187.

Leichtman Research Group. 2010. *On Demand TV: A Nationwide Study on VOD and DVRs.* Durham, NH: Leichtman Research Group.

Lenart, Silvo. 1994. *Shaping Political Attitudes: The Impact of Interpersonal Communication and Mass Media.* Thousand Oaks, CA: Sage.

Lessig, Lawrence. 1999. *Code and Other Laws of Cyberspace.* New York: Basic Books.

———. 2005. *Free Culture: The Nature and Future of Creativity.* New York: Penguin.

———. 2006. *Code: Version 2.0.* New York: Basic Books.

Lessig, Lawrence and Robert W. McChesney. 2006. "No Tolls on the Internet." *Washington Post.* June 8. Retrieved December 9, 2010 (http:// www.washingtonpost.com/wp-dyn/content/ article/2006/06/07/ AR2006060702108.html).

Levin, Murray. 1987. *Talk Radio and the American Dream.* Lexington, MA: Lexington Books.

Levine, Elana. 2001. "Toward a Paradigm for Media Production Research: Behind the Scenes at General Hospital." *Critical Studies in Media Communication* 18 (1): 66–82.

Levy, Steven. 2010. *Hackers: Heroes of the Computer Revolution,* 25th anniversary ed. Cambridge, MA: O'Reilly.

Lewis, Lisa. 1990. *Gender Politics and MTV.* Philadelphia, PA: Temple University Press.

Liacas, Tom. 2005. "101 Tricks to Play With the Mainstream: Culture Jamming as Subversive Recreation." Pp. 61–74 in *Autonomous Media: Activating Resistance and Dissent,* edited by Andrea Langlois and Frédréric Dubois. Montréal, QB: Cumulus Press.

Lichter, S. Robert, Linda S. Lichter, and Stanley Rothman. 1994. *Prime Time.* Washington, DC: Regnery.

Liebes, Tamar, and Elihu Katz. 1993. *The Export of Meaning.* Cambridge, MA: Polity.

Lievrouw, Leah A. 2011. *Alternative and Activist New Media.* Malden, MA: Polity.

Lievrouw, Leah A. and Sonia Livingstone, eds. 2006. *Handbook of New Media. Social Shaping and Social Consequences of ICTs.* London, UK: Sage.

Lind, Rebecca and James A. Danowski. 1998. "The Representation of Arabs in U.S. Electronic Media." Pp. 157–168 in *Cultural Diversity and the U.S. Media,* edited by Yahya R. Kamalipour and Theresa Carilli. Albany, NY: SUNY Press.

Ling, Rich and Scott Campbell, eds. 2009. *The Reconstruction of Space and Time: Mobile Communication Practices.* New Brunswick, NJ: Transaction Publishers.

Lister, Martin, Jon Dovey, Seth Giddings, Iain Grant, and Kieran Kelly. 2009. *New Media: A Critical Introduction.* 2nd ed. New York: Routledge.

Little, Vance. 2008. "Audiovisual Media Services Directive: Europe's Modernization of Broadcast

Services Regulations." *Journal of Law, Technology & Policy* 1: 223–236.

Live Nation Entertainment. 2013. Company Profile. www.livenation.com/investors. Retrieved January 11, 2013.

Long, Elizabeth. 1985. *The American Dream and the Popular Novel.* Boston, MA: Routledge Kegan Paul.

Longley, Lawrence, Herbert Terry, and Erwin Krasnow. 1983. "Citizen Groups in Broadcast Regulatory Policy-Making." *Policy Studies Journal* 12: 258–270.

Lopes, Paul D. 1992. "Innovation and Diversity in the Popular Music Industry, 1969 to 1990." *American Sociological Review* 57: 56–71.

Lopez, Lori Kido. 2011. "Fan Activists and the Politics of Race in The Last Airbender." *International Journal of Cultural Studies* 15 (5): 431–445.

Louw, Eric P. 2010. *The Media and the Political Process.* 2nd ed. Thousand Oaks, CA: Sage.

MacArthur, John R. 2003. "The Lies We Bought. The Unchallenged 'Evidence' for War," *Columbia Journalism Review,* May/June, pp. 62–63.

MacBride Commission. 1980. *Many Voices, One World: Towards a New, More Just, and More Efficient World Information and Communication Order.* London, UK: Kogan Page. Retrieved December 9, 2010 (http://unesdoc.unesco.org/images/0004/000400/040066eb.pdf).

MacBride, Sean and Colleen Roach. 1993. "The New International Information Order." Pp. 3–11 in *The Global Media Debate: Its Rise, Fall, and Renewal,* edited by George Gerbner, Hamid Mowlana, and Kaarle Nordenstreng. Norwood, NJ: Ablex.

Madden, Mary, Amanda Lenhart, Maeve Duggan, and Sandra Cortesi. 2013. "Teens and Technology 2013." Pew Research Center's Internet & American Life Project. Washington, DC (http://www.pewinternet.org/Reports/2013/Teens).

Majoribanks, Tim. 2000. *News Corporations, Technology, and the Workplace.* Cambridge: Cambridge University Press.

Mancini, Paolo. 2013. "Media Fragmentation, Party System, and Democracy." *The International Journal of Press/Politics* 18 (1): 43–60.

Manning, Jennifer. 2013. "Membership of the 113th Congress: A Profile." Washington, DC: Congressional Research Service. Retrieved July 21, 2013 (http://www.fas.org/sgp/crs/misc/R42964.pdf).

Marchetti, Gina. 1989. "Action-Adventure as Ideology." Pp. 182–197 in *Cultural Politics in Contemporary America,* edited by Ian H. Angus and Sut Jhally. New York: Routledge Kegan Paul.

Martin, Christopher. 2003. *Framed! Labor and the Corporate Media.* Ithaca, NY: ILR Press.

Mattelart, Armand. 1979. *Multinational Corporations and the Control of Culture.* Atlantic Highlands, NJ: Humanities Press.

McAdam, Doug. 1982. *Political Process and the Development of Black Insurgency, 1930–1970.* Chicago, IL: University of Chicago Press.

McChesney, Robert W. 1994. *Telecommunications, Mass Media, and Democracy.* New York: Oxford University Press.

_____. 1999. *Rich Media, Poor Democracy: Communications Politics in Dubious Times.* Urbana, IL: University of Illinois Press.

_____. 2004. *The Problem of the Media: U.S. Communication Politics in the Twenty-First Century.* New York: Monthly Review Press.

_____. 2008. *The Political Economy of Media.* New York: Monthly Review Press.

_____. 2013. *Digital Disconnect: How Capitalism Is Turning the Internet Against Democracy.* New York, NY: The New Press.

McChesney, Robert, Russell Newman and Ben Scott, eds. 2005. *The Future of Media: Resistance and Reform in the 21st Century.* New York: Seven Stories Press.

McClelland, Stephen. 2012. "Social Networks and the Second Screen." *Intermedia* 40 (3): 16–21.

McClintock, Pamela. 2013. "Sony Pictures No. 1 in 2012 Worldwide Box Office Market Share." *The Hollywood Reporter.* January 2. Retrieved June 5, 2013 (http://www.hollywoodreporter.com/news/sony-pictures-no-1-2012-407575).

McClure, Robert and Thomas Patterson. 1976. *The Unseeing Eye.* New York: Putnam.

McCombs, Maxwell and Donald L. Shaw. 1972. "The Agenda-Setting Function of the Mass Media." *Public Opinion Quarterly* 36: 176–187.

_____. 1977. *The Emergence of American Political Issues: The Agenda-Setting Function of the Press.* St. Paul, MN: West.

McCombs, Maxwell E. 2004. *Setting the Agenda: The Mass Media and Public Opinion.* Cambridge, MA: Polity Press.

McConahay, John B. 1986. "Modern Racism, Ambivalence, and the Modern Racism Scale." Pp. 91–125 in John F. Dovidio and Samuel L. Gaertner, eds. *Prejudice, Discrimination, and Racism*. Orlando, FL: Academic Press.

McConnell, Ben. 2006. "The 1% Rule: Charting Citizen Participation." *Church of the Customer Blog*. Retrieved December 8, 2010 (http://customere vangelists.typepad.com/blog/2006/05/chart ing_wiki_p.html).

McCracken, Ellen. 1993. *Decoding Women's Magazines*. New York: St. Martin's.

McDermott, Terry. 2010. "Dumb Like a Fox." *Columbia Journalism Review*. 48 (6): 26–32.

McLaughlin, Margaret L., Kerry K. Osborne, and Christine B. Smith. 1995. "Standards of Conduct on Usenet." Pp. 90–111 in *Cybersociety,* edited by Steven G. Jones. Thousand Oaks, CA: Sage.

McLeod, Kembrew. 2010. "How to Make a Documentary About Sampling—Legally." *The Atlantic Monthly*. March 31 (http://www.theatlantic.com/entertainment/archive/2010/03/how-to-make-a-documentary-about-sampling-legally/38189/).

McLuhan, Marshall. 1962. *The Gutenberg Galaxy*. Toronto, ON: University of Toronto Press.

____. 1964. *Understanding Media: The Extensions of Man*. New York: McGraw Hill.

McLuhan, Marshall and Quentin Fiore. 1967. *The Medium Is the Message: An Inventory of Effects*. New York: Bantam.

McMillin, Divya C. 2002. "Choosing Commercial Television's Identities in India: A Reception Analysis." *Journal of Media and Cultural Studies* 16 (1): 123–36.

McNamara, Mary. 2010. "Television Review: 'The Bridge' on CBS." *The Los Angeles Times*. July 10. Retrieved November 8, 2010 (http://articles.lat imes.com/2010/jul/10/entertainment/la-et-theb ridge-20100710).

McQuail, Denis. 2010. *Mass Communication Theory*. 6th ed. Thousand Oaks, CA: Sage.

McQuail, Denis, Rosario de Mateo, and Helena Tapper. 1992. "A Framework for Analysis of Media Change in Europe in the 1990s." Pp. 8–25 in *Dynamics of Media Politics: Broadcast and Electronic Media in Western Europe,* edited by Kareen Siune and Wolfgang Truetzschler. London, UK: Sage.

McRobbie, Angela. 1984. "Dance and Social Fantasy." Pp. 130–161 in *Gender and Generation,* edited by Angela McRobbie and Mica Nava. London, UK: Macmillan.

Media Action Network for Asian Americans (MANAA). n.d. "Restrictive Portrayals of Asians in the Media and How to Balance Them." Retrieved February 22, 2011 (http://www.manaa.org/asian _stereotypes.html).

Media Alliance. n.d. "Mission." Retrieved March 6, 2011 (http://www.media-alliance.org/section. php?id=57).

MediaNews Group. 2013. Audience Reach: Market Leadership. Retrieved January 14, 2013 (http://www.medianewsgroup.com/CONSUMERS/Pages/AudienceReach.aspx).

Meehan, Eileen R. 2005. *Why TV Is Not Our Fault*. Lanham, MD: Rowman and Littlefield.

Messner, Marcus and Marcia Watson DiStaso. 2008. "The Source Cycle: How Traditional Media and Weblogs Use Each Other as Sources." *Journalism Studies* 9 (3): 447–463.

Messner, Michael, Margaret Carlisle Duncan, and Kerry Jensen. 1993. "Separating the Men From the Girls: The Gendered Language of Televised Sports." *Gender & Society* 7 (1): 121–137.

Messner, Michael A. and Cheryl Cooky. 2010. *Gender in Televised Sports: News and Highlights Shows, 1989–2009*. Los Angeles, CA: Center for Feminist Research, University of Southern California.

Meyrowitz, Joshua. 1985. *No Sense of Place*. New York: Oxford University Press.

____. 1994. "Medium Theory." Pp. 50–77 in *Communication Theory Today,* edited by David Crowley and David Mitchell. Stanford, CA: Stanford University Press.

Milan, Stefania and Arne Hintz. 2010. "Media Activists and Communication Policy Processes." Pp. 317–319 In *Encyclopedia of Social Movement Media,* edited by John Downing. Thousand Oaks, CA: Sage.

Miller, Laura J. 2006. *Reluctant Capitalists: Bookselling and the Culture of Consumption*. Chicago, IL: University of Chicago Press.

Miller, Toby, Nitin Govil, John McMurria, Ting Wang, and Richard Maxwell. 2008. *Global Hollywood 2*. London, UK: British Film Institute.

Milliot, Jim. 2013. "Trade Sales Rose 6.9% in 2012." *Publishers Weekly*. May 15. Retrieved June 3 (http://www.publishersweekly.com/pw/by-topic/industry-news/financial-reporting/article/57242-trade-sales-rose-6-9-in-2012.html).

Mills, C. Wright. 1959. *The Sociological Imagination.* New York: Oxford University Press.

Modleski, Tania. 1984. *Loving With a Vengeance.* New York: Methuen.

Morgan, Marcyliena and Dionne Bennett. 2011. "Hip-Hop & the Global Imprint of a Black Cultural Form." *Daedalus* 140 (2): 176–196.

Morgan, Michael. 2009. "Cultivation Analysis and Media Effects." Pp. 69–82 in *The SAGE Handbook of Media Processes and Effects.* Thousand Oaks, CA: Sage.

Morgan, Nick. 2013. "Thinking of Self-Publishing Your Book in 2013? Here's What You Need to Know." *Forbes.* January 8. Retrieved July 14, 2013 (http://www.forbes.com/sites/nickmorgan/2013/01/08/thinking-of-self-publishing-your-book-in-2013-heres-what-you-need-to-know/).

Morley, David. 1980. *The Nationwide Audience.* London, UK: British Film Institute.

_____. 1986. *Family Television.* London, UK: Comedia.

_____. 1992. *Television, Audiences, and Cultural Studies.* London, UK: Routledge Kegan Paul.

Morris, Aldon. 1984. *The Origins of the Civil Rights Movement.* New York: Free Press.

Mosco, Vincent and Dan Schiller. 2001. *Continental Order?* Lanham, MD: Rowman & Littlefield.

Motherjones.com. 2011. "What is Mother Jones?" Retrieved February 21, 2011 (http://motherjones.com/about).

Mowlana, Hamid, George Gerbner, and Herbert Schiller, eds. 1992. *Triumph of the Image: The Media's War in the Persian Gulf.* Boulder, CO: Westview.

Mueller, Milton. 2002. *Ruling the Roost: Internet Governance and the Taming of Cyberspace.* Cambridge, MA: MIT Press.

_____. 2010. *Networks and States: The Global Politics of Internet Governance.* Cambridge, MA: MIT Press.

Mueller, Milton, Brendan Kuerbis, and Christiane Pagé. 2004. "Reinventing Media Activism: Public Interest Advocacy in the Making of U.S. Communication-Information Policy, 1960–2002." The Convergence Center, School of Information Studies, Syracuse University. Retrieved November 15, 2010 (dcc.syr.edu/PDF/reinventing.pdf).

Musgrove, Mike. 2009. "Twitter Is a Player in Iran's Drama." *Washington Post.* June 17. Retrieved November 30, 2010 (http://www.washingtonpost.com/wp-dyn/content/article/2009/06/16/AR2009061603391.html).

Nacos, Brigitte L. and Oscar Torres-Reyna. 2007. *Fueling Our Fears: Stereotyping, Media Coverage, and Public Opinion of Muslim Americans.* Lanham, MD: Rowman & Littlefield.

Nakamura, Lisa. 2009. "Don't Hate the Player, Hate the Game: The Racialization of Labor in *World of Warcraft.*" *Critical Studies in Media Communication* 26 (2): 128–144.

Napoli, Philipp M. 2007. "Public Interest Media Activism and Advocacy as a Social Movement: A Review of the Literature." *McGannon Center Working Paper Series.* Paper 21. Retrieved November 15, 2010 (http://fordham.bepress.com/mcgannon_working_papers/21).

Nardi, Peter. 1997. "Changing Gay and Lesbian Images in the Media." Pp. 427–442 in *Overcoming Heterosexism and Homophobia: Strategies That Work,* edited by James T. Sears and Walter Williams. New York: Columbia University Press.

Naughton, John. 2000. *A Brief History of the Future: From Radio Days to Internet Years in a Lifetime.* Woodstock, NY: Overlook Press.

NBC. 1998. "Will and Grace." Retrieved December 30, 1998 (www.nbc.com).

Negrine, Ralph. 2008. *The Transformation of Political Communication: Continuities and Changes in Media and Politics.* New York: Palgrave MacMillan.

Negrine, Ralph, Paolo Mancini, Christina Holtz-Bacha, and Stylianos Papathanassopoulos, eds. 2007. *The Professionalisation of Political Communication.* Bristol, TN: Intellect.

Negroponte, Nicholas. 1995. *Being Digital.* New York: Vintage.

Nesbitt, Jim. 1998. "Radio Pirates Feel the Heat." *Cleveland Plain Dealer,* July 19, p. 1D.

Netcraft. 2010. "December 2010 Web Server Survey." Retrieved December 9, 2010 (http://news.netcraft.com/archives/category/web-server-survey/).

Neuman, W. Russell. 1991. *The Future of the Mass Audience.* New York: Cambridge University Press.

_____. 1996. "Political Communications Infrastructure." *Annals of the American Academy of Political and Social Sciences* 546 (July): 9–21.

News Corporation. 2012. *Annual Report, 2012.* New York: News Corporation.

News-press.com/watchdog. 2011. *The Watchdog Blog.* Retrieved February 21, 2011 (http://www.news- press.com/watchdog).

Nielsen. 2013a. "Free to Move Between Screens: The Cross-Platform Report, March 2013." New York, NY. Retrieved July 14, 2013 (http://www.nielsen.com/us/en/reports/2013/the-nielsen-march-2013-cross-platform-report--free-to-move-betwe.html).

_____. 2013b. "State of the Media: The Cross-Platform Report, Q3, 2012 US." New York, NY. Retrieved August 23, 2013 (http://www.nielsen.com/us/en/reports/2013/state-of-the-media--the-nielsen-cross-platform-report-q3-2012.html).

_____. 2013c. "The Nielsen Company & Billboard's 2013 Mid-Year Music Industry Report." Retrieved July 23, 2013 (http://www.nielsen.com/content/dam/corporate/us/en/reports-downloads/2013%20Reports/Nielsen-Music-2013-Mid-Year-US-Release.pdf).

Nielsen, Jakob. 2006. "Participation Inequality: Encouraging More Users to Contribute." Retrieved December 8, 2010 (http://www.useit.com/alertbox/participation_inequality.html).

Nightline. 1989. ABC News. September 27.

Noam, Eli M. 2009. *Media Ownership and Concentration in America.* New York: Oxford University Press.

Noam, Eli M., ed. 1985. *Video Media Competition: Regulation, Economics, and Technology.* New York: Columbia University Press.

Norris, Pippa. 2000. *A Virtuous Circle: Political Communications in Post-Industrial Societies.* New York: Cambridge University Press.

NPD Group. 2012. iTunes Continues to Dominate Music Retailing, but Nearly 60 Percent of iTunes Music Buyers Also Use Pandora. Retrieved January 17, 2013 (https://www.npd.com/wps/portal/npd/us/news/press-releases/itunes-continues-to-dominate-music-retailing-but-nearly-60-percent-of-itunes-music-buyers-also-use-pandora/).

Nussbaum, Bruce. 2007. "It's Time to Call One Laptop per Child a Failure." *Business Week.* September 24. Retrieved December 9, 2010 (http://www.businessweek.com/innovate/NussbaumOnDesign/archives/2007/09/its_time_to_call_one_laptop_per_child_a_failure.html).

O'Barr, William. 1994. *Culture and the Ad.* Boulder, CO: Westview.

O'Connor, A., ed. 2004. *Community Radio in Bolivia: The Miners' Radio Stations.* Lewiston, NY: Edwin Mellen Press.

OhmyNews. 2010. "OMNI's New Approach to Citizen Journalism." August 1. Retrieved November 4, 2010 (http://english.ohmynews.com/ArticleView/article_view.asp?menu=A11100&no=386159&rel_no=1&back_url).

O'Neil, Michael. 1993. *The Roar of the Crowd: How Television and People Power Are Changing the World.* New York: Time Books.

Ó Siochrú, Seán and Bruce Girard. 2002. *Global Media Governance.* Lanham, MD: Rowman & Littlefield.

Ott, Brian L. 2004. "(Re)Locating Pleasure in Media Studies: Toward an Erotics of Reading." *Communication and Critical/Cultural Studies* 1 (2): 194–212.

Paik, Haejung and George Comstock. 1994. "The Effects of Television Violence on Antisocial Behavior: A Meta-Analysis." *Communication Research* 21: 516–546.

Palfrey, John and Urs Gasser. 2008. *Born Digital: Understanding the First Generation of Digital Natives.* New York: Basic Books.

Palmer, R. R. and Joel Colton. 1978. *A History of the Modern World.* New York: Knopf.

Papper, Bob. 2010. "Number of Minority Journalists Down in 2009; Story Mixed for Female Journalists." Radio Television Digital News Association. Retrieved November 3, 2010 (http://www.rtdna.org/pages/posts/rtdnahofstra-survey-number-of-minority-journalists-down-in-2009-story-mixed-for-female-journalists1083.php).

Parenti, Michael. 1986. *Inventing Reality: The Politics of the Mass Media.* New York: St. Martin's.

PEJ (Project for Excellence in Journalism). 2007. "The Invisible Primary—Invisible No Longer: A First Look at Coverage of the 2008 Presidential Campaign." October 29. Retrieved November 11, 2010 (http://www.journalism.org/node/8187).

_____. 2009. "Covering the Great Recession: How the Media Have Depicted the Economic Crisis During Obama's Presidency." Retrieved November 29, 2010 (http://www.journalism.org/sites/journalism.org/files/Covering%20the%20Great%20Recession.pdf).

Perks, Lisa Glebatis. 2012. "Three Satiric Decoding Positions." *Communication Studies* 63 (3): 290–308.

Peters, Gerhard and John T. Wooley. 1999. The American Presidency Project. 1996 Presidential Election Speeches and Remarks, Robert Dole, May 31, 1995, "Remarks in Los Angeles: 'Hollywood Speech.'" Retrieved from www.presidency.ucsb.edu/ws/index.php?pid = 85193

Peterson, Richard A. and N. Anand. 2004. "The Production of Culture Perspective." *Annual Review of Sociology* 30: 311–334.

Peterson, Richard A. and David G. Berger. 1975. "Cycles in Symbol Production: The Case of Popular Music." *American Sociological Review* 40: 158–173.

Peterson, Robin T. 2007. "Consumer Magazine Advertisement Portrayal of Models by Race in the US: An Assessment." *Journal of Marketing Communications* 13 (3): 199–211.

Pew Internet and American Life Project. 2013. "Trend Data (Adults)." Washington, DC (http://www.pewinternet.org/Trend-Data-%28 Adults%29).

Pew Research Center. 2012a. "Low Marks for the 2012 Election." Retrieved July 21, 2013 (http://www.people-press.org/files/legacy-pdf/11-15-12%20Post%20Election.pdf).

____. 2012b. *State of the News Media: 2012* (http://stateofthemedia.org/media-ownership/newspapers/?srt = 3&so = -1&compare =).

____. 2012c. "Trends in News Consumption: 1991-2012." Retrieved July 21, 2013 (http://www.people-press.org/files/legacy-pdf/2012%20News%20Consumption%20Report.pdf).

____. 2013. *State of the News Media: 2013.*

Pew Research Center for the People & the Press. 2010. *Americans Spending More Time Following the News.* September 12. Retrieved November 11, 2010 (http://people-press.org/report/652/).

Pfanner, Eric and Amy Chozick. 2012. Random House and Penguin Merger Creates Global Giant. *The New York Times.* October 30. Page B1.

Philips, Angela. 2010. "Old Sources: New Bottles." Pp. 87–101 in Natalie Fenton, ed. *New Media, Old News: Journalism and Democracy in the Digital Age.* Thousand Oaks, CA: SAGE.

Pizzigati, Sam and Fred J. Solowey. 1992. *The New Labor Press.* Ithaca, NY: ILR/Cornell University Press.

Pool, Ithiel de Sola. 1983. *Technologies of Freedom.* Cambridge, MA: Harvard University Press.

Postman, Neil. 1985. *Amusing Ourselves to Death.* New York: Penguin.

Potter, W. James. 2003. *The 11 Myths of Media Violence.* Thousand Oaks, CA: SAGE.

Powell, Walter W. 1985. *Getting Into Print.* Chicago, IL: University of Chicago Press.

Powers, Matthew. 2011. "What's New in the Sociology of News?: Connecting Current Journalism Research to Classic Newsroom Studies." Paper presented at the International Communication Association. Boston, MA.

Powers, William. 2010. *Hamlet's Blackberry: A Practical Philosophy for Building the Good Life in the Digital Age.* New York: HarperCollins.

Pred, Allan R. 1973. *Urban Growth and the Circulation of Information.* Cambridge, MA: Harvard University Press.

Press, Andrea. 1991. *Women Watching Television.* Philadelphia, PA: University of Pennsylvania Press.

Price, Monroe. 2002. *New Role of the State in Media and Sovereignty.* Cambridge, MA: MIT Press.

Prince, Stephen. 1992. *Visions of Empire: Political Imagery in Contemporary American Film.* New York: Praeger.

Prindle, David F. 1993. *Risky Business.* Boulder, CO: Westview.

Prior, Markus. 2007. *Post-Broadcast Democracy: How Media Choice Increases Inequality in Political Involvement and Polarizes Elections.* New York: Cambridge University Press.

Project for Excellence in Journalism. 2012. "How the Presidential Candidates Use the Web and Social Media" Retrieved January 8, 2013 (http://www.journalism.org/analysis_report/how_presidential_candidates_use_web_and_social_media).

Prysby, Charles and David Holian. 2008. "Who Votes On the Basis of the Candidate's Personality? Vote Choice in U.S. Presidential Elections, 1992–2004." Paper presented at the Annual Meeting of the American Political Science Association, Boston, MA, August 28.

Puette, William J. 1992. *Through Jaundiced Eyes: How the Media View Organized Labor.* Ithaca, NY: ILR Press.

Puri, Jyoti. 1997. "Reading Romance Novels in Postcolonial India." *Gender & Society* 11 (4): 434–452.

Quandt, Thorsten and Jane B. Singer. 2008. "Convergence and Cross-Platform Journalism." Pp. 130–144 in *Handbook of Journalism Studies,* edited by Karin Wahl-Jorgensen and Thomas Hanitzsch. New York: Routledge.

Radway, Janice A. 1991. *Reading the Romance: Women, Patriarchy, and Popular Literature.* 2nd ed. Chapel Hill, NC: University of North Carolina Press.

Rawsthorn, Alice. 2009. "Nonprofit Laptops: A Dream Not Yet Over." *New York Times.* November 8. Retrieved December 9, 2010 (http://www.ny times.com/2009/11/09/arts/09iht-design9 .html?ref = nicholas_negroponte).

Regan, Donald. 1988. *For the Record.* New York: Harcourt Brace.

Reisman, David. 1953. *The Lonely Crowd.* Garden City, NY: Doubleday.

Rendall, Steve and Tara Broughel. 2003. "Amplifying Officials, Squelching Dissent." *Extra!* May/June. Retrieved November 1, 2010 (http://www.fair .org/index.php?page = 1145).

Rennie, Ellie. 2006. *Community Media: A Global Introduction.* Lanham, MD: Rowman & Littlefield.

Reporters Without Borders. 2009. "Reporters Without Borders in Rome to Defend Press Freedom." October 5. Retrieved February 11, 2011 (http:// en.rsf.org/italy-reporters-without-borders-in-rome-05–10–2009,34647.html).

———. 2013. *World Press Freedom Index: 2013* (http:// en.rsf.org/press-freedom-index-2013,1054 .html).

Reuters. 1998. "Most Minorities Under-Represented on U.S. TV." December 22, wire.

Rheingold, Howard. 2000. *The Virtual Community. Homesteading on the Electronic Frontier.* Rev. ed. Cambridge, MA: MIT Press.

———. 2002. *Smart Mobs.* Cambridge, MA: Perseus Publishing.

Rhodes, Jane. 1993. "The Visibility of Race and Media History." *Critical Studies in Mass Communication* 20: 184–190.

RIAA (Recording Industry Association of America). 2013. "Parental Advisory" (http://www.riaa .com/toolsforparents.php?content_selector = parental_advisory).

Rideout, Victoria J., Ulla G. Foehr, and Donald F. Roberts. 2010. *Generation M2: Media in the Lives of 8- to 18-Year-Olds.* Menlo Park, CA: Henry J. Kaiser Family Foundation.

Robertson, John W. 2010. "The Last Days of Free Market Hegemony? UK TV News Coverage of Economic Issues in Spring 2008." *Media, Culture & Society* 32: 517–529.

Robinson, Michael J. 1976. "Public Affairs Television and the Growth of Political Malaise: The Case of the 'Selling of the Pentagon.'" *American Political Science Review.* 70: 409–432.

Robinson, Tom, Mark Callister, Brad Clark, and James Phillips. 2009. "Violence, Sexuality, and Gender Stereotyping: A Content Analysis of Official Video Game Web Sites." *Web Journal of Mass Communication Research* 13 (June): 1–17.

Robischon, Noah. 1998. "Browser Beware." *Brill's Content,* August, pp. 40–44.

Rogers, Everett. 1986. *Communication Technology.* New York: Free Press.

Rogers, Everett M., Arvind Singhal, and Avinash Thombre. 2004. "Indian Audience Interpretations of Health Related Content." *The Bold and the Beautiful. Gazette: The International Journal for Communication Studies* 66 (5): 437–458.

Romano, Lois. 2012. "Obama's Data Advantage." *Politico.* Retrieved January 8, 2013 (http://www .politico.com/news/stories/0612/77213.html).

Romer, Daniel, Kathleen Hall Jamieson, and Sean Aday. 2003. "Television News and the Cultivation of Fear of Crime." *Journal of Communication* 53 (1): 88–104.

Rose, Tricia. 1994. *Black Noise.* Hanover, NH: Wesleyan University Press.

Rosen, Jay. 1993. "Who Won the Week? The Political Press and the Evacuation of Meaning." *Tikkun* 8 (4): 7–10, 94.

Rosenblum, Barbara. 1978. *Photographers at Work.* New York: Holmes & Meier.

Rosenfeld, Megan. 1997. "The 'Ellen' Coming Out Club." *Washington Post.* April 24, p. B1.

Ross, Steven J. 1999. *Working Class Hollywood: Silent Film and the Shaping of Class in America.* Princeton, NJ: Princeton University Press.

Ryan, Charlotte. 1991. *Prime Time Activism.* Boston, MA: South End Press.

Sachdev, Ameet. 2010. "FTC Cracks Down on Fake Online Endorsements." *Chicago Tribune.* October 11. Retrieved November 29, 2010 (http://articles .chicagotribune.com/2010–10–11/business/

ct-biz-1011-web-reviews--20101011_1_ftc-cracks-endorsements-mary-engle).

Saleh, Nivien. 2012. "Egypt's Digital Activism and the Dictator's Dilemma: An Evaluation." *Telecommunications Policy* 36 (6): 476–483.

Salganik, Matthew J., Peter S. Dodds, and Duncan J. Watts. 2006. "Experimental Study of Inequality and Unpredictability in an Artificial Cultural Market." *Science* 311: 854–856.

Salzman, Jason. 1998. *Making the News: A Guide for Nonprofits and Activists*. Boulder, CO: Westview.

Sandler, Adam. 1994. "Hollywood: 'R' Kind of Town." *Variety.* September 12, pp. 1, 7.

Sandvine. 2013. "Sandvine Global Report: Internet Data Usage Up 120 Percent In North America" (http://www.sandvine.com/news/pr_detail.asp?ID = 394).

Scardaville, Melissa C. 2005. "Accidental Activists: Fan Activism in the Soap Opera Community." *American Behavioral Scientist* 48 (7): 881–901.

Schell, L. A. 1999. *Socially Constructing the Female Athlete: A Monolithic Media Representation of Active Women*. Unpublished doctoral dissertation, Texas Woman's University, Denton. Retrieved overview and excerpt November 4, 2010 (http://www.womenssportsfoundation.org/Content/Articles/Issues/ Media-and-Publicity/D/DisEmpowering-Images--Media-Representations-of-Women-in-Sport.aspx).

Scheufele, Dietram A. and David Tewksbury. 2007. "Framing, Agenda Setting, and Priming: The Evolution of Three Media Effects Models." *Journal of Communication* 57 (1): 9–20.

Schiffer, Michael. 1991. *The Portable Radio in American Life*. Tucson, AZ: University of Arizona Press.

Schill, Dan. 2009. *Stagecraft and Statecraft: Advance and Media Events in Political Communication*. Lanham, MD: Lexington Books.

Schiller, Herbert. 1971. *Mass Communications and American Empire*. Boston, MA: Beacon.

____. 1989. *Culture, Inc.* New York: Oxford University Press.

____. 1992. *Mass Communications and American Empire*. 2nd ed. Boulder, CO: Westview.

Scholz, Trebor. 2010. "Market Ideology and the Myths of Web 2.0." *First Monday* 13 (3) March 3. Retrieved December 8, 2010 (http://firstmonday.org/htbin/cgiwrap/bin/ojs/index.php/fm/article/view/2138/1945).

Schudson, Michael. 1978. *Discovering the News*. New York: Basic Books.

____. 1984. *Advertising: The Uneasy Persuasion*. New York: Basic Books.

____. 2011. *The Sociology of News*. 2nd ed. New York: W.W. Norton.

Schultz, Julianne. 1998. *Reviving the Fourth Estate*. New York: Cambridge University Press.

Scott, Althaus R., Peter F. Nardulli, and Daron R. Shaw. 2002. "Candidate Appearances in Presidential Elections, 1972–2000." *Political Communication* 19: 49–72.

Screen Actors Guild. 2008. "2007 & 2008 Casting Data Reports." Retrieved November 1, 2010 (http://www.sag.org/content/studies-and-reports).

Seggar, John F., Jeffrey K. Hafen, and Helena Hannonen-Gladden. 1981. "Television's Portrayals of Minorities and Women in Drama and Comedy Drama, 1971–80." *Journal of Broadcasting* 25: 277–288.

Seib, Philip and Dana M. Janbek, 2011. *Global Terrorism and New Media*. New York: Routledge.

Shah, Dhavan V., Nojin Kwak, and R. Lance Holbert. 2001. "'Connecting' and 'Disconnecting' With Civic Life: Patterns of Internet Use and the Production of Social Capital." *Political Communication* 18 (2): 141–162.

Shaheen, Jack G. 2008. *Guilty: Hollywood's Verdict on Arabs After 9/11*. Northampton, MA: Olive Branch Press.

____. 2009. *Reel Bad Arabs: How Hollywood Villifies a People*. Northampton, MA: Olive Branch Press.

Shales, Tom. 1995. "The Fat Cat Broadcast Bonanza." *Washington Post*. June 13, pp. C1, C9.

____. 2003. "Aboard the Lincoln: A White House Spectacular." *Washington Post*. May 2, p. C1.

Shedden, David. 2010. "New Media Timeline, 1969–2010." Poynter Institute. Retrieved November 29, 2010 (poynter.org/content/content_view.asp?id = 75953).

Shiver, Jube, Jr. 1998. "Eye on the Sky: FCC Agents Guard the Crowded Airwaves Against Pirates and Accidental Interference." *Los Angeles Times*. July 20. Retrieved November 29, 2010 (http://articles.latimes.com/1998/jul/20/business/fi-5408).

Sigal, Leon. 1973. *Reporters and Officials: The Organization and Politics of Newsmaking*. Lexington, MA: Lexington Books.

Signorielli, Nancy. 2009. "Race and Sex in Prime Time." *Mass Communication and Society* 12: 332–352.

Simmons, Steven J. 1978. *The Fairness Doctrine and the Media.* Berkeley, CA: University of California Press.

Simons, John. 1998. "Faced with 'Convergence,' FCC Takes Closer Look at Internet Access via Cable." *Wall Street Journal.* September 8, p. B8.

Smith, Stacey and Marc Choueiti. 2011. "Black Characters in Popular Film: Is the Key to Diversifying Cinematic Content Held in the Hand of the Black Director?" Annenberg School for Communication & Journalism. Retrieved March 12, 2013 (http://annenberg.usc.edu/Faculty/Communication%20and%20Journalism/~/media/BlackCharacters_KeyFindings.ashx).

Snow, David A., E. Burke Rochford, Jr., Steven K. Worden, and Robert D. Benford. 1986. "Frame Alignment Processes, Micromobilization, and Movement Participation." *American Sociological Review* 51: 464–481.

Snow, David A., Rens Vliegenthart, and Catherine Corrigall-Brown. 2007. "Framing the French Riots: A Comparative Study of Frame Variation." *Social Forces* 86 (2): 385–415.

Solove, Daniel. 2006. *The Digital Person: Technology and Privacy in the Digital Age.* New York: New York University Press.

Sparta, Christine. 2002. "Emergence from the closet." March 11. *USA Today* (http://usatoday30.usatoday.com/life/television/2002/2002-03-11-coming-out-timeline.htm?iframe=true&width=80%&height=80%).

Spigel, Lynn. 1992. *Make Room for TV.* Chicago, IL: University of Chicago Press.

Squires, James. 1993. *Read All About It! The Corporate Takeover of America's Newspapers.* New York: Times Books.

Sreberny, Annabelle. 2005. "Contradictions of the Globalizing Moment." *Global Media and Communication* 1: 11–15.

Sreberny-Mohammadi, Annabelle. 1997. "The Many Faces of Imperialism." Pp. 48–68 in *Beyond Cultural Imperialism,* edited by Peter Golding and Phil Harris. Thousand Oaks, CA: Sage.

Starr, Paul. 2004. *The Creation of the Media: Political Origins of Modern Communications.* New York: Basic Books.

Statistical Abstract of the United States. 1990. "Table 934. Advertising—Estimated Expenditures by Medium, 1970–1988." Washington, DC: U.S. Census Bureau.

Statistical Abstract of the United States. 2010. "Table 1243: Advertising—Estimated Expenditures by Medium, 1990–2008." Washington, DC: U.S. Census Bureau.

Stecklow, Steve. 2010. "On the Web, Children Face Intensive Tracking." *Wall Street Journal.* September 17. Retrieved December 8, 2010 (http://online.wsj.com/article/SB10001424052748703904304575497903523187146.html).

Steel, Emily. 2010. "Some Data-Miners Ready to Reveal What They Know." *Wall Street Journal.* December 3. Retrieved December 8, 2010 (http://online.wsj.com/article/SB10001424052748704377004575650802136721966.html).

Steiner, Linda. 1988. "Oppositional Decoding as an Act of Resistance." *Critical Studies in Mass Communication* 5 (1): 1–15.

Steinhauser, Paul. 2010. "Majority of Campaign Commercials Are Attack Ads." CNN Political Ticker. August 27. Retrieved November 30, 2010 (http://politicalticker.blogs.cnn.com/2010/08/27/majority-of-campaign-commercials-are-attack-ads/).

Stelter, Brian. 2010. "FCC Is Set to Regulate Net Access." *New York Times.* Retrieved February 16, 2011 (http://www.nytimes.com/2010/12/21/business/media/21fcc.html).

Straubhaar, Joseph. 1991. "Beyond Media Imperialism: Asymmetrical Interdependence and Cultural Proximity." *Critical Studies in Mass Communication* 8 (1): 39–59.

Strauss, Jessalynn R. 2011. "Public (Relations) Disturbances and Civil Disobedience: Why I Use 'The Yes Men Fix the World' to Teach Public Relations Ethics." *Public Relations Review* 37: 544–547.

Street, John. 2002. "Bob, Bono and Tony: the Celebrity as a Politician." *Media, Culture and Society* 24 (3): 422–441.

____. 2004. "Celebrity Politicians: Popular Culture and Political Representation." *The British Journal of Politics and International Relations* 6 (4): 435–452.

Strelitz, L. 2003. "Where the Global Meets the Local: South African Youth and Their Experience of Global Media." Pp. 234–256 in *Global Media*

Studies: Ethnographic Perspectives, edited by Patrick D. Murphy and Marwan M. Kraidy. New York: Routledge.

Sunstein, Cass. 2002. *Republic.com.* Princeton, NJ: Princeton University Press.

Surowiecki, James. 2005. *The Wisdom of Crowds.* New York: Random House.

Tan, See Kam. 2011. "Global Hollywood, Narrative Transparency, and Chinese Media Poachers: Narrating Cross-Cultural Negotiations of *Friends* in South China." *Television & New Media* 12 (3): 207–227.

Tang, Tang, Gregory D. Newton, and Xiaopeng Wang. 2007. "Does Synergy Work? An Examination of Cross-Promotion Effects." *The International Journal on Media Management* 9 (4): 127–134.

Target Market News. 2010. "ABC's 20/20 Takes No. 1 Ranking Among TV Shows in Black Households." July 28. Retrieved October 28, 2010 (http://www .targetmarketnews.com/storyid07281001.htm).

Taylor, Ella. 1989. *Prime Time Families.* Berkeley, CA: University of California Press.

Taylor, Phillip M. 1992. *War and the Media: Propaganda and Persuasion in the Gulf War.* New York: St. Martin's.

The Economist. 2001. "Fit to Run Italy?" Retrieved April 14, 2011 (http://www.economist.com/ node/593654?story_id = 593654).

The Guardian. 2013. "The NSA Files." Retrieved July 23, 2013 (http://www.guardian.co.uk/world/the-nsa-files).

The Leveson Inquiry. 2012. An Inquiry into the Culture, Practices, and Ethics of the Press: Executive Summary. November. London: The Stationary Office.

Thompson, John. 2010. *Merchants of Culture: The Publishing Business in the Twenty-First Century.* New York: Penguin Group.

Thompson, Krissah. 2013. "Yep, we've come a long way." March 26. *Washington Post.* C1.

Tichi, Cecelia. 1991. *Electronic Hearth: Creating an American Television Culture.* New York: Oxford University Press.

Time Inc. 2013. Company Profile. Retrieved January 10, 2013 (http://www.timeinc.com/aboutus/ companyprofile.php).

Tomlinson, John. 1991. *Cultural Imperialism: A Critical Introduction.* New York: Continuum.

____. 2003. "Media Imperialism." Pp. 113–134 in *Planet TV: A Global Television Reader,* edited by

Lisa Parks and Shanti Kumar. New York: New York University Press.

____. 2007. *The Culture of Speed: The Coming of Immediacy.* London, UK: Sage.

Townhall.com. 2011. "Townhall.com—the Leading Conservative and Political Opinion Website." Retrieved February 21, 2011 (http://townhall .com/AboutUs.aspx).

Traugott, Michael W. 1992. "The Impact of Media Polls on the Public." Pp. 125–149 in *Media Polls in American Politics,* edited by Thomas E. Mann and Gary Orren. Washington, DC: Brookings Institution.

Tuchman, Gaye. 1978. *Making News: A Study in the Construction of Reality.* New York: Free Press.

Tuggle, C.A. 1997. "Differences in Television Sports Reporting of Men's and Women's Athletics: ESPN SportsCenter and CNN Sports Tonight." *Journal of Broadcasting & Electronic Media* 41 (1): 14–24.

Tunstall, Jeremy. 1977. *The Media Are American.* New York: Columbia University Press.

____. 1986. *Communications Deregulation: The Unleashing of America's Communications Industry.* Oxford, UK: Basil Blackwell.

Turner, Ted and Bill Burke. 2008. *Call Me Ted.* New York: Grand Central Publishing.

Turow, Joseph. 1997. *Breaking up America: Advertisers and the New Media World.* Chicago, IL: University of Chicago Press.

Turow, Joseph. 2011. *The Daily You: How the New Advertising Industry Is Defining Your Identity and Your Worth.* New Haven: Yale University Press.

Twenge, Jean. 2006. *Generation Me: Why Today's Young Americans Are More Confident, Assertive, Entitled—and More Miserable Than Ever Before.* New York: Free Press.

UNCTAD (United Nations Conference on Trade and Development). 2004. *Creative Industries and Development.* June 4. Retrieved December 9, 2010 (http://www.unctad.org/Templates/Page. asp?intItemID = 5106&lang = 1).

Underwood, Doug. 1993. *When MBAs Rule the Newsroom.* New York: Columbia University Press.

UNESCO (United Nations Educational, Scientific, and Cultural Organization). 2005. "Convention on the Protection and Promotion of the Diversity of Cultural Expressions 2005." October 20.

Retrieved December 9, 2010 (http://portal.unesco.org/en/ev.php-URL_ID = 31038&URL_DO = DO_ TOPIC&URL_SECTION = 201.html).

_____. 2010. "Creative Content: Radio, TV, New Media." Retrieved October 18, 2010 (http://portal. unesco.org/ci/en/ev.php-URL_ID = 5459&URL_DO = DO_TOPIC&URL_SECTION = 201.html).

U.S. Census Bureau. 2010. *Statistical Abstract of the United States*. Washington, DC: Government Printing Office.

Vaidhyanathan, Siva. 2011. *The Googlization of Everything*. Berkeley, CA: University of California Press.

van de Rijt, Arnout, Eran Shor, Charles Ward, and Steven Skiena. 2013. "Only 15 Minutes? The Social Stratification of Fame in Printed Media." *American Sociological Review* 78 (2): 266–289.

Van Dijk, Jan. 1998. "The Reality of Virtual Communities." *Trends in Communication* 1 (1): 39–63.

Verrier, Richard. 2009. "MPAA stops disclosing average costs of making and marketing movies." April 1. *Los Angeles Times*. Retrieved July 24, 2013 (http://articles.latimes.com/2009/apr/01/business/fi-cotown-mpaa1).

Viacom. n.d. "Our Brands." Retrieved December 9, 2010 (http://www.viacom.com/ourbrands/).

Vidmar, Neil and Milton Rokeach. 1974. "Archie Bunker's Bigotry: A Study in Selective Perception and Exposure." *Journal of Communication* 24: 36–47.

Waldrop, Michael. 2001. *The Dream Machine: J.C.R. Licklider and the Revolution That Made Computing Personal*. New York: Penguin.

Wales, Jimbo. 2001. "Neutral Point of View." Retrieved November 30, 2010 (http://web.archive.org/web/20010416035757/http://www.wikipedia.com/wiki/NeutralPointOfView).

Walters, Suzanna D. 1995. *Material Girls*. Berkeley, CA: University of California Press.

Washbourne, Neil. 2010. *Mediating Politics: Newspapers, Radio, Television and the Internet*. New York: Open University Press/McGraw Hill.

Washington Post. 2013a. "NSA Secrets." Retrieved July 23, 2013 (http://www.washingtonpost.com/nsa-secrets).

Washington Post. 2013b. "Top Secret America" (http://projects.washingtonpost.com/top-secret-america/).

Weedon, Alexis. 2007. "In Real Life: Book Covers in the Internet Bookstore." Pp. 117–127 in *Judging a Book by Its Cover*, edited by Nicole Matthews and Nickianne Moody. Burlington, VT: Ashgate.

Weisman, Jon. 2013. "Upfronts: What Are New Shows' Chances for Survival?" *Variety* (http://variety.com/2013/tv/news/upfronts-what-are-new-shows-chances-for-survival-1200482660/).

White, Armond. 2009. "Pride & Precious." *New York Press*. November 4. Retrieved February 24, 2011 (http://www.nypress.com/article-20554-pride-precious.html).

White, David Manning. 1950. "The Gatekeeper: A Case Study in the Selection of News." *Journalism Quarterly* 27: 383–390.

Wible, Scott. 2004. "Media Advocates, Latino Citizens, and Niche Cable: The Limits of 'No Limits' TV." *Cultural Studies* 18 (1): 34–66.

Wikinews.org. 2011. "Wikinews Content Guide." Retrieved February 21, 2011 (http://en.wikinews.org/wiki/Wikinews:Content_guide).

Wiley, Richard E. 1994. "'Fairness' in Our Future?" *Quill*. March, pp. 36–37.

Williams, Dmitri, Nicole Martins, Mia Consalvo, and James D. Ivory. 2009. "The Virtual Census: Representations of Gender, Race and Age in Video Games." *New Media & Society* 11 (5): 815–834.

Williams, Raymond. 1974. *Television, Technology, and Cultural Form*. New York: Schocken Books.

_____. 1983. *Towards 2000*. Harmondsworth, UK: Penguin Press.

Wilson, Clint C., II, Felix Gutierrez, and Lena M. Chao. 2012. *Racism, Sexism, and the Media*. Thousand Oaks, CA: Sage.

Wingfield, Nick. 2010. "Microsoft Quashed Effort to Boost Online Privacy." *Wall Street Journal*. August 2. Retrieved December 3, 2010 (http://online.wsj.com/article/SB10001424052748703467304575383530439838568.html).

Wolf, Edward. 2012. "The Asset Price Meltdown and the Wealth of the Middle Class." New York University. Retrieved (http://appam.confex.com/data/extendedabstract/appam/2012/Paper_2134_extendedabstract_151_0.pdf).

Writers Guild of America, West. 2008. *Comments of the Writers Guild of America, West Regarding the Rampant Use of Embedded Advertising in Television* and Film and the Need for Adequate Disclosure to Viewers. September 22. Los Angeles, CA: Writers Guild of America, West.

____. 2011. "Recession and Regression: The 2011 Hollywood Writers Report." Retrieved July 19, 2013 (http://www.wga.org/uploadedFiles/who_we_are/hwr11execsum.pdf).

Wu, Michael. 2010. "The Economics of 90–9-1: The Gini Coefficient (With Cross-Sectional Analyses)." Lithium Lithosphere. Retrieved December 8, 2010 (http://lithosphere.lithium.com/t5/Building-Community-the-Platform/bg-p/MikeW/label-name/90–9-1).

Zafirau, Stephen. 2008. "Reputation Work in Selling Film and Television: Life in the Hollywood Talent Industry." Qualitative Sociology 31 (2): 99–127.

Zaharopoulos, Thimios. 2003. "Perceived Foreign Influence and Television Viewing in Greece." Pp. 39–56 in The Impact of International Television: A Paradigm Shift, Michael G. Elasmar. Mahwah, NJ: Lawrence Erlbaum.

Zaniello, Tom. 2003. Working Stiffs, Union Maids, Reds, and Riffraff: An Expanded Guide to Films About Labor. Ithaca, NY: Cornell University Press.

Index

About the Authors

David Croteau is an Associate Professor (retired) of Sociology at Virginia Commonwealth University, where he continues to teach. He is the author of *Politics and the Class Divide: Working People and the Middle-Class Left*.

William Hoynes is Professor of Sociology and former Director of the Media Studies Program at Vassar College in Poughkeepsie, New York, where he teaches courses on media, culture, and social theory. He is the author of *Public Television for Sale: Media, the Market, and the Public Sphere*.

Croteau and Hoynes are the coauthors of *Experience Sociology; The Business of Media: Corporate Media and the Public Interest;* and *By Invitation Only: How the Media Limit Political Debate*.

◎SAGE researchmethods

The essential online tool for researchers from the world's leading methods publisher

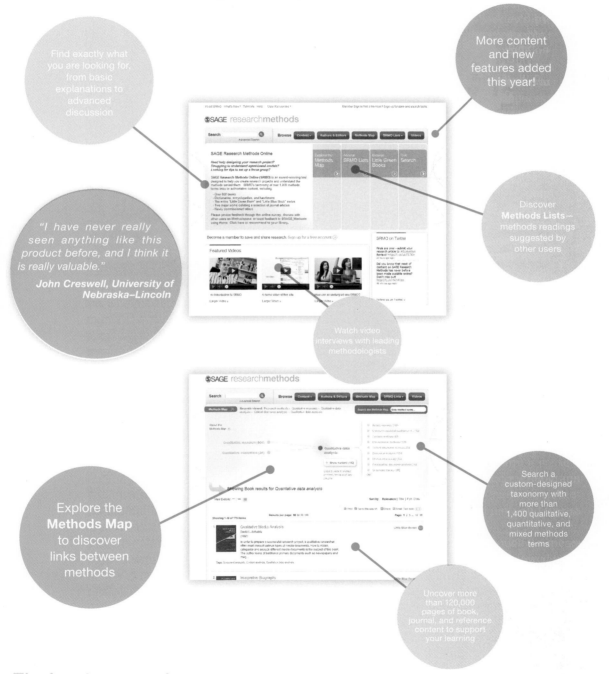

Find exactly what you are looking for, from basic explanations to advanced discussion

More content and new features added this year!

"I have never really seen anything like this product before, and I think it is really valuable."
John Creswell, University of Nebraska–Lincoln

Discover **Methods Lists**— methods readings suggested by other users

Watch video interviews with leading methodologists

Explore the **Methods Map** to discover links between methods

Search a custom-designed taxonomy with more than 1,400 qualitative, quantitative, and mixed methods terms

Uncover more than 120,000 pages of book, journal, and reference content to support your learning

Find out more at
www.sageresearchmethods.com